BRITISH WRITERS

BRITISH WRITERS

Edited under the auspices of the British Council

IAN SCOTT-KILVERT
General Editor

VOLUME II

THOMAS MIDDLETON

TO

GEORGE FARQUHAR

CHARLES SCRIBNER'S SONS / NEW YORK

Library of Congress Cataloging in Publication Data
Main entry under title:

British writers.

Includes bibliographies and index.
CONTENTS: v. 1. William Langland to the English
Bible.—v. 2. Thomas Middleton to George Farquhar.
1. English literature—History and criticism.
2. English literature—Bio-bibliography. 3. Authors,
English—Biography. I. Scott-Kilvert, Ian. II. Great
Britain. British Council.
PR85.B688   820'.9   78-23483
ISBN 0-684-15798-5 (v. 1)
ISBN 0-684-16407-8 (v. 2)

3 5 7 9 11 13 15 17 19   V/C   20 18 16 14 12 10 8 6 4 2
PRINTED IN THE UNITED STATES OF AMERICA

Editorial Staff

List of Subjects in Volume II

Introduction

British Writers is designed as a work of reference to complement *American Writers*, the six-volume set of literary biographies of authors past and present, which was first published in 1974. In the same way as its American counterpart, which first appeared in the form of individual pamphlets published by the University of Minnesota Press, the British collection originates from a series of separate articles entitled *Writers and Their Work.* This series was initiated by the British Council in 1950 as a part of its worldwide program to support the teaching of English language and literature, an activity carried on both in the English-speaking world and in many countries in which English is not the mother tongue.

The articles are intended to appeal to a wide readership, including students in secondary and advanced education, teachers, librarians, scholars, editors, and critics, as well as the general public. Their purpose is to provide an introduction to the work of writers who have made a significant contribution to English literature, to stimulate the reader's enjoyment of the text, and to give students the means to pursue the subject further. The series begins in the fourteenth century and extends to the present day, and is printed in chronological order according to the date of the subject's birth. The articles are far from conforming to a fixed pattern, but speaking generally each begins with a short biographical section, the main body of the text being devoted to a survey of the subject's principal writings and an assessment of the work as a whole. Each article is equipped with a selected bibliography that records the subject's writings in chronological order, in the form both of collected editions and of separate works, including modern and paperback editions. The bibliography concludes with a list of biographical and critical publications, including both books and articles, to guide the reader who is interested in further research. In the case of authors such as Chaucer or Shakespeare, whose writings have inspired extensive criticism and commentary, the critical section is further subdivided and provides a useful record of the new fields of research that have developed over the past hundred years.

British Writers is not conceived as an encyclopedia of literature, nor is it a series of articles planned so comprehensively as to include every writer of historical importance. Its character is rather that of a critical anthology possessing both the virtues and the limitations of such a grouping. It offers neither the schematized form of the encyclopedia nor the completeness of design of the literary history. On the other hand it is limited neither by the impersonality of the one nor the uniformity of the other. Since each contributor speaks with only one voice out of many, he is principally concerned with explaining his subject as fully as possible rather than with establishing an order of merit or making "placing" comparisons (since each contributor might well "place" differently). The prime task is one of presentation and exposition rather than of assigning critical praise or censure. The contributors to the first volume consist of distinguished scholars and critics—later volumes include contributions by poets, novelists, historians, and biographers. Each writes as an enthusiast for his subject, and each sets out to explain what are the qualities that make an author worth reading.

When King James of Scotland became the first Stuart ruler of England, he entered, it has aptly been said, not only a new country but a new era. The interacting forces of politics, religion, economics, science, the spirit of individualism, and the claims of personal inner revelation all combined to make the seventeenth century a period of breathless change, even by modern standards. Protestant England became the laboratory of evolution and experiment, both for church and state: it is worth noting that the proposals of the English Diggers and Levelers for a primitive Christian communist society were being debated and canvassed during the early years of the reign of France's most absolute monarch, Louis XIV—the Sun King.

Publishing records reveal that the appetite of the reading public for religious works was greater than at any other time, before or since; and contemporary Europeans testify that in the middle of James I's reign there was little or no literary scholarship in England and that theology was the dominant interest of educated men. Political controversy was an almost equally intense subject of concern. Posterity has of course made its choice from the literature of the period and, for obvious reasons, has consigned to the vaults the majority of the once avidly read writings of the preachers and pamphleteers. But the fact remains that many of the authors dealt with in this volume were read only by a narrow circle and that, unlike the Elizabethan era, literature was more often identified with courtly than with popular taste. Only in the writings of John Milton and John Bunyan, and at moments in those of John Dryden and Andrew Marvell, are we made aware of the full pressure and turbulence of the *Zeitgeist*. At the other extreme, we see writers who found it prudent to avail themselves of a relative obscurity. Anyone born, say, in the early 1630's would have experienced four major political upheavals in his lifetime, and it is hard not to feel some sympathy for the man of letters who sought to match the talent for survival of the legendary and symbolic vicar of Bray:

> So whatsoever King shall reign,
> I'll still be the Vicar of Bray, Sir.

Critical fashions and methods have changed significantly during the past three decades, and part of the attraction of this series may be found in the diversity of critical approaches that it now provides. This volume of *British Writers* opens with a group of essays that completes the selective survey of the great age of the English drama with studies of the successors of Shakespeare. In the tragedies of this "second wave" of the dramatists, the upward, aspiring Renaissance conception of man has been succeeded by a downward-looking, satirical estimate. The essays on John Marston and Cyril Tourneur and on Thomas Middleton are among the most recent additions to the series and together with that

on Francis Beaumont and John Fletcher pay special attention to the merits of the playwrights in terms of modern performance. As regards the choice of texts for quotations, where a complete and scholarly edition of the writer's works exists in modern spelling, as with the Carey–Fowler edition of Milton's poems, this has been used; otherwise, the best available edition has been employed.

The essays on the lyrical poetry of the pre-Restoration period are divided in the main between "the devout singers" (in Herbert J. Grierson's phrase) and "the courtly love poets." Margaret Willy's critique of the metaphysical poets originally dealt with Richard Crashaw, Henry Vaughan, and Thomas Traherne, to which has been added an article on Abraham Cowley, now chiefly remembered in literary history as a pioneer of the Pindaric ode. T. S. Eliot's appreciation of George Herbert was one of his last critical essays, written two years before his death. Robin Skelton assesses the four cavalier poets, and John Press examines the poetry of Robert Herrick, the most notable of the successors of Ben Jonson, and that of Marvell, the last writer in the metaphysical tradition.

The writings of Milton provide the natural centerpiece for any literary study of this period. E. M. W. Tillyard, one of the earliest contributors to the series, concentrates his attention mainly upon the early poems, *Paradise Lost* and *Samson Agonistes*. His interpretation of *Paradise Lost* contests the widely held view of Satan as the hero of the epic; he argues that the redemption of man is Milton's major theme and the real crux of the poem, and hence the "lost" is an ironical epithet, since mankind can attain another and a better inner paradise. This conclusion that the state of mind outweighs earthly success or failure is also seen as the key to the interpretation of "Lycidas" and of *Paradise Regained*.

The year 1660 provides an unusually distinct historical boundary, marking a frontier in politics and philosophy, as also in aesthetic and social history, and signaling the beginning of the Augustan era in literature. The essay on Dryden by Bonamy Dobrée, a specialist on this period and the original editor of many of the essays in this volume, stresses Dryden's versatility, the range and urbanity of his criticism, and the unsurpassed élan and intellectual vigor of his satire. Vivian de Sola Pinto's study of the Restoration court poets is duly critical of the amateurism of "the mob of gentlemen who wrote with ease," but pays tribute to Rochester's originality and intellectual armory, and makes the topical point that the romanticism of the seventeenth century needed to be deflated no less than that of the Victorian age if poetic diction was to regain a healthy relation to common speech. The volume concludes with four essays on the leading comic dramatists of the Restoration period. The careers of Sir John Vanbrugh and George Farquhar extended into, it is true, and were influenced by the theatrical climate of the succeeding age, but on balance it is preferable to associate them with the Restoration theater than to isolate them in the eighteenth century.

The series was founded by Laurence Brander, then director of publications, at the British Council. The first editor was T. O. Beachcroft, himself a distinguished writer of short stories. His successors were the late Bonamy Dobrée, formerly Professor of English Literature at the University of Leeds; Geoffrey Bullough, Professor Emeritus of English Literature, King's College, London, and author of *The Narrative and Dramatic Sources of Shakespeare*; and since 1970 the present writer. To these founders and predecessors *British Writers* is deeply indebted for the design of the series, the planning of its scope, and the distinction of their editorship, and I personally for many years of friendship and advice, and invaluable experience, generously shared.

—Ian Scott-Kilvert

Chronological Table

1571	Defeat of the Turkish fleet at Lepanto
ca. 1572	Ben Jonson born
1572	St. Bartholomew's Day massacre
	John Donne born
1574	The earl of Leicester's theater company formed
ca. 1575	Cyril Tourneur born
1576	The Theatre, the first permanent theater building in London, opened
	The first Blackfriars Theatre opened with performances by the Children of St. Paul's
	John Marston born
1577–1580	Sir Francis Drake sails around the world
1578	Raphael Holinshed's *Chronicles*
1579	John Lyly's *Euphues: The Anatomy of Wit*
	Thomas North's translation of Plutarch's *Lives*
	John Fletcher born
ca. 1580	John Webster born
1580	Thomas Middleton born
1581	Seneca's *Ten Tragedies* translated
1582	Richard Hakluyt's *Divers Voyages Touching the Discoverie of America*
1584	Francis Beaumont born
1585	First English settlement in America, the "Lost Colony," comprising 108 men under Ralph Lane, founded at Roanoke Island, off the coast of North Carolina
ca. 1586	John Ford born
1586	Thomas Kyd's *The Spanish Tragedy*
	Christopher Marlowe's *Tamburlaine*
	The Babington conspiracy against Queen Elizabeth
	Death of Sir Philip Sidney
1587	Mary Queen of Scots executed
	Birth of Virginia Dare, first English

	child born in America, at Roanoke Island
1588	Defeat of the Spanish Armada
	Marlowe's *Dr. Faustus*
1590	Edmund Spenser's *The Faerie Queen*, Cantos I-III
1591	Robert Herrick born
1593	Death of Christopher Marlowe
	George Herbert born
	Izaak Walton born
1594	The Lord Chamberlain's Men, the company to which Shakespeare belonged, founded
	The Swan Theatre opened
	Death of Thomas Kyd
ca. 1595	Thomas Carew born
1595	Ralegh's expedition to Guiana
1596	The second Blackfriars Theatre opened
ca. 1597	Death of George Peele
1597	Bacon's first collection of *Essays*
1598	Jonson's *Every Man in His Humour*
	The Edict of Nantes
1599	The Globe Theatre opened
	Death of Edmund Spenser
1600	Death of Richard Hooker
1601	Rebellion and execution of the earl of Essex
1602	The Bodleian Library reopened at Oxford; the Stationers' Company agrees to present a copy of every book printed
	Shakespeare's *Hamlet*
1603	John Florio's translation of Montaigne's *Essays*
	Death of Elizabeth I
1603–1625	**Reign of James I**
1604	Shakespeare's *Othello*
ca. 1605	Shakespeare's *King Lear*
	Tourneur's *The Revenger's Tragedy*
1605	Bacon's *Advancement of Learning*

Cromwell is offered and declines the crown

Death of Richard Lovelace

1658 Death of Oliver Cromwell

Richard Cromwell succeeds as Protector

1659 Conflict between Parliament and the army

1660 General Monck negotiates with Charles II

Charles II offers the conciliatory Declaration of Breda and accepts Parliament's invitation to return

Will's Coffee House established

Sir William Davenant and Thomas Killigrew licensed to set up two companies of players, the Duke of York's and the King's Servants, including actors and actresses

Pepys's *Diary* begun

1660–1685 **Reign of Charles II**

1661 Parliament passes the Act of Uniformity, enjoining the use of the Book of Common Prayer; many Puritan and dissenting clergy leave their livings

1662 Peace Treaty with Spain

King Charles II marries Catherine of Braganza

The Royal Society incorporated (founded in 1660)

1664 War against Holland

New Amsterdam captured and becomes New York

John Vanbrugh born

1665 The Great Plague

Newton discovers the binomial theorem and the integral and differential calculus, at Cambridge

1666 The Great Fire of London

Bunyan's *Grace Abounding*

London Gazette founded

1667 The Dutch fleet sails up the Medway and burns English ships

The war with Holland ended by the Treaty of Breda

Milton's *Paradise Lost*

Thomas Sprat's *History of the Royal Society*

Death of Abraham Cowley

1668 Sir Christopher Wren begins to rebuild St. Paul's Cathedral

Triple Alliance formed with Holland and Sweden against France

Dryden's *Essay of Dramatick Poesy*

1670 Alliance formed with France through the secret Treaty of Dover

Pascal's *Pensées*

The Hudson's Bay Company founded

William Congreve born

1671 Milton's *Samson Agonistes* and *Paradise Regained*

1672 War against Holland

Wycherley's *The Country Wife*

King Charles issues the Declaration of Indulgence, suspending penal laws against Nonconformists and Catholics

1673 Parliament passes the Test Act, making acceptance of the doctrines of the Church of England a condition for holding public office

1674 War with Holland ended by the Treaty of Westminster

Deaths of John Milton, Robert Herrick, and Thomas Traherne

1676 Etherege's *The Man of Mode*

1677 Baruch Spinoza's *Ethics*

Jean Racine's *Phèdre*

King Charles's niece, Mary, marries her cousin William of Orange

1678 Fabrication of the so-called popish plot by Titus Oates

Bunyan's *Pilgrim's Progress*

Dryden's *All for Love*

Death of Andrew Marvell

George Farquhar born

1679 Parliament passes the Habeas Corpus Act

Rochester's *A Satire Against Mankind*

1680 Death of John Wilmot, earl of Rochester

1681 Dryden's *Absalom and Achitophel* (part I)

1682 Dryden's *Absalom and Achitophel* (part II)

Thomas Otway's *Venice Preserv'd*

Philadelphia founded

Death of Sir Thomas Browne

1683 The Ashmolean Museum, the world's first public museum, opens at Oxford

Death of Izaak Walton

CHRONOLOGICAL TABLE

1685–1688 Reign of James II
1685 Rebellion and execution of the duke of Monmouth
1686 The first book of Newton's *Principia—De motu corporum*, containing his theory of gravitation—presented to the Royal Society
1687 Dryden's *The Hind and the Panther*
King James issues the Declaration of Indulgence
Death of Edmund Waller
1688 King James reissues the Declaration of Indulgence, renewing freedom of worship and suspending the provisions of the Test Act
Acquittal of the seven bishops imprisoned for protesting against the Declaration
William of Orange lands at Torbay, Devon
King James takes refuge in France
Death of John Bunyan
1689 Parliament formulates the Declaration of Rights
William and Mary accept the Declaration and the crown
The Grand Alliance concluded between the Holy Roman Empire, England, Holland, and Spain
War declared against France
1689–1702 Reign of William III
1690 James II lands in Ireland with French support, but is defeated at the battle of the Boyne

John Locke's *Essay Concerning Human Understanding*
1692 Salem witchcraft trials
Death of Sir George Etherege
1694 George Fox's *Journal*
Death of Mary II
1695 Congreve's *Love for Love*
Death of Henry Vaughan
1697 Vanbrugh's *The Relapse*
War with France ended by the Treaty of Ryswick
1698 Jeremy Collier's *A Short View of the Immorality and Profaneness of the English Stage*
1700 Congreve's *The Way of the World*
Death of John Dryden
1701 War of the Spanish succession
Death of Sir Charles Sedley
1702–1714 Reign of Queen Anne
1702–1704 Clarendon's *History of the Rebellion*
1703 Death of Samuel Pepys
1706 Farquhar's *The Recruiting Officer*
Deaths of John Evelyn and Charles Sackville, earl of Dorset
1707 Farquhar's *The Beaux' Stratagem*
Act of Union joining England and Scotland
Death of George Farquhar
1709 Benjamin Franklin born
1714–1727 Reign of George I
1716 Death of William Wycherley
1726 Death of Sir John Vanbrugh
1727–1760 Reign of George II
1729 Death of William Congreve

List of Contributors

MARGARET BOTTRALL. Formerly Lecturer, Faculty of Education, University of Cambridge. Publications include *George Herbert* and *Every Man a Phoenix: Studies in Seventeenth Century Autobiography*. **Izaak Walton.**

BONAMY DOBRÉE. Professor of English, University of Leeds (1936–1955). Formerly General Editor (with Douglas Bush) of the *Oxford History of English Literature*. Publications include *Restoration Comedy*; *Restoration Tragedy*; *The Lamp and the Lute*; *Variety of Ways*; *English Literature in the Early Eighteenth Century*, vol. VII of the *Oxford History of English Literature*. **John Dryden; William Congreve.**

THOMAS STEARNS ELIOT, O.M. Winner of the Nobel Prize for Literature, 1948. Critical works include *Homage to John Dryden*; *The Use of Poetry and the Use of Criticism*; *Elizabethan Essays*; and *Selected Essays (1917–1932)*. **George Herbert.**

ALBERT JOHN FARMER. Formerly Professor of English Literature, University of Grenoble, University of Bordeaux, and the University of Paris at the Sorbonne. Publications include *Walter Pater as a Critic of English Literature* and *Le Mouvement Aesthetique en Angleterre (1873–1900)*. **George Farquhar.**

IAN FLETCHER. Professor of English Literature, University of Reading. Publications include *Romantic Mythologies*; *The Decadent Movement of the 1890's*; essays on W. B. Yeats and his circle; and an edition of *The Poems of Lionel Johnson*. **Francis Beaumont and John Fletcher.**

REGINALD ANTHONY FOAKES. Professor of English, University of Kent. Publications include *Shake-speare: From the Dark Comedies to the Last Plays*; and editions of *The Comedy of Errors*; *Henry VIII*; *Much Ado About Nothing*; *The Revenger's Tragedy*; and *Henslowe's Diary* (with R. T. Rickert). **John Marston and Cyril Tourneur.**

PETER MORRIS GREEN. Professor of Classics, University of Texas at Austin. Publications include *The Sword of Pleasure* (novel); *Kenneth Grahame*; *Essays in Antiquity*; and *Alexander of Macedon*. **Sir Thomas Browne.**

BERNARD ALOYSIUS HARRIS. Professor of English, University of York; Provost of Goodricke College. Editor (with John Russell Brown) of *Stratford-upon-Avon Studies*, vols. I–X, and *Stratford-upon-Avon Library*, vols. I–VI. Editor of James Shirley's *Cupid and Death*, vol. II of *Musica Britannica* (1965). Associate Editor of *The New Cambridge Shakespeare*. **Sir John Vanbrugh.**

CLIFFORD LEECH. Professor of English Literature, University of Toronto (1963–1974); Visiting Professor, University of Connecticut (1974–1975). General Editor of the Revels Plays series (1958–1970). Publications include *Shakespeare's Tragedies and Other Studies in Seventeenth-Century Drama*; *John Webster: A Critical Study*; and *John Ford and the Drama of His Time*. **John Ford.**

JAMES RONALD MULRYNE. Professor of English, University of Warwick. General Editor of the Revels Plays series. Publications include books and articles on Shakespeare, Thomas Middleton, John Webster, and W. B. Yeats; and editions of Thomas Kyd's *The Spanish Tragedy*; John Webster's *The White Devil*; and Thomas Middleton's *Women Beware Women*. **Thomas Middleton.**

VIVIAN DE SOLA PINTO. Professor of English, University of Nottingham. (1938–1961). Publications include *Enthusiast in Wit: A Portrait of John Wilmot, Earl of Rochester; Crisis in English Poetry, 1880–1940*; and editions of *Poems by John Wilmot, Earl of Rochester* and *Poetic and Dramatic Works of Sir Charles Sedley*. **The Restoration Court Poets.**

JOHN PRESS. Literature Adviser, the British Council. Publications include *The Fire and the Fountain; The Chequer'd Shade; Rule and Energy; A Map of Modern English Verse; The Lengthening Shadows; Uncertainties; Guy Fawkes' Night*; and *Aspects of Paris* (poetry). **Robert Herrick; Andrew Marvell.**

IAN STANLEY SCOTT-KILVERT. Director of Publications, Recorded Sound, and Literature Departments, the British Council (1962–1977). Publications include *A. E. Housman*; and translations of *The Rise and Fall of Athens; Makers of Rome; The Age of Alexander* (Plutarch's *Lives*); and *The Rise of the Roman Empire* (Polybius' *Histories*). **John Webster.**

ROBIN SKELTON. Professor of Creative Writing, University of Victoria, British Columbia. Publications include *Poetic Pattern; The Practice of Poetry; The Writings of J. M. Synge; Patmos, and Other Poems; Country Songs*; and *Hunting Dark* (poetry). Editor (with David R. Clark) of *The Irish Renaissance*. **The Cavalier Poets.**

HENRI A. TALON. Formerly Professor of English, University of Dijon. Publications include *Studies in Milton; The Miltonic Setting; The English Epic and Its Background; The Epic Strain in the English Novel; Shakespeare's History Plays*; and editions of "Comus" and *Paradise Lost*. **John Milton; John Bunyan.**

PAUL FRANK VERNON. Reader in English, Punjab University, Chandigarh, India (1960–1962); Lecturer in English, King's College, London (1962–1969). Publications include "Marriage of Convenience and the Moral Code of Restoration Comedy"; "Wycherley's First Comedy and Its Spanish Source"; and an edition of Nathaniel Lee's *The Rival Queens*. **William Wycherley.**

MARGARET ELIZABETH WILLY. Lecturer in English, Goldsmith's College, University of London (1959–1973) and Morley College, London (1973–   ). Editor of *English* (1954–1975). Publications include *Life Was Their Cry* and *The Invisible Sun: Every Star a Tongue* (poetry). Editor of *The Metaphysical Poets*. **Four Metaphysical Poets; John Evelyn and Samuel Pepys.**

BRITISH WRITERS

THOMAS MIDDLETON

(1580-1627)

J. R. Mulryne

HIS LIFE AND WORK

THOMAS MIDDLETON must be counted one of the most versatile and prolific of the seventeenth-century dramatists, writing, over a long career, comedy, tragicomedy, and tragedy for both the men's companies and the boys', and contributing masques and pageants for civic and other occasions. The two major tragedies, *The Changeling* (with William Rowley) and *Women Beware Women*, have been revived in professional productions of distinction, and there are signs that the professional theater may begin to explore the less celebrated work as well: *A Chaste Maid in Cheapside* has, deservedly, been produced with much success, and the National Theatre in London has produced *A Fair Quarrel*. Other work, especially among the citizen comedies, may well follow. In his own day Middleton attracted wide attention; above all, his political satire *A Game at Chess* excited so much public interest that it enjoyed the first recorded "run" in the history of the English stage. If Middleton's concern with social relationships, and his special insight into feminine psychology, are particularly likely to appeal to present-day audiences, his skills as a dramatic craftsman should earn him a permanent place in the theatrical repertoire.

A short introduction to Middleton confronts an immediate problem. Although the main body of the dramatist's work is known, there is no final agreement over his authorship of certain important plays, nor over the extent of his contribution to others. In the latter case, the task of separating out Middleton's work, while worth attempting, may prove ultimately insignificant. Collaboration between seventeenth-century dramatists appears sometimes to have involved one writer revising a scene already sketched out by his partner; on other occasions, two dramatists seem to have worked together so closely in devising the content and

structure of a scene that whoever wrote the final text could only with license be described as its single author. *The Changeling* and *A Fair Quarrel*, two of Middleton's acknowledged collaborations with Rowley, may have involved cooperation of this kind. Even where the two, or more, dramatists worked independently, the meaning of each scene is so bound up, for the reader or theater audience, with its context that to separate out from the rest and discuss separately what might by inference be considered Middleton's individual work would be a less than helpful exercise. I have therefore, in this introduction, discussed full-length play texts, and not only the Middleton portion of them.

Problems regarding the authorship of complete plays cannot be so conveniently avoided. Here I have adopted an unargued and only partially satisfactory solution. Except in one important case, I have taken over the attributions in David Lake's *The Canon of Thomas Middleton's Plays* (1975), the most complete study in this area. The important exception is *The Revenger's Tragedy*, a play of outstanding merit attributed to Middleton by Lake, in agreement with a number of previous scholars. In the present volume, *The Revenger's Tragedy* is discussed in R. A. Foakes's essay on Marston and Tourneur, and so analysis would be inappropriate here. Yet the question of Middleton's authorship of the play carries considerable weight in an overall assessment of his achievement, and greatly modifies a description of his career. The linguistic and statistical evidence for regarding *The Revenger's Tragedy* as Middleton's has reached impressive proportions. Many sensitive readers find it difficult, however, to reconcile their response to his known work, especially at this early point in his career (*ca.* 1606; not later than 1607), with their response to *The Revenger's Tragedy*. In my own view, the question has not been finally resolved, even now. I have therefore omitted reference to *The Revenger's*

Tragedy from the rest of this essay. This is, of course, unsatisfying. In the case of another play of uncertain attribution, I have had no such qualms. I have gladly accepted Lake's claim (shared with others) that *The Second Maiden's Tragedy* is Middleton's, and have given some pages to what seems to me a play of great theatrical vigor, and one that shows clearly many of Middleton's habits of mind and composition.

I have chosen in the following pages to discuss in detail no more than six representative plays. I have thought it helpful to list at the end of the essay the putative Middleton canon, as drawn up by Lake. The sixteen plays attributed to Middleton alone, with the ten written with other playwrights, make up in anyone's terms an impressively weighty and varied contribution to theater in English.

It is possible to reconstruct parts of Middleton's biography, and to speculate on the connections between the biography and the published work. A picture emerges of the playwright gaining firsthand acquaintance in his early years with the intricate legal disputes that later figure prominently in his comedies; of a young man repeatedly faced with the equation (or contrast) of property and affection, a theme much pondered in the plays; of one greatly concerned, like his characters, with money; and of a man stemming from the class of prosperous citizens and traders, but at least holding acquaintance with more socially elevated groups, thus informing, perhaps, the acute interest the plays take in class and power. It is also possible to speculate that the fatherless boy, brought up from the age of five, it would seem, largely in the company of women, gained in that way his noted concern with female psychology.

Middleton was christened at St. Lawrence in the Old Jewry, London, on 18 April 1580, the child of a prosperous merchant, William Middleton, "citizen and Bricklayer" of London, and his wife, Anne Snow. Just over five years later, William was buried, on 14 January 1586, leaving property and bequests to his wife and children. His widow, Anne, was prompt to remarry, linking herself within eleven months to one "Thomas Harvey of St. Dioniss," a grocer by trade, but one who had beggared himself taking part in the ill-fated expedition of Ralegh and Grenville to Roanoke Island. The following years seem to have been occupied largely by squabbles and lawsuits, sometimes of bizarre ingenuity, as stepfather, mother, and children sought to obtain control over the family money and property. Middleton and his sister Avice (or Alice) were repeatedly involved. The conflict pursued Middleton even to Oxford, and he had to return to London on at least one occasion to intervene.

Middleton subscribed at Queen's College, Oxford, on 7 April 1598, just as he reached his eighteenth birthday. Little is known of his career at the university, except that he sold some of his father's property (in June 1600) to maintain himself in funds. There is no record of his taking a degree, and we learn only a few months later, in February 1601, that "nowe he remaynethe heare in London daylie accompaninge the players." Yet his Oxford years may well have contributed importantly to the direction of his work, and not just in furnishing material for occasional play scenes. About 1603, Middleton married into a distinguished family with strong connections with Oxford, the law, and the theater. His wife was Mary Marbeck, or Morbeck, daughter of Edward Morbeck, a clerk of chancery, and niece of the provost of Oriel College, Oxford, Dr. Roger Marbecke, an author and physician. (Dr. Marbecke had shown his interest in theater by acting on stage and by allowing his lodgings to be used for work on Richard Edwards's *Palamon and Arcite*, in connection with Queen Elizabeth's visit to Oxford in 1566.) Mary Marbeck's grandfather was the famed Elizabethan musician and composer, John Merbeck; her brother was an actor, one of the Admiral's men, the company for whom some of Middleton's earliest dramatic work (now lost) was composed. The marriage produced one son, Edward, of whom we hear some twenty years later, when he was called by the Privy Council to answer in his father's stead during legal proceedings following the production of *A Game at Chess*. Although Middleton's marriage brought him acquaintance with a talented and well-connected family, it seems to have failed to bring him financial security.

Middleton's writing career began even before he reached Oxford, with the publication in 1597 of *The Wisdom of Solomon Paraphrased*, a sententious and lengthy piece of versifying, but showing application and seriousness, and to that extent anticipating work to come. The other early pieces in verse and prose demonstrate a growing ability to write satirically about contemporary moral and social abuses. *Micro-Cynicon, Six Snarling Satires* (1599) focuses on contemporary types, including the usurer and the prodigal, to whom the comedies were also to turn; *The Ghost of Lucrece* (1600) is an exercise, in response to Shakespeare's *The Rape of Lucrece*, in the outworn "Complaint" mode; *The Black Book* (1604) has again a distinctly moral-satiric purpose, dealing with the London underworld with wit and vigor; *The Ant and the Nightingale or Father Hubburd's Tales* enjoyed two editions in 1604 and gives some vivid glimpses of dissipation in contemporary London. Before the date of these last two publications, there are records of Middleton's involvement with writing for the theater. Entries for 22 and 29 May 1602 in the *Diary* or account book of Philip Henslowe, the theater owner and businessman, show Middleton receiving payment with Munday, Drayton, Dekker, and Webster for work on a play that appears to be variously known as "sesers [Caesar's] ffalle" or "too [two] shapes." Later in the same year, he was paid for work on other plays, now lost, and for a prologue and epilogue for Robert Greene's popular *Friar Bacon and Friar Bungay*. Before 14 March 1604, Middleton and Dekker received payment for work on *The Honest Whore, Part I* (Middleton's contribution to this play may not have been very extensive). A further play, *The Viper and Her Brood*, written in 1606, has since been lost.

These early, often collaborative, pieces were written mainly for Henslowe's company, the Admiral's Men; Middleton's career as a successful dramatist was securely launched when he began to write citizen comedy for the boys' companies, especially the Children of Paul's. *Michaelmas Term*, *A Mad World, My Masters*, and *A Trick to Catch the Old One*, all written for the boy players between 1604 and 1606, read like commercial pieces that might be expected to appeal to audiences closely familiar with the life of merchant-class London. The same might be said of *Your Five Gallants*. (Two collaborations with Thomas Dekker, *The Family of Love* and *The Roaring Girl*, also belong, probably, to these years.) But the children's companies declined from 1606, and by 1609 had effectively ceased playing. With them declined the popularity of citizen comedy, its place taken (to simplify a complex topic) by a new interest in tragicomedy, as written by Beaumont and Fletcher. Middleton followed the new development by writing *A Chaste Maid in Cheapside* (ca. 1613) for the Lady Elizabeth's Men, a company that seems to have incorporated one of the children's troupes; the play itself

combines elements of citizen comedy with the new interest in Fletcherian tragicomedy. From this part of Middleton's career come several other plays broadly in the same tragicomic mold: *No Wit, No Help Like a Woman's* (ca. 1611–1612), *More Dissemblers Besides Women* (ca. 1614–1615), *A Fair Quarrel* (ca. 1615–1617; with Rowley), *The Witch* (ca. 1615–1616), and *The Widow* (ca. 1616). The plays vary in depth and adroitness, but all show to greater or lesser extent the influence of Fletcher's concern with sexual emotion and the coup de theatre. The last major phase of Middleton's playwriting, the tragedies, had been anticipated by *The Second Maiden's Tragedy* (ca. 1611). *Hengist, King of Kent* (or *The Mayor of Quinborough*), a play of uneven achievement based on chronicle material and written, probably, between 1616 and 1620, leads toward the great tragedies, *Women Beware Women* (ca. 1621) and *The Changeling* (1622; with Rowley). Middleton's playwriting career closes with the opportunist *A Game at Chess* (1624), a political satire drawing directly on personalities and events from the contemporary political scene, and, by so doing, stirring up overwhelming public interest. (I have omitted from this simplified account a few lesser plays, together with controversial attributions such as *The Yorkshire Tragedy*.)

In addition to his work for the theater, Middleton contributed largely, from 1613 on, to the civic pageantry commissioned annually by the London livery companies to welcome the new lords mayor. From *The Triumphs of Truth* (1613) to *The Triumphs of Wealth and Prosperity* (1626), Middleton contrived in most years to provide material for this important city event. Other commissioned work included *Civitatis Amor* (1616), written in recognition of Prince Charles's assumption of the title of Prince of Wales, and the *Entertainment* (1613) composed for the opening of the New River, a public water system completed by Hugh Middleton during the mayoralty of the playwright's namesake, Sir Thomas Middleton. Middleton also wrote three masques (one with Rowley) and some minor occasional pieces. Perhaps in recognition of this diverse activity, he was granted in 1620 the post of chronologer to the City of London; his tasks seem to have included the preparation of a journal of public events, together with the writing of speeches and entertainments on certain occasions. It appears he carried out his duties with some thoroughness (in contrast to his successor, Ben Jonson), and the post may well have been quite a lucrative one.

Middleton was buried on 4 July 1627, at the parish church of Newington Butts, an area in which he had lived since at least 1609.

THE CITIZEN COMEDIES

MIDDLETON's first distinctive contribution to the theater came in the form of what are now known as "city" or "citizen" comedies. Jonson and Marston in particular shared with Middleton in providing the theater of the early years of the century with a dramatic genre satiric in intent, contemporary and urban in setting, cleverly plotted, spirited, and entertaining. In plays like *Volpone*, *The Alchemist*, and *Bartholomew Fair*, Jonson transformed entertainment into pungent and elaborate images of human greed. Middleton's work also takes an interest in the deceptive relationships between cleverness and power, appetite and identity, language and moral truth. There are no portraits in Middleton as richly conceived as Sir Epicure Mammon, no caricature as sustained and acid as Zeal-of-the-Land Busy; yet Sir Bounteous Progress in *A Mad World, My Masters* shares with Sir Epicure that large vanity that makes both of them memorably comic figures, and Dampit, the drunken usurer of *A Trick to Catch the Old One*, proves that on occasion Middleton can write with some acerbity. Yet, in the main, Middleton's city comedy concentrates—with notable success—not on morality but on intrigue. Few intrigues in the whole range of comedy can be as adroitly managed as the series of tricks by which Follywit robs and deceives Sir Bounteous (*A Mad World, My Masters*), or by which Master Richard Easy is coney-catched[1] (*Michaelmas Term*). Within the intrigue good acting parts abound, sharply etched and consistent (Follywit; Shortyard in *Michaelmas Term*, as active and versatile as Mosca[2]; the Host in *A Trick to Catch the Old One*); situations are often highly contrived, making considerable use of disguise (the culminating scenes in *A Mad World*, as "play" and "reality," mesh inextricably); incidental touches also offer the actor repeated comic opportunities (the Country Wench dressing up in *Michaelmas Term*, full of opportunities for comic business, yet functional too in

[1]Duped.　　[2]Servant to Volpone in Jonson's play.

relation to the play's theme of disguise and self-knowledge).

Perhaps it is in *Michaelmas Term* that Middleton best focuses his personal contribution to entertainment and social commentary. Here, in the figure of Quomodo, the woolen draper, and his group, Middleton manages to express in summary a broad sociocultural movement, as the commercial classes of London seek to displace the gentry as centers of influence and owners of land (not the universalizing of the contemporary, as in Jonson, but an adroit specifying). The play radiates authenticity, whether in what Richard Levin calls "the remarkable series of genre scenes" showing gallants parading their finery in St. Paul's or gaming in a tavern, or in the coney-catching tricks and personal portraits (the tricks may well be transcribed directly from life; Andrew Lethe, the country boy who has, precariously, made the grade in town, may allude, a little covertly, to King James's Scottish followers). But above all, Quomodo's fantasies of the good life exactly catch the note of class envy exuberantly resolved by a conviction of new power (the sexual pleasures, already his own, are intensified and transformed because they are given a new social reference):

A fine journey in the Whitsun holidays, i'faith [to his expected new land in Essex], to ride down with a number of citizens and their wives, some upon pillions, some upon sidesaddles, I and little Thomasine i' th' middle, our son and heir, Sim Quomodo, in a peach-colour taffeta jacket, some horse-length or a long yard before us—there will be a fine show on's, I can tell you—where we citizens will laugh and lie down, get all our wives with child against a bank, and get up again.

(IV. i. 70-77)

The comic detailing shows Quomodo wholly taken in by his own wish-fulfillment (he is aptly tripped up as he pursues fantasy to a point beyond his power to control it). The play is an extraordinarily adroit combination of social document and lively theater.

If *Michaelmas Term* is the most characteristic city comedy, *A Trick to Catch the Old One* is perhaps the most interesting for Middleton's development. The play relies for its plot on an inventive variation of the familiar story of the prodigal and witty young man who has wasted his fortune and now tries to recoup his position by hoodwinking his elders. Thus, Witgood, the young spendthrift, with the help of a genial Host, succeeds in passing off his mistress as a rich widow; his uncle, the avaricious Lucre, is taken in, and in expectation of advantage to himself, returns to Witgood (provisionally as he thinks) the title to his forfeited lands. In the turns and twists of the plot, Lucre's dire enemy, the equally avaricious Hoard, finds himself married to Witgood's mistress, and for the privilege is duped into paying the young man's debts; and Witgood himself succeeds in winning Joyce Hoard, and with her a fortune. A range of minor characters, including Witgood's creditors, Lucre's foolish stepson and the usurer Dampit, complicate the action.

As a theater piece, the play brims with opportunities. A kind of verve and animation radiate out from the language into character and action. Characterization throughout the play is remarkably distinct and actable, even where for economy's sake it must tend toward caricature. Hoard and Lucre emerge vividly: "Two old tough spirits, they seldom meet but fight, . . ./I think their anger be the very fire/That keeps their age alive" (I. i. 109–112). Their quarrelsomeness provides really splendid cartoon action, the pithy, pregnant vocabulary only very occasionally lapsing into the rather precious virtuosity characteristic of the boys' companies. Yet the figures do not remain flat caricatures. Lucre, in particular, is very shrewdly conceived, musing how far he may commit himself and his fortune in his newfound enthusiasm for his nephew's astuteness: Middleton allows us to glimpse, with amusement and a measure of sympathy, the "kind of usurer's love" that struggles in his mind and feelings with his avarice, his caution, and his enmity for Hoard. Hoard, too, subtly suggests a kind of innocent relish and even generosity of spirit dammed up by avarice: as he fantasizes, like Quomodo (though perhaps less gloatingly), on the display of his new wealth when he rides into the country, or as he delights in his new wife's social graces and welcomes distinguished and congenial company to his marriage feast. Neither portrait is fully developed, yet within the compass of a boy player each invites both bold and restrained playing. Even less developed are the drunken usurer Dampit and his usurer-acquaintance Gulf, who shadow Hoard and Lucre and (in Dampit, at least) exemplify how avarice damages the personality to the point where the individual loses contact with his fellows. It would be of great interest to see the part played with full seriousness, sardonically rather

than for ridicule, but the effect might be to overset the balance of the play. Yet the caricature of drunkenness and malign temper is so strong as to suggest the term Hogarthian; and the two main scenes, detachable from the action if not, in its wider sense, from the plot, are so intense as to imply both a specific contemporary target and a boy player who excelled at such cameos.

Perhaps a more interesting figure, less precisely rendered but with more potential for exploratory playing, is Witgood's mistress, the so-called Courtesan. Though her motivation is not always clear, Middleton shows here, for perhaps the first time, his interest in the concealed sources of a woman's feelings: in love with Witgood, she has given herself to him, without benefit of marriage, yet is now prepared to lose him in order to secure his financial advantage and his marriage to another woman; she even risks her own newfound prosperity to do him good. The play's convention will not allow Middleton to develop the Courtesan's inner life; but just occasionally she turns aside from the given action to complain or to consult her own feelings. We may detect an important growing point for Middleton's drama.

Our uncertainty of response toward the Courtesan reflects the characteristically complex balance of moral feeling in these citizen comedies. The bolder attitudes come across plainly enough: usury, an old man's vice, restricts life; wit and vivacity must be freed and their excesses pardoned; folly (Lucre has a foolish stepson) must not marry beauty and sensitivity. More difficult to accept comfortably is the simple assumption, everywhere, that rich marriage is a good to be striven for: so that we must find ourselves approving the marriage of the Courtesan to the foolish old usurer Hoard—not because, as Lucre thinks, it serves Hoard right to marry a whore, but because we must think the Courtesan, a sympathetic figure throughout, well served by her marriage. At the end, we experience her rhymed repentance and that of Witgood not so much as an improbability or an insincerity, nor even as the sort of recantation appropriate to a play written for the boys' companies, but simply as further plot development, a kind of coda, excusable because rarely in the play have moral problems taxed us seriously, and the spirit of fun has predominated. Yet the more serious possibilities are there, and Middleton will consider them in later work.

THOMAS MIDDLETON

A CHASTE MAID IN CHEAPSIDE

A Chaste Maid in Cheapside marks, in Brian Parker's phrase, a watershed among Middleton's plays. First performed, it seems likely, in 1613 by a combined company of adult and boy actors, the play draws on much of Middleton's experience as a writer of citizen comedy, and looks forward to the techniques and interests of the tragicomedies and tragedies. Introducing us, as the play begins, to "the heart of the city of London," Middleton again investigates, with the effect of knowledge at first hand, the life and outlook of people of the merchant class. Again, the stance is satiric, the technique related to caricature, but this time the writing displays an emotional force not evident in the earlier comedies. Some readers (like some among the audiences at William Gaskill's 1966 revival) may find the play distasteful; some may find weak areas in motivation or plotting, such as Sir Walter's repentance, or the theatrical surprise that conveniently ties up the chief love interest; it may even be felt that Middleton sometimes confuses us as to how we should bestow our sympathies (in Touchwood Senior's activities, for example). Yet, even if these views are accepted, *A Chaste Maid* comes over as a powerful piece of theater in which deep sources of feeling are touched, both personal and more widely shared. The play's gusto and seriousness, combined, make it one of theater's richest statements on money, sex, and society.

A Chaste Maid concerns the intricately related affairs of four family groups: the goldsmith Yellowhammer and his wife Maudline, their children Moll (or Mary) and Tim; Allwit and his wife, with the bastards Wat and Nick; Touchwood Senior and his wife; Sir Oliver and Lady Kix. All are in some way affected by the activities of Sir Walter Whorehound: heir to Sir Oliver Kix (whose marriage is barren), he seeks to marry Moll Yellowhammer (for her money) and to find in Tim Yellowhammer a husband for his whore; meanwhile, he begets children on Mrs. Allwit, with the ready connivance of her husband, who thereby escapes the cares and costs of family life; he loses his position as heir when Touchwood Senior, promiscuously fertile, begets a child on Lady Kix. The remaining important character is Touchwood Junior, in love with Moll (and she with him). The set of relationships here established allows Middleton to portray a remarkable range of sexual feeling, to involve his characters in complex, ironic situations (through blindness, hypocrisy, and folly), and to explore with characteristic insight the adjustments of language and tone that come with the social pretensions of the Yellowhammers, or the delicate and unusual relationship Allwit bears to his benefactor Sir Walter Whorehound. Above all, it allows Middleton to show sexual impulse expressing itself without restraints, except for those exerted by social and commercial competitiveness.

The play's most noted scene (Act III, scene ii) stages the christening feast for Mrs. Allwit's child. As a festive event, the episode draws together much of the play's society to celebrate fertility and procreation. Yet, the comic release associated with festivity is qualified by considerations of a moral kind (the child is a bastard, fathered by Sir Walter Whorehound) and by language that refers again and again to physical processes, often of a gross or immodest character. Sweetmeats are gobbled down greedily or pocketed (there are strong phallic associations in this greedy eating); the Puritan gossips in particular are soused in the flood of drink that "pours down" "to wet the gossips'[3] whistles" (one is grossly drunk and "reels and falls" as the scene progresses). At centerstage, Mrs. Allwit lies in bed, recently delivered, we hear, of "a large child," though herself "but a little woman." It is as though Middleton wished to express by word and action this society's values: the christening feast represents a social ritual, the reception into society of a new member; and this is what they make of it. These bourgeois saturnalia end in disarray; as stage action has expressed the greedy egotism and self-indulgence of these people, so the final stage picture expresses their chaotic physicality: Allwit draws attention to the "Fair needlework stools" scattered about the stage, stools laid "E'en as they lie themselves, with their heels up!" and to the rushes on the floor "shuffled up. . . . With their short figging little shittle-cork-heels." Yet this disorder should not be thought of in morality terms only. The scene celebrates the birth of a fair and lusty child, "a chopping girl"; we saw in an earlier scene Allwit's splendidly un-self-conscious delight in her. The christening feast is made possible by the generosity of Sir Walter Whorehound, a sort of Sir Bounteous Progress of sexual activity, begetting children on another man's wife and paying gener-

[3]Godparents.

6

ously for their keep (symbolically, his christening gift takes the phallic shape of "a fair high standing-cup/And two great 'postle-spoons, one of them gilt!"). Middleton's geniality conflates with disapproval and distaste in an expressive tension characteristic of his work and brought to strong focus in the high spirits and disorder of this marvellously theatrical scene.

Among those introduced into the christening scene are the unfortunate Tim Yellowhammer and his Cambridge tutor. The social pretensions of Yellowhammer and his wife provide a focus for the play complementary to that of Sir Walter Whorehound and the Allwits (the romantic attachment of Touchwood Junior and Moll, though important as narrative, and providing a climactic coup de theatre, is less strongly presented). Middleton's enjoyment, as well as shrewd insight, is evident in the portrayal of these rich but socially and culturally limited people: overvaluing "education" as a social advantage, the Yellowhammers nevertheless expose the emptiness of Tim's Latin learning; taken in by Sir Walter's aristocratic title and his claims to landed wealth, they end up marrying their son to his whore. Yet there is a darker side than social vanity, merely, to the portrait of Maudline in particular. Both her children, Moll and Tim, are shown as "bashful" and "shamefaced" in sexual matters; her sexual bullying of them (both are forced in the direction of relationships they dislike; Moll is haled back by the hair from one she chooses) is coupled in Maudline with a salacious interest in her children's sexual affairs (Sir Walter, who has been chosen for Moll, has, she says, "A brave court-spirit makes our virgins quiver/And kiss with trembling thighs"). An actress could well develop a rich stage portrait. Maudline and her husband display the self-concern underlying their professed wish for their children's advancement when, on hearing of Moll's apparent death, they think first of their neighbors' reaction ("All the whole street will hate us") and decide to absent themselves from her burial—though only after "we have given order for the funeral" (the merchant's business sense evident here). Tim's entrance into the christening feast exposes him to acute embarrassment: the gossips smother him with attentions ("O this is horrible,/She wets as she kisses!"; "This is intolerable!/This woman has a villainous sweet breath,/Did she not stink of comfits"). His mother threatens him with whipping, and reminds him of an occasion in the past when he was whipped "at the free-school/in Paul's church-yard"; the social embarrassment caused by the threat is evidenced in the pathetic contemporary story of the twenty-year-old son of the bishop of Bristol, who "killed himself with a knife to avoid the disgrace of breeching." The play's interest in personal and social adjustment is given a very vivid and individual dramatic expression in the treatment of the Yellowhammer family.

A concern with physicality and its relationship to sex and to forms of human order (especially marriage) distinguishes the play throughout. Middleton sets up contrasts and parallels that touch on some of the most sensitive areas of human experience. Sir Oliver and Lady Kix (the name means "dry") have for seven years shared a childless marriage; Sir Oliver is perhaps impotent, but certainly sterile. The remedy he tries, characteristically for this play, involves both farce (five hours of riding a white mare, and various athletic feats, after drinking a "certain water") and irony (when he thinks he has begotten a child he gleefully congratulates himself on his powers, and promises the adulterer "Get children, and I'll keep them"—a new Allwit situation, though he doesn't know it). Yet Lady Kix's suffering over her lack of children is not altogether mocked (though, in Middleton's sardonic way, it is alleged that she has borne bastards elsewhere); nor is the portrait of the brittle and unpredictable relationship between Sir Oliver and his wife wholly unsympathetic. Touchwood Senior is helplessly prolific, where Sir Oliver is sterile; country wenches suffer from his prowess ("every harvest I shall hinder hay-making"); one follows him to town with his bastard (or so she persuades him). It is he who "cures" Sir Oliver by getting children on Lady Kix; not only does this make safe his own financial future and disinherit Sir Walter (the links between money and children are sketched in again and again), it makes possible his own family life, supported by Sir Oliver. Allwit inverts the received truths about family harmony in the most astonishing way. As a contented cuckold, he lives a perfectly well-adjusted life, both toward his wife and family and toward matters of money and property. His coolness over his moral position invites both laughter and amazement; his servility before Sir Walter cloaks derision, as he manipulates the other's lust and (surprisingly perhaps) jealousy to his own advantage; when Sir Walter becomes of no further use as a patron, Allwit and his wife close ranks and throw him out with staggering effrontery ("Cannot our house be private to ourselves/But we must have such guests?"). It is as if this dense and rich play were just reined in, by its own temper and by the busy-ness of its intrigue, from exploring relationships of a most painful kind. To some, the geniality will seem forced. It is not surprising that several critics think of the brilliant cameo of the two "Promoters" as representative of the whole play: "pricking up their ears/And snuffing up their noses, like rich men's dogs/When the first course goes in" as they wait to detect illicit traffic in meat during Lent. But the meat they find, in the end, under "A good fat loin of mutton," and construed successively as a quarter of lamb, a shoulder of mutton, a loin of veal, and a lamb's head, is, in fact, a human child.

The fifth act of the play represents something of a theatrical tour de force, blending caustic and unexpected reversals with emotionally-heightened theater that reminds one of Fletcher (yet always qualified by Middleton's wit). A sardonic first scene shows Sir Walter, wounded in a skirmish with Touchwood Junior, turning deathbed moralist and heaping abusive strictures on his erstwhile liaison with Mistress Allwit; the Allwits, at first doing everything to repair the relationship, come to recognize that Sir Walter has nothing more to give and coldly banish him from their house, planning instead to set up fashionably in the Strand, surrounded by the furniture derived from years of Sir Walter's bounty. Thus Middleton dramatizes the realities underlying the absurdly sunny veneer of the Allwit and Sir Walter menage: conscience and self-interest both declare themselves boldly, as Sir Walter reviews his life and is seized by the terrors of death and damnation; and Allwit, once a lighthearted *mari complaisant*, is revealed as a Tartuffe, a coldhearted manipulator. The dramatic tone is subtly and daringly judged, as the audience's mood is suspended between laughter and shock. In another emotionally complicated action, the apparent deaths of Moll and Touchwood Junior lead to a mock funeral, elaborately staged and an occasion of considerable sentiment, both of a lachrymose and, when the young couple revive, a genial character. The threatened sentimentality is qualified not only by the audience's broader knowledge of events, but also by Middleton's quicksilver varying of focus, as the playing touches in the range of motive and sensibility among all those onstage, and as the complicated plot resolves itself. Such freedom of invention and depth of character perception, over a range of dramatis personae, distinguishes *A Chaste Maid* from the earlier comedies, and ensures its theatrical vitality: a richly conceived and densely particular play made buoyant by the dramatist's skilled manipulation of audience response over a wide emotional area.

THE TRAGEDIES

MIDDLETON's reputation as a writer of tragedy rests chiefly on the great plays of the 1620's, *Women Beware Women* and *The Changeling*. Yet *The Second Maiden's Tragedy*, licensed in 1611, claims attention both in its own right and as an important indicator of its author's developing skills (though anonymously written, it is now widely accepted as Middleton's.) For one thing, *The Second Maiden's Tragedy* brings us closer to the stage life of Middleton's work than any other of his plays; the one surviving early text appears to be the prompt book used by the King's Men (Shakespeare's company) for their 1611 production. We can therefore in places recreate the theatrical life of the play with some vividness. Of great interest, too, is Middleton's response to literary and dramatic fashion; *The Second Maiden's Tragedy* drew for some of its effects on the currently popular tragicomic mode associated with Fletcher. But Middleton's play, while certainly in the popular sense "theatrical," qualifies the sensationalism and moral vacuousness of tragicomedy both by its shrewd character insights and by its serious moral commentary. The play predicts, too, that remarkable variety of styles that in the greater plays fused into a powerful theater language: in *The Second Maiden's Tragedy* symbolic action mingles with naturalism, grandiloquent writing with plain, ironic patterning that offers moments of intense insight into character. It would be wrong to see *The Second Maiden's Tragedy* as a fully achieved play—there is a certain overearnestness and predictability about its temper and plot—yet it would be wrong, too, to neglect its achievements.

It is usual to say that the tragedy's subplot is more strongly conceived than its main action. Certainly, the most compelling character insights are found there (despite the improbabilities and complications of the narrative). For example, Middleton prepares very subtly the growing sexual attraction between the Wife and Votarius. (In the subplot narrative, Anselmus, uncertain of his wife's fidelity, invites Votarius to attempt her seduction). One speech in particular obliquely and very adroitly illuminates the Wife's sense of neglect, her hurt pride and longing for notice, and her (undeclared, unrecognized) sexual availability, implicit in the terms she uses:

> I want his [her husband's] company.
> He walks at midnight in thick shady woods
> Where scarce the moon is starlight. I have watched him
> In silver nights when all the earth was dressed
> Up like a virgin in white innocent beams;
> Stood in my window, cold and thinly clad,
> T'observe him through the bounty of the moon
> That liberally bestowed her graces on me.
> And when the morning dew began to fall,
> Then was my time to weep. 'Has lost his kindness,
> Forgot the way of wedlock, and become
> A stranger to the joys and rites of love.
> He's not so good as a lord ought to be;
> Pray tell him so from me, sir.
>
> (I. ii. 98–111)

Both the Wife and Votarius are at this point innocent of sexual feeling toward each other; but this speech is enough to light a spark of sexual interest in Votarius, and to inform the audience of the Wife's emotional nature. Middleton follows up this first insight with precise acting opportunities: Votarius is a little too vehement in the Wife's defense when Anselmus returns; he is given broken speeches and exclamations to convey his new unease; he begins to perceive emotional self-division in himself and to see the equivocal nature of his role as pretended tempter of the Wife's honor. Gradually, bawdy talk begins to infiltrate the exchanges, and the line becomes blurred between Votarius' assumed role and his genuine feelings. Both he and the Wife recognize they are emotionally ensnared, and have some success in shaking off the entanglement; but they soon recognize they are too deeply committed to be open to reason and propriety. Middleton gives the Wife a subtly written exchange (I. ii. 258–290) to convey her state of mind: she turns impatiently on her servant Leonella, thus solacing her own guilt; the unrest in her feelings makes her talk of buying and selling a woman's honor; the air of abstraction that renders her forgetful of what she has just said consorts with her woman's need to

hide her love, yet reveal it too. Leonella rightly distinguishes the tide of emotion against which her mistress is powerless:

> Life, have I power or means to stop a sluice
> At a high water?
>
> (I. ii. 287–288)

Middleton's dramatization of the emotions of his characters in the subplot does not again reach this level of precision and delicacy; he becomes preoccupied with intrigue and with ironic effects (though the gradual hardening of the Wife's sensibility, and that of Votarius, is persuasively handled). This one scene indicates the developing skills of the dramatist who later contributed to the creation of Beatrice and De Flores in *The Changeling*.

The main plot of *The Second Maiden's Tragedy* complements the secondary plot in dealing with a woman (the Lady) who, despite assaults on her virtue by the usurping king (the Tyrant) and by her father (Helvetius), remains faithful to her chosen lord, Govianus, the rightful king. As the personal names suggest, this plot shares a good deal with the morality play, and with homiletic writing in general; a number of incidents, it has been shown, derive directly from such traditional sources as the lives of the saints. For a sympathetic audience, therefore, much of the enjoyment arises from confirmation of attitudes and beliefs already held. So in the first scene, for example, the Tyrant on a high platform or throne demands the Lady's love, but she, upon entering, prefers to bestow it on Govianus, who stands, deposed, on a lower stage level. The moral truths are familiar ones: goodness is more important than greatness; power does not necessarily confer peace of mind. An audience accustomed to pageant drama, masques, and various forms of allegory and emblem would respond readily to these meanings; they would also appreciate the propriety of Middleton's inserting into this framework allusions to the court of King James, where the nobility is "mightier" and their "styles" are "heavier" than in the previous reign, but where learning has diminished and avarice increased (I. i. 76–98).

Such an audience might even feel no incongruity with the introduction into this scene of the cheerful wittol[4] Sophonirus, a figure more apt, perhaps, to the citizen comedies, and one much developed

[4]Acquiescent cuckold.

within a year or two into Allwit in *A Chaste Maid*. Yet, Sophonirus may represent the immaturity that marks this play. His situation as wittol fits naturally into the play's themes, but the narrative structure fails to support the parallels and contrasts; the cheeky shallowness of his language often sorts oddly with the elevated diction and interests of others—as though Middleton's experience as playwright did not yet fit him to maintain a consistent tone.

But, despite the immaturity and awkwardness, there are notable achievements within the main plot. The sudden conversion of Helvetius, from tempter of his daughter's honor to man of principle, has been much criticized; yet Govianus' speech to him (II. i. 111–153) on the immorality of thinking "greatness" the prime object of life is a powerful one, and likely, perhaps, to be persuasive to a man caught in a shameful attempt to prostitute his own daughter for gain. So that even on realistic grounds, the event may not be implausible. Yet Middleton is not concerned here, in this plot, or not principally, to go beyond homily into the complexities and contradictions of personal feeling. And when the action reaches a crisis, and so renders emotion simple, the dramatic experience can be intensely rendered. One such occasion takes place when the Tyrant sends his men to lay siege, finally, to the Lady's virtue. Even today, we are readily conscious of the literary and dramatic analogues to this besetting of virtue; to a Jacobean audience they would have been much more vivid. The knocking on the stage doors, repeated at least five times, and obviously violent (a stage direction reads "*A great knocking again*"), sharply increases the theatricality of the occasion, embodying in sound and stage action the threat to the Lady's virtue. We may well think that Middleton enters the realms of melodrama, exploiting the situation for pathos; we may think he accedes too readily to the stereotype of the Lady killing herself to preserve her honor (yet the Lucrece stereotype is culturally a very powerful one); and we may think he exaggerates both action (Govianus faints as he attempts to kill the Lady) and words. Yet the scene, given a strong production, must be powerfully effective; and it would be difficult to remain indifferent to the pathos of the Lady's self-description:

> I have prepared myself for rest and silence
> And took my leave of words.
>
> (III. i. 133–134)

It may be more difficult to respond appropriately to the final scenes of the main plot, the tone and content of which are evidently much influenced by Fletcherian melodrama. The Tyrant, cheated of the Lady alive, exhumes her body, and has it "painted" by an artist (Govianus in disguise) to simulate life. Dark lanterns, stealthy movement, and haunting songs cooperate with the soldiers' nervousness as the tomb is opened up, to evoke a highly atmospheric stage situation. The Lady's spirit introduces a supernatural dimension to complement the eeriness of the terrestrial action. The staginess of all this can be accused of being gratuitous sensationalism; or it can be seen as a theatrical statement of the Tyrant's imbalance; or, in a complementary way, it can be said to state, very vividly, the moral commonplaces about the folly of valuing too highly beauty that is merely skin deep. Certainly, there are memorable insights into the deranged mind; and there are stage moments of great power, as the tomb is violated, or the lady's body in its pallor ("She's only pale, the colour of the court,/And most attractive") is contemplated by the fascinated Tyrant (IV. iii. 64–65). These scenes offer remarkable challenges and opportunities to the director, and in the modern theater to the designer; challenges of taste and tact. What emerges most expressively from the stage directions is how seriously the author himself took the pictorial values of these final scenes; for example, from the direction:

> *They bring the body in a chair, dressed up in black velvet which sets out the paleness of the hands and face, and a fair chain of pearl 'cross her breast, and the crucifix above it.*
>
> (V. ii. 13. 1–3)

A more robust piece of stage action is suggested by an earlier direction:

> [*On a sudden, in a kind of noise like a wind, the doors clattering, the tombstone flies open, and a great light appears in the midst of the tomb; his LADY, as went out, standing just before him all in white, stuck with jewels, and a great crucifix on her breast.*]
>
> (IV. iv. 42. 1–4)

A first-class production could explore the effectiveness and the acceptability of such theater writing as this.

Women Beware Women, Middleton's major unassisted tragedy, shows many of the interests, and the skills, first developed in tragicomedy and comedy. Although the play is based on Italian history, supplemented by French romance, the primary sources of feeling are shared with the London comedies. The riches and the glamour of an Italian dukedom are there as contrast to the lives of those in humbler circumstances—the play emphasizes the power of money and social rank—yet the Italianate tradition of Jacobean drama, stressing violence of action and language, is scarcely called on. In its place Middleton offers a spare, austere idiom within an action tightly controlled and richly ironic. Considered structurally, the play offers a most dexterous patterning of similar and contrasted intrigues, focusing on relationship and marriage. It is easy to enjoy the ironic dexterity with which Middleton develops his characters' lives, leading them in ignorance, whether imposed or self-chosen, toward the final masque. It is also easy to relish the cool wit he displays in laying bare the moral self-deceptions and evasions of most of the play's characters. Yet our enjoyment of Middleton's structural skill, and his moral seriousness, should not blind us to the individual life so many of the characters assume, nor to the fullness and density of the milieux they inhabit: the play lives fully on the stage, drawing us into the emotional situations the characters experience, as well as alerting us to the larger design in which they play their parts. It might be said, indeed, that the major achievement of *Women Beware Women* lies in the integrity of the moral and social analysis with the individual lives involved: a tragedy of guilt, not of chance or prejudice.

The tragedy's main plot deals with the life history of Bianca Cappello, a rich Venetian girl who has eloped with and married a struggling Florentine merchant called Leantio; in the course of the play she meets Duke Francesco of Florence, becomes his mistress, and then, after Leantio's murder, his wife. Middleton uses the story to explore the tensions of personality, wealth, and rank inherent in the initial, runaway marriage, and the consequences for Leantio's outlook and behavior, as well as Bianca's, of the duke's intervention. Even in the first scene, the playwright economically dramatizes the difficulties beneath the surface of Leantio's marriage with Bianca. In a tragedy much occupied with relationships, Bianca begins as an outsider attached to her new society by the single, brittle link of her marriage. Her silence in this opening scene is the silence of a woman cautiously observing her new world; as the child of a rich house, the poverty of her surroundings, to which Middleton draws attention, is unfamiliar; as a Venetian, she comes a stranger to the alien society of Florence. Even the structure of the scene, beginning with a long and familiar exchange between mother and son, emphasizes Bianca's apartness in contrast with their intimacy. And Bianca, as the dialogue stresses, is an emotional novice in the state of marriage; of the sincerity of her affection for Leantio, there can be no doubt, and she appears prepared to commit herself fully to her new home:

> I have forsook friends, fortunes, and my country,
> And hourly I rejoice in 't: here's my friends,
> And few is the good number
>
> . . .
>
> I'll call this place the place of my birth now,
> And rightly too: for here my love was born,
> And that's the birth-day of a woman's joys.
>   (I. i. 131–133, 139–141)

Yet that commitment, we see, depends for its truth on her relationship with Leantio; and he seems ill-fitted to offer a response. Where Bianca is vulnerable, Leantio is sententious and priggish; preoccupied with money matters, he tries to conceal from his new wife the real state of his mother's household affairs. While they meet at a sensual level, it seems improbable they will have a great deal else to share; Bianca is only just offstage when Leantio begins to think of her as a jewel to be "cased up from all men's eyes"; his pleasure in her is connected with his merchant's petit bourgeois pride in securing a possession more dazzling than all his competitors. As the portrait develops, we understand how fully Leantio is the product of Middleton's practiced knowledge of merchant-class values. After Bianca's loss, he expresses his sorrow with real feeling (the portrait is not simple caricature); the tendency to moralistic analogy is countered by the emotion of his reply to Livia:

> *Livia*   That deep sigh went but for a strumpet, sir.
> *Leantio*   It can go for no other that loves me.
>   (III. iii. 309–310)

Yet underlying this, and underlying, too, his bitter scorn for the seducer Francesco, is a set of values that allows him to accept the seducer's gifts (while shrewdly assessing his bribe as worth very little) and one that makes clearly understandable his eventual acceptance of Livia's proffered "love":

Livia Do but you love enough, I'll give enough.
Leantio Troth then, I'll love enough, and take enough.
Livia Then we are both pleased enough.
(III. iii. 374–376)

There is a sense in which the separation of Bianca and Leantio is not only humanly understandable, but also just: Leantio's values predicate that the richest man should have the brightest jewel. Out of such ironies Middleton constructs a tragedy that is both sardonic and humanly knowing.

For Bianca, the new position of mistress to the duke means removal from the status of a hidden possession to that of a treasure on display: from merchant-class values to those of the aristocracy. Middleton scarcely troubles to make convincing her change of manner—from self-effacing girl to confident, articulate woman of society. Partly this stems from dramatic compression; in the sources, Bianca has some years to grow into her new role. But partly it is due to Middleton's concern in the play with the effect of social environment and social rank on a character's values and behavior. Certainly, the Mother recognizes at once the new incompatibility between Bianca and her bourgeois surroundings:

She's no more like the gentlewoman at first
Than I am like her that never lay with man yet;
And she's a very young thing where'er she be.
(III. i. 66–68)

Bianca can exchange coquettish pleasantries with the duke, browbeat the Cardinal, and heartlessly ignore her husband's presence at the banquet, because her new social status (in this morally indulgent society) permits her to do so. Characteristically, Middleton writes a scene that summarizes the situation of the new Bianca and the new Leantio (now kept "bed-fellow" to Livia). Act IV, scene i shows them confronting each other, dressed in gaudy finery, in the opulence of Bianca's court lodgings. The contrast with the opening scene is stark, both in the costliness of the surroundings, and in the angry, competitive repartee that takes the place of the opening's affectionate give and take. Yet, in many ways, the two participants remain the same people still. Leantio stays self-justifying and moralistic, too blind to see that the taunts he throws at Bianca apply equally to himself; and under the aggression lie hurt vanity and the need to believe himself a man of principle. Bianca takes command in the battle of wills and insults—she is capable by nature and upbringing of a social poise beyond Leantio's bourgeois experience; yet the diffidence that marked her in the opening scene has merely been transmuted into a vulgar belief in sexual "liberty." Her daughter will be free to wander:

they will come to 't
And fetch their falls a thousand mile about,
Where one would little think on 't.
(IV. i. 38–40)

The tragic irony of Bianca's life is that by escaping from Leantio's imprisonment into the "self-realization" of the duke's society, she has really entered a cul de sac: a society whose values repeatedly offer her "heart's peace," but that in truth destroy her.

The subplot offers parallels and contrasts to the main plot. Here, Guardiano seeks an attractive bride for his uncouth, but rich, Ward; Isabella, the chosen girl, not only reacts with revulsion to the idea of marriage with the Ward but is herself powerfully drawn toward an "incestuous" relationship with her uncle, Hippolito. In the way of this world, a solution is found that allows the participants to enjoy their sexual pleasures without sacrificing the material advantages or the social approval that go with marriage. Livia, who made arrangements for the seduction of Bianca—Middleton is a master of dramatic economy—also plays the role of persuading Isabella that she is not, after all, related to Hippolito (the tale is that she is really the illegitimate child of the Marquis of Coria); and with this assurance that incest is not in question, Isabella agrees to marry the Ward as cover for her relations with her uncle. Hippolito, equally drawn to Isabella, marvels at his sister Livia's skill in changing Isabella's mind, since Isabella had previously rejected his advances. So, for his part, neither incest (he is not told the Marquis of Coria story) nor adultery deter him from enjoyment of his sexual wishes.

In this web of deceit, Middleton allows his audience to enjoy the ironies that attach to ignorance and deception. A festive scene (III. iii), of the kind Middleton creates so well, summarizes the deception and the casual morality of the people of both plots. The duke presents Bianca as his consort, before the admiring court, while her husband Leantio looks on helplessly; at the same banquet Isabella dances first with the Ward, clumsily and absurdly, and then elegantly with Hippolito. The veneer of social approval masks immorality, and the social forms—banqueting, dancing, music—become hollow and ironic: because marriage, society's chief support, is mocked. Yet Middleton complicates and enriches the didacticism by showing how various are the human sources of this immoral situation. Guardiano, "by custom seconded and such moral virtues," sees his proposal of a marriage between Isabella and the Ward as a perfectly usual business transaction, encouraged and sanctioned by society; the grotesque personal consequences of such a relationship are hidden from him, or overlooked. Isabella's love for Hippolito, and his for her, is tender and genuine; Isabella displays self-control and consideration before the Marquis of Coria story deceives her, and her subsequent relationship with Hippolito, even if culpable, also represents a true gain. Perhaps more daringly, Middleton sketches in the human tie that motivates, at least in part, Livia's lie on Hippolito's behalf, and shows, too, the reluctance with which she undertakes it. There are clear indications that Livia feels an unusually powerful attraction toward her brother:

> thou art all a feast,
> And she that has thee a most happy guest.
> (I. ii. 149–150)

And her reluctance to proceed with the deception shows that she is led on by strong emotion:

> Beshrew you, would I loved you not so well.
> I'll go to bed, and leave this deed undone.
> (II. i. 63–64)

We are prepared for her subsequent turning to Leantio for sexual solace, at least to the extent that we have already seen her capacity for strong sexual feeling. Thus Middleton, in a remarkably compressed way, combines moral analysis with convincing documentation of human needs and impulses.

The Ward and his companion Sordido provide a full contrast to the sophistication and cultivated manners of the aristocracy. They also express, in exaggerated form, the mercenary and sexual codes of their betters. The play construes sexual pursuit as a game (in the play's language and in Livia's chess game); the Ward and Sordido are constantly engaged in the rough sport of cat-and-trap, and they allude to the Ward's relationship with Isabella in the terms of that game. In the main plot and the subplots, sexual relationships are associated with money; the Ward and Sordido set up a sort of auction-ring appraisal of Isabella, to assess her worth as a sexual partner. In these ways, the two companions have a role in the narrative—they are convincingly boorish and ridiculous—and at the same time provide a ground base for the play's themes: the values of this society are set off and parodied in their language and behavior.

The play's most famous scene is that of Bianca's seduction, where Middleton uses the chess playing of Livia and the Mother as counterpoint to the off-stage meeting of Bianca and the duke. The scene is characterized by a kind of visual punning, as the moves of the duke and pawn on the chessboard correspond to the activities of the real life figures off-stage; the power of the duke and the powerlessness of the pawn further echo the real life situation. But the episode serves also as dramatic metaphor for the game of love played out in the rest of the play. Equally, the scene displays Middleton's talent for writing persuasive neonaturalist drama (the exchanges between the Mother and Livia during the game and before it are wholly convincing), while endowing the naturalism with symbolic value. The play's concluding masque, in which most of the leading figures contrive each other's deaths, may be less persuasive as naturalism, but fully consorts with the wit that conceived the play's other structures. Livia, who arranges marriages and wrecks marriage, is cast as Juno Pronuba, the marriage goddess; she is poisoned by the woman, Isabella, whose marriage she has helped to falsify. Hippolito, victim of his own desires, dies by Cupid's poisoned arrows, as they are said to "wound" him in love. Isabella, who had acquiesced in a marriage-for-wealth with the Ward, dies in a shower of flaming gold. Guardiano, the contriver, dies in his own trap. In an antimasque, Bianca thinks to give the duke a cup of love, but gives him instead a cup of poison, and then dies of it herself. The ironies are especially adroit, complementing the extensive ironies that surround almost all the action of this remarkable tragedy.

Women Beware Women shows more clearly

perhaps than any other play the distinctive features of Middleton's dramatic craftsmanship. The playwright's skill as a contriver of plots has often, and justly, been admired; but here the dovetailing of Italian history (or gossip) with the subplot's French romance is especially adroit. The placing of Livia as bridge-character between the two narratives (the character representing her is little better than a shadow in either source) is masterly, integrating the main plot and subplots more coherently than is common in Jacobean drama, and securing thereby not merely a singularly lucid narrative line, but a disposition of events that immediately makes clear the parallels and contrasts that serve Middleton's analysis of the play's society. An equal skill shows in the economy with which scenes contribute simultaneously to the action and the significance of the play; it would be difficult (outside the Ward and Sordido scenes, perhaps) to imagine a story more briefly yet completely told, and yet the sparse narrative embodies, besides characters of depth, precise and resonant symbolic statement. Middleton's dramatic language complements this rich austerity. In his plays, metaphor tends to be assumed into the visual statement of theater; we see more than hear those continuities that give a play integrity and life. Accordingly, the verbal idiom is unusually bare for Jacobean drama; and when it offers expansion and eloquence, the effect, where it is not ironic, is normally witty rather than emotionally rich:

> Never were finer snares for women's honesties
> Than are devised in these days; no spider's web
> Made of a daintier thread, than are now practised
> To catch love's flesh-fly by the silver wing.
>
> (II. ii. 397–400)

Out of such dexterity Middleton builds a dramatic oeuvre that is coolly observant, analytical and ironic, while also managing, in the best plays, to be humanly engaged and to engage us.

Middleton wrote *The Changeling* in collaboration with William Rowley, the actor and playwright. The collaboration must have been especially close, for the division of work accepted by most scholars gives Rowley not only the subplot—where his talents as a writer of comedy are particularly called on—but also the play's opening and closing scenes (and a short passage in Act IV, scene ii). It has usually been assumed that Middleton, as the

better-known dramatist, deserves much of the credit for the tragedy's success; and certainly his long-practiced skill as a contriver of plots and his ability to render in dialogue the inner life of his characters must have contributed in a major way to the play's composition. The intellectual force that reduced a leisurely source narrative (John Reynolds' *God's Revenge Against Murder*) into the effective simplicity of the main plot also looks very much like Middleton's, and his is certainly the imagination behind the self-disclosures of the two superb scenes (II. ii and III. iv) between Beatrice-Joanna and De Flores. Yet the theatrical vitality of *The Changeling* arises from more than isolated achievements or good organization; it comes from a Jacobean understanding of the life of the play as a texture of dispersed allusions that resonate together in a complex fashion. Here, both men must have been involved, at a deep level: the plots reinforce each other, and image and symbol, by a kind of osmosis, cross the membrane that separates one writer's work from the other's. Theories about the exact processes of the collaboration are idle, for the details cannot be recovered. What is certain is that the play comes across, astonishingly, as a unity, one of the most powerful tragedies of the Elizabethan-Jacobean theater.

The Changeling is so rich a theater piece that commentary is hard-pressed to reflect even a few of its many facets. Yet, it is not difficult to point to the successes of Rowley's opening scene: the terse economy with which he introduces us to Alsemero, the merchant and man of action, now caught up in the bewilderments of love, and to Beatrice-Joanna, betrothed to Alonzo and very soon to be married, but finding (and losing) herself for the first time, she says, in her new relationship with Alsemero. The wider context is quickly sketched too: Vermandero, Beatrice's father, genially welcoming Alsemero to his house, but anticipating as well, confidently and in an expansive mood, the arrival of Alonzo, Beatrice's fiancé: the first of many in the play to be deceived about the thoughts and feelings of those around them. Even the subsidiary characters are allowed to begin their parts, as Jasperino and Diaphanta pair off in imitation of their betters. (It is noticeable how skillfully Rowley employs the wide Jacobean stage to permit separate but related intrigues to develop side-by-side.) Yet, for those capable of "reading" a Jacobean play, in the study or the theater, much more is in hand than simple development of the narrative, however skilled. Premonitions of the tragic set of events make themselves felt, both in language and in the broad intimations of character and action. We recognize, for instance (though it is easy to be heavy-handed in describing this), the dangers inherent in the instability of Alsemero's feelings and those of Beatrice; in their feelings toward each other, but more especially in the emphasized irrationality of Beatrice's loathing for her father's servant De Flores. The temper of this first scene is not only one of deception, overt or unadmitted, but of emotionality precariously free. Sensitized by such an atmosphere, we begin to pick up ominous words and phrases: the winds that should bear Alsemero from Beatrice are (against the evidence of the senses) "contrary"; words like "infirmity," "poison," "frailty" begin to be heard. We take in the dangerous intensity of Beatrice's impulsive and independent nature. We see the ugliness of De Flores (directly suggestive to the Jacobeans, and not quite neutral even to us) and understand his obsessive impulses, echoing those of Beatrice. Furthermore, associations begin to gather around the castle that is Vermandero's home and Beatrice's, and into which the action is about to move; "our citadels," declares Vermandero,

> Are plac'd conspicuous to outward view,
> On promonts'⁵ tops; but within are secrets.
> (I. i. 165–166)

Alsemero, sensing the dangers of the developing action, begins to find the castle ominous:

> How shall I dare to venture in his castle,
> When he discharges murderers at the gate?
> But I must on, for back I cannot go.
> (I. i. 222–224)

"Murderers" are, for Alsemero, the arrangements for Beatrice's wedding to Alonzo; but the word resonates in the audience's mind with "secrets" and with Alsemero's helpless lack of self-command, to reflect the theatrical experience of the first scene and its anticipations of things to come.

Jacobean tragedies often use the subplot to extend and intensify the experience of the main action. Here, Rowley uses the secondary plot, set in a madhouse run by Alibius and Lollio, to express in

⁵Promontories.

another key the deceptions, the sexual opportunism, and the irrationality of the action in Vermandero's castle. Antonio, disguised as an idiot, and Franciscus, disguised as a madman, become inmates of the madhouse in order to seek access to Isabella, Alibius' wife (and Lollio, too, makes advances to her). It is easy to see how the clandestine atmosphere of the main plot bridges across into this one: Alibius begins by emphasizing the "secret" of his young wife's sexual availability, and Antonio and Franciscus repeatedly remind us of pretense and hiding as they assume and shed their disguises. The deceiving of a foolish old husband is material for comedy, and Rowley treats this action in a generally comic vein. Yet the cross-connections between the two plots ensure that, even while we laugh, we understand that the grotesque comedy of love in a madhouse shares symbolic, and not just narrative, connections with the emotional lives of Alsemero, Beatrice, and De Flores. Cross-references repeatedly occur: Franciscus, for example, we are told, "ran mad for a chambermaid, yet she was but a dwarf neither"; Isabella interprets his mad antics differently: "His conscience is unquiet, sure that was/The cause of this." Antonio lays stress in his self-descriptions and his actions on the irrational power of love to change and deform. Even Isabella, eventually, disguises herself as a madwoman, and behaves so convincingly in her grotesque role as to deceive the eyes of her lover, Antonio. It would be wrong to interpret such lines and incidents as direct allusions to the main plot (though the suggestion that Franciscus kill his rival as the price of Isabella's love almost persuades us to think in that way). The effect is subtler: the incidents and language of the subplot color the mind in such a way as to intensify the experience of irrationality and deceit communicated by the main action. Plainly, the capering and the disfigured language of the genuine fools and madmen complement the behavior of Beatrice and De Flores, or serve as commentary on it. As the lunatics appear onstage "some as birds, others as beasts," they "act out their fantasies in any shapes /Suiting their present thoughts." In the same way, the restraints of morality and reason are slipped in the main plot. Even more, the masque of fools and madmen arranged to celebrate the marriage of Alsemero and Beatrice offers a kind of parody of the Elizabethan wedding masque, just as the marriage itself parodies in its horror and deceit the sanctities it should honor. The modern stage has begun to rediscover how a unified convention of feeling may integrate plays where the narrative connection between the plots is slight. *The Changeling* offers a superb example of imaginative coherence of this kind.

For many critics, and audiences, the center of the tragedy lies in the moral analysis by which "the irresponsible and undeveloped nature" of Beatrice, in T. S. Eliot's words, is made to contemplate the reality of her own wishes and actions. But moral analysis is in this case the product of something much deeper, the creative understanding of a whole nature, indeed of two natures, those of Beatrice herself and De Flores—and especially of the intense emotional chemistry that draws them together. From their first exchange, the play lifts from highly competent writing into a work of originality and power. Each responds to the other with an intensity that defies analysis. For Beatrice, De Flores serves as an incitement to insult and anger. She dignifies her abuse as contempt, but its sources are much more instinctual: De Flores is an "infirmity," his looks affect her like the glance of the basilisk. Later, she is more explicit:

> This ominous ill-fac'd fellow more disturbs me
> Than all my other passions
>
> . . .
>
> I never see this fellow, but I think
> Of some harm towards me, danger's in my mind still;
> I scarce leave trembling of an hour after.
>
> (II. i. 53–54; 89–91)

De Flores, in his turn, is as obsessed by Beatrice as she is by him. His inability to leave her alone ("Must I be enjoin'd/To follow still whilst she flies from me?"; "I know she hates me,/Yet cannot choose but love her") consorts with a determination to persist in this unwelcome servitude until he has his "will." It is often said that De Flores is a "realist"; and certainly he sees his own physical features in an entirely unflattering light; yet with that unsentimental vision of himself goes a readiness to be deluded:

> And yet such pick-hair'd faces, chins like witches',
> Here and there five hairs, whispering in a corner,
> As if they grew in fear one of another
>
> . . .
>
> Yet such a one pluck'd sweets without restraint,
> And has the grace of beauty to his sweet.
>
> (II. i. 40–42; 46–47)

When Beatrice makes her fatal error of thinking she can use him in the murder of Alonzo, with impunity, he is ready to respond to her flattery in the most nakedly emotional fashion: "I'm up to the chin in heaven" (II. ii. 79). Yet such a response does not cancel his egotism, nor his determination:

> I was blest
> To light upon this minute; I'll make use on't.
>
> (II. ii. 90–91)

Equally, Beatrice subdues her impulsive loathing for De Flores in order to "use" him. Both are passionate natures; both are egotists to the point where the moral sense undergoes paralysis. In the intricate, ironic chemistry of that situation, Middleton finds the material for the superb confrontation scenes of the play.

Audiences have found Act III, scene iv one of the most powerful encounters between two antagonistic yet similar personalities in the whole range of theater. The scene is a fairly lengthy one (about 170 lines), and for almost all of it Beatrice and De Flores are alone onstage. Yet so subtle is Middleton's command of the scene's rhythms that the intensity of the psychic struggle between the two never flags. Part of the audience's pleasure derives from the changeover that the scene effects in the power relationship of the two figures: Beatrice begins as the self-assured, contriving lady, able to patronize her servant; she ends being invited by De Flores to rise from kneeling "and shroud your blushes in my bosom." Victory and defeat in a contest between strong personalities represents one of the permanently satisfying formulas of theater. Yet the scene draws on other, and perhaps less usual, sources of satisfaction. In earlier scenes, the audience has been affronted by the brutality of Alonzo's murder, set against the matter-of-fact fashion in which it is suggested by Beatrice and carried out by De Flores. Here, too, the enormity of the act is set against the almost casual language used to refer to it. But when De Flores produces the dead man's finger, with Beatrice's ring still on it, in token of what he has done, the gap between the deed and its significance is suddenly closed. For Beatrice, the moment is one of "realization." Even if we think the production of the finger extravagant and stagey, the action fits with Middleton's practice of using stage events to clarify moral truths. Beatrice tries to shelter behind her old self-image, and to buy off what has happened by flattery and reward. De

Flores remorselessly exposes the inadequacy of this: the jewel she offers is a fine one, but

> 'Twill hardly buy a capcase for one's conscience, though,
> To keep it from the worm, as fine as 'tis.
>
> (III. iv. 44–45)

Yet, the major direction of the scene is to make clear to Beatrice truths not so much about morality as about herself and her impercipience. Her own emotional life so engulfs her, she begins to see, that she has ignored or misinterpreted the emotional lives of others. She could not be ignorant of the strength of De Flores' feelings, yet she has quite mistaken their nature, confounding infatuation toward herself with greed for money:

> Belike his wants are greedy, and to such
> Gold tastes like angels' food.
>
> (II. ii. 125–126)

What De Flores asserts in the course of this scene is the reality of his own feelings and the pride of the man who, once despised, has earned the right to equal consideration. Beatrice tries to fend off his claims on her body by withdrawing to conventional protests of outraged modesty. De Flores trenchantly indicates she can no longer find refuge in such pieties:

> Push, you forget yourself!
> A woman dipp'd in blood, and talk of modesty?
>
> (III. iv. 125–126)

His clarifications come to rest in the bleakest assertion of what she has hitherto been ready to "forget": the moral reality of what has been done, and the claims the deed must make on her:

> Push, fly not to your birth, but settle you
> In what the act has made you, y'are no more now;
> You must forget your parentage to me:
> Y'are the deed's creature; by that name
> You lost your first condition, and I challenge you,
> As peace and innocency has turn'd you out,
> And made you one with me.
>
> (III. iv. 134–140)

The self is made by the actions it undertakes; Beatrice "in a labyrinth" comes to accept that sin is indivisible. If the chief narrative movement of the scene is the victory that De Flores achieves over

Beatrice's self-esteem, its chief moral burden lies in its making plain the reality of sin.

It is one of the play's sharp ironies that the clarifications that form the substance of Act III, scene iv lead in narrative terms, and in terms of theater experience, not into truth but further into deceit. The rest of the play is mainly occupied with the pretenses that follow from Beatrice's acceptance that the truth of her nature lies with De Flores and not with Alsemero. Already, concealment has been made the chief idiom of the action (strengthened of course by the subplot); even Alsemero, in general an honorable man, has had to resort to a clandestine meeting with Beatrice, and in action the murder of Alonzo persistently stresses secrecy and deceit. Delivering the fatal blow, De Flores exclaims:

> Do you question
> A work of secrecy? I must silence you.
>
> (III. ii. 16–17)

And when the deed is done, Middleton once again brings to our attention that emblematic location—the castle—with its narrow, hidden passages:

> So, now I'll clear
> The passages from all suspect or fear.
>
> (III. ii. 25–26)

The "labyrinth" of emotional relations in which Beatrice finds herself trapped is one that De Flores shares too, despite his tough-mindedness and his practical skill. The concealments that the guilty pair must now practice lead ultimately to another murder: of Diaphanta, Beatrice's maid. Many have thought the business of the bed trick, in which Diaphanta supplies her mistress' place on her wedding night, either a mere conventionalism or a desperate resort when convincingly motivated action fails. Even more, modern audiences tend to find embarrassing or silly the physician's closet from which Alsemero selects a potion to test his wife's virginity. Yet, the bed trick and the emotional crisis it visits on Beatrice, as she waits in anger and anxiety for Diaphanta to leave Alsemero's side, merely state in narrative terms the increasingly ridiculous and fragile pretense within which Beatrice and De Flores have chosen to live. The physician's closet is more a matter of pathos than of quaintness or absurdity: the last, technical, resort for a husband when he mistrusts his own judgment of another's feelings, and that other his wife. Even Beatrice can utter the pathetic cry, "I must trust somebody" (V.i.15). This theme of ignorance and unawareness has, of course, been general from the play's beginning; and Middleton keeps it before us, as Tomazo seeks his brother's murderer, and Vermandero, sometimes misled, seeks him too. Ultimately, the action brings us, with the sure instinct of this play for making location confirm theme, to the killing of both De Flores and Beatrice, prisoners hidden offstage in Alsemero's anteroom: the final graphic statement of their isolation. The play elaborates, sometimes perhaps a little too easily, the ironies that knowledge and concealment give rise to; but its main business lies in the suffering brought about by sin. At the end, Vermandero's castle has become, equivocally, a place for game-playing (the game of "barley-brake") and hell itself:

Beatrice	Your bed was cozen'd on the nuptial night, For which your false bride died.
Alsemero	Diaphanta!
De Flores	Yes; and the while I coupled with your mate At barley-brake; now we are left in hell.
Vermandero	We are all there, it circumscribes here.[6]

(V. iii. 160–165)

Such is the power of Middleton's dramaturgy, and Rowley's, that we feel we have experienced that "hell," in the transformation that has overcome the play's setting, as well as all its characters, from the pristine freshness of the first scene. We have moved from the open air, and talk of meetings in a temple, to this confined and sin-ridden place: the movement has been rendered tragic, not merely pathetic, by the insight into human feeling and the nature of sin that accompanies it.

A GAME AT CHESS

MIDDLETON's last play, *A Game at Chess*, opened at the Globe Theatre on Friday, 6 August 1624, and ran for nine consecutive days (excluding Sundays), the first recorded "run" in the history of the English stage. The play's enormous popularity derived from its risky allusiveness to contemporary political

events; its permanent interest stems from Middleton's inventive exploration of a dramatic mode —political allegory—that was little used (from prudential more than artistic motives, perhaps) by his contemporaries.

A Game at Chess has its origins in popular feeling about relationships between Protestant England and Catholic Spain. The turns and twists of international diplomacy over this matter are intricate, but there can be little doubt where popular sympathy lay. A flood of pamphlets appeared, denouncing Spain and Catholic ambition, in particular the Jesuit order, which symbolized for English Protestants the desire of Catholicism for religious and political domination of the world. As an opportunist piece, the play was staged at a moment of particular national feeling: Prince Charles, the heir apparent, had recently returned from Spain without the Spanish bride who, many Englishmen feared, would set in train Spanish and Catholic encroachment on England's national life. Middleton capitalized on the widespread rejoicing to write a play summarizing the contemporary "scene," taking in recent political events (in particular, the prolonged visit of Charles and the duke of Buckingham to Spain), flattering popular prejudice (by vividly staging Catholic perfidy and jingoistically showing England's comprehensive disposal of her enemy Spain), and incorporating vividly realized portraits of current political figures (above all, the brilliant former Spanish ambassador, Count Gondomar, and the "fat bishop," Marco Antonio de Dominis, whose turnabout from leading Catholic to Protestant and back again established him as both a political influence and a popular figure of execration and fun).

There are clear signs that Middleton worked in haste, bringing events to the play almost as they occurred: the surviving manuscripts show Middleton revising to refer, for example, to the impeachment of Lionel Cranfield, earl of Middlesex and former lord treasurer (White King's Pawn in the play), which began in April 1624, just four months before the play opened, and only two before it was approved by the censor. Such vivid contemporaneity brought risks, even if it seems clear that the play enjoyed high-level protection, since it was allowed by the normally cautious censor, Sir Henry Herbert. Timed for presentation at a period when the king and court were away from London, the play nevertheless inevitably led to prosecution. Although in

---

[6]The original quarto and the edition cited here, N. W. Bawcutt's, print this line as above; other editors print "circumscribes us here."

the event the consequences were of no great seriousness for author or players (and they had made very considerable sums of money from the nine-day run) official disapproval was clearly shown—ostensibly because the law had been broken through the portrayal of reigning monarchs onstage, but in fact because the theater had contributed in so pungent, if also perhaps so heart-warming, a fashion to a matter of such extreme political delicacy. The protests of Spain could not be ignored, at least for more than a few days. Middleton had written a play, it must have seemed, not merely offensive in trespassing over the boundaries that in a tightly-governed state divide creative writing from political activism, but actually dangerous in so successfully giving expression to intense popular feeling. Yet the portraits of Charles and Buckingham, for example, are not without their ambivalence, and the visit to Spain, an unhappy initiative of King James himself, is treated with a bold complexity. *A Game at Chess* is a creative, not merely an opportunistic, piece.

The device that makes possible the play's range and complexity is the chess game itself. It is usually said that in employing it Middleton draws on established stage practice. Yet Heywood's use of the game of cards in *A Woman Killed With Kindness*, while inventive, plays a relatively minor role in the play's overall structure; and Middleton's game of chess in *Women Beware Women*, while recognized as a brilliant stage device, also contributes only one feature to the complex set of relationships of which the play is made up. The chess game here, by contrast, articulates the whole action. Throughout *A Game at Chess*, Middleton maintains contact, verbal and visual, with the idiom of the game: the two Houses, dressed appropriately in allusion to their role as black or white pieces, confront each other several times onstage; pieces are taken and lost; at the end the black pieces are bundled into the bag reserved for the losing side. Perhaps most characteristic of Middleton is the bizarre little scene (III. ii) where the black jesting Pawn and two other pawns, black and white, play out the essence of rivalry between their two sides, ending up "for all the world/Like three flies with one straw through their buttocks": a cameo that, in Middleton's fashion, summarizes an important sector of the play's feeling. Yet this fidelity to the chess game structure does not at all inhibit the play's range, but rather orders and disciplines it. Middleton takes in religious

debate, political struggle, personal satire, and historical allusion (there are references to the loss of the Palatinate, for example); and, in the way of successful allegory, the meanings of individual pieces or actions are not fixed: the White Queen, to take one example, refers to the wife of James (the White King), yet frequently the piece makes more sense if regarded as the Church of England, for whose possession the Black King lusts. *A Game at Chess* is the appropriate culmination for Middleton's career as a master craftsman in the art of play construction: a single invention is by a kind of supreme dramatic wit extended and made flexible until it can accommodate a wealth of interests from game-playing to high political events.

A Game at Chess divides into two main actions. One concerns the attempted seduction of the White Queen's Pawn (broadly allegorizing the Protestant soul). The other involves principally the Black Knight (Gondomar), the Fat Bishop (de Dominis), the White Knight (Prince Charles), and the White Duke (Buckingham). The play is organized chiefly, therefore, in terms of a play of pawns and a play of named pieces; and this corresponds to different allegorical levels, one occupying itself with matters of religious controversy, the other alluding to historical events. Yet, the two plots intertwine, as do the allegorical levels; Middleton's skill lies as much in relating the two as in developing them separately.

The play of pawns derives a good deal of its material, and its force, from Protestant anxieties about Jesuits: their typifying hypocrisy, their use of disguise, their Machiavellian cunning, their consuming desire for universal religious and political domination. Middleton gives these stereotypes dramatic credibility chiefly through the figure of the Black Bishop's Pawn (the Jesuit). The sanctimonious deceit associated with Jesuits is expressed in the false lyricism of his courtship of the White Queen's Pawn:

> that eye
> Does promise single life and meek obedience;
> Upon those lips, the sweet fresh buds of youth,
> The holy dew of prayer lies like pearl
> Dropped from the opening eyelids of the morn
> Upon the bashful rose.
>
> (I. i. 75–80)

Middleton is extraordinarily adroit in the way in which he incorporates anti-Jesuit prejudice into a narrative of seduction: the lyrical strain is the language of courtship, but the terms that modify it (obedience, prayer) are the terms of the Jesuit. The Jesuit scenes further elicit Protestant fantasies, especially about the power of the confessional, and the doctrine of obedience. Again, the White Queen's Pawn is at the center of the intrigue. As she is tempted to accept the Jesuit's control, Middleton develops her character in a way reminiscent of Shakespeare's Isabella, anxious for a "more strict restraint" on taking her vows:

> Holy sir,
> Too long I have missed you; oh, your absence starves me!
> Hasten for time's redemption, worthy sir,
> Lay your commands as thick and fast upon me
> As you can speak 'em; how I thirst to hear 'em!
>
> (II. i. 31–35)

The religious and the sexual motives become seriously confused, here and later in the scene. In such ways Middleton permits his actors to convey dramatically the allegorized content of the play; as this scene develops, dramatic tension builds up until the Pawn is almost compromised, and reaches an exciting theatrical climax as an unexpected "noise within" saves, but only just saves, her virtue. So Middleton's theater realizes what was perceived at the time as a serious moral threat.

The play of the named pieces is dominated by two figures, each worthy of standing among Middleton's grandest dramatic creations. Each of them is satirized, but each is delighted in as well as ridiculed. De Dominis, the Fat Bishop, revels in his girth in a manner that recalls Falstaff:

Fat Bishop's Pawn:	I attend at your great holiness' service.
Fat Bishop:	For great I grant you, but for greatly holy,
	There the soil alters, fat cathedral bodies
	Have very often but lean little souls
	. . .
	Of all things I commend the White House best
	For plenty and variety of victuals.
	When I was one of the Black side professed
	My flesh fell half a cubit, time to turn
	When my own ribs revolted.
	(II. ii. 1–4; 27–31)

Middleton may treat de Dominis more sardonically than Shakespeare treats Falstaff; the Fat Bishop becomes mean and self-satisfied, gullible and whining, in a fashion very different from Shakespeare's figure. Yet he remains a formidable presence, a rich caricature for the actor to embody (the part was created at the first performance, probably, by William Rowley, Middleton's coauthor on other occasions). Certainly the Fat Bishop is formidable enough to provoke venomous speeches from the second major figure, the ambassador Gondomar. The real life ambassador was a diplomat of great skill and shrewdness, with a number of remarkable diplomatic achievements to his credit. Middleton transmutes this skill into dramatic terms by rendering him as the Black Knight, a Machiavellian politician in the familiar stage tradition. He is rather fully characterized. He is judicious when others, less far-seeing, want to hasten the action; equally, he is impatient when talk gets in the way of doing; he shows the diplomat's detachment in the respect he gives Charles and Buckingham; he is adroit and inventive in a tight corner; especially, he is energetic and high-spirited and of considerable personality. It is true that the players represented Gondomar in a cruelly specific manner, wearing one of his cast suits, and having him ride in the litter he used because of his fistula (often alluded to in the text). Yet the portrait is far from a coldly contemptuous one; like the great political cartoons, the Black Knight's features derive as much from respect and enjoyment as from more satirical impulses.

These two figures represent very well one part of the spirit of *A Game at Chess*: the sheer enjoyment of dramatic creation. The same relish is evident, verbally, in the confrontation between the Black Knight and the White Knight that leads to the play's end. The lengthy exchange (V.iii) recalls in its embellishment the language of Jonson's Sir Epicure Mammon or Volpone:

> We do not use to bury in our bellies
> Two hundred thousand ducats and then boast on 't,
> Or exercise the old Roman painful-idleness
> With care of fetching fishes far from home,
> The golden-headed coracine out of Egypt,
> The salpa from Eleusis, or the pelamis,
> Which some call summer-whiting, from Chalcedon,
> Salmons from Aquitaine, helops from Rhodes,
> Cockles from Chios, franked and fatted up
> With far and sapa, flour and cocted wine . . .
>
> (V. iii. 6–15)

Whatever the ostensible occasion of this passage, the extravagant relish of the language serves to show not only that Middleton could, when occasion permitted, understudy Jonson, but that behind the moral rigor that some see as Middleton's distinguishing quality there lies an energy of mind that invigorates the concern and the observation. This is the quality not only of *A Game at Chess*, but of the whole range of Middleton's best work.

The bibliography deals only with the plays, since this study is concerned with Middleton as dramatist. The following list derives from David J. Lake, *The Canon of Thomas Middleton's Plays: Internal Evidence for the Major Problems of Authorship* (Cambridge, 1975). An asterisk indicates disputed and controversial ascriptions.

Plays by Middleton alone:
The Phoenix
Michaelmas Term
A Mad World, My Masters
A Trick to Catch the Old One
*The Puritan**
*The Revenger's Tragedy**
Your Five Gallants
*The Second Maiden's Tragedy**
No Wit, No Help Like a Woman's
A Chaste Maid in Cheapside
More Dissemblers Besides Women
*The Widow**
The Witch
Hengist, King of Kent
Women Beware Women
A Game at Chess

Plays written in collaboration:
*The Family of Love** (with Thomas Dekker; revised by Barry)
*The Honest Whore** (with Dekker)
A Yorkshire Tragedy (with one or more unknown collaborators)
The Roaring Girl (with Dekker)
*Wit at Several Weapons** (with William Rowley)
*The Nice Valour** (with Thomas Fletcher)
A Fair Quarrel (with Rowley)
*The Old Law** (with Rowley and one other dramatist)
*Anything for a Quiet Life** (with John Webster)
The Changeling (with Rowley)

SELECTED BIBLIOGRAPHY

I. BIBLIOGRAPHY. S. A. Tannenbaum, *Thomas Middleton: A Concise Bibliography* (New York, 1940); D. Donovan, *Thomas Middleton*, Elizabethan Bibliographies Supplements, no. 1 (London, 1967).

II. COLLECTED EDITIONS. A. Dyce, ed., *The Works of Thomas Middleton*, 5 vols. (London, 1840); A. H. Bullen, ed., *The Works of Thomas Middleton*, 8 vols. (London, 1885–1886); H. Ellis, ed., *Selected Plays of Thomas Middleton*, vol. I (London, 1887), intro. by A. C. Swinburne, includes *A Trick to Catch the Old One, The Changeling, A Chaste Maid in Cheapside, Women Beware Women, The Spanish Gypsy*; vol. II (1890) includes *The Roaring Girl, The Witch, A Fair Quarrel, The Mayor of Queensborough*, and *The Widow*; M. W. Sampson, ed., *Selected Plays of Thomas Middleton* (London, 1915), includes *Michaelmas Term, A Trick to Catch the Old One, A Fair Quarrel*, and *The Changeling*; K. Muir, ed., *Thomas Middleton: Three Plays* (London, 1977), includes *A Chaste Maid, Women Beware Women*, and *The Changeling*; D. L. Frost, ed., *Selected Plays of Thomas Middleton* (London, 1978), includes *A Mad World, My Masters, A Chaste Maid, Women Beware Women*, and *The Changeling*.

III. SEPARATE PLAYS. (Following are the plays available in modern editions; dates after titles are those of original publication.) *Michaelmas Term* (London, 1607), comedy, in R. Levin, ed. (London, 1966) and G. R. Price, ed. (The Hague—Paris, 1976); *The Revenger's Tragedy* (London, 1607), in R. A. Foakes, ed. (London, 1966), L. J. Ross, ed. (London, 1966), B. Gibbons, ed. (London, 1967), and G. Parfitt, ed. (London, 1976); *A Mad World, My Masters* (London, 1608), comedy, in S. Henning, ed. (London, 1965); *A Trick to Catch the Old One* (London, 1608), comedy, in C. Barber, ed. (London, 1968), G. J. Watson, ed. (London, 1968), and G. R. Price, ed. (The Hague—Paris, 1976); *The Roaring Girl* (London, 1611), comedy, in F. T. Bowers, ed., *Dramatic Works of Thomas Dekker*, vol. III (London, 1958) and A. Gomme, ed. (London, 1976); *A Fair Quarrel* (London, 1617), tragicomedy, in R. V. Holdsworth, ed. (London, 1974) and G. R. Price, ed. (London, 1976); *A Game at Chess* (London, 1625), political allegory, in R. C. Bald, ed. (London, 1929) and J. W. Harper, ed. (London, 1966); *A Chaste Maid in Cheapside* (London, 1630), comedy, in A. Brissenden, ed. (London, 1968), C. Barber, ed. (London, 1969), and R. B. Parker, ed. (London, 1969); *The Widow* (London, 1652), tragicomedy, in R. T. Levine, ed., *Salzburg Studies in English Literature* (Salzburg, 1975); *The Changeling* (London, 1653), tragedy, in N. W. Bawcutt, ed. (London, 1958), P. Thomson, ed. (London, 1964), G. W. Williams, ed. (London, 1966), and M. W. Black, ed. (Philadelphia, 1966); *Women Beware Women* (London, 1657), tragedy, in R. Gill, ed. (London, 1968), C. Barber, ed. (London, 1969), and J. R. Mulryne, ed. (London, 1975); *Hengist,*

King of Kent (London, 1661), in A. Lancashire, ed. (London, 1978).

IV. Critical Studies. A. Symons, "Middleton and Rowley" in *Cambridge History of English Literature*, vol. VI (Cambridge, 1910), a general treatment but still worth reading; T. S. Eliot, "Thomas Middleton" (London, 1927), reprinted in Eliot's *Selected Essays* (London, 1932), *Elizabethan Essays* (London, 1934), and *Elizabethan Dramatists* (London, 1962), praises Middleton as "a great comic writer and a great tragic writer" yet one who "has no point of view"; M. C. Bradbrook, *Themes and Conventions of Elizabethan Tragedy* (Cambridge, 1935), includes a sensitive analysis of *The Changeling* and *Women Beware Women*; U. Ellis-Fermor, *The Jacobean Drama: An Interpretation* (London, 1936; rev. ed., 1958), a perceptive study that surveys both comedies and tragedies, noting the range of Middleton's interests and valuing his insight into character; L. C. Knights, *Drama and Society in the Age of Jonson* (London, 1937), includes the chapter "Middleton and the New Social Classes," which places him well below Jonson as a writer of comedy; K. J. Holzknecht, "The Dramatic Structure of *The Changeling*" in A. H. Gilbert, ed., *Renaissance Papers* (Columbia, S. C., 1954), reprinted in M. Bluestone and N. Rabkin, eds., *Shakespeare's Contemporaries: Modern Studies in English Renaissance Drama*, 2nd ed. (London, 1970); M. C. Bradbrook, *The Growth and Structure of Elizabethan Comedy* (London, 1955), summarizes the comedies and offers individual insights but not a systematic study; J. D. Jump, "Middleton's Tragic Comedies," *Pelican Guide to English Literature*, vol. II (Harmondsworth, 1955), studies principally *Women Beware Women* and *The Changeling*, contending against reading them in naturalistic terms; S. Schoenbaum, ed., *Middleton's Tragedies* (New York, 1955), considers *The Revenger's Tragedy* and *The Second Maiden's Tragedy* as well as tragedies commonly ascribed to Middleton, offers full consideration of authorship problems; S. Schoenbaum, "Middleton's Tragi-comedies," *Modern Philology* (1956), looks at *The Witch*, *The Old Law*, *More Dissemblers*, and *A Fair Quarrel* as plays that seek to develop a new kind of ironic and realistic drama; G. R. Hibbard, "The Tragedies of Thomas Middleton and the Decadence of the Drama," *Nottingham Renaissance and Modern Studies* (1957), argues that Middleton tries, unsuccessfully, to break away from conventional tragic forms; R. H. Barker, *Thomas Middleton* (New York, 1958), discusses Middleton's biography and the whole range of his work; S. Schoenbaum, "*A Chaste Maid in Cheapside* and Middleton's City Comedy" in J. W. Bennett et al., eds., *Studies in English Renaissance Drama* (New York, 1959), analyzes the achievement of *A Chaste Maid* as "the grandest, most textured of the city comedies," a complex, vital, and disturbing play; R. Ornstein, *The Moral Vision of Jacobean Tragedy* (Madison, Wisc., 1960), analyzes the achievements of *The Change-*

ling and *Women Beware Women* especially by way of contrast with Beaumont's *The Maid's Tragedy*; R. B. Parker, "Middleton's Experiments with Comedy and Judgement" in J. R. Brown and B. A. Harris, eds., *Jacobean Theatre*, Stratford-upon-Avon Studies 1 (London, 1960), shrewd discussion of the comedies and *Women Beware Women*; C. Ricks, "The Moral and Poetic Structure of *The Changeling*," *Essays in Criticism* (1960); C. Ricks, "Word Play in *Women Beware Women*," *Review of English Studies* (1961), two studies showing the subtle interconnection of wordplay and moral analysis in the tragedies; I. Ribner, *Jacobean Tragedy: The Quest for Moral Order* (London, 1962), sees *The Changeling* and *Women Beware Women* in the light of the "Calvinistic bias" of Middleton's outlook; E. Engleberg, "Tragic Blindness in *The Changeling* and *Women Beware Women*," *Modern Language Quarterly* (1962), emphasizes the harshness of Middleton's tragic universe in which blinded characters stumble; T. B. Tomlinson, *A Study of Elizabethan and Jacobean Tragedy* (London, 1964), considers "naturalistic comedy and tragedy" in *A Chaste Maid* and *Women Beware Women* and "poetic naturalism" in *The Changeling*; R. Chatterji, "Theme, Imagery and Unity in *A Chaste Maid in Cheapside*," *Renaissance Drama* (1965), focuses on the family theme, with particular reference to how this is taken up on the play's language; D. Krook, "Tragedy and Satire: Middleton's *Women Beware Women*," A. Shalvi and A. A. Mendilow, eds., *Studies in English Language and Literature* (Jerusalem, 1966); A. C. Dessen, "Middleton's *The Phoenix* and the Allegorical Tradition," *Studies in English Literature* (London, 1966), shows how Middleton reconciles the methods of the "estates" morality with a more "realistic" dramatic mode; B. Gibbons, *Jacobean City Comedy* (London, 1967), considers Middleton as a writer of satiric comedy in an urban setting; R. Chatterji, "Unity and Disparity: *Michaelmas Term*," *Studies in English Literature 1500–1900* (London, 1968), argues a thematic unity between main plot and subplot and connects the play with *Volpone*; D. L. Frost, *The School of Shakespeare* (London, 1968), sees Middleton as a "blatantly commercial" writer who is at his best when most indebted to Shakespeare, considers a range of plays including *The Revenger's Tragedy*; I.-S. Ewbank, "Realism and Morality in *Women Beware Women*," *Essays and Studies* (1969), argues the moral and theatrical unity of the play, including the masque in Act V; W. W. E. Slights, "The Trickster-Hero and Middleton's *A Mad World*," *Comparative Drama* (1969), emphasizes the "overriding benignity" of the play, but finds it disturbing too; C. A. Hallett, "Middleton's Allwit: The Urban Cynic," *Modern Language Quarterly* (1969), proposes that Middleton's insight into Allwit's cynicism predicts the concerns of *Women Beware Women* and *The Changeling* and shows the dramatist's modernity; A. F. Marotti, "Fertility and Comic Form in *A Chaste Maid in*

Cheapside," *Comparative Drama* (1969), emphasizes festivity and the celebration of life forces as a central principle in the play; D. M. Holmes, *The Art of Thomas Middleton* (Oxford, 1970), emphasizes Middleton's moral preoccupations; R. Jordan, "Myth and Psychology in *The Changeling*," *Renaissance Drama* (1970), finds mythological patterns, such as the wild man and the maiden, in the language of *The Changeling*; R. Levin, *Multiple Plot in English Renaissance Drama* (Chicago, 1971), considers in detail a number of Middleton's plays, including *The Second Maiden's Tragedy, A Chaste Maid*, and *The Changeling*, in a rich study of the structures and functions of the multiple plot; D. George, "Thomas Middleton's Sources: A Survey," *Notes and Queries* (1971); C. Ricks, "The Tragedies of Webster, Tourneur and Middleton: Symbols, Imagery and Conventions" in C. Ricks, ed., *English Drama to 1710*, The Sphere History of Literature in the English Language, vol. III (London, 1971), a searching consideration of language and action in Jacobean plays, questioning comfortable assumptions about dramatic convention; A. C. Kirsch, *Jacobean Dramatic Perspectives* (Charlottesville, Va., 1972), sees Middleton's plays in relation to the techniques of morality drama and the interests of the coterie theaters; J. B. Batchelor, "The Pattern of *Women Beware Women*," *Yearbook of English Studies* (1972), a careful, close reading showing the integrity of the play's theatrical and moral structure; D. M. Farr, *Thomas Middleton and the Drama of Realism* (Edinburgh, 1973), discusses seven plays including *Women Beware Women, The Changeling*, and *A Game at Chess*; A. Leggatt, *Citizen Comedy in the Age of Shakespeare* (Toronto, 1973), Middleton's city comedies provide a central instance of this largely satiric genre, the comedies are grouped according to social issues such as "the prodigal," "money and land," and "adultery"; D. J. Lake, *The Canon of Thomas Middleton's Plays* (London, 1975), the most complete study of authorship problems; M. Heinnemann, "Middleton's *A Game at Chess*: Parliamentary-Puritans and Opposition Drama," *English Literary Renaissance* (London, 1975), the religious and political context of the play, suggests that court protection may have been secured by the earl of Pembroke; J. A. Bryant, Jr., "Middleton as a Modern Instance," *Sewanee Review* (1976), Middleton offers a world of sex and self-interest without redemption by optimism or faith; G. E. Rowe, "Prodigal Sons, New Comedy and Middleton's *Michaelmas Term*," *English Literary Renaissance* (London, 1977), discusses the "disquieting ambiguity" of the play in terms of its employment of earlier comic forms.

JOHN MARSTON
(1576-1634)

CYRIL TOURNEUR
(*ca.* 1575-1626)

R. A. Foakes

MARSTON'S WORLD

IT is not easy to sum up the achievements of John Marston, for though there is general agreement that he was an important figure in the literary and dramatic development of his time, the nature and quality of his work has been much disputed. To understand why this is so it is especially important to appreciate something of his background and social milieu. He was born in 1576, thus belonging to a different generation from that of his older contemporary, William Shakespeare, and he moved in a different social sphere. His father was a lawyer of some consequence and wealth, who kept chambers in the Middle Temple and made provision for his son to follow in his footsteps. Marston was sent to Oxford, where he graduated in 1594; meanwhile he was entered as a member of the Middle Temple from 1592. After graduating, he joined his father in London and shared his chambers in the Inns of Court until his father died in 1599; for some years he continued to reside in the Middle Temple and had rooms there until 1606. He thus came to maturity in a select social group, and this in many ways affected his work as a writer.

The Inns of Court at this time functioned largely as a kind of finishing school for the sons of gentry and wealthy middle-class parents. They resembled the two universities of Oxford and Cambridge in providing something like a college atmosphere, but differed in that no formal instruction was given. The young men, who entered often after having attended a university, could keep terms and study for a career in law, but for many the law was less important than the access the Inns of Court provided to an interesting, cultured society, enjoying great privileges in the heart of London. Marston acquired some knowledge of the law, which is reflected in his writings, but he was probably one of those who attended the theater rather than disputations, and he certainly found the cultural and literary life in the Inns of Court more to his taste than a career like his father's. At his death, his father left him his law books, but with a resigned awareness that, whatever he proposed, God might dispose things differently; and he must have known by then that John, who had already made an impact with the publication of his satires, was not likely to succeed him as a bencher of the Middle Temple.

Among the cultivated and leisured young men attached to the Inns of Court were a number who developed a talent for writing, the best known of them in the 1590's being John Donne, Sir John Davies, and Marston. All wrote satirical verse, and this indicates something about the nature of the society in which they flourished, one that was detached from the workaday concerns of the world of politics or trade, constituting a kind of social and intellectual elite, self-regarding and perhaps a little self-important. The Inns of Court men enjoyed the "liberty" Ben Jonson referred to in his dedication of *Every Man out of His Humour* (1599) to "the Noblest Nurseries of Humanity and Liberty," a license to make sport "when the gown and cap is off, and the Lord of Liberty reigns." This was reflected in their Christmas revels, when a mock court was set up under a lord of misrule, and there was much play with processions, dances, the making of fictitious laws, mock ceremonies, and mock trials. In such a setting, epigram and satire flourished, and Marston's first publications were inevitably of this kind, beginning with what may, to judge by the dedication to Opinion, and the elaborate foolery of its presentation, have been intended as a burlesque of Ovidian amatory poetry in *The Metamorphosis of Pygmalion's Image*. This was published with *Certain Satires* (1598), and *The Scourge of Villainy* (1598, expanded 1599), all issued anonymously, although he signed the address to the reader in *The Scourge of Villainy*, "W. Kinsayder," proclaiming in this: "He that thinks worse of my rhymes than myself, I scorn him, for he cannot; he that thinks better, is a fool."

It is not necessary to take this disclaimer too seriously, but it shows an equivocal attitude to his own writing, something that may be traced in many of his works. In June 1599 came an order prohibiting the publication of satires. The immediate cause of this is not known, but Marston's poems were part of a spate of satiric writing in this period, and some of it was bound to give offense. Either because of this, or, as has been suggested, because of a growing disenchantment with the role of satirist, Marston turned to drama and during the next decade produced a series of plays, all of them for the new professional children's companies, the Children of the Chapel Royal, or the Queen's Revels, who played at Blackfriars, and the Children of Paul's, who played in the precincts of St. Paul's Cathedral. At these small, indoor, so-called "private" theaters, patrons paid much higher entrance charges than at the large, open-air public theaters, and they seem to have constituted a more sophisticated audience. Most of Marston's plays are comedies or tragicomedies with some satiric content, although he attempted to write an ambitious tragedy in *Sophonisba* (1606). He wrote no more after 1608, when he sold the share he had held in the company of the Queen's Revels since 1604, and in 1609 he was ordained. Not much is known about the remaining years of his life, but he became the incumbent of the parish of Christchurch in Hampshire in 1616, a living he held until he resigned in 1631. He died in 1634.

There was a moment in 1599 when Marston was involved in negotiations with Philip Henslowe about writing part of a play for the Admiral's Men, an adult group, and for a few years he was a sharer in the Queen's Revels. To this extent he can be regarded as a professional dramatist, but his career as student at Oxford, Inns of Court man, wit and satirist, dramatist, and finally parson, is more like that of Donne than that of Shakespeare. It is doubtful whether he ever needed to earn a living from the stage, and he was able to give it up and abandon writing in 1608. Marston, then, is better to be understood as a kind of gentleman amateur poet and dramatist; this is no reflection on the quality of his work but explains a good deal about its nature, and his attitude toward it.

MARSTON AS SATIRIST

MARSTON's writings are those of an educated man, and they feed off his reading; their reference to life is, so to speak, filtered through their reference to books. His satires show his knowledge of Juvenal, Persius, and Horace, as well as his reading of Seneca, Aristotle, and Castiglione. His early plays refer to contemporary drama, to the so-called "war of the theaters" (in which Marston seems to have offended Ben Jonson), to the conventions of the popular drama of the day (notably Kyd's *The Spanish Tragedy*), and to Seneca, while his later plays show the impact of other writers, notably Montaigne. His attitude toward his work seems, with the exception perhaps of *Sophonisba* (1606), ambivalent, as if at the same time, he scorns what he is doing and yet believes in it, or he would not do it; so *The Scourge of Villainy* ends with a poem "To Everlasting Oblivion," in which Marston writes:

> Let others pray
> For ever their fair Poems flourish may,
> But as for me, hungry *Oblivion*
> Devour me quick, accept my orison.
>   (3–6)

Satires had, of course, been written in English before the late 1590's, as for instance in the quarrel between Thomas Nashe and Gabriel Harvey a few years earlier, but there was something quite new about the satires of writers like Joseph Hall and John Marston in 1598. Hall made the claim in *Virgidemiarum* (1598),

> I first adventure; follow me who list
> And be the second English satirist.

Marston perhaps is to be thought of as the second, and his satires show a subtler stance than those of

Hall, who assumes a position of right-minded authority from which to attack vice in the world. What is new in both of them is their discovery of the possibilities for using in English the techniques of the Latin satirists, Juvenal, Persius, and Horace especially. The etymology of the word "satire" was confused, since the Latin "satura" meant medley, while the Greek "satyros" denoted something rough and harsh, and the English poets did not realize that Latin satires were written for recitation, which controlled their length. They imitated the Roman satirists by writing groups of poems of moderate length, and Marston wrote in a deliberately rough style, as he indicates in the dedication to *The Scourge of Villainy*, subtitled "Three Books of Satires."

The Latin writers provided a structure for satire, a quasi-dramatic one, with a speaker, the satirist, provoked by a kind of adversary, who embodies some vice or folly. The satirist may adopt a single philosophical position, like the Stoic Persius, who is quoted by Marston on the title page of *The Scourge of Villainy*; but in the eleven satires of this volume Marston chooses rather to explore a range of possible stances, moving right along the spectrum available to the satirist, from the tolerance of the gentle humorist at one end to savage indignation at the other. Although the speaker generally recommends rationality, recalling man to reason in rejection of folly or vice, he can do this in varying degrees and ways.

So in Satire XI, Marston presents himself as a humorist:

> Sleep grim *Reproof*, my jocund Muse doth sing
> In other keys, to nimbler fingering.
>
> (I–2)

Here the satirist sets up a series of adversaries more notable for folly than vice, like the one he starts with, whose affectation is to borrow all his speech from plays he has seen:

> He hath made a common-place book out of plays,
> And speaks in print, at least whate'er he says
> Is warranted by Curtain's *plaudities*.
>
> (43–45)

This fool, who speaks "Naught but pure Juliet and Romeo," is treated, like the other butts in this satire, with "sporting merriment." By contrast,

Satire VIII is headed, "A Cynic Satire," in which the spokesman, the cynic, searches in vain for a man, finding only "swine," men so stained with "vile impiety,/And muddy dirt of sensuality," that they can be regarded as no better than animals. The satire ends with the final cynicism, that men cannot have been created by God to share a divine essence, or if so then our own "slime" or beastliness has choked our pipeline to God; here, in the condemnation of all men, the writer himself is included. Satire II starts off from Juvenal; and the speaker in this bursts out in rage, railing against the wickedness of men:

> Preach not the Stoic's patience to me,
> I hate no man, but man's impiety.
> My soul is vext, what power willeth desist?
> Or dares to stop a sharp-fang'd satirist?
>
> (5–8)

This snarling figure presents one aspect of what by this time had become a well-established type in literature and in life, the malcontent, and Marston's satires provide, perhaps above all, a sense of exploring this. In Satire II he attacks Bruto, who represents the more unpleasant features of one type of malcontent, the discontented traveler, who has seen better things elsewhere, complains his merit is neglected and rails against the corruption he sees around him, yet is just as corrupt himself. Elsewhere, in his address to the readers and in other satires, such as Satire X, Marston himself adopts the stance of a better type of malcontent, the worthy intellectual, undervalued and misunderstood; and so, made bitter, he lashes out at the hypocrisy and vice he sees around him, provoking hatred by his onslaught, yet striving

> in honest seriousness
> To scourge some soul-polluting beastliness,
> (*In Lectores*, 67–68)

and aware too, at times, that it is a kind of folly or madness to waste his energy so, and tax his brain,

> Playing the rough part of a Satirist
> To be perus'd by all the dung-scum rabble
> Of thin-brain'd Idiots, dull, uncapable.
> (Satire X, 13–16)

The variety of stances involves, too, a variety of dramatic relationships with the figures attacked, ranging from loathing to friendly chivying. In all this Marston was showing his virtuosity, but underlying the display of a range of satiric stances, there lies a quality peculiarly characteristic of Marston himself. The main attack of his satires is on various forms of lust, and much of his language has a violence of tone that prompted a sharp comment in the anonymous academic play, *The Return from Parnassus*, part II (1606), on the "great battering ram of his terms," but the violence seems to mark a powerful sense of revulsion at times, a melancholy that has been seen as a dark, pessimistic weariness falling little short of despair. This is to find too consistent an attitude in the satires, which equally refuse to support any particular view. This is their strength, that they are as hostile to self-righteousness and hypocrisy as they are to lust and affectation, and consequently Marston can turn on himself as spokesman and find corruption there too. This is seen in the "Proemium" to book II, where he admits his own blemishes and sins. Marston was perhaps uncertain of his own criteria, or at any rate had an ambivalent attitude toward the stances he enacted, so that his satires are neither wholly serious, nor wholly fooling, written with a harsh force that at times seems to embody an extremity of passion, and yet disclaimed at the outset in his address to the reader. The satires are not great poems, and they are limited not only by their roughness and sense of strain in much of the verse but also by their narrowness of focus, for although, like any good satirist, Marston claims to be attacking vice in general, his specific targets are mainly drawn from gallants and young men about town such as no doubt were familiar in the Inns of Court.

MARSTON AS DRAMATIST

MARSTON's ambivalence of attitude carried over into his plays, and it has provoked considerable disagreement among critics writing about them. While this ambivalence has been the theme of much modern criticism, especially in the wake of T. S. Eliot's influential essay, it has also troubled interpreters, who divide roughly into those who stress what they see as Marston's attempt to embody, not altogether successfully, a serious moral purpose and vision in his dramas, and those who emphasize rather the satiric and comic effects and what they

see as the dramatist's deliberate subversion of potentially tragic situations and of the moralizings of his characters. Such disparate accounts of his central plays, like *The Malcontent* (1604), are perhaps not irreconcilable, insofar as they constitute a response to the presence of conflicting attitudes within Marston's writings, but it is not easy to arrive at a just assessment of so tantalizing and original a dramatist.

Two plays published anonymously, *Histriomastix* (printed 1610), and *Jack Drum's Entertainment* (printed 1601), are thought to be among his first efforts as a dramatist, but if so he acknowledged neither of them as his own, and neither is a good play. The first could have been concocted as a kind of entertainment or pageant for the Inns of Court, and it has some amusing moments, especially in its mockery of a rampum-scampum company of adult players, whose repertory consists of "mouldy fopperies of stale poetry,/Unpossible dry musty fictions."

The play, written, like all of Marston's, for a children's company, also takes a crack at the child actors for playing "musty fopperies of antiquity," so its satire on the theater is more general and may reflect a period when the new, professionally organized children's companies started playing without having a new repertory to match, thereby being forced to use old plays, including some from among those played by the children's companies that had to cease performing about 1589. *Jack Drum's Entertainment* is really a conventional romantic comedy used as a vehicle for satirical attacks on the kinds of gallant pilloried in *The Scourge of Villainy*, with one character, Brabant Senior, acting as a kind of arbiter, or voice of reason. This was a tactic Ben Jonson used, as in the figure of Asper in *Every Man out of His Humour*, and provided a way of locating and distancing satire within a dramatic framework, so circumventing the banning of satires, although the enforcement of this ban may simply have been lax.

The first plays Marston issued as his own were *Antonio and Mellida* and *Antonio's Revenge* (1602), which were probably written for production by the Children of Paul's in 1599–1600. With these plays he seems to have succeeded in creating a new mode of drama, replacing "musty fopperies" with lively, sharp plays peculiarly adapted to the talents and limitations of the boy actors and, probably, to the taste of the private theater audiences. He found, more importantly, a dramatic vehicle for his own ambivalences, in plays that could be at the same time passionate and detached, satiric and self-mocking, serious and absurd. A description of the action of *Antonio and Mellida* would make it sound pretty silly, but Marston used absurdities of stance, character, and dialogue for deliberate effect. The play is written with a deliberate self-consciousness, as is evident from the induction, in which the players discuss their parts. Antonio, the hero, is taken aback to find he will be disguised as an Amazon and cries, "I a voice to play a lady! I shall ne'er do it." Marston is, of course, joking on the normal expectation in adult companies that female parts would be acted by boys. The action proceeds with continual mocking references to a range of dramatic conventions, and an exploitation of the boy actors in a conscious relation to the adults they imitate or "play," and all this works much more subtly, and more interestingly, than the crude satire on players in *Histriomastix*.

The play has a story of sorts, relating the "comic crosses of true love," in which Antonio, who spends much of his time disguised as a girl, is eventually brought together with Mellida, who has for much of the action been disguised as a page, in the promise of marriage. At their recognition of one another in act IV they burst into Italian, which Marston had learned from his Italian mother, in what has been seen as a kind of operatic duet, but was no doubt, like much in the play, a mocking of the extremities of romantic ardor as expressed in some of the fashionable modes of poetry and drama of the time, such as the sonnet. The setting is a court, full of courtiers who display their affected humors in love as "servants" to Rossaline, in contrast to the passion of Antonio and Mellida. One character, Feliche, acts as a kind of arbiter or satirical spokesman, but is himself exposed as full of self-pity and envy in act III. In the course of the play everything comes in for some mockery, within action that is inconsequential and dialogue full of fine speeches that lead to nothing. The play not only satirizes the affectations of gallants and lovers but exposes to a mocking scrutiny, through exaggeration, a whole range of dramatic attitudes, the heroic, the passionate, the stoic, the tragic, the satiric, and makes us see them dispassionately, by reminding us that we are watching boys self-consciously playing adults. The dramatic conventions made familiar by Kyd and other dramatists

are mocked, but then the mockers too are mocked. There is little or no sense of character in the play; the players know they are posturing in roles for the moment, and this is necessary for the overall effect; it is not a question of Marston's ability to create convincing characterization, but rather that in the mode of drama he invented, with some influence from Ben Jonson, character is not necessary.

Antonio's Revenge is a continuation in that it mocks the conventions of heroic tragedy, with special reference to Seneca and to Thomas Kyd's *The Spanish Tragedy*. By the time Marston wrote this play, about 1600, the first wave of the influence of Seneca on English tragedy had spent itself. For several decades, and especially since the publication of a translation of his collected plays in 1581, a series of blood-thirsty tyrants and revengers, speaking with lofty and often bombastic utterance, had appeared on the stage. The melodramatic world of Seneca's tragedies offered a model for the raving out of passion, for sententiousness, for the expression of violence in an age accustomed to violence, and for social acceptance of suffering. The Senecan style combined well with the concept of the villainous intriguer, which the Elizabethans linked with the name of Machiavelli, and the revenge play rapidly established itself as a popular mode. These plays were often set in Italy or southern countries, where popular belief supposed that men were naturally more hot-blooded and where traditions of revenge for honor were known to exist. But this was also a way of distancing what was familiar in England, where death was ever present and dueling to settle a quarrel was common enough. The more sophisticated revenge plays also made much of the ethical dilemma resulting from marrying a classical and pagan mode of tragedy to Renaissance and Christian stories and themes. The most successful revenge plays, those at any rate that are still read or acted, tend to present this dilemma in the sharpest form by presenting a protagonist whose father, son, or mistress has been murdered by a tyrannical ruler who controls or embodies the law. It is therefore not possible to obtain justice by ordinary means, and the protagonist is driven, as by a duty, to seek redress by revenge, although with a troubled conscience, and is likely to straddle the boundary between hero and villain. The early dramatists overworked the conventions, the bombast, the ghosts, the sententiousness, the horror; and even the finest examples of the mode, such as *The Spanish*

Tragedy, were old-fashioned in manner by Marston's time. *Antonio's Revenge*, by its exaggeration of features of earlier revenge plays and the rant and "braggart passion" that it provided for boy actors to declaim, exposed the limitations of what had gone before. With Shakespeare's *Hamlet* (published in the first good text in 1604), it prepared the way for a much more sophisticated treatment of revenge as a motif in Jacobean tragedy, notably in *The Revenger's Tragedy* and *The Atheist's Tragedy*, which are discussed below.

In the working out of Antonio's revenge on Piero for the murder of his father, Andrugio, a series of sensational effects is contrived, designed to shock, such as the discovery of the body of Feliche hung up and "stabb'd thick with wounds," the emergence of the ghost of Andrugio from a tomb, and, most startling of all, the killing by Antonio of Julio, Piero's small son, in a church, at midnight, and the sprinkling of the boy's blood on the tomb of his own father. Here a choirboy actor playing an adult kills another choirboy actor playing a boy, in a church. The contrast between the extreme horror of the act and the innocence of the choirboys doing it must have provided a special kind of frisson for the original audiences at the play. In relation to this action, Marston pushes to an extreme the bombast and violence possible in revenge tragedy and deflates it at the same time in various ways—for example, in the presence of an absurd clown, Balurdo, as the savage Piero's unlikely servant or in the frequent reminders that we are watching boys aping adults. The melodramatic exaggerations of the language in many speeches and the frequent bathos are evidently deliberate, as when Balurdo comes on in act II, summoned by Piero after a particularly bloody speech boasting of a plotted murder:

> O, 'twill be rare, all unsuspected done,
> I have been nurs'd in blood, and still have suck'd
> The steam of reeking gore—Balurdo, ho!
>
> (II. i. 18–20)

At this point Balurdo rushes on trying to glue on his beard, which is "half off, half on," as the stage direction says, and complaining that the "tyring man" has not stuck it on properly—it duly falls off, for a comic effect, and it is not possible to take very seriously the speeches, actions, or passions of characters presented in scenes like this.

At the same time, the play is not simply a burlesque of conventional tragic stances. The tone of it is hard to define, especially given the rarity of good professional productions, and we have to guess at the effect of boy actors playing it; but the undermining of the assumptions of heroic tragedy by discontinuities, incongruous juxtapositions, and effects of bathos may release an underlying bleak sense, as G. K. Hunter puts it, of "the cold realities of power." Certainly Marston was acutely aware of the discrepancy between ideals and realities and found in the boy actors a peculiarly appropriate vehicle for displaying this, as in Pandulpho's speech in act IV:

> Why, all this time I ha' but play'd a part
> Like to some boy that acts a tragedy,
> Speaks burly words and raves out passion;
> But when he thinks upon his infant weakness,
> He droops his eye. I spake more than a god,
> Yet am less than a man.
>
> (IV. ii. 70–75)

The raving out of passion by boys, who are less than men but speak more than gods, allowed some unusual play with tragic stances, as when Antonio murders Julio and is visually identified, by his bloody arms and dagger, with the villain Piero. At the end, the brutal slayers of Piero, who have plucked out his tongue and offered him a Thyestean feast of the limbs of his dead son, are greeted, to their amazement, as saviors and join a holy order, "religiously held sacred," in an extraordinary reversal of conventional expectations. So the satiric and burlesque aspects of the play and the exploitation of the child actors enabled Marston to shock his audience into an awareness of quite different perspectives from those in which heroes and villains are plainly recognizable as such.

The satire in these plays is largely at the expense of conventional literary and dramatic modes and moral assumptions, and perhaps it was a kind of achievement that could not be repeated. In his next work, *What You Will* (written 1601), Marston returned to a lighter kind of comedy that dramatizes the world of the verse satires, depicting a Venice full of follies and vanities. It is a play written for young Inns of Court men and is essentially about their own world; the most interesting part of its action, which may have a reference to the quarrel between dramatists at this time, or "war of the theaters," as a further level of interest for people in the know, concerns the conversion of the character Lampatho Doria by the epicure Quadratus from railing in condemnation of what he sees around him. Again there is a sense that everything is open to mockery, as Marston pokes fun at himself in the play, using the pseudonym "Kinsayder" from *The Scourge of Villainy.*

After this play Marston may have stopped writing for a time or have been affected by the long suspension of dramatic performances because of plague in 1603. Between 1604 and 1608, when he seems to have severed his connection with the stage, he wrote or had a hand in at least five or six plays. His masterpiece, *The Malcontent* (1604), deserves special consideration and is discussed later. Probably his next work after this was *The Dutch Courtesan* (1605), a sprightly satirical comedy informed by a reading of Montaigne. It opposes Malheureux, the man who is unhappy because he thinks he is wise and virtuous, but tries to deny natural impulses and passions to his friend Freevill, who accepts in his freedom of will what men are by nature. Malheureux is captivated by Franceschina, the Dutch courtesan of the title, who embodies passion but speaks in a strange stage accent that seems designed to distance her comically. In the end Freevill rescues his friend from an inevitable fall, and Malheureux loses himself in lust only to emerge in a comic ending with the discovery of a better understanding of himself:

> I am now worthy yours, when, before,
> The beast of man, loose blood, distemper'd us.
> He that lust rules cannot be virtuous.
> (V. iii. 65–67)

The play has a subplot in which the intriguing Cocledemoy, who parallels Freevill as a witty, natural man and satirical spokesman, devises with great relish various ways of tormenting and exposing the money-loving citizen and vintner Mullingrub. It thus belongs with the so-called city comedies of the period, which satirized and mocked the tradesman and merchant from the point of view of the young gentleman or gallant. Marston had a hand in one of the best of all the plays of this kind, sharing the authorship with Ben Jonson and George Chapman. This play, *Eastward Ho!* (1605), in which Marston's contributions are chiefly in the early part, works well because it is not patronizing, but shows an awareness of the follies of the court as well as the city. Its main satiric attack is directed against the usurer, a favorite target of city comedy, but it also exposes other forms of greed masquerading under bourgeois puritanism or disguised as vanity.

The Fawn (ca. 1604–1606) resembles a number of plays of this time, like Marston's own *Malcontent,* Shakespeare's *Measure for Measure,* and Middleton's *The Phoenix,* in showing a duke in disguise commenting sardonically on the follies of a court. In this case, Hercules, duke of Ferrara, disguised as Faunus, ingratiates himself in the court of Urbino and becomes an arbiter of behavior, thereby "fawning," or flattering. He exposes the flatteries of the courtiers by the exaggeration of his own flattery. The court is full of "over-amorous and unconscionable covetous young gallants," who are brought finally to a kind of trial at the "parliament of Cupid" in the last act, with Hercules acting there as a kind of prosecutor. Again the chief targets of the satire are the sexual follies and aberrations of gallants with names like "Amoroso Debile-Dosso," a lover whose back, as his name suggests, is so weak that he cannot beget an heir. In his address to the reader, prefixed to this play, Marston cites Juvenal, and the main intent of the play is to provide an amusing satire for an audience of young men about town. The parliament of Cupid seems especially to belong to the world of Inns of Court revels. There may be a satirical reference to King James I in the figure of the foolish Duke Gonzago of Urbino, who prides himself on his wisdom and his ability to quote from authors he has read. In addition, an overlay of romantic comedy is provided by the excuse Hercules has for going to Urbino in the first place, which is to keep an eye on his son Tiberio, who is supposed to be on a diplomatic mission to seek for his father the hand of Gonzago's daughter Dulcimel. It comes as no great surprise to the audience that Dulcimel prefers Tiberio, although Gonzago is quite unable to see what is obvious, and the young couple end betrothed to one another, with Hercules applauding them.

In his address to the reader published in *The Fawn,* Marston apologized for the slightness of the play and promised, "I will present a tragedy to you which shall boldly abide the most curious perusal." This duly appeared as *The Wonder of Women: or The Tragedie of Sophonisba,* his only tragedy and something of a curiosity. It seems to be a conscious attempt at a masterpiece, but can only be regarded as an interesting failure. Probably the private theaters with their boy actors, whose range of voice and expression must have been limited, were not very suitable for serious tragedy of a conventional kind. Perhaps to compensate for these limitations Marston introduced a good deal of sensational and melodramatic incident. Sophonisba herself is well drawn as representing a serene indifference to misfortune; she even collaborates finally with her husband Massinissa in her own death by poisoning, in order that he will not have to keep a promise to hand her over as a prisoner to Scipio. She is the embodiment of Marston's ideal of stoicism, and her ability to stay unruffled and rise above calamity contrasts both with the more passionate and unsteady nature of Massinissa and with the violence of the jealous Syphax, who also loves her and who thinks she should have preferred him. The middle part of the play concerns his attempt to abduct her and force her to his will. Thwarted by her escape through a vault, he consults Erichtho, an enchantress, who promises to help him "Nice Sophonisba's passion to enforce" (IV. i), but it is the witch herself who enters the bed in place of Sophonisba, and who takes the edge of Syphax's lust. Syphax, horrified to discover what he has done, tries to stab her, but, according to the stage direction, "*Erichtho* slips into the ground as *Syphax* offers his sword to her" (V. i). In spite of the presence of a bed onstage during several scenes—for Massinissa's wedding night at the opening, when he is summoned to fight for Carthage before they can consummate their marriage, and then for Syphax's attempt to ravish her—Sophonisba dies "a Virgin wife," and no doubt this is what Marston was mainly concerned to show. It would be surprising if onstage the melodramatic effects, which include the stabbing of a servant in the bed and the emergence of the ghost of Sophonisba's father, Asdrubal, out of an altar, did not take over. The verse, which is strong and varied, is nevertheless not powerful or memorable enough to counteract these.

Marston was at his best as a satirist and writer of comedies or tragicomedies, and his talents seem to have been exactly suited to the possibilities for drama that could be developed in the private theaters. He wrote part of an indifferent tragicomedy called *The Insatiate Countess*, completed by William Barksted and published in 1613, and he had a hand in one or two masques and entertainments, but after 1606 he seems to have withdrawn from the stage, selling his share in the Queen's Revels in 1608. He had produced a string of witty, entertaining, but loosely structured, and sometimes casually written, satirical comedies, innovatory in technique, and cocking a snook at dramatic and literary conventions of the time, as well as at folly and vice. He also wrote the strange tragedy *Sophonisba*, which is remarkable as an attempt to achieve a kind of heroic grandeur or epic quality on the Jacobean stage, with its setting in the wars of Carthage, and the heroic pomp of much of the verse:

> Then look as when a Falcon towers aloft
> Whole shoals of fowl and flocks of lesser birds
> Crouch fearfully and dive, some among sedge,
> Some weep in brakes: so Massinissa's sword
> Brandisht aloft, toss'd 'bout his shining casque,
> Made stoop whole squadrons.
>
> (II. iii. 69–74)

Heroic similes do not necessarily make a good play, and none of Marston's other works could have the zest and novelty of the two *Antonio* plays, while none of them has the depth and resonance of *The Malcontent*, by which above all he is remembered.

THE MALCONTENT

MARSTON's most important play, and the one on which his reputation chiefly rests, was notable enough when first acted to be "stolen" by an adult company, and performed, with some additions especially written for it by John Webster, at the Globe. It is characteristic of Marston's satirical plays in its exploitation of discontinuities of action and its manipulation of characters for comic or shock effects, with some deliberate use of burlesque and bathos; but it has a depth that makes *The Fawn* and *The Dutch Courtesan* seem slight by comparison, and realizes the potentialities present in the *Antonio* plays. Marston calls the play a comedy in his Address to the Reader, and the characters tend to verge at times on caricature, which is what the very names of some, like Maquerelle, a hideous old bawd, or stinking fish, suggest. But the dialogue contains serious speeches, and a good deal of quasi-philosophical reflection is put into the mouths of Pietro the "villain," who has usurped the dukedom of Genoa, and Malevole, the "malcontent," the disguised true Duke Altofronto, who stalks the court as a satiric commentator and eventually recovers both his throne and his wife Maria, who has been lingering in prison. But however serious the speeches may be, the tendency of the action is to dissipate their effect; railing against vice seems in the end a bit pointless when the vicious are ineffectual and when villainy never achieves its end. Marston chooses rather to emphasize theatricality, as at the climax of the play, when in act IV the villainous Mendoza contrives to hire Malevole and the disguised Pietro to poison one another, a device that leads to the scene in which the two characters echo one another in revealing all:

Pietro:	I am commanded to poison thee.
Malevole:	I am commanded to poison thee, at supper.
Pietro:	At supper?
Malevole:	In the citadel.
Pietro:	In the citadel?
Malevole:	Cross-capers! Tricks!

(IV. ii. 7–11)

The plot does not issue in action but in "cross-capers," and the effect is one of comic bathos, in a ludicrous descent from the grand threats in rhyming couplets with which Mendoza closes the previous scene:

> Then conclude,
> They live not to cry out ingratitude,
> *One stick burns t'other, steel cuts steel alone;*
> *'Tis good trust few; but O, 'tis best trust none.*
> (IV. i. 238–241)

Not content with undoing in the action that follows any serious effect these lines might have, Marston goes on to give Malevole a topical joke that invites the audience not to take such speeches too seriously. Pietro comes on speaking in the same vein as Mendoza, as if he were in a serious revenge play:

Pietro:	O! let the last day fall; drop, drop on our cursed heads! Let heaven unclasp itself, vomit forth flames!
Malevole:	O do not rant, do not turn player—there's more of them than can well live one by another already.

(IV. ii. 2–5)

Here Marston deflates the "serious" speeches of Mendoza and Pietro, in action and in dialogue.

This exploitation of tricks, coincidences, sudden reversals, and surprises for their own sake tends to predominate in performance over the more serious elements in the play, but it would be a mistake to think of this action as merely frivolous. The effect is more complex. The characters take themselves seriously, but inhabit a sort of cartoon version of a corrupt court, in which revenge motifs tend to collapse into comedy. The overall strength of the play, in a curious way, relates to this, for it has the kind of seriousness that caricature can have, releasing the grosser appetites and energies of human beings into inflated and grotesque proportions in character and language, but containing them at the level of gesture by denying them fulfillment; because of this we can be amused and enjoy an exhibition that exposes potential violence and horror but that allows us to contemplate it with pleasure because it is all playful and exaggerated, and because of the satirical commentary provided within the play, mainly by Malevole/Altofronto.

Malevole has been seen as a spokesman for Marston, and it is true that insofar as the play has a controlling voice or vision it is his, since he pulls the strings and arranges much of the action. He does not provide an effective moral vision so much as indulge himself in a kind of variety show, a display of humors and fantasies, bringing to life his wildest chimeras and conceits, as suggested in an exchange of dialogue with Pietro:

Pietro:	I hear thou never sleep'st?
Malevole:	O no, but dream the most fantastical . . . O heaven! O fubbery, fubbery!
Pietro:	Dream? What dream'st?
Malevole:	Why, methinks I see that signior pawn his footcloth, that *metreza* her plate; this madam takes physic that t'other monsieur may minister to her; here is a pander jewelled; there is a fellow in a shift of satin this day that could not shift a shirt t' other night; here a Paris supports that Helen; there's a lady Guinever bears up that Sir Lancelot—dreams, dreams, visions, fantasies, chimeras, imaginations, tricks, conceits!

(I. iii. 85–98)

The world of the play is something like a realization of Malevole's dreams, and however pungently satirical his comments are from time to time, the action betrays his relish in the acting out of his fantasies.

The play is important partly because of this. The daring and range of Marston's dramaturgy mark him an original. The play anticipates the development of tragicomedy. From the first entry of Malevole to "out-of-tune" music, Marston jars his audience with a series of surprises and theatrical cross-capers. The threats of death, which turn out to be empty of danger, climaxed in the "poisoning" by Mendoza of Malevole, who seems to die but jumps up to speak, full of life, a few lines later (V. iii), and the "repentance" of Aurelia, lamenting her sins and wishing for death, when the audience knows she is on her way to the cell of a "hermit" who is in fact her husband, are notable examples of what became the stock in trade of Beaumont and Fletcher, who focus in a more limited way on theatrical gestures that issue in melodramatic effects. *The Malcontent* also influenced later tragedy, especially plays such as *The Revenger's Tragedy* and the work of dramatists such as Webster. For in it Marston showed how to make the most of the malcontent figure in order to create a variety of satirical perspectives. More than this, he revealed new ways in which entertaining stage effects could be achieved by the conscious exploitation of theatrical artifice, and in showing how by exaggeration and discontinuity the conventions of revenge tragedy could become comic, he came near to discovering a drama of the absurd long before the twentieth century.

THE REVENGER'S TRAGEDY

THIS remarkable play was published at the beginning of 1608, some copies bearing the date 1607. No author's name appears on the title page, and it was first ascribed to Cyril Tourneur in a playlist of 1656. Tourneur had written a play with a parallel title, *The Atheist's Tragedy* (1611), which, in spite of some marked stylistic differences, offered enough points of contact with the earlier work to make the ascription seem reasonable, and his authorship of it was generally accepted until the twentieth century. In recent years much attention has been paid to this question, and various studies of the imagery and language of *The Revenger's Tragedy* have con-

siderably weakened the case for assigning the play to Tourneur and convinced many that it was written by Thomas Middleton, whose peculiar linguistic habits can be found in it. As against this, the play was performed by the King's Men, or Shakespeare's Company, according to the title page, and all Middleton's early plays were written for children's companies. Also, in a court case of 1609, Middleton said he had written a tragedy called *The Viper and Her Brood*, which is hardly likely to be the same as *The Revenger's Tragedy*, since this was already in print by then; otherwise he is not known to have written any tragedies during this period. In any case the authorship issue should not be allowed to distract attention from the play itself; whether by Tourneur, Middleton, or someone else, it is something very special, a masterpiece unique in its time, and perhaps of an unrepeatable kind.

It is a play appropriately considered in relation to *The Malcontent*, for it uses many of Marston's techniques, but for a rather different purpose and in a more structurally coherent way. The central figure, Vindice, owes something to the image of the malcontent, as he is educated but poor, the son of a "worthy gentleman" who was disgraced for some unexplained reason at the court that is the play's setting and who died "Of discontent, the nobleman's consumption" (I. ii. 127). However, in a fashion that also owes something to Marston, he plays variations on this theme, appearing in disguise in act IV as a different kind of malcontent, absorbed in melancholy. The action of the play is intricate but easily followed and consistent. Vindice begins by seeking the justice he cannot get for the death of his betrothed, who was poisoned by the duke because she would not yield to his lust. It is useless for him to seek a remedy in law, since the duke himself controls everything. But Vindice, whose situation resembles Hamlet's to the extent that he cannot obtain justice, extends his aims with a kind of missionary zeal to "blast this villainous dukedom vex'd with sin." The opening is brilliant; Vindice, glowering over the skull of his dead mistress, watches as a procession of courtiers led by the duke and his family cross the stage; they may be thought of as gorgeously costumed to indicate the luxury of the court. Clutching his memento mori, like some figure from an emblematic painting, Vindice is not only reminding himself and the audience of the death of his betrothed and of the need to think upon one's end (*respice finem*, the usual motto accompanying the death's head), but, more largely, he stands rather like the figure of Death itself in a dance of Death, about to seize each of the gay figures prancing unaware in front of him. For we see at once that his desire for vengeance spreads out to embrace all:

> Duke, royal lecher; go, grey-hair'd adultery;
> And thou his son, as impious steep'd as he;
> And thou his bastard, true-begot in evil;
> And thou his duchess, that will do with devil . . .
> (I. i. 1–4)

Vindice has appointed himself the moral arbiter of this world, and in this he is related to Marston's satirical spokesmen. But where they tend to act as spectators, or prove ineffectual in plays that move, like *The Malcontent*, to a comic resolution, Vindice initiates right away, with his brother Hippolito, a series of schemes designed not only to bring the duke to his death but to rid the court of all corruption.

He is so appalled by the viciousness of his world that he fails to notice what is happening to himself; in plotting to bring the duke to an assignation with a "lady," who is in fact the skull of his dead mistress dressed up, and then poisoning the lips of the skull so that the duke will die from kissing her, Vindice shows that he is no better than the rest. In this he differs from Hamlet, who wrestles all along with his conscience; yet his moral passion, directed against a corrupt world, carries great force, and it is largely through this, embodied as it is in magnificent poetry, that *The Revenger's Tragedy* impresses itself as a serious and disturbing play. This passion is one facet of Vindice, who can forget it in the sheer pleasure of manipulating others. He is a master of intrigue, always ready with a witty device, an actor who loves disguise and pretense, and the pleasure of teasing, and finally tormenting, others. He twice takes service with Lussurioso, the duke's eldest son and heir to the throne, as a means of effecting his revenge; and his most brilliant stroke is to dress the body of the murdered duke in the clothes of his first disguise as Piato, so ridding himself of an identity he no longer has a use for and diverting suspicion from himself. The action is full of lesser intrigues, as Lussurioso seeks to seduce Castiza, Vindice's sister, ironically employing him as a go-between, and the duchess' sons seek to have Lussurioso, the duke's son by a previous marriage, executed so as to ease their path to the throne. Behind these characters is the more shadowy figure of Antonio, whose wife was raped by the duchess' younger son and committed suicide. Antonio stands, like Castiza, as a moral figure in a generally vicious world, surviving at the end to take over the dukedom and announcing a new hope:

> May I so rule that heaven may keep the crown.
> (V. iii. 89)

Vindice is both part of this world, as the arch-intriguer, cleverer, wittier, more aware of what he is about than the others, and at the same time a satiric spokesman, commenting on the world, making us see through his eyes the full scope of its monstrous lust, greed, and ambition. The play's central irony stems from the contrast between his sharp insight into the nature of what he sees around him and his growing inability to relate this to what he is himself doing. As satiric spokesman he can chill the audience by making us see ourselves reflected, in however distorted a fashion, in the world of the play. So, in the central scene in act III, when he brings on the skull of his betrothed, dressed up to look like a lady to satisfy the duke's lust, he meditates on it in relation to all of us:

> Does every proud and self-affecting dame
> Camphor her face for this? And grieve her maker
> In sinful baths of milk, when many an infant starves
> For her superfluous outside—all for this?
> Who now bids twenty pound a night, prepares
> Music, perfumes, and sweetmeats? All are hush'd;
> Thou mayst lie chaste now. It were fine, methinks,
> To have thee seen at revels, forgetful feasts,
> And unclean brothels; sure, 'twould fright the sinner,
> And make him a good coward, put a reveller
> Out of his antic amble,
> And cloy an epicure with empty dishes.
> Here might a scornful and ambitious woman
> Look through and through herself;—see, ladies, with
>   false forms
> You deceive men, but cannot deceive worms.
> (III. v. 84–98)

Here the general comments, in the form of rhetorical questions demanding our uncomfortable assent, suddenly become an outright attack on the audience, or the women in it, as he faces us with the skull, the death's head grinning just under the makeup and the handsome clothes. The speech relates to the court, but at the same time is daring in its wilder challenge, its confidence that in the theater we "All are hush'd." Vindice assumes the role almost of preacher here, with his social conscience about starving children, and his comment on the proud woman who grieves "her maker."

Yet he fails to link this notion of what is "sinful" with what he is at this moment putting into effect—his plan to poison the duke and torture him even as he is dying. By this time he has come to enjoy his own intellectual control, his wit, his manipulation of others so much that, in the sheer self-congratulation and excitement generated by his inventiveness, he loses sight of the nature of his actions. In this scene he bursts in at the beginning, longing to display his latest device to Hippolito, high in triumph at his own skill:

> O sweet, delectable, rare, happy, ravishing!
> (III. v. 1)

This delight in his own intelligence makes for some amusing moments in the play, which at times verges on farce, although always with an undertone of savagery; Vindice is self-consciously controlling others and enjoying his success; and, as we recognize the total viciousness of the court, we are prepared to enjoy the games he plays and to share his pleasure in his wit, which is also the wit of the dramatist. Simply by being more intelligent, and starting with the moral advantage of being sinned against rather than sinning, Vindice carries us with him, even though long before act III we have seen that his pursuit of revenge has become merely vindictive, and is corrupt, if not as nasty as the combination of malice, greed, and lust common in the court. It is at the end of this scene that the full horror of what Vindice is about is brought home to the audience. With Hippolito, he is making the duke, who is dying from the poisoned kiss, watch his wife, the duchess, meet his own bastard son Spurio in a lustful assignation. He holds a dagger at the duke's heart, while Hippolito pins down the duke's tongue with another dagger to keep him quiet, and Vindice cries:

> Let our two other hands tear up his lids
> And make his eyes, like comets, shine through blood:
> When the bad bleeds, then is the tragedy good.
> (III. v. 203–205)

Here the combination of wanton cruelty and a moralizing that has become a cliché is revolting and reminds us of the irony Vindice has lost sight of—that he has become "the bad" himself as much as the duke.

Perhaps this is, nevertheless, to treat the play too realistically. The bizarre and gruesome humor of scenes like this one is far removed from any ordinary level of realism or credibility. Most of the characters have emblematic names, as "Vindice" simply means "revenger," his sister Castiza's name is from the Italian "Casta," or chaste, and "Lussurioso" means lecherous or riotous. The piece has often been seen as related to the medieval morality play in its conventional nature, but it is a morality sophisticated and brought up to date through the satirical impact of Marston. The action consists of a series of intrigues and ironic reversals that may border on farce, but the comic elements work, as in some powerful forms of caricature art, to make it possible for the audience to watch without revulsion what on a naturalistic level would be merely horrible. The world of the play is grotesque, and Vindice's apparent exaggerations in act I describe, as it turns out, pretty well what is going on in the court:

> Some father dreads not (gone to bed in wine)
> To slide from the mother, and cling the daughter-in-law;
> Some uncles are adulterous with their nieces,
> Brothers with brothers' wives. O, hour of incest!
> Any kin now, next to the rim o' th' sister,
> Is man's meat in these days . . .
> (I. iii. 58–63)

The humor and conventional distancing of the play make contemplation of this world possible. Vindice acts for most of the play as a commentator, and we see the action through his eyes, his macabre joking and sense of artistry pointing up our awareness of the grotesque nature of the action. As manipulator, puppetmaster, he displays for us the rottenness of the court, as he is intellectually, if not morally, aware of and critically hostile to the world around him.

Where in Marston's plays the author intrudes to joke with the audience and mock the conventions of the play or indulge in self-parody, in *The Revenger's Tragedy* the author never shows his hand but projects the action through Vindice, whose intellectual control is matched by his inability to see his own actions morally. Yet his view of the court around him is sharp and perceptive, as he edges us into visualizing the possibility of a world controlled by greed and lust, a vision not far from that purveyed by a good deal of modern television and cinema. In a justly celebrated speech, Vindice provides an especially subtle and forceful image of such a world, when he recognizes and projects for us the perversion of values in the pursuit of beauty, sex, and wealth:

> And now methinks I could e'en chide myself
> For doting on her beauty, though her death
> Shall be reveng'd after no common action.
> Does the silk-worm expend her yellow labours
> For thee? for thee does she undo herself?
> Are lordships sold to maintain ladyships
> For the poor benefit of a bewitching minute?
> Why does yon fellow falsify high-ways,
> And put his life between the judge's lips,
> To refine such a thing? keeps horse and men
> To beat their valours for her?
> Surely we are all mad people, and they
> Whom we think are, are not; we mistake those:
> 'Tis we are mad in sense, they but in clothes.
>
> (III. v. 69–82)

This speech exemplifies the most remarkable feature of the play, the superb compression and explosive force of its poetry. Here the vivid metaphors, with the boldly suggestive activity of the verbs "expend," "undo," "falsify," and "beat," convey a rich vitality, a sense of exuberance and delight in the play of language that is quite original, and characteristic of the poetic texture of the play. At the same time these lines are full of the energy of Vindice's moral passion, brilliantly translated into dramatic terms, as he addresses a death's head grotesquely clothed, and through that embraces all of us in the image of madness. To be able to judge his world mad shows a better balance in Vindice, and yet he too is bound up in the madness (as his generalizing "we" suggests), not by the willful pursuit of grossly immoral ends but because, absorbed in the pleasure of his craft, the success of his cunning intrigues, he loses sight of their moral nastiness, to the point where at the end he boasts to the new Duke Antonio of the murder of the old duke: "Twas somewhat witty carried, though we say it" (V.iii.97). Antonio sees at once what Vindice and Hippolito have become blind to—that murder is merely a game to them and that they will do anything "witty." He cries: "You that would murder him, would murder me" (V. iii. 105), and sends Vindice to the scaffold.

By comparison with him and with the actions in which he is involved, especially with Lussurioso, who has his own splendidly hideous vitality, Antonio is a cipher, and Castiza is little more than a representative of chastity, even though she has her moments of dramatic power in saying no to temptation. Yet the intensity and vigorous imagery of the play's astonishing poetry, with its wit, suppleness, and richness of metaphor, can give even these figures dignity and stature, as in Castiza's fine rebuff to the lure of wealth and lust: "Your tongues have struck hot irons on my face" (II. i. 238). Because of this the play may properly be seen as a revenge tragedy, belonging to a tradition that includes *Hamlet*, which it echoes occasionally—notably when Vindice and Hippolito threaten their morally lax mother (IV.iv) with daggers in their hands, and, like Gertrude threatened by Hamlet, she cries: "What, will you murder me?" In setting the action in a court dedicated to lust and greed and showing a protagonist who becomes a villain without seeing it, the play provides an original treatment of a convention with a limited range of possibilities. The features that recall Marston—the frequent use of disguise, the masque that brings about the catastrophe (as in *Antonio's Revenge*), the self-consciousness of the characters in the roles they play, the elaborate intrigues—are all made to serve a more rigorous design and controlled purpose than in *The Malcontent*, a design reinforced by the tough splendors of the verse, which gives the play an extraordinary power in the theater. It is not a play that moves us, for it lacks pathos and depth of character, but it can grip modern audiences, entertaining them and making them uneasy, as a tragic satire penetratingly exposing in its exaggerations not only "the skull beneath the skin," but the full monstrosity of those passions that are precariously kept in control in a society in which people with rank and wealth can obtain anything they want. After this, perhaps the only really new development in the revenge play had to take the form of *The Atheist's Tragedy*, in which the protagonist abandons the idea of revenge altogether.

TOURNEUR'S LIFE AND WORK

CYRIL TOURNEUR is known chiefly for his play *The Atheist's Tragedy*, and the long association of his name with *The Revenger's Tragedy*. Like Marston, he did not seek to make a career as a professional writer. His date of birth can only be conjectured, and almost nothing is known about his early life. He may have been related to a Captain Richard Turnor, who was in the service of the Vere and Cecil families and who died in 1598, for Cyril Tourneur too served these same families. At some time he was secretary to Sir Francis Vere, who commanded English forces in the Netherlands during the wars with Spain in the closing years of Elizabeth's reign. Cyril Tourneur played some part in that campaign, and in *The Atheist's Tragedy* the hero, Charlemont, goes off to fight at the siege of Ostend (1601-1604). It is probable that Tourneur was the author of "A Funeral Poem Upon the Death of the Most Worthy and True Soldier Sir Francis Vere" in 1609. In 1612 Tourneur published *The Character of Robert Earl of Salisbury*, after the death of Robert Cecil in May of that year, and he also wrote a poem addressed to Lady Anne Cecil, Lord Burleigh's daughter. The former is his one prose work, unless the pamphlet *Laugh and Lie Down*, or *The World's Folly*, issued in 1605 over the initials "C.T.," is by him. What prompted his first publication, the obscure long poem *The Transformed Metamorphosis* (1600), is not known. This shows the influence of Marston in its satirical vision of the world as given over to vice:

> Black Avarice, makes sale of Holiness,
> And steaming Luxury doth broach her lust;
> Red-tyrannizing wrath doth souls oppress
> And canker'd Envy falsifies all trust . . .
>
> (64-68)

The images of a world dominated by lust and greed, and transformed into the "tragic scenes of woe" with which the poem begins, might be seen as providing a link with the world of *The Revenger's Tragedy* and *The Atheist's Tragedy*. The latter part of the poem becomes an allegorical tale in which a knight, Mavortio, overcomes a monster on the island of Delta. It is tempting to identify Mavortio as Sir Francis Vere, but the meaning has not been satisfactorily explained. The ending celebrates the purifying of the world in the triumph of Queen Elizabeth:

> Come, come you wights that are transformed quite,
> *Eliza* will you retransform again.
>
> (596-597)

The satirical opening of the poem shows the marked influence of Marston, but the intention of the whole work remains unclear.

These publications constitute a meager list, and none of them is of much literary interest. Probably Tourneur would be virtually forgotten now if it were not for a few years he practiced as a dramatist. Apart from a possible connection with *The Revenger's Tragedy*, he wrote *The Atheist's Tragedy* (published 1611) and *The Nobleman*, a lost tragicomedy that is known to have been performed at court in 1612. He may have had a hand in other plays, for in June 1613 the writer Robert Daborne, who cobbled plays together for the theater owner Philip Henslowe, wrote that he had given an act of an otherwise unknown play, *The Arraignment of London*, to Tourneur to write. Tourneur's association with the theater and theater people at this time is also suggested by the inclusion of his elegy "A Grief on the Death of Prince Henry" in a volume printed in 1613, containing elegies also by the dramatists John Webster and John Heywood.

At the end of 1613 Tourneur was in government service, taking official letters to Brussels, and he may well have spent most of his remaining years abroad. He is known to have been in England in 1617, when he was arrested for some unknown cause and released on the intercession of Sir Edward Cecil, who had fought in the Netherlands under Sir Francis Vere. Presumably Cecil remained his patron, for in 1625, when, as Viscount Wimbledon, he was appointed commander of a naval action aimed at seizing Spanish treasure ships off Cadiz, Tourneur was employed as secretary to his council of war. The expedition failed, and the fleet turned back. Many of the men aboard the *Royal Anne*, Cecil's flagship, fell ill and were put ashore at Kinsale, Ireland. Tourneur was among these, and he died there in February 1626. The work by which he is most securely known, *The Atheist's Tragedy*, is thought to have been written about 1610-1611, and it may constitute a response to George Chapman's *The Revenge of Bussy D'Ambois* (published 1613, but written some years earlier), which is also set in France, and in which the stoic hero Clermont (whose name resembles Tourneur's Charlemont) ends by carrying out reluctantly a revenge for the death of his brother. The title of Tourneur's play links it with *The Revenger's Tragedy*, and it belongs more in the tradition exemplified by that play than it does with Chapman's mode of drama.

THE ATHEIST'S TRAGEDY

THE central figure in the play is D'Amville, who proclaims himself, in effect, an atheist at the beginning by agreeing with his "instrument," as the list of characters describes his servant Borachio, that "Wealth is lord of all felicity" (I.i.30). D'Amville sees no higher good than nature and has no criterion for action other than a selfish rationalism that permits any deed that furthers his interest and those of his two sons, Rousard and Sebastian, whom he regards as projections of himself into the future. Opposed to him is the young Charlemont, his nephew, who embodies the kind of honor that leads him to want to fight in the wars of Ostend, although his father, Montferrers, would prevent him. Charlemont cries out:

> Shall I serve
> For nothing but a vain parenthesis
> I'th' honour'd story of your family?
> Or hang but like an empty scutcheon
> Between the trophies of my predecessors
> And the rich arms of my posterity?
>
> (I. ii. 18–23)

Here is a different conception of the family from that of D'Amville, and the imagery is appropriate, for as Charlemont embodies martial valor, so Castabella (chaste beauty), to whom he is betrothed, represents true love, what she calls the "chaste affection of the soul" (II.iii.1). To describe these characters in such emblematic terms is to accord them less life than they have in the action, but it points to something central in the play.

The setting is vaguely French, but Tourneur recalls his own service with Sir Francis Vere in the Netherlands in making Charlemont seek to fight in the siege of Ostend, an action that ended in 1604. D'Amville supplies the money to equip Charlemont as a soldier and forces Montferrers to allow his son to go to the wars, thus putting Charlemont under an obligation to him. With Charlemont safely away, D'Amville then has Borachio dress up as a soldier returned from Ostend and report the young hero's death in a fine narrative speech:

> He lay in's armour as if that had been
> His coffin, and the weeping sea, like one
> Whose wilder temper doth lament the death
> Of him whom in his rage he slew, runs up

> The shore, embraces him, kisses his cheek,
> Goes back again, and forces up the sands
> To bury him, and ev'ry time it pars,
> Sheds tears upon him . . .
>
> (II. i. 79–86)

The report is credited and enables D'Amville, with the aid of Castabella's father and stepmother, Belforest and Levidulcia, to force her into a marriage with his elder son, Rousard. Under cover of a servants' quarrel, D'Amville and Borachio also engineer the murder of Montferrers, whose wealth D'Amville inherits, since Charlemont is supposed dead. It seems that everything is going D'Amville's way, and he does not notice the dramatic irony of the thunder and lightning that mark his triumph in the death of Montferrers or the irony of the false protestations of woe that he makes at the "news" of the death of Charlemont:

> Drop out
> Mine eye-balls, and let envious Fortune play
> At tennis with 'em—Have I liv'd to this?
> Malicious Nature! Hadst thou born me blind,
> Th'hadst yet been something favourable to me . . .
>
> (II. iv. 25–29)

It is a little while before D'Amville discovers just how malicious nature can be. The complications of the third and fourth acts include a good deal of comic knockabout stuff, involving various minor characters like Languebeau Snuffe (a candlemaker —hence "snuff"—turned Puritan priest), and the lecherous Levidulcia, as well as much violence. Warned by the ghost of his father that all is not well, Charlemont returns to quarrel with Sebastian and kill Borachio, who is attempting to murder him at the instigation of D'Amville. Most of act IV takes place in a churchyard, with a charnel house and a number of skulls onstage. Here Charlemont finds a ghost's costume, a "sheet, hair and beard," discarded by Languebeau Snuffe, and uses it at the critical moment to frighten away D'Amville when he is about to rape Castabella. Charlemont and Castabella, who puts her trust in God, lie down with death's heads for pillows, unperturbed by their ghoulish surroundings, while D'Amville, the rationalist who appeals to nature, is distracted as he meditates on a skull.

Here D'Amville's vulnerability is seen. He attempts to force Castabella because Rousard fell sick on marrying her and cannot consummate the marriage, so incest becomes a means to ensure the continuance of his line; but the intervention of Charlemont, thought by D'Amville to be the ghost of the murdered Montferrers, and his encounter with a death's head, startle him for the first time into a sense of the horror of his deeds:

> Why doest thou stare upon me? Thou art not
> The skull of him I murder'd. What hast thou
> To do to vex my conscience? Sure thou wert
> The head of a most dogged usurer,
> Th'art so uncharitable . . .
>
> (IV. iii. 211–215)

He dismisses his conscience and recovers his wits by the beginning of act V when, with the gold he has inherited from Montferrers in his possession and with Charlemont and Castabella in prison as suspected murderers of Borachio, he seems to be at the zenith of his fortunes. At this point Rousard is brought in, dying from the illness that struck him down on his marriage. Sebastian, his other son, has been pursuing an adulterous affair with Levidulcia, and when he is found with her by her husband, Belforest, at the end of act IV, the two men fight and kill each other. So now the body of Sebastian too is carried on stage, and, faced with the end of that posterity (I.i.43) for whose benefit all his labors had been intended, D'Amville at last concedes that there is a power above nature:

> Now to myself I am ridiculous.
> Nature, thou art a traitor to my soul.
> Thou hast abus'd my trust. I will complain
> To a superior court to right my wrong.
> I'll prove thee a forger of false assurances.
> In yond' Star Chamber thou shalt answer it.
> Withdraw the bodies. O the sense of death
> Begins to trouble my distracted soul.
>
> (V. i. 115–122)

D'Amville, "distracted" again at the trial of Charlemont and Castabella, who leap on the scaffold and call for water (emblem of purity and temperance), cannot comfort himself by drinking wine, as the thought of death congeals his blood. He insists on acting as executioner and answers his own crimes in God's star chamber when, as the stage direction puts it, he "strikes out his own brains" with the axe. He does not do this so thoroughly as to prevent him from making a full confession of his misdeeds, and Charlemont is left

to enjoy Castabella and to proclaim "That *Patience is the honest man's revenge*" (V. ii. 278).

To recount the action of the play in this way is also to comment on it, for a good deal of the play's thematic design is expressed in the narrative. The progress of D'Amville, from the assurance of his "atheism" to the recognition of defeat when both his sons are dead, and to the admission that "Nature" is not all-powerful, is matched by Charlemont's growing confidence once he accepts the advice given to him supernaturally by the ghost of his father, that he should not seek revenge. The various emblematic features of the play contribute to the working out of this tragicomic theme. Act III begins with the funeral processions of Montferrers, who was murdered by D'Amville, and Charlemont, who is reported dead. D'Amville's triumph here is set visually against his dismay at the introduction of the dead bodies of Rousard and Sebastian in act V. The skulls in the churchyard, on which Charlemont and Castabella sleep peacefully, frighten D'Amville into an awareness of the "loathsome horror" of his sin. The wine he drinks at the end cannot unfreeze his blood, while Charlemont cheerfully drinks water on the scaffold.

It may be that Tourneur also intended us to see a contrast between the superior atheism of D'Amville, who is rational in seeking wealth not for mere sensual gratification but for power and for the sake of his family, and the cruder immorality of Sebastian and Levidulcia, who pursue sensual pleasure for its own sake. If so, this contrast is muddied by Sebastian's good qualities, which are shown when he comes to the aid of Charlemont, and by the fact that D'Amville's attempt to rape Castabella, with its implications of incest, is more revolting than Levidulcia's attempted adultery with Sebastian. The issue is further clouded by Levidulcia's instant repentance and suicide after her husband and Sebastian kill one another. Here the differences from *The Revenger's Tragedy* are most noticeable. The plays have something in common: the graveyard humor, the skulls, the acceptance of lust, even incest, by many characters as normal. *The Revenger's Tragedy* generates its power through the quality of its poetry, which sustains the finely engineered structure of intrigues through the verbal and imaginative dominance of Vindice. By contrast, *The Atheist's Tragedy* works chiefly through its action, which embodies its thematic oppositions.

The interest of *The Atheist's Tragedy* lies largely

in these oppositions and in the novel twist to the conventions of the revenge play, whereby the "revenger" is a Christian who decides not to seek revenge, confronting an atheist who in the end finds his philosophy insufficient. Its weakness lies in the verse, which can rise to fine moments, as in some of the passages quoted above, but at its best has a more relaxed and elegiac note than *The Revenger's Tragedy*, relying on simile rather than metaphor, and lacking the vigor or memorable density of image that would carry the extravagances of the action. So most critics have felt that the divine vengeance shown in D'Amville's knocking out his own brains is not saved from absurdity and would be very difficult to stage. The argument and action provide the main strength of the play; it lacks the passion and visionary power of *The Revenger's Tragedy*, which opens up vistas into the hideous possibilities latent within ourselves and our society. *The Atheist's Tragedy* is more abstract, a more philosophical play. But as an original and occasionally very powerful treatment of revenge it has its enduring importance.

SELECTED BIBLIOGRAPHY

I. BIBLIOGRAPHY. S. A. Tannenbaum, *John Marston: A Concise Bibliography* (New York, 1946); S. A. Tannenbaum, *Cyril Tourneur: A Concise Bibliography* (New York, 1946); C. A. Pennel, ed., *Cyril Tourneur*, Elizabethan Bibliographies Supplements, no. 2 (London, 1967); C. A. Pennel, ed., *George Chapman and John Marston*, Elizabethan Bibliographies Supplements, no. 4 (London, 1967).

II. GENERAL CRITICISM. M. C. Bradbrook, *Themes and Conventions of Elizabethan Tragedy* (London, 1935); T. Spencer, *Death and Elizabethan Tragedy* (Cambridge, Mass., 1936); U. Ellis-Fermor, *The Jacobean Drama* (London, 1936); F. Bowers, *Elizabethan Revenge Tragedy* (Princeton, 1940; repr. 1966); R. Ornstein, *The Moral Vision of Jacobean Tragedy* (Madison, Wisc., 1960); I. Ribner, *Jacobean Tragedy: the Quest for Moral Order* (London, 1962); T. B. Tomlinson, *A Study of Elizabethan and Jacobean Tragedy* (London, 1964); R. B. Heilman, *Tragedy and Melodrama* (Seattle, Wash., 1968).

JOHN MARSTON

I. COLLECTED EDITIONS. W. Sheares, ed., *The Workes of Mr. John Marston: Being Tragedies and Comedies Collected Into One Volume* (London, 1633); A. H. Bullen, ed., *The Works*, 3 vols. (London, 1887; repr. 1970); H. Harvey Wood, ed., *The Plays*, 3 vols. (Edinburgh, 1934–1939); A. Davenport, ed., *The Poems* (Liverpool, 1961).

II. SEPARATE WORKS. Plays: *Jack Drum's Entertainment* (1601), comedy, published anonymously but attributed to Marston, in R. Simpson, ed., *The School of Shakespeare* (London, 1878); *The History of Antonio and Mellida: the First Part* (1602), comedy, in W. W. Greg, ed., Malone Society Reprints (London, 1921), and G. K. Hunter, ed., Regents Renaissance Drama series (London, 1965); *Antonio's Revenge: the Second Part* (London, 1602), tragedy, in W. W. Greg, ed., Malone Society Reprints (London, 1921), and G. K. Hunter, ed., Regents Renaissance Drama series (London, 1965); *The Malcontent* (1604), tragicomedy, in G. B. Harrison, ed. (London, 1933), M. L. King, ed., Regents Renaissance Drama series (London, 1964), B. Harris, ed., New Mermaids series (London, 1967), and G. K. Hunter, ed., The Revels Plays series (London, 1975); *Eastward, Ho!* (1605), comedy, mainly the work of Chapman and Jonson, with Marston a minor collaborator; *The Dutch Courtesan* (1605), comedy, in M. L. King, ed., Regents Renaissance Drama series (London, 1965), T. Davison, ed., Fountainwell Drama Texts (Edinburgh, 1968); *Parasitaster: or The Fawn* (1606), comedy, in G. A. Smith, ed., Regents Renaissance Drama series (London, 1965); *The Wonder of Women: or The Tragedie of Sophonisba* (1606), tragedy; *What You Will* (1607), in C. W. Dilke, ed., *Old English Plays*, vol. II (London, 1814); *Histriomastix: or The Player Whipt* (1610), comedy, published anonymously but attributed to Marston, in Tudor Facsimile Texts (London, 1912); *The Insatiate Countess* (1613), tragicomedy, begun by Marston and completed by William Barksted.

Poems: *The Metamorphosis of Pigmalions Image and Certain Satyres* (1598), in E. S. Donno, ed., *Elizabethan Minor Epics* (New York, 1963); *The Scourge of Villanie: Three Bookes of Satyres* (1598), in G. B. Harrison, ed. (London, 1925).

Criticism: William Hazlitt, *Lectures on the Dramatic Literature of the Age of Elizabeth* (London, 1820), the lecture on Marston praises him as a dramatic satirist; J. H. Penniman, *The War of the Theatres* (Philadelphia, 1897), still the best account of the so-called war; H. N. Hillebrand, *The Child Actors* (Urbana, Ill., 1926), remains the standard history; T. S. Eliot, *Selected Essays* (London, 1934), stimulated new interest in Marston and Tourneur; O. J. Campbell, *Comicall Satyre and Shakespeare's Troilus and Cressida* (San Marino, Calif., 1938), first, and still an important, study of dramatic satire in relation to Marston, Jonson, and Shakespeare; L. Babb, *The Elizabethan Malady* (East Lansing, 1951), on melancholy and the malcontent as a type; A. Harbage, *Shakespeare and the Rival Traditions* (New York, 1952), schematic treatment of the rivalry between adult and children's companies; G. Cross, "Some Notes on the Vocabulary of John Marston" in *Notes and Queries*, nos. 199–206, 208 (London, 1954–1961; 1963); A. Axelrad, *Un* malcontent élisabéthain: John Marston (Paris, 1955); J. Peter, *Complaint and Satire in Early English Literature* (Oxford, 1956), especially useful for literary background; A. Kernan, *The Cankered Muse* (New Haven, 1959), on satire generally, helpful in relation to Marston; G. K. Hunter, "English Folly and Italian Vice: The Moral Landscape of John Marston" in J. R. Brown and B. Harris, eds., *Jacobean Theatre*, Stratford-upon-Avon Studies I (London, 1960); A. Caputi, *John Marston, Satirist* (Ithaca, 1961), an important study, emphasizing Marston's stoicism; B. Gibbons, *Jacobean City Comedy* (London, 1968), includes an essay on Marston's comedies and *The Malcontent*; P. Finkelpearl, *John Marston of the Middle Temple* (Cambridge, Mass., 1969), the fullest biography, with a critical account of Marston emphasizing his connections with the Inns of Court; J. Kaplan, "John Marston's *Fawn*: A Saturnalian Satire" in *Studies in English Literature 1500-1900*, vol. IX (London, 1969); R. A. Foakes, "Tragedy of the Children's Theatres After 1600: A Challenge to the Adult Stage" in D. Galloway, ed., *The Elizabethan Theatre*, vol. II (London, 1970); Geoffrey Aggeler, "Stoicism and Revenge in Marston" in *English Studies*, vol. I (London, 1970); Ejner Jensen, "Theme and Imagery in *The Malcontent*" in *Studies in English Literature 1500-1900*, vol. X (London, 1970); R. A. Foakes, *Shakespeare: From the Dark Comedies to the Last Plays* (London, 1971), argues that Marston's satirical comedy and tragedy influenced Shakespeare's development; B. G. Lyons, *Voices of Melancholy* (London, 1971), claims Marston's treatment of melancholy was innovative and original; M. Shapiro, *Children of the Revels: The Boy Companies and Their Plays* (New York, 1971), on the companies operating after 1599, with special emphasis on Marston as the major dramatist writing for them; T. F. Wharton, "*The Malcontent* and 'Dreams, Visions, Fantasies'" in *Essays in Criticism*, vol. XXIV (London, 1974); R. A. Foakes, "On Marston, *The Malcontent*, and *The Revenger's Tragedy*" in G. R. Hibbard, ed., *The Elizabethan Theatre*, vol. VI (Toronto, 1978).

CYRIL TOURNEUR

I. COLLECTED EDITIONS. J. Churton Collins, ed., *The Plays and Poems of Cyril Tourneur*, 2 vols. (London, 1878); Allardyce Nicoll, ed., *The Works of Cyril Tourneur* (London, 1930); G. R. Parfitt, ed., *The Plays of Cyril Tourneur* (Cambridge, 1978).

II. SEPARATE WORKS. *The Transformed Metamorphosis* (1600), poem; *The Revenger's Tragedy* (1607), repr. in A. J. Symonds, ed., *Webster and Tourneur*, Mermaids series (London, 1888; repr. 1954); H. Fluchère, ed. and tr., *La tragédie du vengeur* (Paris, 1960); G. Salgado, ed., *Three Jacobean Tragedies* (London, 1965), R. A. Foakes, ed., Revels Plays (London, 1966), and B. Gibbons, ed., New Mermaids series (London, 1967); *A Funerall Poeme upon the Death of the Most Worthy and True Soldier Sir Francis Vere* (1609); *The Atheist's Tragedy* (1611), repr. in A. J. Symonds, ed., *Webster and Tourneur*, Mermaids series (London, 1888; repr. 1954), I. Ribner, ed., Revels Plays (London, 1964), A. H. Gomme, ed., *Jacobean Tragedies* (London, 1969), and B. Morris and R. Gill, eds., New Mermaids series (London, 1976); *The Character of Robert Earle of Salesburye* (1612), prose; *A Grief on the Death of Prince Henrie. In Three Elegies on the Most Lamented Death of Prince Henrie* (1613).

III. CRITICISM. T. S. Eliot, *Selected Essays* (London, 1932), a seminal study of Tourneur; U. Ellis-Fermor, "The Imagery of *The Revenger's Tragedy* and *The Atheist's Tragedy*" in *Modern Language Review*, vol. XXX (London, 1935); L. G. Salingar, "*The Revenger's Tragedy* and The Morality Tradition" in *Scrutiny*, vol. VI (London, 1938); R. A. Foakes, "On the Authorship of *The Revenger's Tragedy*" in *Modern Language Review*, vol. XLVIII (London, 1953); S. Schoenbaum, "*The Revenger's Tragedy*: Jacobean Dance of Death" in *Modern Language Quarterly*, vol. XI (London, 1954); L. G. Salingar, "Tourneur and the Tragedy of Revenge" in *The Age of Shakespeare*, Pelican Guide to English Literature (London, 1955); S. Schoenbaum, *Middleton's Tragedies: A Critical Study* (New York, 1955); Inga-Stina Ewbank (Ekeblad), "An Approach to Tourneur's Imagery" in *Modern Language Review*, vol. LIV (London, 1959); Inga-Stina Ewbank, "On the Authorship of *The Revenger's Tragedy*" in *English Studies*, vol. XLI (London, 1960); George R. Price, "The Authorship and the Bibliography of *The Revenger's Tragedy*" in *The Library*, 5th ser., vol. XV (London, 1960); Allardyce Nicoll, "*The Revenger's Tragedy* and the Virtue of Anonymity" in *Essays on Shakespeare and Elizabethan Drama in Honor of Hardin Craig* (London, 1962); P. Murray, *A Study of Cyril Tourneur* (Philadelphia, 1964), fullest general study, written in the belief that Middleton was the author of *The Revenger's Tragedy*; S. Schoenbaum, *Internal Evidence and Elizabethan Dramatic Authorship* (London, 1966), judicious study of the difficulties of using internal evidence, with a full treatment of *The Revenger's Tragedy*; Daniel Jacobsen, *The Language of The Revenger's Tragedy* (Salzburg, 1974), brings linguistics to bear on a detailed study of the play's imagery; D. J. Lake, *The Canon of Middleton's Plays* (London, 1975), comprehensive array of statistics relating to spelling, word usage, etc., designed to prove that Middleton wrote *The Revenger's Tragedy*; S. Schuman, *Cyril Tourneur*, Twayne's English Authors series, no. 221 (Boston, 1977), a general intro. to the work of Tourneur; P. Ayres, *The Revenger's Tragedy*, Studies in English Literature (London, 1977), a useful short critical account of the play; Stanley Wells, "*The Revenger's Tragedy* Revived" in G. R. Hibbard, ed., *The Elizabethan Theatre*, vol. VI (Toronto, 1978), a valuable analysis of the production by the Royal Shakespeare Company in 1966.

FRANCIS BEAUMONT
(1584-1616)

JOHN FLETCHER
(1579-1625)

Ian Fletcher

Ian Fletcher

CRITICAL HISTORY

OF all Shakespeare's fellow dramatists, Beaumont and Fletcher have suffered the strangest fortune. The fifty-two plays with whose authorship they are credited have touched the extremes of commendation and contempt. In 1647, and again in 1679, they were honored by collection in folio, and so ranked with Shakespeare and Jonson among the most distinguished practitioners of their art. Commonly, at this period, they were judged to have combined the virtues and abstained from the weaknesses of their two older contemporaries. Acted or privately read, their plays gave pleasure. Indeed, until the close of Charles II's reign, they were staged frequently and with applause. Like Shakespeare, they survived in adaptation through the eighteenth to the middle part of the nineteenth century, when Victorian taste began to find their bold speaking offensive.

The reaction of readers against their work set in with romanticism. In his marginalia, Samuel Coleridge missed no opportunity of comparing, to their disadvantage, Beaumont and Fletcher with Shakespeare. It was part of that romantic bardolatry that regarded Shakespeare as moral philosopher, demigod even: "Merciful, wonder-making Heaven, what a man was this Shakespeare." Much of twentieth-century criticism has been as obliquely disparaging as Coleridge's comments: a trenchant paragraph from T. S. Eliot, a sour aside here and there, have conspired to reduce the two authors' status, as if by appeal to some undisclosed consensus. Victorian attitudes have subtly lingered. Their most severe and persuasive critic, M. C. Bradbrook, has firmly associated Beaumont and Fletcher's aesthetic with

their moral lapses and pronounced their tragedies hollow, their tragicomedies "stunningly factitious," their comedies engagingly minor.

The aesthetic decline of English tragedy after Shakespeare has largely been blamed on Beaumont and Fletcher. Yet, if it is absurd to blame Milton for some of the inert diction of his eighteenth-century imitators, it is as absurd to blame Beaumont and Fletcher for the narrow, complacent cavalier drama that succeeded them. Far more than Milton, or Beaumont and Fletcher, it was Shakespeare who built a "Chinese wall": his greatness exhausted the tragic form. He was indeed "the great actuality of the current imagination" down to the beginning of this century. "He did too much for us ever to leave us free—free of judgement, free of reaction"; what Henry James remarked of Charles Dickens' effect on the later nineteenth century is as true of the effect of Shakespeare on the whole course of English tragedy.

The comparison with Shakespeare, mechanically made in the case of Beaumont and Fletcher, though less frequently in the case of their contemporaries, can only work to their harm. Their reputation has become involved with that of the master, but only in a derogatory sense. Neither Beaumont and Fletcher, nor Shakespeare, was the first to practice in English the "middle mood" of tragicomedy, but in 1901 an American scholar suggested that the collaborators had influenced Shakespeare's late "Romances," though it is now more reasonably inferred that all three were responding to a shift in their audience's taste, or perhaps modulating it. The suggestion was regarded as implausible, if not blasphemous and, as a matter of necessity, critics set out to depreciate Beaumont and Fletcher. The facts are that Fletcher succeeded Shakespeare as principal dramatist at the Blackfriars Theatre, and that both he and Beaumont show themselves intensely aware of Shakespeare's work: on occasions they imitate or parody it. Fletcher sometimes inverts or "outdoes" his master: *The False One* gives us Cleopatra before Antony (and Bernard Shaw); *The Sea Voyage* is a feeble pendant to *The Tempest*, though *The Woman's Prize* is barely clouded by its archetype, *The Taming of the Shrew*. Most damaging to Fletcher has been the suggestion that he was Shakespeare's collaborator in *Henry VIII* and the ascription to him of a share in *The Two Noble Kinsmen* and the lost *Cardenio*. Fletcher's hand in *Henry VIII* was detected by nineteenth-century scholars at a moment when the taste for disintegration, triumphant already in the classical and theological field, was beginning to affect literary studies. Superficially at least, *Henry VIII* displays a static, pageantlike structure and a tendency to fragment into scenes, while it lacks a clearly defined central figure or a coherent "philosophy of history": and all those characteristics suggest affinities with Fletcher's talent for romantic and spectacular dramatizing. The high proportion of blank verse with feminine endings also suggests Fletcher's presence.

Since the early part of this century, a reaction against disintegrators in both classical and literary studies has set in. It is fashionable now to reassert the unity of *Henry VIII*, and criticism of that play will probably multiply and lead to sharp revaluation. There are plausible arguments that connect the structural peculiarities of the play to Shakespeare's concerns in his last plays with "archaising," and the main source material, Edward Hall's *Chronicles*, imposes its own limitations, abstaining generally as it does from any direct reference to high politics. The question of joint authorship is still open. The title page of *The Two Noble Kinsmen* (1634) announced it as a joint production of Fletcher and Shakespeare. It was consequently printed in the second Beaumont and Fletcher folio (1679). In the nineteenth century, the play was scrutinized for Shakespearean passages. Metrical tests were applied, not to the 1634 edition, but to a text based on Seward's 1750 edition, where prose (infrequent in Fletcher's work) was printed as irregular verse with a high proportion of feminine endings. A recent book has set out to prove that the play is entirely by Shakespeare. The thesis is barely convincing, though it is very possible—should some scholars accept it—that the play will undergo revaluation.

A first impression of Beaumont and Fletcher's work is likely to be confused. This is the largest single body of dramatic poetry from the Elizabethan-Jacobean period. The work of at least six other authors has been traced in it, while it includes one or two plays in which neither Beaumont nor Fletcher had a hand. The fifty-two plays contain only one unequivocal masterpiece—and that a burlesque. Given such a medley, it remains surprising that the folio should leave a uniform impression. These plays read with almost suspicious ease and contain much lucid and sustained blank verse, broken by songs that rank second only to Shakespeare's in variety and quality, if not in dramatic effect. Such songs contribute to a central theme, but rarely edge it as do Shakespeare's with disquieting double ironies. In structure, the plays sometimes seem calculated to satisfy William Archer's demands for well-made drama. They offer strong scenes with conventional morality, quite in the problem play manner, challenged but not actually exposed. Such dramatic opportunism will come about when values are known to be hollow, but are clung to from moral fatigue. Beaumont and Fletcher rely on coincidence, surprise, and recognizable theatrical types. Their plays often suggest the party game of "consequences" in the ingenuity with which they manipulate predicament. To dismiss them, nonetheless, as mere anticipations of "Sardoodledom," that flimsy kingdom of nineteenth-century French melodrama, would be patently unfair. What is now taken for granted in dramatic construction barely existed before the time of Beaumont and Fletcher, though they obviously owe much to their reverence for Jonson. The tense construction of a play such as *A King and No King* contrasts still with the rambling evolution of some of Shakespeare's work. Still, they seem to be less interested in the inflexible laws that have exercised men, whether in Argos or in England, than in peripheral puzzles, or remote casuistries. To gauge the tone of these plays is difficult, for the dramatists give the impression that they are not deeply involved with their characters. Indeed they degrade their heroes, and sometimes by a species of nasty, even sick, humor. Their characters are deflected deliberately in the direction of the small, the mean, the average, and placed in unfamiliar, at times perverse, situations.

Such characters act with little motivation and seem not to pay for whatever mistakes or crimes they commit. Death is accidental rather than meaningful. Morally, their universe is a void, peopled by individuals who are lost in their "solitary dream of a world." They do not communicate, therefore, though they harangue one another and even convince one another—momentarily. To an age that sometimes sees itself as having passed or retreated from the tragic frontier, these are not qualities that by definition disqualify Beaumont and Fletcher from serious consideration. Plays, moreover, that were popular for generations are not likely to be so devoid of the higher qualities of drama as the recent fortunes of Beaumont and Fletcher might suggest. Is it not possible that the wrong questions have been asked of them; the wrong criteria applied?

COLLABORATION

BETWEEN the plays and ourselves lie further difficulties. First, the psychological response to the coupled names, for few masterpieces issue from two minds simultaneously engaged. The combination will suggest, at the highest, opera: Verdi and Boito, say; or, to descend, Rodgers and Hammerstein. It is in the areas of burlesque, melodrama, farce, operetta, and parody that collaboration tends to success, where the idiom is surface and hazard is king. Moreover, tragedy, however defined, concerns itself with man in the final solitude, the victim of irrational laws exposed to "the murderous caprice of the inhuman." Such a form can rarely be the product of two minds since it demands that the artist himself submit to that solitude: the insights that bring the solitary hero to self-knowledge and destruction must be won by the author. Of tragedy, in its purest form, there is no true example in Beaumont and Fletcher. Their plays are deflected toward tragicomedy, or, should the outcome be tragic, the accent tends to fall not on the privileged, doomed individual but, as in comedy, on the group. Moreover, the plays are concerned not with the exceptional man who, paradoxically, becomes representative of humanity, but with persons who in other plays would be minor characters. This generalization holds even for *The Maid's Tragedy*, which most nearly touches the tragic requirement. Plays in which Fletcher collaborated with authors other than

Beaumont edge into melodrama. In Clifford Leech's phrase: "there is no sign in Fletcher's work that he needed to be alone."

The relationship, nonetheless, between the minds of Beaumont and Fletcher was so intimate that it has proved difficult to distinguish their hands. And the skills Beaumont and Fletcher learned together are repeated, if less commandingly, in later plays where Beaumont had no part. The resources of modern scholarship have still not determined the authorship of a number of plays in the canon. The grounds that determined attribution in the nineteenth century were confined to metrical tests and parallels in vocabulary: Fletcher's mannerisms made this tempting. He habitually ends lines with trisyllables and dissyllables, the stress falling on the first syllable; and he will often pad the end of the line with an unemphasized word (such as "Sir") to induce this effect. He uses dactyls and anapests as substitute feet, so that on occasions his lines are thirteen or more syllables long. This leads him to revert—after Shakespeare's energetic enjambments—to an end-stopped line. The aim was to render the lines as rapidly speakable as possible. Identification of authors tends now to rest on the selective study of syntactical forms: on Fletcher's fondness for the pronominal form "ye," for example, where others would write "you," or on Beaumont's archaic preference for "hath." The text of the two folios is more complicated than mere division between Beaumont and Fletcher might suggest, for Beaumont was on occasion responsible for the final text. Elsewhere Fletcher seems to have revised Beaumont's part in a play, or, at a still later date, Beaumont's final revision of a play; or, Fletcher's original work or revision may itself have been revised by Philip Massinger and in one instance by James Shirley.

Apart from such complications, some works survive as truncated by the actors. Criticism of the plays will hardly be commanding until the completion of the new edition in which Fredson Bowers and his associates have employed all the latest sophistications of bibliography. According to seventeenth-century tradition, Beaumont brought "the *ballast* of judgement, Fletcher the *sail* of phantasie; both compounding a poet to admiration" and certainly the works in which the two collaborated possess a structure firmer than that of Fletcher's work with other collaborators. Beaumont probably learned more from Jonson than did Fletcher: his burlesque *Knight of the Burning Pestle* (1607) uses parody to more moral ends than does Fletcher in his comedy. Beaumont's verse in its high proportion of male endings and sharper syntax is Jonsonian also. His virtues counterpart Fletcher's, yet he seems to have needed as stimulus Fletcher's fertile, irresponsible gift.

Fifteen plays can, with moderate certainty, be ascribed to Fletcher alone. These include the tragedies *Bonduca* and *Valentinian*, the tragicomedies *The Mad Lover*, *The Island Princess*, *The Loyal Subject*, and *The Humorous Lieutenant*; the pastoral drama *The Faithful Shepherdess*, which also has a tragicomic structure; and the sparkling, if unambitious, comedies *Monsieur Thomas*, *Rule a Wife and Have a Wife*, *The Wild Goose Chase*, *A Woman Pleased*, and *A Woman Tamed*. The joint productions of Beaumont and Fletcher include the most famous works in the canon: *The Maid's Tragedy*, *Philaster*, and *A King and No King*. In such plays, Beaumont's appears to have been the controlling role.

After Beaumont's retirement from the stage, Philip Massinger, whose hand has been traced in at least eleven of the plays, succeeded as Fletcher's main coadjutor. That collaboration was not altogether fortunate: it was one of unfruitfully antithetical talents, and Massinger hardly worked as Fletcher's equal. Nathaniel Field and Robert Daborne also collaborated with Fletcher (Field's contributions are particularly interesting), while recent scholarship divides that brisk melodrama *Rollo, Duke of Normandy* between four highly diverse dramatists: Chapman, Jonson, Fletcher, and Massinger. No other author collaborated as intensively as Fletcher. We can connect his skill, facility, and acumen with some of the great painters of the time: a Rubens, for example, whose individuality imposes itself on his followers and whose energy demands multiplicity.

The three dramatists most concerned in the canon came from a social class distinctly higher than that of most of their contemporaries. Beaumont was the son of a judge; Fletcher, of a bishop; Massinger, of the house steward and agent of the second earl of Pembroke. Beaumont, Fletcher, and Massinger were all, in a sense, déclassé: writing for the playhouse, professionally, determined that. The aristocracy and the gentry held aloof from anything that might resemble professional writing: indeed to publish at all was regarded as a kind of taint. Beau-

mont was a younger son, and so, without expectations; Fletcher's father, a handsome courtier and a favorite of Queen Elizabeth, had been disgraced by a late second marriage and died soon after, leaving his son to make his way in the world. Beaumont and Massinger were both products of Oxford; Fletcher probably went to Cambridge. All possessed something of the graceful reading of their class.

By about 1605, Beaumont and Fletcher had come to London and been admitted to the friendship of Ben Jonson, then and for many years the dominant personality in the literary world. Both young men contributed prefatory verses to Jonson's *Volpone* (1605). The seventeenth-century gossip writer John Aubrey vividly evokes their friendship and "marriage of minds":

> There was a wonderful consimility of phansey between him (Beaumont) and Mr. John Fletcher which caused that dearnesse of friendship between them. They lived together on the Banke side, not far from the Playhouse, both batchelors; lay together; had one Wench in the house between them, which they did so admire, the same cloathes and cloake, &c between them.

Fletcher's image, as prefixed to the 1647 folio, reveals a handsome, dandyish, slightly effeminate-looking figure. His modesty and geniality resembled what tradition has preserved of Shakespeare's character. Fletcher's attitude to his own work was deliberately detached, though at the successful performance of his comedy *The Wild Goose Chase* he was startled into applause. We have a further glimpse of him from Thomas Fuller's *Worthies of England*, written a quarter of a century or so after his death: "Meeting once in a Tavern to contrive the rude draught of a Tragedie; Fletcher undertook to *kill the King* therein; whose words being overheard by a listener . . . he was accused of High Treason; till, the mistake soon appearing, that the plot was onely against a Dramatick and scenical King, all wound off in merriment." The story serves to remind us of Fletcher's delight in the knotting of a plot, sometimes at the expense of structure.

Beaumont remains a more shadowy personality. Jonson, hardly given to postures of humility, is reported to have relied on Beaumont's literary judgment. A glimpse of their life in London's literary bohemia may be caught in Beaumont's Horatian verse letter to Jonson "written before he and Mr Fletcher came to London with two of the precedent comedies then not finished."

What things have we seen
Done at the *Mermaid!* heard words that have been
So nimble, and so full of subtle flame,
As if that every one from whence they came,
Had meant to put his whole wit in a jest,
And had resolved to live a fool, the rest
Of his dull life . . .

The poem deviates into an ironic pastoralizing defense of the dull country against the witty city, with its bar talk, for which both young men were obviously longing.

EARLY PLAYS

THE earliest plays in the Beaumont and Fletcher canon are of an experimental kind and date from about 1606. *The Woman Hater* (Beaumont with some revision by Fletcher), is a brash Jonsonian piece with one accomplished song: "Come, sleep, and with thy sweet deceiving," and one remarkable scene where the title figure is tormented by the caresses of a group of girls, an early instance of the interest in abnormal psychology that is frequent in their plays. *Cupid's Revenge*, an immature work of Fletcher's, is a grim cartoon of their first joint tragicomedy, *Philaster*. Jonsonian once more, this comedy also focuses on the grotesque, the abnormal: a princess falls in love with a dwarf. Two further early plays, though failures when first given, are among their finer work: *The Knight of the Burning Pestle* (1607) and *The Faithful Shepherdess* (1608). Their collaboration was altogether to last about six years. Beaumont then married an heiress, Ursula Isley of Sundridge, Kent, and, retiring from the theater, died on 6 March 1616. After Beaumont and Shakespeare had ceased to be active, Fletcher became the leading dramatist for the King's Men, the most popular playwright indeed in London. He died in August 1625 of plague. According to Aubrey:

John Fletcher invited to goe with a Knight into Norfolke or Suffolke in the Plague-Time 1625, stayd but to make himself a suite of cloathes, and while it was makeing, fell sick of the Plague and dyed. This I had (1668) from his Tayler, who is now a very old man, and Clarke of St Mary Overy's in Southwark. Mr Fletcher had an issue in his arm. . . . The Clarke (who was wont to bring him ivy-leaves to dresse it) when he came, found the Spotts upon him. Death stopped his journey and laid him low there.

The last sentence takes us into the area of the medieval Dance of Death: poor Fletcher paid for his anxious dandyism.

Beaumont and Fletcher were born into the gentry at a moment of rapid social change. They were caught between two worlds—the "golden" world of the Elizabethan Great House, where secure, paternalist values and a Renaissance ideal of "contemplation and valour" could be cherished, and a more painfully complex Jacobean world, where the court was disrupting the social and cultural balance between country and town. The change might have been dealt with satirically by authors who were less directly involved. Beaumont and Fletcher wrote for those who, like themselves, had been educated above their prospects; they were forced to combine bitterness and reassurance. Some of the features of their work reflect those of the private theater tradition of the time: for example, the satire on conventional bourgeois morality; Petrarchan theorems of love, the detritus of Renaissance ideals, with their opposite, a raw cynicism; the notion of male friendship surviving the caprice of fortune; the cleansing anarchy of war in the pacific England of James I. In the transmission of such themes, a degree of fantasy was necessarily involved. While the poet of the Great House, Sir Philip Sidney, for example, wrote gratuitously and from a context in which the Great House ideals were at least partially embodied, Beaumont and Fletcher wrote for money and for an audience that wanted protection against too painful a sense of change and yet wished its resentments to find expression.

Beaumont and Fletcher's early tragicomedies, then, dramatize the moment of division between those opposing forces in the state that was to issue finally in the Civil War. On the one hand, we find a class that professed magnanimity, a conscious artistry of conduct, a sometimes hysterical chivalry, a tenuous doctrine of love; and, on the other, that always rising urban class, devoted to the good works of commerce, and serious-minded small gentry from the countryside. "Radical self-division and clashing absolutes," as J. F. Danby puts it, "a world split in every way," yet clung to despairingly for that very reason, or surrounded with protective mockery. Beaumont and Fletcher are unique among Jacobean dramatists in anticipating actual historical figures who, like their heroes, searched for their appropriate role. There seems to be no coherence, for example, in the character of the boastful Lord

Herbert of Cherbury, who was at once master of the "great horse" and of gallantries in France, unsuccessful ambassador and tired traitor to the royalist cause, accomplished minor poet, and serious, enquiring metaphysician. There were similar inconsistencies in a Sir Kenelm Digby of a later generation: at once a virtuoso, defiant devotee of the lascivious Venetia Stanley, and initiate into the mysteries of Platonic love, commentator on Spenser, and searcher after the "powder of Sympathy." Or, to turn from the tragifarcical to the tragic, we may cite two men who had a superb sense of the role required for the ritual moment: Lord Falkland arranging for his own death in battle with the sad formality of one of the self-conscious victims of a Fletcherian tragedy, or his master, King Charles I, who impressed on future ages the pattern of a picturesque martyrdom.

Thus, far from being, as Coleridge put it, servile de jure royalists, Beaumont and Fletcher possess some of the skeptical, probing attitude toward political problems of the Inns of Court tradition. If we complain that, unlike Shakespeare, they appear to present no coherent political philosophy, it may be argued that they reflect more sensitively the changing opacity of contemporary politics. In his English history plays Shakespeare did not evade their swarm of assassinations, judicial murders, usurpations, civil wars, and disputed titles; but his reliance on metaphors of macrocosmic order (still present as the norm in *Troilus and Cressida*) must have seemed irrelevant, even archaic, in the early years of the seventeenth century. Moreover there is just a tinge of the mere Tudor propagandist in the master's presentation of the English past. We are allowed to rest in the image of Henry VII as Richmond, the young rose of state, the rising sun of a temperate new order, but he appears to have flinched from devoting a play to the acts of that efficient and repellent monarch—no Tudor order; no coat of arms; no place for the middle classes; no affluent return to Stratford.

Some critics have related these peculiarities of Beaumont and Fletcher's work to changes that took place in the theater audience about the year 1608. In that year, the King's Men, for whom Shakespeare had written and Beaumont and Fletcher were to write, took over the private Blackfriars Theatre. (The only theater in Elizabeth's reign had been served by boy actors who performed in intensely sophisticated plays.) Although the King's Men

maintained the public Globe Theatre, Blackfriars became more and more their center of operations. Indeed, after 1608 the dramatic current ran more and more toward the private theaters. The divergence between two types of audience was thus accentuated. Up to 1608, the London theater audience had included a complete cross section of society that ranged from students, courtiers, and merchants down to servants, pickpockets, and prostitutes.

In 1600 a literary feud known as "The War of the Theatres" broke out between the learned authors of private theater plays—Jonson, Marston, and Chapman—and the popular theater dramatists—Henry Chettle, Thomas Heywood, and William Dekker. The dramatists of the private theater concentrated on satire, often bawdy and pessimistic, which echoed their reading in classical satire; they derided the citizens and, anticipating the Restoration dramatists, presented an aggrandized reflection of their audience on the stage. The popular authors, on the other hand, expressed their naive idealism in sprawling chronicle plays and crude domestic dramas, though Shakespeare used and transformed the popular mediums. The audience was the final determinant, but the various dramatic categories often overlapped. Jonson wrote plays in the popular mode and Heywood wrote at least one tragicomedy verging on the manner of Fletcher. Where the public theater audience, including the London citizenry, demanded wholesome, chauvinistic fare, the private theater audience was more adventurous; it looked for novelty. But we must be cautious about sentimentalizing the one and depreciating the other.

The staging conditions of the two types of theater may have influenced dramatic form and tone. The popular theaters were modeled on the enclosed courtyard, with a thrust stage. Relations were warm and close between actors and audience, particularly on the part of the clowns, much in the manner of the music hall. Rant abounded. Simpleminded persons in the audience were caught up at once in the stage world of illusion. The private theaters, such as Whitefriars (1605–1614) and Blackfriars (1600–1655), were covered, small, candlelit. This affected, the argument runs, the relation of actor and audience, encouraging perhaps a muted style of performance, so that the audience had the sensation almost of eavesdropping on the actors, even though there were boxes at the back and sides of the theater for the wealthier patrons and some stools actually onstage. Inwardness, pathos rather than passion, and rhetoric made up the idiom. Both theater conditions and a sophisticated audience emphasized the unreality of the dramatic images and movements, while music, masque, and triumph were frequent, being part of the spectacular court influence on the private theaters. Other features in demand were literary conceits and virtuosity in acting.

A more recent criticism, though, has been skeptical of any sharp, causative link between the style of staging and the type of play offered. One of the first plays actually written for Blackfriars was Jonson's *Alchemist*, which was of a traditional public theater type. Moreover, the romance type of play, so popular in the private theaters, had already been witnessed by public theater audiences—Shakespeare's *Pericles*, for example, was produced before the Blackfriars was available. The audience, though, is still viewed as the determining factor, and particularly its taste for "romance": Greek romances were enjoyed by a considerable public, as was Sidney's *Arcadia*, and both were freely used by dramatists as sources for their plots.

Unlike Shakespeare and Jonson, Beaumont and Fletcher passed their whole careers in the private theater. To that theater the two dramatists brought exactly the required qualities: adroit stagecraft; lucid, graceful language intended as an idealized version of the language of gentlemen, with elegant casuistries that derived from the Roman *controversiae* (these were arguments about special, even fantastic, cases of law that must have appealed particularly to the young Inns of Court men who made up a large proportion of their audiences).

The Knight of the Burning Pestle, their first major offering, is a play acted by boys that mocks the adult theater. From those earlier plays, it differs in its freedom from bitterness. The satire is sometimes trenchant, but the note also suggests a detached relish for the crude vigor of the popular theater. Something of that vigor certainly informs *The Knight*. The plays admired by the citizenry contrasted with their own discreet lives, being full of swirling incident and old-fashioned chivalric story. The title of Heywood's *Four Prentices of London With the Conquest of Jerusalem* gives some notion of their rambling structure. That play is satirized in *The Knight*, along with Dekker's citizens and sentimental lovers: old Merrythought, awash with

song and ale, is a typical Dekker character. *The Knight* begins with the Citizen, a grocer (a typical, ignorant patron of the public theater), his wife, and his apprentice, Ralph, taking their places as though to witness a play. The Citizen and his wife are complacent, though likeable—patterns of all bourgeois censors of the arts. The Prologue-Speaker announces the performance of *The London Merchant*, but the grocer and his wife interrupt and demand that the actors perform instead a play in which a grocer shall do "admirable things"; adding that their apprentice Ralph, of whom both are extravagantly fond, can easily play the chief part. Throughout this action, which encloses the style of Dekker and Heywood, the Citizen and his wife constantly attempt to alter the action and find a larger role for Ralph in a play that will move from the merely domestic to the chivalric. Two plays run at once before a stage audience. The original play, a satire on Dekker, recounts how the apprentice Jasper woos and finally wins his master's daughter Luce, but this action is checkered by the improvisations of Ralph as hero of one of Heywood's chronicle romances, relics of medieval cycles about knights and derring-do that still pleased vulgar taste. The two plays interact at the moment when Ralph gives help to Mrs. Merrythought and fights unsuccessfully with Jasper (II.v); but in the remainder of the play Ralph's role is purely episodic. The epilogue may be quoted as illustrative of the general tone:

> *Citizen.* Come *Nel*, shall we go, the Plaies done.
> *Wife.* Nay by my faith George, I have more manners than so, I'le speake to these Gentlemen first: I thanke you all Gentlemen, for your patience and countenance to *Ralph*, a poor fatherless child, and if I might see you at my house, it should go hard, but I would have a pottle of wine and a pipe of Tobacco for you, for truely I hope you do like the youth, but I would bee glad to know the truth: I referre it to your owne discretions, whether you will applaud him or no, for I will winke, and whilst you shall do what you will, I thanke you with all my heart, God give you good night; come in *George*.

The old punctuation catches the breathless, continuous speech of this remote kinswoman of James Joyce's Molly Bloom. The grocer's wife is so naive that she constantly mistakes the stage show for reality and urges her husband to intervene and protect Ralph in his fantastic adventures. The Citizen soothes her with a variety of bourgeois endearments: "honeysuckle," "bird." Beaumont's method (the play is mainly, perhaps entirely, his work) is to juxtapose bombastic and commonplace; vulgar realism and false romance: conscious incongruities. The satire operates finally by comic exploitation of the stage as illusion that can subdue "reality," and by means of a complex, perspicuous device of a play within a play. As Clifford Leech has pointed out, *The Knight of the Burning Pestle* gives us a simultaneous, triple apprehension of the lovers, Jasper and Luce: on the one hand, as romantic figures who demand sympathy, but are presented so extravagantly as to constitute a parody of popular dramatic types; and, on the other, seen through citizens' eyes, as a dangerously ambitious apprentice (telescoping too much the Dick Whittington model) and a girl who neglects her duty to her father. Other incidental targets of satire are foppishness, the "tobacco" habit, and the popular interest in puppet shows. The notion of satirizing old romances such as *Palmerin of England* might well derive from *Don Quixote*. Shelton's translation appeared in 1612, some years after the *Knight* was written, but Fletcher most certainly had some knowledge of Spanish. The ascending curve of Beaumont and Fletcher's popularity began in the second decade of the seventeenth century, and could barely have been foreseen from their principal earlier works. Before proceeding to consider first the works jointly accomplished, and then Fletcher's unaided work and his collaboration with dramatists other than Beaumont, *The Faithful Shepherdess* will be discussed, for its form, tragicomedy, prefigures that of the successful collaboration between Beaumont and Fletcher in this mode.

THE FAITHFUL SHEPHERDESS

The Faithful Shepherdess, Fletcher's first considerable offering, was acted, probably, in 1608. Like *The Knight*, unsuccessful when first presented, it was successfully revived before a more decidedly coterie audience—the court—in 1633. Couched in the pastoral idiom, the play has connections with the sophisticated romances of late Greek literature, full of coincidences and surprising reversals of fortune, and with the courtly romances of the Renaissance.

The necessary idiom of pastoral is the Golden Age, embodied in the lives of shepherds, who are not the rustics of our history, but natural aristocrats, owning their own flocks, taught wisdom by Nature herself. This Golden Age may be envisaged as one that existed in reality before our own corrupt history set in or, in an ideal sense, as a standard for nostalgic or satiric comparison. The major theme of pastoral drama is Nature, particularly in relation to Love. Much of Beaumont and Fletcher's drama veers between two extreme conceptions of love— the one as a spiritual disturbance, madness, or disease (often treated comically), the other as noble, refining, without sexual fulfillment, a late Petrarchanism.

Torquato Tasso began the analysis, its kinds and states, in his *Aminta*, and both Guarino Guarini's *Il Pastor fido* and Fletcher's *The Faithful Shepherdess* are elaborations and variations on Tasso's work. For Tasso, the law of love is indeed ideal, a voluptuous innocence, *s'ei piac' ei lice*: "that is lawful which doth please, love if you will." Tasso's play has two contrasting pairs of lovers, an older pair whose self-conscious disenchantment makes them delight in the sexual duel; a youthful pair, the chaste Silvia and the passionate, equally innocent Aminta. Tasso recreates the intense, simplified world of adolescence, with its absolutes and indignities, and, after a potentially tragic situation has been created, the play is genially resolved, yet with all that Tassesque ambiguity, that sense of the near-identity of fulfillment and death. Tasso's appeal to love is based on the pastoral premise that man is part of Nature, and natural law decrees that all should love their kind. Guarini's *Il Pastor fido* of 1585 reverses Tasso's situation: a young hero, passionate, chaste, reluctant, is educated in love's wisdom by an older, experienced shepherd who makes the same appeal to Nature. But Guarini's is a plot of high complexity. For present purposes, focus may rest on his importation into his Arcadia of a corrupt woman character who plots against the chaste lovers (she has herself fallen in love with the hero), but protects herself against the advances of a satyr. Guarini explicitly corrects Tasso's "love if you will" by an appeal to the law not of Nature but of God and Man. In Sir Richard Fanshawe's translation:

Not Nature's law perchance, *Love where thou Wilt*:
But that of Man and Heaven, Love without guilt.

Love only if it is lawful. Guarini recognizes that the golden world, if psychologically renewed, is still governed by Christian law: there husband and lover signify one thing. Guarini divides his lovers into pairs: Amarilli, absolute for death in love, separated by law; the obdurate Sylvio and the distracted Dorinda (comically slanted), whose love he repulses till he has almost killed her. The satyr represents irredeemable lust (as does the satyr in *Aminta*), but is no match for Corsica, who seems a stray from the town. Guarini's play follows a trajectory almost tragic through Acts III and IV, but ends happily in "the middle mood," having touched the extremes of sententiousness and absurdity. In various theoretical writings, Guarini defended his tragicomic method. Fletcher, in a tantalizingly brief introduction to *The Faithful Shepherdess*, shows himself aware of these. This introduction expresses his disgust with an audience that should have possessed sufficiently sophisticated literary awareness to distinguish between the Dresden china figurines of Italian pastoral and the Hardyesque rustics whose presence would have fractured all stylized illusion:

If you be not reasonably assured of your knowledge in this kind of poem, lay down the book, or read this, which I would wish had been the prologue. It is a pastoral tragicomedy, which the people seeing when it was played, having ever had a singular gift in defining, concluded to be a play of country hired shepherds in gray cloaks, with curtailed dogs in strings, sometimes laughing together and sometimes killing one another; and missing Whitsun-ales, cream, wassail and morris dances, began to be angry.

A tragicomedy, he continues

is not so called in respect of mirth and killing, but in respect it wants deaths, which is enough to make it no tragedy, yet brings some near it, which is enough to make it no comedy, which must be a representation of familiar people, with such kind of trouble as no life be questioned; so that a god is as lawful in this as in a tragedy, and mean people as in a comedy.

And with a final tilt at the audience:

Thus much I hope will serve to justify my poem, and make you understand it; to teach you more for nothing, I do not know that I am in conscience bound.

Curt and vulgarized as the introduction is, it defines a characteristic part of Beaumont and Fletcher's (and later Massinger's) work, even though the supernatural tends (in Fletcher particularly) to be muted and the personages are rarely mean.

Like its Italian predecessors, *The Faithful Shepherdess* presents a map of love, ranging from the frontiers of lust, true chaste love, both physical and spiritual, to a new extreme, positive virginity, Fletcher's version of Italian platonizing. It is announced in the opening soliloquy by its embodiment, the shepherdess Clorin, who, in terms to be echoed in Milton's *Comus*, expounds the magical powers of chastity:

> if I keep
> My virgin flower uncropt, pure, chaste, and fair,
> No goblin, wood-god, faery, elf or fiend,
> Satyr, or other power that haunts the groves,
> Shall hurt my body, or by vain illusion
> Draw me to wander after idle fires,
> Or voices calling me in dead of night,
> To make me follow, and so tole [entice] me on,
> Through mire and standing pools to find my ruin.
> (I. i. 112–120)

As an emblem of that supernatural power that governs instinctive nature, Clorin is adored by Pan's votary, a satyr. This creature, part man and part beast, is tamed by her beauty and chastity and stands as a witness to the Neoplatonic powers of sympathy that bind the universe (the source is probably in Spenser's episode of Una and the satyrs in book II of the *Faerie Queen*. This satyr's liquid eight-syllabled lines recall Puck and anticipate Ariel, and will sound behind the music of the Attendant Spirit in *Comus*. In the light of Clorin's fidelity to her dead lover, the play's other relationships are judged. Pairs of lovers, in Guarini's manner, are established in other scenes: Perigot and Amoret, agreeing on a tryst for the interchange of chaste kisses and garlands, are followed by Amaryllis hungering for Perigot. This announces that, in Fletcher's Arcadia, love is a dangerous passion of the blood, requiring the strictest control. Amaryllis (modeled on Guarini's Dorinda) attempts to court Perigot, but she is repulsed. There enters the Sullen Shepherd, like Amaryllis, incontinent, but cynically libertine; he personifies intellectualized lust, and, like his female counterpart Cloe, is prepared for indiscriminate sensual pleasures. But Cloe displays a comically innocent unscrupulousness that sets her off from the Sullen Shepherd. Comedy stems from the successive disappointments of her aggressive wooing first of Thenot, an idealist in love, devoted to the unattainable Clorin, and then Daphnis, who is faithful but so simple that he agrees to a rendezvous with Cloe, who, to ensure success by numbers, arranges another meeting with the sensual but amiable Alexis. The first act presents us with the scale of love that ranges from Clorin's first words "Hail, holy earth," an earth vibrating with religious awe, down to Cloe's opportunistic sensuality:

> My grief is great if both these boys should fail:
> He that will use all winds must shift his sail.
>
> (I. iii. 177–178)

All the characters present extreme states, for, like Tasso's pair, these are adolescent lovers, and, like the lovers in Shakespeare's *A Midsummer Night's Dream*, they perform ballet suites of misunderstandings. Fletcher's drama has nothing to correspond to Theseus' civil, daylight world and the nightwood of the fairies, which so marvelously interact on the world of the young lovers. "Pastoral" in Shakespeare's play is a licensed "holiday" from reality, a dwelling in the fantasy world of love-at-first-sight, youthful mythologizing. Fletcher's lovers, like Shakespeare's, are individualized only by the passions to which they are victim. Though his characters are distinguished by their attitudes to love, Fletcher is less interested in the conditions under which love may be licit in his Arcadia than in the complications the lovers' situations afford. Amaryllis, for instance, knowing that Perigot's chaste love for Amoret is firm, persuades the Sullen Shepherd to use his dark arts to transform her into the image of Amoret and so enable her to make love to Perigot. Perigot, however, rejects this figment of Amoret, for he can only love her so long as she plays within the rules of prenuptial chastity.

Fletcher is making the same point that Shakespeare makes about the lovers in *A Midsummer Night's Dream*, though not of course with such subtlety. A parallel to the Perigot-Amoret-Amaryllis action is provided by Thenot's somewhat masochistic calf love for Clorin. That love conflicts with Clorin's vow of fidelity to the dead. She decides on a drastic remedy: she will cure him by pretending to abandon herself to him. This disgusts Thenot, and he leaves her disillusioned.

The basis of *The Faithful Shepherdess* is ironic juxtaposition. As Eugene Waith puts it: "in every scene characters are (or imagine themselves to be) moral opposites and the disguising of vice as virtue or the appearance of virtue heightens the implicit contrasts in these situations." Clorin's white counterparts the dark art of the Sullen Shepherd.

Clorin cures the wounds of sensuality with herbs and waters from her spring. Nature in this play is shown as a blend of good and evil (as in *A Midsummer Night's Dream*, a sharp antithesis is drawn between night and day, while the unity of time is observed). Love is presented as Nature's motive force, and thus shares this dual character: it may lead to animal darkness or to a bodiless radiance, as with Milton's Sabrina. It is at "the holy well" that Amaryllis is given the appearance of Amoret and where Amoret's seemingly lifeless body is rescued by the River God. His waters will only heal a virgin; they cannot drown her.

The episode, with its subdued Christian symbolism, also looks forward to Milton's Sabrina. Supernatural power is required to tame the passions of the blood; the cold water that the Priest of Pan sprinkles on these warm adolescents is perfectly ineffectual. Between the two extremes of Clorin and the Sullen Shepherd lie the other lovers, none of whom is irredeemable, whose incontinence is that of youth and folly. When they have learned to subdue their desires to the rule of premarital chastity, they can be forgiven and united, except for Amaryllis; she has not yet found some "good shepherd" and must persist in "virgin state" until she does. In this Arcadia, as in Guarini's Counter-Reform, love is permitted under condition of marriage. The recalcitrant are expelled: the Sullen Shepherd, naturalistic, emotionally skeptical to the last, tries to suggest some return to the voluptuous innocence of Tasso's world of adolescence:

> Yet tell me more;
> Hath not our mother Nature, for her store
> And great increase, said it is good and just,
> And will that every living creature must
> Beget his like?

But the Priest of Pan returns this dusty answer:

> Ye are better read than I,
> I must confess, in blood and lechery.
>
> (V. iii. 131–136)

The Sullen Shepherd, indeed, is an experienced lover (unlike Cloe, and like Tasso's Dafne) who is clearly out of place in this Arcadia of the young. He cannot respond to the awareness of guilt that pervades this veiled Christian pastoral.

Adolescent sex and, particularly, feminine aggression are continuously mocked (male timidity is more mildly mocked in Perigot's reaction to Amaryllis, and more disturbingly in Thenot's to Clorin). Mockery distinguishes between a precocious Cloe's attraction to Thenot and to the Sullen Shepherd— "yon shaggy man"—a vitality altogether unqualified by ceremony. But the mockery of ungainly adolescent love tends to fracture the fragile and stylized pastoral tone. Fletcher is well aware of the paradoxes of love, but, as Clifford Leech has pointed out, he never presents human experience simultaneously like Shakespeare, but in successive and schematized modes as though arguing first on one side and then on another. Such abstention enables him to arrive at peculiar effects, as for example in Thenot's supposed spiritual love for the Faithful Shepherdess herself. Thenot addresses a virtual love song to Clorin, though it is qualified by an overture: it is her impossible sanctity that attracts him. Yet the descriptive terms drift beyond platonizing to a barely subdued, autoerotic fantasy, reinforced by lingering patterns of sound, near-pleonasms, and dangerous plays on what Milton would have noted as "fallen" interpretations of such words as "error" and "curious," not the innocent "golden world" root meanings of the visually wandering and visually attractive:

> Your hair wove into many a curious warp,
> Able in endless errour to enfold
> The wandering soul.
>
> (II. iii. 126–128)

If this is almost the only work of Fletcher's in which the supernatural is active, it still operates equivocally and its powers (as expressed through the Priest) are limited. The paradox of characterizing Pan as the guardian of Virginity and the satyr as the agent of virtue and servant of Pan's mistress Syrinx (though he also serves Clorin) is clearly deliberate, and again illustrates the theme of an ambiguous "Nature."

PHILASTER

THIS method of stylized patterning and contrasting of characters in *The Faithful Shepherdess* points forward to the two tragicomedies *Philaster* (1608–1610) and *A King and No King* (1611). Yet the texts of these two plays as we have them suggest that the dominant influence was that of Beaumont. The plot of *Philaster* shows a superficial affinity to that of *Hamlet*, especially in the predicament of the hero. Before the action begins, Philaster, the young prince, has been deprived of his throne. He is in love with Arethusa, the usurping king's only daughter. Euphrasia, a nobleman's daughter, is in love with Philaster and disguises herself as his page, Bellario; and Philaster sends her in this disguise to Arethusa as go-between. Pharamond, a Spanish prince, arrives at court to ask the hand of Arethusa. A group of courtiers are stung into action as this suit, if successful, may well extinguish all Philaster's chances of regaining his lost kingdom. Pharamond, a near-buffoon, begins womanizing, almost as soon as he is onstage, with the overeager Megra. When their affair is discovered, Megra accuses Arethusa of adultery with the disguised Euphrasia to preserve herself by blackmailing the king. This is made plausible by Arethusa's innocent affection for the supposed boy, partly for his winning self, partly because, as Philaster's page, he is a substitute of her love for the prince. The lie about Arethusa's carnality is repeated to Philaster by Dion, Euphrasia's father, who wishes Philaster to lead a revolt against the usurper and break with Arethusa, using the lie as one more cause of grievance. The mob rises, captures Pharamond and the king, is persuaded by Philaster to return peacefully home, and the prince's right of succession is assured.

The final twist of the knife comes when Philaster offers Pharamond honorable return to Spain and the services of Megra. Megra then accuses Arethusa of being as sensually adventurous as herself, and the page Euphrasia–Bellario is forced to reveal herself as Dion's long-lost daughter. Euphrasia refuses the king's offer of an honorable match and accepts Arethusa's invitation to continue life as servant to Philaster and herself, in an oddly platonized ménage à trois. The close of the play is "tragicomic" in the strict sense, but the margin between the characters and death remains large. Great persons inhabit this play, but do not act greatly: they move at the mercy of chance, which dwarfs them.

Philaster shows an advance on *The Faithful Shepherdess* in counterpointing scenes of the enclosed forest world of adolescence with the high political context of the adult world, but such a political context is hollow. This remains the most romantic, the most genially improbable, play of the Beaumont and Fletcher partnership. The principal characters all become absurd at different moments and to such a degree as to suggest a parody of some of the stage conventions of the time, in particular those of the revenge drama. At his first appearance Pharamond is established as a baroque buffoon, when he offers a speech to Arethusa of clotted pomp. He loses further dignity at his lodgings when he is surprised with Megra by king and court, and his fears at being captured by the mob diminish him to a point beneath contempt. The king himself, when Arethusa has been lost in the wood and cannot be found, rants in a way that can only mock "Divine Right":

Where is she? Mark me all, I am your King,
I wish to see my daughter, shew her me:
I do command you all, as you are subjects,
To shew her me: what, am I not your King?
If ay, then am I not to be obeyed?
  Dion. Yes, if you command things possible, and honest.
  King. Things possible and honest? Hear me, thou—
Thou traitor—that dar'st confine thy King to things
Possible and honest. . . .

                              (IV. ii. 108-116)

Similarly, when the king begs Philaster to quieten the mob:

They will not hear me speak, but fling dirt at me, and call me Tyrant. Oh run dear friend, and bring the Lord *Philaster*: speak him fair, call him Prince, do him all the courtesy you can, commend me to him. Oh my wits, my wits!

                                (V. iv. 156-160)

All this in common prose. But Philaster, Arethusa, and Bellario, the three adolescent lovers, are equally, if more engagingly, absurd. Philaster appears to mock the king in this passage where absolute loyalty to the usurper collides with absolute loyalty to his father's memory:

    A dangerous spirit . . . bids me be a King,
    And whispers to me, these are all my subjects:
    Tis strange, he will not let me sleep, but dives
    Into my fancy, and there gives me shapes
    That kneel, and do me service, cry me King. . . .
                              (I. i. 278-283)

But Philaster finds that the only role possible is one that achieves nothing, or only breeds suspicion in the king:

    But I'le suppress him, he's a factious spirit.

The king considers him mad; the passage seems intended to recall *Hamlet*. This conflict of roles grows more acute later in the next scene (I.ii) when Arethusa sends for Philaster. Both Philaster and the audience expect that she will use the occasion to express hatred for him. But Arethusa loves Philaster and believes that love will work to redeem political injustice. This scene is deliberately juxtaposed with its predecessor, which proclaims the first absolute: Divine Right. With pure propriety, Arethusa declares her love. Philaster, as her subject, cannot woo her, but declared love itself provokes an opposite; adolescent Petrarchan idealism has another face—adolescent cynicism:

    But how this passion should proceed from you,
    So violently, would amaze a man,
    That would be jealous.
                              (I. ii. 94-96)

Philaster (like Thenot in *The Faithful Shepherdess*) loved Arethusa because of her "impossibility." As in Act I where, in J. F. Danby's words, "the loyalty of the subject is absolute, since it can only be maintained by an actively willed suppression of the disloyalty he (Philaster) shares in," so here, similar paralyzing incompatibles work. And in Act III, scene i, the new absolute demands of love and honor entrap both Bellario and Philaster. Philaster acts out a comedy of reality and appearance, mistaking Bellario for the consummate player of the role of innocent, when Bellario really is innocent, but imprisoned by the demands of an absolute "honor" that forbids tattling.

Like Perigot in *The Faithful Shepherdess*, Philaster is adept at swordplay with women; both Arethusa and Bellario feel his touch. But so clean a cut through the tangle of absolutes would be untrue both to the prince and to tragicomic "chance." As he wounds Arethusa with the cry "Are you at peace?" a "countrey fellow" appears and rebukes Philaster for striking a woman.

  Philaster. Leave us, good friend.
  Arethusa. What ill-bred man art thou, to intrude thy selfe/Upon our private sports, our recreations?
  Countrey Fellow. God uds me, I understand you not; but/I know the rogue has hurt you.

                                (IV. iii. 89-93)

The vulgar and pragmatic must not intrude on this attempt to act out an episode from Sidney's *Ar-*

cadia. To show how far off he is from that ideal world, Philaster fights the boor and is worsted. He should have recalled his Castiglione, whose ideal Renaissance courtier never fights with an inferior, in case just such an indignity occurs. Later Philaster wounds Bellario, who loves him all the more for this noble violence. The scene of the play is a wood, and in this familiar Renaissance pastoral setting "only the feet of the plot" will somehow find a way and make the adolescent dream mysteriously come true.

All the characters in *Philaster*, indeed, are helpless, from the courtly figures to the mob who, led by their captain in the dramatic Act V, scene iv, gather to free Philaster from prison. Like the "Church and King" mobs of the eighteenth century, this one has been manipulated by the aristocrats for their own ends. Fletcher's attitude toward it is genially paternalistic. The mob is good-humoredly ferocious toward Pharamond and is easily persuaded to disperse by Philaster, who being a naïf prefers the orderly process of succession to a coup d'etat. This scene is both concrete and extravagant. Its gamey slang looks forward to similar scenes in the delightful *Beggar's Bush*, with its beggars' argot.

Such indecorum of language is a usual device for "placing" the lower orders. So the mob's captain roars out indecipherable menace:

                                                    Talk
No more such Bugs-words, or that solder'd Crown
Shall be scratched with a Musket: Dear Prince Pippin,
Down with your noble bloud, or as I live,
I'll have you coddled . . .
And with this washing blow, do you see sweet Prince,
I could hock your grace, and hang you up cross-legged,
Like a Hare at a Poulters.

                                            (V. iv. 28–37)

If we must have rulers, let them be of our own race. The scene reads like a parody of other mob scenes and earlier theatrical styles.

THE MAID'S TRAGEDY AND A KING AND NO KING

The Maid's Tragedy (1611) represents Beaumont and Fletcher's nearest approach to formal tragedy. It is their most trenchant work. Amintor, a young noble, is solemnly engaged to the maid herself, Aspatia, daughter of the sour and senile Calianax,

lord chamberlain and commander of the citadel. The king forces Amintor, a servile de jure royalist indeed, to break off his match with Aspatia and marry Evadne, a sister of Amintor's close friend Melantius, the king's general. The first act establishes the familiar absolutes of Heroic Virtue, the masculine simplicity and sanctioned anarchy of war as exemplified in the person of Melantius, and Divine Right, with its split between loyalty to king and to kingdom, to the king's political and his natural body, along with notions of Petrarchan love. This act progresses toward a contrast between the desolation of Aspatia and the maturing joy of Evadne and Amintor, Aspatia's famous lament being also an elegy for a melting world of value:

And you shall find all true but the wild Island;
Suppose I stand upon the Sea beach now,
Mine arms thus, and mine hair blown with the wind,
Wild as that desert, and let all about me
Tell that I am forsaken. Do my face
(If thou hadst ever feeling of a sorrow)
Thus, thus, Antiphila, strive to make me look
Like sorrow's monument; and the trees about me,
Let them be dry and leaveless; let the Rocks
Groan with continual surges, and behind me
Make all a desolation; see, see Wenches,
A miserable life of this poor picture.

                                            (II. ii. 66–77)

Aspatia is the first in a gallery of Fletcher's self-conscious unfortunates, who assume postures appropriate for pathos.

The consummation of Amintor and Evadne's marriage is preceded by a nuptial masque, whose symbolic persons include Night, Cynthia, the Moon-goddess, and Neptune. Neptune is commanded to loose the winds (with their suggestions of fertility) but to confine Boreas, wind of destruction. But Boreas breaks his chain. Three nuptial songs evoke the wakefulness and painful brevity of the lovers' night. Boreas raises a storm, but this is diffused by Neptune's imposing calm. Night (reluctantly) and Cynthia vanish. The masque's position in the play emphasizes its ironic role: the lovers' night, as we shall shortly discover, will be wakeful and, in a different sense to that proclaimed, painful. Day will bring not concord but tension.

In *The Maid's Tragedy*, precisely because the audience is behind the events onstage, the masque is enabled to furnish such dramatic ironies. In Shakespeare's plays, the audience is abreast of the plot even before the stage action, and this constrains the use of the masque. In *The Tempest* the masque does induce suspense, but elsewhere both verse and effect are archaic, distanced, static: a diagrammatic glimpse of the supernatural.

It is significant that in his conversations with William Drummond, Ben Jonson declared that besides himself only Chapman and Fletcher could make a masque. It is also significant that scholarship has been sufficiently prejudiced to assume that a fuddled Jonson could mistakenly have substituted the name of Beaumont for that of Fletcher on the ground that no masques by Fletcher are extant. But both Beaumont and Fletcher sensed the affinities between masque and tragicomedy with its shifts of mood; indeed such shifts are sometimes signaled by scaled-down versions of masque. In *Philaster*, the news of Arethusa's love for and marriage to the hero are broken to the king by Bellario in the guise of a reported wedding masque. Arethusa then responds to the king's testy enquiry as to the occasion:

Sir, if you love it in plain truth
(For now there is no masquing in't) this gentleman,
The prisoner that you gave me is become
My Keeper,

. . .
                                    and at length
Arrived here by dear husband.
                                    (V. iii. 46–52)

The king's response is to transform verbally the celebratory masque into the masque of death:

Your Hymen turn his saffron into a sullen coat . . .
Blood shall put out your torches, and instead
Of gaudy flowers about your wanton neck
An axe shall hang, like a prodigious meteor.
                                    (V. iii. 55–60)

More elaborately, in Act IV, scene i of Fletcher's *The Mad Lover*, the attempt is made to cure Memnon of his love madness by means of an antimasque, which invokes the orphically medicinal powers of music. Indeed, the latter part of this play, like *The Prophetess*, responds to this instability of current dramatic forms in the 1620's by melting into the operatic. Beaumont and Fletcher's use of masque, it may be concluded, is more inventive than Shakespeare's.

In Act II, scene i, Aspatia's complaint is made in the actual presence of Evadne and her ladies, and the lewd song, which Evadne's maid sings by request, after Aspatia's "Lay a garland on my Hearse/Of the dismal yew," together with Evadne's lack of sympathy for Aspatia, prepares us for coming events. When Amintor and Evadne are left alone, a dialogue of naturalistic directness ensues, which anticipates Middleton's writing of this kind. Amintor finds Evadne reluctant to go to bed and presumes it an effect of innocence. The dialogue points up the ironic discrepancy between Amintor's naiveté and his assumption that it is Evadne who is innocent, not himself. Amintor, like Aspatia, is a mere sentimentalist. He is treated half comically, half pathetically:

Amin.   To bed then; let me wind thee in these arms,
                Till I have banished sickness.
Evadne.   Good my Lord, /I cannot sleep.

The last word introduces a pun that is to be played on ironically:

Amin.   Evadne, we will watch. /I mean no sleeping.
Evadne.   I'll not go to bed.
                                    (II. i. 134–138)

A little later, Amintor's Edwardian archness irritates Evadne to an acrid candor.

Amin.   How? Sworn, Evadne?
Evadne.   Yes, sworn, Amintor, and will swear again
If you will wish to hear me.
Amin.   To whom have you sworn this?
Evadne.   If I should name him, the matter were not great.
Amin.   Come, this is but the coyness of a Bride.
Evadne.   The coyness of a Bride!
Amin.   How prettily that frown becomes thee! . . .
If you have sworn to any of the Virgins
That were your old companions, to preserve
Your Maidenhead a night, it may be done
Without this means.
Evadne.   A Maidenhead *Amintor*/At my years!
                                    (I. ii. 140–145; 175–179)

Evadne mocks Amintor's own vapid style:

                                    If thou dost love me,
Thou weigh'st not anything compar'd with me;
Life, Honour, Joys Eternal, all Delights
This world can yield, or hopeful people feign,
Or in the life to come, are light as air,
To a true Lover when his Lady frowns,

FRANCIS BEAUMONT AND JOHN FLETCHER

And bids him do this: wilt thou kill this man?
Swear my Amintor, and I'll kiss the sin
Off from thy lips.

(II. i. 157–165)

The man, of course, is Amintor himself, for the marriage has been one of convenience to mask the king's adultery with Evadne, though Amintor is still ignorant of that. Evadne begins the process of enlightenment:

'tis not for a night
Or two that I forbear thy bed, but ever.
   Amin.   I dream,—awake, Amintor!
   Evadne.   You hear right,
I sooner will find out the beds of snakes,
And with my youthful blood warm their cold flesh,
Letting them curl themselves about my Limbs,
Than sleep one night with thee; this is not feigned,
Nor sounds it like the coyness of a Bride.

(II. i. 190–197)

The root of this impatience, aggression even, has not yet been shown. An ironic premonition sounds when Amintor tries to extort his marital rights:

   Amin.   Come to bed!
Or by those hairs, which if thou hast a soul
Like to thy looks were threads for Kings to wear
About their arms.
   Evadne.   Why so perhaps they are.

(II. i. 257–260)

When Amintor histrionically demands who the man is, Evadne replies, "Why, 'tis the King." At this his manhood falters:

in that sacred word
The King, there lies a terror: what frail man
Dare lift his hand against it.

Both resolve to act as if they had indeed spent the night in love, and the following morning, when Evadne's brothers come to visit the couple, the complex game of appearances and realities is emphasized by the punning dialogue:

Diphylus.   You look as you had lost your eyes to night;
I think you ha' not slept.
Amintor.   I'faith I have not.
Diphylus.   You have done better then.

(III. i. 20–22)

In the sense of sleeping with Evadne, Amintor indeed has not. He and Evadne act out their roles so well that when the king enters they succeed in rousing his jealous suspicions that they have slept together: the king ironically enough finds himself in the role of cuckold rather than intending cuckolder.

The remainder of the play is less satisfactory, though it is carried by its initial momentum. Melantius extorts Amintor's secret and decides to revenge himself: his instrument will be Evadne. The means by which Calianax, Melantius' old enemy, is persuaded to hand over the citadel provide a comic version of the appearance-reality theme. The oddly uneven scene where Evadne murders the king is Fletcher's work. Fletcher insists on diminishing her, though to this point she has been magnificent. Finding the king asleep, she trusses him up, and when he wakes he thinks it merely some sophisticated variant of love play. Evadne hints perversity to the last. She represents herself as a fatal woman:

I have begun a slaughter on my honour
And I must end it there . . .

(V. ii. 12–13)

but at the same time finds it necessary to convince the audience that she can execute the murder:

nor bear I in this breast
So much cold Spirit to be call'd a Woman:
I am a Tiger: I am any thing
That knows not pity: stir not.

(V. ii. 51–54)

Indeed, as critics have pointed out, when she reveals herself in the role of tigress, the king's helplessness becomes almost an embarrassment. There follows a veritable carnage. Aspatia is killed at Amintor's hands, an episode that underlines the themes of masochism and sadism, and Amintor, already wounded by Aspatia, stabs himself. All ends with the conventional moral of the revenge play as a new king succeeds, with Melantius as his support.

It is difficult to persuade ourselves that the deaths of Evadne and the king flow inevitably from some violation of immutable law; nor by dying do they display any increase either in moral awareness or in human dignity. Yet, flawed though it is, *The Maid's Tragedy* remains a far more complex and ambitious play than *Philaster*. The absolutes—Melantius' soldierly honor, friendship, Divine Right, and Petrarchan love—are not simply placed in juxtaposition, but are dryly challenged by Evadne's nihilizing clarity of mind. Though the play comes to rest in the formulation of commonplaces, Melantius is not punished. Killing a king, even a vile one, onstage, was never more tricky than in the reign of James I, and the ending of this play is the more daring.

A King and No King, though written about the same time, represents a retreat from the relatively complex moral world of *The Maid's Tragedy*. It is more carefully constructed than any other play in the canon: the subplot of Tigranes and Spaconia balancing and echoing the main plot. Beaumont seems once more to have been the dominant partner. The theme, incest between brother and sister, is treated with far more detachment than in Ford's *'Tis Pity She's a Whore*: until the last act it seems that the usual tragic values will triumph and that sin must be paid for. The resolution is tragicomic. In place of Ford's sympathy with the incestuous lovers, who yet pay the moral and social debt, we have a curious undercutting of any moral sanctions: incestuous dreams become lawful.

Arbaces, king of Iberisa, conquers Tigranes, king of Armenia, in single combat. Like many of the kings in this canon, Arbaces is arbitrary and emotionally immature, his conduct toward Tigranes wavering between arrogance and magnanimity. He offers the defeated king freedom, if Tigranes will marry Arbaces' sister, Panthea. Brother and sister have been separated for some years: Arbaces has been about his wars. Already vowed to Spaconia, Tigranes promises his fiancée that he will try and dissuade Panthea from the match; but Panthea's beauty subdues not only Tigranes but Arbaces also. Struck with jealousy and fear, he imprisons Tigranes and confines Panthea closely, so that he will not be tempted by her presence; but, haunted by her absence, he sends for her. A familiar figure, the bluff, disinterested soldier, Mardonius, who acts as Arbaces' good angel in this odd morality, refuses to play the pander. Arbaces is more successful with Bessus, a swaggering braggart, who recalls at moments both Falstaff and Parolles, but also acts as a comic caricature of Arbaces himself. Bessus' false reputation for courage and the difficulties in which this involves him provide at once comment on and protection for Arbaces' entanglement with his sister. The response of Bessus, Arbaces' "Bad Angel," to the king's request is:

'Tis no matter how I look; I'll do your business as well as they that look better, and when this is despatched, if you have a mind to your mother, tell me, and you shall see I'll set it in hand.

(III. iii. 168–171)

This flat, comic profession disgusts Arbaces and he dismisses Bessus roughly. As usual, love operates as an absolute force, and Arbaces wavers helplessly. He interviews Panthea in secret. She is as strongly attached to him as he to her. Fletcher plays with the concepts of Petrarchan love in terms that remind us of Philaster's relationship to Arethusa: if Panthea is not chaste, it will be easier to reject her; if she is chaste, she will reject him. The casuistry works itself out as Arbaces offers Panthea freedom:

> There is a way
> To gain thy freedom, but 'tis such a one
> As puts thee in worse bondage.

As this scene drives to its climax, Panthea confesses:

> Sir, I will pray for you, yet you shall know
> It is a sullen fate that governs us
> For I could wish as heartily as you
> I were no sister to you, I should then
> Embrace your lawful love sooner than death.
>   *Arbaces.* Could'st thou affect me then?
>   *Panthea.* So perfectly,
> That as it is, I ne'er shall sway my heart
> To like another.

Once temptation appears to have been subdued, tension fades. Arbaces and Panthea coquet with one another. Arbaces remarks:

> Brothers and sisters may
> Walk hand in hand together. So will we.
> Come nearer, is there any hurt in this?

Panthea suggests they may go further:

> But is there nothing else
> That we may do, but only walk? Methinks
> Brothers and sisters lawfully may kiss.
>   *Arbaces.* And so they may Panthea, so will we
> And kiss again too. We were scrupulous
> And foolish but we will be so no more. (*They embrace*)
>   *Panthea.* If you have any mercy, let me go
> To prison, to my death, to anything:
> I feel a sin growing upon my blood
> Worse than all these, hotter I fear than yours.
> (IV. iv. 58–60; 102–109; 141–143; 150–158)

Anxiously, they part. By another turn of the screw, Gobrias, regent of the kingdom, reveals that Arbaces is really his own son, adopted by Panthea's mother Arane, the queen dowager. The love affair is not incestuous but natural after all. Arbaces and Panthea can marry; the "no king" becomes king indeed. Tigranes marries Spaconia and is restored to his throne. The revelation of Arbaces' own parentage is prepared for in Act I by a casual reference to Arane's apparently unmotivated plots against her supposed son and an enigmatic conversation between Arane and Gobrias in the following scene. Gobrias has to prepare the ground carefully before the secret of Arbaces' birth can be revealed. The king is too willful; he must be broken, and the instrument Gobrias uses is Panthea. This is witty theater. The dry examination of Arbaces' adolescent conduct helps to conserve the tragicomic middle tone through most of the play, with its "little people in great positions who suffer distress but not the ultimate disaster," and thus act out their limited and limiting roles. To speak of dramatic irony in connection with a play that so elegantly baffles its audience may well seem paradoxical. But for the reader such ironies certainly involve the principal characters, as when Panthea promises Arbaces she will not fall in love with Tigranes.

FLETCHER'S TRAGEDIES

FLETCHER wrote two tragedies unaided: *Valentinian*, in about 1614, and *Bonduca*, probably a year or two earlier. Both are, typically, set in the decadence of the empire, rather than in the austere climate of Republican Rome. Both display certain differences from and affinities with *The Maid's Tragedy*. Like that play, *Valentinian* proceeds from climax to climax, each climax being virtually autonomous, not part of a single ascendant rhythm of action. Such a method enables Fletcher to vary the tempo of his scenes: slow in scenes of persuasion, rapid when decisive action occurs. Like *The Maid's Tragedy* also, *Valentinian* escapes the pattern of the orthodox revenge play with its mechanism of tyranny, assassination, and retribution. The young emperor, Valentinian, is enervated by flatterers and panders. An unnatural peace hangs over the empire, which is decaying, like its nominal head, from within. Valentinian is violently attracted to Lucina,

the wife of a distinguished general, Maximus, and fruitlessly employs all his usual engines of seduction: insinuating bawds, gifts, bland and vicious courtiers. He wins Maximus' ring at dice and uses this to lure Lucina to the palace. The first movement of the play comes to its climax in Act II, scene iv: Lucina, nervous but trusting an assurance that Maximus is somewhere in the palace, and will shortly appear, is led in with the somewhat frail accompaniment of her two serving women. The scene is arranged in fact like a play within a play, a Triumph, though Lucina protests "I bring no triumph with me." The courtiers comment:

> *Chilax.* She's come.
> Is the music placed well? . . .
> *Licinius.* Excellent.
> *Chilax.* Licinius, you and Proculus receive her
> In the great chamber; at her entrance,
> Let her alone; and do you hear, Licinius?
> Pray, let the ladies ply her further off,
> And with much more discretion. One word more. . . .
> Are the jewels, and those ropes of pearl,
> Laid in the way she passes?
>
> (II. iv. 1–9)

All this increases anticipation. Valentinian effectively remains offstage for most of the next two scenes, also set in this labyrinthine palace, to descend, not like the rescuing deity in a masque but like some amorous deus ex machina, at the climax of this assault on Lucina's senses. We are wound still further into the perspectives of the palace:

> *Licinius.* She is coming up the stairs. Now, the music:
> And, as that stirs her, let's set on. Perfumes there!
> *Proculus.* Discover all the jewels!
>
> (II. v. 1–3)

Here is comic overplus, as in Satan's temptation by banquet in *Paradise Regained*. Music assists jewels and perfumes in a cumulative "feast of the senses":

> Yet the lusty spring hath stayed,
> Blushing red and purest white
> Daintily to love invite
> Every woman, every maid.
> Cherries kissing as they grow
> And inviting men to taste,
> Apples even ripe below,
> Winding gently to the waist:
> All love's emblems, and all cry:
> "Ladies, if not plucked, we die."

A comic riot of ripeness, the nature–woman–fertility equation is compacted in metaphor. Yet these are some of the most intense moments in the play, springing from a sharp deployment of dramatic conventions in which moral rigor has been replaced by an aesthetic that allows for a double awareness. This is art, not life; but our involvement with the action denies the possibility of a remote distancing. The differences between Volpone's attempted seduction of Celia and the duke's of Bianca in *Women Beware Women* and Valentinian's of Lucina are wide indeed, but it must be said that what is often put forward as a criticism of Beaumont and Fletcher (their manipulative technique) is in fact description of their art. An atmosphere of sick desire drenches the court and the last line of the first inviting song is ironic, for Lucina is plucked and still dies (the serving women merely die in the well-known Elizabethan figurative sense of sexual climax). Lucina professes formal anxiety concerning her reputation, but the world to which she belongs is no more morally sensitive than the court:

> Hear, ye ladies that despise,
> > What the mighty love has done;
> Fear examples, and be wise:
> > Fair Calisto was a nun;
> Leda, sailing on the stream
> > To deceive the hopes of man,
> Love accounting but a dream,
> > Doted on a silver swan;
> Danae, in a brazen tower,
> Where no love was, loved a shower.
> Hear, ye ladies that are coy,
> > What the mighty love can do;
> Fear the fierceness of the boy:
> > The chaste moon he makes to woo;
> Vesta, kindling holy fires,
> > Circled round about with spies,
> Never dreaming loose desires,
> > Doting at the altar dies;
> Ilion, in a short hour, higher
> He can build, and once more fire.

A sensual warning underlies these more than decorative songs. Love is presented as a cosmic force, which brings absurdity and disaster on those who repudiate it, particularly when it strikes through Jove's deputy, the emperor. Lucina's serving women disappear to be pleasured by the courtiers, and the following scene unfolds like the false perspectives of a masque into further recesses of the palace. One corrupt courtier observes:

> The women by this time are worming of her;
> If she can hold out them, the Emperor
> Takes her to task.
>
> > (II. vi. 2–4)

Valentinian and Lucina then appear. Citing her husband's service to the state, Lucina eloquently appeals to Valentinian's compassion. But her eloquence is formal, not human, and it remains part of the plan of this play that room should be allowed for such speeches: the mode has its tradition, the outcome has not. The scene concludes with Valentinian wavering between conflicting roles, the magnanimous and the lustful. He was, he protests, merely trying her temper, and will now lead Lucina to "your lord and give you to him." Duplicity lurks in this phrase, for Valentinian, politically speaking, is also Lucina's lord, and the scene concludes with a proverb that is enigmatic rather than authoritative: its rhyme is indecisive (even if a potentially perfect rhyme were available) and does not clinch the sentiment, as such couplets normally do:

> He that endeavours ill,
> May well delay, but cannot quench his hell.
> > (II. vi. 41–42)

This does not diminish the theatrical stroke that instantly follows: "'Tis done Licinius," one courtier says to another. And by rape, it is gradually revealed, not by seduction. As ever, Fletcher cannot resist deflation:

> a good whore
> Had saved all this and haply as wholesome.
> > (III. i. 21–22)

The comment protects the audience against too keen a sense of the absurd and so points to the fact that it is not true. The antiethic of the play (the insistence that it is a play, not life) requires the rape of the eloquently chaste: we are indulged but not committed. Valentinian and Lucina then appear:

> *Lucina.* As long as there is motion in my body,
> And life, to give me words, I'll cry for justice!
> *Valentinian.* Justice shall never hear you: I am Justice.
> > (III. i. 33–35)

Lucina replies with a traditional image that anticipates the manner of Valentinian's death by an agonizing poison. Her suicide follows, a climax that virtually truncates the play. While Maximus' friend, Aecius, half-heartedly dissuades her, Maximus actively encourages her. The manner in which the two alternatively urge her on to death and call her back has an air of deliberate comedy. In *The Maid's Tragedy*, though the screw is turned more and more tightly, the focus still remains on the group of Melantius, Amintor, and Evadne, but in *Valentinian* attention is fixed on each character only as his or her most intense moments of experience take place. Aecius becomes the center of interest in this way when he dares tell Valentinian some home truths (I.iii), although his extravagant loyalty emerges also. The ground is prepared for Maximus' plot against his friend. Aecius represents that familiar type in Fletcher's work: the bluff soldier, contrasted with the parasitic civilian, whose only course in the more complex moral world of peace is a passive obedience that is allowed a compensatory candor of speech. Aecius' stubborn loyalty convinces Maximus that his friend must be killed before any attempt on the emperor's life can succeed. In one of Fletcher's rare soliloquies, which subtly suggests the ebb and flow of the will, Maximus argues and counterargues the rival claims of honor and friendship. Finally he betrays Aecius by sending an anonymous letter to Valentinian, who is now presented as the classical, neurotically guilty tyrant: Aecius has been frank with the emperor in reporting the army's unfavorable sentiments, and this rough honesty now tells against him. An officer is sent to dispatch him, but Aecius prefers to fall on his own sword. Maximus incites Aecius' servants to revenge their master's death by poisoning the emperor. Valentinian expires slowly, mocked by one of the poisoners, Aretus, who, having already poisoned himself, can enact the torments that the emperor will shortly suffer. Valentinian approaches a moment of truth when he questions the separation between his abstract political entity and his natural body. It is a more serious version of the king's questioning of his position in *Philaster*, and it also echoes Valentinian's triumphant "I am Justice":

> O flattered fool,
> See what thy Godhead's come to. . . .
> I' the midst of all flames, I'll fire the Empire
> (V. ii. 27–28; 43)

and the metaphor of fire ironically recalls Love's destruction of Ilion in the second song.

The main characters in this play, Valentinian, Maximus, Aecius, like the characters in earlier plays, are much concerned, in adolescent fashion, with the "image" they present to others. This has little to do with any soldierly concept of honor and, as Clifford Leech has shown, indicates Fletcher's awareness of how the naked man searches for an identity and a role. And the immediate impulse behind Lucina's suicide is not so much the injury to her private self or any tragic realization that part of her consents to rape, but rather a concern in a narrow sense for her reputation.

Fletcher's other unaided tragedy, *Bonduca*, involves the Jonsonian theory of humors, a physical determinism that governs character. This is coldly applied to a play that does not want deaths. The focus is once more distributed among individuals, both British and Roman, in the story of the fierce Queen Boadicea, her virago daughters, the absurdly chivalrous Caratach, and the young British prince Hengo. Both sides are treated with decidedly sick humor, though Hengo's death displays high pathos. His hope for Britain quenched, Caratach surrenders to the Romans he so admires, subdued, he proclaims, by Roman courtesy, not by force. These fine words cannot mask the fact that he is to provide the centerpiece for a Roman triumph, "gilding their conquest," in words that echo those of Richard II and Bolingbroke:

Caratach: I am for Rome./*Suetonius*: You must.

Caratach's extravagant chivalry, besides exhibiting a "humour," accords with some of the exemplary gestures recorded by Roman historians as illustrative of the republican virtues: the episode in Livy, for example, where the Roman general Camillus sends back the children of the general commanding the enemy, who have been betrayed to him by their tutor. Caratach, however, is chivalrous to men only; war and love are once more represented as opposed processes of self-annihilation. The verse of this powerful, if repellent, play is more masculine and metrically ornate than is usual with Fletcher.

FLETCHER'S COMEDIES

The Humorous Lieutenant and the romantic *Island Princess*, with its unstable but attractive heroine, illustrate the range of Fletcher's tragicomedy. Inflicted on the lieutenant is a Jonsonian "humour" of fighting well when ill and playing the coward when well. The main action involves Demetrius, the king's son, and Celia, whom he loves and intends to marry. Demetrius leads his father's army to war and Celia catches the king's eye. The scenes between him and Celia are particularly well managed. Unlike Lucina, Celia reduces the ruler to virtue by her spirit, sweetness, and eloquence. To seduce Celia, the king works through a madam, Leucippe. Her establishment, run on brisk, businesslike lines (II.iii), is reminiscent of *Measure for Measure*, in which the brothel is a microcosm of the kingdom, and in Act II, scene iii, Fletcher gives a coolly naturalistic picture of its working. More or less gratuitous in terms of structure, the scene leaves an impression of a genuine sense of evil rare in Fletcher's work and is all the more intense for being presented without rhetoric.

1st Maid.	I have wrought her . . .
Leucippe.	These kind are subtle.

Did she not cry and blubber when ye urg'd her?
1st Maid.   O most extremely: and swore she would rather perish—
Leucippe.   Good signs: very good signs; symptoms of easy nature . . .

(*enter a woman and a girl*)
Would you aught with us, good woman?
I pray be short, we are full of business.
Woman.   I have a tender girl here, and 't please your honour—
Leucippe.   Very well.
Woman.   That hath a great desire to serve your worship.
Leucippe.   It may be so: I am full of maids.
Woman.   She is young, forsooth;
And for her truth, and, as they say her bearing—
Leucippe.   Ye say well: Come hither, maid: let me feel your pulse;
'Tis somewhat weak, but Nature will grow stronger;
Let me see your leg: she treads low i' the pasterns.
Woman.   A cork-heel, madam.
Leucippe.   We know what will do it
Without your help. Good woman, what do you pitch her at?
She's but a slight toy, cannot hold out long.
Woman.   Even what you think is meet.
Leucippe.   Give her ten crowns: we are full of business:
She's a poor woman; let her take a cheese home:
Enter the wench i' the office.   (*Exit woman*)
2nd Maid.   What's your name, sister?

Phoebe.   Phoebe, forsooth.
Leucippe.   A pretty name: 'will do well:
Go in, and let the other maid instruct ye, Phoebe, (*exeunt*)
Let my old velvet skirt be made fit for her
(I'll put her into action) for a waistcoat,
And when I've rigged her up once, this small pinnace
Shall sail for gold, and good store too . . .
                    (II. iii. 24; 27–30; 58–78)

Leucippe prepares an aphrodisiac for Celia, but it is drunk by the "humorous" lieutenant, who in scenes of sparkling farce proceeds to fall in love with the king (as intended) and wishes himself "a wench of fifteen" for the royal use.

Fletcher's unaided comedies are full of verve, and suspense is, as usual, skillfully exploited. They do not, however, provide that combination of darkness and beauty that we find in Shakespeare's comedy. Fletcher's plot and subplot reinforce but rarely contrast with each other and there is no fool to suggest ranges of experience beyond the scope of the young lovers. His role is tepidly supplied by the older generation. The settings are more remote from contemporary life than those of Middleton's comedies, and it is Fletcher's colloquial language, rather than his ideas or situations, that supplies vitality. *Monsieur Thomas* has an amusingly absurd plot. It presents a father who is anxious for his son to prove himself a man by sowing wild oats; a son who is doing just that, but mistakenly believes that he will only inherit his father's riches if he assumes a mask of sobriety and preciseness; and a servant who reports how wicked the son is, but is constantly foiled by the young man's quick hypocrisies.

The Wild Goose Chase offers one of Fletcher's favorite themes, the sexual duel expressed through witty argument and stratagem. This comedy anticipates the course of the genre for the next hundred years, from cavalier comedy to the heroes of Farquhar with their "good hearts" and venial vices. Less savage than much Restoration comedy, *The Wild Goose Chase* has much in common with that, though only Oriana possesses the percipience of the Restoration "true wit," but is too simple to make a Millamant. Oriana starts at a disadvantage, for she has already ingenuously acknowledged her love for Mirabel, "the wild goose," to himself and his friends. Her determination to be married rather than entered in Mirabel's pocket register of seductions carries little conviction even with her brother, Du Garde. The general terms of the battle are stated as Mirabel returns from Italy to his father's house in France.

> *Mirabel.* I know thou art a pretty wench; I know thou lov'st me;
> Preserve it till we have a fit time to discourse on't,
> And a fit place; I'll raise thy heart, I warrant thee:
> Thou seest I have much to do now.
> *Oriana.* I am answered sir;
> With me you shall have nothing on these conditions.
>
> (I. iii. 57–61)

To be natural is impractical, humiliating, for a woman. Through the succeeding acts Oriana devises, with the help of her brother and Lugier, a suite of stratagems to trap Mirabel into marriage. Du Garde disguises himself as a wealthy Savoyard and publicly courts Oriana, so kindling Mirabel's jealousy until he discovers the trick. Oriana then simulates madness and is carried onto the stage elegantly raving, but Mirabel sees through this, just as he sees through Oriana's disguise as an Italian noblewoman with a large dowry sent by a brother grateful to Mirabel for having once saved his life. By now, though, "the wild goose" has tired of being chased and allows himself to be tricked into a promise of marriage by the veiled lady, and so capitulates to Oriana and marrying. The humor lies in situation rather than speech. Mirabel is only crudely, if forcibly, cynical.

> Why should I be at charge to keep a wife of mine own,
> When other honest married men will ease me,
> And thank me too, and be beholding to me?
> Thou thinks't I am mad for a maidenhead; thou art cozened:
> Or, if I were addicted to that diet,
> Can you tell me where I should have one? thou art eighteen now,
> And, if thou hast thy maidenhead yet extant,
> Sure, 'tis as big as cod's head; and those grave dishes
> I never love to deal withal.
>
> (II. i. 144–152)

Here, the deliberate artificiality of the sentiment works against Fletcherian comedy. What is brutal is distracting also because its effect—of inviting our participation—even while acknowledging this to be art, not life—fails. Failed manipulation is a more serious fault in comedy than in tragedy.

The play succeeds through spruce plotting, revolving entirely around marriage. It contains nothing gratuitous—not an episode, scarcely indeed a sentence, that is not in some way related to this theme. The most farcical moments of *The Wild Goose Chase* concern disguise of one kind or another, and the note of artifice in relation to the civilized personality. The natural demands of sex and the demands of a necessarily artificial society reach a compromise in marriage.

CONCLUSION

CRITICISM has done less than justice to Beaumont and Fletcher by its failure to distinguish between the description and the evaluation of their drama and by the unimaginative comparisons it has made between them and other Jacobean playwrights. The art and achievement of these collaborators were unique and look forward to twentieth-century practice. This fact has been obscured because the test of staging has been consistently withheld from their work. Their most important contribution lies in exploiting the paradoxes of drama and life, and it is not surprising that Pirandello should have found them absorbing. They are keenly interested in a topic that fascinates the modern world, that is, the problem of identity and the playing out of roles, or, to put it in another way, the refusal of the average human being to live as an individual when faced with painful challenges. As Clifford Leech observes, "Men avoid nakedness by doing what they feel the codes and traditions of society demand from them." Yet the moving images on the stage are always subordinated to the effect that Beaumont and Fletcher aim to produce on the audience: it is with the audience that they are predominantly concerned.

The special tone, which critics have recognized as peculiar to Beaumont and Fletcher, signifies a challenge and invitation to involvement on the part of the audience, which the dramatists then proceed to contradict by whipping the carpet away; so that their audience is quite literally never on safe ground in assuming it has detected the appropriate stance or response. Such a method is announced in *The Knight of the Burning Pestle* and was clearly learned from the failure of *The Faithful Shepherdess*. A good deal of the success or failure of such a tone depends on how the pretense of a self-enclosed dramatic world is maintained, that is, one that is unaware of any effect on the audience. If this pretense falters (exploitation becomes too knowing, manipulation too coarse), so disturbing the internal equilibrium of the dramatic world, then the play begins to fail. Beaumont and Fletcher's remains an art of the most severe virtuosity, and, in at least four or five of these plays, commandingly sustained.

SELECTED BIBLIOGRAPHY

I. General Bibliographical and Textual Discussions. W. W. Greg, "Nathan Field and the Beaumont and Fletcher Folio of 1679," *Review of English Studies*, 3 (1927); E. H. C. Oliphant, *The Plays of Beaumont and Fletcher: An Attempt to Determine Their Respective Shares and the Shares of Others* (London, 1927); E. H. C. Oliphant, "The Plays of Beaumont and Fletcher: Some Additional Notes," *Philological Quarterly*, 9 (1930); R. C. Bald, "Bibliographical Studies in the Beaumont and Fletcher Folio of 1647," *Transactions of the Bibliographical Society Supplement*, 13 (1938); S. A. Tannenbaum, *Beaumont and Fletcher: A Concise Bibliography* (New York, 1938), also a *Supplement* (New York, 1948); J. Gerritsen, "The Printing of the Beaumont and Fletcher Folio of 1647," *The Library*, 5th ser., 3 (1948); C. Hoy, "The Shares of Fletcher and His Collaborators in the Beaumont and Fletcher Canon," *Studies in Bibliography: Papers of the Bibliographical Society of the University of Virginia*, 8, 9, 11, 13, 14, 15 (1956–1962); S. Henning, "The Printers and the Beaumont and Fletcher Folio of 1647," *Studies in Bibliography*, 22 (1969); T. P. Logan and D. S. Smith, eds., *The Later Jacobean and Caroline Dramatists: A Survey and Bibliography of Recent Studies in English Renaissance Drama* (Lincoln, Nebr.–London, 1978).

II. Collected Works. *Drama: Comedies and Tragedies . . . Never Printed Before* (London, 1647), contains 34 plays and Beaumont's *The Masque of the Inner Temple and Grayes Inn*; *Fifty Comedies and Tragedies . . . All in One Volume* (London, 1679), contains 52 plays and *The Masque*; G. Langbaine the younger, ed., *The Works*, 7 vols. (London, 1711); L. Theobald et al., comp., *The Works*, 10 vols. (London, 1750); G. Colman, ed., *The Dramatick Works*, 10 vols. (London, 1778); *The Works of Beaumont and Fletcher*, 14 vols. (London, 1812), with an intro. and explanatory notes by H. W. Weber, *The Faithful Friends* first appears here; *The Works*, 2 vols. (London, 1840), with an intro. by G. Darley, this is Weber's text with additions to *The Humorous Lieutenant* from A. Dyce, ed., *Demetrius and Enanthe* (London, 1830); A. Dyce, ed., *The Works . . . the Text Formed from a New Collation of Early Editions*, 11 vols. (London, 1843–1846), with notes and a bibliographical memoir, the best of the earlier eds.; J. St. Loe Strachey, ed., *Beaumont and Fletcher* (London, 1887; last repr., 1949), with an in-

tro. and notes, 10 of the plays including *Valentinian, Bonduca*, and *The Wild Goose Chase*; A. H. Bullen, gen. ed., *The Works*, vols. I–IV (London, 1904–1912), only four of the projected twelve vols. in the Variorum ed. were completed; A. Glover and A. R. Waller, eds., *The Works*, 10 vols. (Cambridge, 1905–1912), with the Variorum, this constitutes the standard text, but it is being superseded by the work of F. Bowers et al.; G. P. Baker, ed., *Beaumont and Fletcher. Select Plays* (London, 1911); M. C. Bradbrook, ed., *Beaumont and Fletcher. Select Plays* (London, 1962), a surprisingly appreciative intro.; F. Bowers, gen. ed., *The Dramatic Works in the Beaumont and Fletcher Canon* (Cambridge, 1966–), comprises to date: *The Knight of the Burning Pestle, The Masque of the Inner Temple and Gray's Inn, The Woman Hater, The Coxcomb, Philaster*, and *The Captain*, vol. I (1966); *The Maid's Tragedy, A King and No King, Cupid's Revenge, The Fearful Lady, Love's Pilgrimage*, vol. II (1970); *The Faithful Shepherdess, The Tragedy of Thierry and Theodoret, Beggar's Bush, The Noble Gentleman, Love's Cure*, vol. III (1976).

Verse: *Salmacis and Hermaphroditus* (London, 1602), an early Ovidian exercise by Beaumont, discussed in H. Hallett-Smith, *Elizabethan Poetry: A Study in Conventions* (London, 1952), authorship is discussed by P. Finkelpearl in *Notes and Queries*, 16 (1969) and by R. Sell in *Notes and Queries*, 19 (1972); F. Beaumont, *Poems* (London, 1640), this contains a number of poems certainly not by Beaumont, reprinted in 1653 with additions and as *The Golden Remains of Francis Beaumont and John Fletcher* (London, 1660), also found in A. Chalmers, ed., *The Work of the English Poets*, vol. VI (London, 1810) and in Darley's ed. of *The Works* (above); H. Macdonald, ed., *Songs and Lyrics from the Plays of Beaumont and Fletcher* (London, 1928).

Miscellaneous Prose: M. Eccles, ed., "Grammar Lecture," *Review of English Studies*, 16 (1940).

III. General Scholarship and Criticism. C. Lamb, *Specimens of English Dramatic Poets* (London, 1808); G. C. Macaulay, *Francis Beaumont, A Critical Study* (London, 1883); A. C. Swinburne, "Beaumont and Fletcher" in *Encyclopaedia Britannica*, 9th ed. (London, 1875), this essay has been replaced in the 1964 ed. by an essay by P. Ure, Swinburne's essay is reprinted in his *Studies in Prose and Poetry* (London, 1894); J. A. Symonds, *In the Key of Blue, and Other Prose Essays* (London, 1893), contains the essay "Some Notes on Fletcher's Valentinian" first printed in the *Fortnightly Review*; A. H. Thorndike, *The Influence of Beaumont and Fletcher on Shakespeare* (Worcester, Mass., 1901), suggests that Beaumont and Fletcher influenced Shakespeare's tragicomic "romances" such as *Cymbeline*; J. W. Tupper, "The Relation of the Heroic Play to the Romances of Beaumont and Fletcher," *PMLA*, 20 (1905); O. L. Hatcher, *John Fletcher: A Study in Dramatic Method* (Chicago, 1905); "Fletcher's Habits of Dramatic Collaboration" in *Anglia*, 33 (1910); F. H. Ristine, *English Tragicomedy: Its Origin and History* (London, 1910); G. Macaulay, "Beaumont and Fletcher" in *The Cambridge History of English Literature*, vol. VI (Cambridge, 1910); C. M. Gayley, *Francis Beaumont, Dramatist* (London, 1914); W. Farnham, "Colloquial Contractions in Beaumont, Fletcher, Massinger and Shakespeare as a Test of Authorship" in *PMLA*, 31 (1916); S. Lindley, "The Music of the Songs in Fletcher's Plays," *Studies in Philology*, 21 (1924); A. C. Sprague, *Beaumont and Fletcher on the Restoration Stage* (Cambridge, Mass., 1926); J. H. Wilson, *The Influence of Beaumont and Fletcher on Restoration Drama* (Columbus, 1928); E. S. Lindsey, "The Original Music in Beaumont's Play, *The Knight of the Burning Pestle*," *Studies in Philology*, 26 (1929); J. Isaacs, *Productions and Stage Management at the Blackfriars Theatre* (London, 1933); U. M. Ellis-Fermor, *The Jacobean Drama: An Interpretation* (London, 1936), contains a fine essay on Beaumont and Fletcher that stresses the coherent unreality of their work; D. M. MacKeithan, *The Debt to Shakespeare in the Beaumont and Fletcher Plays* (Austin, Tex., 1938), privately published; B. Maxwell, *Studies in Beaumont, Fletcher and Massinger* (Chapel Hill, N.C., 1939); G. E. Bentley, *The Jacobean and Caroline Stage*, 7 vols. (London, 1941–1968); L. B. Wallis, *Fletcher, Beaumont and Company, Entertainers to the Jacobean Gentry* (New York, 1947); M. K. Mincoff, *Baroque Literature in England* (Sofia, 1947), the plays in the canon do to some degree fit this difficult literary category; D. J. Rules, "Beaumont and Fletcher on the London Stage, 1776–1833," *PMLA*, 63 (1948); E. M. Wilson, "Did John Fletcher Read Spanish?" *Philological Quarterly*, 27 (1948); M. K. Mincoff, "The Social Background of Beaumont and Fletcher," *English Miscellany*, 1 (Rome, 1950); I. A. Shapiro, "The Mermaid Club," *Modern Language Review*, 46 (1950), a rejoinder by P. Simpson in *Modern Language Review*, 46 (1951) brushes aside Shapiro's doubts about the attribution of the famous verse to Beaumont; E. M. Waith, *The Pattern of Tragicomedy in Beaumont and Fletcher* (New Haven, 1952), claims that Beaumont and Fletcher significantly stylize experience and relates their work to the Roman art of declamation and to the classical controversiae; A. Harbage, *Shakespeare and the Rival Traditions* (New York, 1952), a learned but moralistic and somewhat melodramatic account of the war between the theaters and the distinction between popular and coterie drama and audience; J. F. Danby, *Poets on Fortune's Hill. Studies in Sidney, Shakespeare, Beaumont and Fletcher* (London, 1952), contains some brilliant criticism of Beaumont and Fletcher, republished as *Elizabethan and Jacobean Poets* (London, 1964); M. Abend, "Shakespeare's Influence in Beaumont and Fletcher," *Notes and Queries*, 197 (21 June–16 August 1952); W. Bryher [W. Ellerman], *The Player's Boy* (London, 1953), Beaumont's life in fictional form; M. C. Bradbrook, *The Growth and Structure of Elizabethan Comedy* (London, 1955), has a chapter on Fletcher's comedies; R. F. Brinkley, ed., *Coleridge on the Seventeenth Century* (Durham, N.C., 1955); M. T. Herrick, *Tragicomedy: Its Origin and Development in Italy, France and England* (Urbana, Ill., 1955), useful for background but of little critical value; W. W. Appleton, *Beaumont and Fletcher* (London, 1956), useful summary of plots and some shrewd comment; G. E. Bentley, *The Later Jacobean and Caroline Stage*, vol. III (London, 1956), cites early sources for Fletcher's life; W. A. Armstrong, *The Elizabethan Private Theatre, Facts and Problems* in Society for Theatre Research, 6 (London, 1957–1958); C. Barber, *The Idea of Honour in the English Drama 1592–1700* (Goteburg, 1957); J. Masefield, "Beaumont and Fletcher," *Atlantic Monthly* (June 1957); W. E. Miller, " 'Periaktoi' in the Old Blackfriars," *Modern Language Notes*, 74 (1959); J. R. Brown and B. Harris, eds., *Jacobean Theatre* in Stratford-upon-Avon Studies, 1 (1960), contains P. Edwards' "The Danger Not the Death," which dismisses *Valentinian* and praises one or two of the tragicomedies; K. Muir, *Shakespeare as Collaborator* (London, 1960); R. Ornstein, *The Moral Vision of Jacobean Tragedy* (Madison, Wisc., 1960), a major work of criticism though unsympathetic to Beaumont and Fletcher; C. Leech, *The John Fletcher Plays* (London, 1962), acute and sympathetic, singles out *The Humorous Lieutenant* as Fletcher's masterpiece; G. E. Bentley, *Shakespeare and His Theatre* (Lincoln, Nebr., 1964); T. B. Tomlinson, *A Study of Elizabethan and Jacobean Tragedy* (Cambridge, 1964), chapter 12 deals with Beaumont and Fletcher, a neo-Leavisian approach but contains some brilliant pages on *The Maid's Tragedy*; S. Schoenbaum, ed., *Renaissance Drama*, vol. VII (London, 1964), contains M. K. Mincoff, "Fletcher's Early Tragedies," an interesting analysis of *Valentinian* with Aecius seen as the real but passive hero, and N. Rabkin, "The Double Plot: Notes on the History of Conventions"; S. Schoenbaum, *Internal Evidence and Elizabethan Dramatic Authorship* (London, 1966), an able account of the history of a dangerous game, which has incidental reference to the Beaumont and Fletcher canon; J. R. Brown and B. A. Harris, eds., *Later Shakespeare*, Stratford-upon-Avon Studies, 8 (1966), contains R. Proudfoot's "Shakespeare and the New Dramatists of the King's Men, 1608–1613"; D. L. Frost, *The School of Shakespeare* (Cambridge, 1967); H. Berry, "The Stage and Boxes at Blackfriars," *Studies in Philology*, 63 (1969); J. H. Long, ed., *Music in English Renaissance Drama* (London, 1968), contains "Patterns of Music and Action in Fletcherian Drama"; D. Galloway, ed., *The Elizabethan Theatre* (Toronto, 1969), contains R. Hosley's "A Reconstruction of the Second Blackfriars"; P. J. Finkelpearl, "Beaumont, Fletcher, and 'Beaumont and Fletcher': Some Distinctions," *English Literary Renaissance*, 1 (1970); G. E. Bentley, *The Profession of Dramatist in Shakespeare's Time* (Princeton, 1972); S. Gossett, "Masque Influences on the Dramaturgy of Beaumont and Fletcher," *Modern Philology*, 69 (1972); M. Cone, *Fletcher Without Beaumont* (Salzburg, 1976), usefully resumes the history of Fletcher criticism.

IV. CRITICISM OF INDIVIDUAL PLAYS. W. Graham, "The Cardenio-Double Falsehood Problem," *Modern Philology*, 14 (1916); V. M. Jeffers, "Italian Influence in Fletcher's *The Faithful Shepherdess*," *Modern Language Review*, 21 (1920); T. P. Harrison, "A Probable Source of Beaumont and Fletcher's *Philaster*," *PMLA*, 41 (1926); A. W. Upton, "Allusions to James I and His Court in Marston's *Fawn* and Beaumont's *Woman-Hater*," *PMLA*, 44 (1929); E. Castle, "Theobald's 'Double Falsehood'" in *Archiv für das Studium der neueren Sprachen*, 169 (1936); T. Spencer, "The Two Noble Kinsmen," *Modern Philology*, 36 (1939); A. Mizener, "The High Design of *A King and No King*," *Modern Philology*, 38 (1941); W. C. Powell, "A Note on the Stage History of Beaumont and Fletcher's *Love's Pilgrimage* and *The Chances*," *Modern Language Notes*, 56 (February 1941); M. G. M. Adkins, "The Citizens in *Philaster*: Their Function and Significance," *Studies in Philology*, 43 (1946); J. E. Savage, "Beaumont and Fletcher's *Philaster* and Sidney's *Arcadia*" in *English Language History*, 14 (1947); J. E. Savage, "The Date of Beaumont and Fletcher's *Cupid's Revenge*," *English Literary History*, 15 (1948); A. C. Partridge, *The Problem of Henry VIII Reopened* (Cambridge, 1949); J. E. Savage, "The 'Gaping Wounds' in the Text of *Philaster*," *Philological Quarterly*, 28 (1949); P. Simpson, "Beaumont's Verse Letter to Ben Jonson," *Modern Language Review*, 46 (1951); M. K. Mincoff, "The Authorship of *Two Noble Kinsmen*," *English Studies*, 33 (1952); H. S. Wilson, "*Philaster* and *Cymbeline*," *English Institute Essays* (1952); "Extra Monosyllables in *Henry VIII* and the Problem of Authorship," *Journal of English Germanic Philology*, 52 (1953); "The Effects of Reunion in the Beaumont and Fletcher Play *Wit at Several Weapons*," University of Mississippi *Studies in English* (1960); M. K. Mincoff, "*Henry VIII* and Fletcher," *Shakespeare Quarterly*, 12 (Summer 1961); D. Mehl, "Beaumont and Fletcher's *The Faithful Friends*," *Anglia*, 80 (1962); E. A. Armstrong, "Shakespearean Imagery in *The Two Noble Kinsmen*" in appendix to *Shakespeare's Imagination*, 2nd ed. (Lincoln, Nebr., 1963); P. Davison, "The Serious Concerns of *Philaster*," *English Literary History*, 30 (1963); I. Lemberg, "'Das Spiel mit der dramatischen illusion' in Beaumont's *The Knight of the Burning Pestle*," *Anglia*, 81 (1963); P. Bertram, *Shakespeare and the Two Noble Kinsmen* (New Brunswick, N.J., 1965), attempts to show that Shakespeare was the sole author and succeeds in impeaching previous scholarship for inaccuracy, but does not make its case; L. L. Steiger, "'May a Man Be Caught with Faces?' The Convention of 'Heart' and 'Face' in Fletcher and Rowley's *The Maid in the Mill*" in M. Holmes, ed., *Essays and Studies* (London, 1967); J. Doebler, "Beaumont's *Knight of the Burning Pestle* and the Prodigal Son Plays," *Studies in English Literature*, 5 (1965); M. K. Mincoff, "*The Faithful Shepherdess*: A Fletcherian Experiment," *Renaissance Drama*, 9 (1966); J. Freehafer, "'Cardenio,' by Shakespeare and Fletcher," *PMLA*, 84 (1969); M. Neill, "'The Simetry, Which Gives a Poem Grace': Masque, Imagery and the Fancy of *The Maid's Tragedy*," *Renaissance Drama*, 3 (1970); J. Doebler, "The Tone of the Jasper and Luce Scenes in Beaumont's *The Knight of the Burning Pestle*," *English Studies*, 16 (1975).

V. SEPARATE WORKS. *Plays by Fletcher*: *The Faithful Shepherdess* (quarto ed., London, 1609), in F. W. Moorman, ed. (London, 1896); *Monsieur Thomas* (quarto ed., London, 1639); *Rule a Wife and Have a Wife* (quarto ed., London, 1640), in G. Saintsbury, ed. (London, 1914). The folio of 1647 contained the following: *Bonduca*, in W. W. Greg, ed. (London, 1951); *The Chances*, in G. Villiers, ed. (London, 1682); *The Humorous Lieutenant*, appears later as A. Dyce, ed., *Demetrius and Enanthe* (London, 1830) and in E. M. Cook and F. P. Wilson, eds. (London, 1951); *The Island Princess*, in C. F. T. Brooke and N. B. Paradise, eds., *English Drama 1580–1642* (London, 1933); *The Loyal Subject*; *The Mad Lover*; *The Pilgrim*; *Valentinian*; *Wife for a Month*; *Woman Pleased*; *The Woman's Prize or the Tamer Tamed*, in G. B. Ferguson, ed. (The Hague, 1966); *The Wild Goose Chase* (quarto ed., London, 1652).

Plays Probably by Beaumont: *The Knight of the Burning Pestle* (quarto ed., London, 1613), in F. W. Moorman, ed. (London, 1898), H. S. Murch, ed. (London, 1908), R. M. Alden., ed. (London, 1910), W. T. Williams, ed. (London, 1924), W. J. Sergeaunt, ed. (London, 1928), J. W. Peel, ed. (London, 1929), M. T. Jones-Davies, ed. (London, 1958), with useful comments on diction, syntax, and poetic technique, J. W. Lever, ed. (London, 1962), J. Doebler, ed. (London, 1967), A. Gurr, ed. (London, 1967), M. Hathaway, ed. (London, 1971). Most scholars are agreed in assigning this to Beaumont, but it is possible that the love scenes are by Fletcher.

Plays by Beaumont and Fletcher: *The Woman Hater* (quarto ed., London, 1607), probably an early work, the major role was Beaumont's but revised in at least five scenes by Fletcher; *Cupid's Revenge* (quarto ed., London, 1615); *The Scornful Lady* (quarto ed., London, 1616), according to Hoy, Fletcher's is the major share; *A King and No King* (quarto ed., London, 1619), in R. M. Alden. ed. (London, 1910), R. K. Turner, ed. (London, 1964), Hoy allots only five scenes to Fletcher, Beaumont gave the play its final form; *The Maid's Tragedy* (quarto eds., London, 1619, 1622, 1630, etc.), in A. H. Thorndike, ed. (Boston, 1906), C. Morley, ed. (London, 1929), A. E. McIlwraith, ed., *Five Stuart Tragedies* (London, 1953), H. B. Norland, ed. (London, 1968), A. Gurr, ed. (London, 1969), according to Hoy, Fletcher contributed only four scenes; *Philaster* (quarto eds., London, 1620, 1622), F. S. Boas, ed. (London, 1898), A. H. Thorndike, ed. (Boston, 1906), A. Gurr, ed. (London, 1969), and D. M. Ashe, ed. (London, 1975), Beaumont's was the greater share; *The Captain* (folio ed., London, 1647), Hoy gives the major portion to Fletcher; *Love's Pilgrimage* (folio ed., London, 1647), includes a total of 132 lines that are identical with a similar number of lines in Jonson's *New Inn*; *The Noble Gentlemen* (London, 1647), Hoy argues that this is Fletcher's revision of an early work of Beaumont's.

Plays by Beaumont, Fletcher, and Massinger: *Beggar's Bush* (folio ed., London, 1647), a MS from the prompt book in the Folger Library, Washington, D. C., has been edited by H. H. Donnenkemp (The Hague, 1967), who eliminates Beaumont from the collaboration; *The Coxcomb* (folio ed., London, 1647), revised when restaged; *Love's Cure* (folio ed., London, 1647), highly complex division between authors, Massinger is mainly present as reviser, according to Hoy; *Thierry and Theodoret* (ca. 1621), Hoy assigns to Beaumont Act III and Act V, scene i, and to Fletcher five scenes altogether.

Plays by Fletcher and Massinger: *The Tragedy of Sir John Van Olden Barnavelt*, in A. H. Bullen, ed., *A Collection of Old English Plays*, vol. II (London, 1884) and W. P. Frijlinck, ed. (Amsterdam, 1922), acted in August 1619 but not published, MS prompt book at British Museum, Hoy gives Fletcher thirteen scenes and Massinger about nine, text seems to indicate a play hastily assembled for its contemporary relevance; *The Elder Brother* (quarto ed., London, 1637), in W. H. Draper, ed. (London, 1916), highly entertaining comedy, Hoy assigns Fletcher Acts II, III, IV, and Massinger the other two; *The Custom of the Country* (folio ed., London, 1647), according to Hoy, Massinger's share predominates but Fletcher's may be obscured in the final state of the text; *The Double Marriage* (folio ed., London, 1647), Fletcher's share slightly predominates; *The False One* (folio ed., London, 1647), Fletcher is assigned Acts II, III, IV and Massinger Acts I and V, Oliphant suggests the play has been absurdly underrated, entirely because of its Shakespearean connections; *The Little French Lawyer* (folio ed., London, 1647), rather dull though much praised by Coleridge, Massinger seems to have given the final form to the extant text, according to Hoy; *The Lover's Progress* (folio ed., London, 1647), a revision by Massinger of Fletcher, rather than a final revision by Massinger of a play in which Massinger had earlier collaborated with Fletcher; *The Prophetess* (folio ed., London, 1647), Hoy assigns broadly equal shares to both; *The Sea Voyage* (folio ed., London, 1647), Hoy assigns Acts I and IV to Fletcher and Acts II, III, and V to Massinger; *The Spanish Curate* (folio ed., London, 1647), Hoy assigns broadly equal shares to both; *A Very Woman*, in *Three New Plays* (octavo ed., London, 1655), according to Hoy, this is a Massinger revision of a Fletcher original.

Plays by Fletcher and Field: *Four Plays in One* (folio ed., London, 1647), Hoy assigns *The Induction, Triumph of Love*, and *Triumph of Honour* to Field and *Triumph of Death* and *Triumph of Time* to Fletcher.

Plays by Fletcher, Field, and Massinger: *The Honest Man's Fortune* (folio ed., London, 1647), in J. Gerritson, ed. (Groningen, 1952), a MS scribal transcript is preserved in MS Dyce 9 at the Victoria and Albert Museum, both the MS of 1625 and the folio text appear to derive from the same MS; Field, in Hoy's view, has the dominant part in this play; *The Knights of Malta* (folio ed., London, 1647), Field seems to have been responsible for the splendid "Fatal Woman" Zanthea and Fletcher for the boring Norandine; *The Queen of Corinth* (folio ed., London, 1647), a skillful play, Hoy gives Field and Massinger two acts each and Fletcher one act.

Plays by Fletcher and Middleton: *The Nice Valour* (folio ed., London, 1647), the shortest play in the canon and an unsatisfactory text, Hoy relates the play to Middleton's tragicomedies of the 1620's.

Plays by Fletcher and Rowley: *The Maid in the Mill* (folio ed., London, 1647), Rowley's part in the folio text slightly predominates over that of Fletcher.

Plays by Fletcher and Shakespeare: *The Double Falsehood*, written originally by Shakespeare and revised by L. Theobald (London, 1728), in W. Graham, ed. (Cleveland, 1920), it has been conjectured that this represents L. Theobald's revision of the lost *Cardenio* apparently acted at court by the King's Men in 1613 and entered in the Stationers' Register on 9 September 1653. The suggested identification of two hands, one being Fletcher's, was first made by Gamaliel Bradford in *Modern Language Notes*, 25 (1910). See also E. H. C. Oliphant, *Notes and* Queries (Feb., March, Apr., 1919) and K. Muir, *Shakespeare as Collaborator* (London, 1960); *Henry VIII* (folio ed., London, 1623), in D. Nichol Smith, ed., *Shakespeare Folio* (London, 1899), and in C. K. Pooler, ed. (London, 1915), J. M. Berdan and C. F. T. Brooke, eds. (New York, 1925), R. A. Foakes, ed. (rev. ed., London, 1964); *The Two Noble Kinsmen* (quarto ed., London, 1634), in H. Littledale, ed. (London, 1885), W. J. Rolfe, ed. (New York, 1891), C. H. Herford, ed. (London, 1897), C. Leech, ed. (New York–London, 1966), C. R. Proudfoot, ed. (London, 1970), also in C. F. T. Brooke, ed., *The Shakespeare Apocrypha* (London, 1908).

Plays in Which Fletcher and James Shirley Are Involved: *The Night Walker* (quarto ed., London, 1640), it is known from the office book of the Revels that Shirley reissued the original text by Fletcher, Hoy finds only three scenes substantially unaltered.

Plays in Which Fletcher Is Involved with an Unidentified Reviser: *Wit Without Money* (quarto ed., London, 1639).

Plays of Multiple Authorship, Including That of Fletcher: *The Fair Maid of the Inn* (folio ed., London, 1647), this has been divided among Fletcher, Ford, Massinger, and Webster, the Websterian element has been questioned and the Fletcherian element is slight; *Rollo, Duke of Normandy* (quarto ed., London, 1639), attributed to "B. J. F." in J. D. Jump, ed. (Liverpool, 1948). Four authors have been tentatively identified: Chapman, Fletcher, Jonson, and Massinger. The consensus is that Fletcher and Massinger are present in this play, and that there are probably two other hands. This ed. has the title *The Bloody Brother* and that of 1640 has the present title; *Wit at Several Weapons* (London, 1647). Hoy suggests that this is a revision by Middleton and Rowley of an original text by Fletcher and an unknown collaborator.

Plays with Status in Doubt: *The Laws of Candy* (folio ed., London, 1647), a magnificent, Pirandellesque play, following Oliphant, Hoy gives it entirely to Ford, but Schoenbaum suggests that his grounds are slender.

Lost Plays: *The Jeweller of Amsterdam, or The Hague*, suggested limits are 1616–1619, by Fletcher, Field, and Massinger; *The Devil of Dowgate, or Usury Put to Use*, licensed on 17 October 1623, by Fletcher; *The History of Madan*, by Beaumont.

Plays Probably Not Belonging to the Canon: *The Faithful Friends* (1613–*ca*. 1621), published in H. W. Weber, ed. (London, 1812), attributed to Beaumont and Fletcher in the Stationers' Register. Daborne, Massinger, and Field have been suggested as authors; derives from MS Dyce 10 at the Victoria and Albert Museum; also in G. M. Pinciss and G. R. Proudfoot, eds. (London, 1975).

JOHN WEBSTER

(ca. 1580-ca. 1638)

Ian Scott-Kilvert

LIFE

APART from the approximate date of publication of his works, we know very little about Webster's life. It is unlikely that he can have been born much later than 1580. He may have been the John Webster who was admitted to the Middle Temple on 1 August 1598. If so, this might account for the many legal allusions in his plays and for his skill in creating the courtroom scenes of *The White Devil, The Devil's Law-Case,* and *Appius and Virginia.* Alternatively he may have been an actor.

The first mention of his dramatic career is dated 1602, in which year an entry in Henslowe's diary refers to his collaboration with Middleton, Drayton, Munday, and others in the play *Caesar's Fall.* For the next six or seven years he worked for a variety of companies. Later in 1602 he collaborated with Dekker, Heywood, and Chettle on *Lady Jane*—an historical drama concerning the ill-fated Lady Jane Grey—and *Christmas Comes But Once A Year.* Two years later we find him working with Dekker on two comedies of city life, *Westward Ho* and *Northward Ho,* and in the same year he published the induction to Marston's *The Malcontent.* This was a comic curtain-raiser written in prose and full of topical jokes, somewhat in the manner of the induction to Shakespeare's *Taming of the Shrew.*

In 1607 he was again collaborating with Dekker, and published *Sir Thomas Wyatt,* possibly a revised version of *Lady Jane.* By this time he may already have begun work on *The White Devil,* which is believed to have taken him several years to write. The early months of 1612 are the most likely date for the first performance, which was given by the Queen's Men at the Red Bull, a surprisingly lowbrow playhouse for a piece of this kind. In his note to the first edition, Webster pays tribute (the first time that a poet had ever done so) to the play-

ing of an actor: this was Richard Perkins, then at the beginning of his career and later to become the most famous member of the company. "The worth of his action," writes Webster, "did crown both the beginning and the end," which makes it almost certain that he played the part of Flamineo.

The production of *The White Devil* evidently enhanced Webster's reputation, and at the end of 1612 he published "A Monumental Column," an elegy inspired by the death of the eighteen-year-old Prince Henry, James I's much admired eldest son. Both the dramatic technique and the versification of *The Duchess of Malfi* suggest that Webster's two great tragedies were written in close succession, and it is likely that *The Duchess* belongs to the year 1613. His next work was probably the lost historical play *The Guise,* and it is now generally agreed that in 1615 he contributed a new set of Characters to the highly successful volume of this title that had been posthumously published for Sir Thomas Overbury. The *Characters* is a collection of epigrammatic, often satirical prose portraits of contemporary types; it is modeled on the *Ethical Characters* of the Greek philosopher Theophrastus, a work that had been translated into Latin by Casaubon and enjoyed great popularity during this period.

Webster's last indisputably independent play, a tragicomedy of bourgeois life (again placed in an Italian setting) entitled *The Devil's Law-Case,* followed some two years later, and he is also the author of "Monuments of Honour," an elaborate occasional poem written on behalf of the Merchant Taylor's Company for the Lord Mayor's Pageant and published in 1624. After this his most notable work is the Roman tragedy *Appius and Virginia,* which some scholars have ascribed to the earliest phase of his career, while others judge it to have been written in partnership with Heywood in the late 1620's. Other plays in which Webster's collaboration is discernible are *Anything for a Quiet Life*, a comedy originally attributed to Middleton, which Lucas dates about 1621, *The Fair Maid of the Inn*, shared with Massinger and Ford, and *A Cure for a Cuckold* with Rowley, both these latter pieces probably belonging to the year 1625. Recently R. G. Howarth has claimed several new attributions for Webster, notably *A Speedy Post* (1624), *The Valiant Scot* (1637), and several more of the Overburian Characters.

Our picture of Webster's life remains conjectural in the extreme. The sequence of his published works suggests that he was not a particularly inventive playwright, but was influenced by current theatrical fashion. After writing his two great tragedies he seems to have experimented with a variety of topical themes, but never again found a subject that could rekindle his inspiration: certainly in his later plays of bourgeois life his interest seems to be engaged only in an intermittent and perfunctory fashion. The closing years of his life are again veiled in obscurity, but there is at least a strong presumption that the dramatist was the John Webster who died in 1637–1638, and was buried in the churchyard of St. James, Clerkenwell, which is also the resting place of his colleagues Dekker and Rowley.

TRAGEDY IN ENGLAND

TRAGEDY deals in absolutes. The typically tragic image is that of Thomas Hardy's poem "The Convergence of The Twain," which describes the collision of the *Titanic* with its fated iceberg. The typically tragic situation is the act of self-will pursued, whether in ignorance or knowledge, *à outrance*, the determination of the tragic hero, Oedipus or Faustus or Macbeth, to refuse compromise and to hold his course. Comedy accepts our weaknesses as ultimately controllable within a human norm: tragedy springs from the paradox that men's desires and ambitions vastly exceed their limitations. Tragedy's central theme is the meaning of suffering and the mystery of evil —"Is there any cause in nature that makes these hard hearts?" But it is not, as John Dennis, the Augustan critic, believed that it should be, "a very solemn lecture, inculcating a particular Providence, and showing it plainly protecting the good and chastising the bad."

It is not a sermon or a philosophical enquiry, but an art that strives to arouse a particular kind of emotion, and only certain kinds of situation will produce this effect—neither the downfall of an innocent hero nor of an out-and-out villain, for example. The true material of tragedy is the fate, in the Aristotelian phrase, of "the man in the middle," the hero who is allowed no unsullied choice, but is torn by conflicting impulses, and is forced to act, to suffer, to bear the load of guilt, and finally to attain self-knowledge. Thus tragedy makes its impact not as doctrine but as discovery, however unwelcome or unpleasant, by virtue of its truth to our experience and its uncompromising confrontation of the worst that life can do to man. But in order to arrive at this knowledge, it is necessary that the conflict between the forces of good and evil should be left free to play itself out, not be predetermined in the interests of divine or poetic justice.

So at least it seems to the modern reader, but this freedom of the imagination has not been acceptable to every age. Restoration audiences could not endure the ending of *King Lear*, and the death of Cordelia was banished from the English stage for a century and a half. But the drama is above all a communal art, a sharing of experience, and the tragic writer is concerned with the extremes of human potentiality. Among the Elizabethans and Jacobeans we find the desire to explore the heights and depths of men's conduct, to encompass the mysterious contradictions of human nature, more highly developed than in any other dramatic literature. The inspiration of the early Elizabethan drama sprang from the Renaissance mood of delight in the splendor of the mortal world, and its exhilaration at the sense of power derived from the newly won knowledge of the time. Marlowe's *Tamburlaine* echoes the Renaissance boast, "Men can do all things if they will," for the intellectual vitality of the age led directly from enquiry to action. But this impulse to rise above man's "middle state" soon turns to disillusion at the discovery of his limitations.

Such, in crude outline, was the spiritual crisis that brought English tragedy to its maturity; and the period in which its distinctive masterpieces were created was as short-lived as it was rich in achievement. It was preceded by a decade or more of such plays as *The Spanish Tragedy*, *The Jew of Malta*, and *Titus Andronicus*, pieces created to satisfy the robust appetites of a confident society; it was succeeded by a drama of detachment, exemplified in the tragicomedies and romances of Beaumont and Fletcher and their successors. The great era includes—apart from Shakespeare's four major tragedies—*Timon of Athens, Coriolanus,* and *Antony and Cleopatra;* Tourneur's *The Revenger's Tragedy* and *The Atheist's Tragedy;* Chapman's Bussy and Biron plays; and Webster's *The White Devil* and *The Duchess of Malfi.* It also embraces plays of such near-tragic outlook as *Troilus and Cressida, Measure for Measure, Volpone,* and *The Malcontent,* and it is concentrated within the first dozen years of the seventeenth century. Middleton's work belongs essentially to the same period, although he did not begin to write tragedy until late in his career. Shakespearean tragedy pursues a more profound, less nihilistic line of development, but in the work of his immediate juniors, such as Tourneur and Webster, we see the fulfillment of the process already foreshadowed in the later plays of Marlowe. The upward, aspiring, humanistic conception of man is replaced by a downward, realistic, satirical estimate, and the dominant tragic theme becomes the misdirection of humanity's most admired qualities: authority, courage, love, and intelligence in men; beauty, devotion, and civilization in women. *Troilus and Cressida* gives warning of the fearful consequences to mankind "when degree is shak'd," but what Shakespeare's successors call in question is the fitness of the human hierarchy itself. These writers, in C. Leech's phrase, know little of heaven, much of hell, and the kind of consolation that their tragedy offers might be summed up in a line from *The White Devil*: "Through darkness diamonds spread their richest light."[1]

THE PHILOSOPHY OF TRAGEDY

THE rebirth in Western Europe of the pagan literary form of tragedy was in itself an indication of a much wider historical process—the replacement of the theocratic values of the Middle Ages by a conception of life based partly upon the rediscovered ideals of the ancient world, partly upon man's growing sense of mastery over nature. In particular the revival of tragedy bore witness to the revolution that had taken place in men's beliefs concerning death, the afterlife, and the power of the individual to shape his own destiny. The attitude of the Greek tragedians had been paradoxical—at once rational and fatalistic. Solon's famous warning, "Call no man happy until he is dead," at least implied that if man refrained from excess and hubris, he had a chance of avoiding calamity. On the other hand, disaster, when it came, had to be accepted as the will of the gods, although, as with Oedipus or Hippolytus, the punishment might be out of all proportion to the offense.

The medieval view is conveniently summarized for us in Chaucer's *Prologue of The Monk's Tale*:

Tragedie is to seyn a certeyn storie,
As olde bokes maken us memorie,
Of hym that stood in greet prosperitee,
And is y-fallen out of hegh degree
Into myserie, and endeth wrecchedly.

In other words, man is merely the victim of the unpredictable movements of Fortune's wheel. But behind this simple definition lies the far more important Christian belief that death is a punishment for man's sin, that it represents not the end but the beginning of the true life, and hence that earthly triumphs and disasters are of no account, save as a preparation for the world to come. Thus a medieval drama such as *Everyman* is not a tragedy, because the hero, although sorely tried, knows that his salvation is assured provided that he makes himself the willing instrument of God's purposes, and hence the tribulations of this life are seen as no more than the first act of a "divine comedy," in the sense that Dante uses the term. But tragedy foreshortens, as it were, the perspective of the hereafter, and deliberately creates the impression of finality: every action seems eternal and irrevocable, and although we are conscious of the influence of higher powers, we believe that the hero is to a great extent responsible for his choice and so for its consequences.

As the new learning spread, so the assumptions of medieval Christianity were first challenged, then undermined. In statecraft, in commerce and the use of wealth, in science and the arts, in short in every sphere of human intercourse, the new education encouraged a civilized and active self-development that began to compete more and more insistently

---

[1] Act III, scene ii, line 292. Quotations from *The White Devil* and *The Duchess of Malfi* are taken from *Webster and Tourneur* (1959), in the Mermaid series. All other quotations from Webster are taken from F. L. Lucas, ed., *The Complete Works of John Webster*, 4 vols. (1927).

with the contemplative ideal. The doctrines of Machiavelli, transmitted to England in a distorted form, came to exercise a peculiar fascination upon the Elizabethans, and seemed to provide a technique for overcoming the vicissitudes of fortune and the hazards of the struggle for power. At the same time the Stoic philosophy, with its emphasis upon dying well, especially as it is presented in the plays of Seneca, offered yet another guide to conduct in misfortune. Very few Elizabethan dramatists could read Greek, and the inspiration that they drew from the great themes of the ancient drama—the jealousy of Medea, the pride of Oedipus, the revengeful cruelty of Atreus—reached them almost entirely through the medium of Seneca. Seneca draws upon much the same mythological material as the Greeks, but he gives it an altogether coarser, more crudely theatrical treatment. His taste for realistic descriptions of bloody actions and physical torture, combined with his sententious moralizing, appealed strongly to the Elizabethans, and his most popular plays were those in which he dramatizes a spectacular sequence of crime and revenge, such as the *Thyestes*, the *Agamemnon*, and the *Medea*. The consolation he offers is philosophical rather than religious. While the Greeks had believed that calamity might be avoidable through right action, Seneca regards it as inseparable from the human condition and seeks rather to find a way of triumphing over it. The new element that he introduces into tragedy is the defiant courage of the hero, which enables him to preserve his integrity and thus win a Pyrrhic victory over an unjust fate:

> Though in our miseries Fortune hath a part,
> Yet in our noble sufferings she hath none:
> Contempt of pain, that we may call our own.
> (*The Duchess of Malfi*, V. iii. 54–56)

It is worth noting that the influence of Seneca in England is closely connected with that of Machiavelli, for Senecan tragedy became known to the Elizabethans not only in Latin but through the plays of Seneca's Italian imitators. It was these dramatists, and especially Giraldi Cinthio (from whom Shakespeare borrowed the plot of *Othello*), who first created the character of the Machiavellian intriguer and who thus provided the link between the Senecan tyrant (Atreus or Lycus) and the Elizabethan Machiavellian villain.

All these conceptions played a vital part in the creation of the tragedy of the period. But perhaps its most exceptional characteristic is its almost obsessive preoccupation with death. Of course death is always likely to provide the climax of a tragedy, but to the Elizabethans and Jacobeans it was often the play's very raison d'être, the end of human achievement and the embodiment of the final and the terrible. They regarded a man's attitude toward death as a uniquely significant clue to his character, and they explored every means to dramatize the sight of death upon the stage. Death haunted the imagination of the Elizabethans to a degree that it is difficult for us to appreciate. The emblems and disguises of death, the memento mori encountered in the jewelry, the churches, the public signs, and many other everyday objects were familiar to every member of the audience. These associations enabled the playgoer to follow the poet without difficulty on the furthest flights of his imagination, from the simple images of the skull, the worm, and the taper to the "fell sergeant" of Shakespeare's *Hamlet*, or, strangest of all, the "lean, tawny-face tobacconist" of Dekker's *Old Fortunatus*.

THE JACOBEAN ERA

THE years of Webster's apprenticeship in the theater coincided with a period of intense disillusion in the national life. The decline of landed wealth and the pursuit of moneymaking in its place, the downfall of the brilliant but erratic earl of Essex, the death of Queen Elizabeth and the conspicuous absence of the magic of sovereignty in her successor, the disgrace and imprisonment of Ralegh, the series of conspiracies aimed at the throne and culminating in the Gunpowder Plot—these and many parallel events combined to produce a sense of the breakdown of established standards and beliefs, which was quickly reflected in the drama. Shakespeare and Chapman, survivors of the Elizabethan age, approach tragedy by way of the historical play, and we find them at all times keenly aware of the sanctity of kingship and the hierarchy of degree. Their protagonists are men and women of unquestioned authority, whose public life is brought to ruin by private weaknesses. The tragedy of Othello or of Antony lies not only in the hero's betrayal—real or imaginary—by his beloved, but also in the collapse of his soldiership.

But with the younger generation of tragedians, Marston, Webster, Tourneur, and Middleton, we feel at once the absence of this ideal order. These new playwrights were oppressed by an apparently irreconcilable conflict between the world of earthly experience and the world of the spirit:

> While we look up to heaven, we confound
> Knowledge with knowledge. O, I am in a mist!
> (*The White Devil*, V. vi. 256–257)

Humanity, they are compelled to recognize, is no better for its newfound knowledge, but rather more inhuman: indeed what marks out the tragedy of this period is the ingenuity and elaboration of the dramatists' conception of evil. The bond of nature is cracked, and the pragmatic creed of Machiavelli, with its assumption of the natural weakness and wickedness of men and its insistence upon *la verità effetuale della cosa*, has become the reality that forces itself upon the playwright's vision. Beyond this code of self-seeking, all is uncertainty, "a mist," as Webster repeatedly describes it; the divine powers are indifferent, and the heavens far off and unsearchable.

By comparison with the Elizabethan approach, the new dramatic poetry is noticeably more skeptical, more sophisticated, more aware of inner contradictions. The very title *The White Devil* contains a multiplicity of meanings, which begin with the Elizabethan proverb, "the white devil is worse than the black," and may be applied not only to Vittoria but to the hero, Bracchiano, and indeed to the society in which the play is set. The new poetry is also more condemnatory and satirical in tone, and in the case of Webster (although not of Marston and Tourneur, who caricature and distort to intensify the effect of their satire) it is more naturalistic in its handling of character and event. For Webster's audience *The White Devil* was a strikingly topical play: the actions that it depicts had taken place barely a quarter of a century before. And just as a subject that is remote in legend or history seems to emphasize the influence of fate upon the outcome, so the choice of a modern theme creates the opposite illusion: the more contemporary the characters, the greater their apparent freedom of action. Certainly by comparison with such plays as *Romeo and Juliet* or *Othello* the plots of Webster's

tragedies owe very little to chance: at first glance his characters strike us as willful to the last degree in courting their own downfall. Of course freedom and compulsion are necessarily the coordinates upon which all tragedy is plotted, and every dramatist of consequence discovers, as it were, a new equation for the act of choice, which is the starting point for a tragic situation. But a closer study suggests that Webster differs from most of his contemporaries in choosing *not* to make this issue explicit. When Bosola exclaims

> We are merely the stars' tennis-balls, struck and banded
> Which way please them.
> (*The Duchess of Malfi*, V. iv. 53–54)

we know that this is only a half-truth in the design of the tragedy, and in fact the continuous uncertainty as to whether fate or chance rules the world contributes powerfully to the horror that the play inspires in us.

What perhaps most astonishes the modern reader of Jacobean tragedy is the divergence between the avowed purpose of the dramatists and the actual effect of the drama, between the impression intended and the impression conveyed. Both the poets and the critics of the time were convinced that Renaissance tragedy was more improving than Greek. They found fault with the latter for its rebellious protest against divine providence, and praised the former for demonstrating, in Puttenham's phrase, "the just punishment of God in revenge of a vicious and evil life." Similarly the playwrights constantly defend the theater against the attacks of the Puritans by stressing its reformative value. Yet in *The White Devil* it is perfectly clear that Webster's sympathies are strongly drawn toward the guilty lovers, while in *The Duchess of Malfi* the sufferings inflicted upon the heroine are out of all proportion to her offense. It was this discrepancy between the precept and the practice of Elizabethan and Jacobean tragedy that prompted Rymer's indignant question—which he might as well have applied to Webster's tragedies as to *Othello*—"If this be our end, what boots it to be virtuous?" Webster's sympathy, not only in his tragedies but also in his later plays, consistently goes out to what he calls "integrity of life," that is, the determination to remain what you are, in the face of suffering, misfortune, and death: admiration for this quality can scarcely be reconciled with conventional notions of good and evil.

THE WHITE DEVIL

WEBSTER's contribution to the comedies written with Dekker is hardly distinguishable from his collaborator's. But in his first independent play, *The White Devil*, he suddenly emerges as a highly sophisticated writer who has succeeded in forging an original masterpiece out of the theatrical fashions of the moment. *The White Devil* brings together an astonishing number of these. It is in part a tragedy of revenge, with the customary accompaniments of ghosts, madness, treachery, and sudden violence: it is in part a tragedy of love, centered upon the brilliant figures of a Renaissance prince and a renowned adulteress. It is also an Italianate tragedy, complete with Machiavellian plotters, and new and horrifying methods of assassination. It has something of the pageantry of a chronicle play, with its papal election and its dramatic trial scene. Finally, it provides a satirical commentary upon courtly life by means of the fashionable creation of a malcontent observer, the total effect being seasoned with the type of formal moralizing, the "elegant and sententious excitation to virtue," which the serious writers and critics of the day regarded as indispensable to tragic writing.

It was a recognized convention of the period that tragedy should be based upon incidents taken from real life, the theory being that audiences would be more deeply impressed by a catastrophe based upon fact than by an invented plot. The events described by Webster in *The White Devil* were drawn from a recent cause célèbre in Italy. Vittoria Accorombona (Vittoria Corombona) was a strikingly beautiful girl who had been married at the age of sixteen to Francesco Peretti (Camillo), a nephew of Cardinal Montalto (Monticelso), who later became Pope Sixtus V. The duke of Bracchiano, Paolo Orsini, a member of one of the noblest Roman families and a soldier who had distinguished himself at Lepanto, met Vittoria in Rome in 1580, when she was twenty-three, and fell passionately in love with her. He was believed to have murdered his wife Isabella on the ground of her infidelity, and he now procured the murder of Vittoria's husband and soon afterward married her in secret. The suspected couple had been expressly forbidden to marry by Pope Gregory XIII; Peretti's murder was investigated, and Vittoria arrested. But she was soon released, and when Pope Gregory died in 1585, Bracchiano married her openly. On the same day Cardinal Montalto, the uncle and protector of Peretti, was elected pope and lost no time in excommunicating Bracchiano. Later in that year the duke fell sick and died, but not before making generous provision for Vittoria. The Orsini family was determined to deprive her of this legacy in the interests of the young heir (Giovanni), and when Vittoria resisted their efforts, she was brutally murdered in Padua by a band of assassins led by one of Bracchiano's kinsmen (the Lodovico of the play).

These events were recorded in innumerable chronicles of the time. The Swedish scholar Gunnar Boklund has traced over a hundred separate accounts—the most interesting, and one that shows many correspondences with minor incidents of the play, being a newsletter written in German for the famous banking house of Fugger. But whatever Webster's source, which has never been conclusively identified, he drastically reshaped both the details and the motivation of the original straggling narrative. Lodovico, who is credited with a secret passion for Bracchiano's murdered wife, is transformed from a minor character into the principal agent of retribution, whose consuming desire for revenge hangs over the play from beginning to end. The young Peretti is given the unsympathetic role of a middle-aged cuckold, Isabella becomes a virtuous wife, while Bracchiano, far from dying peacefully in his bed, is first poisoned by mercury smeared on the mouthpiece of his helmet and then strangled on his deathbed by assassins disguised as Capuchin friars, a horrifying scene that provides one of the climaxes of the action.

But by far the most important addition to the play is the character of Vittoria's brother. The roles of Flamineo in this play and of Bosola in *The Duchess of Malfi* are peculiarly Websterian creations and represent two of his most original contributions to Jacobean tragedy. Each is in one sense a topical character, a Renaissance "forgotten man," who is amply endowed with intelligence and courage, but lacks preferment. Each is in critical parlance "a tool villain," who, as in other Jacobean plays, bears a grudge against his master, but whose motives have been subtly humanized, and who thus brings a new dimension to the tragedy, because he is capable of the pangs of conscience:

I have lived
Riotously ill, like some that live in court,
And sometimes when my face was full of smiles,
Have felt the maze of conscience in my breast.
                    (*The White Devil*, V. iv. 115–118)

Each is also given the role of satirical observer: he exercises an important influence upon the action and the emotional tone of the play, but at the same time stands apart, mocking, criticizing, and uttering many of the dramatist's sharpest comments upon the other characters and the human condition in general.

The drama of that age commonly achieves its most powerful effects by violent contrasts, the contrast between Hamlet and the gravediggers, Cleopatra and the clown, murders that take place on wedding nights. The first impression left by *The White Devil* is that Webster is aiming at a similar kind of contrast between outward magnificence and inward corruption. His purpose, as implied in the play's title, is apparently to juxtapose the splendor and the horror of a Renaissance court, and to exploit the paradox, so potent in the minds of his audience, that the loveliest and most civilized country in the world was also, as a contemporary describes it, "the Academie of manslaughter, the sporting-place of murther, the Apothecary's shop of poyson for all Nations," where a man such as Lodovico could pride himself upon a murder as a work of art. *The White Devil* is a tragedy of worldliness, of the desires of the flesh embraced with the courage of utter abandon. Abandon is the keynote of Bracchiano's first speech, "Quite lost, Flamineo!," and it is clear from the outset that here there will be no struggles of conscience, no question of a noble character weakened or overthrown by misfortune. The protagonists of this play are bent on earthly pleasures and rewards, and they show themselves to be shameless and often heartless: they may appeal to our reluctant admiration, but not to our pity. Perhaps the sharpest irony of the play is found in its message that man, even at his most calculating and self-willed, cannot be master of his fate. Bracchiano, the soldier-prince of the cinquecento, still represents in our eyes something of the magnificence and assurance of his age, but the poisoned helmet that reduces this former hero of Lepanto to delirium and an unsanctified death may be seen as an apt symbol for the spiritual corruption that had infected the Renaissance ideal of greatness.

As soon as the play is studied more closely, the contradictions and ambiguities of its values begin to appear. In the opening scenes we find Lodovico, a man of blood already guilty of several murders in Rome, swearing vengeance before any crime has been committed. Francisco, the brother of the murdered Isabella, pursues his revenge with such Machiavellian lack of scruple that he taints the justice of his cause, and at the end of the play is condemned by his nephew Giovanni, whose rights he is supposed to be vindicating. On the other hand, when Isabella and Camillo are murdered, Webster, by representing their deaths in dumbshow, contrives to distance the crime and diminish its horror, and thus to avoid alienating our sympathy for Bracchiano and Vittoria. In the trial scene we are shown for the first time the full measure of Vittoria's courage, when alone and abandoned by her lover, she not only faces but dominates a completely hostile court. At the same time we know that this is the courage of impenitence and bravado, not of a clear conscience, for there is little doubt that even if she has not actually procured her husband's murder, she is at least an accessory after the fact. Yet when she shows herself equally undaunted by the lawyer's pedantry and the cardinal's animosity, admiration for her courage proves stronger than evidence, so that the audience can almost accept her denials:

For your names
Of whore and murderess, they proceed from you
As if a man should spit against the wind
The filth returns in's face . . .
                    (*The White Devil*, III. ii. 146–149)

or the outrageous profession of innocence with which she greets her sentence of imprisonment in a house of correction:

It shall not be a house of convertites.
My mind shall make it happier to me
Than the Pope's palace, and more peaceable
Than thy soul, though thou art a cardinal.
                    (*The White Devil*, III. ii. 287–290)

In this play Webster takes up a position that is quite different from that of Kyd or of Shakespeare in their revenge tragedies, where the duel between the avenger and his antagonist can be identified as a struggle between good and evil; and there is in fact a fundamental difference in his conception of tragedy. In *Hamlet* the avenger is not only technically the hero, but in a very real sense the moral center of the play. In *The White Devil* there is no moral center, and no set of values is held up as the right one. Yet the play, its author might well argue, possesses a strongly moral theme, which is stated in the opening lines, the theme of "courtly reward and punishment." Where Webster differs from Shakespeare is in pursuing his moral purpose by condemnation and exposure, by focusing attention not upon the hero but upon the social setting, the corruption of which is held up as a warning; in short, by teaching man "wherein he is imperfect." The play is much concerned with the situation of prince and courtier and the vicious nature of their relationship. On the prince's side, power leads to ruinous extravagance, the guilty recollection of which haunts Bracchiano on his deathbed, and to tyrannous injustice: he refuses to reward Flamineo's faithful service but heaps privileges upon Mulinassar, who is in reality his deadly enemy, the duke of Florence, in disguise. On the courtier's side, the system encourages unscrupulous flattery and disloyalty at the first opportunity: Bracchiano is mocked and ignored the moment that he is dead.

In spite of the powerful impetus of the action, this satirical approach produces a discordant and at times disjointed impression both in the construction and the characterization, with the result that individual scenes are intensely vivid but the total effect is confused. In its general design the plot lacks the unifying power of a single dominant motive: it moves forward in a succession of loosely connected episodes and with the help of casually introduced supernumeraries such as the doctor, the conjuror, the lawyer, and the ambassadors. The poetry displays abrupt changes of feeling and a perpetual conflict of moods, so that the most eloquent and passionate protestations may be called into question or rendered ambiguous by some ironical comment, which makes us doubt the motives of the speaker.

This ambiguity applies principally to the character of Vittoria. Here, as the play's title suggests, Webster has aimed at creating an image of fatal fascination, a character who combines treachery and loyalty, cowardice and courage, infidelity and devotion to a degree that baffles judgment. But equally the minor characters are not

what they at first appear: we find on closer scrutiny that Isabella is by no means totally unselfish and that even Cornelia and the upright Marcello are quite ready to accept Bracchiano's patronage. Above all, this ambivalence makes itself felt in the relationship between Bracchiano and Vittoria. The duke's "Quite lost, Flamineo!" leaves us in no doubt as to the depth of his infatuation, but this declaration is immediately followed by Flamineo's sneers, which cheapen not only Bracchiano's passion in itself but Vittoria as the object of it. Later in the play the effect of the otherwise moving quarrel and reconciliation scene in the house of convertites is offset by our knowledge that the lovers have themselves been outwitted by Francisco. And in Bracchiano's death scene, the audience's sympathy for Vittoria, at first aroused by the tenderness of the duke's

> Where's this good woman? Had I infinite worlds
> They were too little for thee: must I leave thee?
> (*The White Devil*, V. iii. 18–19)

is later dispelled by his delirious ravings, which repeatedly hint at her wantonness and falsehood, and from this point onward Webster offers no hint that theirs is a union that can transcend death. When Vittoria faces her own end, the quality that emerges supreme is her defiant courage, not her tenderness. The love that she and Bracchiano have shared is destructive in its essence, and in the superb simile with which she confronts her fate,

> My soul, like to a ship in a black storm,
> Is driven I know not whither,
> (*The White Devil*, V. vi. 245–246)

it may not be fanciful to detect a parallel to Dante's image of the lovers in the second circle of the Inferno, who have abandoned salvation for passion and who, yielding to the strength of their desires, are forever "blown with restless violence about the pendent world." Paradoxically *The White Devil* offers us the most brilliant and spirited picture of "the busy trade of life" that Webster ever created. Compared with its successor it gives off a vitality, a confidence, and a dramatic impetus that he could never afterward sustain through a whole play. But it remains a tragedy of despair.

THE DUCHESS OF MALFI

The Duchess of Malfi was first performed not later than the end of 1614. It clearly belongs to the same creative phase of *The White Devil*, for Webster's powers, unlike Shakespeare's, did not pass through a prolonged and many-sided development: his art rose swiftly to its zenith and swiftly declined. In *The Duchess of Malfi* there are many striking parallels with its predecessor, but the contrast in tone and in tempo is unmistakable. These resemblances, it may be, are the product of Webster's peculiar and laborious methods of composition, which often led him to refashion or to transpose situations that he had already handled. Thus he once more takes for his theme a woman's passion pursued in defiance of the social code, the unwritten law of "degree." On this occasion the heroine marries beneath her station rather than above it, but the result is the same: she suffers the persecution of powerful enemies, namely her brothers (again a cardinal and a duke), who act as the supposed champions of moral orthodoxy and family interest. Once more the author dwells upon the corruption of high place, and once more he gives a major role to a satirical malcontent, a down-at-the-heel scholar and soldier, who is forced by poverty to make himself the creature of an unscrupulous patron.

But from the outset the mood of the play is more chastened and melancholy, the texture of the poetry more delicate, less rhetorical, the tempo of events less strenuous, more world-weary. *The White Devil* delivers a crushing indictment of courtly society, but at the same time it depicts a world of exuberant animation and self-assertion. Although its characters fail in their worldly ambitions, they still desire passionately to live. By contrast, the cardinal as he dies asks to be laid by and never thought of, and Antonio reckons life but the good hours of an ague. A malevolent stillness and secrecy brood over the action and behind it lurk the terrors of madness, witchcraft, and the supernatural. The play seems to be set in a somber half-world, poised between death and life, and this oppressive atmosphere is intensified by the nightmarish rhythm of the duchess' persecution, which seems to be now suspended, now pursued with demoniac cruelty. The duchess' torment of being continually watched and prevented from sleeping was a recognized method of dealing with witches. Ferdinand, when he vows

never to set eyes on her more, is in effect calling down a curse upon his sister. The duchess in the agony of her imprisonment solemnly curses her brothers, and elsewhere we learn of the hereditary curse that dooms the House of Aragon. By comparison with the earlier tragedy, in which man is seen as a sinning but potentially magnificent creature, his stature has terrifyingly shrunk: "deformity" is a key word in Webster's vocabulary for this play.

The plot is again based on historical events, but it reached Webster in fictional form through one of Bandello's novels adapted into French by Belleforest: this version was in turn translated into English by William Painter and included in his *Palace of Pleasure*, published in 1566, which was Webster's direct source. Painter treats his subject as a cautionary tale, the story of a woman of royal birth who, after being widowed early in her youth, "was moved with that desire that pricketh others that be of flesh and blood," and contracted a secret marriage to her steward, a commoner. In doing this she chose to ignore the wishes of her family, and so, the novelist concludes, her fate was not undeserved. Webster, however, found in this tale of suffering a further development of his conception of tragedy. Previously he had shown his admiration for the courage that was the saving grace of characters who were otherwise unscrupulous or morally insensitive. Here the ordeal he imposes on his heroine is not confined to violence and death: it is a remorseless attempt to annihilate her soul, and the courage of the duchess is the more spiritually profound because she is capable of self-judgment. None of the characters of *The White Devil* had possessed sufficient self-judgment to be capable of altering the course of his life. Webster's moral scheme demanded that the duchess' murder should be avenged, and he proves the keenness of his moral sense by his control of Bosola's gradual awakening to the iniquity of his service. Bosola's dying words,

> Let worthy minds ne'er stagger in distrust
> To suffer death or shame for what is just:
> Mine is another voyage,
> *(The Duchess of Malfi*, V. v. 102–103)

contain the agonized discovery that *he* has suffered death and shame to no purpose. But dramatically speaking, the pursuit of the duchess' murderers introduces a shift of interest that is fatal to the tension of the play, and after the greatness of the fourth act the closing scenes are inevitably felt as an anticlimax.

A great deal of critical comment has been devoted to the motives of the cardinal and of Ferdinand in persecuting their sister, and again to the question of how far Webster considered the duchess' conduct as blameworthy. The cardinal is, no doubt, concerned in his aloof and haughty fashion with the question of family honor, and the news of the duchess' feigned pilgrimage to Loreto can rouse him to anger. But he never speaks to her save in Ferdinand's company, and his behavior is so much that of the self-sufficient Machiavellian that it is difficult at times to remember that he is her brother at all. With Ferdinand the case is very different. It is he who takes the initiative and invents every refinement of cruelty in the torture of his sister. It is he who obscenely threatens her in the first scene, and who is thrown into a frenzy of rage at every mention of the pleasures of her marriage. Certainly Webster hints at an intense physical awareness of his sister, which some critics have gone so far as to interpret as an incestuous passion. But while Webster repeatedly stresses the pain and the fury that lie behind Ferdinand's outbursts, he consistently declines to interpret them, and it is at least arguable that the peculiar effect of terror and suffering that he sought to convey demanded that this issue should remain a mystery: in fact the duchess' ordeal becomes the more horrifying because of the very lack of an explicit motive on the part of her tormentors.

As for the duchess, a modern audience naturally tends to see her as the innocent victim of her brothers' jealousy, suspicion, and greed. The fact remains, however, that in choosing to disregard their warnings and marry beneath her she compromises her integrity and finds herself involved with Antonio in a web of deceit and subterfuge from which she is delivered only by her imprisonment. According to the public opinion of the time, she had not only flouted the secular and religious concept of degree but had added to her offense by concealing it. Besides this, there was a strong current of disapproval against the remarriage of widows; Webster in his "Character of a Virtuous Widow" indicates the strength of this sentiment:

For her children's sake she first marries, for she married that she might have children, and for their sakes she marries no more. She is like the purest gold, only employed for Princes' medals, she never receives but one man's impression . . . .

The Swedish scholar Inga Stina Ekblad has put forward the theory, supported by a close analysis of the text, that the consort of madmen introduced by Ferdinand as a final torment for his sister was intended as a masque in mockery of her marriage to Antonio, and that its form is derived from the charivari or "marriage-baiting," a ceremony of French origin, which dates from the late Middle Ages and was performed as a gesture of public disapproval of a reprehensible or unequal marriage. This interpretation certainly lends a deeper and more intelligible purpose to an episode that has often been criticized as a crude attempt to intensify the horror of the duchess' "mortification by degrees." According to the same theory, Bosola's famous dirge:

> Hark, now everything is still
> The screech-owl and the whistler shrill
> Call upon our dame aloud
> And bid her quickly don her shroud . . .
>
> Strew your hair with powders sweet:
> Don your clean linen, bathe your feet,
> And (the foul fiend more to check)
> A crucifix let bless your neck:
> 'Tis now full tide, 'tween night, and day
> End your groan, and come away,
> (*The Duchess of Malfi*, IV. ii. 175–178; 187–192)

represents both in its context and its imagery a mock epithalamion, performed to bring the duchess not to her wedding chamber but to her death.

Nevertheless, in this play there is far less moral ambiguity than we find in *The White Devil*. In the character of the duchess, Webster creates for the first time a tragic figure who in the process of suffering develops in stature. At the beginning of the play we are made aware of her youthful beauty, her grace, her impulsiveness, her craving for love, and her isolation, while the scene in which she woos and marries Antonio strikes a note of tenderness and devotion that is entirely new in Webster's work. Throughout her relationship with Antonio it is the duchess' courage that keeps the initiative, and when her secret is discovered, it is she who faces her brother's dagger and contrives Antonio's pretended disgrace. The turning point in her development is reached with her separation from Antonio, when she declares that "nought made me e'er/Go right but Heaven's scourge-stick . . ." and this scene leads directly to the fourth act, which may claim to be regarded as one of the supreme achievements of Jacobean drama.

Here the play suddenly opens into a wider universe that transcends common experience: the action moves on the psychological plane to the frontiers of madness, and on the spiritual to a limbo of suffering in which the duchess undergoes her purgatory. As in the storm scenes of *Lear*, time and place seem to be suspended, and in these few pages it is as if the duchess passes through a lifetime. The conflict within her nature between "the spirit of greatness" and "the spirit of woman," which has persisted throughout the play, is now brought to its climax. When she is deprived of all that she cherishes most—her husband, her children, her position, her very identity—she loses all desire to live, her mind totters, and it is Bosola's deliberate alternation of mockery and compassion that helps her to cling to sanity and to see her situation without illusion. She has passed beyond the state of defiant self-assertion, which had earlier wrung from her the Senecan outcry "I am Duchess of Malfi still,"[2] and in her last words to the executioners who are to strangle her, she has put behind her not only despair but pride:

> Pull, and pull strongly, for your able strength
> Must pull down Heaven upon me:
> Yet stay; Heaven-gates are not so highly arched
> As princes' palaces; they that enter there
> Must go upon their knees.
> (*The Duchess of Malfi*, IV. ii. 226–230)

This declaration of humility stands out in contrast to the self-conscious resolve shown by Webster's other heroes and heroines in the face of death, and it is unique in Webster's writing: it suggests that in the creation of the duchess he lays hold for once of a spiritual assurance and exaltation that elsewhere escape him.

FORMS OF TRAGEDY

In the history of literature, tragedy is generally regarded as an exceptionally stable form, which has

somehow preserved throughout the centuries a recognizable resemblance to its Greek originals. But these resemblances are deceptive. Greek drama is essentially religious. Its primary concern is not to study the personality of the hero but to interpret the regulation of human affairs by the actions of the gods: its plots are drawn from a single body of mythology and its form is rigidly stylized. Elizabethan tragedy is essentially secular. The playwrights abandoned the scriptural or allegorical material that had supplied the themes of the medieval drama, and turned their attention instead to English and Roman histories or French and Italian novellas. The mysteries that they explore are those "Of fate and chance and change in human life," and this change of direction has never been reversed. But if Elizabethan and modern tragedies share some resemblances in theme, they share very few in form or technique, and the reader will be led far astray if he expects the Elizabethan play to conform to the dramatic methods of Ibsen and his successors, themselves strongly influenced by the techniques of modern fiction.

The vital point to be grasped here—admirably developed by M. C. Bradbrook in her *Themes and Conventions of Elizabethan Tragedy*—is that the Elizabethan playwright did not set out to devise a plot in the form of a logical or internally consistent narrative. The essential ingredients for his drama were striking episodes and memorable language. He could not, as his modern counterpart can, conceal his lack of poetic inspiration by attention to the details of construction. Yeats's criticism of the speech of modern dramatic characters is well-known: "When they are deeply moved, they look silently into the fire-place," and he was referring to the modern playwright's assumption that he can achieve his emotional effect through the placing and sequence of events, rather than through the eloquence of his dialogue. To Elizabethan audiences eloquence was the very breath of drama, and they were interested above all in how a character spoke and acted in a moment of crisis, rather than in how he arrived there. In this respect an Elizabethan tragedy is more like the score of an opera than the text of a novel. The elements of place and time, for example, are treated as freely and flexibly as possible. If they lend themselves to dramatic exploitation, well and good, but they possess few rights of their own. Much of the sustained effect of terror and anguish that is built up in the fourth act of *The*

---

[2]An echo of a famous phrase from Seneca's *Medea*: "Medea superest."

Duchess of Malfi depends on the vagueness of the location and the suspension of time during the duchess' imprisonment.

This is not to say that the Elizabethans were incapable of the kind of mechanical dexterity that was so much admired by William Archer. Shakespeare achieved something of this cogwheel effect in *Othello*, as did Jonson in *Volpone*, while Beaumont and Fletcher were still more adroit in the plotting of their material. But most of the playwrights of the period were not thinking along the lines of the Aristotelian whole, and it would be difficult to select any play as a typical specimen of Elizabethan or Jacobean dramatic structure. Since the source material varied so widely, and since plays tended to be conceived as a series of striking situations, every major playwright developed a dramatic form of his own, the mold of which was shaped by the nature of his poetic gifts. At its best, the imaginative pressure and concentration of the language of Jacobean tragedy sweep away the problems of dramatic illusion. The poets created a speech that could be simple or ceremonious by turns, and was at once direct in its elementary sense and rich in secondary meanings. In *The White Devil*, for example, Webster achieves one of the most powerful openings in the whole range of Jacobean drama. Lodovico's cry of "Banish'd!" not only sums up the initial situation of the play and casts the shadow of the revenger over all that follows, but in a deeper sense it suggests the self-excommunication of this blood-crazed figure from the normal instincts of humanity. It is at once followed by other metaphors central to the play's meaning, such as those that hint at Vittoria's career—"Fortune's a right whore" and "an idle meteor soon lost i'th'air." The best of Webster's poetry, like that of Shakespeare, Tourneur, and Middleton, preeminently possesses this power of prophesying the action by means of dramatic images that leap from the particular to the general and reveal the moral universe that surrounds the characters and the setting.

WEBSTER'S DRAMATIC IDIOM

WEBSTER was one of those rare dramatists who in his first independent play achieved at a single bound the height of his poetic powers. *The White Devil* offers us Jacobean verse in its full maturity: here Webster is exploiting after his own fashion many of the developments in style and versification that Shakespeare had first introduced into his great tragedies. The end-stopped blank-verse pentameter has been completely remolded, passages of any length are frequently enjambed, the rhythms of colloquial speech are counterpointed against the regular beat of the line, and the style and tone of the dialogue clearly reflect the demand for a greater naturalism in expression and performance. Like the best of his rivals in the theater, Webster quickly established a dramatic idiom that is unmistakably his own. Unlike his fellow satirists Marston and Tourneur, he shows himself sympathetic even to the most villainous of his characters and keenly aware of their individual and unpredictable qualities, and he shares something of Shakespeare's gift for coining images that can project a character within a single line of verse or prose.

The tone of his verse is at once witty, sardonic, allusive, full of nervous energy. His handling of meter is often as harsh and irregular as Donne's, and his frequent habit of introducing resolved feet reflects the complexity of deliberate outlandishness of his figures of speech:

> Mark her, I prithee: she simpers like the suds
> A collier hath been washed in . . .
> (*The White Devil*, V. iii. 238–239)

Elsewhere, when he aims at a sententious effect, he produces a rallentando through a sequence of heavily stressed monosyllables:

> This busy trade of life appears most vain
> Since rest breeds rest, where all seek pain by pain.
> (*The White Devil*, V. vi. 270–271)

If he lacks the architectonic sense, he comes nearest of all his contemporaries to Shakespeare in his power to produce striking yet subtle variations of mood, of strength, and of pace within a scene. Some of his finest effects are achieved by sudden transformations of this kind, as in *The White Devil* with the entry of the boy Giovanni in mourning for his mother immediately after the passion and tumult of the court scene, or with Ferdinand's eavesdropping upon the careless jesting of the lovers in *The Duchess of Malfi*. While other dramatists employ song to great effect, Webster, without invoking the aid of music in *The White Devil* and *The Duchess of Malfi*, uses the dramatic lyric in a completely original fashion to introduce a different emotional dimension. Of Cornelia's lines:

> Call for the Robin-red-breast and the wren,
> Since o'er shady groves they hover,
> And with leaves and flowers do cover
> The friendless bodies of unburied men
> (The White Devil, V. iv. 91–94)

Lamb wrote:

I never saw anything like this dirge, except the ditty which reminds Ferdinand of his drowned father in *The Tempest*. As that is of the water, watery, so this is of the earth, earthy. Both have that intenseness of feeling which seems to resolve itself into the elements which it contemplates.

These achievements represent the peaks of Webster's art. On the other hand he is curiously unenterprising in his use of the soliloquy, which he normally employs merely to give notice of his characters' intentions rather than to explore their inmost qualities. And besides his didactic habit of rounding off an episode with a conventional platitude, he is apt to interrupt the progress of a scene with a tedious moral fable, thus destroying much of the tension that he has carefully built up.

This habit brings us to his borrowings from other authors. Commentators long ago remarked that his plays, especially *The White Devil* and *The Duchess of Malfi*, contain many sentiments, images, and even whole sentences that have been lifted from contemporary writers, in particular from Montaigne, Sidney, and the Scottish dramatist William Alexander. Of course originality was less highly prized in Webster's age than it is today. Quotation or adaptation from classical or foreign authors was regarded as a mark of erudition, and plagiarism was even to some extent encouraged by the educational system of the time, which required students to keep a commonplace book. Lucas defends Webster's imitation and contends that he almost always transmuted what he borrowed into something different and better. This is often the case, but it does not tell us the whole story. Certainly Webster excels in the final stroke, the expansion of some hitherto unremarked detail, which transforms a second-hand perception into a touch of perfect aptness. He was not the kind of author who plagiarized in order to save himself mental effort. On the contrary he was an exceptionally laborious artist who took

great pains to weave his borrowings into the texture and atmosphere of his plays. Nevertheless his borrowings so far exceeded the normal that they came to affect his methods of composition. If we analyze the sequence of his dialogue in passages where the borrowing can be traced, it becomes clear that his imagination was often prompted by what he had read rather than by his own invention. This habit of working from a commonplace book explains the peculiarly conceit-laden and disjointed style that Webster employs in a passage such as the following, which contains images drawn from three different authors:

Thou shalt lie in a bed stuffed with turtle-feathers, swoon in perfum'd linen like the fellow was smothered in roses. So perfect shall be thy happiness that as men at sea think land and trees and ships go that way they go, so both heaven and earth shall seem to go thy voyage. Shalt meet him, 'tis fixed with nails of diamonds to inevitable necessity.

In the same way his longer verse passages do not flow as Shakespeare's do with an opulent succession of metaphors, in which each image springs naturally from its predecessor. Instead they often consist of a series of undeveloped metaphors or similes so loosely strung together that any one might be removed without damage to the rest, and the borrowing habit also seems to be responsible for the abrupt transitions of thought and feeling that so often occur in his verse. But when all this has been said, the fact that Webster's finest flights are often launched with the help of a borrowed idea does not diminish their effect. The study of his sources is valuable not in a derogatory sense, but because the identification of the original often helps to penetrate a meaning, clarify a dramatic effect, or define the qualities of a character that the commentators have missed.

Webster's use of figures of speech is closely related to his conception of tragedy, and his imagery throws much light upon the inner meaning of his plays. Both *The White Devil* and *The Duchess of Malfi*, for example, are pervaded by images of the fair show that masks inward corruption or poison, and the calm weather that hides an impending storm, and each of these sequences of metaphor is skillfully woven into the play so as to suggest the deceitfulness of fortune. The Elizabethan delight in the familiar objects and traditional beauties of the created world lies far behind him, and in his choice of metaphor and simile he deliberately singles out the curious, the grotesque, and the sinister. His universe is a place of fear—it is noticeable that he is one of the few Elizabethans who does not celebrate the sublime and healing qualities of music. The birds that figure in his poetry are visualized in captivity or awaiting death. In nature it is the deformed and the deadly that fascinate him—witness his reference to hemlock, mildew, poison, snakes, and the mysterious properties of the mandrake. Often his visual symbols suggest a fearful immediacy, an icy touch, a suffocating embrace, a physical contact with the horrible. He strives to express and reconcile incongruity, above all that of the mortality of the graveyard and the sensuality of the living body. The symbolic act to which his imagination continually returns is that of tearing away the mask and uncovering the dreadful shape in the effort to resist the horror of death.

His poetry and prose follow two distinct styles of expression. The first is sophisticated, intellectually agile, staccato and restless in rhythm. In the second we find his imagination working at white heat, for he is a poet of brief and blinding insight rather than of steady illumination. This is the style that is reserved for the climaxes of his plays and that pervades his most highly wrought passages:

> Your beauty! O, ten thousand curses on't
> How long have I beheld the devil in crystal!
> Thou hast led me, like an heathen sacrifice,
> With music and with fatal yokes of flowers
> To my eternal ruin. Woman to man
> Is either a god or a wolf.
> (*The White Devil*, IV. i. 84–89)

> I am not mad yet, to my cause of sorrow:
> The Heaven o'er my head seems made of molten brass,
> The earth of flaming sulphur, yet I am not mad.
> I am acquainted with sad misery
> As the tanned galley-slave is with his oar;
> Necessity makes me suffer constantly
> And custom makes it easy.
> (*The Duchess of Malfi*, IV. ii. 25–31)

At these moments Webster's language is unadorned. His vocabulary becomes predominantly Anglo-Saxon, enriched by the rare Latin word, his rhythm steady, his tone prophetic: his words seem to wield an absolute power, with which they suddenly gather together the thought and emotions of the whole play, state the tragic issue, and create the moment of vision.

THE CHARACTERS

WEBSTER's contribution to the Overbury collection of *Characters* is of interest because the character as a literary genre noticeably influenced the dramatic writing of the time. Theories of psychological classification such as the doctrine of the humors were in the air, and Theophrastus' treatise aroused an interest in a similar analysis of manners and sociology. Bishop Hall was the pioneer of the form and in his *Characterismes of Vertues and Vice* he handles the subject in broader and more concrete terms than his Greek model. Thus, while Theophrastus remarks that "The Flatterer is a person who will say as he walks with another. 'Do you observe how people are looking at you?,'" Hall individualizes his portrait as follows: "The Flatterer is blear-eyed to ill and cannot see vices . . . . Like that subtle fish, he turns himself into the colour of every stone. . . . He is the moth of liberal men's coates, the earewig of the mightie, the bane of courts, a friend and slave to the trencher, and good for nothing but to be factor for the Divell."

Webster develops his character writing along similar lines. Clearly the form was congenial to him: it demanded a mannered, compressed, carefully cadenced prose, gave scope for ingenious and extravagant imagery, and lent itself equally to satirical commentary and moral exhortation. It is noticeable that in his two major tragedies, Webster puts almost all this type of prose into the mouths of his two satirical commentators, Flamineo and Bosola. Among the Overbury *Characters* connoisseurs of Webster's powers of invective will appreciate his sketch of "A Jesuit," and of "A Rimer" ("A Dung-Hille not well laid together"), but in general he succeeds better in praise than in blame. The best pieces written in his happier vein are the characters of "An Excellent Actor," "A Franklin," and—a surprising contribution for Webster—"A Fayre and Happy Milke-Mayd." This last may be seen as the complete antithesis of his tragic heroines, and in fact Bosola, when he finally urges the duchess to lay aside her youth, her beauty, and her desire to live, tells her (IV. iii):

Thou art some great woman sure; for riot begins to sit on thy forehead (clad in grey hairs) twenty years sooner than on a merry milkmaid's.

WEBSTER's work is often criticized as episodic and lacking in architectonic power. Certainly the plots of *The White Devil* and *The Duchess of Malfi* are overloaded with detail, and there are moments when the playwright willfully abandons dramatic truth for the sake of an immediately striking effect. Nevertheless each of these tragedies embodies a dramatic idea that is sufficiently powerful to hold it together. It is impossible to say the same of his later plays. At least five years separate *The Duchess of Malfi* from Webster's next play, and in that interval the changing mood of the theater has been at work. Both Jacobean tragedy and comedy at their best had been bent on the pursuit of reality. The characteristics of the "new wave" of tragicomedy, of which the most skillful practitioners were Beaumont and Fletcher, had been sketched as early as 1609 in the latter's preface to *The Faithful Shepherdess*:

> A tragie-comedie is not so called in respect of mirth and killing, but in respect it wants deaths, which is inough to make it no tragedie, yet brings some near it, which is inough to make it no comedie.

This was a formula with insidious possibilities. Shakespeare, it is true, turned it to sublime use in his final romances. There he contrived to raise the action to a higher plane, on which at the end of each play the confused purposes of sinful humanity are transcended by a divine forgiveness. But in other hands the new mode suggests little more than a weary longing to lay aside the ultimate questions and seek relief from the painful integrity of great art, whether tragic or comic. Suspense or surprise in an exotic setting, sudden reversals of situation or transformations of sentiment—in short, entertainment of an agreeably romantic kind—now become the dramatist's principal aim, and to achieve the unforeseen he must be prepared to distort character, confuse motive, and ignore the normal consequences of human actions. These tendencies become increasingly apparent in Webster's later plays, the more regrettably so, because his genius was obviously so unsuited to satisfy the new taste. John Fletcher, the originator of the tragicomic mode, was a sufficiently ingenious and versatile playwright to make this irresponsible treatment of the drama plausible. When Webster attempts such effects the result seems as unnatural as it is clumsy: in fact, as one might expect, the scenes that redeem his post-tragic plays are those in which his instinct prompts him to work against the prevailing fashion.

This division of purpose is most apparent in his last independent play, *The Devil's Law-Case*. Here he abandons courtly for bourgeois life and makes no attempt to draw a coherent moral. Nevertheless, a number of recognizable characteristics survive from his earlier work. Once again it is a woman's passion that dominates the plot and asserts an even more astonishing defiance of conventional standards. The play opens with Leonora, a sixty-year-old widow, cynically arranging with her son, Romelio, a marriage of convenience for her daughter, Jolenta. Mother and son are well aware that Jolenta is in love with another aristocratic wooer, Contarino, but have no compunction in allowing a duel to take place between the suitors. But when Romelio tries to make certain of the wounded Contarino's death by disguising himself as a Jewish physician and stabbing his supposed patient, it transpires that Leonora has fallen in love with Contarino, and in revenge hires an unscrupulous lawyer to prove her own son illegitimate and thus disinherit him. The climax is reached in the trial scene—Webster excels throughout his career in the drama of the courtroom—in which the corrupt eloquence of the prosecuting lawyer is matched by the resource of Romelio and the perspicacity of the upright advocate Crispiano. Leonora's case collapses, but this does not prevent a grotesque denouement whereby she is matched "happily ever after" with the young Contarino, Jolenta with her prescribed husband Ercole, and Romelio with a nun whom he had seduced years before.

The figure who dominates the play and links it with the world of the tragedies is the Neapolitan merchant Romelio. This character represents yet another of Webster's Machiavellian studies, shrewder and more experienced than Flamineo, as quick-witted and resolute as the cardinal. When Romelio disguises himself as a Jewish physician, Webster is clearly evoking the memory of Marlowe's Barabas, the Jew of Malta, and appears to be depicting Romelio as a thorough-paced villain. But later, when he is visited in prison by a Capuchin friar to prepare him for death—an episode strongly reminiscent of the death cell scene in *Measure for Measure*—the humor and steadiness of temper that underlie Romelio's courage make a powerful appeal to our sympathy:

> *Friar:* Pray tell me, do you not meditate of death?
> *Rom:* Phew, I tooke out that lesson
> When once I lay sicke of an Ague: I do now
> Labour for life, for life! Sir, can you tell me
> Whether your Toledo or your Millain blade
> Be best temper'd?
>
> (*The Devil's Law-Case*, V. iv. 60–65)

Romelio is by far the most vital of Webster's tragicomic creations and it is certainly the role into which he poured the best of his later dramatic poetry.

Anything for a Quiet Life, a comedy written mainly in prose in collaboration with Middleton, is the least interesting play of any in which Webster took a hand. It makes fun of the marriage of an elderly knight to a young, capricious, and self-willed girl. Lady Cressingham bullies her husband into parting with his estate, disinheriting his eldest son, and sending away his younger children; but at the end of the play she is suddenly presented in a completely different light as a sensible wife, who has rid her husband of his ruinous obsessions with alchemy and gambling. *A Cure for a Cuckold*, attributed to Webster and Rowley and probably written some four years later, at least provides more dramatic tension. The hero, Lessingham, is told by his mistress that he will succeed in his wooing only if he kills his best friend for her sake. Although he is prepared to comply, both parties contrive to evade this harsh condition, and the unscrupulousness of Lessingham's action is forgotten in a conventionally happy ending. The play is chiefly memorable for its dueling scene on the sands at Calais, for its sequel when Lessingham pretends that he has fulfilled his mistress' command, and last but not least for Rowley's comic creation of the returned mariner, Compass. In the following year appeared *The Fair Maid of the Inn*, which is generally regarded as the joint work of Webster, Massinger, and Ford. In this play Webster returns to a theme that resembles that of *The Devil's Law-Case*, the disowning of a son (Cesario) by his mother (Mariana), though on this occasion the object is to save him from danger. But once again we find a hero whose shifts of affection and equivocations in his dealings with the heroine are finally rewarded by marriage. Webster's contribution to this play is mainly limited to the second act and the last three scenes, and his sardonic style

shows itself most plainly in a satirical creation, the fantastic charlatan Forobosco.

With *Appius and Virginia* Webster returned finally to tragedy—that is, if we follow those scholars who place the play at the end rather than the beginning of his career. There is evidence for either conclusion, but Lucas makes a strong case when he argues that the portrait of the Roman lawyer in this play is such an accomplished creation that it is far more likely to have followed the equally sophisticated Cantilupo of *The Devil's Law-Case* than to have preceded the crude caricature of an advocate that we find in *The White Devil*. There is also the argument from topical allusion, which suggests that the starving of the Roman army, which plays an important part in the plot, refers to the scandalous neglect and hardships suffered by an English contingent dispatched to the Low Countries in 1624–1625. Those critics who prefer the later date attribute only a minor share of collaboration to Heywood. The play reflects something of the blunt, unsophisticated quality of early Roman history. The action is straightforward, the sequence of emotions easily predictable, the characters drawn with rigid, somewhat elementary strokes: in particular the character of the martyred Virginia possesses far too little freedom of choice to stand comparison with Webster's earlier heroines. But amid the artificiality of Caroline tragedy the rough simplicity of Virginia's farewell to his daughter stands out powerfully. And in Appius' speech before execution, Webster expresses for the last time the tribute he can never withhold from courage—especially in a villain:

> Think not, lords
> But he that had the spirit to oppose the gods
> Dares likewise suffer what their powers inflict . . .
> Now with as much resolved constancy
> As I offended will I pay the mulct . . .
> Learn of me, Clodius,
> I'll teach thee what thou never studieds't yet
> That's bravely how to dy . . .
>
> (*Appius and Virginia*, V. ii. 125–127; 134–135; 138–140)

CONCLUSION

*Webster was much possessed by death
And saw the skull beneath the skin*

wrote T. S. Eliot. Certainly in his tragedies the menace and the mystery of death become the preoccupation that in the end overpowers all others, so that the dramatist seems deliberately to hold his characters on the brink of eternity as he questions them in their dying moments. Time and again his imagination returns to study the different responses of humanity to this ordeal which none can escape: now it is the sudden, uncontrollable dread voiced by Bracchiano:

> O thou soft natural death, that art joint-twin
> To sweetest slumber: no rough-bearded comet
> Stares on thy mild departure: the dull owl
> Beats not against thy casement: the hoarse wolf
> Scents not thy carrion. Pity winds thy corse
> Whilst horror waits on princes

and

> On pain of death, let no man name death to me,
> It is a word infinitely terrible.
> (*The White Devil*, V. iii. 30–35; 39–40)

or Flamineo's wry mockery, which masks a total and desperate uncertainty in all things spiritual:

> *Lod:* What dost think on?
> *Fla:* Nothing; of nothing: leave thy idle questions
> I am i'th' way to study a long silence.
> To prate were idle, I remember nothing.
> There's nothing of so infinite vexation
> As man's own thoughts . . .
> We cease to grieve, cease to be fortune's slaves
> We cease to die by dying . . .
>
>   I do not look
> Who went before, nor who shall follow me;
> No, at myself I will begin and end
> (*The White Devil*, V. vi. 203–208; 255–256; 259–261)

or the Duchess of Malfi's resolution and assurance:

> What would it pleasure me to have my throat cut
> With diamonds, or to be smothered
> With cassia, or to be shot to death with pearls?
> I know death hath ten thousand several doors
> For men to take their exits: and 'tis found
> They go on such strange geometrical hinges
> You may open them both ways: any way, for heaven's
>   sake
> So I were out of your whispering: tell my brothers
> That I perceive death, now I am well awake,
> Best gift is they can give, or I can take.
> I would fain put off my last woman's fault,
> I'll not be tedious to you
> (*The Duchess of Malfi*, IV. ii. 212–223)

or, as a final comment, the stoical fatalism of Bosola:

> Yes, I hold my weary soul in my teeth,
> 'Tis ready to part from me . . .
>   O, I am gone.
> We are only like dead walls or vaulted graves
> That, ruined, yield no echo. Fare you well—
> It may be pain, but no harm to me to die
> In so good a quarrel: O this gloomy world,
> In what shadow, or deep pit of darkness
> Doth womanish and fearful mankind live.
> Let worthy minds ne'er stagger in distrust
> To suffer death, or shame, for what is just
> Mine is another voyage.
> (*Duchess of Malfi*, V. v. 74–75; 95–104)

Webster was also "possessed" by the contrast between the willful pretensions and desires of men and women and the reality that lies in wait for them. He does not follow Shakespeare's conception of tragedy as a fateful and exceptional conjunction of character and circumstance, whereby a man

> Carrying, I say, the stamp of one defect . . .
> His virtues else, be they as pure as grace . . .
> Shall in the general censure take corruption
> From that particular fault.
> (*Hamlet*, I. iv. 30–35)

for to Webster corruption is a matter of the general doom, not the particular fault. The world, as he sees it, is a pit of darkness through which men grope their way with a haunting sense of disaster, and the ordeal to which he submits his characters is not merely the end of life but a struggle against spiritual annihilation by the power of evil: it is noticeable that none of them, however intolerable the blows of fate, seeks refuge in suicide. The nature of this struggle is beset by a terror that is Webster's most original contribution to tragic art. At the end of a Shakespearean tragedy the forces of evil have spent themselves, the hero has in some measure learned wisdom. At the end of *The White Devil*, death merely interrupts the worldly concerns of the protagonists, leaving them face to face with damnation. Only in *The Duchess of Malfi* do we receive a suggestion of a further vision, a hint that the spiritual chaos of the early seventeenth century is not eternity.

Webster is not an easy dramatist to appreciate, nor does he yield up his best at a first reading. His plots lack the unity and the impetus that are the reward of devotion to a single dominant theme. But judged by his individual scenes he remains, after Shakespeare, the most profound and theatrically accomplished tragedian of his age, who excels equally in the sudden coup de theatre or in the gradual heightening of tension and the capacity to play upon the nerves of his audience. He surpasses Middleton and Ford in the imaginative depth and concentration of his poetry, and Chapman and Tourneur as a creator of living men and women and of roles that can still hold the stage. He succeeds better than any of his contemporaries in recreating the color and the spiritual climate of Renaissance Italy—in *The White Devil*, as Lucas says, we know at once that we have crossed the Alps. On the strength of his two great plays, he stands second only to Shakespeare in the history of English tragedy.

SELECTED BIBLIOGRAPHY

I. Bibliography. W. W. Greg, *A Bibliography of the English Printed Drama to the Restoration*, 4 vols. (London, 1939–1959); S. A. Tannenbaum, *A Concise Bibliography* (New York, 1941).

II. Collected Works. A. Dyce, ed., *The Works of J. Webster* (London, 1830); W. C. Hazlitt, ed., *The Dramatic Works of J. Webster* (London, 1857); F. L. Lucas, ed., *The Complete Works of John Webster*, 4 vols. (London, 1927), the standard ed. and a monument of scholarship; vols. I–II, which contain *The White Devil* and *The Duchess of Malfi*, were reprinted in 1958 and include a revised intro. and a commentary; the original intro. and bibliography are drastically abridged.

III. Selections. J. A. Symonds, ed., *Webster and Tourneur* (London, 1888; new ed., 1959); *Webster and Ford* (London, 1954). Both works contain *The White Devil* and *The Duchess of Malfi*.

IV. Separate Works. *Commendatory Verses Prefixed to the Third Part of Munday's Translation of Palmerin of England* (London, 1602); *Ode Prefixed to S. Harrison's Arches of Triumph Erected in Honour of James the First* (London, 1604); *The Malcontent . . . With the Additions Plaied by the King's Majesties Servants* (London, 1604), includes Webster's induction, also included in A. H. Bullen, ed., *The Works of John Marston* (London, 1887); *The Famous History of Sir Thomas Wyat. With the Coronation of Queen Mary and the Coming in of King Philip* (London, 1607), title page attributes the play to Dekker and Webster, repr. in W. J. Blew, *Two Old Plays* (London; facs. ed., 1914); *West-Ward Hoe* (London, 1607), title page attributes play to Dekker and Webster (facs.

repr., London, 1914); *North-Ward Hoe* (London, 1607), title page attributes play to Dekker and Webster (facs. repr., London 1914); *The White Devil, or the Tragedy of Paulo Giordano Ursini, Duke of Brachiano. With the Life, and Death, of Vittoria Corombona, the Famous Venetian Curtizan* (London, 1612; repr. 1631, 1665, 1672), modern eds. include G. B. Harrison (London, 1933), G. H. W. Rylands, ed. (London, 1933), J. R. Brown (London, 1960), the most important ed. since Lucas, Elizabeth M. Brennan, ed. (London, 1966), J. R. Mulryne, ed. (Lincoln, Nebr., 1970); *Commendatory Verses. Prefixed to Heywood's Apology for Actors* (London, 1612); *A Monumental Column. Erected to the Living Memory of the Ever-Glorious Henry, Late Prince of Wales* (London, 1613); *New Characters (Drawne to the Life) of Severall Persons, in Severall Qualities* (London, 1615), a group of thirty-two Characters added, with a separate title page, to the 6th ed. of the Overbury collection, included in E. F. Rimbault, ed., *The Miscellaneous Works in Prose and Verse of Sir Thomas Overbury, Knt.* (London, 1856; repr., 1890); *The Tragedy of the Dutchess of Malfy* (London, 1623; repr. 1640, 1664, 1668, 1708); C. Vaughan, ed. (London, 1896); F. Allen, ed. (London, 1921), new ed. with introductory essays by G. H. W. Rylands and C. Williams (London, 1945); A. K. MacIlwraith, ed., in *Five Stuart Tragedies* (London, 1953); J. R. Brown, ed. (London, 1965), the most important ed. since Lucas; Elizabeth M. Brennan, ed. (London, 1964); and C. Hart, ed. (Edinburgh, 1972); *The Devil's Law-Case, or, When Women Go to Law the Devil Is Full of Business* (London, 1623); *Monuments of Honour* (London, 1624), poem commissioned by the Merchant Taylors Company for the Lord Mayor's Show, 1624; *The Fair Maid of the Inn* (London, 1647); published in the Beaumont and Fletcher first folio (London, 1626; repr. 1679), and included in A. Glover and A. R. Waller, eds., *The Works of Beaumont and Fletcher* (London, 1905–1912), Lucas accepts the view that the play is the work of Massinger, Webster, and Ford; *Appius and Virginia* (London, 1654; repr. 1659, 1679), title page attributes play to Webster alone, but most modern scholars accept Heywood's collaboration; *A Cure for a Cuckold* (London, 1661), title page lists Rowley as collaborator; *Anything for A Quiet Life* (London, 1662), title page attributes this play to Middleton, but Sykes and Lucas assign most of the scenes to Webster, included in A. Dyce, ed., *Works of Thomas Middleton* (London, 1840), and in A. H. Bullen, *Works of Thomas Middleton* (London, 1885).

R. G. Howarth, to whose scholarship this essay and bibliography are indebted, assigns to Webster *A Speedie Poste* (1624) and *The Valiant Scot* (1637). Webster's dedication to *The Devil's Law-Case* (1623) mentions *The Guise*, a lost play probably written between 1614 and 1623. Other references of the period mention Webster's collaboration in *Caesar's Fall* (with Munday, Middleton, and Drayton), *Christmas Comes But Once a Year* (with Heywood, Dekker, and Chettle), and *The Late Murder in Whitechapel or Keep the Widow Waking* (with Ford, Dekker, and Rowley).

V. Biographical and Critical Studies. Charles Lamb, *Specimens of English Dramatic Poets* (London, 1808); William Hazlitt, *Lectures on the Dramatic Literature of the Age of Elizabeth* (London, 1821); D. Gnoli, *Vittoria Accoramboni* (Florence, 1870), a study of the historical background of *The White Devil*; W. W. Greg, "Webster's *White Devil*, an Essay in Formal Criticism," in *Modern Language Quarterly*, 3 (1900), an important discussion both of the text and of the act and scene divisions of the play; E. E. Stoll, *John Webster* (London, 1905); C. Crawford, *Collectanea* (London, 1906), reprints from *Notes and Queries*; F. Morellini, *Giovanna d'Aragona, Duchess D'Amalfi* (Cesena, 1906), the standard work on the historical background of the play; A. C. Swinburne, *The Age of Shakespeare* (London, 1908); Rupert Brooke, *John Webster and the Elizabethan Drama* (London, 1916), a pioneer work, but dated; W. Archer, *The Old Drama and the New* (London, 1923); H. D. Sykes, *Sidelights on Elizabethan Drama* (London, 1924), contains essays on *Appius and Virginia, The Fair Maid of the Inn*, and *Anything for a Quiet Life*; G. Murphy, *A Cabinet of Characters* (London, 1925), a useful intro. to the Overbury collection of Characters; T. S. Eliot, *Selected Essays* (London, 1932), especially "Four Elizabethan Dramatists," "Seneca in Elizabethan Translation," and "Shakespeare and the Stoicism of Seneca"; M. C. Bradbrook, *Themes and Conventions of Elizabethan Tragedy* (London, 1934); U. M. Ellis-Fermor, *The Jacobean Drama* (London, 1936); T. Spencer, *Death and Elizabethan Tragedy* (Cambridge, Mass., 1936); F. T. Bowers, *Elizabethan Revenge Tragedy* (London, 1940); T. Spencer, *Shakespeare and the Nature of Man* (New York, 1942); F. P. Wilson, *Elizabethan and Jacobean* (London, 1945); F. S. Boas, *Stuart Drama* (London, 1946); C. Leech, *Shakespeare's Tragedies and Other Studies in Seventeenth-Century Drama* (London, 1950); C. Leech, *John Webster* (London, 1951); A. Harbage, *Shakespeare and the Rival Traditions* (New York, 1952); M. Doran,

Endeavors of Art: A Study of Form in Elizabethan Drama (Madison, Wis., 1954); T. Bogard, *The Tragic Satire of John Webster* (London, 1955); B. Ford, ed., *The Pelican Guide to Literature, II: The Age of Shakespeare* (London, 1955), contains L. G. Salingar, "Tourneur and the Tragedy of Revenge"; G. Boklund, *The Sources of The White Devil* (London, 1957); A. Kernan, *The Cankered Muse: Satire of the English Renaissance* (New Haven, 1959); J. R. Brown and B. Harris, eds., *Jacobean Theatre*, Stratford-upon-Avon Studies I (London, 1960), contains G. K. Hunter, "English Folly and Italian Vice" and J. R. Mulryne, "*The White Devil*" and "*The Duchess of Malfi*"; R. W. Dent, *John Webster's Borrowing* (London, 1960), an important study of Webster's methods of composition and indebtedness to other authors; R. Ornstein, *The Moral Vision of Jacobean Tragedy* (London, 1960); R. Kaufmann, ed., *Elizabethan Drama: Modern Essays in Criticism* (London, 1961), contains essays on Webster by H. T. Price and I. Ekblad; G. Boklund, *The Duchess of Malfi: Sources, Themes and Characters* (London, 1962); I. Ribner, *Jacobean Tragedy* (London, 1962); C. Leech, *Webster: The Duchess of Malfi* (London, 1964), a short appreciation designed for students in the Studies in English Literature series; T. B. Tomlinson, *A Study of Elizabethan and Jacobean Tragedy* (Cambridge, 1964); C. O. Macdonald, *The Rhetoric of Tragedy: Form in Stuart Drama* (Amherst, Mass., 1966); D. D. Moore, *John Webster and His Critics* (Baton Rouge, La., 1966); J. M. R. Margeson, *The Origins of English Tragedy* (Oxford, 1967); R. B. Heilman, *Tragedy and Melodrama: Versions of Experience* (Seattle—London, 1968); N. Rabkin, ed., *Twentieth Century Interpretations of "The Duchess of Malfi"* (Englewood Cliffs, N.J., 1968); G. K. and S. K. Hunter, eds., *John Webster*, Penguin Critical Anthologies (Harmondsworth, 1969); P. B. Murray, *A Study of John Webster* (The Hague—Paris, 1969); B. Morris, ed., *John Webster*, Mermaid Critical Commentaries (London, 1970); C. Ricks, ed., *Sphere History of Literature in the English Language*, vol. III (London, 1971), contains "The Tragedies of Webster, Tourneur and Middleton; Symbols, Imagery, Conventions"; R. Berry, *The Art of John Webster* (Oxford, 1972).

JOHN FORD

(ca. 1586–ca. 1639)

Clifford Leech

THE theater of Charles I's reign is not to be sharply divided from the theater of his father, James I. It was about 1610 that the King's Men, Shakespeare's company, became the first adult group of actors to occupy a private theater—the Blackfriars—a small, roofed theater, functioning by artificial light, and catering to the tastes of an audience limited by its ability to pay the relatively high prices for admission. It was this event that began a bifurcation of the London audience continuing until the outbreak of the Civil War in 1642, when all theaters closed. When, in earlier years, the boys' companies had occupied the private theaters, the adult players continued to attract a wide audience from almost all classes of society. But as other companies followed the example of the King's Men in the years after 1610, the public theater became the home of audiences and of playwrights who gave themselves to a taste for simple spectacle, homespun sentiment, and unambitious comedy, while the private theaters moved closer to the court and specialized in a drama of sophisticated enquiry.

The man who left his mark most strongly on this adult private theater was John Fletcher. Collaborating first with Beaumont, then almost certainly with Shakespeare in *The Two Noble Kinsmen* and probably in *Henry VIII* and the lost *Cardenio* (partially preserved, it seems, in Lewis Theobald's adaptation called *Double Falsehood*, published in 1728), and later with Massinger and others, Fletcher not only found an appropriate audience in the private theaters but powerfully influenced all private theater drama until it came to an end in 1642. He died in 1625, the year of Charles I's accession. The new king's reign saw Massinger continuing as a leading playwright, and saw too the last plays of Ben Jonson (still vigorously satirical, still ready to experiment, still a master of language,

but now out of key with his audience's sense of fashion). And along with these men of an older generation, the Caroline private theater saw the rise of a new group of dramatists—William Davenant, Richard Brome, James Shirley, and above all John Ford. All addressed themselves to a small audience on the fringe of the court; all were in different ways disciples of Fletcher; all anticipated the drama of the Restoration; Ford alone among them was touched by what we call "genius."

Neither Ford nor his immediate contemporaries can be understood without reference to the achievement of Fletcher. Fletcher brought a new simplicity of language to the English theater, and simultaneously drove English drama to a concern with the periphery of the human condition—or, to change the metaphor, with situations remote from the normal current of life but recognizable as possible and therefore as legitimate matter for our consideration. To turn to him from the later Shakespeare, or from Chapman, Webster, Tourneur, or Marston, is to move from a complex to a direct style. Fletcher's language is the language of the polite gentleman of James I's reign: he can be lyrical, he can be eloquent, but he rarely makes us pause as we read. His blank verse has neither the rigidity of the Elizabethans nor the packed content, the close texture, of the early Jacobeans. He loves the feminine ending, the falling cadence, the casualness of polite speech. But he uses this easy language in the depiction of scenes where unlikelihood is the regular datum. Let us take, he seems to say, an improbable situation, and let us work out from there the sequence of events that in human probability will ensue. Strangeness of character was not his concern: there is not in any Fletcher play a figure comparable to Webster's Ferdinand of Calabria, of Tourneur's Vindice, or Shakespeare's Othello. The stress is on the initial situation, and a curious counterpoint is established between the peripheral pattern of event and the simplicity of both character and language. The peculiar and major talent of Fletcher is now beginning to be recognized after two and a half centuries of denigration, but we must still acknowledge that Fletcher's drama was basically a drama in which human nature was explored in too clinical a fashion for a sense of tragic dignity to emerge. The special contribution of Ford to English drama is his modification of the Fletcherian pattern in a way that made tragedy again possible. And Ford's tragedies are perhaps the last in the English language until very recent years. He could genuinely admire human nature, as no Restoration dramatist could; he could sense the difficulty of doing so more surely than any other dramatist from his time until ours. And for tragedy something near admiration and the realization of its near-impossibility are both necessary.

There was a reinforcement of Fletcher's influence on Ford—the publication of Robert Burton's *The Anatomy of Melancholy* in 1621. Here in nondramatic form was an encyclopedic survey of the periphery of the human condition. One is abnormal, sick, because one is in an abnormal situation. Burton traces the history of the sickness and relates it to kindred instances. All his subjects are victims of melancholy, a broad enough term in the early seventeenth century to include every possibility of mental suffering emerging into mental disorder. Ford recognizes his indebtedness to Burton in a marginal note to *The Lover's Melancholy*, perhaps his earliest play, but the debt can be traced in every one of his writings subsequent to the publication of Burton's book.

The close relation of the Caroline private theater to the court entailed a further influence, though at times the importance of this has been exaggerated, or at least seen in too simple a fashion. Queen Henrietta Maria encouraged a cult of "Platonic Love," which exalted a love-sentiment existing apart from a physical relationship. In *The Queen; or, The Excellency of Her Sex*, a play probably by Ford but published anonymously in 1653, Colonel Valasco is wooing Salassa and indicates in act II that the height of his ambition is a kiss:

> Oh, fear not,
> For my affections aim at chast contents;
> Not at unruly passions of desire.
> I onely claim the title of your servant,
> The flight of my ambitions soars no higher,
> Than living in your grace, and for incouragement

> To quicken my attendance now and then
> A kinde unravisht kiss.

But the action of the play demonstrates the absurdity of Valasco's wooing and the arrogance of Salassa in accepting the kind of devotion he offers. In *Love's Sacrifice*, Fernando enters into a relationship with the Duchess Bianca that hovers on the edge of adultery: they are able to half-persuade themselves that their love is platonic and guilt-free, but the special edge of Ford's treatment of the situation depends on his and our realization that the courtly code was at odds with human nature and its demands. Indeed, Ford's plays are, commonly, studies of a passion that is inclusive and destructive: insofar as he reflects the modish concept, it is only as a means of demonstrating its illusory character. His lovers may talk of their passion in ideal terms, but there is always in them a full drive toward coition: it is this that commonly destroys them.

Ford was born about 1586 in Devonshire, and was admitted to the Middle Temple in 1602. We know he was still residing in the Temple in 1617, and, though there is no record of his having been called to the bar, he may have concerned himself in some capacity with the law during the years when he was writing for the stage. His earliest known compositions are nondramatic. There is a verse elegy on Charles Mountjoy, earl of Devonshire, husband of Penelope Devereux. This appeared in 1606, and was followed by three prose pamphlets: *Honour Triumphant* (1606), describing the ceremonial challenge of four knights on the occasion of the Danish king's visit to England, and *The Golden Mean* (1613) and *A Line of Life* (1620), which urge a stoical facing of adversity. To these we may probably add a poem *Christe's Bloody Sweat* (1613), extravagantly baroque in its imagery, unexpectedly Calvinist in its theology: its title page and dedication give the author as "I.F.," and the paradox of manner and matter—in addition to the similarity of its picture of hell to that given by the friar to Annabella in *'Tis Pity She's a Whore* —makes Ford's authorship at least tenable.[1] The dramatist later wrote several sets of commendatory and other verses,[2] but from the beginning of

---

[1] The case for Ford's authorship is argued by M. J. Sargeaunt in her *John Ford* (1935).

[2] For a complete list of certain and probable nondramatic writings, see *John Ford and the Drama of His Time* (London, 1957), pp. 124–126.

Charles' reign it was to the theater that nearly all Ford's writing was directed.

In 1660 the publisher Humphrey Moseley entered in the Stationers' Register a play that he attributed to Ford with the title *An Ill Beginning Has a Good End, and a Bad Beginning May Have a Good End.* A play with a similar title was acted by the King's Men at court in 1612–1613. Moseley's attributions are unreliable, and it appears likely that Ford's beginnings in the drama were in collaboration with Thomas Dekker (*ca.* 1572–*ca.* 1632). Certainly we have evidence that the two dramatists worked together on the lost plays, *The Fairy Knight* (1624) and *The Bristow Merchant* (1624), and on *The Witch of Edmonton* (1621) and *The Sun's Darling* (1624). In addition Ford collaborated with Dekker, Webster, and Rowley (also a part-contributor to *The Witch of Edmonton*) on another lost play, *A Late Murder of the Son Upon the Mother*, or *Keep the Widow Waking* (1624), which brought together the stories of two topical crimes and involved its authors in legal proceedings.[3] Dekker was a dramatist of substantial experience, author of *The Shoemaker's Holiday* (1599), *Old Fortunatus* (1599), *The Honest Whore* (Part I, 1604; Part II, *ca.* 1630), and a series of other plays written for both adult and boys' companies. In many ways a strange collaborator for Ford, Dekker represents an older and simpler strain in the drama, free from the complexity of thought and language that marked the major writers of the early seventeenth century, and with nothing of the special austerity that was to characterize Ford's later preoccupation with strange and perilous human conduct. Yet it was doubtless from him that Ford learned the elements of his craft. *The Witch of Edmonton* is one of the most powerful domestic dramas of its time: its title refers to the story of Mother Sawyer, an old woman who becomes a witch because her neighbors accuse her of being one, so that traffic with the devil seems a mode of escape from persecution. Ford's share in the play was perhaps limited to the story of Frank, a young countryman whom circumstances drive to bigamy and murder, to self-betrayal and remorse and execution. Although Dekker's hand is to be felt as well as Ford's in the handling of this story, the sense of an inevitable sequence of events anticipates what we find in the independent plays of the younger dramatist, and the homespun verse of Dek-

ker, so different from the more ambitious writing of his contemporaries, perhaps helped to provide a foundation for Ford's mature manner—though that was to be given a precision of its own.

Of the plays written by Ford alone, we can date *The Lover's Melancholy* (1628) and *The Lady's Trial* (1638): it is likely that the rest were written within this ten-year period. He wrote for the King's Men at the Blackfriars (*The Lover's Melancholy, The Broken Heart*) and for the Queen's Men and for Beeston's boys' company at the Phoenix (*'Tis Pity She's a Whore, Love's Sacrifice, Perkin Warbeck, The Fancies, Chaste and Noble, The Lady's Trial*). Whether he changed his allegiance from one theater to the other at one point in his career,[4] or whether the place of performance has no relation to date, we cannot be sure. But all seven of these plays belong to the reign of Charles I, as most probably does *The Queen; or, The Excellency of Her Sex*, now commonly accepted as Ford's. When he had become a dramatist working on his own, the last phase of pre-Civil War drama had begun.

Of Ford's life apart from his writings and his association with the Middle Temple, we know almost nothing, not even the date of his death. It is likely enough that he either left London (perhaps for his native Devonshire) or died soon after the publication of *The Lady's Trial* in 1639: certainly no firm evidence of his being alive is dated later than this.

FORD'S VERSE

In a performance of a Ford play the first requisite is that the actors should make the audience fully conscious of the verse. Certainly this is necessary with any verse play of the late sixteenth and early seventeenth centuries, but with Ford the need is special. His plays have a good deal of violent action onstage and off. In *The Broken Heart*, Penthea starves herself to death; her lover, Orgilus, stabs her brother Ithocles in the presence of her dead body; Orgilus is condemned and ceremonially executes himself by opening a vein; the Princess Calantha successfully commands her own heart to break. In *'Tis Pity She's a Whore*, Grimaldi kills Bergetto by mistake for Soranzo; Hippolita poisons herself in-

---

[3]See C. J. Sisson, *Lost Plays of Shakespeare's Age* (1936), pp. 80–124.

[4]See G. E. Bentley, *The Jacobean and Caroline Stage*, III (London, 1956), p. 437.

stead of Soranzo; Soranzo drags his wife, Annabella, across the stage by the hair; Putana is blinded and finally condemned to death; Giovanni stabs Annabella and displays the heart he has taken from her body; Giovanni kills Soranzo and is himself killed by Soranzo's hired banditti. The themes, moreover, most used by Ford are repellent or at least disturbing—madness, incest, impotence, jealousy. It is easy, then, for his plays to seem mere lurid exercises, and the term "decadent" was long thrown at them.[5] But the ready application of this label can disguise their special quality. This emerges at once if the verse is allowed to assert itself. Its general simplicity is deceptive. Except in a few places where the text is probably corrupt, Ford can be read quickly: there is not, any more than in Fletcher, the love of involution, of compression, of a developing series of images, that marks Webster and Chapman and the later Shakespeare. Yet it is different writing from Fletcher's, for at its most characteristic it is formal rather than familiar, with a heavy weight on its stresses and a consequent slowness. Because of this deliberateness Ford can use the run-on line more frequently than Fletcher, who retains a blank verse pattern principally by a fairly consistent use of an end-stop. There is imagery, of course, but it is usually of a conventional sort. Here, for example, is Giovanni speaking in the last scene of 'Tis Pity. He has just entered with Annabella's heart upon his dagger, and he now tells of their incest and of murdering her when he realized they were both doomed:

> The glory of my deed
> Darken'd the mid-day sun, made noon as night.
> You came to feast, my lords, with dainty fare:
> I came to feast too; but I digg'd for food
> In a much richer mine than gold or stone
> Of any value balanc'd; 'tis a heart,
> A heart, my lords, in which is mine entomb'd:
> Look well upon't; d'ye know't?
>   *Vas.* [*aside*]   What strange riddle's this?
>   *Gio.*   'Tis Annabella's heart, 'tis:—why d'ye startle?—
> I vow 'tis hers: this dagger's point plough'd up
> Her fruitful womb, and left to me the fame
> Of a most glorious executioner.[6]
>
>   (V. vi. 20–32)

In the first of these speeches Giovanni uses a sequence of four images—the sun made to seem dark by the birth of a greater splendor; the feasting that the company expected in relation to the feasting that he himself has made; the so rich mine into which he has dug; the heart as a tomb for another heart. The first three are linked through their use of terms of comparison for Giovanni's act, but only the second and third are more than sequentially related (the food image becoming incorporated in the mine image). Thus the current of thought is hardly at all impeded by cross-reference. In the second speech there is only one image, and that is for Ford a rather complex one: the common phallic image of ploughing is here transformed through its association with "dagger." The total effect is of a weighted yet perspicuous utterance, with a frequent use of repetition. For contrast one could look at Bosola's words to the Duchess of Malfi when, in the fourth act of Webster's tragedy, he urges her to see the frailty of her condition.[7]

We can see Ford's weighted simplicity from another angle, by comparing the use made by him and by Richard Crashaw of the same Latin poem. In The Lover's Melancholy, Menaphon is telling Amethus how in Thessaly he heard a contrast between a lute player and a nightingale: as the man played, the bird sought to outdo him. The affair is described in terms of plain wonderment, with well-worn adjectives ("best-skill'd," "well-shap'd," "quaking") and with imagery almost absent:

>   A nightingale,
> Nature's best-skilled musician, undertakes
> The challenge, and for every several strain
> The well-shap'd youth could touch, she sung her own;
> He could not run division with more art
> Upon his quaking instrument than she,
> The nightingale, did with her various notes
> Reply to: for a voice and for a sound,
> Amethus, 'tis much easier to believe
> That such they were than hope to hear again.
>
>   (I.i. 121–130)

Ford inserted a note in the text, acknowledging indebtedness to a Latin poem of Famiano Strada. This was also the source of Crashaw's poem *Musicks Duell*, which is more than three times as long as the passage in The Lover's Melancholy. The

---

[5]See S. P. Sherman, "Forde's Contribution to the Decadence of the Drama," *John Fordes Dramatische Werke*, I, W. Bang, ed. (Louvain, 1908).

[6]Quotations from Ford's plays are from H. Ellis, ed., *John Ford* (London, 1888).

[7]I have attempted a brief analysis of this passage in *Webster: The Duchess of Malfi* (London, 1963), pp. 45–46.

JOHN FORD

poem has all the ingenious violence of Crashaw, as in these lines:

Then starts shee suddenly into a Throng
Of short thicke sobs, whose thundering volleys float,
And roll themselves over her lubricke throat
In panting murmurs, still'd out of her Breast
That ever-bubbling spring; the sugred Nest
Of her delicious soule, that there does lye
Bathing in streamers of liquid Melodie;
Musicks best seed-plot, whence in ripen'd Aires
A Golden-headed Harvest fairely reares
His Honey-dropping tops, plow'd by her breath
Which there reciprocally laboureth
In that sweet soyle.

We are quickly startled by the use of "Throng" as a collective with "sobs," which become cannon fire and then immediately waves, and then return to the throat (made strange by "lubricke") from which they came. The throat becomes a distilling apparatus, the liquid it works on coming from the breast that is also a spring. Yet the breast is then the "sugred Nest/Of her delicious soule" (again the characteristic and challenging adjective); and this nest is both a meetingplace of waters where the soul bathes and a seed-plot from which music is brought to ripeness. For the harvest to be won, the land must be ploughed by the bird's breath. The total movement of the passage has become, in a fashion, circular—as we begin and end with the bird's violent breath—although the sequence of images is arbitrary in its complexity, arbitrary too in its final movement of return. Ford goes straight on, and relies for his effect on a strong but not too obtrusive metrical beat and on a discreet use of common emotive words and phrases. Crashaw always challenges in his language, he defies "discretion," "taste," "decorum." The idea that Ford is a lurid writer is given a noticeable jolt when we come to recognize that no one in his time was more discreet in language.

It was this restraint, along with the marked beat of his lines, that made possible a revival of tragedy despite the powerful influence of Fletcher, which had taken drama into a nontragic direction.

ANATOMY OF THE MIND

In *The Lover's Melancholy*, at or near the outset of Ford's career as an independent dramatist, we have

a play almost devoid of incident. Eroclea, daughter of Meleander, was loved by Palador but coveted by his father, the reigning prince of Cyprus. So she fled; Palador succeeded to the throne on his father's death, but both he and Meleander are plunged into melancholy through the loss of Eroclea. When the play begins, she has returned to Cyprus in male disguise: the action concerns only the curing of Palador and Meleander through her reunion with them. Corax, the court physician, stages a masque of melancholy, with the purpose of diagnosing the particular kind of sickness that afflicts Palador, but although there is a hint that this has aroused the prince to a more active mental state, it is the sight of Eroclea in her disguise that decisively brings him alive. The play is moving in its calm expression of grief and of final happiness, and with the meeting of Eroclea and her father we have a manifest echo of Lear's reunion with Cordelia. We are given the typical Ford blend of sadness and quietness, and the concern with the mastering of sickness that appears in several others of his plays—most notably in *The Lady's Trial*, where Auria is given evidence of his wife's adultery but examines the situation soberly and convinces himself, rightly, of her innocence. In *The Queen*, Alphonso's rejection of his wife's love is cured by Muretto, who makes him jealous, and Colonel Valasco is cured of his subjection to Salassa when she outrages his honor by making him vow not to fight for two years. In each of these instances Ford takes a condition of sickness as his datum (potential sickness in Auria's case) and traces the path of its curing. Only in *The Queen* among these plays is there a surprising revelation (when Muretto declares to Alphonso both the queen's innocence and the reason for his accusation of her), and there, in Fletcherian fashion, Ford drops an occasional hint of what will finally emerge.

There is a facile imitation of the Fletcher pattern in *The Fancies, Chaste and Noble*, where Livio, for the sake of advancement, is persuaded by Troyolo-Savelli, nephew of Octavio, marquis of Sienna, to have his sister Castamela enter the society of the Fancies, three young women whom the marquis is said to keep for his impotent delight. At the end of the play it is suddenly revealed that the Fancies are the marquis' virtuous nieces, that he is concerned only with their education, and that Castamela was induced to join them, so that Troyolo-Savelli could woo her more easily, away from Livio and her suitor Romanello. This is a strange play, in which

91

the resolution is more incredible than the original situation. We are given every reason to believe that things are as Troyolo-Savelli has described them to Livio, and there is a certain distorted dignity in the marquis, whose conduct is presented as far less culpable than that of many great men in Italy. We may guess that Ford at first intended to present the marquis as a "patient," like the disturbed Palador and Meleander of *The Lover's Melancholy*, like Alphonso and Valasco in *The Queen*, like Auria as he could easily have become in *The Lady's Trial*. The difficulty of finding a cure for old age, and the difficulty, on the other hand, of presenting a conversion from the marquis' form of delight, may have led the dramatist to use a means of ending his play in what he could think of as the Fletcherian mode. But Fletcher at his best did not aim at total surprise, only at the momentary shock that quickly becomes a realization that the truth has all along been available. *The Fancies* could perhaps have been one of Ford's most impressive plays if he had faced the fact that cure is not always possible. He did recognize that when he wrote tragedy, but *The Fancies* has nowhere a tragic tone: it needed an ironic ending, with perhaps Livio deceived into believing that things were as the dramatist has forced his audience to believe them to be. But, as it stands, the forcing negates all the evidence, and an audience must just cease to credit the dramatic action.

It is in the four tragedies—*'Tis Pity She's a Whore*, *The Broken Heart*, *Love's Sacrifice*, and *Perkin Warbeck*—that Ford has most successfully absorbed Fletcher's influence and given us plays of high authority and of a special kind. In each instance he takes a strange situation as a datum. In *'Tis Pity* Giovanni and Annabella are brother and sister, and love each other. Giovanni, struggling with his passion, argues the case with Friar Bonaventura. Then he reveals his love to Annabella, and finds it reciprocated. They become lovers. Pregnant, she agrees to marry her suitor Soranzo, who discovers the incest and plans to kill them both. Giovanni anticipates this by killing Annabella himself, and then defies all the company assembled at a banquet in Soranzo's house. Both he and Soranzo die in the last scene's violence. The datum is their incestuous love, a peripheral phenomenon in human experience: what follows is a demonstration of the probable consequences. Ford arouses our sympathy for the lovers, partly by

the intensity of their language, partly by showing them isolated from help (the friar, in panic, deserting them even when Annabella has repented), partly—as in *The Fancies*—by showing the norm of behavior in the Parma of the play's action. The two subplots, closely related to the main action and to each other, exhibit folly and vice frankly and sharply. Soranzo has abandoned his mistress, Hippolyta, the wife of Richardetto; she tries to poison him and is promised help by his servant Vasques, but Vasques ensures that she is poisoned instead. Richardetto, who has been thought dead, has returned to Parma disguised as a physician; his niece Philotis captures the fancy of Annabella's witless suitor Bergetto; Richardetto agrees to the match, but Bergetto is stabbed, in mistake for Soranzo, by Grimaldi, another suitor of Annabella. The church, in the person of the cardinal, is shown protecting Grimaldi despite his murder of Bergetto, seizing all the property of Giovanni's father, Florio, who has died of grief on learning of the incest and of Annabella's death, and finally offering a sentence of pity and condemnation:

> Of one so young, so rich in nature's store,
> Who could not say, 'TIS PITY SHE'S A WHORE?
> (V. vi. 158–159)

In the context of the play we must understand this as meaning 'tis pity she could not have become a faithful wife to the vicious Soranzo, the murderous Grimaldi, or the simpleton Bergetto. The cardinal's sentence on Annabella's nurse, Putana, receives a public approval that we are not likely to share:

> First this woman, chief in these effects,
> My sentence is, that forthwith she be ta'en
> Out of the city, for example's sake,
> There to be burnt to ashes.
>   *Don.*   'Tis most just.
> (V. vi. 133–136)

The way of the lovers' world, the world that destroyed them, is rendered more repellent when both Vasques and Soranzo take pleasure in the thought of incestuous lovemaking immediately before Giovanni and Annabella are to be killed.

But the sympathy with Giovanni goes along with a probing into his mind. We see his incestuous love driving him both to atheism and to a belief in an unavoidable fate. Neither of these is explicitly condemned, though of course the friar expresses horror at the atheism and Richardetto can speak of Providence ("there is One/Above begins to work"). But Giovanni's atheism is not fixed: before he kills her, he wonders if he and Annabella will meet in another world; and his belief in fate is ironic in that he is the most active and self-assertive figure in the play. But he is led also into lying, telling Annabella as he woos her: "I have ask'd counsel of the holy church,/Who tells me I may love you." And we find him taking a new pleasure in love when the thrill of incest is sharpened by adultery:

> Busy opinion is an idle fool,
> That, as a school-rod keeps a child in awe,
> Frights th' unexperienc'd temper of the mind:
> So did it me, who, ere my precious sister
> Was married, thought all taste of love would die
> In such a contract; but I find no change
> Of pleasure in this formal law of sports.
> She is still one to me, and every kiss
> As sweet and as delicious as the first
> I reap'd, when yet the privilege of youth
> Entitled her a virgin.
>
> (V. iii. 1–11)

Annabella is distinguished from her brother by her remorse. The friar induces in her a fear of hell before she marries Soranzo; then her husband's brutality apparently drives her to accept Giovanni again as a lover (this emerges from the action, though her relapse is not commented on); then she repents once more and tries to persuade Giovanni of his guilt in their last scene together. Even so, her thoughts are much more for his safety on earth, or at least on his being prepared to face a violent end, than on his salvation. The firm rebelliousness of Giovanni is not in her, but she is a passionate woman whom the friar can browbeat but not win securely from her brother.

Ford is nearer to Middleton than any other dramatist in his exploration of the lovers' minds here: we can think of the way that Beatrice-Joanna and De Flores, in *The Changeling*, grow together through the association that De Flores insists on, and of the sense of the dramatist's deep involvement with these characters. Fletcher was more wryly equivocal, in tragedy as in comedy or tragicomedy. But Ford differs from both of these writers in the degree of his sympathy (which never raises the question of condonement) and in the authority of utterance that he gives to his lovers. Moreover, despite the complex interweaving of the subplots, this is a firmly composed play, with proper subordination of minor to major action and with each part of the minor action contributing its implied and necessary comment. Ford's title, using the already quoted words with which the cardinal ends the play, has a manifest but inexplicit irony. In his dedication Ford expresses the hope that "the gravity of the subject may easily excuse the lightness of the title," but of course does not explain why he did not match gravity with gravity. It is a play that accepts Giovanni's and Annabella's love as sickness, as involving further corruption with the passage of time, but it affirms a measure of nobility in them that distinguishes them from their world. The title is both plain statement and irony.

By far the most complicated of Ford's plays is *The Broken Heart*. In the concluding section of this essay we shall be concerned with its achievement of an effect of frozen and monumental grief, but this achievement is all the more remarkable in view of the psychological complexities that we may observe briefly here. The prologue asserts that the play is written with the dramatist's "best of art," and the praise seems deserved. The scene is a historically unrecognizable Sparta, where Calantha is princess and heir to the throne. She is officially wooed by Nearchus, prince of Argos, but loves the young and victorious general, Ithocles. He has forced his sister Penthea to leave Orgilus, to whom she was betrothed in her father's lifetime, and to marry Bassanes. This to her constitutes adultery and, together with Bassanes' jealousy, it induces her to starve herself to death. Orgilus kills Ithocles as they sit together with her body, this sudden end coming immediately after Calantha's acceptance of Ithocles as a suitor and the way to their marriage seems plain. Calantha, now Sparta's sovereign since her father's death, condemns Orgilus to death, and dies of a broken heart at her coronation.

There is much strange conduct here, and it will be well to concentrate on the figures of Orgilus, Penthea, and Bassanes. Orgilus tells his father in the first scene that he must leave Sparta because of his thwarted love for Penthea, and he extracts a promise from his sister Euphranea that she will not marry without his consent. But he then stays in Sparta in disguise, and explains in soliloquy that he will thus be able to "hearken after Penthea's usage and Euphranea's faith"—as if he is equally concerned with these two matters. He eavesdrops on a love scene between Euphranea and Prophilus, a friend of Ithocles, and exclaims: "There is no faith in woman." He is shocked by Prophilus' use of the word "desires," and is apparently determined against the marriage:

> Put out thy torches, Hymen, or their light
> Shall meet a darkness of eternal night!
> (I. iii. 176–177)

Yet when he abandons his disguise he quickly gives his consent to the marriage. Ford here seems to suggest that Orgilus is impelled to exercise the same frustrating control over his sister as Ithocles had exercised over Penthea (there being in both men a touch of incestuous feeling), and that his dislike of her marriage is increased by his own loss and, of course, by Prophilus' being a friend of Ithocles. Nevertheless, he wants to act well, and so gives his consent. At this point in the play there is no indication that he will take revenge on Ithocles. At least he assures both the sage Tecnicus and his father that no thought of violence is in his mind. Yet he plays with fire by remaining in Sparta, by spying on Penthea and Euphranea. Then he sees Penthea distracted shortly before her death, and from that point he is resolved on the murder of her brother. He does not attempt to hide his guilt, and dies with dignity.

Orgilus is a man of strong passions who is acted on by circumstance. Penthea begins as the victim of others, but becomes the most active figure in the play. In the second act, before we have seen her with either Ithocles or Orgilus, she seems almost reconciled to her position as Bassanes' wife. When her husband brings himself to speak gently to her she says:

> if your opinion, nobly plac'd,
> Change not the livery your words bestow,
> My fortunes with my hopes are at the highest.
> (II. i. 103–105)

But when she has seen Orgilus and dismissed him forever, she hears that Ithocles has a sudden indisposition. Though Bassanes makes light of it, she immediately thinks of death:

> In vain we labour in this course of life
> To piece our journey out at length, or crave
> Respite of breath; our home is in the grave.
> (II. iii. 145–147)

In the third act, she is visiting Ithocles, and he admits to her that he is in love. His heart, he says, is "now a-breaking." Her reply is that for him to die now would be too easy:

> Not yet, heaven,
> I do beseech thee! first let some wild fires
> Scorch, not consume it! may the heat be cherish'd
> With desires infinite, but hopes impossible!
> (III. ii. 30–33)

When he tells her that it is Calantha he loves, she asks him to imagine what it would be like if he were contracted to her and then lost her:

> Suppose you were contracted to her, would it not
> Split even your very soul to see her father
> Snatch her out of your arms against her will,
> And force her on the Prince of Argos?
>   *Ith.*   Trouble not
> The fountains of mine eyes with thine own story;
> I sweat in blood for't.
>   *Pen.*   We are reconcil'd.
> Alas, sir, being children, but two branches
> Of one stock, 'tis not fit we should divide:
> Have comfort, you may find it.
> (III.ii. 108–115)

Here the "We are reconcil'd" can be ambiguous: he is to take it he is forgiven, but it could mean "we are as one in our misfortunes": the ambiguity is continued in "tis not fit we quarrel" and "we should not be separate in our fates." Then she goes to Calantha, talks of her own approaching death, and reveals Ithocles' love. She calls him "this lost creature," which can be taken as a courtly phrase for a lover but may hint at his coming destruction. She reminds Calantha of Ithocles' responsibility for her own suffering:

>   *Cal.*   You have forgot, Penthea,
> How still I have a father.
>   *Pen.*   But remember
> I am a sister, though to me this brother
> Hath been, you know, unkind, O, most unkind!
> (III.v. 100–103)

When Calantha gives no indication of her love for Ithocles, Penthea ends the scene with a couplet that may suggest that she has achieved retribution for her sufferings:

My reckonings are made even; death or fate
Can now nor strike too soon nor force too late.
(III.v. 108–109)

In approaching Calantha, Penthea may believe either that Calantha will reject Ithocles or that the king will forbid the marriage, as she had suggested to Ithocles in their scene together. But she finds that neither of these things happens.

In her mad scene, Penthea continually draws Orgilus' attention to Ithocles. She presses and kisses her former lover's hand, though in their earlier scene together she had behaved with utter coldness. She makes it clear that Ithocles, unlike herself, unlike Orgilus, is on the point of winning all his desires:

alas, his heart
Is crept into the cabinet of the princess;
We shall have points and bride-laces.   Remember,
When we last gather'd roses in the garden,
I found my wits; but truly you lost yours.
That's he, and still 'tis he.
(IV.ii. 217–222)

The reference to Orgilus' losing his wits in the garden may hint that on the occasion of their meeting there Orgilus ought to have determined on revenge or on a violent taking of her from Bassanes. Certainly Orgilus accepts from her a cue for revenge: "She has tutor'd me"; "If this be madness, madness is an oracle." A notable thing in this mad scene is that Penthea does not speak in the disordered prose almost invariably used for deranged characters on the early seventeenth-century stage. She uses always blank verse, a verse controlled in diction and regular in meter. A doubt whether she is really mad may be reinforced by Orgilus' words just quoted, with their echo of Polonius' "Though this be madness, yet there is method in't."

That Penthea did not begin the play with thoughts of retribution on her brother seems evident in her words to Bassanes quoted above. But then she sees Ithocles returning victorious from the war, she painfully dismisses Orgilus when they meet in the garden, she has to endure Bassanes'

suspicion of an incestuous relationship between her and Ithocles. The third of these comes after her loaded words to her brother when she learns of his love for Calantha, but it may reinforce her desire to make things even. When Calantha accepts Ithocles' love, Penthea turns to the rejected Orgilus and makes him her instrument. Then she dies, a monument indeed, patiently waiting for revenge. That does not mean hatred for her brother, any more than Orgilus' murder of Ithocles means hatred: simply, as they see it, the balance of things must be maintained. In appearance the most pathetic of seventeenth-century stage women, Penthea is simultaneously the most ruthless.[8]

Bassanes first appears as a comically or melodramatically jealous figure. In planning to have the window of his wife's room "damm'd-up," he is like the jealous husband Corvino in Jonson's *Volpone*. Yet when he realizes that his wife is lost to him, he declares himself determined to cultivate "composure." He loses his calm, however, when he sees Penthea mad:

Fall on me, if there be a burning Aetna,
And bury me in flames! sweats hot as sulphur
Boil through my pores! affliction hath in store
No torture like to this.
(IV.ii. 95–98)

Yet he recovers, adjuring himself:

Keep in, vexation,
And break not into clamour.
(IV.ii. 124–125)

Then he grows distracted for a while, thinking of fantastic cures for Penthea. Only when all the deaths—of Penthea, of Ithocles, of the king—are known does he also achieve an immutable calm:

mark me, nobles,
I do not shed a tear, not for Penthea!
Excellent misery!
(V.ii. 164–166)

So he qualifies himself for the superintending of Orgilus' execution and for appointment as Sparta's marshal in Calantha's testament. Thus in Bassanes—and in Nearchus, who was first angry

---

[8]In this discussion of Ford's presentation of Penthea, I am indebted to suggestions made to me by Sir Laurence Olivier.

and jealous at Ithocles' love for Calantha, but controls his passion magnanimously—Ford has shown in this play the same winning of mastery as he was to exhibit in the Auria of *The Lady's Trial*. This was his ideal, it appears, most supremely achieved by Calantha here, when she refuses to show grief at the deaths of Ithocles, Penthea, and her father, but bids her heart break at a monument fully consonant with royal decorum. But Bassanes and Nearchus win a kindred mastery with more difficulty.

Love's Sacrifice is a play with a slighter impact than *The Broken Heart*, but in it the Duchess Bianca has some resemblance to Penthea. Her husband's friend Fernando loves her. When she rebukes him for this, he swears never to trouble her again. But in the next scene she goes to his room at night and offers herself to him: but if he accepts the offer, she says she will kill herself in the morning. So he abandons his suit. Then she grows reckless, freely admitting her love for him. In the presence of her husband, she asks: "Speak, shall I steal a kiss? believe me, my lord, I long." Later we see them exchanging kisses while they still talk of remaining faithful to husband and friend. Fernando would master his love, as Orgilus in *The Broken Heart* would master his resentment against Ithocles, but Bianca will not allow this to happen. She wants to enjoy both her love for Fernando and her sense of fidelity to the duke. Though Ford could dramatize the idealizing of women, he could also present them as the cause of men's destruction—as he very probably did in a less extreme way with Salassa in *The Queen*. In *Love's Sacrifice* and *The Broken Heart* there is an irony in the ceremonial mourning at the woman's death.

But in *Perkin Warbeck* the dramatic interest lies chiefly in the male characters. The impostor Warbeck never admits his imposture, even in soliloquy, and acts with a persistent nobility of bearing, winning the wholehearted devotion of Lady Katherine Gordon, whom he marries, and going to his death with resolution. Throughout he is contrasted with the successful King Henry VII, who triumphs now just as in the past when he was merely earl of Richmond and defeated Richard III at Bosworth Field. Henry is passionate, grieving when his friend Stanley is revealed as a traitor and delighting in his own skill. We have reference, too, to his notorious forced subsidies; and the defection of Stanley and the support for Perkin in Cornwall show that he has a precarious hold on the throne.

When he is told that the Spanish marriage of his son will not be consummated "as long/As any Earl of Warwick liv'd in England,/Except by new creation" (and there is irony in this, when we remember what was to follow from this Spanish marriage for Prince Arthur), he broods ominously: later we learn that Warwick has joined Perkin's party and must die for it. Henry is the successful gamester; Perkin shows always magniloquence and a refusal to abase himself. When the king of Scotland signifies the withdrawal of his help, Perkin replies in his usual courtly terms. And at the end even Henry is impressed by the impostor's firmness, as is Perkin's reluctant father-in-law, the earl of Huntley. Perkin could have his life if he submitted to the humiliation that Lambert Simnel, a former pretender who accepted Henry's pardon along with a menial position in his household, gave precedent for.

Perkin Warbeck is a history play, but different in many ways from the dramatic histories of the last decade of the sixteenth century, when almost all of Shakespeare's plays of this kind were written. Ford is hardly concerned with the state of the kingdom: rather, the character of the pretender is the puzzling center of the play. That he is an impostor seems evident enough, yet his ideal of royalty is contrasted with the successful pragmatism of the man who was victorious at Bosworth Field. Perkin was not born for success, but he has convinced himself of the need to live and die in a manner truly royal. There seems irony in Henry's last words, which also conclude the play:

> Perkin, we are inform'd, is arm'd to die;
> In that we'll honour him.   Our lords shall follow
> To see the execution; and from hence
> We gather this fit use,—that public states,
> As our particular bodies, taste most good
> In health when purged of corrupted blood.
>
> (V. iii. 214–219)

W. Gifford pointed out that the word "use" here seems to be employed in the puritanical sense of "doctrinal or practical deduction": for Ford, as a dramatist writing close to the beginning of the Civil War, this may imply a measure of hypocrisy in the speaker. Henry pays his tribute, but indicates the profit gained from Perkin's overthrow. On the play's title page, *Perkin Warbeck* is described as "A Strange Truth"—strange in its paradoxes, of the kingly impostor and the intriguing king and of the resemblance in their respective bids for power. Perkin is too kinglike a pretender to win kingship itself.

Men and women alike were, for Ford, material for wondering contemplation. He did not condemn, at least as far as his major characters were concerned. Giovanni and Penthea and Bianca are engineers of catastrophe, but they are also seen as subject to impulses not to be controlled. And in *The Broken Heart* he achieved what he worked toward elsewhere, the disastrous impingement of character on character, so that human beings destroy each other through merely existing together. It is a complex world of the mind that he exhibits and that he looks at with sad compassion.

THE MOMENT OF STILLNESS

THERE is a line in the *Phaedra* of Seneca that was frequently echoed in the English drama of the early seventeenth century, "*Curae leves loquuntur, ingentes stupent*" ("Light sorrows speak, great sorrows strike us dumb"). Thus in *Macbeth*, when Macduff learns that his wife and children have been slaughtered by Macbeth, Malcolm urges him to give utterance to his grief:

> Give sorrow words: the grief that does not speak
> Whispers the o'erfraught heart and bids it break.
> (IV.iii. 209–210)

In Tourneur's *The Revenger's Tragedy*, when Antonio is contemplating the dead body of his ravished wife, Hippolito assures him:

> We have grief too, that yet walks without tongue;
> *Curae leves loquuntur, majores stupent.*
> (I.iv. 22–23)

And in Webster's *The White Devil*, Isabella, the deserted wife of Bracchiano, pretends that she no longer loves her husband, so that he may be saved, she thinks, from her brothers' enmity; then, as she leaves the stage after her scene of pretense, she exclaims: "Those are the killing griefs which dare not speak" (II.i. 277).

In Elizabethan and Jacobean tragedy the sufferers are generally eloquent enough, but we can find moments, recurrent in all literature concerned with the ultimate anguish, when the characters realize

that utterance is not only inadequate but unworthy, not only unworthy but impossible. As Thomas Mann put it, "You are indeed inexperienced in grief if you think the deepest would be loud."[9] And Mann in the same novel expressed the quality of full defiance that can be manifested in silence:

> when she revived a second time her eye was dry and her bearing rigid. She had herself informed by the squire what had happened to her lord and then said: "Good." This "good" was not good at all. Such a "good" is by no means submission to God's will, rather it is a word of recalcitrance and perpetual denial of God's counsel and it means: "As you choose, Lord God, I draw my own conclusions from your dispensation, to me unacceptable. You had in me a female, a sinful one, certainly. Now you will have in me no female at all but for ever a rigid bride of affliction, closed and defiant, to amaze you."[10]

Ford does not offer so explicit a challenge, but in his plays we find the fullest expression in English drama of the early seventeenth century of a grief that must be silent. This stands in strange relationship to his probing into aberrant behavior, but it is in full conformity with his simple and restrained verse.

Each of his tragic plays moves through violent action to stillness—as the dead Bianca in *Love's Sacrifice* is offered tributes by her husband and her lover in the last act, as Perkin Warbeck goes to his execution with a refusal to weep or to ask for mercy. But above all we find this phenomenon in *The Broken Heart*. Calantha goes on with her courtly dance when news is brought to her of the deaths of Penthea, her father, and her lover. Orgilus, acting as his own executioner, faces death with neither defiance nor regret nor anticipation of a better world:

> On a pair-royal do I wait in death;
> My sovereign, as his liegeman; on my mistress,
> As a devoted servant; and on Ithocles,
> As if no brave, yet no unworthy enemy:
> Nor did I use an engine to entrap
> His life, out of a slavish fear to combat
> Youth, strength, or cunning; but for that I durst not
> Engage the goodness of a cause on fortune,
> By which his name might have outfac'd my vengeance....
> When feeble man is bending to his mother,
> The dust he was first fram'd on, thus he totters.

[9]*The Holy Sinner*, trans. H. T. Lowe-Porter (London, 1961), p. 49.
[10]*Ibid.*, p. 48.

Bass.　Life's fountain is dried up.
Org.　　　　　　　　　　So falls the standard
Of my prerogative in being a creature!
A mist hangs o'er mine eyes, the sun's bright splendour
Is clouded in an everlasting shadow;
Welcome, thou ice, that sitt'st about my heart,
No heat can ever thaw thee.　　　　　　*[Dies.]*
Near.　　　　　　　　　Speech hath left him.
Bass.　He has shook hands with time.

　　　　　　　　　　　　　　　(V.ii. 143–158)

Bassanes' comment here is wholly appropriate for so restrained a leave-taking. We have already seen how Bassanes and Nearchus master their passions, how Bassanes marvels at his own hard-won restraint. And when Calantha's coronation has taken place with Ithocles' dead body onstage, she arranges for the future conduct of government in Sparta and then addresses the dead man she loved:

　　　　　　　　　now I turn to thee, thou shadow
Of my contracted lord!　Bear witness all,
I put my mother's wedding-ring upon
His finger; 'twas my father's last request.
　　　　　[Places a ring on the finger of Ithocles.]
Thus I new-marry him whose wife I am;
Death shall not separate us.　O, my lords,
I but deceiv'd your eyes with antic gesture,
When one news straight came huddling on another
Of death! and death! and death! still I danc'd forward;
But it struck home, and here, and in an instant.
Be such mere women, who with shrieks and outcries
Can vow a present end to all their sorrows,
Yet live to court new pleasures, and outlive them:
They are the silent griefs which cut the heart-strings;
Let me die smiling.

　　　　　　　　　　　　　　　(V.iii. 62–76)

Here the echo of Seneca's *"ingentes stupent"* is given all of Ford's simple authority. The princess dies as a dirge is sung at her command.

In this play we have murder done, but the mode of killing is sober and reverent. The deaths of Penthea, Orgilus, and Calantha, moreover, are all self-willed. They choose to die because only by death can they find the stillness, the freedom from empty action, empty speech, that they crave. They seem to move throughout the play with slowness and deliberation to the condition of immobility that they finally achieve. They do not despair, they merely abandon a life that has become meaningless to them. Penthea starved in her chair, Orgilus holding himself upright with a staff as he bleeds to death, Calantha bidding her own heart break—all give us the impression of sculptured figures who have won the silence that was at last their only desire. The things that we remember most in the play are these moments of death, and the words that stay most securely in our minds are "He has shook hands with time" and "Let me die smiling." Even Ithocles, robbed of his hope of Calantha when he feels Orgilus' dagger, can speak of finding a "long-look'd-for peace." So the play is like a frieze on which a series of figures mourn for a life that could not be. Calantha's apparent indifference, when she danced onward despite the threefold news of death, becomes in retrospect a proud refusal to unpack the heart with words, a proud refusal even to die until all things have been done fittingly.

Few readers are attracted to *The Broken Heart* when they first come to know it. That is partly because they expect it to give them the same kind of interest as the plays of Ford's predecessors give. Perhaps, too, they may find it difficult to stomach so much quiet nobility in suffering. They may feel chilled by Calantha's self-control, and find her a little arrogant in her self-induced heartbreak. It is indeed a world remote from common life that Ford offers us. Its nearest analogue is to be found not in English literature but in the *Bérénice* of Racine, where suffering nobly borne is also unremittingly displayed. The final *"Hélas!"* of Racine's play strikes a note similar to that of the controlled lamentations of *The Broken Heart*. Ford has not Racine's fullness of achievement, his paring away of inessentials, his delicate variations on the simplest of patterns, his resolute avoidance of striking action; but in *The Broken Heart* we have the nearest English approach to the pure form of French classical tragedy. Neither Ford's play nor *Bérénice* could become a work much loved by the multitude, but close familiarity with either of them induces not only fascination but respect. Men and women do not behave, we know, like Calantha and Ithocles and Orgilus, or like Bérénice and Titus and Antiochus, but these dramatic figures represent an ideal of conduct that demands esteem. There is strong feeling here, and a refusal to let that feeling overflow into indignity. It is a narrow ideal, but nonetheless remarkable.

Nowhere else did Ford realize so fully the idea of a quiet confrontation of disaster, but we can find frequently in his plays the suggestion of a special nobility in the avoidance of an easy utterance, a wanton display. In *The Lover's Melancholy*, Meleander thinks of the need for simplicity in death:

> When I am dead,
> Save charge; let me be buried in a nook:
> No guns, no pompous whining; these are fooleries.
> If whiles we live, we stalk about the streets
> Jostled by carmen, footposts, and fine apes
> In silken coats, unminded and scarce thought on,
> It is not comely to be haled to the earth,
> Like high-fed jades upon a tilting-day,
> In antic trappings.   Scorn to useless tears![11]
>
> (II.ii. 109–117)

Spinella's silence in *The Lady's Trial* when she is accused of adultery, like Perkin's refusal to admit, even to himself, the fact of his imposture, bears witness to a similar ideal. We can link this to Annabella's refusal to name her lover to Soranzo in *'Tis Pity*, and to Bianca's refusal in *Love's Sacrifice* to avow her innocence when her husband assumes that Fernando has committed adultery with her. And we could indeed wish that the marquis in *The Fancies, Chaste and Noble* had similarly been allowed a final silence, in which he might face the fact of the perversion that age has induced in him, without the facile and unconvincing explaining away of his "Bower of Fancies."

It is evident that Ford could not have achieved his characteristic effect of a sculptured stillness if his language were not of the simple and direct kind that we have noticed. And we may end by observing how, even in the fevered action of *'Tis Pity She's a Whore*, Annabella, near her death, comes close to the plain eloquence that was fully achieved by so many of the characters in *The Broken Heart*. She urges her brother to face the fact that death will almost at once be upon them:

> Brother, dear brother, know what I have been,
> And know that now there's but a dining-time
> 'Twixt us and our confusion: let's not waste
> These precious hours in vain and useless speech.
> Alas, these gay attires were not put on
> But to some end; this sudden solemn feast
> Was not ordain'd to riot in expense;
> I, that have now been chamber'd here alone,
> Barr'd of my guardian or of any else,
> Am not for nothing at an instant freed

To fresh access.   Be not deceiv'd, my brother;
> This banquet is an harbinger of death
> To you and me; resolve yourself it is,
> And be prepar'd to welcome it.
>
> (V.v. 16–29)

Repeatedly here she addresses him as "brother," remembering the relationship that was theirs long before sexual love grew between them. The term "dining-time" also brings her speech close to everyday experience, as she would have Giovanni abandon his wild dreams and think, as she now does, of common duties and demands. Of their coming death she says, in all simplicity, "be prepar'd to welcome it." She longs for an end of revolt. Though she laments death's coming, though her speech includes an "Alas" that the Calantha of *The Broken Heart* would not condescend to utter, she moves toward the paradoxical pride in total submission that is the ultimate stance of Ford's dramatic figures. And she could not do this if her language were in any way inflated, if it had anything of magniloquence. We may remind ourselves again of Calantha's simplicity in her final speeches: "Thus I new-marry him whose wife I am;/Death shall not separate us." By the bareness of this, the juxtaposition of the homely words "whose wife I am" with the proud, direct boast "Death shall not separate us," aided perhaps by the only slightly odd and invigorating coinage "new-marry," we are made ready to accept the dream image of Princess Calantha as one not outside our capacity to entertain. For Ford's men and women at their best are always dream images, emblems of an exalted submission, products of a fancy at its most chaste and noble.

Tragedy, by its nature, is paradoxical. It induces wonder along with terror; it may urge on us a sense of human greatness while insisting also on human littleness, weakness, absurdity; it asserts our kinship with characters who are simultaneously presented as exceptional; it uses the strange event as an image of a universal human situation. Some of these paradoxes exist in Ford's writing, but there we find too a combination of eloquence with the notion of silence as an ideal. We move in his plays through an action frequently violent to a condition of stillness that seems always to have been its goal. And as the characters work their way to this point, they speak of common things, they use our everyday words, but with an economy and control and dignity.

---

[11]For a close modern analogue, we may note the will of Celestino Marcilla in Henry de Montherlant's *Chaos and Night*, trans. Terrence Kilmartin (1966), pp. 103–104.

SELECTED BIBLIOGRAPHY

I. BIBLIOGRAPHY. W. W. Greg, *A Bibliography of the English Printed Drama to the Restoration*, 4 vols. (London, 1939–1959); S. A. Tannenbaum, *Ford: A Concise Bibliography* (New York, 1941).

II. COLLECTED WORKS. H. Weber, ed., *The Dramatic Works*, 2 vols. (Edinburgh, 1811); W. Gifford, ed., *The Dramatic Works*, 2 vols. (London, 1827), revised eds. by A. Dyce, 3 vols. (London, 1869) and A. H. Bullen, 3 vols. (London, 1895); H. Coleridge, ed., *The Dramatic Works of Massinger and Ford* (London, 1839; repr. 1840, 1848, 1851); H. Ellis, ed., *John Ford* (London, 1888), contains *The Lover's Melancholy*, *'Tis Pity*, *The Broken Heart*, *Love's Sacrifice*, *Perkin Warbeck*; W. Bang and H. de Vocht, eds., *John Ford's Dramatic Works*, 2 vols. (Louvain, 1908–1927), a type-facsimile reprint.

III. SEPARATE WORKS. *Fames Memoriall, or the Earle of Devonshire Deceased* (London, 1606; repr. 1810); *Honour Triumphant, or the Peeres Challenge* (London, 1606; repr. 1843); *Christe's Bloodie Sweat* (London, 1613; repr. 1616), good evidence for accepting Ford's authorship; *The Golden Meane* (London, 1613; repr. 1614, 1638), good evidence for accepting Ford's authorship; *A Line of Life* (London, 1620; repr. 1843); *The Lover's Melancholy* (London, 1629), licensed by the master of the Revels in 1628; *'Tis Pity She's a Whore* (London, 1633), in S.P. Sherman, ed., (Boston, 1915), A. K. McIlwraith, ed., *Five Stuart Tragedies* (London, 1953), N. W. Bawcutt, ed. (London, 1966), and B. Morris, ed. (London, 1968); *Love's Sacrifice* (London, 1633); *The Broken Heart* (London, 1633), in O. Smeaton, ed. (London, 1906), S. P. Sherman, ed. (Boston, 1915), B. Morris, ed. (London, 1965), and D. K. Anderson, Jr., ed. (London, 1968); *The Chronicle Historie of Perkin Warbeck. A Strange Truth* (London, 1634), in M. C. Struble, ed. (Seattle, 1926), D. K. Anderson, Jr., ed. (London, 1965), and P. Ure, ed. (London, 1968), with an outstanding intro.; *The Fancies, Chaste and Noble* (London, 1638); *The Ladies Triall* (London, 1639), licensed by the master of the Revels in 1638; *The Queen; or, The Excellency of Her Sex* (London, 1653), in type-facsimile ed. by W. Bang (Louvain, 1906), who attributes this to Ford on stylistic grounds; *The Sun's Darling. A Moral Masque* (London, 1656), published as the work of Dekker and Ford, licensed by the master of the Revels in 1624; *The Witch of Edmonton. A Known True Story* (London, 1658), published as the work of Rowley, Dekker, and Ford, acted in 1621.

Note: Ford's hand has been commonly seen in *The Spanish Gipsy*, acted 1623, and published as the work of Middleton and Rowley (London, 1661), and less certainly seen in *The Welsh Ambassador* (London, 1620) and in several plays in the Beaumont and Fletcher folios. Seventeenth-century references give Ford as sole or part author of the following lost plays: *An Ill Beginning Has a Good End, and a Bad Beginning May Have a Good End*, probably acted 1612–1613; *The Fairy Knight*, licensed in 1624 (Ford and Dekker); *A Late Murder of the Son Upon the Mother, or Keep the Widow Waking*, licensed in 1624 (Ford, Webster, Dekker, and Rowley); *The Bristow Merchant*, licensed in 1624 (Ford and Dekker); *Beauty in a Trance*, acted 1630; *The Royal Combat*. It has been argued by Alfred Harbage in *Modern Language Review* (July 1940) that *The Great Favourite, or the Duke of Lerma*, published as the work of Sir Robert Howard in 1668, is an adaptation of a lost play by Ford. Ford was also the author of various commendatory and other occasional verses.

IV. SOME CRITICAL AND BIOGRAPHICAL STUDIES. C. Lamb, *Specimens of the English Dramatic Poets* (London, 1808); W. Hazlitt, *Lectures Chiefly on the Dramatic Literature of the Age of Elizabeth* (London, 1820); A. C. Swinburne, *Essays and Studies* (London, 1888), contains an essay on Ford; H. Ellis, ed., *John Ford* (London, 1888), contains a critical intro.; H. Sykes, *Sidelights on Elizabethan Drama* (London, 1924); T. S. Eliot, *Selected Essays* (London, 1932), contains an essay on Ford repr. in *Elizabethan Essays* (London, 1934); M. C. Bradbrook, *Themes and Conventions of Elizabethan Tragedy* (Cambridge, 1935), the discussion in ch. 10 represents the shrewdest Ford criticism of the preponderantly unsympathetic kind; M. J. Sargeaunt, *John Ford* (Oxford, 1935), one of the most important contributions to Ford criticism, also valuable for its discussion of the nondramatic writings; U. M. Ellis-Fermor, *The Jacobean Drama* (London 1936), among the best of the favorable appreciations of the plays; C. J. Sisson, *Lost Plays of Shakespeare's Age* (Cambridge, 1936); T. Spencer, *Death and Elizabethan Tragedy* (Cambridge, Mass., 1936); S. B. Ewing, *Burtonian Melancholy in the Plays of John Ford* (Princeton, 1940); G. F. Sensabaugh, *The Tragic Muse of John Ford* (Palo Alto, Calif., 1944), argues for the importance of the "Platonic Love" cult in Ford's plays, and stresses the "modern" note in them; F. P. Wilson, *Elizabethan and Jacobean* (London, 1945); M. Praz, *Il dramma elisabettiano* (Rome, 1946); J. Wilcox, "On Reading John Ford," *Shakespeare Association Bulletin*, 21 (London, 1946); P. Ure, "Cult and Initiates in Ford's *Love's Sacrifice*," *Modern Language Quarterly*, 11, (1951); L. Babb, *The Elizabethan Malady: A Study of Melancholia* (East Lansing, Mich., 1951); R. Davril, *Le Drame de John Ford* (Paris, 1954), the fullest treatment the dramatist has received, done with wide learning, sympathy, and no narrow thesis; H. J. Oliver, *The Problem of John Ford* (Melbourne, 1955); G. E. Bentley, *The Jacobean and Caroline Stage*, 7 vols. (Oxford, 1941–1968), for Ford see vol. III (1956); C. Leech, *John Ford and the Drama of His Time* (London, 1957); R. Ornstein, *The Moral Vision of Jacobean Tragedy*, (Madison, Wis., 1960); G. H. Blaney,

"Convention, Plot and Structure in *The Broken Heart*," *Modern Philology*, 56 (1958); C. Hoy, "Ignorance in Knowledge: Marlowe's Faustus and Ford's Giovanni," *Modern Philology*, 57 (1960); R. J. Kaufmann, "Ford's Tragic Perspective," *Texas Studies in Literature and Language* (1960); R. Ornstein, *The Moral Vision of Jacobean Tragedy* (Madison, Wis., 1960); I. Ribner, *The Quest for Moral Order* (London, 1962); T. B. Tomlinson, *A Study of Elizabethan and Jacobean Tragedy* (Cambridge, 1964); R. B. Heilman, *Tragedy and Melodrama: Versions of Experience*, (Seattle, Wash.—London, 1968); M. Stavig, *John Ford and the Traditional Moral Order* (Madison, Wis., 1968), aims at presenting Ford as an orthodox man of his time.

ROBERT HERRICK

(1591-1674)

John Press

I

HERRICK'S reputation, which fluctuated considerably even in his lifetime, has enjoyed mixed fortune since his death. In 1625 Richard James, in "The Muses Dirge" (on the death of James I), ranked Herrick with Drayton and Ben Jonson, yet the publication of his collected poems in 1648, Herrick then being fifty-seven years old, aroused little interest at a time when the vogue was for metaphysical verse. This decline in his fame lasted until the early nineteenth century, but, in 1810, John Nott edited the first volume to be devoted to Herrick's poetry since 1648. Nott, like other contemporary critics, was troubled by the coarseness of some of the poems and, as late as 1891, the publishers who printed *The Hesperides and Noble Numbers* (Muses' Library edition) followed the example of Byron's learned men confronted with the grosser parts of the classical poets:

> They only add them all in an appendix,
> Which saves, in fact, the trouble of an index.[1]

Herrick's popularity increased throughout the nineteenth century, rising to its peak when, in *Studies in Prose and Poetry* (1894), Swinburne hailed him, with characteristic extravagance, as "the greatest song-writer—as surely as Shakespeare is the greatest dramatist—ever born of English race." *The Oxford Book of English Verse* (1900) allots twenty-one pages to Herrick, thereby placing him on a level with Keats and with Shelley, who receive twenty-four and twenty-one pages respectively, while Blake gets only nine pages and Donne is dismissed with a mere seven.

The climate of opinion has altered in the past seventy years, and in *The Pelican History of English Literature*, which represents fairly accurately the

[1]*Don Juan*, I. xliv.

academic taste of the 1950's and 1960's, Herrick is thought to merit no more than a few unenthusiastic sentences. J. B. Broadbent is even harsher in his judgment: he calls Herrick a "specialist in decadent Spenserianism" and refers to the "snuggling infantilism" of his poems, which he describes as being "crammed with fetichistic superficies." Such a verdict is no more balanced than Swinburne's rhapsodic eulogy; and to wave Herrick aside as the author of a few hackneyed poems about rosebuds, daffodils, and young girls argues either an ignorance of his verse or an indifference to the art of poetry. We should not overlook the robust elements in his work; the complexity of attitude in which pagan hedonism is modified by Christian humanism; the unifying power of his art, which enables him to celebrate the world of labor and of pleasure, the annual cycle of decay and renewal, the richness and vigor of human life played out beneath the shadow of death. The brief survey of his life and of his verse that follows is designed to show the variety, subtlety, and accomplishment of his finest poems, and to suggest that he deserves more respect than is commonly accorded him nowadays.

II

ROBERT HERRICK, the son of Nicholas Herrick, who had married Juliana Stone, was baptized on 24 August 1591. His father died in 1592 after a fall from a window of his house in Goldsmith's Row, London. Although suicide was suspected, which would have entailed the forfeiture of the dead man's property to the Crown, the bishop of Bristol, as high almoner, charitably granted the estate to Nicholas' widow and six children as provided in the will. Since Juliana renounced the third part of the inheritance bequeathed to her, the children inherited just over £800 apiece. We do not know for

102

certain where Robert passed his infancy or where he went to school, but we find that in 1607 he was apprenticed to his uncle, Sir William Herrick, a prosperous goldsmith. In 1613 he entered St. John's College, Cambridge, migrating to Trinity Hall, from which he graduated in 1617.

We know almost nothing about his life between then and 1629, when he was appointed to the living of Dean Prior in Devonshire. He took holy orders in 1623, accompanied the duke of Buckingham on his expedition to the Isle of Rhé in 1627 as his chaplain and, presumably, spent much of his time in London, where he acquired some influential patrons, mingled with literary friends in taverns, became acquainted with the musicians William Lawes and Henry Lawes, and won a reputation as a fashionable poet, although his poems circulated only in manuscript. Among the manuscripts collected by Sir Thomas Phillipps (1792–1872), and sold at Sotheby's on 29 June 1965, was the *Commonplace Book of Robert Herrick*, which contained twelve pages of verse in the poet's hand; verbatim reports of the divorce case that dissolved Frances Howard's marriage to the earl of Essex, thus permitting her to marry the earl of Somerset; and a number of poems about the divorce case, the remarriage of Frances Howard, and the trial of herself and her new husband, in 1616, for the murder by poisoning of Sir Thomas Overbury (the accused were found guilty and condemned to death, but pardoned by James I). It has been conjectured that some of the more scurrilous poems about Lady Howard were the work of the young Robert Herrick.

Some of Herrick's poems, notably "To Deanbourn" and "His Returne to London," suggest that he was often bored and wretched in Devonshire, which he elsewhere terms "dull" and "loathed." He was remembered in the village of Dean Prior long after his death, as Barron Field discovered when he paid a visit there in 1809. He met in the village an old woman in her ninety-ninth year, named Dorothy King, who repeated five of Herrick's *Noble Numbers*, which she had learned from her mother. The mother had served Herrick's successor at the vicarage and had passed on to her daughter various anecdotes about Herrick. He had, so Dorothy King reported, kept a tame pig, which he taught to drink from a tankard; and he once threw his sermon at his inattentive congregation.

In or around 1640 Herrick seems to have been lodging in London, since a private note by Archbishop Laud's secretary (supposedly written in 1640) alleges that he has come to live in Westminster without leave of absence from Devonshire, and that he has fathered the illegitimate child of Thomasine Parsons, daughter of John Parsons, organist and master of the choristers at Westminster Abbey in the reign of James I. There is no evidence to prove whether this charge was justified, nor can we tell whether his erotic poems reflect his own sexual experience. Despite the numerous mistresses whom he celebrates in his verse, his assertion at the close of *Hesperides* (1648) may have been true:

> To his Book's end this last line he'd have plac't,
> *Jocund his Muse was; but his Life was chast.*

Herrick's long residence in Devonshire was broken in 1647, when he was expelled for refusing to subscribe to the Solemn League and Covenant. After the Restoration of King Charles II in 1660 he returned to his vicarage, where he remained until his death in 1674. The only poem that he is known to have written after 1648 is the elegy on Lord Hastings (1649), although a tradition dating back to 1701 attributes to him the epitaph on the tomb of Sir Edward Giles and his wife in Dean Prior Church, said to have been composed when Herrick was "very Aged." Four years after Herrick's death his faithful maidservant, Prewdence Baldwin, was buried at Dean Prior. More than three decades earlier, her master had paid her a beautiful and tender tribute:

> These *Summer-Birds* did with thy Master stay
> The times of warmth; but then they flew away;
> Leaving their Poet (being now grown old)
> Expos'd to all the comming Winters cold.
> But thou *kind Prew* did'st with my Fates abide,
> As well the Winters, as the Summers Tide:
> For which thy Love, live with thy Master here,
> Not two, but all the seasons of the yeare.[2]

III

MANY modern critics find Herrick uncongenial, if only because he gives them so little opportunity to show their paces. We can find in him no daring

---

[2]Although Prewdence Baldwin lived until 1678, Herrick included in *Hesperides* an epitaph on her that runs: "In this little Urne is laid/*Prewdence Baldwin* (once my maid)/From whose happy spark here let/Spring the purple Violet."

strokes of metaphysical wit to analyze at length; no ingenious paradoxes and dark ambiguities demanding to be unraveled and elucidated; no borrowings from books of Emblems, no debts to recondite neo-Platonic treatises, which the learned commentator can trace back to their hidden sources. Moreover, we must acknowledge that, compared with, say, Donne, Crashaw, Herbert, Vaughan, and Marvell, he is deficient in deep religious feeling, emotional intensity, intellectual power, high moral seriousness, and civilized poise. We should also recognize the fact that many of the poems that fill nearly 450 pages in the handsome Oxford edition of his poetical works are trivial and insipid. Even so, there remains a substantial body of verse that, for cunning artistry and musical delight, is barely surpassed by any other poetry of his time.

Herrick is offensive to modern taste for two main reasons, distinct from each other and yet allied: the coarseness of some of his epigrams and the nature of certain of his love poems. There are indeed passages in many eminent English writers that surpass anything written by Herrick in their frankness and indecency, but even the most obscene passages in Chaucer, Shakespeare, Donne, Dryden, Swift, Pope, and Byron contribute something to the whole design of the work in which they occur. Herrick frequently contrives to be pointless and dull as well as dirty. It is possible that he included grubby little poems in *Hesperides* to counterbalance the excessive sweetness and prettiness that characterize so many of his verses; or he may have published them to display his unruffled acceptance of life as he had found it among the rude and churlish savages of Devonshire.

Far more disconcerting and significant than the occasional vulgarity of his epigrams is Herrick's attitude to physical love. The daring licentiousness of Donne and the insolent sensuality of Carew may offend strict moralists, but most of us accept without fuss their erotic poems because of the passion and the intensity that inform them. Herrick, on the contrary, is faintly unpleasant because his sensuality is lukewarm and adulterated with a self-conscious roguishness. He is one of those who, in Meredith's phrase, "fiddle harmonics on the strings of sensualism"; and when we are surfeited with poems about petticoats or about kissing paps and insteps, we may feel tempted to apply to the girls and mistresses who flit through the pages of *Hesperides* the judgment passed by Millet on Boucher's nudes:

that they were not naked women but little things undressed.

Although we should not blind ourselves to the presence of this prurient quality in Herrick's verse, we should try to understand its nature and to see it in its true perspective. Even the fascinated attention that he devotes to the study of women's clothes is not invariably a sign of a slightly perverse eroticism: sometimes he indulges in harmless fancies about contrived negligence in clothes ("Delight in Disorder"); occasionally his meditations on the psychology of dress are a mark of his interest in aesthetic theory and a pointer to the nature of his temperamental endowment.

"The Lilly in a Christal," for example, treats a theme that had attracted Martial, Montaigne, and Ben Jonson. It is, in part, a discourse on variety and contrast, a problem much discussed in seventeenth-century aesthetics, and Herrick argues that beautiful objects become still lovelier if their tinctures are set off by contrasting shades and textures:

> Thus Lillie, Rose, Grape, Cherry, Creame,
> And Straw-berry do stir
> More love, when they transfer
> A weak, a soft, a broken beame;
> Then if they sho'd discover
> At full their proper excellence;
> Without some Scean cast over,
> To juggle with the sense.

Herrick develops his argument for six stanzas, coolly, precisely, and delicately, in the manner of a metaphysical poet; then, in a final stanza, suddenly changing his tone, he speaks with an easy freedom and directness, urging the girl whom he is addressing in the poem to draw the appropriate lesson from his analogies:

> So though y'are white as Swan, or Snow,
> And have the power to move
> A world of men to love:
> Yet, when your Lawns & Silks shal flow;
> And that white cloud divide
> Into a doubtful Twi-light; then,
> Then will your hidden Pride
> Raise greater fires in men.

It would be hypocrisy to pretend that Herrick is examining in a detached way an interesting aesthetic problem, when he is so clearly displaying a sensuality that we may term either sophisticated or unpleasant, and a knowledge of erotic psychology that is both cynical and acute. This is not the place to discuss the ways in which, as a general rule, aesthetic sensibility is linked with sexual feeling: our particular concern is with Herrick, whose sensuality is diffused over the whole range of his physical experiences and is not concentrated upon the flesh of women. Indeed, throughout his verse, we are conscious of a sensuality that is at once powerful, all-pervasive, discriminating, and exact. We are constantly encountering his love of precious stones, his delight in glittering surfaces and in varying textures, his strong sense of smell, his lively joy in the pleasures offered by the visible world to man's five senses. Herrick is a lesser poet than Marvell and Tennyson, not to mention Shakespeare, Pope, and Keats, but he resembles these five masters in his invariable responsiveness to the sensuous quality of things, his eagerness to receive and to absorb into himself all kinds of physical sensations.

It is clear that Herrick derives intense satisfaction from contemplating whiteness, softness, sweetness, and smoothness, qualities on which he often dwells with a luxurious, lingering appreciation. His brilliant deployment of these motifs can best be studied in "A Nuptiall Song, or Epithalamie, on Sir Clipseby Crew and his Lady," one of his longest, richest, and most finely sustained pieces. In the twelfth stanza, for example, without describing the charms of the bride or referring in any detail to the act of love, he makes almost palpable the voluptuous quality of the marriage bed and thus, by implication, suggests the delicious nature of the amorous play to be enjoyed there by "the youthful Bridegroom, and the fragrant Bride":

> And to your more bewitching, see, the proud
> Plumpe Bed beare up, and swelling like a cloud
>   Tempting the too too modest; can
>   Ye see it brusle like a Swan,
>   And you be cold
> To meet it, when it woo's and seemes to fold
>   The Armies to hugge you? throw, throw
> Your selves into the mighty over-flow
>   Of that white Pride, and Drowne
>   The night, with you, in floods of Downe.

He uses a similar device in "To Electra":

> More white then whitest Lillies far,
> Or Snow, or whitest Swans you are:

> More white then are the whitest Creames,
> Or Moone-light tinselling the streames:
> More white then *Pearls*, or *Juno's* thigh;
> Or *Pelops* Arme of *Yvorie*.
> True, I confesse; such Whites are these
> May me delight, not fully please:
> Till, like *Ixion's* Cloud you be
> White, warme, and soft to lye with me.

It is typical of Herrick, as Aldous Huxley has said, that he should turn Juno's cloud, which is normally employed as a symbol of deprivation and of punishment, into a symbol of exquisite pleasure. The popular legend that Herrick was a purveyor of well-turned commonplaces about pretty young girls and time passing ignores the playful, civilized wit and subtlety of observation that again and again lurk almost unobserved in the lightest and gayest of his lyrics.

Moreover, Herrick can command at times a gentleness, a delicacy, and a gravity in his approach to women. A second poem "To Electra," far from celebrating her physical charms, is in part a graceful compliment to her and in part an avowal of the poet's unworthiness to draw near her, still less to touch her:

> I dare not ask a kisse;
>   I dare not beg a smile;
> Lest having that, or this,
>   I might grow proud the while.

> No, no, the utmost share
>   Of my desire, shall be
> Onely to kisse that Aire,
>   That lately kissed thee.

His famous declaration, "To Anthea, who may command him any thing" epitomizes the Cavalier ideal of love between the sexes at its noblest and firmest, untainted by any false, cloying extravagance, free of licentious bravado, and unmarred by erotic innuendo:

> Bid me to live, and I will live
>   Thy Protestant to be:
> Or bid me love, and I will give
>   A loving heart to thee.

> A heart as soft, a heart as kind,
>   A heart as sound and free,
> As in the whole world thou canst find,
>   That heart Ile give to thee.

Bid that heart stay, and it will stay,
   To honour thy Decree:
Or bid it languish quite away,
   And't shall doe so for thee.

Bid me to weep, and I will weep,
   While I have eyes to see:
And having none, yet I will keep
   A heart to weep for thee.

Bid me despaire, and Ile despaire,
   Under that *Cypresse* tree:
Or bid me die, and I will dare
   E'en Death, to die for thee.

Thou art my life, my love, my heart,
   The very eyes of me:
And hast command of every part,
   To live and die for thee.

It is worth observing that even in this poem, which seems to ring with the accents of personal conviction, Herrick may well be drawing upon his recollection of a passage from Robert Burton's *Anatomy of Melancholy,* under the heading "Symptoms of Love." As we shall see later in this essay, it is characteristic of his genius that he should weave into his verse reminiscences and echoes of older writers.

Having acknowledged that Herrick's love poetry is not exclusively physical and erotic, we may nevertheless conclude this section by glancing at two further examples of the organic sensibility that lends his verse such vitality and distinction. Just as in "A Nuptiall Song" he avoids all detailed physical description of the bride, so in "Upon Julia's Unlacing Herself" he conveys the intensity of sexual desire by evoking the sense of smell. The reference to the gods serves a double purpose, both endowing the figure of Julia with a divine mystery and grace and hinting that in complete sensual bliss there resides an element of the supernatural:

Tell, if thou canst, (and truly) whence doth come
This *Camphire, Storax, Spiknard, Galbanum*:
These *Musks*, these *Ambers*, and those other smells
(Sweet as the *Vestrie of the Oracles.*)
Ile tell thee; while my *Julia* did unlace
Her silken bodies, but a breathing space:
The passive Aire such odour then assum'd,
As when to *Jove* Great *Juno* goes perfum'd.
Whose pure-Immortall body doth transmit
A scent, that fills both Heaven and Earth with it.

A tiny poem called "The Amber Bead," though it is in quite a different vein, offers yet another proof of Herrick's power to evoke a world of sensuous vitality and harmony in a small compass:

I saw a Flie within a Beade
Of Amber cleanly buried:
The Urne was little, but the room
More rich then *Cleopatra's* Tombe.

IV

So far we have examined only one aspect of Herrick's verse, the warm, vibrant sensuality that colors and molds poem after poem in *Hesperides.* We must now glance at an equally significant facet—the consummate technical skill that he brings to the practice of his art. He is not only responsive to the colors, shapes, smells, sounds, tastes, and textures of the world, but acutely sensitive also to the properties and potentialities of language: the weight of words; the sensuous values of consonants and vowels; the melodic flow of verse; the varied shapes of metrical patterns; the way in which verbal rhythms can be adjusted to correspond with a shift of emotional mood; the means whereby a poem's tone can be made lighter or darker; the extent to which a poem's texture can change in sympathy with the unfolding of its logical and emotional argument; the orchestral resources of our tongue, which draws upon Anglo-Saxon and Romance elements. A knowledge of these and kindred factors must be inborn in a poet or acquired by constant labor; and few verse writers have shown more accomplishment than Herrick in the management of those devices that all need to master if their poems are to survive the whirligig of fashion and the collapse of political systems.

His poetic technique is, on the surface, lucid and straightforward, exhibiting little of the daring ingenuity and complexity so much prized by the metaphysicals, or of the learned artistry that distinguishes Milton's early work. In his diction an easy grace and fluency mingle with a homely strength, although in his more formal poems his vocabulary tends to be richer and more elaborate than in his personal lyrics. One of his favorite devices is to introduce a Latinism quite unexpectedly into a passage largely made up of common everyday words, thereby varying the simplicity of the language and breaking the gentle flow of mono-syllables by a heavy polysyllable. In "To Dianeme," the lazy sensuality of the verse is lent a certain weight and solemnity by the dignity of *Principalities* and by the wholly unforeseen use of the word *Assention*:

> Shew me thy feet; shew me thy legs, thy thighes;
> Shew me Those *Fleshie Principalities*;
> Shew me that Hill (where smiling Love doth sit)
> Having a living Fountain under it.
> Shew me thy waste; Then let me there withall,
> By the *Assention* of thy Lawn, see All.

We meet a similar device in "Upon Julia's Fall," where Herrick conveys the intense whiteness and smoothness of Julia's legs by talking of their sincerity, reminding us that the root meaning of the Latin word "sincerus" is "pure" or "unmixed." It is typical of Herrick that he should indulge in this stroke of pedantic wit in a faintly low and rustic context:

> *Julia* was careless, and withall,
> She rather took, then got a fall:
> The wanton *Ambler* chanc'd to see
> Part of her leggs sinceritie.

Again, in one of his best-known pieces, "Upon Julia's Clothes," Herrick makes the poem turn upon two Latinate words that are, at the same time, splendidly resonant and remarkably precise in their sensuous delineation:

> When as in silks my *Julia* goes,
> Then, then (me thinks) how sweetly flowes
> That liquefaction of her clothes.
>
> Next, when I cast mine eyes and see
> That brave Vibration each way free;
> O how that glittering taketh me!

Herrick's technical prowess reveals itself in tiny strokes of artistry rather than in any virtuosity of language, metrical invention, or mastery of complex imagery. It is above all in the handling of texture, the control of vowel and consonant, the harmony of his numbers, the felicity of phrase, and the sense of design that Herrick excels. "Upon Julia's Voice" is an instance of his power to convey the quality of sensuous experience by using imagery derived from one sense to illustrate the operation of another—touch, taste, and sight are all employed to evoke our responsiveness to sound:

> So smooth, so sweet, so silv'ry is thy voice,
> As, could they hear, the Damn'd would make no noise,
> But listen to thee (walking in thy chamber)
> Melting melodious words, to Lutes of Amber.[3]

Moreover, the reference to "the Damn'd" cunningly reinforces the sense imagery by conjuring up the vision of souls in torment enraptured by the supernatural melody of Julia's singing.

In "Lovers How They Come and Part," we find a quality distinct from metaphysical wit, and yet resembling it, in the play of intelligence that strengthens and irradiates the poem. Herrick has solved the problem of how to portray the voluptuous pleasure that we take in natural objects, without declining into mawkishness or prettiness; and the complementary problem of how to convey the delicate nuances of relationships between lovers without becoming dryly analytical. The poem is a minor triumph of ordered sensibility and of technical accomplishment:

> A *Gyges* Ring they beare about them still,
> To be, and not seen when and where they will,
> They tread on clouds, and though they sometimes fall,
> They fall like dew, but make no noise at all.
> So silently they one to th'other come,
> As colours steale into the Peare or Plum,
> And Aire-like, leave no pression to be seen
> Where e're they met, or parting place has been.

Every reader can find for himself dozens of examples of Herrick's quality as a miniaturist. Here is a little-known poem, only four lines long, which tells us much about Herrick's delighted acceptance of chance pleasures, his keen observation of the world, and his concern for poetic form:

> So Good-luck came, and on my roofe did light,
> Like noyse-lesse Snow; or as the dew of night:
> Not all at once, but gently, as the trees
> Are, by the Sun-beams, tickel'd by degrees.
> *(The Comming of Good Luck)*

V

For all its deceptive simplicity on the surface, Herrick's verse is more complex and learned than has sometimes been allowed. Thanks to the labors of

---

[3]The reference is probably to lutes inlaid with the resin amber, rather than to lutes made of amber.

scholars over the past eighty or ninety years we can trace many of Herrick's borrowings from the poetry and prose of other writers, ancient and modern, sacred and profane. There has been much debate about which of the Latin authors influenced Herrick most deeply, and to follow the chronological development of his art in detail is impossible, because we can assign an exact date to only fifty or so of his poems. The probabilities are that in his earlier work he draws extensively upon Catullus, Horace, and Ovid, whereas his later poetry, which is more economical and terse, bears the imprint of Martial and of Tacitus. He owes something to the *Elegies* (book 1) of Johannes Secundus (1511–1536), from which he may have derived the name of the heroine, Julia; he may also have studied Jean de Bonnefon (1554–1614), who was much admired by Herrick's revered master, Ben Jonson.

Of all the classical poets, Horace seems to have been the most sympathetic to Herrick, but we need not suppose that he was a profound student of Latin literature. In recent years scholars have shown the extent to which Herrick was an heir to the multifarious inheritance of Renaissance humanism, which embraced pagan and Christian elements in its manifold complexity; and even in the narrow field of literary allusion it seems likely that Herrick owes as much to the compilers of translations from the ancient writers as to a close study of the original texts. It is to Florio's version of Montaigne and to Burton's miscellany *The Anatomy of Melancholy* that we must often look for the source of Herrick's borrowings from Latin authors. Above all, we must remember that, like all good poets, Herrick borrows only those elements that he finds congenial and that even these fragments he transforms, shaping them to his own ends and steeping them in the characteristic flavor and color of his own verse.

Herrick's adaptation of Catullus, *Carmina V*, reveals the nature of his debts to classical poets and the lineaments of his sensibility. The opening lines of "To Anthea" develop a neat set of variations upon the theme "Da mi basia mille," which inspires Herrick to an extravagant rhapsody:

Ah my *Anthea*! Must my heart still break?
(*Love makes me write, what shame forbids to speak.*)
Give me a kisse, and to that kisse a score;
Then to that twenty, adde an hundred more:
A thousand to that hundred: so kisse on,
To make that thousand up a million.

Treble that million, and when that is done,
Let's kisse afresh, as when we first begun.

There is, in the verse of Catullus, another strain, an agonized contemplation of mortality that reverberates through the poem and sets the enjoyment of erotic pleasure in its true perspective:

Soles occidere et redire possunt:
Nobis cum semel occidit brevis lux
Nox est perpetua una dormienda.[4]

Herrick chooses to ignore this note of intense anguish, preferring to dwell upon the delicious prospect of meeting Anthea in bed:

But yet, though Love likes well such Scenes as these,
There is an Act that will more fully please:
Kissing and glancing, soothing, all make way
But to the acting of this private Play:
Name it I would; but being blushing red,
The rest Ile speak, when we meet both in bed.

This poem indeed confirms our suspicions that there is a coarse fiber in Herrick and that his element is earth rather than fire.

Two of Herrick's best-known poems resound with echoes from antiquity. "To the Virgins, to Make Much of Time" recapitulates the old advice "Carpe diem," which is so commonplace that we cannot hope to single out the passages that were in Herrick's mind when he wrote this poem. It may well be that he was shaping into verse a reflection from *The Anatomy of Melancholy* about the need for fathers to arrange their daughters' marriages in due time:

For if they tarry longer to say truth, they are past date, and no body will respect them. . . . A Virgin, as the Poet holds, . . . is like a flower, a Rose withered on a sudden . . . . Let them take time then while they may, make advantage of youth. . . . Let's all love . . . whiles we are in the flower of years, fit for love matters, and while time serves.

There is an obvious similarity between those phrases (reinforced as they are by quotations from Ausonius and Catullus) and Herrick's lines:

[4] "Suns may set and rise again:/But when our brief light is once put out/We must sleep in an unending night."

Gather ye Rose-buds while ye may,
　　Old Time is still a flying:
And this same flower that smiles to day,
　　To morrow will be dying.

The glorious Lamp of Heaven, the Sun,
　　The higher he's a getting;
The sooner will his Race be run,
　　And neerer he's to Setting.

That Age is best, which is the first,
　　When Youth and Blood are warmer;
But being spent, the worse, and worst
　　Times, still succeed the former.

Then be not coy, but use your time;
　　And while ye may, goe marry:
For having lost but once your prime,
　　You may for ever tarry.

One of Herrick's finest achievements is "Corinna's Going a Maying," which is worth quoting in full as an example of his abundant richness and vitality. The first four stanzas describe the celebration of May Day in the country, and require no commentary. It is enough to notice how eagerly he relishes brightness, glittering light, freshness, whiteness, all that is youthful and flowering; we may also observe how uncensoriously he accepts the wanton sportiveness inherent in the May Day customs, which the Puritans later tried to stamp out on the grounds that they encouraged drunken revelry and lasciviousness:

Get up, get up for shame, the Blooming Morne
Upon her wings presents the god unshorne.
　　See how *Aurora* throwes her faire
　　Fresh-quilted colours through the aire:
　　Get up, sweet-Slug-a-bed, and see
　　The Dew bespangling Herbe and Tree.
Each Flower has wept, and bow'd toward the East,
Above an houre since; yet you not drest,
　　Nay! not so much as out of bed?
　　When all the Birds have Mattens said,
　　And sung their thankfull Hymnes: 'tis sin,
　　Nay, profanation to keep in,
When as a thousand Virgins on this day,
Spring, sooner than the Lark, to fetch in May.

Rise; and put on your Foliage, and be seene
To come forth, like the Spring-time, fresh and greene;
　　And sweet as *Flora*. Take no care
　　For Jewels for your Gowne, or Haire:
　　Feare not; the leaves will strew

Gems in abundance upon you:
Besides, the childhood of the Day has kept,
Against you come, some *Orient Pearls* unwept:
　　Come, and receive them while the light
　　Hangs on the Dew-locks of the night:
　　And *Titan* on the Eastern hill
　　Retires himselfe, or else stands still
Till you come forth. Wash, dresse, be briefe in praying:
Few Beads are best, when once we goe a Maying.

Come, my *Corinna*, come; and comming, marke
How each field turns a street; each street a Parke
　　Made green, and trimm'd with trees: see how
　　Devotion gives each House a Bough,
　　Or Branch: Each Porch, each doore, ere this,
　　An Arke a Tabernacle is
Made up of white-thorn neatly enterwove;
As if here were those cooler shades of love.
　　Can such delights be in the street,
　　And open fields, and we not see't?
　　Come, we'll abroad; and let's obay
　　The Proclamation made for May:
And sin no more, as we have done, by staying;
But my *Corinna*, come, let's goe a Maying.

There's not a budding Boy, or Girle, this day,
But is got up, and gone to bring in May.
　　A deale of Youth, ere this, is come
　　Back, and with *White-thorn* laden home.
　　Some have dispatcht their Cakes and Creame,
　　Before that we have left to dreame:
And some have wept, and woo'd, and plighted Troth,
And chose their Priest, ere we can cast off sloth:
　　Many a green-gown has been given;
　　Many a kisse, both odde and even:
　　Many a glance too has been sent
　　From out the eye, Loves Firmament:
Many a jest told of the Keyes betraying
This night, and Locks pickt, yet w'are not a Maying.

It is only in the final stanza that Herrick turns away from his portrayal of rural ceremonies and country matters to a poignant elegy on the transience of life:

Come, let us goe, while we are in our prime;
And take the harmlesse follie of the time.
　　We shall grow old apace, and die
　　Before we know our liberty.
　　Our life is short; and our dayes run
　　As fast away as do's the Sunne:
And as a vapour, or a drop of raine
Once lost, can ne'er be found againe:
　　So when or you or I are made
　　A fable, song, or fleeting shade;

All love, all liking, all delight
Lies drown'd with us in endlesse night.
Then while time serves, and we are but decaying;
Come, my *Corinna*, come, let's goe a Maying.

Here again, it is likely that Herrick owes a debt to Burton's bringing together of many classical echoes into a cunningly devised amalgam:

Our life is short and tedious, and in the death of a man there is no recovery, neither was any man knowne that hath returned from the grave, for we are borne at all adventure, and we shall bee hereafter as though wee had never beene; for the breath is as smoke in our nostrils, &c. and the spirit vanisheth as the soft aire. Come let us enjoy the pleasures that are present, let us chearfully use the creatures as in youth, let us fill our selves with costly wine and ointments, let not the flower of our life passe by us, let us crowne our selves with rose buds before they are withered, &c. Vivamus mea Lesbia et amemus, &c. Come let us take our fill of love, and pleasure in dalliance, for this is our lot.
Tempora labuntur tacitisq; senescimus annis.[5]

Burton's meditations possess a stately dignity, but Herrick's verse moves with an exquisite grace and perfection of melody that far surpass the measured tread of Burton's prose. In these lines we may recognize how poetry, catching up and transfiguring a statement in prose, may endow it with an emotional intensity and a rhythmical energy that raise it to a higher power.

In the first poem of *Hesperides*, entitled "The Argument of His Book," Herrick indicates the range of his poetic themes:

I sing of *Brooks*, of *Blossomes*, *Birds*, and *Bowers*:
Of *April*, *May*, of *June*, and *July*-Flowers.
I sing of *May-poles*, *Hock-carts*, *Wassails*, *Wakes*,
Of *Bride-grooms*, *Brides*, and of their *Bridall-cakes*.
I write of *Youth*, of *Love*, and have Accesse
By these, to sing of cleanly-*Wantonnesse*.
I sing of *Dewes*, of *Raines*, and piece by piece
Of *Balme*, of *Oyle*, of *Spice*, and *Amber-Greece*.
I sing of *Times trans-shifting*; and I write
How *Roses* first came *Red*, and *Lillies White*.
I write of *Groves*, of *Twilights*, and I sing
The Court of *Mab*, and of the *Fairie-King*.
I write of *Hell*; I sing (and ever shall)
Of *Heaven*, and hope to have it after all.

[5]"Time slips by; and we grow old with the silent years" (Ovid, *Fasti*, book 6, 771).

We have already glanced at his treatment of certain themes, and we must now attempt a brief survey of his work as a whole.

Like Ben Jonson, Herrick admires the aristocratic ideal, symbolized by the great country house—a center of high civilization, a home of virtue, ceremonious order, learning, and hospitality. Although Herrick lacks Jonson's intellectual force, massive integrity of mind, deep seriousness, and fine moral perceptiveness, he too feels the need for justice in the social order and in "A Panegerick to Sir Lewis Pemberton" he explicitly commends Sir Lewis for his lack of greed and harshness as a landlord:

Safe stand thy Walls, and Thee, and so both will,
Since neithers height was rais'd by th'ill
Of others; since no Stud, no Stone, no Piece
Was rear'd up by the Poore-mans fleece:
No Widowes Tenement was rackt to guild
Or fret thy Seeling, or to build
A *Sweating-Closset*, to annoint the silke-
soft-skin, or bath in *Asses milke*.

This type of reflection is rare in Herrick, whose response to the world is immediate and intuitive rather than deeply considered and analytical. He loves, as we have seen, the glittering beauty of the countryside and, in particular, the teeming fertility of the earth whose flowers and fruits are no less delicious and savory than the maidens who pluck them. In "The Apron of Flowers" the girl and the blossoms are so closely intertwined that they have almost become one flesh:

To gather Flowers *Sappha* went,
And homeward she did bring
Within her Lawnie Continent,
The treasure of the Spring.

She smiling blusht, and blushing smil'd,
And sweetly blushing thus,
She lookt as she'd been got with child
By young *Favonius*.

Her Apron gave (as she did passe)
An Odor more divine,
More pleasing too, then ever was
The lap of *Proserpine*.

Herrick is the poet of fruition as well as of burgeoning. One of his most characteristic poems, "The Hock-Cart, or Harvest Home," addressed to

"The Right Honourable Mildmay, Earle of Westmorland," celebrates the joys of feasting and merrymaking in traditional style after a good harvest:

> Come Sons of Summer, by whose toile,
> We are the Lords of Wine and Oile:
> By whose tough labours, and rough hands,
> We rip up first, then reap our lands.
> Crown'd with the eares of corne, now come,
> And, to the Pipe, sing Harvest home.

Herrick's love of life reveals itself in his praise of bounty, of hospitality, in his wish that all creatures and fruits of the earth should multiply. His vigor and high spirits overflow into his poem "Happinesse to Hospitalitie, or a Hearty Wish to Good House-keeping," where he desires abundance in all things. The poem ends in a burst of exuberant frankness tinged with an exulting gaiety and wit:

> Last, may the Bride and Bridegroom be
> Untoucht by cold *sterility*;
> But in their springing blood so play,
> As that in *Lusters* few they may,
> By laughing too, and lying downe,
> People a *City* or a *Towne*.

Although Herrick prefers to dwell upon the pleasant things of life, he is sufficiently honest and robust to acknowledge that even in the placid English countryside the forces of darkness and destruction lurk hidden and menacing in the shadows. He can assure his mistress, in "The Night-piece to Julia," that she may come to him safely:

> Her Eyes the Glow-worme lend thee,
> The Shooting Starres attend thee;
>   And the Elves also,
>   Whose little eyes glow,
> Like the sparks of fire, befriend thee.
>   . . .
> Let not the darke thee cumber;
> What though the Moon do's slumber?
>   The Starres of the night
>   Will lend thee their light,
> Like Tapers cleare without number.

Yet, in "The Hag," he conjures up an image of terror and of fear, the hag who rides at midnight:

> A Thorn or a Burr
> She takes for a Spurre:

> With a lash of a Bramble she rides now,
>   Through Brakes and through Bryars,
>   O're Ditches, and Mires,
> She followes the Spirit that guides now.

> No Beast, for his food,
> Dares now range the wood;
> But husht in his laire he lies lurking:
>   While mischiefs, by these,
>   On Land and on Seas,
> At noone of Night are a working.[6]

Nor does Herrick retreat from the world into artificial paradises. His poems about elves and fairies are means by which he comes to terms with the folk tales, legends, and superstitions of the country people among whom he worked and in whose daily life there still lingered relics of pagan beliefs and observances of pagan customs. Even in his recourse to sack he is not seeking a means of escape from problems that he is too frail or neurotic to face, but searching for an elixir that will aid him to enjoy the world with greater vigor and intensity. In "The Welcome to Sack," he demands goblets of sack's "gen'rous blood" so that he may live more fiercely:

> Swell up my nerves with spirit; let my blood
> Run through my veines, like to a hasty flood.
> Fill each part full of fire, active to doe
> What thy commanding soule shall put it to.

And in "His Fare-well to Sack," Herrick invokes his beloved wine with fervent eloquence:

> O thou the drink of Gods, and Angels! Wine
> That scatter'st Spirit and Lust; whose purest shine,
> More radiant then the Summers Sun-beams shows;
> Each way illustrious brave . . .
>   . . .
> 'Tis thou, alone, who with thy Mistick Fan,
> Work'st more then Wisdome, Art, or Nature can,
> To rouze the sacred madnesse; and awake
> The frost-bound-blood, and spirits; and to make
> Them frantick with thy raptures, flashing through
> The soule, like lightning, and as active too.

Herrick's joy in the abundance of life does not prevent him from facing steadily the fact of man's mortality, his daily experience as a Christian priest

[6]The meters of these contrasting poems are both to be found in Ben Jonson, in *Gypsies Metamorphos'd* and in *Masque of Queenes* respectively. The phrase "noone of Night" (from *meridies nocti*) was perhaps first used in English by Jonson.

reinforcing his intuitive acceptance of the Horatian truism that the years are bearing us inexorably to the grave. In "To Daffodills," "To Blossoms," and "The Mad Maids Song," the blossoms, the flowers, the fruits, and the dew bring with them a reminder of death. Gently but firmly Herrick contrasts the decaying of flesh with the permanence of a jewel and warns Dianeme to put no trust in her physical charms:

> When as that *Rubie*, which you weare,
> Sunk from the tip of your soft eare,
> Will last to be a precious Stone,
> When all your world of Beautie's gone.
> ("To Dianeme")

When Herrick speaks to the daffodils he is rehearsing the common fate of all living creatures:

> We have short time to stay, as you,
> We have as short a Spring;
> As quick a growth to meet Decay,
> As you, or any thing.
> We die,
> As your hours doe, and drie
> Away,
> Like to the Summers raine;
> Or as the pearles of Mornings dew
> Ne'er to be found againe.
> ("To Daffodills")

It is noteworthy that the *eheu fugaces* theme often evokes in Herrick an unwonted depth of feeling. The long, eloquent poem "His Age, Dedicated to his Peculiar Friend, M. John Wickes," contains a fine adaptation of some famous lines by Horace, and the prospect of death in "An Ode to Master Endymion Porter, Upon his Brothers Death" moves Herrick to a grave autumnal elegy through which the tones of personal grief resound:

> Alas for me! that I have lost
> E'en all almost:
> Sunk is my sight; set is my Sun;
> And all the loome of life undone:
> The staffe, the Elme, the prop, the shelt'ring wall
> Whereon my Vine did crawle,
> Now, now, blowne downe; needs must the old stock fall.[7]

[7]Herrick is probably referring to the death of his brother, William Herrick. The poem that follows "An Ode" is entitled "To his Dying Brother, Master William Herrick."

The constant awareness of our mortality casts its shadow upon the pages of *Hesperides*, yet our abiding impression is of Herrick's resolve to grasp the full richness of life, to revel in the variety of experiences that it offers to those who explore it unhesitatingly. In the face of the frank, intuitive paganism that stamps so much of *Hesperides*, we must now consider the question of Herrick's religious beliefs, and the quality of his spiritual life as he reveals it in *His Noble Numbers*.

VI

WE need not doubt the sincerity of Herrick's belief in Christianity or the devotion with which he discharged his priestly duties. He seems to be speaking the truth in "Mr. Robert Herricke His Farewell unto Poetrie," where he proclaims his resolve to renounce poetry, in obedience to "the God of Nature," or at least to subordinate verse to higher ends:

> Knowe yet (rare soule) when my diviner Muse
> Shall want a Hand-mayde, (as she ofte will use)
> Bee readye, thou In mee, to wayte uppon her
> Thoughe as a servant, yet a Mayde of Honor.

But the inferiority of *His Noble Numbers* to the religious poetry of Donne, Crashaw, Vaughan, Traherne, Milton, and Herbert (and to Herrick's profane verse) is so marked as to call for some explanation. "Julia's Churching, or Purification" may yield a clue. After detailing the ceremonies that she must perform, beginning with the burning of incense, Herrick concludes:

> All Rites well ended, with faire Auspice come
> (As to the breaking of a Bride-Cake) home:
> Where ceremonious *Hymen* shall for thee
> Provide a second *Epithalamie*.
> *She who keeps chastly to her husbands side*
> *Is not for one, but every night his Bride:*
> *And stealing still with love, and feare to Bed,*
> *Brings him not one, but many a Maiden-head.*

Anybody who turns from these verses to that portion of the Book of Common Prayer containing the order of service for The Thanksgiving of Women after Childbirth will be tempted to murmur: "Very pretty, Mr. Herrick, but you must not call it Anglicanism." We shall, indeed, not find in him Donne's passionate apprehension of Christian dogma, Crashaw's fervent devotional mysticism, Milton's exaltation of God's majesty, or Herbert's unfeigned desire to attune himself to God's will. Nor does Herrick ever display the Puritan humility and sense of grace that inform that most touching of Marvell's religious poems, "The Coronet." Herrick is, above all else, a ritualist: he had been raised in a family where pomp and circumstance were accepted as part of daily life (two of his aunts had been lady mayoresses), and he retained to the end the ritualistic view of human existence.

His gorgeous marriage songs are primarily concerned with the ritual of sex; his epitaphs for himself and for others stress the importance of making the correct ritual libations, of performing the due ceremonies—"To Perilla," "To the Reverend Shade of His Religious Father," "To His Lovely Mistresses," "On Himself." In "The Temple" he details the ornaments of Oberon's Chapel with the same minuteness, seriousness, and loving care that a Christian priest should bring to his study of Church furnishings. One of his poems bears the significant title "To Julia, the Flaminica Dialis, or Queen-Priest," and we feel that Herrick himself would have made an admirable priest of a Roman temple or of a Hindu shrine, that he was more fitted to be a devout guardian of holy mysteries than an apostle of Christ.

Herrick's concept of heaven is that we shall fly to "The White Island: or Place of the Blest":

> In that *whiter Island*, where
> Things are evermore sincere;
> Candor here, and lustre there
>   Delighting.

This is simply the Earthly Paradise indefinitely prolonged and rendered a shade more edifying by the apparent absence of wine and sex; even so, the verse is tepid and the vision unconvincing compared with the wonderful pagan sensuality that pulsates in "The Apparition of His Mistresse Calling Him to Elizium":

> Where ev'ry tree a wealthy issue beares
> Of fragrant Apples, blushing Plums, or Peares:
> And all the shrubs, with sparkling spangles, shew
> Like Morning-Sun-shine tinsilling the dew.
> Here in green Meddowes sits eternall May,

> Purfling the Margents, while perpetuall Day
> So double gilds the Aire, as that no night
> Can ever rust th'Enamel of the light.
> Here, naked Younglings, handsome Striplings run
> Their Goales for Virgins kisses; which when done,
> Then unto Dancing forth the learned Round
> Commixt they meet, with endlesse Roses crown'd.
> And here we'l sit on Primrose-banks, and see
> Love's *Chorus* led by *Cupid*; and we'l be
> Two loving followers too unto the Grove,
> Where Poets sing the stories of our love.

"To Julia, the Flaminica Dialis, or Queen-Priest" is yet another proof that for Herrick the due performance of rites constitutes a major part of religion. It is characteristic also of Herrick that he should envisage his mistress as a queen-priest ministering in the temple of love and thereby winning redemption for those who fail to observe the prescribed rituals:

> Thou know'st, my *Julia*, that it is thy turne
> This Mornings Incense to prepare, and burne.
> The Chaplet, and *Inarculum* here be,
> With the white Vestures, all attending Thee.
> This day, the *Queen-Priest*, thou art made t'appease
> Love for our very-many Trespasses.
> One chiefe transgression is among the rest,
> Because with Flowers her Temple was not drest:
> The next, because her Altars did not shine
> With daily Fyers: The last, neglect of Wine:
> For which, her wrath is gone forth to consume
> Us all, unlesse preserv'd by thy Perfume.
> Take then thy Censer; Put in Fire, and thus,
> O *Pious-Priestesse*! make a Peace for us.
> For our neglect, Love did our Death decree,
> That we escape. *Redemption comes by Thee.*

Even when Herrick attempts a Biblical theme or turns to Christian devotion, the pagan cast of his mind reveals itself. "The Dirge of Jephthah's Daughter: Sung by the Virgins" is not so much a Hebrew lamentation for one who has been sacrificed to Jehovah as an elegy for a young Greek or Roman maiden on whom the flowers of the spring are strewn:

> Sleep in thy peace, thy bed of Spice;
> And make this place all Paradise:
> May Sweets grow here! & smoke from hence,
>   Fat Frankincense:
> Let Balme, and Cassia send their scent
> From out thy Maiden-Monument.

It is instructive to compare Donne's "Hymne to God My God, in My Sickness" with Herrick's "His Letanie, to the Holy Spirit." Whereas Donne contemplates the significance of Calvary, the redemption of Man, the Communion of Saints, Herrick can scarcely pass beyond the natural fear of death to which we are all subject. There is in his poem a genuine pathos, tempered by a wry, humorous recognition that doctors cannot save him:

> When the artlesse Doctor sees
> No one hope, but of his Fees,
> And his skill runs on the lees;
> Sweet Spirit comfort me!

There is also a childlike cry, for mercy and for help, to the "Sweet Spirit"; but there is no deep spiritual perception, no profound vision of heaven, no sense of God's terrifying majesty and love.

Herrick's poem on the crucifixion, "Good Friday: Rex Tragicus, or Christ Going to His Crosse," is even feebler and more superficial. Christ is reduced to the level of an actor in a spectacle:

> Thou art that *Roscius*, and that markt-out man,
> That must this day act the Tragedian.

Herrick presents for us a stage performance, a moderately well-composed pageant, disinfected of the agony and bloody sweat. The spectators are mere lay figures whose prime concern is to ensure that the proper burial rites are observed:

> And we (Thy Lovers) while we see Thee keep
> The Lawes of Action, will both sigh, and weep;
> And bring our Spices, to embalm Thee dead;
> That done, wee'l see Thee sweetly buried.

Herrick is far more convincing when, avoiding the shoals of Christian dogma, he moves safely in the calmer waters of personal piety. We can observe in such a poem as "Cockcrow" a humble consciousness of moral frailty and a sincere desire to walk in God's holy ways:

> Bell-man of Night, if I about shall go
> For to denie my Master, do thou crow.
> Thou stop'st S. *Peter* in the midst of sin;
> Stay me, by crowing, ere I do begin;
> Better it is, premonish'd, for to shun
> A sin, then fall to weeping when 'tis done.

In the lines "To His Sweet Savior" (a characteristic title) where Herrick asks Christ to comfort him and to illuminate his soul, we feel that he is expressing a genuine, unaffected devotion to the person of Jesus:

> Sick is my heart; O Saviour! do Thou please
> To make my bed soft in my sicknesses:
> Lighten my candle, so that I beneath
> Sleep not for ever in the vaults of death:
> Let me Thy voice betimes i'th morning heare;
> Call, and I'le come; say Thou, the when, and where:
> Draw me, but first, and after Thee I'le run,
> And make no one stop, till my race be done.

The sophistication and subtlety that color so much of Herrick's best profane verse are markedly absent from his sacred poems, their place often being taken by the childlike naiveté that we noted in "His Letanie." It is not surprising that in "Another Grace for a Child" he should have reproduced so faithfully and with such sympathetic understanding the grave solemnity of a child's petition to God:

> Here a little child I stand,
> Heaving up my either hand;
> Cold as Paddocks though they be,
> Here I lift them up to Thee,
> For a Benizon to fall.
> On our meat, and on us all. *Amen.*

Yet the presence of a few decent, well-ordered poems scarcely compensates for the succession of dull, mechanical pieces that make up the bulk of *His Noble Numbers*. Herrick's intellectual and emotional resources are too meager to sustain him when he exiles himself from the delicious pagan landscape and attempts to survey the divine order of the universe.

VII

To claim that Herrick is a major poet would be false; to despise him, to dismiss him as an elegant trifler, would be equally injudicious and far more stultifying. Within certain limits he is a consummate artist: this essay has tried to indicate that these limits are broader than is commonly supposed and that his poetry is stronger, more complex, and more finely balanced than censorious judges have been willing to grant. He lacks the visionary power and insight that enable Blake to proclaim, "Everything that lives is holy"; but how many of us can honestly maintain this tenet when we consider the liver-fluke, the anopheles mosquito, the blow-fly, the tarantula, and the hyena? Herrick speaks for the normal sensual man in his avowal, made with such accuracy and zest, that many things that live are delightful.

His verse survives because of its lyrical perfection, a quality that continues to be admired by the common reader in every generation, no matter how literary fashion may veer. He is Elizabethan not only in sensibility but also in the relationship of his lyrics to the art of music. It is significant that in the eighteenth century, when he was largely forgotten, some of his poems were known in musical settings, and even today a lyric such as "Cherry-ripe" is familiar as a song to many who are not normally readers of Herrick. Indeed, certain of his poems, sacred and profane, were originally designed to be sung, for Herrick, who in his youth had been a friend of the most gifted court musicians, belongs in spirit to the age of the masque, even of the lutanists, to the time when a song was an indissoluble marriage of words and music.

This concept of the song is one that Herrick shares with his revered master, Ben Jonson, whose memory he invokes in a famous ode:

> My *Ben*
> Or come agen:
> Or send to us,
> Thy wits great over-plus;

Scattered throughout *Hesperides* are echoes and imitations of Jonson, such as the poem "Upon a Child That Dyed," which recalls an epitaph by Jonson on one of his own children:

> Here she lies, a pretty bud,
> Lately made of flesh and blood:
> Who, as soone, fell fast asleep,
> As her little eyes did peep.
> Give her strewings; but not stir
> The earth, that lightly covers her.

We know, by comparing poems in *Hesperides* with earlier readings in manuscripts and in printed books published before 1648, how carefully Herrick revised and polished his verse. In doing so he both followed the Jonsonian tradition of careful workmanship and sought to attain the immortality assured to Homer, Virgil, Ovid, Catullus, Propertius, and Tibullus, whose health he pledges in "To Live Merrily, and to Trust to Good Verses." In "Poetry Perpetuates the Poet," he claims with a rumbling Horatian sonority that

> eternall Poetrie
> Repullulation gives me here
> Unto the thirtieth thousand yeere.

Thirty thousand years is a great span for any poet to endure, but it seems likely that so long as men care for the art of English poetry their admiration for Herrick's verse will ratify the judgment that he passed "On Himself":

> Live by thy Muse thou shalt; when others die
> Leaving no Fame to long Posterity:
> When Monarchies trans-shifted are, and gone;
> Here shall endure thy vast Dominion.

SELECTED BIBLIOGRAPHY

I. Bibliography. M. MacLeod, *A Concordance to the Poems of Robert Herrick* (New York, 1936); S. A. and D. R. Tannenbaum, *Robert Herrick: A Concise Bibliography*, Elizabethan Bibliographies no. 40 (New York, 1949), Supplement no. 3 to the series adds a section on Herrick compiled by G. R. Guffey and covering the years 1949–1965.

II. Collected Works. *Hesperides*: or, *The Works Both Humane & Divine of Robert Herrick Esq.* (1648), includes, with separate title and pagination, *His Noble Numbers . . . , 1647*; J. N[ott], ed., *Select Poems from the Hesperides* (Bristol, [1810]), the first reprinting of Herrick's verse in book form for over 150 years, includes 284 poems; T. Maitland, ed., *The Works*, 2 vols. (Edinburgh, 1823), with a biographical notice; William C. Hazlitt, ed., *Hesperides: the Poems and other Remains now first Collected*, 2 vols. (London, 1869), the first collection to include poems not in the original edition of 1648, and the first to include letters; Rev. A. B. Grosart, ed., *The Complete Poems*, 3 vols. (London, 1876), introduction and notes, though not always accurate, add considerably to what was previously known about Herrick's life and works; A. W. Pollard, ed., *The Hesperides and Noble Numbers*, 2 vols. (London, 1891), with a preface by A. C. Swinburne, in the Muses' Library, second ed. (1898) has the poems numbered for the first time

(*Hesperides* and *His Noble Numbers* separately); G. Saintsbury, ed., *The Poetical Works*, 2 vols. (London, 1893), in the Aldine edition of the British Poets, numbers the poems in a single sequence; F. W. Moorman, ed., *The Poetical Works* (Oxford, 1915); L. C. Martin, ed., *The Poetical Works* (Oxford, 1956), the definitive edition in the Oxford English Texts, based upon the 1648 edition, includes 41 pages of additional poems, some of which had not been previously ascribed to Herrick, extensive biographical and critical commentary; J. Hayward, ed., *Poems* (London, 1961), a paperback selection with a critical introduction; J. M. Patrick, ed., *The Complete Poetry* (New York, 1963); L. C. Martin, ed., *Poems* (London, 1965), the Oxford Standard Authors edition, based on the Oxford English Texts edition of 1956.

III. SOME BIOGRAPHICAL AND CRITICAL STUDIES. A. C. Swinburne, *Studies in Prose and Poetry* (London, 1894), contains a eulogy of Herrick that now seems extravagant; F. W. Moorman, *Robert Herrick: A Biographical and Critical Study* (London, 1910), a pleasant study, but inaccurate in places and not particularly illuminating as literary criticism; F. Delattre, *Robert Herrick: Contribution a l'étude de la poésie lyrique en Angleterre au dix-septième siècle* (Paris, 1912), admirable scholarship, with an excellent chapter on Herrick's debts to Roman and to Renaissance poets, still the best and most thorough study of Herrick; P. Aiken, *The Influence of the Latin Elegists on English Lyric Poetry, 1600–50, with Particular Reference to the Works of R. Herrick* (Orono, Maine, 1932); E. I. M. Easton, *Youth Immortal: A Life of Robert Herrick* (Boston, New York, 1934); F. R. Leavis, *Revaluation* (London, 1936), contains an important essay, "The Line of Wit," which takes a low view of Herrick's achievements; M. J. Ruggles, "Horace and Herrick," in *Classical Journal*, 31 (London, 1936); K. A. McEuen, *Classical Influence Upon the Tribe of Ben: A Study of Classical Elements in the Non-dramatic Poetry of Ben Jonson and His Circle* (Cedar Rapids, 1939), devotes many pages to Herrick and to his borrowings from earlier poets; A. H. Gilbert, "Herrick on Death," in *Modern Language Quarterly*, 5 (London, 1944), a discussion of the more serious and somber elements in Herrick's poetry; G. W. Regenos, "The Influence of Horace on Herrick," in *Philological Quarterly*, 26 (London, 1947); S. Musgrove, *The Universe of Robert Herrick* (Auckland, 1950), argues that Herrick owes more to the complex inheritance of Renaissance humanism than to the example of any single poet; M. Chute, *Two Gentlemen: The Lives of George Herbert and Robert Herrick* (London, 1960); J. B. Broadbent, *Poetic Love* (London, 1964), contains a few sharp comments on Herrick; R. B. Rollin, *Robert Herrick* (New York, 1966), argues that Herrick is a major poet; R. H. Deming, *Ceremony and Art* (The Hague, 1974); A. L. Deneef, *"This Poetick Liturgie": Robert Herrick's Ceremonial Mode* (Durham, N. C., 1974); G. W. Scott, *Robert Herrick 1591–1674* (London, 1974); G. Braden, *The Classics and English Renaissance Poetry: Three Case Studies* (New Haven—London, 1978), includes a survey of Herrick's work, with particular reference to his use of classical authors.

GEORGE HERBERT

(1593-1633)

T. S. Eliot

LIFE

THE family background of a man of genius is always of interest. It may show evidence of powers that blaze forth in one member, or it may show no promise of superiority of any kind. Or it may, like that of George Herbert, show distinction of a very different order. There is a further reason for knowing something of the ancestry of George Herbert: it is of interest to us because it was important to him.

The family of Herbert was, and still is, notable among the British aristocracy. I say British rather than English because one branch of the family, that to which the poet belonged, had established itself in Wales and had intermarried with Welsh landed families. The Herberts lay claim to being of Norman-French origin, and to having been landholders since the Norman conquest. At the time of the Wars of the Roses, the Herberts of Wales had supported the Yorkist cause; but after the battle of Bosworth they transferred their allegiance to the new monarch, the Lancastrian Henry Tudor, himself a Welshman on his father's side, who ascended the throne as Henry VII. Under the new dynasty the Herberts continued to flourish. Henry VII was determined to exert in Wales the same authority that he enjoyed in England—a control to which the local chieftains of Wales were not accustomed. Among those Welshmen of position and authority who supported and advanced King Henry's law and order in Wales was Sir Richard Herbert of Montgomery Castle. Montgomery lies in North Wales; in the South another Herbert was (and is) earl of Pembroke; and still another branch of the family is represented by the earl of Carnarvon.

George Herbert's ancestors and kinsmen were active both in the service of the king and in local affairs. Their rank was among the highest. Several of the family were distinguished for their courage, their prowess in war and duel, and their astonishing feats of arms. An exceptional race, but giving no in-dication of literary tastes and ability before the time of George Herbert and his brother Edward. That two poets, brothers, should appear in a family so conspicuous for warlike deeds, administrative gifts, and attendance at court can be accounted for only by the fact that their mother, the wife of Sir Richard Herbert of Montgomery, was a woman of literary tastes, of strong character, and of exceptional gifts of mind as well as beauty and charm. She was Magdalen, daughter and heiress of Sir Richard Newport, a wealthy landowner in Shropshire.

George Herbert was born at Montgomery Castle on 3 April 1593. Three years later his father died, leaving the mother with ten children, seven boys and three girls. Edward was the eldest son; the younger sons would have, of course, to make their own way in life—presumably, as other Herberts had done, in the wars or in some public service—but Lady Herbert's standards were high and she was determined to give them all a good education. Edward, the heir to the estates, was fourteen and already an undergraduate at Oxford when his father died. At sixteen he was married off to an heiress (a Herbert of another branch) but continued at Oxford, where his mother moved her family to be near him and to supervise his education. There she made friends, and even held a kind of salon, among the more brilliant of the learned dons.

It is worthwhile to say something of Edward Herbert, not merely to mention his poetry but also to point out the striking contrast between the two gifted brothers. Edward was ambitious to live abroad, to enjoy court life in foreign capitals, and to engage in rather dilettante diplomacy; and to this end he learned French, Italian, and Spanish. He seems to have been a man of great physical strength, and was noted for his address at sports and success in lovemaking: in short, he was a man of abounding vitality. He was later raised to the peerage as Lord Herbert of Cherbury, by which name he is known as author of at least two very fine poems familiar to readers of anthologies. He was not only a poet, but also something of a philosopher, and entertained distinctly heretical views in religious matters. On the other hand, John Donne spoke well of him, and Ben Jonson was a friend and correspondent. He enjoyed the society of men of letters, among whom he moved as an equal, as he did among the courtiers of Europe and among ladies and gentlemen of fashion. In Edward the characteristic traits of the Herberts and some of the particular traits of Magdalen Herbert appear to have been combined. In George, of frailer constitution and contemplative mind, we seem to find more of Magdalen; yet he was as proudly conscious of being a Herbert as was any other Herbert, and at one period had the family inclination to life in the world of public affairs.

By far the most important for our study of George Herbert, of the men of letters and the scholars who delighted in the company of Magdalen Herbert, was John Donne. He was older enough in years to have the admiration of the younger man and to influence him: he was enough beneath Lady Herbert in rank to be almost a protégé. The friendship between Donne and Lady Herbert is commemorated in one of Donne's best-known and most loved poems, "The Autumnall," in which is found the couplet that every lover of Donne's poetry knows by heart:

No Spring, nor Summer Beauty hath such grace
As I have seen in one autumnal face.

To the influence of Donne's poetry upon that of Herbert we shall return presently. Meanwhile, it is in place to provide a brief survey of Herbert's life and a sketch of his character.

At the age of twelve George Herbert was sent to Westminster School, where he became proficient in the usual disciplines of Latin and Greek, and also gained—what is equally important here—an advanced practice in music: not only in the choral singing for which that famous school was well known because of its association with the services in Westminster Abbey, but also with a difficult instrument—the lute. If we remember Herbert's knowledge of music and his skill at the instrument, we appreciate all the better his mastery of lyric verse. From Westminster he went on to Trinity College, Cambridge, being one of three boys from Westminster School who were given scholarships to that college at that time.

At Westminster School, Herbert had an exemplary record. The relation of the school to the abbey had familiarized him with the church offices, in which the boys took part. (Their close attention to the sermon was ensured by the requirement that they should afterward compose a summary of it in Latin.) At the university Herbert was equally forward; sober and staid in his conduct and diligent in his studies, he was given particular attention by the master. It was said of him, however, that he was careful to be well, even expensively, dressed; and that his attitude toward his fellow undergraduates of lower social position was distant, if not supercilious. Even Izaak Walton (his most nearly contemporary biographer), who tends to emphasize Herbert's saintliness, admits that Herbert, at this stage of his life, was very much aware of the consideration that he thought due to his exalted birth.

At the age of twenty-three Herbert was made a fellow of Trinity College. He began by instructing the younger undergraduates in Greek grammar; later he taught rhetoric and the rules of oratory. His health was never good, and the climate of Cambridge was somewhat harsh for a young man of frail constitution. His income as fellow and tutor was eked out by a small allowance from his brother Edward (the head of the family) and occasionally by gifts from his stepfather. (His mother had, in middle age, married again, and was now the wife of Sir John Danvers.) But Herbert's poor health meant doctors' bills and occasional absences from Cambridge; as a learned scholar with an active and curious mind he needed constantly to purchase books, and books were expensive, especially those that had to be imported from the Continent. He therefore sought to improve his finances, and at the same time attain a position of considerable dignity, by obtaining appointment as public orator to the university.

Herbert had not yet formed the design of passing his life as a country parson. Indeed, the post of public orator was one that would bring him into the great world and even into contact with the court of James I. He achieved his aim; and during his tenure of this office acquired an extensive acquaintance, which his family connections and his own wide sympathies helped to enlarge. He greatly admired Sir Francis Bacon, a man of a type of mind very different from his own; another elder friend with whom he was on affectionate terms was the saintly Bishop Lancelot Andrewes. Nor did a wide divergence of religious attitude and belief diminish the warm regard between him and his elder brother Edward.

A fellow of a college was expected to take holy orders in the Church of England within seven years of his appointment, or resign his fellowship. Herbert was, like his mother, a practicing and devout Anglican, but at this time his ambition looked toward the world of court and government. His violent attack, in the form of a Latin thesis, upon the Puritan position in the person of one of its most outrageous zealots, Andrew Melville, was his only sortie into religious controversy; though undoubtedly wholly sincere, Herbert probably aimed at winning the approval of King James. He would certainly have liked public office, but had neither the wiles of ingratiation nor the means or the wish to buy his way in. His next step was to become member of Parliament for Montgomery—an election that came to him almost as a matter of course as a member of the Herbert family. But this period of his life was not marked by success: two great noblemen of whose patronage he felt assured died, and the death of King James, in the following year, seems to have left him with little hope of a secretaryship of state.

It was necessary to review this much of his early life to make the point that Herbert, though from childhood a pious member of the Anglican church, and a vigorous opponent of the Puritans and Calvinists, felt no strong vocation to the priesthood until his thirty-first year. There were at least four persons in his life who may, by precept or example, have influenced him to this decision. His mother, to whom he was devotedly attached, was, we know, a woman not only of strong character, but also of great piety. Two friends much older than himself have already been mentioned: Dr. John Donne and Bishop Andrewes. And finally, there was his dear friend Nicholas Ferrar of Little Gidding, an exemplar of High Churchmanship, whose domestic life approached that of a religious community. It was to Ferrar that Herbert consigned, upon his death, the manuscript collection of verse upon which his fame is founded, *The Temple*, which we should not know had Ferrar not chosen to publish it. This he did in the same year that Herbert died.[1]

Herbert's mother died in 1627. George Herbert was for a time a guest in the house of his stepfather's elder brother, Lord Danvers, and in 1629, having already taken holy orders, he married Jane Danvers, the daughter of a cousin of Lord Danvers. It was a happy marriage. Six years after Herbert's death, his widow married Sir Robert Cook. In her widowhood, Izaak Walton says:

. . . She continued mourning, till time and conversation had so moderated her sorrows, that she became the happy wife of Sir Robert Cook of Highnam in the County of Gloucester, Knight. And though he put a high value on the excellent accomplishments of her mind and body; and was so like Mr Herbert, as not to govern like a Master, but as an affectionate Husband; yet she would even to him take occasion to mention the name of Mr George Herbert, and say that name must live in her memory, till she put off mortality.

George Herbert died of consumption on 3 March 1633. For the last years of his life he had been rector of the parish of Bemerton in Wiltshire, where he was buried. That he was an exemplary parish priest, strict in his own observances and a loving and generous shepherd of his flock, there is ample testimony. And we should bear in mind that, at the time when Herbert lived, it was most unusual that a man of his social position should take orders and be content to devote himself to the spiritual and material needs of a small parish of humble folk in a rural village. From Walton's *Life* I must quote one anecdote:

---

[1]Four editions of *The Temple* appeared within three years of its first publication; its popularity continued to the end of the century. In the eighteenth century Herbert's poems were generally disparaged: William Cowper, for instance, though he found in them a strain of piety that he admired, regarded them as "gothick and uncouth," and this was the universal opinion of that age. The restoration of Herbert's reputation was begun by Coleridge, who, in a letter to William Collins, dated 6 December 1818, writes: ". . . I find more substantial comfort now in pious George Herbert's 'Temple' which I used to read to amuse myself with his quaintness—in short, only to laugh at—than in all the poetry since the poems of Milton. If you have not read Herbert, I can recommend the book to you confidently. The poem entitled 'The Flower' is especially affecting; and, to me, such a phrase as 'and relish versing' expresses a sincerity, a reality, which I would unwillingly exchange for the more dignified 'and once more love the Muse' &c. And so, with many other of Herbert's homely phrases" (*Letters*, IV, edited by Earl Leslie Griggs, 1959). Writing to Lady Beaumont in 1826, Coleridge says: "My dear old friend Charles Lamb and I differ widely (and in point of taste and moral feeling this is a rare occurrence) in our estimate and liking of George Herbert's sacred poems. He greatly prefers Quarles—nay he dislikes Herbert" (*The Letters of Charles Lamb*, edited by E. V. Lucas, I, 1935).

In another walk to *Salisbury*, he saw a poor man, with a poorer horse, that was fall'n under his Load; they were both in distress, and needed present help; which Mr *Herbert* perceiving, put off his Canonical Coat, and help'd the poor man to unload, and after, to lead his horse: The poor man blest him for it: and he blest the poor man; and was so like the *good Samaritan* that he gave him money to refresh both himself and his horse; and told him, *That if he lov'd himself, he should be merciful to his Beast.* Thus he left the poor man, and at his coming to his musical friends at *Salisbury*, they began to wonder that Mr *George Herbert* which us'd to be so trim and clean, came into the company so soyl'd and discompos'd; but he told them the occasion: And when one of the company told him, *He had disparag'd himself by so dirty an employment*; his answer was, *That the thought of what he had done, would prove Musick to him at Midnight; and that the omission of it would have upbraided and made discord in his Conscience, whensoever he should pass by that place; for, if I be bound to pray for all that be in distress, I am sure that I am bound so far as it is in my power to practise what I pray for. And though I do not willingly pass it is in my power to practise what I pray for. And though I do not wish for the like occasion every day, yet let me tell you, I would not willingly pass one day of my life without comforting a sad soul, or shewing mercy; and I praise God for this occasion:* And now let's tune our instruments.

In this context it is worth mentioning a prose treatise of Herbert's entitled *A Priest to the Temple, or, the Country Parson His Character etc.* In this treatise he sets forth the duties and responsibilities of the country parson to God, to his flock, and to himself; and from what we know of Herbert, we can be sure that he practiced, and always strove to practice, what he here prescribes to other priests. The story of the poor man and his horse is all the more touching when we read that the parson's apparel should be

plaine, but reverend, and clean, without spots, or dust, or smell; the purity of his mind breaking out, and dilating it selfe even to his body, cloaths, and habitation.

We are told elsewhere in the same treatise that a priest who serves as domestic chaplain to some great person is not to be

over-submissive, and base, but to keep up with the Lord and Lady of the house, and to preserve a boldness with them and all, even so farre as reproofe to their very face, when occasion calls, but seasonably and discreetly.

The pride of birth natural to Herbert is transformed into the dignity of the servant of God. The parson, he continues, should be a man of wide reading: Herbert mentions the Church Fathers and the Scholastics, and tells us that the parson should be attentive to later writers also. The parson must give careful attention to his sermon, taking due account of the needs and capacities of his parishioners, and keeping their attention by persuading them that his sermon is addressed to this particular congregation and to one and all of them. And he should, especially when visiting the sick or otherwise afflicted, persuade them to particular confession, "labouring to make them understand the great good use of this antient and pious ordinance."

We are not to presume that George Herbert was naturally of a meek and mild disposition. He was, on the contrary, somewhat haughty; proud of his descent and social position; and, like others of his family, of a quick temper. In his poems we can find ample evidence of his spiritual struggles, of self-examination and self-criticism, and of the cost at which he acquired godliness.

> I struck the board, and cry'd, No more.
> I will abroad.
> What? Shall I ever sigh and pine?
> My lines and life are free; free as the rode,
> Loose as the winde, as large as store.
> Shall I be still in suit?
> Have I no harvest but a thorn
> To let me bloud, and not restore
> What I have lost with cordiall fruit?
> Sure there was wine
> Before my sighs did drie it: there was corn
> Before my tears did drown it.
> Is the yeare onely lost to me?
> Have I no bayes to crown it?
> No flowers, no garlands gay? all blasted?
> All wasted?
> Not so, my heart: but there is fruit
> And thou hast hands.
> Recover all thy sigh-blown age
> On double pleasures: leave thy cold dispute
> Of what is fit and not. Forsake thy cage,
> Thy rope of sands,
> Which pettie thoughts have made, and made to thee
> Good cable, to enforce and draw,
> And be thy law,
> Whilst thou didst wink and wouldst not see.
> Away; take heed;
> I will abroad.

Call in thy deaths head there: tie up thy fears.
He that forbears
To suit and serve his need
Deserves his load.
But as I rav'd and grew more fierce and wilde
At every word,
Me thought I heard one calling, *Child!*
And I reply'd, *My Lord.*
("The Collar")

To think of Herbert as the poet of a placid and comfortable easy piety is to misunderstand utterly the man and his poems. Yet such was the impression of Herbert and of the Church of England given by the critic who wrote the introduction to the World's Classics edition of Herbert's poems in 1907. For this writer the Church of England, in Herbert's day as well as in his own, is typified by a peaceful country churchyard in the late afternoon:

Here, as the cattle wind homeward in the evening light, the benign, white-haired parson stands at his gate to greet the cowherd, and the village chimes call the labourers to evensong. For these contented spirits, happily removed from the stress and din of contending creeds and clashing dogmas, the message of the gospel tells of divine approval for work well done. . . . And among these typical spirits, beacons of a quiet hope, no figure stands out more brightly or more memorably than that of George Herbert.

This rustic scene belongs to the world of Tennyson and Dickens, but no more to the world of George Herbert than to our world today. It is well that the 1961 World's Classics edition (the text based on that established by F. E. Hutchinson) has a new introduction by a learned and sensitive critic, Helen Gardner. The earlier introduction gave a false picture of Herbert and his poetry, and of the church itself in an age of bitter religious conflict and passionate theology: it is worth quoting in order to point out how false a picture this is.

HERBERT'S POEMS

THE poems on which George Herbert's reputation is based are those constituting the collection called *The Temple*. About *The Temple* there are two points to be made. The first is that we cannot date the poems exactly. Some of them may be the product of careful rewriting. We cannot take them as being necessarily in chronological order: they have another order, that in which Herbert wished them to be read. *The Temple* is, in fact, a structure, and one that may have been worked over and elaborated, perhaps at intervals of time, before it reached its final form. We cannot judge Herbert, or savor fully his genius and his art, by any selection to be found in an anthology; we must study *The Temple* as a whole.

To understand Shakespeare we must acquaint ourselves with all of his plays; to understand Herbert we must acquaint ourselves with all of *The Temple*. Herbert is, of course, a much slighter poet than Shakespeare; nevertheless, he may justly be called a major poet. Yet even in anthologies he has for the most part been underrated. In Sir Arthur Quiller-Couch's *Oxford Book of English Verse*, which was for many years unchallenged in its representative character, George Herbert was allotted four pages—the same number as Bishop Henry King and far fewer than Robert Herrick, the latter of whom, most critics today would agree, is a poet of very much slighter gifts. For poetic range Herbert was commonly considered more limited than Donne, and for intensity he was compared unfavorably with Richard Crashaw. This is the view even of Herbert J. C. Grierson, to whom we are greatly indebted for his championship of Donne and those poets whose names are associated with that of Donne.

And here we must exercise caution in our interpretation of the phrase "the school of Donne." I once contemplated writing a book under that title, and the title has in fact been used by a distinguished younger critic for a study covering the same ground. The phrase is legitimate and useful to designate that generation of men younger than Donne whose work is obviously influenced by him, but we must not take it as implying that those poets who experienced his influence were for that reason lesser poets. (Grierson, indeed, seems to consider Andrew Marvell the greatest, greater even than Donne.) That Herbert learned directly from Donne is self-evident. But to think of "the school of Donne," otherwise "the metaphysical poets," as Donne's inferiors, or to try to range them on a scale of greatness, would be to lose our way. What is important is to apprehend the particular virtue, the unique flavor, of each one. Comparing them with any other group of poets at any other period, we observe the characteristics they share; when we compare them with each other, their differences emerge clearly.

Let us compare a poem by Donne with a poem by Herbert; and since Herbert's poetry deals always with religious matter, we shall compare two religious sonnets. First Donne:

Batter my heart, three person'd God; for, you
As yet but knocke, breathe, shine, and seeke to mend;
That I may rise, and stand, o'erthrow mee, and bend
Your force, to breake, blowe, burn and make me new.
I, like an usurpt towne, to 'another due,
Labour to 'admit you, but Oh, to no end,
Reason your viceroy in mee, mee shall defend,
But is captiv'd, and proves weake or untrue.
Yet dearely 'I love you,' and would be loved faine,
But am betroth'd unto your enemie:
Divorce mee, 'untie, or break that knot againe;
Take mee to you, imprison mee, for I
Except you 'enthrall mee, never shall be free,
Nor ever chast, except you ravish mee.

And here is George Herbert:

Prayer the Churches banquet, Angels age,
    Gods breath in man returning to his birth,
    The soul in paraphrase, heart in pilgrimage,
The Christian plummet sounding heav'n and earth;
Engine against th' Almightie, sinners towre,
    Reversed thunder, Christ-side-piercing spear,
    The six-daies world transposing in an houre,
A kinde of tune, which all things heare and fear;
Softnesse, and peace, and joy, and love, and blisse,
    Exalted Manna, gladnesse of the best,
    Heaven in ordinarie, man well drest,
The milkie way, the bird of Paradise,
    Church-bels beyond the starres heard, the souls bloud,
    The land of spices; something understood.
                    ("Prayer I")

The difference that I wish to emphasize is not that between the violence of Donne and the gentle imagery of Herbert but, rather, a difference between the dominance of intellect over sensibility and the dominance of sensibility over intellect. Both men were highly intellectual, both men had very keen sensibility; but in Donne thought seems in control of feeling, and in Herbert feeling seems in control of thought. Both men were learned, both men were accustomed to preaching—but not to the same type of congregation. In Donne's religious verse, as in his sermons, there is much more of the orator; whereas Herbert, for all that he had been successful as public

orator of Cambridge University, has a much more intimate tone of speech. We do not know what Herbert's sermons were like; but we can conjecture that in addressing his little congregation of rustics, all of whom he knew personally, and many of whom must have received both spiritual and material comfort from him and from his wife, he adopted a more homely style. Donne was accustomed to addressing large congregations (one is tempted to call them audiences) out-of-doors at Paul's Cross; Herbert, only the local congregation of a village church.

The difference I have in mind is indicated even by the last two lines of each sonnet. Donne's

                    . . . for I
Except you 'enthrall mee, never shall be free,
Nor ever chast, except you ravish mee

is, in the best sense, wit. Herbert's

Church-bels beyond the starres heard, the souls bloud,
The land of spices; something understood

is the kind of poetry that, like Keats's

        magic casements, opening on the foam
Of perilous seas, in faery lands forlorn
                    ("Ode to a Nightingale")

may be called magical.

Of all the poets who may be said to belong to "the school of Donne," Herbert is the only one whose whole source of inspiration was his religious faith. Most of the poetry upon which the reputation of Donne rests is love poetry, and his religious verse is of a later period in his life; his reputation, and his influence upon other poets, would have been as great had he written no religious poetry at all. Crashaw, who had frequented the community of Nicholas Ferrar at Little Gidding before his conversion to the Church of Rome, might still have been a notable poet had he written no religious verse —even though his devotional poems are his finest. Herbert, before becoming rector of Bemerton, had never been a recluse; he had, in his short life, wide acquaintance in the great world, and he enjoyed a happy marriage. Yet it was only in the faith, in hunger and thirst after godliness, in his self-questioning and his religious meditation, that he was inspired as a poet. If there is another example since his time of a poetic genius so dedicated to God, it is that of Gerard Hopkins. We are certainly justified in presuming that no other subject matter than that to which he confined himself could have elicited great poetry from George Herbert. Whether we regard this as a limitation or as the sign of solitary greatness, of a unique contribution to English poetry, will depend upon our sensibility to the themes of which he writes.

It would be a gross error to assume that Herbert's poems are of value only for Christians—or, still more narrowly, only for members of his own church. For the practicing Christian, it is true, they may be aids to devotion. When I claim a place for Herbert among those poets whose work every lover of English poetry should read and every student of English poetry should study, irrespective of religious belief or unbelief, I am not thinking primarily of the exquisite craftsmanship, the extraordinary metrical virtuosity, or the verbal felicities, but of the content of the poems that make up *The Temple*. These poems form a record of spiritual struggle that should touch the feeling, and enlarge the understanding, of those readers also who hold no religious belief and find themselves unmoved by religious emotion. L. C. Knights, in an essay on George Herbert in his *Explorations*, both expresses this doubt on the part of the non-Christian and dispels it:

Even Dr Hutchinson, whose superbly edited and annotated edition of the Complete Works is not likely to be superseded . . . remarks that "if to-day there is a less general sympathy with Herbert's religion, the beauty and sincerity of its expression are appreciated by those who do not share it." True, but there is much more than the "expression" that we appreciate, as I shall try to show. Herbert's poetry is an integral part of the great English tradition.

Whether the religious poems of Donne show greater profundity of thought, and greater intensity of passion, is a question that every reader will answer according to his own feelings. My point here is that *The Temple* is not to be regarded simply as a collection of poems, but (as I have said) as a record of the spiritual struggles of a man of intellectual power and emotional intensity who gave much toil to perfecting his verses. As such, it should be a document of interest to all those who are curious to understand their fellow men; and as such, I regard it

as a more important document than all of Donne's religious poems taken together.

On the other hand, I find Herbert to be closer in spirit to Donne than is any other of "the school of Donne." Since the personal bond, through Lady Herbert, was much closer, this seems only natural. Other powerful literary influences formed the manner of Crashaw, the Roman Catholic convert: the Italian poet Giambattista Marino and the Spanish poet Luis de Góngora, and, we are told by Mario Praz (whose *Seicentismo e marinismo in Inghilterra* is essential for the study of Crashaw in particular), the Jesuit poets who wrote in Latin. Henry Vaughan and Thomas Traherne were poets of mystical experience: each appears to have experienced early in life some mystical illumination that inspires his poetry. And the other important poet of the "metaphysical" school, Andrew Marvell, is a master of secular and religious poetry equally. In my attempt to indicate the affinity of Herbert to Donne, and also the difference between them, I spoke earlier of a "balance" between the intellect and the sensibility. But equally well (for one has recourse to diverse and even mutually contradictory metaphors and images to express the inexpressible) we can speak of a "fusion" of intellect and sensibility in different proportions. In the work of a later generation of "metaphysicals"—notably John Cleveland, Edward Benlowes, and Abraham Cowley—we encounter a kind of emotional drought and a verbal ingenuity that, having no great depth of feeling to work upon, tend toward corruption of language, and merit the censure that Samuel Johnson applies indiscriminately to all the "school of Donne."

To return to the import of *The Temple* for all perceptive readers, whether they share Herbert's faith or no: Knights quotes with approval F. E. Hutchinson's description of the poems as

colloquies of the soul with God or self-communings which seek to bring order into that complex personality of his which he analyses so unsparingly,

but goes on to make a qualification that seems to me very important. Hutchinson believes that Herbert's principal temptation was ambition. We need not deny that Herbert had been, like many other men, ambitious; we know that he had a hot temper, that he liked fine clothes and fine company and would have been pleased by preferment at court. But beside the struggle to abandon thought of the attractions offered to worldly ambition, Knights finds "a dejection of spirit that tended to make him regard his own life, the life he was actually leading, as worthless and unprofitable." Knights attributes the cause partly to ill health, but still more to a more ingrained distrust. It was perhaps distrust of himself, or fear of testing his powers among more confident men, that drove Herbert to the shelter of an obscure parsonage. He had, Knights suggests, to rid himself of the torturing sense of frustration and impotence and to accept the validity of his own experience. If this is so, Herbert's weakness became the source of his greatest power, for the result was *The Temple*.

I have called upon Knights's testimony in evidence that Herbert is not a poet whose work is significant only for Christian readers; that *The Temple* is not to be taken as simply a devotional handbook of meditation for the faithful, but as the personal record of a man very conscious of weakness and failure, a man of intellect and sensibility who hungered and thirsted after righteousness. And that by its content, as well as because of its technical accomplishment, it is a work of importance for every lover of poetry. This is not to suggest that it is unprofitable for us to study the text for closer understanding, to acquaint ourselves with the liturgy of the church, with the traditional imagery of the church, and to identify the biblical allusions. One long poem that has been subjected to close examination is "The Sacrifice." There are sixty-three stanzas of three lines each, sixty-one of which have the refrain "Was ever grief like mine?" I mention this poem, which is a very fine one, and not so familiar as are some of the shorter and more lyrical pieces, because it has been carefully studied by William Empson in his *Seven Types of Ambiguity*, and by Rosamund Tuve in her *A Reading of George Herbert*. The lines are to be taken as spoken by Christ upon the cross. We need, of course, enough acquaintance with the New Testament to recognize references to the Passion. But we are also better prepared if we recognize the Lamentations of Jeremiah, and the reproaches in the Mass of the Presanctified that is celebrated on Good Friday.

Celebrant: I led thee forth out of Egypt, drowning Pharaoh in the Red Sea: and thou hast delivered me up unto the chief priests.
Deacon & Subdeacon: O my people, what have I done unto thee, or wherein have I wearied thee? Testify against me.

It is interesting to note that Empson and Tuve differ in their interpretation of the following stanza:

O all ye who passe by, behold and see;
Man stole the fruit, but I must climbe the tree;
The tree of life to all, but onely me:
                    Was ever grief like mine?

Empson comments: "He climbs the tree to repay what was stolen, as if he were putting the apple back," and develops this explanation at some length. Upon this interpretation, Tuve observes rather tartly: "All [Empson's] rabbits roll out of one small hat—the fact that Herbert uses the time-honoured 'climb' for the ascent of the Cross, and uses the word 'must', to indicate a far deeper necessity than that which faces a small boy under a big tree." Certainly, the image of replacing the apple that has been plucked is too ludicrous to be entertained for a moment. It is obvious that Christ "climbs" or is "lifted" up on the cross in atonement for the sin of Adam and Eve, the verb "climb" being used traditionally to indicate the voluntary nature of the sacrifice for the sins of the world. Herbert was, assuredly, familiar with the imagery used by the pre-Reformation church. It is likely also that Donne, learned in the works of the Scholastics, and also in the writings of such Roman theologians contemporary with himself as Cardinal Bellarmine, set a standard of scholarship that Herbert followed.

To cite such an instance as this is not to suggest that the lover of poetry needs to prepare himself with theological and liturgical knowledge before approaching Herbert's poetry. That would be to put the cart before the horse. With the appreciation of Herbert's poems, as with all poetry, enjoyment is the beginning as well as the end. We must enjoy the poetry before we attempt to penetrate the poet's mind; we must enjoy it before we understand it, if the attempt to understand it is to be worth the trouble. We begin by enjoying poems, and lines in poems, that make an immediate impression; only gradually, as we familiarize ourselves with the whole work, do we appreciate *The Temple* as a coherent sequence of poems setting down the fluctuations of emotion between despair and bliss, between agitation and serenity, and the discipline of suffering that leads to peace of spirit.

GEORGE HERBERT

The relation of enjoyment to belief—the question whether a poem has more to give us if we share the beliefs of its author—is one that has never been answered satisfactorily: I have made some attempt to contribute to the solution of the problem, and remain dissatisfied with my attempts. But one thing is certain: that even if the reader enjoys a poem more fully when he shares the beliefs of the author, he will miss a great deal of possible enjoyment and of valuable experience if he does not seek the fullest understanding possible of poetry, in reading which he must "suspend his disbelief." (I am very thankful for having had the opportunity to study the *Bhagavad Gita* and the religious and philosophical beliefs, so different from my own, with which the *Bhagavad Gita* is informed.)

Some of the poems in *The Temple* express moods of anguish and a sense of defeat or failure:

At first thou gav'st me milk and sweetnesses;
      I had my wish and way:
My dayes were straw'd with flow'rs and happinesse;
      There was no moneth but May.
But with my yeares sorrow did twist and grow,
And made a partie unawares for wo. . . .

      . . .

Yet, though thou troublest me, I must be meek;
      In weaknesse must be stout.
Well, I will change the service, and go seek
      Some other master out.
Ah my deare God! though I am clean forgot,
Let me not love thee, if I love thee not.

The foregoing lines are from the first of five poems that bear the title "Affliction." In the first of two poems entitled "The Temper," Herbert speaks of his fluctuations of faith and feeling:

How should I praise thee, Lord! how should my rymes
    Gladly engrave thy love in steel,
      If what my soul doth feel sometimes,
        My soul might ever feel!

The great danger, for the poet who would write religious verse, is that of setting down what he would like to feel rather than be faithful to the expression of what he really feels. Of such pious insincerity Herbert is never guilty. We need not look too narrowly for a steady progress in Herbert's religious life, in an attempt to discover a chronological order. He falls, and rises again. Also, he was ac-

customed to working over his poems; they may have circulated in manuscript among his intimates during his lifetime. What we can confidently believe is that every poem in the book is true to the poet's experience. In some poems there is a more joyous note, as in "Whitsunday":

    Listen sweet Dove unto my song,
      And spread thy golden wings in me;
    Hatching my tender heart so long,
    Till it get wing, and flie away with thee. . . .

    Lord, though we change, thou art the same;
      The same sweet God of love and light:
    Restore this day, for thy great name,
    Unto his ancient and miraculous right.

In "The Flower" we hear the note of serenity, almost of beatitude, and of thankfulness for God's blessings:

    How fresh, O Lord, how sweet and clean
    Are thy returns! ev'n as the flowers in spring;
      To which, besides their own demean,
    The late-past frosts tributes of pleasure bring.
        Grief melts away
        Like snow in May,
    As if there were no such cold thing.

      . . .

    And now in age I bud again,
    After so many deaths I live and write;
      I once more smell the dew and rain,
    And relish versing: O my onely light,
        It cannot be
        That I am he
On whom thy tempests fell all night.[2]

I cannot resist the thought that in this last stanza—itself a miracle of phrasing—the imagery, so apposite to express the achievement of faith that it records, is taken from the experience of the man of delicate physical health who had known much illness. It is on this note of joy in convalescence of the spirit in surrender to God that the life of discipline of this haughty and irascible Herbert finds conclusion: *In His will is our peace.*

[2]A. Alvarez, in *The School of Donne*, says justly of this stanza: "This is, I suppose, the most perfect and most vivid stanza in the whole of Herbert's work. But it is, in every sense, so natural that its originality is easily missed." (See also Coleridge on this poem: letter to William Collins of 6 December 1818.)

GEORGE HERBERT

HERBERT AND DONNE

Of all the "school of Donne," Herbert is the closest to the old master. Two other fine poets of the group might just as well be said to belong to the "school of Herbert." The debt of Vaughan to Herbert can be shown by quotation; Herbert's most recent and authoritative editor, Dr. F. E. Hutchinson, says: "There is no example in English literature of one poet adopting another poet's work so extensively." As for Crashaw, he undoubtedly admired Herbert. Nevertheless, in spite of a continuity of influence and inspiration, we must remember that these four poets, who form a constellation of religious genius unparalleled in English poetry, are all highly individual, and very different from each other.

The resemblances and differences between Donne and Herbert are peculiarly fascinating. I suggested earlier that the difference between the poetry of Donne and that of Herbert shows some parallel to the difference between their careers in the church. Donne the dean of St. Paul's, whose sermons drew crowds in the City of London; Herbert the shepherd of a little flock of rustics, to whom he labored to explain the meaning of the rites of the church, the significance of holy days, in language that they could understand. There are lines that might have come from either, where we seem to hear the same voice—Herbert echoing the idiom or reflecting the imagery of Donne. There is at least one poem of Herbert's in which he plays with extended metaphor in the matter of Donne. It is "Obedience," where he uses legal terms almost throughout:

> My God, if writings may
> Convey a Lordship any way
> Whither the buyer and the seller please;
> Let it not thee displease,
> If this poore paper do as much as they.
>
> . . .
>
> He that will passe his land,
> As I have mine, may set his hand
> And heart unto this Deed, when he hath read;
> And make the purchase spread
> To both our goods, if he to it will stand.

Such elaboration is not typical of Herbert. But there is wit like that of Donne in "The Quip." One feels obliged to quote the whole poem:

> The merrie world did on a day
> With his train-bands and mates agree

> To meet together, where I lay,
> And all in sport to geere at me.
>
> First, Beautie crept into a rose,
> Which when I pluckt not, Sir, said she,
> Tell me, I pray, Whose hands are those?
> But thou shalt answer, Lord, for me.
>
> Then Money came, and clinking still,
> What tune is this, poore man? said he:
> I heard in Musick you had skill.
> But thou shalt answer, Lord, for me.
>
> Then came brave Glorie puffing by
> In silks that whistled, who but he?
> He scarce allow'd me half an eie.
> But thou shalt answer, Lord, for me.
>
> Then came quick Wit and Conversation,
> And he would needs a comfort be,
> And, to be short, make an Oration.
> But thou shalt answer, Lord, for me.
>
> Yet when the houre of thy designe
> To answer these fine things shall come;
> Speak not at large; say, I am thine:
> And then they have their answer home.

Knights observes very shrewdly: "the personifications here have nothing in common with Spenser's allegorical figures or with the capitalised abstractions of the eighteenth century: 'brave Glorie puffing by in silks that whistled' might have come straight from *The Pilgrim's Progress*." How audible are these silks "that whistled"! 'Puffing' is equally apt: the same participle is used, to produce another but equally striking effect, elsewhere:

> Sometimes Death, puffing at the doore,
> Blows all the dust about the floore: . . .
> ("The Churche-Floore")

Herbert is a master of the simple, everyday word in the right place, and charges it with concentrated meaning, as in "Redemption," one of the poems known to all readers of anthologies:

> Having been tenant long to a rich Lord,
> Not thriving, I resolved to be bold,
> And make a suit unto him, to afford
> A new small-rented lease, and cancell th'old.
>
> In heaven at his manour I him sought:
> They told me there, that he was lately gone

About some land, which he had dearly bought
Long since on earth, to take possession.

I straight return'd, and knowing his great birth,
   Sought him accordingly in great resorts;
   In cities, theatres, gardens, parks, and courts:
At length I heard a ragged noise and mirth

Of theeves and murderers: there I him espied,
Who straight, *Your suit is granted*, said, & died.

The phrase "ragged noise and mirth" gives us, in four words, the picture of the scene to which Herbert wishes to introduce us.

There are many lines that remind us of Donne:

What though my bodie runne to dust?
Faith cleaves unto it, counting evr'y grain
With an exact and most particular trust,
   Reserving all for flesh again.
               ("Faith")

My God, what is a heart?
   Silver, or gold, or precious stone,
   Or starre, or rainbow, or a part
Of all these things, or all of them in one?
              ("Mattens")

         . . . learn here thy stemme
And true descent; that when thou shalt grow fat,
          . . .
And wanton in thy cravings, thou mayst know,
That flesh is but the glasse, which holds the dust
That measures all our time; which also shall
Be crumbled into dust. . . .
          ("Church-monuments")

Lord, how can man preach thy eternall word?
   He is a brittle crazie glasse: . . .
         ("The Church Windows")

My bent thoughts, like a brittle bow,
      Did flie asunder: . . .
          ("Deniall")

Herbert must have learned from Donne the cunning use of both the learned and the common word, to give the sudden shock of surprise and delight.

But man is close, reserv'd, and dark to thee:
    When thou demandest but a heart,
      He cavils instantly.
    In his poore cabinet of bone

Sinnes have their box apart,
Defrauding thee, who gavest two for one.
          ("Ungratefulnesse")

The fleet Astronomer can bore,
And thred the sphere with his quick-piercing minde:
He views their stations, walks from doore to doore,
    Surveys, as if he had design'd
To make a purchase there: he sees their dances,
       And knoweth long before
Both their full-ey'd aspects, and secret glances.
          ("Vanitie")

My thoughts are all a case of knives . . .
         ("Affliction IV")

The following lines are very reminiscent of Donne:

How soon doth man decay!
When clothes are taken from a chest of sweets
   To swaddle infants, whose young breath
      Scarce knows the way;
Those clouts are little winding sheets,
Which do consigne and send them unto death.
          ("Mortification")

Here and there one can believe that Herbert has unconsciously used a word or a rhythm of Donne's, in a very different context from that of the original, as perhaps in the first line of "The Discharge":

Busie enquiring heart, what wouldst thou know?

Donne begins "The Sunne Rising" with the line

Busie old foole, unruly Sunne . . .

If Herbert's line be an echo and not a mere coincidence—the reader must form his own opinion—it is all the more interesting because of the difference in subject matter between the two poems. If Herbert, in writing a poem of religious mortification, could echo a poem of Donne's that is an aubade of the lover's complaint that day should come so soon, it suggests that the literary influence of the elder man upon the younger was profound indeed.

Herbert's metrical forms, however, are both original and varied. To have invented and perfected so many variations in the form of lyrical verse is evidence of native genius, hard work, and a passion for perfection. Two of his poems are such as would be considered, if written by a poet today, merely elegant trifles: "The Altar" and "Easter Wings." In each there is a disposition of longer and shorter lines so printed that the poems have the shape of an altar and of a pair of wings, respectively. Such a diversion, if employed frequently, would be tedious, distracting, and trying to the eyesight, and we must be glad that Herbert did not make further use of these devices; yet it is evidence of Herbert's care for workmanship, his restless exploration of variety, and of a kind of gaiety of spirit, a joy in composition that engages our delighted sympathy. The exquisite variations of form in the other poems of *The Temple* show a resourcefulness of invention that seems inexhaustible, and for which I know no parallel in English poetry. Here, we can only quote a stanza from each of a brief selection to suggest the astonishing variety:

> O my chief good,
> How shall I measure out thy bloud?
> How shall I count what thee befell,
> And each grief tell?
> ("Good Friday")

> O blessed bodie! Whither are thou thrown
> No lodging for thee, but a cold hard stone?
> So many hearts on earth, and yet not one
> Receive thee?
> ("Sepulchre")

Poems in such measures as these, and more obviously "The Sacrifice," quoted earlier, seem to indicate an ear trained by the music of liturgy.

> Rise heart; thy Lord is risen. Sing his praise
> Without delayes,
> Who takes thee by the hand, that thou likewise
> With him mayst rise:
> That, as his death calcined thee to dust,
> His life may make thee gold, and much more, just.
> ("Easter")

The slow movement of the last line quoted above has something of the movement of the exquisite line that ends Donne's "Nocturnall upon S. Lucies Day":

> Both the yeares, and the dayes deep midnight is.

Somewhat similar to the movement of "Good Friday" (quoted above) is

> Since, Lord, to thee
> A narrow way and little gate
> Is all the passage, on my infancie
> Thou didst lay hold, and antedate
> My faith in me.
> ("Holy Baptisme I")

Close enough to the form of "Holy Baptisme" for its difference to be all the more striking is

> Lord, I confesse my sinne is great;
> Great is my sinne. Oh! gently treat
> With thy quick flow'r, thy momentarie bloom;
> Whose life still pressing
> Is one undressing,
> A steadie aiming at a tombe.
> ("Repentance")

The next quotation has a solemn liturgical movement suited to the subject matter and the title:

> O Do not use me
> After my sinnes! look not on my desert,
> But on thy glorie! then thou wilt reform
> And not refuse me: for thou onely art
> The mightie God, but I a sillie worm;
> O do not bruise me!
> ("Sighs and Grones")

Herbert knows the effect of denying a rhyme where it is expected:

> When my devotions could not pierce
> Thy silent eares;
> Then was my heart broken, as was my verse:
> My breast was full of fears
> And disorder:
> ("Deniall")

The roughness of meter of the line

> Then was my heart broken, as was my verse

is exactly what is wanted to convey the meaning of the words. The following stanza has an apparent artlessness and conversational informality that only a great artist could achieve:

> Lord, let the Angels praise thy name.
> Man is a foolish thing, a foolish thing,

Folly and Sinne play all his game.
His house still burns, and yet he still doth sing,
Man is but grasse,
He knows it, fill the glasse.
("Miserie")

The next poem to be quoted is one of several poems by Herbert that, while being, like all the rest of his work, personal, have been set to music and sung as hymns:

King of Glorie, King of Peace,
I will love thee:
And that love may never cease,
I will move thee.
("Praise II")

The same masterly simplicity is visible in

Throw away thy rod,
Throw away thy wrath;
O my God,
Take the gentle path.
("Discipline")

I wish to end by giving in full the poem that, significantly, I think, ends *The Temple.* It is named "Love III," and indicates the serenity finally attained by this proud and humble man:

Love bade me welcome: yet my soul drew back,
Guiltie of dust and sinne.
But quick-ey'd Love, observing me grow slack
From my first entrance in,
Drew nearer to me, sweetly questioning,
If I lack'd any thing.

A guest, I answer'd, worthy to be here:
Love said, You shall be he.
I the unkinde, ungratefull? Ah my deare,
I cannot look on thee.
Love took my hand, and smiling did reply,
Who made the eyes but I?

Truth Lord, but I have marr'd them: let my shame
Go where it doth deserve.
And know you not, sayes Love, who bore the blame?
My deare, then I will serve.
You must sit down, sayes Love, and taste my meat:
So I did sit and eat.

SELECTED BIBLIOGRAPHY

I. BIBLIOGRAPHY. G. H. Palmer, comp., *A Herbert Bibliography* (Cambridge, Mass., 1911), a privately printed catalog of Palmer's collection of books by and about Herbert, useful but incomplete; C. Mann, *A Concordance to the English Poems of George Herbert* (Boston—New York, 1927); S. A. and D. R. Tannenbaum, *Elizabethan Bibliographies* 35 (New York, 1946); L. E. Berry, comp., *A Bibliography of Studies in Metaphysical Poetry, 1939-1960* (Madison, Wisc., 1964); M. A. Di Cesare, ed., *A Concordance to the Complete Writings of George Herbert* (Ithaca, N.Y.—London, 1977).

II. COLLECTED EDITIONS. *The Works*, 2 vols. (London, 1835-1836), with preface by W. Pickering and notes by S. T. Coleridge; A. B. Grosart, ed., *The Complete Works*, 3 vols. (London, 1874), textually most unreliable, but the first ed. to make use of the Williams MS; G. H. Palmer, ed., *The English Works Newly Arranged*, 3 vols. (London, 1905-1907), an important ed., despite some editorial liberties and speculations; F. E. Hutchinson, ed., *Works* (Oxford, 1941), the definitive ed., in the Oxford English Texts series, the World's Classics reprint (London, 1961) has a valuable intro. by H. Gardner.

III. SELECTIONS. D. Brown, ed., *Selected Poems of George Herbert* (London, 1960); M. M. McCluskey and P. R. Murphy, trans., *The Latin Poetry of George Herbert: A Bilingual Edition* (Athens, Ohio, 1964); *Select Hymns Taken Out of Mr. Herbert's Temple* (London, 1967); J. H. Summers, ed., *Selected Poetry of George Herbert* (New York, 1967); R. S. Thomas, ed., *A Choice of George Herbert's Verse* (London, 1967).

IV. SEPARATE WORKS. *The Temple, Sacred Poems and Private Ejaculations* (Cambridge, 1633), had 13 eds. published before 1709 but none thereafter until 1799, the Nonesuch Press ed. (London, 1927), edited by F. Meynell with a bibliographical note by G. Keynes, is based on the Bodleian MS (Tanner 307), which was the copy licensed in 1633 for the printer by the Cambridge vice-chancellor and his assessors; *Witts Recreations. With a Thousand Outlandish Proverbs Selected by Mr. G. H.* (London, 1640), the proverbs attributed to Herbert were published separately as *Jacula prudentum* (London, 1651); *Herbert's Remains* (London, 1652), contains most of *A Priest to the Temple* and *Jacula prudentum*; *A Priest to the Temple, or, the Country Parson, His Character, and Rule of Holy Life* (London, 1671), from which G. M. Forbes edited a selection (London, 1949). Herbert contributed Latin and Greek poems to the following memorial collections: *Epicedium Cantabrigiense, in obitum Henrici Principis Walliae* (Cambridge, 1612), 2 Latin poems; *Lacrymae Cantabrigienses, in obitum Reginae Annae* (Cambridge, 1619), 1 Latin poem; *Oratio qua Principis Caroli reditum ex Hispaniis celebravit Georgius Herbert* (Cambridge,

1623), 1 Latin oration; *True Copies of the Latin Orations, Made at Cambridge on the 25 and 27 of Februarie Last Past* (London, 1623), 1 Latin oration, with English translation; *Memoriae Francisi, Baronis de Verulamio, sacrum* (London, 1626), 1 Latin poem; *A Sermon of Commemorations of the Lady Danvers by John Donne. Together with Other Commemorations of Her, Called Parentalia by Her Sonne, G. Herbert* (London, 1627), 19 Latin and Greek poems.

V. SOME CRITICAL AND BIOGRAPHICAL STUDIES. I. Walton, *The Life of Mr. George Herbert* (London, 1670), reprinted in Walton's *Lives* (London, 1670), which is also in a World's Classics ed. (London, 1923); H. Walpole, ed., *The Life of Lord Herbert of Cherbury* (London, 1764), see also Herbert's *Poems*, Moore Smith, ed. (Oxford, 1923); S. T. Coleridge, *Biographia literaria* (London, 1817), chs. 19 and 20; H. Grierson, ed., *Metaphysical Poems and Lyrics of the Seventeenth Century* (Oxford, 1921), with an intro. by Grierson; M. Praz, *Seincentismo e marinismo in Inghilterra* (Florence, 1925); W. Empson, *Seven Types of Ambiguity* (London, 1930); G. Williamson, *The Donne Tradition* (Cambridge, Mass., 1930); J. Bennett, *Four Metaphysical Poets* (Cambridge, 1934; rev. ed., 1953), reissued with a new section on Herbert as *Five Metaphysical Poets* (Cambridge, 1959); J. B. Leishman, *The Metaphysical Poets* (Oxford, 1934); F. E. Hutchinson, "George Herbert: A Tercentenary," in *The Nineteenth Century*, 113 (1933), repr. in *Seventeenth Century Studies Presented to Sir Herbert Grierson* (Oxford, 1938); M. Praz, *Studies in Seventeenth Century Imagery* (London, 1939; rev. and enl. ed., 1964); L. C. Knights, "George Herbert," *Scrutiny*, 12 (1943–1944), repr. in *Explorations* (London, 1946); R. Freeman, *English Emblem Books* (London, 1948); A. Warren, *Rage for Order: Essays in Criticism* (Chicago, 1948); M. Mahood, *Poetry and Humanism* (London, 1950); R. Tuve, "On Herbert's 'Sacrifice,'" *Kenyon Review*, 12 (1950); R. Tuve, *A Reading of George Herbert* (Chicago—London, 1952); M. Bottrall, *George Herbert* (London, 1954); J. H. Summers, *George Herbert: His Religion and Art* (Cambridge, Mass.—London, 1954); H. C. White, *The Metaphysical Poets* (New York, 1956); D. C. Allen, *Image and Meaning* (Baltimore, 1960); M. Chute, *Two Gentle Men* (New York, 1959; London, 1960), biographies of Herbert and Herrick; R. Ellrodt, *Les Poètes Metaphysiques Anglais* (Paris, 1960); A. Alvarez, *The School of Donne* (London, 1961); W. R. Keast, ed., *Seventeenth Century English Poetry: Modern Essays in Criticism* (New York, 1962); H. R. Swardson, *Poetry and the Fountain of Light: Observations on the Conflict Between Classical and English Traditions in Seventeenth Century Poetry* (London, 1962); G. Williamson, *A Reader's Guide to Six Metaphysical Poets* (New York, 1967), also published as *A Reader's Guide to the Metaphysical Poets* (London, 1968); A. Stein, *George Herbert's Lyrics* (Baltimore, 1968).

IZAAK WALTON

(1593-1683)

Margaret Bottrall

REPUTATION

THE mention of Izaak Walton's name immediately suggests *The Compleat Angler*, the contemplative man's recreation, the peaceful fisherman, book in hand, depicted in the memorial window in Winchester Cathedral. It seems almost treasonable to allege that the extraordinary popularity of the book has resulted in a distorted picture of its author; but extraordinary is the mildest word that can be applied to its reputation. Its real vogue only began well over a hundred years after Walton's death. True, it was well received, and was reissued, with various alterations and additions, four times during his life; but it then had to wait more than seventy years to be rescued from obscurity, and it was not until after 1823 that the spate of reissues began in earnest. Whereas in the eighteenth century there were only ten editions of the book, in the nineteenth century there were a hundred and fifty-nine; and in the first half of the twentieth century more than a hundred reprints have appeared. *The Compleat Angler* is more than a minor classic; in its way it is a best-seller. The ingredients of the book—its combination of practical advice with pastoral fantasy and good-humored piety—are of a kind to commend it, even today, to English palates; and among the devotees of Walton are a number of readers who might not relish so heartily works of greater literary pretensions.

To Walton himself the book was, explicitly, a recreation, written during the Cromwellian ascendancy, to solace himself for the loss of happy bygone days. The work to which he devoted much patient labor through many years was the compilation of his five *Lives*; and these received on their appearance quite as warm a welcome as that accorded to *The Compleat Angler*. Each individual biography was reissued more than once during Walton's lifetime (Hooker's no less than six times) and he continued to enlarge and correct them until he was satisfied that they were as good as he could make them. That they were published collectively in 1670 (another edition of this volume appearing five years later) demonstrates that they were recognized as having merits quite beyond those of the ordinary prefatory Life. Primarily Walton was an amateur historian, whose lively interest in the fortunes of the Church of England and in the personalities of some of its illustrious sons was matched by his diligence in accumulating material for their biographies. Only incidentally was he a fisherman; he was not even a very great authority on angling.

If *The Compleat Angler* had been, from a professional point of view, an exhaustive treatise, it would not have been necessary for Charles Cotton to supplement it in 1676 with "Instructions how to angle for a Trout or Grayling in a Clear Stream," or for Colonel Robert Venables in the same year to add, with Walton's approval, a third section. Nor did *The Compleat Angler* at its first appearance fill a long-felt want, for two years previously, in 1651, Thomas Barker had published his little handbook, *The Art of Angling*, reprinted as *Barker's Delight* in 1657 and 1659. Walton's own angling editor, R. B. Marston, admits that Barker was Walton's superior as a fly-fisher, and that his experience was far more varied. He was, moreover, an enthusiastic cook, and included a number of excellent recipes in his book. Walton, who acknowledges his debt to Barker, very sensibly followed his example in this respect, and cheerfully drew on him and on earlier handbooks on angling to supplement his own firsthand experience. He also incorporated all sorts of fabulous lore in *The Compleat Angler*, thus drawing down upon himself the wrathful contempt of a Cromwellian trooper named Richard Franck, whose *Northern Memoirs* (1658) prove him to have been an expert fisherman, even if a pedantic and disagreeable person. Franck says that Walton "lays the stress of his arguments upon other men's observations, wherewith he stuffs his indigested octavo"; and when it is suggested that *The Compleat Angler* "may pass muster among common mudlers," the curt rejoinder is, "No, I think not." Franck seems to stand alone in his insensibility to the charm of the book, which lies precisely in the fact that it is the production of an amateur. Its aim is quite as much to delight as to instruct, and its merits lie more in its digressions and fanciful disquisitions than in its usefulness as a fisherman's manual. There is enough sound, practical experience included in it to commend it to actual anglers, but it excels in being a conspicuously friendly book, in which an enthusiast is seeking to persuade others to share his various enjoyments.

LIFE

IT was by chance, not training, that Walton became a writer. Had Sir Henry Wotton fulfilled his intention of writing a Life of Donne and "a Discourse of the Art, and in praise of Angling," it is possible that Walton might never have ventured into literature. His references to his education and to his fitness to chronicle the lives of distinguished men are always deprecating; and the little we know of his origins shows that he was a man who rose quite remarkably above the social setting into which he was born.

His father, Jervis Walton, was an alehouse-keeper in the neighborhood of Stafford; his mother, Anne, whose maiden name has not been traced, married another Stafford innkeeper in 1598, a year after the death of Izaak's father, when the little boy was five years old. He was baptized at St. Mary's, Stafford, on 21 September 1593, and his birth date has often been assumed to be 9 August, which is the date, in his ninetieth year, when he began to draft his will. Nothing is known of his childhood and schooling, and one wishes that he, with his insatiable interest in personal anecdote, had thought it worthwhile to preserve, if only for his descendants, a record of his upbringing and early life. Somehow he acquired a love of books, and the ability to express himself with ease and grace; his script was beautiful and scholarly, though his spelling was eccentric, even by seventeenth-century standards.

By the time he was twenty he was in London, ap-prenticed to a kinsman, Thomas Grinsell. The tradition that Walton was some kind of a clothier has been confirmed by the recent discovery of records describing Grinsell as a sempster and Walton as a draper. He appears to have rented half a shop in Fleet Street and to have lived in Chancery Lane. In 1618 he was admitted a free brother of the Ironmongers' Company, to which Grinsell also belonged, and in the license for his first marriage he is described as "of the Cittie of London Ironmonger." By 1637, the company had appointed him warden of their yeomanry. This connection does not imply that he was ever engaged in the ironmongery trade. Donne's father had at one time been warden of this same company, and this may possibly have been one of the links that drew the two men together when Donne became vicar of St. Dunstan's in the West, a living he held, in conjunction with the deanery of St. Paul's, from 1624 until the time of his death. This was Walton's parish church, and he held various parochial offices, including that of vestryman.

There is evidence that as quite a young man Walton was interested in literature, for a volume of verse, *The Loves of Amos and Laura*, by one S.P., was dedicated to him in 1619, with very flattering lines suggesting that he was a connoisseur of poetry if not a poet himself. Enough of Walton's occasional verse has survived to make this plausible; although it never rises above mediocrity, it is sufficiently accomplished to suggest that he had practiced the craft with some diligence and discrimination.

In 1626 Izaak Walton married, at Canterbury, Rachel Floud, who was maternally descended from Archdeacon Cranmer, brother of the archbishop. Her uncle, George Cranmer, had been one of Hooker's favorite pupils at Oxford, and an aunt had married Hooker's literary executor, John Spencer, president of Corpus Christi College, Oxford. If Walton was not already moving in clerical circles, his marriage connected him with them. Rachel Walton bore him seven children, all of whom died young, she herself dying in 1640. It was in this year that Walton's *Life of Dr. Donne* was published, prefacing an edition of his sermons. Sir Henry Wotton, who had intended to write a commemorative Life of Donne, had himself died in 1639. Walton's many bereavements may have impelled him to move his house and business. His name disappears from the registers of St. Dunstan's after 1644, but he seems to have remained in London.

By this time he was evidently a quite well-to-do man, for in 1643 he had paid £30 in parliamentary levies, and in 1646 he lent £50 to Edmund Carew of the Inner Temple—substantial sums in seventeenth-century currency. Later in his life he was described in legal documents as "Gentleman," though on the title page of the fifth edition of *The Compleat Angler*, the last that Walton revised, a careful differentiation is made between Mr. Izaak Walton and Charles Cotton, Esq.

In 1646 Walton married, at Clerkenwell, Anne Ken, whose half-brother Thomas was later to become the famous bishop and hymnwriter. There were three children of this marriage, two of whom survived, a son Isaac and a daughter Anne.

After the defeat of the royalist forces at Worcester, in 1651, occurred the one episode in Walton's career that has a touch of excitement in it. One of Prince Charles's jewels, the lesser George, which had been hidden for safety by a royalist officer taken prisoner near Stafford, was eventually conveyed to the same officer, by now in the Tower of London, "by the trusty hands of Mr. Isaac Walton." The Waltons appear to have lived for a while in the neighborhood of Stafford about this time, when London was an unpleasant place for shopkeepers of outspoken royalist sympathies; but the publication of the *Life of Sir Henry Wotton* in 1651 and of *The Compleat Angler* in 1653 suggests that Walton was not away for long.

After the Restoration (which moved him to write a joyful eclogue), he was appointed steward to Dr. George Morley, who was bishop of Worcester from 1660 to 1662. Mrs. Walton died in the latter year and was buried in Worcester Cathedral, with a touching epitaph composed by her husband. When Morley was transferred to the see of Winchester, Walton went with him. Whether he continued to act as his steward is not certainly known, but he undoubtedly spent a great deal of his time at Farnham Castle and was on the best of terms with the bishop. It was with Morley's encouragement, though at the bidding of Bishop Sheldon, that Walton published his *Life of Mr. Richard Hooker* in 1665. Five years later he brought out his *Life of Mr. George Herbert*, the one *Life* that seems to have been written at nobody's instigation, though it may be that his acquaintance at Worcester with Barnabas Oley, Herbert's editor, gave him the impetus to celebrate the man he so much admired.

The year that saw the publication of the *Life of Herbert* saw also a collected edition of the four *Lives* that had been written up to this date. In 1678, when Walton was eighty-five, he brought out the *Life of Dr. Robert Sanderson*, which is scarcely inferior to the others in spite of the author's great age. Dr. Morley had urged him to undertake this task, and helped him with his reminiscences.

Walton's later life seems to have been very serene. His son Isaac went to Oxford and took holy orders, traveling abroad with Ken for a while, and eventually becoming a canon of Salisbury. His daughter Anne married William Hawkins, a prebendary of Winchester, who was also rector of Droxford, a parish in the neighborhood. The old man made his home with his children and grandchildren in both places.

In his ninetieth year, Walton took on the responsibility of editing a poem, *Thealma and Clearchus*, by John Chalkhill, some of whose verses are quoted in *The Compleat Angler*. This occasion drew from Thomas Flatman some pleasant lines addressed to Walton:

> Happy old man, whose worth all mankind knows
> Except himself, who charitably shows
> The ready road to Virtue and to Praise,
> The road to many long, and happy days;
> The noble arts of generous piety,
> And how to compass true felicity.
> . . . he knows no anxious cares,
> Thro' near a Century of pleasant years;
> Easy he lives, and cheerful shall he die,
> Well spoken of by late posterity.

Walton's will, drawn up when he was ninety, is a characteristic document. By that time he owned two houses in London, a cottage near Stafford, and a farm near Winchester. All his property was most carefully disposed of, his favorite books (foremost among them Donne's *Sermons*) being specially mentioned. He remembered his native town in various benefactions, including a bequest of money

to buie coles for some pore people, that shall most neide them in the said towne; the saide coles to be delivered the last weike in Janewary, or in every first weike in Febreary: I say then, because I take that time to be the hardest and most pinching times with pore people.

Among various small bequests, his son is asked to look after his "Ante Beacham" and to allow her "about fiftie shilling a yeare in or for bacon and cheise (not more)." He left many mourning rings as tokens to his friends, among them one for Bishop Morley with the posy "A mite for a million." Three months after making this will, Izaak Walton died, on 15 December 1683, during a great frost, and his remains were buried in Winchester Cathedral.

The two portraits of Walton that have come down to us confirm the impression that we get from all his writings. Here is a strong, honest, humorous, and serious man; a man both shrewd and kindly. He may have been inferior in birth, education, and opportunity to many of the men with whom he associated, but he was by no means a pious sycophant, as some of his hostile critics have suggested. Rather, in the words of Charles Cotton: "My father Walton will be seen twice in no man's company he does not like, and likes none but such as he believes to be very honest men."

Among such honest men and firm friends were John Donne, who sent to Walton (as he did to George Herbert) one of his specially designed emblematic seals—with which both Waltons, father and son, successively signed their own wills. There was Henry King, bishop of Chichester, another recipient of a Donne seal, himself a fine poet, whose friendly letter prefixed to the *Life of Hooker* speaks of "a Familiarity of more then Forty years continuance, and the constant experience of your Love, even in the worst of the late sad times." There was Sir Henry Wotton, the renowned diplomatist, poet, and provost of Eton, who not only went fishing with Walton but enlisted his help in various literary projects. There were, among many others, Michael Drayton the poet, William Cartwright the dramatist, Dr. John Hales of Eton, Dr. Thomas Warton, the distinguished physician, Charles Cotton, another considerable poet and something of a rake, besides a bevy of bishops and ecclesiastics, among whom George Morley, the bishop of Winchester, was certainly the closest friend and the intermediary by whom Walton got to know so large a clerical circle.

Such men would not have honored Walton with their friendship if they had not found in him a singular degree of integrity and intelligence. As for his geniality, it smiles out from every page of *The Compleat Angler*, and is often to be discerned in the *Lives*, though they are pitched in a sober key. Without ever intruding himself, Walton manages to convey to his readers his personal feelings, whether of enjoyment of his pastime or of veneration and af-

fection for the subjects of his biographies, and thus he leaves an indelible impression of his own disposition.

BELIEFS

WALTON's religious and political sympathies were strong and undeviating. His conduct and his associates prove him a staunch Anglican and royalist, and, naturally, his writings bear this out. Especially interesting in this connection are the two letters published in 1680 under the title *Love and Truth*. Walton did not publicly acknowledge their parentage, but the internal evidence that he wrote them is overwhelming.[1] They purport to be written "from a quiet and conformable citizen of London, to two busie and factious shopkeepers in Coventry" and both deal with "the distemper of the present times." The first, written in 1667, taxes the dissenters with fostering schism and sedition and argues that the penalties enforced against them are no more severe and no less justified than they were "in the very happy days of our late and Good Queen Elizabeth." It defends the Anglican form of public worship and begs the Nonconformist busybodies to repent their indiscreet zeal and "study to be quiet" (one of Walton's favorite scriptural quotations).

The second letter, written some twelve years later, is more humorous and unmistakably Waltonian.[2] Conceding that all the faults are not on one side, it gives a glimpse of the Restoration cleric "in a long, curled, trim *Periwig*, a large *Tippet*, and a silk *Cassock*," and of clergy wives "striving for Precedency and for the highest places in Church Pews," decked out in "silk Cloaths, be-daub'd with lace, and their heads hanged about with painted Ribands." Nevertheless, the author rejoices at having been bred in the Church of England, and warns his correspondents to be on their guard against Papists, who would be the chief gainers if there were a schism between the Anglicans and the Dissenters. If popery came back, "farewell the liberty and care of tender Consciences; there would be an end of that cajoling and flattery." In very similar terms to those

---

[1]Included in Zouch, *Lives* (3rd ed., London, 1817) and in G. L. Keynes, *Collected Works of Izaak Walton* (London, 1929).
[2]Archbishop Sancroft, in his copy now in the Library of Emmanuel College, Cambridge, attributes the letters to Izaak Walton.

that Walton uses in the *Life of Hooker*, the women and shopkeepers "and the middlewitted people" of "this sinful Nation" are warned against meddling in "Divinity, and the Government of the *Church* and *State*." There is another account of Anglican church services, and a defense of the prayer book, "so pathetically and properly worded." Charles I is extolled as a pattern of the Christian graces, and the author laments that "Almighty God hath appointed me to live in an Age, in which Contention increases and Charity decays."

It is not often, even in the *Lives*, which gave him ample opportunity to reflect on the mysteries of change and chance and death, that Walton makes any comment that seems to spring from a deep religious experience. There is a fine passage in the *Life of Hooker*:

Affliction is a Divine diet, which though it be not pleasing to Mankind, yet Almighty God hath often, very often, imposed it as good, though bitter Physick, to those children whose Souls are dearest to him.

Such aphorisms are exceptional in Walton. No reader of the *Lives* can doubt that he was a thoughtful and sensitive man, but his reflections usually led him to accepted conclusions. He was a conformist who neither asked awkward questions himself nor approved of those who did. He is at his best when he recommends thankfulness, humility, and patience as Christian duties; but sometimes his devout simplicity is combined with a good deal of sententiousness. This is markedly so in the long discourse on the duty of thankfulness that leads up to the conclusion of *The Compleat Angler* in its revised version. Piscator wishes his scholar to join him

in thankfulness to the Giver of every good and perfect gift, for our happiness. And that our present happiness may appear to be the greater, and we the more thankful for it, I will beg you to consider with me how many do, even at this very time, lie under the torment of the stone, the gout, and tooth-ache; and this we are free from. And every misery I miss is a new mercy; and therefore let us be thankful.

Though Walton's churchgoing, conforming type of piety may seem dull and limited when it is contrasted with the spiritual agonies and ecstasies of his contemporaries George Fox and John Bunyan, it must in justice be remembered that he lived through

a period when the steadfastness of devout Anglicans was thoroughly put to the test. Walton regarded all Dissenters as dangerous schismatics. His own respect for authority made it impossible for him to sympathize in the least with their pleas for liberty of conscience and the right of private judgment. Lay folk, in his opinion, should know their place. Several times in his writings he inveighs against the "too many foolish meddlers in physick and divinity that think themselves fit to meddle with hidden secrets, and so bring destruction to their followers." It cannot be doubted that the Church of England provided the right niche for a man of Walton's equable temperament and essentially reverent cast of mind.

STYLE

Throughout the *Lives* we find scattered remarks that betray Walton's nostalgia for the peaceful reign of James I. Though his loyalty to the monarchy was unquestionable and he celebrated the Restoration in rollicking stanzas, he realized that the England of his youth had vanished forever. In 1665 he spoke of "this weak and declining Age of the World," and, thirteen years later, in the *Life of Sanderson*, he says:

But when I look back upon the ruine of Families, the bloodshed, the decay of common honesty, and how the former piety and plain dealing of this now sinful Nation is turned into cruelty and cunning, I praise God that he prevented me from being of that party which help'd to bring in this Covenant, and those sad Confusions that have follow'd it.

Born in the year when Shakespeare's *Venus and Adonis* was published, Izaak Walton died a year after the publication of Dryden's *Religio Laici* and *MacFlecknoe*. Although most of his writing was done in the post-Restoration years, its spirit is of an earlier epoch. When in *The Compleat Angler* he introduces the pastoral songs of Marlowe and Ralegh, he remarks: "They were old-fashioned poetry, but choicely good; I think much better than the strong lines that are now in fashion in this critical age." The happy, tranquil tone of the whole book, with its many interludes of "innocent, harmless mirth," may incline the reader to think of Walton as a belated Elizabethan; but its style and conception belong to a soberer age. It is worth remembering that Izaak Walton was born in the same year as George Herbert, though he survived him by half a century. Herbert, by a merciful providence, died before the outbreak of the Great Rebellion; Walton must sometimes have wished that he himself had lived no longer. Yet, in spite of his heartaches, he was evidently a happy old man, and certainly an uncommonly active and productive one.

The earliest extant piece by Walton is *An Elegy on Dr. Donne*, dated a week after Donne's death. This is more notable for its warmth of feeling than for genuine poetic merit, but it is interesting that Walton's first cry of lament is not for the loss that England has sustained of a man eminent in piety, but of a man

> where Language chose to stay
> And shew her utmost power. I would not praise
> That, and his great Wit, which in our vain days
> Make others proud; but, as these serv'd to unlock
> That Cabinet his mind, where such a stock
> Of knowledge was repos'd, that I lament
> Our just and general cause of discontent.

A fair number of Walton's songs and occasional verses have survived; those in *The Compleat Angler* are pleasantly adequate to the occasion, and so are his various dedicatory epistles and elegies; but prose was his proper medium.

He was a careful workman, and probably a slow one. The autograph manuscript of his notes for a *Life of John Hales* (written when he was already eighty) is full of cancellations and emendations, suggesting that words and phrases did not flow freely from his pen. Nevertheless, Walton's finished style is remarkably flexible and unaffected. When he has facts to convey, he sets them down straightforwardly; when he has a story to tell, he handles both narrative and digression with great skill; when there is need of a lyrical description or a piece of impressive eloquence, his style rises to the occasion. The famous peroration to the *Life of Donne* may be cited as an example of his finest, most impassioned prose:

> He was earnest and unwearied in the search of knowledge; with which his vigorous soul is now satisfied, and employed in a continual praise of that God that first breathed it into his active body; that body, which once was a *Temple of the Holy Ghost*, and is now become a small quantity of *Christian dust*:
> But I shall see it reanimated.

It may be worth remarking that the final word originally was "reinanimated." The correction of even single words in Walton's constant revisions is proof of his conscientious artistry.

No less carefully wrought, though altogether lighter and brighter in texture, is this passage from *The Compleat Angler*:

> But the Nightingale, another of my airy creatures, breathes such sweet loud musick out of her little instrumental throat, that it might make mankind to think miracles are not ceased. He that at midnight when the very labourer sleeps securely, should hear, as I have very oft, the clear airs, the sweet descants, the natural rising and falling, the doubling and redoubling of her voice, might well be lifted above earth and say, "Lord, what musick hast thou provided for the Saints in Heaven, when thou affordest bad men such musick on Earth!"

Walton is fond of the balanced sentence, using alliteration to stress symmetry:

> Thus *variable*, thus *vertuous* was the Life: thus *excellent*, thus *exemplary* was the Death of this memorable man.

Another favorite device is his use of parenthesis, often for humorous effect. Walton's style is never intrusive, and his humorous asides are particularly unstressed, so that they sound almost demure, as in the comment:

> His late Majesty King *Charles* the *First*, that knew the value of Sir Henry *Wottons* pen, did by a perswasive loving violence (to which may be added the promise of 500 l. a year) force him to lay *Luther* aside, and betake himself to write the History of *England*.

In *The Compleat Angler*, Walton naturally allows his humor more play, and sometimes becomes quite frolicsome: "If Mr. Pike be there, then the little fish will skip out of the water at his appearance." But all in all, his is a sober, persuasive, lucid style that seldom draws the reader's attention upon itself but focuses it on the matter under discussion.

To appreciate Walton's mastery of extended narrative it is of course essential to read at least one of the *Lives* in its entirety; but a good example of his anecdotal style can be extracted from the *Life of Sanderson*:

About the time of his printing this excellent Preface, I met him accidentally in London in sad-coloured clothes, and God knows, far from being costly: the place of our meeting was near to *Little Britain*, where he had been to buy a book, which he then had in his hand: we had no inclination to part presently; and therefore turn'd to stand in a corner under a Penthouse (for it began to rain) and immediately the wind rose, and the rain increased so much, that both became so inconvenient as to force us into a cleanly house, where we had *Bread, Cheese, Ale & a Fire* for our money.

It is to the many anecdotes embedded in them that the *Lives* owe much of their vivacity. Nobody who has read them will forget George Herbert's encounter with the carter on his way to the music party at Salisbury, or Hooker's clerk protesting against the rearrangement of the church furniture. In a few telling phrases, too, Walton can hit off a man's appearance or disposition; witness his account of Donne's "winning behaviour (which when he would intice, had a strange kind of elegant, irresistible art)," and the glimpse of Hooker, so vivid though necessarily taken from hearsay: "His Body worn out, not with Age, but Study and Holy Mortification; his Face full of Heat-pimples, begot by his inactivity and sedentary life."

Walton's digressions are an essential part of his narrative technique, and he often draws attention to them by such remarks as:

But the Reader may think that in this digression, I have already carried him too far from *Eaton-Colledge,* and therefore I shall lead him back as gently and as orderly as I may to that place, for a further conference concerning Sir *Henry Wotton.*

In this particular *Life,* some of the digressions might be called aimless, but usually Walton only leaves his main story in order to fill in the historical background or to give an account of someone closely connected with his chief character.

In *The Compleat Angler,* also a very digressive work, Walton shows such a fondness for the fabulous natural history derived from Pliny the Elder via Gesner and Topsel (whose *Foure-footed Beastes* appeared in 1607) that we might question whether so credulous a man could be a trustworthy biographer. He does mention that the Royal Society has listed thirty-three species of spider, and refers to the collections of contemporary naturalists, such as John Tradescant and Elias Ashmole; but where

fishes or insects are concerned, he is quite content to accept and pass on all kinds of legendary information. For modern readers, of course, it is this unsophisticated and uncritical inclusiveness of Walton that constitutes one of the great charms of *The Compleat Angler,* combined as it so engagingly is with his accurate firsthand observation and practical knowledge. When he deals with the careers of men, Walton takes considerable pains to check his facts, and each one of his *Lives* was subjected to repeated revision.

THE COMPLEAT ANGLER

THIS striving for perfection extended to *The Compleat Angler,* by-product though it was of his leisure hours. For the 1655 edition he practically rewrote the version of 1653, increasing its length by about a third; and the final edition, brought out under his own supervision in 1676, was far more extensive than the first, containing as it did the supplements of Cotton and Venables. The additions to the original edition include several passages of conscious fine writing, and a great deal of moralizing; they make the treatise appear less of a handbook and widen its appeal.

Formally, the book is a dialogue. There are, in the revised version, three speakers in the opening scene—the huntsman, the falconer, and the angler. The falconer, having duly pleaded the merits of his sport, goes off to practice it; the hunter becomes a convert to the fisherman, and thereafter is addressed as "scholar." From time to time, minor characters—such as Maudlin the milkmaid and her mother, and the anglers Peter and Coridon—are introduced. When Walton has several people on the scene, he writes in a racy and colloquial way:

Piscator: . . . Well met, gentlemen; this is lucky that we meet so just together at this very door. Come, hostess, where are you? is supper ready? Come, first give us a drink; and be as quick as you can, for I believe we are all very hungry. Well, brother Peter and Coridon, to you both! Come, drink: and then tell me what luck of fish: we two have caught but ten trouts, of which my scholar caught three. Look! Here's eight; and a brace we gave away. We have had a most pleasant day for fishing and talking, and are returned home both weary and hungry; and now meat and rest will be pleasant.

Peter: And Coridon and I have not had an unpleasant day: and yet I have caught but five trouts; for, indeed, we went to a good honest ale-house, and there we played at shovel-board half the day; all the time that it rained we were there, and as merry as they that fished. And I am glad we are here now with a dry house over our heads; for hark! how it rains and blows. . . .

For the major part of the book, the dialogue convention is abandoned in favor of long instructional speeches by Piscator; but when Walton suspects that his readers have had enough information, he introduces dialogue again, and sometimes puts his characters in motion:

Piscator: . . . But, come, now it hath done raining, let's stretch our legs a little in a gentle walk to the river, and try what interest our angles will pay us for lending them so long to be used by the Trouts; lent them indeed, like usurers, for our profit and their destruction.

Venator: Oh me! look you, master, a fish! a fish! Oh, alas, master, I have lost her.

Another favorite device of Walton's to alleviate the weight of factual (or fabulous) description is to insert, on some pretext, a poem. *The Compleat Angler* includes verses by Christopher Marlowe, Sir Walter Ralegh, John Donne, Michael Drayton, Sir Henry Wotton, Guillaume Du Bartas, George Herbert, Christopher Harvey, Phineas Fletcher, and Edmund Waller, not to mention a number of less well-known names. Walton himself provides a cheerful catch and a "composure" (or composition) entitled *The Angler's Wish*, which refers to the time he spent at Shallowford near Stafford with his second wife Anne Ken ("my Kenna").

In his prefatory epistle to the reader, Walton expressly says that he devised the book so that it should "not read dull and tediously," seeing that the writing of it had been to him "a recreation of a recreation." He goes on:

I am the willinger to justify the pleasant part of it, because though it is known I can be serious at seasonable times, yet the whole Discourse is, or rather was, a picture of my own disposition. . . .

This picture he provides by a characteristically modest and indirect method. He does not talk about the man Izaak Walton, but allows Piscator to be his mouthpiece. Piscator is not simply the champion and expositor of the art of angling; he is markedly pious, a considerable moralizer, a man who relishes verse and song as well as good food and drink, a great lover of the countryside, above all a man of tranquil and contented temper.

Walton's piety is so pervasive that it scarcely needs illustrating. His duty to God is never very far from his mind. His reliance on the Bible is exemplified in a most disarming way in the arguments that Piscator uses in defense of angling against the counterattractions of hunting and hawking. He reminds his hearers of Christ's close fellowship with fishermen and of his miracles in connection with fish. Jonah is not forgotten—"Almighty God is said to have spoken to a fish, but never to a beast." He conjectures that the prophet Amos was not only a shepherd but a fisherman too, for his "humble, lowly, plain style" reminds him of "the affectionate, loving, lowly, humble Epistles of St. Peter, St. James and St. John, whom we know were all fishers": these he compares with "the glorious language and high metaphors of St. Paul, who we may believe was not."

No writer is more thoroughly English than Walton; and that, presumably, is why the English reading public took *The Compleat Angler* so warmly to their hearts, lavishing on it an abundance of praise that may be perplexing to foreign readers. Walton's delight in his favorite sport commends him, in the first place, to all amateurs; even non-fishermen can share in the enjoyment with which he expounds the mysteries of his craft. Next, he is a genuine lover of country sights and sounds, and it is well known that town-bred Englishmen often have a hankering for the countryside that is not shared by urban Europeans. Lastly, the Angler himself embodies the temperamental qualities on which Englishmen place a perhaps inordinate value; he is a kindly, tolerant, humorous, patient old man, who interferes with nobody and asks nothing better than to be allowed to enjoy his hobby in peace.

The reader who has never angled in his life may yet be beguiled by Walton's descriptions of the different kinds of freshwater fish and of the bait and flies by which they may be taken, for he speaks of all created things—even grubs and caddisworms—with a hearty appreciation of their natural qualities. He is very far, however, from restricting himself to the description of what he has actually observed. Some of his speculations remind us of the "unnatural natural history" of *Euphues*. The slow growth and great size of the carp suggest to him comparisons with the bear, the elephant, and the crocodile; he adduces authority for the belief that pike are bred from pickerel weed, quotes Pliny on the generation of caterpillars from dewdrops, and tells us (this time perhaps with his tongue in his cheek) that

a person of honour, now living in Worcestershire, assured me that he had seen a necklace, or collar of tadpoles, hang like a chain or necklace of beads about a Pike's neck, and to kill him; whether it were for meat or malice, must be, to me, a question.

When Walton has his eye on the object, he sets it before his readers with deft and vivid touches:

The Minnow hath . . . a kind of dappled or waved colour, like to a panther, on its sides, inclining to a greenish or sky colour.

Walton's descriptions of nature are sometimes so artfully contrived that we are transported into Arcadia rather than to the banks of the Lea or the Thames. Some years before he wrote *The Compleat Angler*, he had tried his hand at pastoral fantasy, in the brief introduction that he wrote to Francis Quarles's *The Shepheards Oracles*. Though his style is more parenthetical and clumsy than in the later book, the idyllic note is the same:

He in a Sommer's morning (about that howre when the great eye of Heaven first opens it selfe to give light to us mortals) walking a gentle pace towards a Brook (whose Spring-head was not far distant from his peacefull habitation) fitted with Angle, Lines and Flyes: Flyes proper for that season (being the fruitful month of *May*); intending to beguile the timrous Trout (with which that wat'ry element abounded) observ'd a more than common concourse of Shepheards. . . .

There were shepherdesses, too, "strewing the footpaths with Lillies, and Ladysmocks, so newly gathered by their fair hands, that they smelt more sweet then the morning. . . ." This vein is exploited in *The Compleat Angler*, notably in Venator's long musing on the nature of true riches. Though this deserves to be quoted in its entirety, an extract must serve to indicate the quality of Walton's deliberately pastoral writing:

I could there sit quietly; and looking on the water, see some fishes sport themselves in the silver streams, others leaping at flies of several shapes and colours; looking on the hills, I could behold them spotted with woods and groves; looking down the meadows, could see, here a boy gathering lilies and ladysmocks, and there a girl cropping culverkeys and cowslips, all to make garlands suitable to this present month of May.

No less delightful than these elaborations are the brief references to "yonder high honey-suckle hedge" or to the rain-washed grass—"how pleasantly that meadow looks; nay, and the earth smells so sweetly, too." Piscator and his pupil, for all their flights of eloquence, move in a countryside that is recognizably English.

About All-hallantide, and so till frost comes, when you see men ploughing up heath ground, or greenswards, then follow the plough, and you shall find a white worm, as big as two maggots, and it hath a red head: you may observe in what ground most are, for there the crows will be very watchful and follow the plough very close. . . .

They speak with warm approval of inns where they have been well treated, like the Thatched House at Hoddesdon; they expect from their hostesses comfortable beds, where "the linen looks white, and smells of lavender," besides demanding plenty of good drink and excellent cooking. Walton's relish for well-cooked food is unmistakable and endearing:

Come, my friend Coridon, this Trout looks lovely; it was twenty-two inches when it was taken; and the belly of it looked, some part of it, as yellow as a marigold, and part of it as white as a lily; and yet, methinks, it looks better in this good sauce.

For all his moralizing, Piscator is a thoroughly likeable old fellow, and so, we conclude, was Izaak Walton; but we must remember that he was a man of many dimensions, whereas his Angler has but one.

It is for his literary craftsmanship that Walton is truly remarkable, not for his skill as a fisherman, or for his homely piety and quiet contentment. He could not write a handbook on his favorite sport without making it a kind of anthology of his delights, and lovingly revising it paragraph by paragraph; and the *Lives* he took very much more seriously.

THE LIVES

THE spirit in which he approached the task of biographer reveals itself in the introduction to the *Life of Hooker*, where he speaks of its preparation as "a work of much labour to enquire, consider, research and determine what is needful to be known concerning him." There can be no doubt of his "well-meaning and diligence" when we note how he supplements personal recollections (either his own or those of persons well acquainted with his heroes) by references to records, letters, and wills. When he can ascertain an exact date, he gives it, and his constant revisions show his wish to make his biographies as full and accurate as possible. The appendix that he added to the *Life of Hooker* proves his anxiety in this respect. This *Life* probably gave him more trouble than any of the others, for not only was its subject a very eminent man, he also belonged to a generation of which there were almost no survivors at the time when Walton was writing.

It is probable that his interest in biography developed from the habit of collecting notes and anecdotes in the jackdaw spirit of John Aubrey. We know from the *Life of Hooker* that he had begun to collect information about the great man at the time when he was first acquainted with the Cranmer family—that is, at the time of his first marriage, some forty years before Bishop Sheldon commissioned him to write a biography that would be a corrective to John Gauden's memoir. Walton must have kept a diary of sorts, unless he had an absolutely prodigious memory for dates and conversations. But if the *Lives* owe their origin to an antiquarian's interest in the details relating to famous worthies, it is to an artist's conscious skill in the manipulation of his material that they owe their enduring merit.

Walton's attitude to all five of his subjects is that of the portrait painter. He does not walk all around his subjects, observing them from every point of view; or if he does, this is a preliminary process. Having made up his mind which are the most striking lineaments in each man, and from what angle they appear to the best advantage, Walton sets up his easel and works steadily. He uses different techniques—with Wotton he is more impressionistic, with Hooker and Sanderson he pays special attention to the background—but always he feels himself at liberty to treat some facts as more relevant to his purpose than others. This explains the apparent disproportion in the *Lives* of Donne and Herbert, in both of which the emphasis is overwhelmingly on their latter years. Though all five *Lives* were commemorative tributes, these two especially were written in a spirit of veneration. Walton was not a monumental mason, any more than he was an anatomist. His eulogies are worked into the texture of the extended study. While it is possible to pick out from the *Lives* anecdotes and digressions that can be enjoyed out of their context, it is impossible to extract epitomes of the characters of the men whom Walton is portraying. Until we have looked at each picture in its totality, we cannot get the impression that he was working to convey.

Walton never willfully misleads, even when he takes liberties that would be impossible today. If he makes a synthesis of several letters of Donne, presenting them as one continuous epistle, he gives the reader due warning that it is "an extract collected out of some few of his many Letters." If he paraphrases passages from Herbert's works and presents them as speeches uttered by Herbert, he is acting on the same principle that he acknowledges in the preface to the *Life of Sanderson*—an artistic principle, enabling him to add life and variety to his narrative: "I have been so bold, as to paraphrase and say what I think he (whom I had the happiness to know well) would have said upon the same occasion." Walton did not actually know Herbert, but he knew his writings intimately, and when he puts words into Herbert's mouth, they are always beautifully in character. We may, indeed, rely on Walton's honesty and regard for truth, even though later investigators have established his occasional inaccuracy about circumstance or chronology. When he issued his revised *Life of Donne* in 1658, he set forth plainly his intentions and methods as a biographer:

I either speak of my own knowledge, or from the testimony of such as dare do any thing, rather than speak an untruth. And for that part of it which is my own observation or opinion, if I had a power I would not use it to force any man's assent, but leave him a liberty to disbelieve what his own reason inclines him to.

Walton succeeds in investing all five of his *Lives* with a sense of intimacy because he so consistently relies on personal testimony. Donne and Wotton had been his friends, and Bishop Morley had made him acquainted with Dr. Sanderson; but Herbert he had only seen once, and Hooker had died while Walton was a child. These two *Lives*, however, are not inferior to the others in verisimilitude, for Walton turned for information about Herbert to men who had known him well, including Edmund Duncon and Arthur Woodnoth, who visited Herbert at Bemerton, and the man who ordained him, Dr. Humphrey Henchman, who "tells me, He laid his hand on *Mr. Herberts* Head, and, (alas!) within less then three years, lent his Shoulder to carry his dear Friend to his Grave." Donne, too, may have talked about Herbert, whom he had known from childhood, and so may have Henry King, who had been Herbert's schoolfellow at Westminster. Barnabas Oley, too, who included a brief account of Herbert in his edition of *A Priest to the Temple*, was treasurer of Worcester Cathedral at the time when Walton was Bishop Morley's steward there. For the *Life of Hooker* he drew upon the information he had collected years earlier, at the time of his connection with the Cranmer family and Dr. John Spencer; he mentions also his conversations with Archbishop Usher, Bishop Morton, and "the learned John Hales of Eaton-Colledge," all of whom "loved the very name of Mr. Hooker."

Walton was far from being a mere retailer of personal gossip. There are some notes extant that he sent to Aubrey, who had asked for his recollections of Ben Jonson. He confesses that he scarcely knew him, but supplies some reminiscences that Bishop Morley, in conversation, had summoned up, making quite clear that none of the material is more than hearsay. Even when Walton could speak at first hand, and might legitimately have introduced himself into the narrative, his sense of decorum made him refrain. For example, we know from *The Compleat Angler* that he used to go fishing with Sir Henry Wotton, and had many discourses with him about the art of angling; but in the *Life of Wotton*, we find only this passage:

Nor did he forget his innate pleasure of *Angling*, which he would usually call, *his idle time, not idly spent*: saying often, he would rather live five *May months*, then forty *Decembers*.

A still more striking example of self-effacement may be observed in the *Life of Donne*. From the letter that Bishop King, one of Donne's executors, wrote many years later to "Honest Izaak," it appears that Walton was present at Donne's bedside three days before his death, when he entrusted his sermons to his friend King; but Walton himself makes no mention of the incident. His love and veneration for Donne were too great to allow him to intrude himself into his deeply moving account of the great man's last days. Notwithstanding Walton's regard for personal testimony and firsthand observation, he was no Boswell, rushing in where angels fear to tread. His attitude has more in common with that of John Roper, who in his *Life* of his father-in-law, Sir Thomas More, conveys a wonderful sense of intimacy without sacrifice of reverence.

Walton has been criticized for an excess of reverence toward the subjects of his biographies, and also for reducing them all to a sameness of gentle piety. Certainly he took no liberties with any of them, but it would have been as much against the conventions of his age as against his own good instincts if he had done so. It is true that he celebrates Dr. Donne the dean of St. Paul's and pays scant attention to Jack Donne the poet and amorist; true that he spends far more time on the three years of Herbert's pastorate at Bemerton than on the rest of his career. But he was commemorating in both men the qualities and achievements that they themselves would have wished to endure in the minds of posterity. By the time of his death, Donne's fame as a divine and preacher had made the exploits of his youth seem of little account. Walton was not in the least idiosyncratic in valuing his sermons and sacred poems, together with his theological and devotional prose writings, far above the poems that during his lifetime he had never troubled to collect, some of which he would gladly have disowned. Walton's own verdict is made quite explicit in the lines that he wrote for the 1635 edition of Donne's poems. They appear beneath William Marshall's portrait of Donne at eighteen, and run:

This was for youth, Strength, Mirth and wit that Time
Most count their golden Age: but t'was not thine.
Thine was thy later yeares, so much refind
From youth's Drosse, Mirth & wit; as thy pure mind
Thought (like the Angels) nothing but the Praise
Of thy Creator, in those last, best Dayes.
   Witnes this Booke, (thy Embleme) which begins
   With Love; but endes, with Sighes, & Teares for sins.

Walton could scarcely have anticipated that in three hundred years' time both Donne and Herbert would owe their reputation primarily to their poetry. He saw them, as all his contemporaries did, as ornaments of the Anglican church. If he regarded them both with veneration, he did not, in fact, minimize the contrast between Donne's headstrong, unsettled youth and the penitential gravity of his later years, any more than he failed to record young Herbert's ambitions of worldly success.

It is in the *Life of Sir Henry Wotton*, delightful as it is in its rambling way, that Walton's limitations are most clearly seen. He had not the experience of the world to enable him to write an adequate biography of a very remarkable diplomatist and statesman. He could appreciate the scholarly and pious aspects of Wotton's character, but could not convey his brilliance. The *Life* was apparently written in haste in order to serve as a preface to the *Reliquiae Wottonianae* which was published in 1651 (and frequently reprinted). Walton apologizes for his own shortcomings, but loyalty to the memory of a friend evidently operated as it did with the *Life of Donne*. Rather than see Donne's *Sermons* appear without a prefatory biography, Walton hastily wrote one. He and Wotton had been collecting the material for some time, but the actual composition seems to have taken Walton less than two months. Similarly, in default of a worthier biography to introduce Wotton's collected writings to the public, Walton supplied one.

The *Life of Mr. George Herbert* was written out of pure regard for "that great example of holiness," and was printed as an independent biography, not attached to any edition of Herbert's works. The *Lives* of Hooker and Sanderson were both commissioned by bishops and had a more polemical intention than the other three. Both men had contended at different epochs with the policies of Puritan extremists, and in order to set their achievements in the right perspective, Walton related their individual careers to the general politico-religious background.

These two *Lives* are especially well documented. Walton's main authorities for the Elizabethan survey were William Camden (to whom he refers constantly throughout the *Lives*) and John Spottiswoode's *History of the Church of Scotland* (1655). Fuller was another historian to whom he was indebted. He is usually careful to cite his sources. Conscientiousness, indeed, was the impelling force behind his practice of constant revision.

Walton had few English predecessors in the art of biography; indeed, the term "biographer" first occurs in the 1660's, though "historiographer" was current earlier. He lived at a time when men's minds, besides turning inward to self-scrutiny, were pursuing the study of character through the observation of their fellows. Among Walton's contemporaries were the great introspectives: Bunyan, Fox, Sir Thomas Browne; there was Richard Baxter, who could look both inward and outward and report reliably on all his findings; there were the diarists, Samuel Pepys and John Evelyn; and there was the earl of Clarendon, who was compiling his incomparable gallery of Civil War "characters"; yet as an artist in pure biography, there is nobody in the seventeenth century to touch Izaak Walton.

He had, in the first place, an unusual appreciation of the value of factual material, and was a diligent searcher after dates and documents. He was not the first biographer to use letters, but he made an exceptionally intelligent use of them in his *Lives* of Donne and Herbert. (Incidentally, we owe to Walton the preservation of the two sonnets that the seventeen-year-old Herbert sent to his mother as a gift.) Walton also realized that personal impressions were both immensely valuable and very perishable, and he accordingly took pains to include as many as he considered trustworthy.

He was much more than a conscientious collector of biographical material and much more than an ingenious arranger of that material; he was an artist with a great gift of human sympathy. It is his own personal feeling of reverent affection that animates the studies of Donne, Wotton, Hooker, Herbert, and Sanderson, and unifies the five *Lives* that were written at such different times and for such different purposes. Subordinating himself completely, yet maintaining a consistent and characteristic point of view, Walton produced a series of portraits that were as true and as beautiful as he was able to make them. He excelled in the faculty that Dr. Johnson singled out for particular praise when he wrote in *The Rambler* of the art of the biographer (in which he was himself a master); the discrimination "to pass slightly over those performances and incidents which produce vulgar greatness, to lead the thoughts into domestic privacies, and to display the minute details of daily life." It is small wonder that Johnson reckoned Walton's *Lives* "one of his most favourite books."

In common with the *Lives*, *The Compleat Angler* also commended itself to Johnson's acute judgment, and it was at his instigation that Moses Browne rescued it from neglect and reissued it in 1750. Sir John Hawkins, who ten years later brought out a more accurate edition, which included a life of Walton, was also a friend of Johnson's. The rather whimsical charm of the book was fully appreciated only by later generations. It was a volume after Charles Lamb's own heart, and none of its innumerable eulogists has praised it better. Recommending the book to Samuel Coleridge, he wrote: "It breathes the very spirit of innocence, purity, and simplicity of heart; . . . it would sweeten a man's temper at any time to read it; it would Christianise every angry, discordant passion; pray make yourself acquainted with it."

Since that time, Izaak Walton has become the object of a cult. *The Compleat Angler* has been printed again and again, sometimes very sumptuously, and the little handbook written for his own pleasure to celebrate his favorite pastime has become Walton's chief guarantee of immortality. In spite of all those who connect Walton's name with angling, only a few have read the *Lives*.

Fate is apt to play odd tricks with a man's literary remains, so that what he valued most is left unread, and his unconsidered trifles are treasured. Something of the kind has happened with Donne, and we see it with Walton too. But whereas Donne's sermons and theological works call for a degree of perseverance that the twentieth-century reader is loath to give, Walton's serious works commend themselves by being brief and delightfully readable. Anyone who is attracted to "honest Izaak," in the guise of Piscator, will find his qualities displayed to even better advantage in the *Lives*; and he will also make the acquaintance, on intimate terms, of five very memorable worthies of the seventeenth century.

SELECTED BIBLIOGRAPHY

I. BIBLIOGRAPHY. T. Westwood, *The Chronicle of the Compleat Angler* (London, 1864), reprinted with additions by T. Satchell in R. B. Marston, ed., *The Compleat Angler* (London, 1888); A. Wood, *A Bibliography of The Compleat Angler* (New York, 1900); J. E. Butt, "A Bibliography of Izaak Walton's Lives," *Proceedings of the Oxford Bibliographical Society* II (London, 1930), records only seventeenth-century eds.; P. Oliver, *A New Chronicle of The Compleat Angler* (London, 1936), records 284 eds.; B. S. Horne, *A Bibliography of The Compleat Angler 1653–1967* (Pittsburgh, 1970).

II. COLLECTED WORKS. *The Lives of Dr. John Donne, Sir Henry Wotton, Mr. Richard Hooker, Mr. George Herbert* (London, 1670), reprinted in T. Zouch, ed. (York, 1796; 3rd ed., 1817), with notes and the life of the author; *The Life of Dr. Sanderson* was added to the 1st ed., *Love and Truth* was added to the 3rd ed.; also reprinted in Pickering Diamond Classics ed. (London, 1827), in the Society of the Promotion of Christian Knowledge ed. (London, 1833), in W. Dowling, ed. (London, 1857), with memoir of Walton by the editor, in A. H. Bullen, ed. (London, 1884), in Bohn's Illustrated Library, in A. Dobson, ed. (London, 1898), in the Temple Classics series, in the World Classics ed. (London, 1927), with intro. by G. Saintsbury; R. H. Shepherd, ed., *Waltoniana* (London, 1878), contains all but two of Walton's prose and verse remains; G. L. Keynes, ed., *The Compleat Walton* (London, 1929), a 1-vol. ed. with bibliographical notes.

III. SEPARATE WORKS. *The Life and Death of Dr. Donne* (London, 1640), prefixed to *LXXX Sermons, Preached by . . . John Donne*, a 2nd, enl. ed. appeared separately as *The Life of John Donne* (London, 1658); *The Life of Sir Henry Wotton* (London, 1651), prefixed to *Reliquiae Wottonianae*, 2nd ed. with additions and alterations appeared in the 1654 ed. of *Reliquiae Wottonianae*; *The Compleat Angler or the Contemplative Man's Recreation* (London, 1653; enl. ed., 1655; last rev., 1676), reprinted at least 385 times, including M. Browne, ed. (London, 1750); Sir J. Hawkins, ed. (London, 1760), with "Notes Historical, Critical and Explanatory"; J. Major, publ. (London, 1823), intro. by R. Thompson, profusely illustrated; Pickering's Diamond Classics (London, 1825), the ed. of 1836 has important memoir and notes by Sir H. Nicolas and many illustrations; G. W. Bethune, ed. (New York, 1847); E. Stock, publ. (London, 1876; first facs. ed., 1896), reissue has preface by R. Le Gallienne; R. B. Marston, ed., 2 vols. (London, 1888); J. R. Lowell, ed. (Boston, 1889), with intro.; A. Lang, ed. (London, 1896), with intro., the Everyman ed.; G. A. B. Dewar, ed. (London, 1902), with essay by Sir E. Gray; G. Keynes, ed. (London, 1929), the Nonesuch ed.; Penguin Books ed. (London, 1939); Folio Society ed. (London, 1949); M. Bottrall, ed. (London, 1962), new intro. to Everyman ed.; *The Life of Mr. Richard Hooker* (London, 1665); *The Life of Mr. George Herbert* (London, 1670); *The Life of Dr. Sanderson* (London, 1678); *Love and Truth* (London, 1680), published anonymously.

IV. SOME CRITICAL AND BIOGRAPHICAL STUDIES. W. Teal, *Lives of English Laymen* (London, 1842), draws on Sir Harris Nicolas and other editors of Walton's work; G. M. Tweddell, *Izaak Walton and the Earlier English Writers on Angling* (London, 1854); R. B. Marston, *Walton and Some Earlier Writers on Fish and Fishing* (London, 1894); Stapleton Martin, *Izaak Walton and His Friends* (London, 1903); E. Marston, *Thomas Ken and Izaak Walton* (London, 1908); L. Lambert, *Izaak Walton and the Royal Deanery of Stafford* (London, 1926); H. Nicolson, *The Development of English Biography* (London, 1927), disparages Walton; D. A. Stauffer, *English Biography Before 1700* (Cambridge, Mass., 1930), contains a valuable chapter on Walton; H. J. Oliver, "Izaak Walton's Prose Style," *Review of English Studies*, XXI (1945); J. E. Butt, *Biography in the Hands of Walton, Johnson, and Boswell* (Los Angeles, 1966); J. R. Cooper, *The Art of the Compleat Angler* (Chapel Hill, N.C., 1968); F. Costa, *L'oeuvre d'Izaak Walton* (Paris, 1973).

SIR THOMAS BROWNE

(1605-1682)

Peter Green

PHYSIC AND METAPHYSIC

THERE is a peculiarly paradoxical flavor about Sir Thomas Browne's position in English letters. Few writers of his distinction have shown less professional interest in literature as such: what primarily concerned Browne were the twin themes of scientific research and religious exploration. He fell into public authorship by accident; and, with paradoxical irony, he is remembered today less for his experiments in embryology or even his antisectarian mysticism than for his unique style. We know that, as Georges Louis Leclerc, comte de Buffon said, *le style c'est l'homme même*; and it is true that Browne's hypnotic, haunting rhythms, the rich texture of his prose, his idiosyncratic vocabulary and imagery are indissolubly bound up with the beliefs he held no less than his professional vocation of medicine. But to read Browne for his style alone, as though his work were some religious incantation, the meaning of which had long fallen into oblivion, is to lose the greater part of what he has to offer us. Few prose writers have achieved such associative denseness of texture: the strands that compose his web cannot be separated without damaging the whole.

To recover the atmosphere—emotional no less than intellectual—in which Browne composed his works requires some effort today. Very early the pressing problems that confronted him had changed or were forgotten: Pepys records how already in his day the *Religio Medici* was bracketed with Osborne's cynical *Advice to a Son* and Samuel Butler's *Hudibras*—a collocation that would not, probably, occur to most modern readers—and how "these three books were the most esteemed and generally cried up *for wit* in the world": an equally surprising verdict. Browne had a talent for making unconscious prophecies about himself: in a letter to his son Thomas he remarked, apropos Lucan: "I

hope you are more taken with the verses than the subject, and rather embrace the expression than the example." Subsequent generations were not slow to apply the precept to Browne's own work. Yet his style has in the last resort acted as the preservative of his ideas; without it the chances are that he would not now be read at all. It is his pregnant imagery rather than his rational argument that sends our imagination soaring: "Those images that yet/ Fresh images beget. . . . " And it is, without doubt, his most famous passages that have most to offer today.

Sir Thomas Browne's life spans the most troubled years of an exceedingly troubled century—troubled politically, socially, and above all by the increasing tension between religious transition and scientific discovery. The fugal counterstresses set up by this tension affected every thinking person, in particular every writer of the period. Browne, Janus-like, faced both ways, at some cost to himself. Sweet reasonableness is never popular with passionate sectarians; and Browne had further to contend with the subtle temptations of his scientific training. "The Devill, that did but buffet Saint *Paul*, playes mee thinkes at sharpe with me," he wrote. "There is another man within mee, that's angry with mee, rebukes, commands and dastards mee." His deep faith was only equaled by his unquenchable experimental curiosity; and it was the two in combination that crystallized his unique mystical prose poems, as a precipitate forms in the retort from two powerful chemical substances forced together by an external agent. He stood, literally, at the crossroads of history: past and future fused in him. He could have written at no other time than when he did.

As Professor B. Willey puts it, "how to fit a supernaturalist and poetic scripture into the new world-scheme, how to reconcile . . . the whole miraculous structure of Christianity with the new 'philosophy'"—this was the problem facing writers as diverse as Bacon and Donne. The tradition of classical skepticism had been renewed by Pierre Gassendi; fresh Aristotelian manuscripts had come to light that proved exceedingly hard to reconcile with Scholastic doctrine; and hardly was the Anglican rupture with Rome settled when the old cosmology was torn from top to bottom by the theories of Galileo and Copernicus. The possibility that the earth was not, after all, the stable center of the universe produced a violent psychological shock on all thinking and religious people. Where were the limits of human knowledge to be set? How was belief to be squared with the new revolutionary advances in natural science?

Browne's training as a physician exposed him to such doubts in their most naked form. After a normal English education at Winchester and Pembroke College, Oxford, he left for the Continent in 1630, to pursue his medical studies successively at Montpellier, Padua, and Leyden. Montpellier was a half-Catholic, half-Protestant town: the medical school, though backward in anatomy, breathed a liberal atmosphere independent of ecclesiastical authority, and pursued a deliberately revolutionary policy of keeping science and religion in distinct compartments. William Harvey had recently graduated from Padua, which was under Venetian protection and in diametrical opposition to papal control: as a result there was no embargo on clinical dissection, and the anatomy school was the finest in Europe. At Leyden students of all faiths were freely admitted, and the town was, as a result, a hotbed of religious controversy. It was here, in December 1633, that Thomas Browne received his degree of doctor of medicine: possibly with a thesis on syphilis, which casts an interesting light on his obsessive imagery relating to death and physical corruption.

In any case it is clear that the new scientific and medical methodology, viewed at close quarters, made an extremely powerful impact on Browne's mind. He, like many of his contemporaries, suffered periods of intense melancholic depression. He clearly came near to losing his faith early in his pursuit of scientific knowledge:

The Devill played at Chesse with mee, and yeelding a pawne, thought to gaine a Queen of me, taking advantage of my honest endeavours; and whilst I laboured to raise the structure of my reason, hee striv'd to undermine the edifice of my faith.

(*Religio Medici*, Part I, sec. xix)

Browne found a solution; but it was one more common among Roman Catholics than Anglicans, and tinged with heresy at that: the doctrine known as fideism.

Fideism was expressed concisely by Pietro Pomponazzi a century or more earlier: the Bolognese philosopher defended himself against a charge of heresy by declaring: "I believe as a Christian what I cannot believe as a philosopher." The doctrine had plausible classical antecedents and became popular with writers such as Montaigne, Pico della Mirandola, and Pascal, chiefly through reconciling free intellectual skepticism with an ultimate adherence to religious orthodoxy. It lies at the heart of Sir Thomas Browne's philosophy of life and scientific method. He formulated his principles of thought and belief in his earliest work, the *Religio Medici*, and applied them, diversely, to all his subsequent activities, literary or scientific. The merit of fideism, from Browne's viewpoint, was that it released his energies for scientific experiment without ever imperiling his religious faith. So sure was he of his ground, in fact, that he could afford to indulge in remarkably trenchant Higher Criticism of the Scriptures. This, together with his profession, is quite enough to explain his reputation, with some of his contemporaries, as an atheist.

Few books, surely, can have so quickly become a classic yet remained so thoroughly misunderstood as the *Religio Medici*. Its very title appeared a paradox; and certainly its spiritual tolerance and charity—travel had left Browne with a friendly respect for all creeds and customs—must have struck oddly on the ears of that dogmatic and sectarian age:

I am, I confesse, naturally inclined to that which misguided zeale terms superstition . . . at my devotion I love to use the civility of my knee, my hat, and hand, with all those outward and sensible motions, which may expresse or promote my invisible devotion. . . . At a solemne Procession I have wept abundantly, while my consorts, blinde with opposition and prejudice, have fallen into an excesse of scorne and laughter . . . I could never divide my selfe from any man upon the difference of an opinion, or be angry with his judgement for not agreeing with mee in that, from which perhaps within a few dayes I should dissent my selfe.

(*Rel. Med.*, Part I, secs. iii, vi)

On the basis of the *Religio Medici* Browne was not only attacked for atheism but claimed, with some show of plausibility, both by Catholics and Quakers, as a de jure convert.

His approach to Christian dogma is, indeed, somewhat eclectic, not to say muddled. He makes an initial declaration of allegiance to the Church of England; but his subsequent ramblings in Hermetic mysticism, Roman Stoicism, and near-Manichee heresies make it clear that his Anglican faith was infinitely elastic. His favorite doctrine, the Platonic theory of ideas, hardly figures in Church of England theology. It should be remembered that the book was conceived as a private summing up of the author's spiritual and philosophical position after his continental experiences; it was never intended for publication, and only appeared after a text pirated from Browne's manuscript had attracted considerable publicity—mainly through the attentions of Sir Kenelm Digby. Perhaps for this reason it offers a remarkably early example of spiritual self-analysis, un-self-conscious to a degree Browne might well have failed to attain if deliberately aiming at an unrestricted public.

In this sense *Religio Medici* possesses, quite apart from its literary or mystical value, much interest considered purely as an autobiographical document. It is fascinating to learn that Browne knew six languages, "beside the *Jargon* and *Patois* of several provinces"; that he could "look a whole day with delight upon a handsome Picture, though it be but of an Horse"; and that he wished "we might procreate like trees, without conjunction." (He married Dorothy Mileham in 1641, and had ten children; what Dame Dorothy made of this passage, history does not relate.) His ironic self-appraisal, however, keeps us perpetually on the alert:

There is I think no man that apprehends his owne miseries lesse than my selfe, and no man that so neerely apprehends anothers. I could lose an arme without a teare, and with a few groans, mee thinkes, be quartered into pieces; yet can I weepe most seriously at a Play, and receive with a true passion, the counterfeit griefes of those knowne and professed impostours . . . I thank the goodnesse of God, I have no sinnes that want a name; I am not singular in offences; my transgressions are Epidemicall, and from the common breath of our corruption. . . .

(*Rel. Med.*, Part II, secs. v, vii)

The questions Browne discusses are those most pressing at the time—the creation or eternity of the world, the nature of the soul, the truth of God's ex-

istence, the rival claims of faith and reason, the veracity of demons, witches, astrology, and miracles. But his conclusions and his autobiographical method (which blends St. Augustine's *Confessions* with the relaxed temperament of an English Montaigne) are worlds away from the prevalent theological temper of Anglican England, more fairly represented by the rational *Ecclesiastical Polity* of Richard Hooker. It is no coincidence that *Religio Medici* was better understood, and more fully appreciated, on the Continent: it is full of continental ideas. Montaigne and Pascal would have recognized its premises instantly.

Browne's fideism at one stroke disposes of sectarian wrangling and, by establishing a double criterion of truth, opens the door to his beloved scientific experiments:

As for those wingy mysteries in Divinity, and ayery subtilties of Religion, which have unhing'd the braines of better heads, they never stretch the *Pia Mater* of mine; mee thinkes there be not impossibilities enough in Religion for an active faith; the deepest mysteries ours containes have not only been illustrated, but maintained, by syllogisme and the rule of reason: I love to lose my selfe in a mystery, to pursue my Reason to an *o altitudo!* . . . I can answer all the objections of Satan, and my rebellious reason with that odde resolution I learned of *Tertullian, Certum est, quia impossibile est.*

(*Rel. Med.*, Part I, sec. ix)

His faith, in fact, flourishes on mystical paradox: it is hardly surprising that he should relish and repeat the Hermetic definition of God as a circle whose center is everywhere and whose circumference is nowhere.

Those who look for strict consistency in the *Religio Medici* will be disappointed—and ill-advised. The principle of dual reality once established, Browne can relax into his natural temper: what may best be described as religioscientific romanticism. He ranges like a bee over the whole variegated garden of contemporary thought, sipping where he will, integrating what he needs into his own personal, creative interpretation of the universe. He is at heart a poet: his vision has the direct, symbolic intensity we associate with Vaughan, Traherne, Crashaw, or—above all—Donne, whose famous declaration that "all divinity is love or wonder" echoes exactly Browne's own attitude. What drew, and continues to draw, readers to this idiosyncratic spiritual testament is the creative unity that it imposes on apparently irreconcilable modes of thought; the harmony that can embrace science and faith alike, gather together the scattered, broken symbols and from them strike, clear and complete, the lost music of the spheres.

THAT GREAT AMPHIBIUM

BROWNE's eclectic theology explains why, on the basis of his own utterances, various critics can, with equal plausibility, claim him as a serious scientist, a disciple of Aquinas, or a latter-day Gnostic. (Others, again, have accused him of deliberate duplicity or schizoid thought, the metaphysical equivalent of doublethink.) None of these interpretations seems wholly justified; they all approach Browne from a limited and partial viewpoint. "I attained my purpose," he wrote, "and came to reach this port by a bare wind, much labour, great paynes and little assistance." The squaring of his medical with his religious conscience was not achieved by an easy piece of casuistry. One is reminded of T. S. Eliot's famous remark about the seventeenth century's "dissociation of sensibility." In Browne this dissociation can be observed in embryo. His whole creative energy was directed toward the reintegration of already rapidly diverging intellectual and spiritual elements: but it was a vain endeavor. He lived to see his unity of awareness finally destroyed, split apart by the wedge of scientific inquiry unmodified by moral considerations.

Though he knew and approved the work of such pioneers as Descartes, Vesalius the anatomist, and Harvey—whose treatise on the circulation of the blood he valued more highly, he declared, than Columbus' discovery of America—the framework of Browne's thought remained, inevitably, dependent on the pre-Copernican cosmology. It is no accident that the poet from whom he quotes most often, and who influenced him more than any other literary source except the Bible, is Dante. *The Divine Comedy* presented a model of the stable cosmos, mystically conceived, that matched exactly Browne's own temperament: it offered the combination of precise (and often exotic) antiquarianism and a passionate sense of divine order and pattern. Browne might have had the *Paradiso* in mind when he wrote, in the final chapter of *The Garden of Cyrus*: "All things began in order, so shall they end, and so shall they begin again; according to the or-

dainer of order and mysticall Mathematicks of the City of Heaven."

The ultimate responsibility for truth, then, Browne resigns to God; and the medieval Divine Ladder of Being, with its immutable hierarchy, is used by Browne as a pattern and background for his investigation of natural phenomena. Nature, he declares in a pregnant phrase, is the art of God (an excellent way, incidentally, of avoiding his natural tendency to slip into pantheism); and all physical phenomena are mere Platonic shadows of ideal and absolute reality. At the highest point of the Ladder is God, with the Angels a little below; at the bottom lie the vegetable and mineral worlds. But in the central position, poised between physical and divine, and partaking of both, stands man—"that great and true *Amphibium*," as Browne describes him, "whose nature is disposed to live, not onely like other creatures in divers elements, but in divided and distinguished worlds." Browne, in fact, applies the traditional concepts of macrocosm and microcosm to the world; and man, for him, represents the focal point of potential knowledge:

Wee carry with us the wonders we seeke without us: There is all *Africa* and her prodigies in us; we are that bold and adventurous piece of nature, which he that studies wisely learnes in a *compendium* what others labour at in a divided piece and endlesse volume.

(Rel. Med., Part I, sec. xv)

In considering Browne we are all too apt to forget the physician while analyzing his faith. At least half of Browne's creative mind depends for its conceptual imagery on his medical and scientific awareness; and this awareness often accords more nearly with his notions of universal harmony than we might suppose. He allows his intellect to follow up innumerable isolated phenomena, but carefully avoids coordinating his research in the modern sense. This is his method of saving appearances. He can collect innumerable data as long as no dangerous general law is allowed to emerge from his findings: which explains the piecemeal character of much in his work. He resembles in this the victim of the old music hall joke, who has never seen an inference and therefore cannot draw one.

Thus when he speaks of the "strange and mystical transmigrations of silkworms," Browne is, at one level, applying the results (as we know from his notes) of painstaking laboratory observation; but on a higher plane he is shaping the visible manifestation into his a priori Platonic scheme of things. For him this implies no inconsistency; he finds no difficulty in accommodating to his religious tenets the scientific credo that he poses:

Let thy Studies be free as thy Thoughts and Contemplations, but fly not only upon the wings of Imagination; joyn Sense unto Reason, and Experiment unto Speculation, and so give life unto Embryon Truths, and Verities yet in their Chaos. There is nothing more acceptable unto the Ingenious World, than this noble Eluctation of Truth; wherein, against the tenacity of Prejudice and Prescription, this Century now prevaileth.

(Christian Morals, Part II, sec. v)

Nor does Browne find any trouble in reconciling this advice (which, within limits, he follows scrupulously himself) with an acceptance of demonology and witchcraft. To deny the existence of the Devil and his agents is to deny, by implication, the whole of the fixed spiritual hierarchy, and thus lay oneself open to a charge of atheism. Following the same double standard, Browne experiments in detail with the atomic theory, but sternly warns his son, on religious grounds, against reading Lucretius.

It is against this background that Browne's first deliberate venture into the world of authorship must be considered. *Pseudodoxia Epidemica*, commonly known—though not by its author—as *Vulgar Errors*, appeared in 1646, and proved immensely popular during Browne's lifetime. Despite its summary dismissal by modern critics—few of whom appear to have read it with any care—as a jumble of old wives' tales and *idées reçues* culled from the pages of Pliny the Elder or Dioscorides, it was planned and executed with a perfectly serious scientific purpose. Far from perpetuating myths, it aimed to remove the worst of those superstitions, irrational fancies, and popular legends then current regarding the natural world; and in the process to deal a blow at the deadening influence of so-called classical "authorities." Of course, Browne had a generous share of all the vices he attacked; he was, besides, severely handicapped by his religious scruples. But the intention was there.

Pseudodoxia Epidemica makes fascinating reading, not only for the devotee of curiosa, but also for anyone interested in the popular (as opposed to the "advanced") beliefs current in the seventeenth century. The subtitles of sections tell their own story: "That an Elephant hath no joints"; "That a Badger hath the Legs of one side shorter than of the other"; "That Storks will only live in Republicks and free States"; and, with ingenuous honesty, "Of some Relations whose truth we fear." But, wherever theology permitted, the matter was put to scientific proof: "That Flos Affricanus is poison, and destroyeth dogs," Browne observes tranquilly, "in two experiments we have not found."

The obvious inspiration for a work of this nature is Bacon's *Advancement of Learning*; but Browne's scheme for the extirpation of popular error differs materially from Bacon's Idols. He seems to owe more to the classical tradition of skepticism. Many of the experiments are surprisingly sound; and Browne's biological observations supply revealing glosses to the imagery of his more literary works. The life cycle was never far from his mind.

Pseudodoxia Epidemica has suffered neglect for two main reasons. It is scientifically obsolete, and not composed, on the whole, in that heightened mystical style that is the main attraction for Browne's readers today. But the style, plain and serviceable in the main though it be, is still underrated: again and again Browne enriches his text with a memorable phrase or associative image—as when, discussing the properties of crystal, he credits it with "the seeds of petrification and Gorgon within itself." And as for the experimental research—the hours spent observing the slow growth of duckweed or fetus, the behavior of electrified bodies, the swarming creatures gyrating in a drop of rainwater—all this was for Browne simply a physical demonstration of the ideal reality embodied in the ultimate macrocosm. Yet the traffic of suggestion moved in both directions: it seems certain that the miracle of the developing embryo, which so fascinated Browne, also led him to formulate large generalities, by analogy, about the universe.

Browne saw the microcosm in the microscope: throughout his life he preserved a passion for the minute intricacies of the insect or plant world, which he found more to his taste than the Creator's larger and clumsier pieces of handiwork. There is the closest possible interrelationship between his work in biology, his religious beliefs, his general philosophy, his well-known thematic preoccupations, and his use of metaphor, image, and symbol (including his obsession with the mystical numerology of Pythagoreanism and the Cabbala). His literary achievement owes its power, depth, and associative richness precisely to this interaction of widely differing modes of apprehension and thought. A stale literary theme is transmuted in Browne's laboratory; his symbols hatch from eggs or frog spawn to soar into the cosmos, and his mysticism makes poetry of gestation.

Browne, as we might expect, adhered to the "vitalistic" school of biology, according to which all living creatures shared in a "vegetal or nutritive soul," the nature of which was akin to fire or light. He also believed in panspermatism, the doctrine that taught that at the creation, seminal particles were diffused through the world, where they continue to cause generation by direct entry into the organism. After death this "seminal principle" leaves the corpse and becomes available once more: it is a kind of indestructible élan vital.

It is not hard to see how from this pseudoscientific theory a more general cosmology could be inferred. It was a short step (on the principle, again, of microcosm and macrocosm) from panspermatic vitalism to the divinity of the World Soul; from the unseen nutritive fire to the Invisible Flame of Life. The intersecting point of matter and spirit could be conceived as lying in the generative seminality of the womb: "Parts of the seed," Browne noted, "do seem to contain the Idea and power of the whole." Again, from the human womb an easy transference could be made (with good literary precedent) to Chaos as the Universal Womb; and the departure of the "seminal principle" at death also fostered a paradoxical connection between the grave and rebirth, this life and the next. Womb and tomb achieved a kind of mystical identity.

Meanwhile, in the womb of Browne's imagination, all these elements slowly fused and germinated. Image, theme, and interpretation came together to form a single creative entity; and fifteen years later Browne produced his unquestioned masterpiece.

URN AND QUINCUNX

Pseudodoxia Epidemica appeared in 1646, the year that saw the Parliamentarians' final triumph in the Civil War. *Hydriotaphia*, or *Urn Burial*, and *The Garden of Cyrus* were published together in 1658, the year of Cromwell's death. Thus the gestation of the later works coincided almost exactly with the Protectorate; and this is not without its signifi-

cance. Browne was an ardent royalist in a town that favored the protector: his political views probably underlay his one marked intolerance, for:

> that great enemy of reason, vertue and religion, the multitude; that numerous piece of monstrosity, which taken asunder seeme men, and the reasonable creatures of God; but confused together, make but one great beast, and a monstrosity more prodigious than Hydra.
>
> (*Rel. Med.*, Part II, sec. i)

During the whole of those fifteen years he must have been under violent emotional and psychological stress.

He did not, as is so often supposed, withdraw himself in Epicurean isolation: as his letters show, he took a keen interest in politics and world affairs. Nothing could be further from the truth than the popular conception of Browne as a shy, solitary, unworldly recluse. To the end of his life he remained a practicing physician, in close contact (if any man was) with the intimate realities of birth, suffering, and death.

It was a century, too, when death was cheap, and memento mori was stamped on all men's minds. Battle and famine raged through the land; plague and syphilis were perennial visitors. The graveyard temper that these conditions engendered was hardly lightened by gloomy Calvinist talk of predestination and hellfire. From the Jacobean dramatists onward, grisly symbols of charnel corruption and morbid psychology formed an integral element in every seventeenth-century writer's creative equipment; and Browne, notoriously, had his full share of them.

His obsession with death wavers between fear and desire. A cancelled[1] passage preserved in two manuscripts of the *Religio Medici* is revealing: "It is a symptom of melancholy to be afraid of death, yet sometimes to desire it; this latter I have often discovered in my selfe, and thinke no man ever desired life, as I have sometimes death." And again: "For the world, I count it not an Inne, but an Hospitall, and a place, not to live, but to die in." Where he differs from, say, Donne, is in his medical detachment from the physical unpleasantness of death: he never flinches in mere horror or nausea. He is not immune, even, from hard-boiled medical

---

[1]Denonain (p. 51) prints this passage in Part I, sec. xxxviii, as an integral part of the established text.

jokes: "Death hath spurs," he remarks in the *Pseudodoxia*, "and carcasses have been courted."

Vitalistic biology, fideism, embryology, antiquarianism; mystical numerology, the precepts of Pythagoras and the Cambridge Platonists; Dante's paradisal vision, Gnostic eschatology, the medieval hierarchy, microcosm and macrocosm; the ravages of disease and civil war, the ubiquitous signs of transient mortality—all these passed through the creative alembic of Browne's mind to produce that single immortal volume. There has been a fashion among modern critics to study *Hydriotaphia* and *The Garden of Cyrus* as though they were separate, independent works. In fact—as Browne himself makes clear—they form a single, indivisible unity:

That we conjoyn these parts of different Subjects, or that this [*The Garden of Cyrus*] should succeed the other; Your judgement will admit without impute of incongruity; Since the delightfull World comes after death, and Paradise succeeds the Grave. Since the verdant state of things is the Symbole of the Resurrection, and to flourish in the state of Glory, we must first be sown in corruption. Beside the ancient practise of Noble Persons, to conclude in Garden-Graves, and Urnes themselves of old, to be wrapt up in flowers and garlands.

(Dedicatory Epistle to *The Garden of Cyrus*)

These two essays, then, are in structure an echo of Dante's *Purgatorio* and *Paradiso*.

The symbolic framework chosen to sustain such a meditation is curious in every sense of the word. *Hydriotaphia* ostensibly discusses a cache of ancient burial urns unearthed at Old Walsingham; *The Garden of Cyrus* revolves around the various aspects of the quincunx—five points arranged in such a way (:·:) that, connected, they form an X, or Greek *chi*. Again, Browne makes an explicit statement as to the reason for going at his theme in such an odd way:

In this multiplicity of writing, bye and barren Themes are best fitted for invention; Subjects so often discoursed confine the Imagination, and fix our conceptions unto the notions of fore-writers. Beside, such Discourses allow excursions, and venially admit of collaterall truths, though at some distance from their principals.

By concentrating, almost like a hypnotist, on this pair of unfamiliar symbols, Browne paradoxically releases the reader's mind into an infinite number of associative levels of awareness, without any preconceptions. Emphasis on particularities gives shape and substance to quite literally cosmic generalizations.

Both essays are constructed according to the same formula: four chapters of examples and instances, much in the tradition of the *Pseudodoxia* (types of burial, categories of urn, variations on the quincuncial pattern) rise cumulatively to a fifth, in which theme and variations are gathered up and resolved in an exalted climax, a mystical and poetic *O altitudo*. The two works are interlinked by a dualistic pattern of opposed symbols—death and life, body and soul, substance and form, accident and design, time and space, darkness and light, earth and heaven. They can no more be separated than the voices of a fugue: taken together they form one of the deepest, most complex, most symbolically pregnant statements ever composed on the great double theme of mortality and eternity.

We feel the shadow of devouring time fall across every page. *Fugit hora*: "our Fathers finde their graves in our short memories . . . old Families last not three Oaks." Vanity of vanities, all is vanity, and mere human attempts to achieve immortality are doomed to ludicrous failure. Browne foreshadows the lesson of Shelley's *Ozymandias:*

The iniquity of oblivion blindely scattereth her poppy, and deals with the memory of men without distinction to merit of perpetuity. Who can but pity the founder of the Pyramids? *Herostratus* lives that burnt the Temple of *Diana*, he is almost lost that built it; Time hath spared the Epitaph of *Adrian's* horse, confounded that of himself. In vain we compute our felicities by the advantage of our good names, since bad have equall durations; and *Thersites* is like to live as long as *Agamemnon*. . . . Without the favour of the everlasting Register the first man had been as unknown as the last, and *Methuselah's* long life had been his only Chronicle. . . .

Man is a Noble Animal, splendid in ashes, and pompous in the grave, solemnizing Nativities and Deaths with equall lustre, nor omitting Ceremonies of bravery, in the infamy of his nature.

(*Hydriotaphia*, ch. v)

Mere human knowledge, too, is a poor and pitiful substitute for divine reality. Browne's parade of dubious antiquarian knowledge in *Hydriotaphia* seems almost designed to highlight the futility of scholarship. "Than the time of these Urnes deposited," he admits, "or precise Antiquity of these Reliques, nothing of more uncertainty"—and underlines the point by identifying obviously Saxon pots as Roman. He had (as is often forgotten) already delivered a scathing verdict on the value of antiquities generally, in the *Religio Medici*.

Throughout the *Hydriotaphia* (as F. L. Huntley has pointed out in a brilliant essay) the subject remains "small, temporal, local, *sui generis*, mutable, pathetic, nameless"—in sharp contrast to the soaring eternal universalities of *The Garden of Cyrus*:

> But these are sad and sepulchral Pitchers, which have no joyful voices; silently expressing old mortality, the ruines of forgotten times, and can only speak with life, how long in this corruptible frame, some parts may be uncorrupted.
>
> (Dedicatory Epistle to *Hydriotaphia*)

Yet the burial urn, the symbol of death, is also the symbol of birth. Browne's practiced medical eye at once saw its odd resemblance to the human womb:

> The common form with necks was a proper figure, making our last bed like our first; nor much unlike the Urnes of our Nativity, while we lay in the nether part of the Earth, and inward vault of our Microcosme. . . .
>
> (*Hydriotaphia*, ch. iii)

In the final chapter this cosmo-biological conceit is given a fresh twist: "Death," Browne writes, "must be the Lucina of life." As the seminal particles leave the dead body and enter the living, so the grave itself becomes the womb of our rebirth. Here is the vital connecting image between the two essays, the bridge leading from mortality to eternity. Thus the doctrine of panspermatism is transformed into Christian eschatology:

> Life is a pure flame, and we live by an invisible Sun within us. . . .
>
> And if any have been so happy as truly to understand Christian annihilation, extasis, exolution, liquefaction, transformation, the kisse of the Spouse, gustation of God, and ingression into the divine shadow, they have already had an handsome anticipation of heaven; the glory of the world is surely over, and the earth in ashes unto them.
>
> To subsist in lasting Monuments, to live in their productions, to exist in their names, and praedicament of *Chymera's*, was large satisfaction unto old expectations and made one part of their *Elyziums*. But all this is nothing in the Metaphysicks of true belief. . . .

When we turn from urn to quincunx, from rational to mystical apprehension of reality, the tone insensibly changes. Though the quincuncial figure is used (as the urns were) as a kind of hieroglyph, which enables the reader to grasp its several aspects simultaneously, the method of development pursues a Platonic rather than an Aristotelian course. We first consider "artificial" manifestations of the quincunx—that is, man's use of the figure in imitation of nature; next, nature's own quincuncial phenomena; lastly, the "mystical" prototype—the idea or form of quincunciality in the Creator's mind.

As to the reason for Browne's having chosen this particular symbol and no other in such a context, a clue is to be found in that passage where he discusses the related Platonic emblem of the two circles bisecting one another at right angles. Huntley interprets the meaning of this emblem as follows:

> The circle is God, perfection, immortality; the horizontal that crosses the circle represents the corporal, divisible, death; where the two lines meet we perceive the "mystical" decussation, the cross, or quincunxial [*sic*] figure, i.e. the systasis of the main opposition between "death" and "life."

Seen from one angle, that is, the intersecting circles appear as a cross, thus: +. If they are then rotated through 90° on a vertical axis they will be changed into the Greek θ, *theta*, standing for *thanatos* or death.

Mystical symbolism of this kind is woven throughout the texture of Browne's work and adds, often subconsciously, to its associative power of impact. Only a highly superficial critic[2] could have described *The Garden of Cyrus* as "about as nondescript a piece of Pythagorean madness as ever bewildered the wits of man." It is anything but nondescript; there is nothing vague or woolly about Browne's mysticism, any more than Pascal's. Every symbol is interrelated with the overall pattern—"according to the ordainer of order and mysticall Mathematicks of the City of Heaven."

The development of *The Garden of Cyrus* is in one sense closely parallel to the ascent of the Ladder of Being. Browne's early examples are chosen from man-made gardens, his next from natural growth; he closes with the quincunx of heaven itself. Gardens suggest the additional symbolism of

[2]See bibliography: Paul Elmer More, p. 158.

paradise; natural growth allows an organic digression into embryology and theories of generation. Just as *Hydriotaphia* smells of darkness, death, the futility of human endeavor when man attempts to stand alone (at one level it could be read as an epitaph on the angry dead of the civil and religious wars), so *The Garden of Cyrus* is irradiated with the symbols of growth and fertility: it is seminal in every sense, flooded with physical and spiritual light.

But Browne's favorite, all-embracing metaphor is that of the circle (everything, from God to the revolutions of the arterial blood, he somehow subordinated to the circular concept) and his paradisal picture does not remain in a static blaze of unchanging glory. Neither as biologist, astronomer, mystic, nor artist could he allow this. The wheel of time must turn, the circle of generation must proceed. Even eternity has its seasons: the darkness of death is also the darkness of life, as night follows day:

But Seeds themselves do lie in perpetual shades, either under the leaf, or shut up in coverings; And such as lye barest, have their husks, skins, and pulps about them, wherein the nebbe and generative particle lyeth moist and secured from the injury of Ayre and Sunne. Darknesse and light hold interchangeable dominions, and alternately rule the seminal state of things. Light unto *Pluto* is darknesse unto *Jupiter*. Legions of seminal *Idaea's* lie in their second Chaos and *Orcus of Hipocrates*; till putting on the habits of their forms, they show themselves upon the stage of the world, and open dominion of *Jove*. . . . Life it self is but the shadow of death, and souls departed but the shadows of the living: All things fall under this name. The Sunne it self is but the dark *simulachrum*, and light but the shadow of God.

(*The Garden of Cyrus*, ch. iv)

So on the drowsy, opiate stroke of midnight ("To keep our eyes open longer were but to act our Antipodes") *The Garden of Cyrus* draws to a muted, andante close. With *Hydriotaphia* it indeed fulfills a theme, as Browne put it, "not impertinent unto our profession, whose study is life and death"; and— quite incidentally, one suspects, from the author's viewpoint—crystallizes that theme in language and imagery seldom matched in the English language.

Browne's other works may be briefly mentioned here. *A Letter to a Friend*—probably composed in 1656, and not, as generally supposed, 1672, and therefore in one sense a preliminary study for

Hydriotaphia—is an idiosyncratic exercise in a familiar form, the *consolatio*. A young patient under Browne's care had recently died of tuberculosis; the friend is treated to a clinical account of his death and a homily on how to live. *Christian Morals*, the product of Browne's old age, is a collection of rigid, if illuminating, aphorisms, variously described as "sermonettes on the conduct of life," "a collection of the noblest thoughts, drest in the uncouthest language possible," and "an elaborate and magnificent parody of the Book of Proverbs": it shows—despite some brilliant flashes in Browne's old style—how age had formalized and stereotyped his talents.

The list is rounded off with a collection of miscellaneous scholarly tracts, chiefly remarkable for the light they shed on Browne's exceedingly wide interests: these ranged from ornithology to comparative linguistics. But he will remain, for future generations, one of those rare and special writers whose whole creative effort was crystallized and subsumed in two or three slender volumes. The two essays of 1658 are the focal point for a mind that may properly be compared with those of Coleridge and Leonardo da Vinci.

WHAT SONG THE SYRENS SANG

THOUGH he subsequently became the favorite of literary men such as William Hazlitt, Charles Lamb, and Robert Louis Stevenson, Browne himself never made any claim to be a man of letters (in the modern sense). He actually expressed the opinion—and repeated it—that "it were no loss like that of Galen's library if these [i.e., poets and "poetical" writers generally] had found the same fate; and would in some way requite the neglect of solid Authors, if they were less pursued." The attitude to "fiction" is Platonic; the solidly professional motive is very much Browne's own. Some critics, finding this hard to swallow, have made great play with a dozen or two works of English literature found in the catalog of Browne's library; but they omit to mention the two thousand other volumes in four or five languages, on medicine, theology, physics, mathematics, biology, and travel. Browne's was primarily a working library.

Clearly, he did read pure literature; but it most often seems to have been with an ulterior end in view. We have already seen the debt he owed to Dante. He was, too, exceedingly well read in Greek and Latin classics; yet though his own work was permeated by classical influences of style, cadence, language, and thought, he did not appear to read ancient authors so much for aesthetic satisfaction as for factual information. His attitude to the classics (despite the *Pseudodoxia*) is comparable to his attitude to Holy Writ: the main object in view seems to be the citation of chapter and verse on controversial issues. Browne was not, and never pretended to be, a professional litterateur—a fact that saved him from many literary vices. His wide reading was largely technical, and he achieved the final chapters of *Hydriotaphia* and *The Garden of Cyrus*, one suspects, in much the same tranced condition as Coleridge composing *Kubla Khan*. (Despite the polished state of the published version, early drafts in the British Museum confirm this suspicion. The pen is driven across the page in a white-hot, illegible frenzy, scarcely able to keep up with the succession of thoughts and images that crowded into the author's mind.)

The comparison with Coleridge is a generally profitable one. Both were obsessed by dream imagery and dream symbolism. Both, in their finest work, display an exactly analogous process of absorption and crystallization. (Did Browne take laudanum? It seems very likely. He had free access to drugs and used opiates in various experiments.) Both were widely read in nonliterary sources, travel books in particular, and had strong scientific interests. Browne took his original material on the quincunx, for example, from two excessively dry Italian treatises on agriculture. One of these gave him the notion of nature's domination by the quincuncial figure, and his imagination used this supposition as a springboard to the cosmos.

Browne had an extremely well-stocked mind, but took little account of his immediate literary predecessors. No one, as an American scholar remarked despairingly, has yet discovered a model for the *Hydriotaphia*. All this explains both Browne's strength and his weaknesses. He was honestly indifferent to literary art as an end in itself; he lacked (except in a metaphysical sense) any architectonic imagination on the large scale—his basic unit always remained the commonplace-book citation; he was a busy practicing doctor, and his medical duties absorbed the bulk of his creative energies. But his profession was also his strength in

that it offered his creative imagination an abundance of raw material to work on. His mystical reverence for the processes of life and death was reinforced by his scientific awareness of these processes in every minuscule detail: it is symbolically appropriate that in his numerical meditations on the quincunx he should also embody a vital botanical principle—the quinary arrangement of leaves.

Two basic literary sources did have a vast influence on Browne's prose: Latin oratory and the Authorized Version of the Bible. From the first he borrowed, among other things, his *clausulae*—those superbly rhythmic sentence endings that appear whenever his subject matter heightens in intensity,[3] echoes of Cicero and Seneca. "Pyramids, arches, obelisks, were but the irregularities of vainglory, and wild enormities of ancient magnanimity"; . . . and cannot excusably decline the consideration of that duration, which maketh Pyramids pillars of snow, and all that's past a moment"; or, perhaps most striking of all—to complete an earlier quotation:

Life is a pure flame, and we live by an invisible Sun within us. A small fire sufficeth for life, great flames seemed too little after death, while men vainly affected precious pyres, and to burn like *Sardanapalus*; but the wisedom of funerall Laws found the folly of prodigall blazes, and reduced undoing fires unto the rule of sober obsequies, wherein few could be so mean as not to provide wood, pitch, a mourner, and an Urne.
(*Hydriotaphia*, ch. v)

The five-beat rhythm predominates at moments of greatest intensity; and perhaps it is not fanciful to suppose (as Basil Anderton does) that this, too, can be related to the ubiquitous quincuncial pattern.

Perhaps Browne's greatest single debt is to the Authorized Version, for language, imagery, and cadence. From the Book of Proverbs he acquired the habit of making pregnant aphorisms—a trait especially apparent in *Christian Morals*. From the Book of Psalms he borrowed the Hebrew device of antiphonal statement—the repetition, that is, of the sense of a phrase in different terms. With Browne this involved juxtaposing Latinate and Anglo-Saxon vocabulary—another exercise in fugal con-

[3] Sir Herbert Read observed memorably of prose style that "it is born, not with the words, but with the thought, and with whatever confluence of instincts and emotions the thought is accompanied"—a statement peculiarly applicable to Browne.

trasts: "Chaos of preordination and night of their forebeings"; "Areopagy and dark Tribunal of our Hearts"; or, in a slightly different but no less striking contrast, "To well manage our Affections and Wild Horses of Plato."

Browne's heavy use of classical loan-words (what Coleridge called his "hyperlatinism") has an exceedingly far-reaching effect on his symbolism as well as the texture of his prose. There are whole centuries of associative meaning contained in the well-placed Latinate term. For obvious historical reasons many classical words, with their factual allusiveness and rich verbal harmonics, carry plangent overtones and echoes that our bare Anglo-Saxon could never achieve. Browne, in fact, is once again employing hieroglyphs, this time in a linguistic sense, to pack his prose with as much concentrated symbolic meaning as it will stand: he turns, instinctively, to the poetic method. As with Milton, this is most immediately appreciable in his skillful use of proper names. Janus, Alcmene, Pythagoras, Osiris: their significance germinates and expands in the reader's mind like an opening seed:

But in this latter Scene of time we cannot expect such Mummies unto our memories, when ambition may fear the Prophecy of *Elias*, and *Charles* the fifth can never hope to live within two *Methusela's* of *Hector*.
(*Hydriotaphia*, ch. v)

What saves Browne's prose style and imagery from the euphuistic excesses that ruined so many other writers drawing on similar sources? Primarily, perhaps, the tension constantly generated between his scientific intellect and his artistic imagination, his sensuous feeling for words and the religious austerity of his subject matter. (The same phenomenon may be observed later in Hopkins.) Browne never lets his style run away with his sense, never writes ornamental Latinate prose for the mere pleasure of achieving an unrelated verbal effect or paradoxical humor. Sometimes he writes purely as a scientist, sometimes as scientist and artist together; but never as artist alone. In his letters, and for the bulk of the *Pseudodoxia*, he writes a plain, serviceable, functional prose: this has disconcerted some of his aesthetic admirers,[4] who apparently expected him to write in a perpetual state of exalta-

[4]See bibliography: Austin Warren, pp. 678–679.

tion. But Browne's type of inspirational flash-point is reached, with luck, twice in a lifetime; Coleridge wrote only one *Kubla Khan*, and Traherne, in all the *Centuries of Meditation*, never recaptured the mescalinate ecstasy of his "orient and immortal wheat."

This is not to suggest that Browne did not have a superb natural ear for rhythm and language: he obviously did. (By the same token, as an auditory type he is markedly deficient in visual imagery.) Many of the words he coined have stuck in the language: "hallucination," "umbrella," "medical," "antediluvian," "opaline," and, ironically enough, "literary." But the instinct to form neologisms is due as much to a need for scientific terminology as a vigorous imagination: we are not so conversant with some of his other, more technical, inventions: "stillicidious," "chylifactive," and the weird "retromingent."

It is noticeable that Browne's hypnotic, incantatory effect, which we associate with his highest flights of prose, is generally accompanied by a slight blurring of mental focus, what one critic sourly characterized as "a certain ambiguity or recalcitrant recession of sense, of the sort that we normally associate with poetry." At the same time the imagery achieves a peak of fragmentary, dreamlike allusiveness that reminds us of De Quincey rather than Coleridge, and we remember that drugs can be soporific as well as stimulating:

But the Quincunx of Heaven runs low, and 'tis time to close the five ports of knowledge; We are unwilling to spin out our awaking thoughts into the phantasmes of sleep, which too often continueth praecogitations; making Cables of Cobwebbes and Wildernesses of handsome Groves. Beside, *Hippocrates* hath spoke so little, and the Oneirocriticall Masters have left such frigid Interpretations from plants, that there is little encouragement to dream of Paradise it self. Nor will the sweetest delight of Gardens afford much comfort in sleep; wherein the dulnesse of that sense shakes hands with delectable odours; and though in the Bed of *Cleopatra*, can hardly with any delight raise up the ghost of a Rose.
(*The Garden of Cyrus*, ch. v)

If we shake ourselves into wakefulness, we realize that those superb final lines merely mean that you cannot smell flowers when you are asleep; but poppy-and-mandragora confidence tricks have by then been worked on our imaginations. The Coleridgean dream symbolism has quietly invaded that no-man's-land where science, theology, and imagination meet, and alchemized them into something rich and strange—yet familiar as an echo. A point is reached where the meaning, as in all lyrical poetry, cannot be divorced from the words: the words are the meaning.

Sir Thomas Browne is his own most fascinating subject of study, and knows it:

> That world which I regard is my selfe; it is the Microcosme of mine owne frame that I cast mine eye on; for the other, I use it but like my Globe, and turne it round sometimes for my recreation.
>
> (*Rel. Med.*, Part II, sec. xi)

His antiquarian tinge of mind and his obsessional devotion to serious study recall that prodigious Roman polymath, Pliny the Elder. His personal temperament remains quintessentially English: ironic, melancholy, learned, humorous,[5] eccentric; he is, as Leslie Stephen remarked, Uncle Toby and Mr. Shandy rolled into one. But at a deeper level, his extraordinary use of birth–death, light–dark, growth-decay imagery, and the intense religious love suffusing all his work with a reverent tenderness for created life—these look forward, strikingly, to a Bible-cadenced modern poet who also composed in love of man and in praise of God. It might have been of Browne that Dylan Thomas wrote in "The Force That Through the Green Fuse Drives the Flower":

> The lips of time leech to the fountain head;
> Love drips and gathers, but the fallen blood
> Shall calm her sores.
> And I am dumb to tell a weather's wind
> How time has ticked a heaven round the stars.

In that stanza we can trace the whole paradigm of Sir Thomas Browne's creative achievement, and the whole quality of his faith.

SELECTED BIBLIOGRAPHY

I. BIBLIOGRAPHY. G. L. Keynes, *A Bibliography of Sir Thomas Browne, K. T., M.D.* (Cambridge, 1924; 2nd ed., rev. and aug., Oxford, 1968); O. Leroy, *A French Bibliography of Sir Thomas Browne* (Paris, 1931); D. G. Donovan, *Sir Thomas Browne 1924–1966; Robert Burton 1924–1966* (London, 1968).

II. COLLECTED WORKS. *The Works* (London, 1685–1686), contains little of the posthumous work and none of the correspondence; S. Wilkin, ed., *The Works*, 4 vols. (London, 1833–1836; repr. New York, 1968), the first critical ed., which laid the foundations for all future work, includes biography by Samuel Johnson, supplementary memoir by Wilkin, additional opuscula, and the bulk of the correspondence; C. E. Sayle, ed., *The Works*, 3 vols. (London, 1904–1907), textually unreliable, but makes use for the first time of the author-annotated copy of *Hydriotaphia*; G. L. Keynes, ed., *The Works* (London, 6 vols., 1928–1931; rev. ed., 4 vols., 1964), vol. I: *Religio Medici. A Letter to a Friend. Hydriotaphia* and *The Garden of Cyrus. Brampton Urns. Christian Morals*; vol. II: *Pseudodoxia Epidemica*; vol. III: *Miscellany Tracts. Repertorium. Latin Writings with Translations. Miscellaneous Writings*; vol. IV: *Letters*. The standard ed. revises Wilkin's text from MSS in the British Museum and the Bodleian Library; L. C. Martin, ed., *Religio Medici and Other Works* (London, 1964), the major works with the exception of *Pseudodoxia Epidemica*.

III. SEPARATE WORKS. *Religio Medici* (London, 1642), see "The First Edition of *Religio Medici*," *Harvard Library Bulletin*, 2 (1948), for an authoritative ruling on the priority and status of the two eds. of 1642 and 1643 respectively; the most valuable critical eds. are W. A. Greenhill, ed. (London, 1881), W. Murison, ed. (Cambridge, 1922), J. J. Denonain, ed. (Cambridge, 2nd ed., rev., 1955), V. Sanna, ed. (Cagliari, 1959), and J. Winny, ed. (Cambridge, 1963); see also J. J. Denonain's ed. of a MS discovered at Pembroke College, *Une Version Primitive de Religio Medici* (Paris, 1958); *Pseudodoxia Epidemica* (London, 1646; repr. 1972); *Hydriotaphia and The Garden of Cyrus* (London, 1658), modern critical eds. of *Hydriotaphia* include Sir J. Evans, ed. (London, 1893), W. Murison, ed. (Cambridge, 1922), and R. F. Pande, ed. (London, 1963), modern critical eds. of both works include W. A. Greenhill, ed. (London, 1896) and J. Carter, ed. (2nd ed., rev., Cambridge, 1958), limited ed. but still the standard; T. Tenison, ed., *Miscellany Tracts* (London, 1683), no separate modern ed.; *A Letter to a Friend* (London, 1690), in G. L. Keynes, ed. (Boston, 1971), also reprinted in W. A. Greenhill's ed. of *Religio Medici*, in C. H. Herford, ed., *Religio Medici*, and in G. L. Keynes, *Sir Thomas Browne: Selected Writings* (London, 1968); *Posthumous Works* (London, 1712), superseded by Wilkin and Keynes; J. Jeffery, ed., *Christian Morals* (Cambridge, 1716), modern eds. include W. A. Greenhill, ed. (London, 1881) and S. C. Roberts, ed. (Cambridge, 1927).

IV. SELECTIONS. G. L. Keynes, ed., *Sir Thomas Browne: Selected Writings* (London, 1968), includes

---

[5]In *Pseudodoxia Epidemica* he remarks dryly: "We shall not, I hope, disparage the Resurrection of our Redeemer, if we say the Sun doth not dance on Easter day."

Religio Medici, A Letter to a Friend, Hydriotaphia, The Garden of Cyrus, and selections from other writings; L. C. Martin, Religio Medici and Other Works (Oxford, 1964); M. R. Ridley, Religio Medici and Other Writings (London–New York, 1965); N. Endicott, ed., The Prose of Sir Thomas Browne: Religio Medici, Hydriotaphia, Garden of Cyrus, Letter to a Friend, Christian Morals, with Selections from Pseudodoxia Epidemica, Miscellany Tracts, and from MS Notebooks and Letters (New York, 1968); A. Whyte, Sir Thomas Browne, An Appreciation with Some of the Best Passages of the Physician's Writings (Port Washington, N.Y., 1971); P. H. A. Robbins, Religio Medici, Hydriotaphia, Garden of Cyrus (Oxford, 1972).

V. SOME CRITICAL AND BIOGRAPHICAL STUDIES. Sir K. Digby, Observations upon "Religio Medici" (London, 1643); A. Ross, Medicus Medicatus . . . (London, 1645) and Arcana Microcosmi . . . (London, 1651), two tracts that represent the extreme, almost lunatic, fringe of theological conservatism; Ross was largely responsible for Browne's reputation as an atheist; S. Johnson, Life of Sir Thomas Browne (London, 1756); L. Stephen, Hours in a Library, 2nd ser. (London, 1876); W. Pater, Appreciations (London, 1899); A. White, Sir Thomas Browne: An Appreciation (Edinburgh, 1898); E. Dowden, Puritan and Anglican (London, 1900); E. Gosse, Sir Thomas Browne (London, 1905), superficial and inaccurate, but the first attempt at a critical biography since Samuel Johnson's; P. E. More, Studies of Religious Dualism, 6th ser. (Cambridge, Mass., 1909), Shelburne Essays; W. Schonack, Sir Thomas Browne's "Religio Medici": Ein verschollenes Denkmal des englischen Deismus, &c. (Tübingen, 1911), one of the first attempts to place Browne's religious thought in its proper historical context; C. Whibley, Essays in Biography (London, 1913); B. Anderton, Sketches from a Library Window (Cambridge, 1922), contains an excellent preliminary investigation of Browne's prose rhythms; L. Strachey, Books and Characters French and English (London, 1922); J. A. Symonds, "Sir Thomas Browne," Modern English Essays, 3 (1922); R. Sencourt, Outflying Philosophy (Hildesheim, 1924), a suggestive but chronically inaccurate study of Browne's religious thought, especially in relation to his knowledge of Aquinas; M. L. Tildesley, Sir Thomas Browne, His Skull, Portraits, and Ancestors (London, 1927); O. Leroy, Le Chevalier Thomas Browne: 1605–1682; sa vie, sa pensée, et son art (Paris, 1931); J. Needham, The Great Amphibium (London, 1931); R. R. Cawley, "Sir Thomas Browne and His Reading," PMLA, 48, no. 1 (1933); B. Willey, The Seventeenth-Century Background (London, 1934); J. N. Cline, "Hydriotaphia," in Five Studies in Literature, University of California Publications in English ser. no. 8 (1940); J. S. Finch, "Early Drafts of The Garden of Cyrus," PMLA, 55, no. 2 (1940); J. S. Finch, "Browne and the Quincunx," Studies in Philology, 37 (1940); D. K. Ziegler, In Divided and Distinguished Worlds (Cambridge, Mass., 1944), attempts to show that Browne kept his scientific and religious concepts separate; stimulating but improbable; C. E. Raven, English Naturalists (Cambridge, 1947); M. L. Wiley, "Browne and the Genesis of Paradox," Journal of the History of Ideas, 9 (1948); E. S. Merton, Science and Imagination in Sir Thomas Browne (New York, 1949); W. P. Dunn, Sir Thomas Browne: A Study in Religious Philosophy (2nd ed., Minneapolis, 1950); J. S. Finch, Sir Thomas Browne: A Doctor's Life of Science and Faith (New York, 1950), popular and disappointingly lightweight, superseded by F. L. Huntley, below; M. A. Heideman, "Hydriotaphia and The Garden of Cyrus: A Paradox and a Cosmic Vision," University of Toronto Quarterly, 19 (1950); A. Warren, "The Style of Browne," Kenyon Review, 13 (1951); F. L. Huntley, "Sir Thomas Browne and the Metaphor of the Circle," Journal of the History of Ideas, 14 (1953); F. L. Huntley, "Sir Thomas Browne: The Relationship of Urn Burial and The Garden of Cyrus," Studies in Philology, 53 (1956), the most fruitful single piece of criticism on Browne's work; M. Bottrall, Every Man a Phoenix: Studies in Seventeenth-Century Autobiography (London, 1958), includes a discussion of Religio Medici considered as an autobiographical document; J. J. Denonain, La Personnalité de Sir Thomas Browne, essai d'application de la caractérologie à la critique et l'histoire littéraires (Paris, 1959); F. L. Huntley, Sir Thomas Browne. A Biographical and Critical Study (London, 1962); J. Bennett, Sir Thomas Browne: A Man of Achievement in Literature (London, 1962); R. P. Pande, Sir Thomas Browne, with a Detailed Study and Text of Urn Burial (Allahabad, India, 1963); R. R. Cawley and G. Yost, Studies in Sir Thomas Browne (Eugene, Ore., 1965); J. R. King, Studies in Six 17th-Century Writers (Athens, Ohio, 1966); L. Nathanson, The Strategy of Truth: A Study of Sir Thomas Browne (Chicago, 1967); A. Loeffler, Sir Thomas Browne als Virtuoso. Die Bedeutung der Gelehrsamkeit für sein literarisches Alterswerk (Nürnberg, 1972); J. N. Wise, Sir Thomas Browne's Religio Medici and Two Seventeenth-Century Critics (Columbia, Mo., 1973).

JOHN MILTON
(1608-1674)

E. M. W. Tillyard

I

In *Paradise Lost*, Milton described his Adam as formed for "contemplation and valour." He could thereby have been describing both his own nature and his own ideals. Milton was a natural Platonist, a natural seeker after perfection by high contemplation; but he also believed, with Sidney, that the "ending end of all earthly learning" was "virtuous action." Living before Rousseau and the age when men dreamed of human perfectibility, he believed that in this world action would always fall short of the high aims to which contemplation pointed, and he would have followed Sidney in maintaining that "our erected wit maketh us know what perfection is, and yet our infected will keepeth us from reaching unto it." Nevertheless, Milton's nature both craved forms of action that would not be quite unworthy of their moving principles and was sanguine enough to make him think that a great betterment of earthly conditions was possible despite the entrance of sin into the world. That he could combine and harmonize the elements of contemplation and of action in himself and in his poetry is one of his chief claims to greatness. But his high hopes of approximating action to ideals and of living to see a better England than the one into which he was born exposed him more nakedly to the cruelty of fate than someone more skeptical and pessimistic. His final greatness consists both in the primary wealth and vitality of his nature and in the way he adjusted to the worst that fate could bring him.

Gifted with that ultimate simplicity of mind that Thucydides in his history and Mencius in his aphorisms called the mark of the truly great man, desiring to see life in strong, clear outline, more attracted by the gold pieces than by the small change of thought, Milton was unlucky in the period of history that his life covered. It was an age of transition, belonging neither to the Renaissance confidence that went before nor to the Augustan confidence that came after, an age in England of political division, philosophical skepticism, and a literature ingenious, ornate, and sophisticated rather than strong and simple. Milton was very close to his age; and the more scholars discover about him, the more sensitive they find him to the currents of contemporary thought. Yet behind this sensitivity we can detect the impression of Milton's not being spiritually attuned to his setting. Fundamentally he was a Christian humanist, a kind of rear guard of the great Renaissance army, prolonging the Renaissance faith in man into a less noble age, as Thomas Hardy, though bred in an England by then predominantly industrial, succeeded in using the relics of an older rural England for the material of his novels.

But if Milton's life span proved thus unfortunate, it was long before it definitively revealed itself to be so. Looking back, we may note that he was born three years after the ominous Gunpowder Plot of 1605, that the ill-starred Charles I came to the throne at the time Milton entered college, and that Milton's early manhood coincided with the gradual split of the active elements of the nation into two hostile parties. But in thus looking back and knowing what those various happenings actually led up to, we are in a different position from Milton, who was no more aware of the approach of civil war and all its accompanying ills than an Englishman born in 1885 was aware of the coming outbreak of war in 1914. To those living in them, the years in England before 1639 and 1914 seemed good years and full of hope for better things to come. And most of Milton's poems from before the Civil War breathe not only the vitality of youth but also contentment with the England he inhabits. In no poems more than "L'Allegro" and "Il Penseroso" does this contentment show itself. He wrote them probably near the end of his college career at Cambridge, when he

JOHN MILTON

was an important figure there, and in them he describes the joys first of the cheerful, and then of the thoughtful, man. And the England that provides these joys is still the united England of the days of Elizabeth, the England that, in the words of Shakespeare, was "true to herself":

> Sometimes with secure delight
> The upland hamlets will invite,
> When the merry bells ring round,
> And the jocond rebecks sound
> To many a youth, and many a maid,
> Dancing in the chequered shade;
> And young and old come forth to play
> On a sunshine holy day. . . .
> ("L'Allegro," 91–98)

Nor does the young Anglican Puritan yet see anything wrong in the artistic and musical adornments of the church service:

> But let my due feet never fail,
> To walk the studious cloisters pale,
> And love the high embowed roof,
> With antique pillars' massy proof,
> And storied windows richly dight,[1]
> Casting a dim religious light.
> There let the pealing organ blow,
> To the full-voiced choir below,
> In service high, and anthems clear,
> As may with sweetness through mine ear,
> Dissolve me into ecstasies,
> And bring all heaven before mine eyes.
> ("Il Penseroso," 155–156)

A little later, in "Arcades" and *Comus*, Milton seems to have enjoyed writing the words for that costly and aristocratic entertainment of mixed poetry, music, dancing, and scenic ingenuity called the masque. This is how he turns his delicate lyric vein to compliment the countess dowager of Derby, ancestress of many grandchildren, in whose honor "Arcades" was performed:

> Mark what radiant state she spreads,
> In circle round her shining throne,
> Shooting her beams like silver threads,
> This this is she alone,
> Sitting like a goddess bright,
> In the center of her light.

[1]Adorned.

> Might she the wise Latona be,
> Or the towered Cybele,
> Mother of a hundred gods;
> Juno dares not give her odds;
> Who had thought this clime had held
> A deity so unparalleled?
> (14–25)

Though a strong minority of the English nobility was on the side of Parliament against the king, the masque, along with other dramatic shows, came to be countenanced by the royalists alone. Milton, the future Cromwellian, writing the words for two masques so gaily and serenely, shows that men little understood the storm that threatened.

Comus, by far the longer of the two masques and the longest of Milton's early poems, reveals not only the still-persisting harmony of contemporary England but also the two poles of Milton's own nature, the contemplative and the active. The Attendant Spirit first pictures the earth from without, from the point of view to be reached only through meditation, talking of

> . . . the smoke and stir of this dim spot,
> Which men call earth, and, with low-thoughted care
> Confined, and pestered in this pinfold here,
> Strive to keep up a frail, and feverish being
> Unmindful of the crown that virtue gives
> After this mortal change, to her true servants
> Amongst the enthroned gods on sainted seats
> (5–11)

But he turns into an active character and rescues the benighted children from their danger. The Lady, at her first entrance, varies her speech from pure, active drama:

> This way the noise was, if mine ear be true,
> My best guide now, methought it was the sound
> Of riot, and ill-managed merriment,
> (170–172)

through the shudders of romantic superstitions

> What might this be? A thousand fantasies
> Begin to throng into my memory
> Of calling shapes, and beckoning shadows dire,
> And airy tongues, that syllable men's names
> On sands, and shores, and desert wildernesses
> (205–209)

to the contemplative rapture of

O welcome, pure-eyed Faith, white-handed Hope,
Thou hovering angel girt with golden wings,
And thou unblemished form of Chastity,
I see ye visibly . . . .

(213–216)

Comus may not succeed completely as a whole, but it shows Milton free to indulge the wealth of his nature and full of the promise of great things. Indeed, in many details he has attained greatness. The second passage quoted from the Lady's speech is a poem in its own right, legitimately anthologized by Robert Bridges in *The Spirit of Man*. Only a major poet could have thought of using "syllable" as a verb in this context. "Syllable" is very effective onomatopoeia, but, through its uniqueness in verbal use, it also startles and makes a climax that gives the whole passage a convincing shape.

"Lycidas," published in 1637, is a rhymed poem lamenting the death of a college friend by drowning, in the strict tradition of the pastoral elegy of Greece and Rome. In it Milton at once achieves poetry of the highest order and expresses an incidental foreboding of the bitter times that are to come. There are the same large elements as in *Comus*. The element of rapturous contemplation, expressed in Lycidas' apotheosis, is there just as surely and more intensely:

So Lycidas sunk low, but mounted high,
Through the dear might of him that walked the waves;
Where other groves, and other streams along,
With nectar pure his oozy locks he laves,
And hears the unexpressive nuptial Song,
In the blest kingdoms meek of joy and love.

(172–177)

Milton indulges his vein of romantic description with the utmost brilliance in imagining where the body of his drowned friend may have drifted:

. . . Whilst thee the shores, and sounding seas
Wash far away, where 'er thy bones are hurled,
Whether beyond the stormy Hebrides
Where thou perhaps under the whelming tide
Visit'st the bottom of the monstrous world;
Or whether thou to our moist vows denied,
Sleep'st by the fable of Bellerus old,
Where the great vision of the guarded Mount
Looks toward Namancos and Bayona's hold. . . .

(154–162)

And the urge to action, the will to match ideals with deeds, comes out with all the force of Milton's now mature power in the description of fame and its precariousness in this world:

Fame is the spur that the clear spirit doth raise
(That last infirmity of noble mind)
To scorn delights, and live laborious days;
But the fair guerdon[2] when we hope to find,
And think to burst out into sudden blaze,
Comes the blind Fury with th' abhorred shears,
And slits the thin-spun life.

(70–76)

But there is another side to "Lycidas," not found in *Comus*: the political. And this side is the more important because it comes out not only in a direct manner through St. Peter's attack on the degenerate clergy of the day and his grim reference to the inroads of the Roman church:

Besides what the grim wolf with privy paw
Daily devours apace, and nothing said,
(128–129)

but also through a mere hint in another context: proof that Milton's mind was running on politics at this time. The two resounding lines from the end of the passage quoted about the drifting of Lycidas' body, sometimes cited to prove Milton's love of the mere sound of grandiose names, are actually packed with meaning, political included. The "guarded Mount" is the rock fortress of St. Michael's Mount in Cornwall and the "great vision" is the archangel himself, so called because he appeared in a vision to some fishermen at this site. Namancos and Bayona, unidentified for many years after Milton's death, are in Galicia, the Spanish Land's End. Michael, the chief warrior-angel in heaven, is on duty on his own mount near the English Land's End, fixing his defensive gaze on the Spanish Land's End to prevent both a recurrence of the Spanish Armada and the spread through Continental influence of popery in England, of which the Puritan wing of the English church thought there was danger through the High Church doctrines of William Laud, then at the height of his power as archbishop of Canterbury.

In "Lycidas," then, Milton hints at the troubles to come but is far from believing them inevitable. These enrich rather than overshadow the poem.

[2]Reward.

The troubles are, indeed, an important item in the matters that burdened Milton's mind at that time and made him wonder whether his hopes for the future were justified. But they are subordinate to the great theme of the poem, the theme that coexists with the elegiac theme and of which the elegiac theme is the symbol. Milton saw that action in this world is precarious, that the good die young, that great preparations for high and virtuous deeds often miscarry, that the wicked often prosper. It was a painful vision, but he faced it and overcame it by the hard-won admission that results in this world do not matter and that what does matter is the state of mind behind the attempt, whether successful or not, to achieve results. Lycidas died young and achieved little; yet his state of mind was one of integrity, and his "mounting high" into heaven symbolizes the ultimate victory of that state over what he failed to achieve by earthly action. Such were the mental conflict and the victory Milton achieved in "Lycidas." He was destined to fight the same fight more than once in his life—and it is a fight that cannot be avoided by anyone who believes in the necessity at once of contemplation and of action—but having won it on the first occasion, he was not likely to be defeated thereafter.

II

SHORTLY after writing "Lycidas" (and the last line of the poem, "To-morrow to fresh woods, and pastures new," may refer to it), Milton set out to complete his education in the Renaissance manner through the grand tour. His journey was a happy interlude between the anxieties revealed in "Lycidas" and the imminent Civil War, and its circumstances help us to understand Milton himself. He had no liking for France and did not linger there, and his anxiety about political events at home prevented him from carrying out his plan to visit Greece. Thus his grand tour pretty well resolved itself into a long residence in different parts of Italy. There is every indication that Milton adored Italy and that he was a great success there. Certainly the actual country left its mark on his later poetry. Here, for instance, is a reference to a scene in Tuscany: in the first book of *Paradise Lost*, Satan, having painfully reached the beach of the fiery lake where he had lain prone:

> . . . stood and called
> His legions, angel forms, who lay entranced
> Thick as autumnal leaves that strew the brooks
> In Vallombrosa, where the Etrurian shades
> High overarched imbower . . . .
>
> (300–304)

It has been argued very plausibly that the landscape of Milton's Hell derives its details from the volcanic region near Naples known as the Phlegraean Fields; and I have little doubt, though I have not met the notion elsewhere, that the garden of the Villa d'Este at Tivoli, with its abundance of water drawn from the Anio, its slopes and terraces, and its luxuriance, was at the back of Milton's mind when he created his Paradise. But there were more things than the landscape to attract Milton to Italy. By 1638, when Milton reached Italy, the cultural center of Europe had shifted to France; and Italy was living on its past rather than facing the future. The spirit of the Renaissance, prevalent so much earlier in Italy than in the rest of western Europe, lingered there the longest; and it was here above all that Milton could find an intellectual temper really to his taste. Not that we should make Milton's success in Italy a small matter or underestimate his remarkable powers of adaptation to a foreign setting. It speaks very highly indeed for the flexibility and richness of his temperament that he, bred in a Puritan family and in the more Puritan of the two English universities, strongly opposed politically to the Roman church and to any romanizing tendencies in his own, and professing an austere morality, should have grown so much at home in the center of Catholicism and in a land where morals were far from austere. And he did so at no sacrifice whatever of his own private standards.

Upon returning to England in 1639, Milton was caught in the uprush of enthusiasm that carried away the Parliamentary party and the reforming wing of the English church. There was the chance, he believed, that food might after all be provided for the "hungry sheep" of England, who, he had complained in "Lycidas," "look up" and are "not fed." So believing, he could not hold back. "Virtuous action" for him now lay in the region of politics, and not of poetry, where he had wanted it to be. When Milton committed himself, he did so with all his heart, and he devoted himself to politics instead of poetry for many years to come. And his return to poetry was along the sad road of political disillusionment.

But at first his hopes ran high. He believed, with other sincere and ardent men, that if the English church could be further reformed—if, in particular, the episcopacy could be abolished—a new golden age would be established in England; and he pictured himself as the poet chosen to celebrate the new order:

Then, amidst the hymns and hallelujahs of saints, some one may perhaps be heard offering at high strains in new and lofty measures to sing and celebrate thy divine mercies and marvellous judgments in this land throughout all ages; whereby this great and warlike nation, instructed and inured to the fervent and continual practice of truth and righteousness, and casting far from her the rags of her old vices, may press on hard to that high and happy emulation to be found the soberest, wisest, and most Christian people . . . .

("Of Reformation")

This is superbly said, but it shows the weakness of Milton as politician. Such fervor befits ideals, but not acts of Parliament. And when the Presbyterian superseded the Episcopal form of church government in England, Milton was forced to admit that the change did not bring in the millennium and that "new Presbyter was but old Priest writ large." Under the Commonwealth, Milton worked for what we now call the Foreign Office and, after the precedent of Chaucer and Spenser, was an efficient government servant; but he was too much of an idealist to be able to hedge and compromise over the large issues that concern the high politician and that have to be reduced from their utopian potentialities to the scanty proportions of what will work in the shabby, mean-principled world of every day. Milton's pamphlets, his major expression of high political opinion, are not successful as practical tracts for the times. When he is exalted, he is too remote from the real world; when he forces himself to be controversial and lowers his tone, he carries abuse too far to be effective. Nevertheless, considered not as effective political writing but as independent prose works, Milton's pamphlets, uneven as they are, form a wonderful body of vivid and varied and powerful prose, illustrating, like his earlier poetry, his belief in both contemplation and action, and presenting certain sides of his character that might not, though surely there, have been detected in his verse.

I need not dwell on the theme of action in Milton's prose, for most of it is in itself a form of action, and efforts to persuade men to follow this or that course. What is to the point is to show how Milton's belief in contemplation keeps breaking out in contexts that should be severely practical. Thus, in one of his pamphlets against the bishops, *The Reason of Church Government Urg'd Against Prelaty* (1641–1642), he inserts a long personal passage in which he talks of his poetic plans and of his conception of the poet's high office. A true poem, he holds, is

. . . not to be raised from the heat of youth, or the vapours of wine, like that which flows at waste from the pen of some vulgar amorist or the trencher fury of a rhyming parasite; nor to be obtained by the invocation of Dame Memory and her siren daughters, but by devout prayer to that eternal Spirit, who can enrich with all utterance and knowledge and sends out his Seraphim with the hallowed fire of his altar to touch and purify the lips of whom he pleases . . . .

And if the "eternal Spirit" is ready to inspire, he will inspire the man who has, by the act of contemplation, prepared his heart for the inspiration, for Milton goes on to talk of "beholding the bright countenance of truth in the quiet and still air of delightful studies." Milton is here remote indeed from the grasping and opportunist world of political action.

What are the sides of Milton's nature that his prose makes especially clear, and that readers might overlook in his verse?

First, the man's uncommon exuberance. Milton's total poetic output is not large, and we might be tempted to think that he wrote slowly and painfully. If we heed the torrent of his prose, with its immensely wealthy vocabulary, we can be sure that Milton wrote comparatively little poetry only because he rejected so much and selected so fastidiously. By nature he had the exuberance of a Rubens, but it was checked and compressed by the severity and the scrupulousness of a Racine. In prose, however, Milton felt no obligation to curb his magnanimity or to comb out his vocabulary. He bursts out into vivid metaphors and allows his sentences to grow to great lengths through sheer sustention of vitality. Here, for instance, is his invective, from his tract *Of Education* (1644), against the system of studies still prevalent at the universities with its disastrous effect on the undergraduates' future careers:

And for the usual method of teaching arts, I deem it to be an old error of universities, not yet well recovered from the scholastic grossness of barbarous ages, that instead of beginning with arts most easy (and those be such as are most obvious to the sense) they present their young unmatriculated novices at first coming with the most intellective abstractions of logic and metaphysics, so that they having but newly left those grammatic flats and shallows, where they stuck unreasonably to learn a few words with lamentable construction, and now on a sudden transported under another climate to be tossed and turmoiled with their unballasted wits in fathomless and unquiet deeps of controversy, do for the most part grow into hatred and contempt of learning, mocked and deluded all this while with ragged notions and babblements while they expected worthy and delightful knowledge, till poverty or youthful years call them importunately their several ways and hasten them with the sway of friends either to an ambitious and mercenary or ignorantly zealous divinity: some allured to the trade of law, grounding their purposes not on the prudent and heavenly contemplation of justice and equity, which was never taught them, but on the promising and pleasing thoughts of litigious terms, fat contentions, and flowing fees; others betake them to state affairs with souls so unprincipled in virtue and true generous breeding that flattery and court-shifts and tyrannous aphorisms appear to them the highest points of wisdom instilling their barren hearts with a conscientious slavery, if, as I rather think, it be not feigned; others, lastly, of a more delicious and airy spirit retire themselves, knowing no better, to the enjoyments of ease and luxury, living out their days in feast and jollity, which indeed is the wisest and safest course of all these unless they were with more integrity undertaken—and these are the errors, these are the fruits of misspending our prime youth at the schools and universities as we do, either in learning mere words or such things chiefly as were better unlearned.

This is at once a single sentence and a whole paragraph. Milton's ardor presses on, unremitting to the end.

Second, there appears in Milton's prose—fitfully, it is true—a sense of humor. This comes out at odd moments and in chance phrases, at times when his feelings have cooled and he is not concerned with a main argument. At the end of *Colasterion* (1645), a hot piece of controversy on the subject of divorce, Milton says how glad he is to have done with his adversary:

At any hand I would be rid of him; for I had rather, since the life of man is likened to a scene, that all my entrances and exits might mix with such persons only whose worth erects them and their actions to a grave and tragic deportment and not to have to do with clowns and vices. But if a man cannot peaceably walk into the world but must be infested, sometimes at his face with dorrs and horseflies, sometimes beneath with bawling whippets and shin-barkers . . . have I not cause to be in such a manner defensive as may procure me freedom to pass unmolested hereafter . . . ?

The general tone is scornful, but no man without a sense of humor could have coined the phrase "bawling whippets and shin-barkers." In *Areopagitica* (1644), the most lively and varied and readable of all the pamphlets, there occurs a delightfully humorous description of the wealthy merchant who finds "religion to be a traffic so entangled . . . that . . . he cannot skill to keep a stock going upon that trade" and who solves his problem by hiring a tame clergyman to deputize, resigning "the whole warehouse of his religion, with all the locks and keys, into his custody . . . ."

If the prose tells us certain things about Milton, so do his sonnets, written, like the prose, mostly between "Lycidas" and *Paradise Lost*. Like some of Horace's *Odes* (on which they are partly modeled) and many of Thomas Hardy's lyrics, they are occasional poems dealing with people or contemporary events. That Milton should write sonnets to Thomas Fairfax, Cromwell, and other Parliamentary leaders is not surprising, and accords with his prose. What most adds to our knowledge of the man are the feelings he displays in the personal sonnets: his tenderness toward his second wife, now dead; his uncomplaining humility in the sonnet on his blindness; the urbanity with which, in the following, he invites his friend Lawrence to dinner:

> Lawrence, of virtuous father virtuous son,
>> Now that the fields are dank, and ways are mire,
>> Where shall we sometimes meet, and by the fire
>> Help waste a sullen day; what may be won
> From the hard Season gaining: time will run
>> On smoother, till Favonius reinspire
>> The frozen earth; and clothe in fresh attire
>> The lily and rose, that neither sowed nor spun.
> What neat repast shall feast us, light and choice,
>> Of Attic taste, with wine, whence we may rise
>> To hear the lute well touched or artful voice
> Warble immortal notes and Tuscan air?
>> He who of those delights can judge, and spare
>> To interpose them oft, is not unwise.
>
> (Sonnet 17)

JOHN MILTON

I have written thus far of the pamphlets and the sonnets as isolated works possessing certain literary qualities and telling us things about Milton's nature. They also, when taken in sequence, tell the story of how his hopes of national betterment through high action came to grief, and of his personal disasters or disappointments. Milton did not abandon his hopes lightly. It is true that the defeat of the episcopacy and the victory of Presbyterianism did not produce the wonderful betterment he expected. But Presbyterianism had not come to stay, and better things might issue from the professions of greater religious toleration put out by the Independents. Moreover, the richness and fervor of religious controversy gave Milton grounds for hope. *Areopagitica*, written after the first decisive victory of the Parliamentarians at Marston Moor and when there was the promise of opposition to the now-established Presbyterians, utters this hope. This pamphlet, the classic plea in literature for liberty of the press, is also an utterance of hope that England is about to enter a new era of free vitality when, unrestricted by the harsh decrees of ecclesiastical orthodoxy, she may both face the full truth of God's word and be strong and virtuous enough to draw sustenance and life from it:

Methinks I see in my mind a noble and puissant nation rousing herself like a strong man after sleep and shaking her invincible locks: methinks I see her as an eagle mewing her mighty youth and kindling her undazzled eyes at the full midday beam, purging and unscaling her long-abused sight at the fountain itself of heavenly radiance . . . .

Note once again in this passage the union of action and contemplation: the references first to Samson with his uncut hair, the man of great deeds, and then to the eagle, symbolizing, in its supposed power to envisage the sun, the mind that has the strength to contemplate the Platonic ideas or God himself.

The story of Milton's disillusion is the story of England between *Areopagitica*, written in 1644, and the Restoration in 1660. Parliament won the war but failed to win the hearts of the English people. Representing at first a majority of the population, the Parliamentary rulers became fewer and represented an ever-dwindling minority. Of that minority Milton was an absolutely loyal member, his high idealism drawing him to those who, for whatever

reason, were willing to go to extremes. Here, he felt, were real men and not time-servers or Laodiceans; and in some of his sonnets and in his great Latin prose work, *The Second Defence of the People of England*, he celebrated their virtues and gave them high advice. But all the time Milton knew that these heroic men did not have the country behind them, and he experienced a great revulsion from the sentiments expressed in the passage quoted from *Areopagitica*. He believed that lethargy was the besetting vice of most of his countrymen. It was lethargy, he thought, that caused them to sympathize with Charles for all his misdeeds and to withdraw their support from the men who had dared to put him to death; for lethargy cannot bear change, however called for, and the desire for a king was of long and rooted growth. Not that Milton despaired when men regretted Charles; on the contrary, he vented his hopes and his energies in writing in support of the regicides. His vehement efforts were the final reason for his loss of sight. But he never regretted the sacrifice, as he told Cyriack Skinner in a sonnet; nor did he argue

Against heaven's hand or will, not bate a jot
Of heart or hope; but still bear up and steer
Right onward. . . .
(Sonnet to Mr Cyriack Skinner Upon His Blindness)

This is indeed to apply the lesson of "Lycidas," the lesson that the motive of the deed, not its result, matters.

III

MILTON's blindness had the effect of detaching him gradually from his position as government servant. Through his Latin defenses of the regicides he earned the gratitude of the government at home and fame abroad; but as a blind man he could no longer be of the same use. Released from regular employment, though still good for an occasional pamphlet, he returned to his plans for a great poem some four years before the Restoration.

His other personal trouble was the unhappy beginning of his first marriage. His wife returned to her parents probably a little more than a year after the wedding. But we must remember that she returned to him and bore him children, and that his two other marriages were happy. With little knowledge of the feminine heart before marriage, he acquired a sufficiency by the time he came to write *Paradise Lost*.

With Cromwell's death and the plain imminence of the restoration of the Stuarts, Milton still refused to give up hope, and risked his life by writing last-minute appeals to the English people not to submit their necks to a tyrant. The actual shock of the Restoration must have been terrible. There is no record of his feelings unless, as has been conjectured, he composed *Samson Agonistes*[3] while in hiding and in danger of execution. But if Samson's dejection reflects, as it may well do, feelings that Milton at one time experienced, it may plausibly concern the loss of sight that was common to them both. We shall be safer if we reconstruct Milton's feelings at the time of the Restoration from his more firmly dated works. However great the shock of the Restoration (and its magnitude must have corresponded roughly with the vehemence of Milton's pamphleteering immediately before it), I believe he must have faced beforehand the failure of his hopes, just as a good commander will have faced the problem of extricating his troops, should the victory he so passionately desires be denied him.

The evidence is the general scheme of *Paradise Lost*, begun, and hence, we may be certain, in the case of so rigorously architectonic a poet as Milton, already planned, some four years before the Restoration. The general scheme of *Paradise Lost* embodies the moral of "Lycidas": that results matter less than states of minds. Satan's apparently decisive act in causing man's fall, an act based on an envious and cruel state of mind, ends by being less strong than the small, sound human acts of mutual generosity and of repentance performed by Adam and Eve after they have fallen. If Milton had staked everything on the results of his political hopes, he could never have framed his poem in this way. That he cared greatly about the Restoration is proved by his pamphlets; that he had also learned not to care is proved by the scheme of *Paradise Lost*. That it cost him dear to learn not to care, and that he did suffer mental torment when his hopes failed, we cannot doubt.

Milton planned to make a single great poem the

crown of his life, to do for his own country what Homer, Virgil, Luís de Camões, and Torquato Tasso had done for theirs. I believe that in *Paradise Lost* he succeeded, and hence I have intended my remarks so far to lead up to this poem. All the qualities so far enumerated find a place there. As I shall point out in detail, it largely concerns action and the proper grounds for it. The side of contemplation is included partly through the many shifts of distance from which action is viewed, partly through descriptions that suggest a static condition of eternity rather than the shifting phenomena of this world. The pageants of earthly history that Michael shows to Adam are seen as if from a distance, and Adam's comment on them at the end fixes this impression:

> "How soon hath thy prediction, seer blest,
> Measured this transient world, the race of time,
> Till time stand fixed: beyond is all abyss,
> Eternity, whose end no eye can reach. . . ."
> (XII. 553–556)

The account of Paradise, though in the first instance borrowed from an actual garden, ends by speaking of an imagined world of incredible static beauty and felicity. Politics, though subordinated to a moral theme that goes far beyond it, is included through the infernal debates in the second book and through the characters of the different speakers. I shall refer later to instances of humor and generally to the diversity of the poem, to Milton's success in including in its compass all experience as he knew it.

Up to *Paradise Lost* the facts of Milton's life sometimes help us to understand his writing; and *Paradise Lost* itself is clearer if we know the conditions that led up to it. But after 1660, Milton lived anything but a public life, and there is little profit in connecting poetry and biography. Thus, from now on, I am concerned with his poetry alone.

The fall of man was not Milton's first choice for the subject of his great poem. At the time of his Italian journey he intended to write on King Arthur, and there are passages in his earliest pamphlets that show the kind of poem it would have been. It would have been partly religious and moral, partly patriotic. Arthur would have borne something of the character of Spenser's Prince Arthur in the *Fairie Queene*, uniting the contemplative and active virtues; but unlike Spenser's prince, he would have

---

[3]The date of composition of *Samson Agonistes* has been much disputed among modern scholars. The case for an early dating (1647–1653?) is set out by W. R. Parker, *Philological Quarterly*, 23 (1949) and *Notes and Queries*, 5 (1958).

been the center of action in defeating the heathen Saxon invaders. British history, again as in Spenser, would have been narrated in prophecy, culminating in the defeat of the Spanish Armada. The main emphasis would have been on heroic action. If there had been no civil war and Milton had been free to write his Arthuriad around the time of *Areopagitica*, he would have given us a divinely energetic poem, but one less varied and less mature than *Paradise Lost*. He might have gone on to a second, more mature poem; and the two together might have had an even wider scope than *Paradise Lost*. But if the choice were between an Arthuriad and *Paradise Lost*, we should be content with what we have.

Milton's very earliest critics served him well. Sir Henry Wotton, commenting on *Comus* in 1638, spoke of "a certain Dorique delicacy in your Songs and Odes, whereunto I must plainly confess to have seen yet nothing parallel in our Language." Wotton was thinking of all the parts of *Comus* not in dramatic blank verse, but "Dorique delicacy" describes, like no other phrase, the mixture of austerity and sensuous sweetness that generally marks Milton's early poetry. Andrew Marvell supplied a set of commendatory verses to the second edition of *Paradise Lost* that show a just appreciation of its scope and versification. He described the scope of Milton's subject thus:

> Messiah crowned, *Gods* reconciled decree,
> Rebelling angels, the forbidden tree,
> Heav'n, hell, earth, chaos, all: . . .

This shows that Marvell saw that the actual loss of Paradise was but a fraction of the whole. His account of Milton's style follows:

> At once delight and horror on us seize,
> Thou singst with so much gravity and ease;
> And above human flight dost soar aloft
> With plume so strong, so equal, and so soft.

Softness and ease: these are the qualities of style in *Paradise Lost* often unrecognized by those who are too intent on Milton's gravity and sublimity. Dryden, who praised *Paradise Lost* unstintingly, was also the first critic to interpret it wrongly. He said in 1697 that Milton would have a better claim to have written a genuine epic "if the Devil had not been his hero instead of Adam, if the giant had not

foiled the knight and driven him out of his stronghold to wander through the world with his lady errant." There you have that undue narrowing of the poem's scope to the episode of the Fall and the triumph of Satan: a narrowing that has become traditional and still continues to close the eyes of many readers and critics to the full significance of the poem. It is true that Milton himself gave countenance to this narrowing by the title he gave his epic, though I sometimes think that he was being ironical and meant us to think of *Lost* as in quotation marks. But Dryden's witty contention that the giant foiled the knight is quite at odds with the poem itself.

Paradise Lost in its grand outlines is founded on a simple irony. And we need not be surprised, for irony is one of the qualities Milton gives to God the Father. When, near the beginning of the third book, the Father looks down and sees Satan "coasting the wall of Heav'n" and about to penetrate the universe, he addresses the Son as follows:

> "Only begotten Son, seest thou what rage
> Transports our adversary, whom no bounds
> Prescribed, no bars of hell, nor all the chains
> Heaped on him there, nor yet the main abyss
> Wide interrupt can hold? . . ."
>
> (III. 80–84)

One critic accused Milton of inconsistency here because when, in the first book, Satan raised himself from the burning lake, Milton tells us he did so only through the "will and high permission of all-ruling Heaven." Of course there is no inconsistency, for in the passage quoted the Father speaks ironically, adopting Satan's foolish assumption that he raised himself from the lake and set out to ruin mankind on his own initiative and responsibility alone. If we grasp God's ironical words at Satan's expense, we may be the readier to believe that irony is central to the whole plot. The irony is as follows. Satan succeeds in tempting mankind to transgress God's commandment, and he believes that his success can have only one result: as Satan and his fellows have brought complete ruin on themselves by disobedience, so must Adam and Eve by theirs. But he has made a false comparison. Satan's sin was self-motivated; that of Adam and Eve was partly motivated from without. For Satan there is no hope, for he is corrupt throughout his whole being; for Adam and Eve there is hope, because theirs was not the whole responsibility. And in the end humanity finds itself able to attain an inner paradise better than the paradise it must give up; Dryden's knight and lady errant have in fact the key to a better stronghold than the one from which the giant has driven them. Such is the irony at Satan's expense. There is the further irony that Adam and Eve are as mistaken as Satan about their ultimate fate. When, exhausted by their quarrels and bereft of their pride, they become reconciled in very simple human companionship and fellow feeling, they are quite unaware that they are following the promptings both of heaven and of the residue of good thoughts that have survived the Fall, and that, by so following, they have attained salvation: just as the Ancient Mariner blessed the watersnakes unaware, not knowing that thereby he had broken the evil spell.

There are important consequences of this fundamental irony. First, the weight of the plot is put not on the mere episode of Eve eating the apple in the ninth book but on the whole process of temptation, Fall, the judgment by the Son of the Serpent, Adam, and Eve; on the corruption of the world through the entry of Sin and the consequent despair of Adam and Eve; and then, unexpectedly evolved out of all these varied and vast happenings, their mutual reconciliation, their penitence before God, and their salvation. These happenings occupy the whole of books IX and X. Such a weighting of the plot is of the first moment. The fall of Eve, adequate enough in a larger ironic context, is nowhere near weighty enough, as described by Milton, to be the center of the poem, the point to which all earlier happenings lead and from which all subsequent happenings derive.

But read books IX and X as a unit, treat the events after the Fall not as appendixes to a completed climax but as a sequence leading up to the real climax in man's regeneration, and you find them a brilliantly diversified and massive area of high poetry, a principal glory of the English tongue. It may be asked whether the climax as thus described will really bear the weight put on it any more than will the traditionally assumed climax, the eating of the apple. Can this purely human scene of man and wife forgetting their quarrels, coming together again, and confessing their sin to God stand the tremendous test? First, it can be retorted that Milton undoubtedly intended it to do so. Near the end of the poem there is a conversation

between Adam and Michael that follows the vision of future world history Michael has given to Adam for his instruction. From its all-important position and its intensely concentrated and earnest tone, it is clearly crucial to the meaning of the poem. Adam has at last learned wisdom, and this is his statement of some of the things hard experience has taught him:

"Henceforth I learn, that to obey is best,
And love with fear the only God, to walk
As in his presence, ever to observe
His providence, and on him sole depend,
Merciful over all his works, with good
Still overcoming evil, and by small
Accomplishing great things, by things deemed weak
Subverting worldly strong, and worldly wise
By simply meek . . . ."

(XII. 561–569)

This is high moralizing verse that would be irrelevant in a narrative poem if it did not repeat in its own abstract form what had already been transacted in concrete, dramatic action; and it points precisely to the true climax of the poem, where by their "small" decent action Adam and Eve accomplish great things and in their apparent weakness subvert the apparently "strong" machinations of the prince of this world. Whether Milton not only intended to make this part of the poem his climax but also succeeded in making it a worthy one can be decided only by the verdict of competent readers. But to me, at least, the account of Adam's black despair, his ferocious and cruel repulse of Eve, her persistence, Adam's softening toward her, their coming together, Eve's still distraught state of mind and inclination to suicide, Adam's strong and comforting words, and their final resolution to confess their sins to God is true to the fundamental simplicities of human nature and composes one of the most moving dramatic episodes in literature; it can bear a very heavy weight.

The second consequence of recognizing the fundamental irony of the poem is that it puts Satan in his proper place. Dryden has had many distinguished successors in his heresy that Satan is the hero; and as long as Adam and Eve were denied heroic action in their recovery after the Fall, it was natural to fill the resulting vacuum with any other action that had heroic pretensions. And that action was the escape of Satan from the fiery lake in Hell, and his courage in undertaking alone the journey to

167

Earth for the ruin of mankind. But Milton's Satan is never a hero; he is an archangel ruined: that terrible thing—a being with great potentialities of good corrupted; graced, indeed, to heighten the drama, with some relics of good feelings but doomed to turn those relics to even greater evil. Those who have sentimentalized Satan have failed to see the coarseness and the vulgarity that accompany and darken these lingering relics of good feelings. Here is Milton's description of Satan reviewing the army of devils now mustered in Hell:

> . . . he through the armed files
> Darts his experienced eye, and soon traverse
> The whole battalion views, their order due,
> Their visages and stature as of gods;
> Their number last he sums. And now his heart
> Distends with pride, and hardening in his strength
> Glories . . . .
>
> (I. 567–573)

It is a most damning description. How significant the juxtaposition of number and pride. Satan is revealed as the vulgarian who is thrilled by mere quantity. No wonder he commits a fundamental error in his estimate of what fate awaits disobedient man. All this is not to deny Satan's grandeur. It is just because he combines grandeur with vulgarity, a commanding intellect with a fundamental stupidity, not to speak of other discrepant qualities, that he is so true to life and so eternally fascinating a figure.

The fundamental irony at Satan's expense and at the apparent expense—but to the ultimate profit—of Adam and Eve is surpassingly powerful because it grew out of Milton's life experience and provided the most authentic material for his supreme poetic gift, a gift both congenial and improved by intense study. Milton condemns pride with such authority because he was himself strongly tempted to it. Compare him in this matter with Shakespeare. There is in literature no finer indictment of pride than Isabella's speech to Angelo in *Measure for Measure*:

> Could great men thunder
> As Jove himself does, Jove would ne'er be quiet,
> For every pelting, petty officer
> Would use his heaven for thunder;
> Nothing but thunder . . . Merciful heaven,
> Thou rather with thy sharp and sulphurous bolt
> Split'st the unwedgeable and gnarled oak
> Than the soft myrtle; but man, proud man,

> Drest in a little brief authority,
> Most ignorant of what he's most assured—
> His glassy essence—like an angry ape,
> Plays such fantastic tricks before high heaven
> As make the angels weep . . . .
>
> (II.ii. 111–122)

In his history plays, too, Shakespeare gives convincing pictures of proud and ambitious and unscrupulous men. But Isabella's speech and Shakespeare's quarreling nobles are passionately observed, not created out of the personal stuff of Shakespeare's mind. He could objectify them from the beginning, unhampered by any unusual personal involvement. But, as his pamphlets clearly show, Milton did suffer from that impatient pride that revolts against the nature of things and demands quick results; he had an element of Satan in him, and he experienced the despairing bafflement in which such pride is bound to end. But, as "Lycidas" showed, he was also aware of this side of his nature and hated it, believing even more passionately in the need for humility. And always the victory of humility was complete. It is because of this personal conflict, absent from Shakespeare in this acute form, that the basic irony of *Paradise Lost* has its peculiar power. Milton did objectify his material: we do not, in reading *Paradise Lost*, think of Milton the man. But he objectified with greater difficulty and at a later stage of the poetic process than Shakespeare did; and his poetry makes a different impression. Shakespeare was very close to life; Milton, to his own life. And the Miltonic closeness has its own superb authenticity.

I have asserted that the basis of *Paradise Lost* is a great irony expressive of a great piece of simple morality and that Milton's own total experience of this morality makes his poem authentic. We are reluctant, however, to accept a piece of simple morality as authentic unless it is supported by a great mass of detail. We require a poet to talk about many things before we are ready to accept what he most has to say. So I come now by a quite natural sequence to the various parts of *Paradise Lost*. These are so many that I will have to select; and I will do so by dealing only with those things that have either been denied to Milton or, if granted to him, ignored or slurred over or deprecated.

First, there is the theology. While the eighteenth century was too prone to see in *Paradise Lost* a simple orthodoxy, the late nineteenth and early twentieth centuries were too prone to cut out the theology altogether as an unfortunate accretion dictated by the conditions of seventeenth-century England. The truth is that Milton's theology is not entirely orthodox and that it is inseparable from the poem. If, as I assert, the main theme of the poem has to do with pride and humility, these qualities are not independent and uncircumstantiated, but bear the form, inescapable in the postclassical tradition in Europe, given them by Christianity. However much Milton had tried to free himself from theological ties, Pride, as he presented it, would in some sort have remained the chief of the Seven Deadly Sins, and humility a quality exemplified in the story of Christ as told in the New Testament. When Milton implies the doctrine of disinterestedness in "Lycidas," he gives us neither the abstracted doctrine nor the form of it found in the *Bhagavad-Gita*. However universal the doctrine, Christian and Indian writers had to present it in the ways they had inherited. Readers today are better placed to accept Milton's theology because recent scholarship has been teaching them a great deal about the theological tradition Milton inherited. So long as readers conceived it as a narrow fundamentalism of the kind described in the Mark Rutherford novels, they had to free Milton the poet from it. But if they realize that for Milton, as for his predecessors, theology included all philosophy and a great deal of natural science, they will see that such severance is not only unnecessary but also disastrously weakening to the range of Milton's interests.

One of the great theological doctrines was that a main way to approach God was through studying the beautiful variety of his creation. I have already mentioned the exuberance of Milton's nature as something fundamental. Possessing it, he was bound to find the bounty of nature both exciting and satisfying. Living when he did and brought up as he was, he could conceive of this bounty in other than theological terms. He must see it in terms of the great orderly arrangement of the total creation pictured as a great hierarchical chain stretching from the seraph nearest the throne of God to the meanest speck of inanimate matter. Even when Comus, the champion of disorder, speaks of the bounty of God's creation, that he may tempt the Lady to license, he does so with an enthusiasm that can best be matched in the panegyrics of orthodox divinity:

> Wherefore did Nature pour her bounties forth,
> With such a full and unwithdrawing hand,
> Covering the earth with odors, fruits, and flocks,
> Thronging the seas with spawn innumerable. . . .
> (710–713)

And when, in *Paradise Lost*, Milton writes of free will, he colors a doctrine that was essential to his own nature with traditional disputes over predestination and with the special Protestant doctrine of Christian liberty based on the writings of St. Paul. Milton's theology, far from being a tie, an alien thing, was a great world of thought where an immensely wide range of passions could find their natural embodiments.

Great poets are often the subject of large popular misconceptions. Chaucer has been thought of as hearty, Shakespeare as uneducated and unacademic, Shelley as weakly neurotic, Milton as inhuman and humorless. And these misconceptions die hard. It may be difficult, therefore, to gain the reader's ear if one points to humor and a delicate human perception in *Paradise Lost*. Humor, indeed, is not what one is led to expect in the straight epic from Virgil onward; nor could humor be advertised in the uniform meter of the epic with the clarity possible in a play using both verse and prose like Shakespeare's *Henry IV*. But Milton expects his readers to be fit as well as few; and fitness indicates close reading, which in its turn reveals, perhaps as a great surprise, these qualities of humor and delicate human perception. I mentioned earlier as a humorous figure the wealthy city merchant in *Areopagitica*, who hired a divine to manage his religion for him; and I fancy he reappears in a passage of *Paradise Lost* that has been cited as an example of Milton's seeking to be funny with disastrous results. It occurs just before the great description of Paradise and is a comparison with the way Satan overleaped the leafy barriers of that place, scorning entry by the proper way:

> Or as a thief bent to unhoard the cash
> Of some rich burgher, whose substantial doors,
> Cross-barred and bolted fast, fear no assault,
> In at the window climbs, or o'er the tiles . . . .
> (IV. 188–191)

The point of the passage is to lower the dignity of Satan, who a little earlier has struck a highly dramatic attitude, by homely comparisons, so that the reader may have his mind cleared for the coming description of Paradise; but the actual lines are a piece of satirical humor at the expense of the rich merchant who is imaginative enough to guard against direct assault but not imaginative enough to forestall a cat burglar.

I remarked earlier that Milton acquired a knowledge of women during the years of the Commonwealth, and in *Paradise Lost* this knowledge comes, as we might expect, in the later books, where the action has converged from Hell and Heaven to the universe and finally to the narrow human stage of the mount of Paradise. It is in the long scene near the beginning of book IX, when Adam and Eve discuss whether they shall garden separately or jointly, that the human comedy is most evident. That Milton dared to introduce comedy immediately before the great disaster in human history is quite amazing; and, if that disaster had been irreparable, comedy would have been out of the question. But I do not see how any careful and honest reader can miss the comedy; and I fancy Milton introduced it because he wished to relieve the disaster of the Fall itself of too stark an emphasis and to prepare for the basic irony of the poem.

The dispute between Adam and Eve is as delicate a piece of domestic comedy as you could find. Eve proposes separate gardening on this particular morning, not because she really wants that but because she wants Adam to say that he loves her too much to bear separation from her. Adam falls into the trap and replies with a heavy piece of moralizing. Eve gets her own back by saying that Adam does not trust her. Adam grows seriously concerned and argues earnestly, even impressively; and, if only he could see it, Eve is by now quite satisfied with the effect that her stratagem has produced. But Adam does not see, and refuses the responsibility of keeping Eve at his side. Finally Eve feels that after all this she cannot refuse the offer of a freedom she did not really want at any time, and now less than ever. And so they part, and Eve is exposed alone to the wiles of Satan. It is a perfect picture of the sort of misunderstanding that can afflict any ordinary, well-intentioned married couple; and it is proof that Milton had an eye for ordinary human traffic as well as for God's empyrean. Most remarkable is the stylistic skill by which he keeps the comedy from being cheap, so that it can slide into the tragic; for Adam's failure to assert himself at the right moment is not only comedy but also a tragic moral lapse.

But Milton's success in passing from comedy to tragedy is possible only within a restricted area of contrast. Obliged by writing in the epic form to observe a certain kind of uniformity, he has to pitch his comedy in a higher style than is required for the drama; his conversational cadences have to blend with a modicum of pomp. The conversational cadence of Eve's reprimand to Adam:

> But that thou shouldst my firmness therefore doubt
> To God or thee, because we have a foe
> May tempt it, I expected not to hear.
>
> (IX. 279-281)

with its stresses on "thou" and "my" is perfect, but it is delicately, not blatantly, conveyed; and the dignity of the passage does not fall below the standard expected from epic writing in the seventeenth century. It is this delicacy and lack of blatancy that both separates Milton's art from that of the metaphysical poets and exaggerates that separation. The metaphysicals founded their art on surprise and advertised what they were doing with much emphasis. Milton resembled them in being full of surprises, but he was extremely discreet about them. Had he not been full of surprises, he would have been untrue to the age in which he lived; had he paraded the fact, he would have been intolerable as an epic poet.

The matter of surprise is connected with another: that of realism. Milton's epic has the remotest possible setting, yet he wished its application to be entirely modern. To achieve his end he constantly refers in passing to contemporary events or interests, and slips the homely and the sensuous into contexts that are grandiose and remote. In the high description of Satan's lieutenants in book I, Milton suddenly inserts his reference to the riotous young men who made the streets of London dangerous in the later years of his life:

> . . . and when night
> Darkens the streets, then wander forth the sons
> Of Belial, flown with insolence and wine.
>
> (I. 500-502)

It is a startling piece of realism, but slipped in so coolly and quietly that it does not impair the epic texture. In the last lines of the poem, which give the vast picture of the angels thrusting Adam and Eve out of the gates of Paradise, occurs a reference of the greatest possible homeliness: to an ordinary peasant returning home to supper on a misty evening. I give it in its setting.

> So spake our mother Eve, and Adam heard
> Well pleased, but answered not; for now too nigh
> The archangel stood, and from the other hill
> To their fixed station, all in bright array
> The cherubim descended; on the ground
> Gliding meteorous, as evening mist
> Risen from a river o'er the marish glides,
> And gathers ground fast at the laborer's heel
> Homeward returning. High in front advanced,
> The brandished sword of God before them blazed
> Fierce as a comet; which with torrid heat,
> And vapor as the Lybian air adust,
> Began to parch that temperate clime; whereat
> In either hand the hastening angel caught
> Our lingering parents, and to the eastern gate
> Led them direct, and down the cliff as fast
> To the subjected plaine; then disappeared.
> They looking back, all the eastern side beheld
> Of Paradise, so late their happy seat,
> Wav'd over by that flaming brand, the gate
> With dreadful faces thronged and fiery arms. . . .
> (XII. 624–644)

I quote this passage to illustrate how successfully Milton could insinuate the homely and the realistic into the grandiose, but it will serve also to prompt a final general comment on *Paradise Lost*. It is one of the great passages, and it is typical of the poem generally in uniting so many strands and grades of feeling: the huge, almost monstrous picture of the thronged gate and the miniature picture of the two human beings; the archangel matched by the peasant; the particularity of description of the "eastern gate" set against the symbolic significance of the "subjected plaine." And these many strands are made to cooperate through their common subordination to a unifying though never monotonous type of verse. Such is the general nature of *Paradise Lost*, and it corresponds to the primary wealth and vitality of Milton's own nature, as well as to the mental discipline through which he accepted and held together the good and the ill that life brought him.

Paradise Lost is exacting because it is a long, highly concentrated poem, but not so exacting as to be beyond the reach of a wide public. In the eighteenth century it was extremely popular, partly because, along with the Bible and *The Pilgrim's Progress*, it was legitimate Sunday reading for Puritans, but also partly because readers of that time were willing to give steady attention to a few great works. And it could regain such a vogue whenever a wide public cared to give it similar attention; the potential attraction, the perennial human appeal, are there all the time. *Paradise Regained* is a different case; it has always been a poem for the few. But those few have found it, in some strange way, immensely attractive. Why Milton wrote it we do not know. The old idea that it is a sequel to *Paradise Lost* does not work, because the earlier poem had included the recovery of Paradise through Christ in its scope and had taken world history far beyond the period of time to which *Paradise Regained* is confined. What is certain is that *Paradise Regained* deals once again with the dominant Miltonic theme of the prime importance of the state of mind and the dependence of action on that state.

Paradise Regained is a narrative version of Christ's temptation by the Devil in the wilderness; and in choosing this episode as the chief one in the gospels, Milton was following an earlier tradition particularly dear to Puritan thought. Puritanism loved to picture the Christian life and the chief events leading up to it as a battle. The Christian was a warrior, clad in the spiritual armor listed by St. Paul; and there had been two principal battles that had decided his fate. First, the Devil had fought with and defeated Adam, the Old Man, in the Garden of Eden; and second, Christ, the New Man, had fought with and defeated the Devil in the wilderness. And the wilderness was necessary for the proper correspondence. As Adam had lost a garden for a wilderness, so must Christ conduct his battle in a wilderness to win back the paradisiac garden. Milton accepted this rather surprising preference of the Temptation to the Crucifixion partly because he liked to work in the tradition of the religious party to which, generally, he belonged and partly because the Temptation was, in his view, the episode that marked the formation of the state of mind that governed all Christ's subsequent action, the acceptance of crucifixion included. Once Christ had acquired that state of mind, he had only to act in accordance with it, and action would take care of itself—or, rather, God in heaven would take care of it. Christ's victory in the wilderness symbolized the general moral truth that the state of mind comes first and results are subordinate.

Milton's heart was therefore thoroughly in his theme, and in his treatment of it he seems to have consulted his own inclination rather than his readers' applause, in a way different from *Paradise Lost*. There are long speeches and few deeds. The poem is more of a debate than a narrative; and it is likely that the Book of Job was Milton's model here. The language is less ornate and more restricted to simple words than that of *Paradise Lost*, and the rhythm more subdued and closer to quiet conversation. This is the cool, quiet, and yet passionately concentrated way in which Milton ends the first book. Satan has just asked, with assumed humility, permission to come and talk with Christ in the wilderness:

> To whom our Saviour with unaltered brow.
> Thy coming hither, though I know thy scope,
> I bid not or forbid; do as thou find'st
> Permission from above; thou canst not more.
>   He added not; and Satan bowing low
> His gray dissimulation, disappeared
> Into thin air diffused: for now began
> Night with her sullen wing to double-shade
> The desert, fowls in their clay nests were couched;
> And now wild beasts came forth the woods to roam.
>   (I. 493–502)

It is those already familiar with Milton who will appreciate this kind of writing. For them the leanness of Christ's speech will not indicate starvation or poverty, but the leanness of the perfectly trained athlete whose body is free from every trace of superfluous fat and consists of operant bone and muscle. It will further resemble the athlete's body when in gentle, not violent, motion—gentle, but containing the promise of the fiercest violence, should violence be required. It is also those already familiar with Milton who will appreciate the delicate conversational cadence of many of the speeches. This is Christ speaking of worldly glory:

> But why should man seek glory? who of his own
> Hath nothing, and to whom nothing belongs
> But condemnation, ignominy, and shame?
> Who for so many benefits received
> Turned recreant to God, ingrate and false,
> And so of all true good himself despoiled,
> Yet, sacrilegious, to himself would take
> That which to God alone of right belongs;
> Yet so much bounty is in God, such grace,
> That who advance his glory, not their own,
> Then he himself to glory will advance.
>   (III. 134–144)

There is no unusual word here, no simile, scarcely a metaphor. The effect depends on the verse, the rise and fall of emphasis within narrow limits, the occasional flicker of feeling as in the word "sacrilegious," as if the poet were addressing an intimate reader, one who could catch much meaning from mere hints, one who could take so very much for granted.

If the conversations are quiet and delicately cadenced, the landscape is of twilight and suggests less a real scene than a symbol of the working of the mind. But into this dimness Milton projects brilliant visions that, whether by accident or by design, resemble the infernal creations that in medieval romance tempted Sir Galahad in his quest for the Holy Grail. Here is the description of the phantoms that attended the banquet Satan raised in the wilderness.

> And at a stately sideboard by the wine
> That fragrant smell diffused, in order stood
> Tall stripling youths rich-clad, of fairer hue
> Then Ganymede or Hylas; distant more
> Under the trees now tripped, now solemn stood
> Nymphs of Diana's train, and Naiades
> With fruits and flowers from Amalthea's horn,
> And ladies of the Hesperides, that seemed
> Fairer then feigned of old, or fabled since
> Of fairy damsels met in forest wide
> By Knights of Logres, or of Lyonesse,
> Lancelot or Pelleas, or Pellenore,
> And all the while harmonious airs were heard
> Of chiming strings, or charming pipes and winds
> Of gentlest gale Arabian odors fanned
> From their soft wings, and Flora's earliest smells.
>   (II. 350–365)

Paradise Regained is unusually compounded of twilight, trancelike descriptions, conversations remote from the marketplace or senate house or inn, yet delicately suggesting the cadences of real talk, and brilliant visions. It is a varied and startling composition, but it is strange too; and it is not surprising that in general readers have not been able to take *Paradise Regained* to their hearts.

The case is very different with the other poem published along with *Paradise Regained* in 1671, *Samson Agonistes*. Milton's Samson, blind and in Philistine captivity, is, like Chaucer's Wife of Bath or Shakespeare's Macbeth or Dickens' Mrs. Gamp, one of those figures that helps to compose what can be called a nation's literary mythology. Anthony

Trollope, in *The Last Chronicle of Barset*, makes Mr. Crawley, himself a tragic figure, talk of Milton's Samson as if he were an accepted national inheritance, the common property of all intelligent readers. Mr. Crawley has been making his daughter read about the blinded Polyphemus in the *Odyssey*, and he stops her and comments:

The same story is always coming up; we have it in various versions, because it is so true to life.

> Ask for this great deliverer now, and find him
> Eyeless in Gaza, at the mill with slaves.

It is the same story. Great power reduced to impotence, great glory to misery, by the hand of Fate. At the mill with slaves! Can any picture be more dreadful than that? The mind of the strong blind creature must be so sensible of the injury that has been done to him! The impotency, combined with his strength, or rather the impotency with the memory of former strength and former aspirations, is so essentially tragic.

Aldous Huxley chose *Eyeless in Gaza* for the title of one of his novels. And T. S. Eliot assumed a response he could not assume if he had referred to *Paradise Regained* when he wove references to "*Samson Agonistes* into the texture of "East Coker":

> O dark dark dark. They all go into the dark,
> The vacant interstellar spaces, the vacant into the
>   vacant . . . .

Trollope's Mr. Crawley was right. Milton's Samson is a terrible yet compelling figure of human suffering, reminding one of Sophocles' Philoctetes, Shakespeare's Lear, and one or two of Hopkins' most poignant sonnets. Milton is surely thinking of the physical pangs of Philoctetes when he makes his Samson burst into this lyrical complaint:

> O that torment should not be confined
> To the body's wounds and sores
> With maladies innumerable
> In heart, head, breast, and reins;
> But must secret passage find
> To the inmost mind,
> There exercise all his fierce accidents,
> And on her purest spirits prey,
> As on entrails, joints, and limbs,
> With answerable pains, but more intense,

> Though void of corporal sense.
>   My griefs not only pain me
> As a lingering disease,
> But finding no redress, ferment and rage,
> Nor less then wounds immedicable
> Rankle, and fester, and gangrene,
> To black mortification.
> Thoughts my tormentors armed with deadly stings
> Mangle my apprehensive tenderest parts,
> Exasperate, exulcerate, and raise
> Dire inflammation which no cooling herb
> Or med'cinal liquor can assuage,
> Nor breath of vernal air from snowy alp.
> Sleep hath forsook and given me o'er
> To death's benumbing opium as my only cure.
> Thence faintings, swoonings of despair,
> And sense of heaven's desertion.
>   (606–632)

But if Samson the sufferer is part of English literary mythology, what of the whole play? Here the answer is in some doubt. Milton cannot have written the play to be acted; Samuel Johnson accused it of defective action, and a general notion has prevailed that as a whole it is insufficiently dramatic. And yet *Samson Agonistes* has been played in amateur performances with great success. The general notion and the specific event do not concur. The truth is that Samson is indeed dramatic, but in a way unusual in English drama. There is little action on the stage, the most important being reported. But there is sufficient action in Samson's mind. Even so, that action is unusual. Motives on the stage are usually more obvious than they would be in life. However, mental action in Samson does not consist in obvious changes and transitions, but in the spread of an unconscious temper into consciousness. At the beginning of the play Samson is in the same case as Adam is in book X of *Paradise Lost*, when he is in despair and thinks God has quite cast him off. Actually, both Adam and Samson have accepted complete responsibility for what they have done, and thereby have touched the humility that means salvation. *Samson Agonistes* reveals the mind of its protagonist in its various stages of testing, awakening, comprehension, and finds its end in the death of a forgiven and redeemed hero. As a psychological drama it is a wonderful and satisfying piece of work. And now that the technique of choric speech has been improved (mainly through productions of T. S. Eliot's verse drama), there is no reason why *Samson Agonistes* should not take its place as one of the great acted English classics.

I have written of *Samson Agonistes* after *Paradise Regained* as if the facts of simultaneous publication and the sequence within that publication indicated the same order of composition. But, as already stated, there is no certain proof of when *Samson* was written. Nevertheless, it does supplement *Paradise Regained* very remarkably; and even if Milton wrote *Samson* earlier, he may have recast it for publication. In any case, if he chose to publish the two poems together, we are safer in considering them together than in plumping for earlier dates of composition for which there is no scrap of firm evidence. Like *Paradise Regained*, *Samson Agonistes* deals with the regions of reflection and action. Christ rejected all temptations to achieve quick results. He knew his own powers and wondered whether he should lead Israel to revolt against Rome. But he knew too that such was not his true fate. And he waited until, in the fullness of time, he achieved a state of mind that insured that all his actions would be soundly based. Samson, on the other hand, chose a life of physical action; and up to a point he was right, because he had been gifted with unusual strength. But success corrupted him and made him overvalue his gift. Through this pride he fell into misfortune, but he recognized his error and fell into the extremes of despair and humility:

> O impotence of mind, in body strong!
> But what is strength without a double share
> Of wisdom, vast, unwieldy, burdensome,
> Proudly secure, yet liable to fall
> By weakest subtleties, not made to rule,
> But to subserve where wisdom bears command.
>
> (52–57)

Once Samson has realized that the state of mind comes first, once his own state of mind is sound, God allows him yet again to put his gift of unusual physical strength into action. The idea of the two poems is the same; but in the first the climax is the achievement of a state of mind implying perfect actions to come, while in the second it is a piece of action based on a sound state of mind already achieved.

I think that *Paradise Lost* is worth more than all the rest of Milton's works put together, but fewer readers than in former times have the patience to master a long poem. The almost superstitious reverence for the successful epic has disappeared. It may be that for some years to come the early poems, fragments of *Paradise Lost*, *Samson Agonistes*, and perhaps *Areopagitica* will be the operant portions of his works. It is to be regretted if this should be so; but even if thus truncated, Milton survives as a major poet of surpassing power and variety.

SELECTED BIBLIOGRAPHY

I. Bɪʙʟɪᴏɢʀᴀᴘʜʏ. J. Bradshaw, ed., *A Concordance to the Poetical Works of John Milton* (London, 1894; repr. 1965); W. A. Wright, pub., *Facsimile of the Manuscript of Milton's Minor Poems Preserved in the Library of Trinity College, Cambridge* (Cambridge, 1899), partly reproduced by F. A. Patterson (New York, 1933; Menton, 1970); L. E. Lockwood, *Lexicon to the English Poetical Works of John Milton* (New York, 1907); *Milton, 1608–1674: Facsimile of the Autographs and Documents in the British Museum* (London, 1908); E. N. S. Thompson, *John Milton: A Topical Bibliography* (New Haven, 1916); A. H. Gilbert, *A Geographical Dictionary of Milton* (New Haven, 1919); L. Cooper, ed., *A Concordance of the Latin, Greek and Italian Poems of John Milton* (Halle, 1923); J. H. Hanford, *A Milton Handbook* (New York, 1926; 5th rev. ed., 1970); D. H. Stevens, *Reference Guide to Milton from 1800 to the Present Day* (Chicago, 1930); H. F. Fletcher, ed., *Contributions to a Milton Bibliography, 1800–1930: Being a List of Addenda to Stevens's Reference Guide* (Urbana, Ill., 1931); V. de S. Pinto, *The English Renaissance 1510–1688* (London, 1938; 3rd rev. ed., 1966), contains a bibliography; C. Huckabay, *John Milton: A Bibliographical Supplement, 1929–1957* (Pittsburgh—Louvain, 1960), also in rev. ed., *John Milton: An Annotated Bibliography, 1929–1968* (1969); E. S. Le Comte, *A Milton Dictionary* (New York, 1960; English ed., 1961); William Ingram and Kathleen Swain, eds., *A Concordance to Milton's English Poetry* (Oxford, 1972).

II. Cᴏʟʟᴇᴄᴛᴇᴅ Wᴏʀᴋs. J. Tolland, ed., *A Complete Collection of the Historical, Political, and Miscellaneous Works of Milton*, 3 vols. (London, 1694–1698); P[atrick] H[ume], ed., *Poetical Works, Together with Explanatory Notes on Each Book of the Paradise Lost, and a Table Never Before Printed*, 5 pts. (London, 1695), the first collected ed. of the poetry; H. J. Todd, ed., *Poetical Works. With the Principal Notes of Various Commentators*, 6 vols. (London, 1801; 7 vols., 1809, with additions and a verbal index), a variorum ed. using the work of some of the best-known eighteenth-century editors of Milton, including R. Bentley, T. Newton, and Thomas Warton, and critical appreciations of Milton by Andrew Marvell, John Dryden, Joseph Addison, James Thomson, Samuel Johnson, Thomas Gray, William Cowper, and others; W. Hayley, ed., *Cowper's Milton, with Notes by William Cowper*, 4 vols. (Chichester, 1810); J. A. St. John, ed., *Prose Works*, 5 vols. (London, 1848–1853); J. Mitford, ed., *Works, in Verse and Prose*, 8 vols. (London, 1851), complete except for "Of Christian Doctrine" and minor items; R. C. Browne, ed., *English Poems* (London, 1866), also with notes by H. Bradley (London, 1894); D. Masson, ed., *Poetical Works*, 3 vols. (London, 1874; rev. ed., 1890), the Globe one-volume ed. has an intro. by Masson (London, 1877); A. W. Verity, ed., *The Cambridge Milton for Schools*, 11 vols. (London, 1891–1899); H. C. Beeching, ed., *The Poetical Works of John Milton* (Oxford, 1900; rev. ed., 1938); W. Aldis Wright, ed., *Poetical Works* (London, 1903); H. J. C. Grierson, ed., *The Poems of John Milton, Arranged in Chronological Order*, 2 vols. (London, 1925); M. W. Wallace, ed., *Milton's Prose*, (London—New York, 1925); F. A. Patterson, ed., *The Student's Milton* (New York, 1930), contains the complete poetry and most of the prose, plus early biographies of Milton—the revised edition (1933) contains annotations to the poetry and prose; F. A. Patterson, gen. ed., *Works*, 18 vols. (New York, 1931–1938), issued by Columbia University, is the only complete edition of Milton's works, the last vol. contains previously uncollected writings and marginalia, and there is a two-vol. index, F. A. Patterson and F. R. Fogle, eds. (New York, 1940), that forms an invaluable work of reference; *Private Correspondence and Academic Exercises*, P. B. Tillyard, trans. (Cambridge, 1932), with intro. and commentary by E. M. W. Tillyard; J. H. Hanford., ed., *The Poems of John Milton* (New York, 1936); E. H. Visiak, ed., *Complete Poetry and Selected Prose* (London, 1938); H. F. Fletcher, ed., *Complete Poetical Works* (Boston, 1941), a new text ed., with intro. and notes, of the Cambridge ed., W. V. Moody, ed.; H. F. Fletcher, ed., *Complete Poetical Works*, 4 vols. (Urbana, Ill., 1943–1948), reproduced in photographic facs.: M. Y. Hughes, *John Milton, Complete Poems and Major Prose* (New York, 1957), with notes by Hughes; K. M. Burton, ed., *Milton's Prose Writings* (London—New York, 1958); Helen Darbishire, ed., *Poetical Works* (London, 1958), in the Oxford Standard Authors ed.; J. T. Shawcross, ed., *The Complete English Poetry of John Milton* (London, 1963); D. M. Wolfe et al., eds., *The Complete Prose Works*, 5 vols. (New Haven, 1953–1970); D. Bush, ed., *Complete Poetical Works* (Boston, 1965; English ed., 1966); J. Carey and A. Fowler, eds., *The Poems of John Milton* (London, 1968).

III. SELECTED WORKS. *Poems of Mr. John Milton. Both English and Latin. . . . Printed . . . for H. Moseley* (London, 1645; facs. repr. of English poems, 1968), the minor poems: "On the Morning of Christ's Nativity," "L'Allegro," "Il Penseroso," sonnets, and others; *Poems, Etc. upon Several Occasions. By Mr. John Milton: . . . With a Small Tractate of Education to Mr. Hartlib* (London, 1673); W. Hayley, ed., *Latin and Italian Poems of Milton*, William Cowper, trans. (Chichester, 1808), also W. MacKellar, ed., *Latin Poems*, MacKellar, trans. (New Haven, 1930); O. Elton, ed., *Minor Poems*, 5 vols. (Oxford, 1893–1900); J. S. Smart, ed., *Sonnets* (Glasgow, 1921; repr. 1966), with original notes and new biographical matter; M. Y. Hughes, ed., *Paradise Regained, the Minor Poems and Samson Agonistes* (New York, 1937); D. Bush, ed., *The Portable Milton* (New York, 1949), with intro. by Bush; *Poems of Mr John Milton* (New York, 1951; reiss. London, 1957), the 1645 ed., with analytical essays by Cleanth Brooks and J. E. Hardy; N. Frye, ed., *John Milton: Paradise Lost and Selected Poems* (London–New York, 1951); E. Le Comte, ed., *"Paradise Lost" and Other Poems* (New York, 1961); M. Y. Hughes, ed., *Paradise Lost* (New York, 1962); I. G. MacCaffrey, ed., *John Milton: Samson Agonistes and the Shorter Poems* (New York–London, 1966); C. Ricks, ed., *John Milton: Paradise Lost and Paradise Regained* (New York–London, 1968).

IV. SEPARATE WORKS. "An Epitaph on the Admirable Dramaticke Poet, W. Shakespeare," first published in the Second Folio of Shakespeare's *Plays* (London, 1632); "A Maske Presented at Ludlow Castle, 1634. . . . " (London, 1637), the title *Comus* was first used in the stage version of 1738; "Lycidas," in *Obsequies to the Memory of Mr. Edward King* (London, 1638), a collection of memorial verses in Latin, Greek, and English; *Epitaphium Damonis* (London, ca. 1640), unique copy in British Museum; *Of Reformation Touching Church-Discipline in England: . . .* (London, 1641); *Of Prelatical Episcopacy . . .* (London, 1641); *Animadversions upon the Remonstrants Defence Against Smectymnuus* (London, 1641); *The Reason of Church-Government Urg'd Against Prelaty* (London, 1641); *An Apology Against a Pamphlet Call'd A Modest Confutation of the Animadversions upon the Remonstrant Against Smectymnuus* (London, 1642); *The Doctrine and Discipline of Divorce . . .* (London, 1643; 2nd ed., rev. and enl., 1644); *Of Education. To Master Samuel Hartlib* (London, ca. 1644); *The Judgement of Martin Bucer . . .* (London, 1644); *Areopagitica . . .* (London, 1644); *Colasterion: A Reply to a Nameles Answer Against the Doctrine and Discipline of Divorce* (London, 1645); *Tetrachordon: Expositions upon the Foure Chief Places in Scripture Which Treat of Mariage, or Nullities in Mariage* (London, 1645); "Sonnet to Henry Lawes," in Henry and William Lawes, *Choice Psalmes, Put into Musick for Three Voices* (London, 1648); ΕΙΚΟΝΟΚΛΑΣΤΗΣ: In Answer to a Book Intitl'd Εἰκὼν Βασιλικὴ, the Portraiture of His Sacred Majesty in His Solitudes and Sufferings (London, 1649; 2nd ed., enl., 1650); *Observations upon the Articles of Peace with the Irish Rebels* . . . (London, 1649); *The Tenure of Kings and Magistrates* (London, 1649); *Pro Populo anglicano defensio* . . . (London, 1651), translated by J. Washington (London, 1692); *A Letter Written to a Gentleman in the Country, Touching the Dissolution of the Late Parliament and the Reasons Thereof* (London, 1653); *Pro populo anglicano defensio secunda* (London, 1654), translated by F. Wrangham (London, 1816); *Joannis Miltonii pro se defensio* . . . (London, 1655); *Considerations Touching the Likeliest Means to Remove Hirelings out of the Church* (London, 1659); *A Treatise of Civil Power in Ecclesiastical Causes* . . . (London, 1659); *Brief Notes upon a Late Sermon, Titl'd, The Fear of God and the King* . . . (London, 1660); *The Readie & Easie Way to Establish a Free Commonwealth* . . . (London, 1660); *Paradise Lost* (London, 1667; 2nd ed., 12 bks., rev. and enl., 1674), facs. of 1st ed. with intro. by D. Masson (London, 1877), also in A. Fowler, ed. (London, 1971), MS of bk. I edited by H. Darbishire (Oxford, 1931); *The History of Britain* . . . (London, 1670); *Paradise Regained* (London, 1671), to which is added "Samson Agonistes"; *Of True Religion, Haeresie, Schism, Toleration, and What Best Means May Be Us'd Against the Growth of Popery* (London, 1673); *Mr. John Milton's Character of the Long Parliament and Assembly of Divines* . . . (London, 1681), originally part of bk. III of *The History of Britain*; *A Brief History of Moscovia* . . . (London, 1682); *Letters of State, Written by Mr. John Milton* . . . *from the Year 1649 till 1659* . . . (London, 1694), includes a biography by E. Phillips, several poems, and a catalog of the works; C. R. Sumner, ed., *De doctrina christiana* (Cambridge, 1825), also translated by Sumner (Cambridge, 1825).

V. Some Biographical and Critical Studies. Early biographies of Milton by John Aubrey, Anthony Wood, Edward Phillips, John Toland, Jonathan Richardson, and Thomas Ellwood are collected in *The Student's Milton* (1930). See also Helen Darbishire, *Early Lives of Milton* (London, 1932).

Works of the seventeenth and eighteenth centuries are Andrew Marvell, "On Paradise Lost," a poem in praise of Milton prefixed to the 1674 ed. of *Paradise Lost*; John Dryden, "Apology for Heroic Poetry" (1677), in W. P. Ker, ed., *Essays* (Oxford, 1900); Joseph Addison, papers on *Paradise Lost*, in *Spectator* from 31 December 1711 to 3 May 1712 (no. 267, and on Saturdays until no. 369), twelve papers discuss the beauties of each of the twelve books, and six discuss *Paradise Lost* as a whole; Jonathan Richardson, *Explanatory Notes and Remarks on Milton's Paradise Lost* (London, 1734); J. Warton, *An Essay on the Genius and Writings of Pope* (London, 1756), an interesting estimate of Milton in relation to Pope; Samuel Johnson, "Life of Milton," in his *Lives of the Poets* (London, 1779).

Nineteenth-century writings include W. S. Landor, *Imaginary Conversations* (London, 1824–1829), contains two "conversations" between Milton and Marvell, which were edited by C. G. Crump (London, 1891); S. T. Coleridge, *Literary Remains*, H. N. Coleridge, ed. (London, 1836–1839), contains a lecture on Milton delivered in 1818, also see Coleridge's comparison of Milton and Shakespeare in his *Biographia literaria* (London, 1817), ch. XV; D. Masson, *The Life of John Milton*, 7 vols. (London, 1858–1881; with index, 1894); T. B. Macaulay, *Critical and Historical Essays, Contributed to the Edinburgh Review*, 3 vols. (London, 1843), contains the famous essay on Milton published in August 1825, also see his *Miscellaneous Writings* (London, 1860); M. Arnold, *Mixed Essays* (London, 1879), see also his *Essays in Criticism, Second Series* (London, 1888); W. Bagehot, *Literary Studies*, R. H. Hutton, ed. (London, 1879), contains a study of Milton; M. Pattison, *Milton* (London, 1879), in the English Men of Letters series; R. Garnett, *Life of John Milton* (London, 1890); R. Bridges, *Milton's Prosody* (Oxford, 1893; rev. ed., 1901), a revised version of two essays (1887 and 1889), also another ed. with a chapter on accentual verse, and notes (1921).

During the first three decades of the twentieth century appeared Sir W. A. Raleigh, *Milton* (London 1900); C. G. Osgood, *The Classical Mythology of Milton's English Poems*, Yale Studies in English no. 8 (New Haven, 1900; repr. Oxford, 1925); Lascelles Abercrombie, *The Epic* (London, 1914), contains important criticism of Milton's epics; R. D. Havens, *The Influence of Milton on English Poetry* (Cambridge, Mass., 1922); Denis Saurat, *Milton: Man and Thinker* (New York, 1925), a translation and adaptation of essays earlier published in French that contains a bibliography of criticism of Milton; J. H. Hanford, *A Milton Handbook* (New York, 1926; 5th rev. ed., 1970), see also Hanford's *The Youth of Milton*, in the series University of Michigan Studies of Shakespeare, Milton, and Donne (New York, 1925); H. J. C. Grierson, *Cross Currents in English Literature of the XVIIth Century* (London, 1929), the Messenger lectures, delivered at Cornell University, 1926–1927.

Works of the 1930's are E. E. Stoll, *Poets and Playwrights: Shakespeare, Jonson, Spenser, Milton* (Minneapolis, 1930); E. M. W. Tillyard, *Milton* (London, 1930; rev. ed., 1966), a full treatment of Milton's literary and mental development; T. S. Eliot, *Selected Essays, 1917–1932* (London, 1932), contains observations on Milton that were later amplified in the British Academy's "Annual Lecture on a Master Mind" (1947); Rose Macaulay, *Milton* (London, 1934; rev. ed., 1957); B. Willey, *The Seventeenth Century Background: Studies in the Thought of the Age in Relation to Poetry and Religion* (London, 1934); F. R. Leavis, *Revaluation* (London, 1936), contains an important essay on Milton, see also his *The Common Pursuit* (London, 1952); H. J. C. Grierson, *Milton and Wordsworth, Poets and Prophets: A Study of*

Their Reactions to Political Events (Cambridge, 1937); J. H. Finley, *Milton and Horace: A Study of Milton's Sonnets*, Harvard Studies in Classical Philology, XLVIII (1937); E. M. W. Tillyard, *The Miltonic Setting, Past and Present* (Cambridge, 1938), a study of Milton's seventeenth-century setting and his present poetic status; J. S. Diekhoff, ed., *Milton on Himself* (London, 1939; new ed., 1965).

During the 1940's there appeared W. R. Parker, *Milton's Contemporary Reputation* (Columbus, Ohio, 1940); G. McColley, *Paradise Lost: An Account of Its Growth and Major Origins* (Chicago, 1940); M. Kelley, *This Great Argument: A Study of Milton's De doctrina christiana as a Gloss upon Paradise Lost* (Princeton, 1941); D. Wolfe, *Milton in the Puritan Revolution* (New York, 1941), a study of the political significance of Milton's work; A. E. Barker, *Milton and the Puritan Dilemma, 1641–1660* (Toronto, 1942; repr. 1956); C. S. Lewis, *A Preface to Paradise Lost* (London, 1942), a study of the Christian background of the poem; C. M. Bowra, *From Virgil to Milton* (London, 1945; New York, 1946); D. Bush, *Paradise Lost in Our Time: Some Comments* (Ithaca, N. Y., 1945), a defense of Milton against his modern detractors; C. R. Buxton, *Prophets of Heaven and Hell: Virgil, Dante, Milton, Goethe: An Introductory Essay* (Cambridge, 1945); J. S. Diekhoff, *Milton's Paradise Lost: A Commentary on the Argument* (New York, 1946); B. Rajan, *Paradise Lost and the Seventeenth Century Reader* (London, 1947); I. Samuel, *Plato and Milton* (Ithaca, N.Y., 1947); A. J. A. Waldock, *Paradise Lost and Its Critics* (Cambridge, 1947), an able and coolly provocative statement of doubt whether the poem is a consistent whole; R. Warner, *John Milton* (London, 1949); J. M. French, ed., *The Life Records of John Milton*, 4 vols. (New Brunswick, N.J., 1949–1958); J. H. Hanford, *John Milton, Englishman* (New York, 1949; London, 1950).

Works of the 1950's include: M. M. Mahood, *Poetry and Humanism* (London, 1950); J. Thorpe, ed., *Milton Criticism: Selections from Four Centuries* (New York, 1950; London, 1951); B. Rajan, *The Lofty Rhyme: A Study of Milton's Major Poetry* (London – Coral Gables, Fla., 1970); E. M. W. Tillyard, *Studies in Milton* (London, 1951), aims largely at supplementing and correcting some matters in Tillyard's *Milton*, while a study on the crisis of *Paradise Lost* corrects a common assumption and advances a general interpretation of books IX and X; S. E. Sprott, *Milton's Art of Prosody* (Oxford, 1953); A. Stein, *Answerable Style: Essays on Paradise Lost* (Minneapolis–London, 1953); D. C. Allen, *The Harmonious Vision: Studies in Milton's Poetry* (Baltimore–London, 1954; enl. ed., 1970); J. Arthos, *On a Mask Presented at Ludlow Castle* (Ann Arbor, Mich., 1954); F. T. Prince, *The Italian Element in Milton's Verse* (Oxford, 1954), an original study, embodying new discoveries; R. M. Adams, *Ikon: Milton and the Modern Critics* (Ithaca,

N.Y.–London, 1955); A. E. Dyson, "The Interpretation of Comus," in *Essays and Studies*, 21 (London, 1955); W. Haller, *Liberty and Reformation in the Puritan Revolution* (New York–London, 1955); K. Muir, *John Milton* (London–New York, 1955; rev., 1960); W. B. Watkins, *An Anatomy of Milton's Verse* (Baton Rouge, La., 1955); L. A. Cormican, *Milton's Religious Verse*, in B. Ford, ed., *From Donne to Marvell* (New York–Harmondsworth, England, 1956); H. F. Fletcher, *The Intellectual Development of John Milton*, 2 vols. (Urbana, Ill., 1956–1961); E. M. W. Tillyard, *The Methaphysicals and Milton* (London, 1956); D. Daiches, *Milton* (London–New York, 1957); J. F. Kermode, *Romantic Image* (London, 1957); R. Tuve, *Images and Themes in Five Poems by Milton* (Cambridge, Mass., 1957); A. Stein, *Heroic Knowledge: An Interpretation of Paradise Regained and Samson Agonistes* (Minneapolis–London, 1957); I. MacCaffrey, *Paradise Lost as Myth* (Cambridge, Mass.–London, 1959).

During the 1960's there appeared J. B. Broadbent, *Some Graver Subject: An Essay on Paradise Lost* (London, 1960), a penetrating analysis of the way *Paradise Lost* evolves; J. F. Kermode, ed., *The Living Milton: Essays by Various Hands* (London, 1960), an honest and erudite attempt to define what is left of *Paradise Lost* when its many defects are taken into account; W. Empson, *Milton's God* (London, 1961; rev. ed., with new appendix, 1965); J. B. Broadbent, *Milton, Comus and Samson Agonistes* (London, 1961); E. S. Le Comte, *A Milton Dictionary* (New York, 1961); J. Hollander, *The Untuning of the Sky: Ideas of Music in English Poetry, 1500–1700* (Princeton, N.J., 1961); G. Williamson, *Seventeenth Century Contexts* (Chicago–London, 1961); G. A. Wilkes, *The Thesis of Paradise Lost* (Melbourne, 1961); D. Bush, *English Literature in the Earlier Seventeenth Century, 1600–1660* (vol. 5 of *The Oxford History of English Literature*, New York–Oxford, 1962); J. H. Summers, *The Muse's Method; An Introduction to Paradise Lost* (London, 1962); J. H. Sims, *The Bible in Milton's Epics* (Gainesville, Fla., 1962); B. A. Wright, *Milton's Paradise Lost* (London, 1962); D. A. Ferry, *Milton's Epic Voice: The Narrator in Paradise Lost* (Cambridge, Mass., 1963); J. Arthos, *Dante, Michelangelo and Milton* (London, 1963); C. Ricks, *Milton's Grand Style* (Oxford, 1963); R. Daniells, *Milton, Mannerism and Baroque* (Toronto, 1963); M. H. Nicolson, *John Milton: A Reader's Guide to His Poetry* (New York, 1963); J. Blondel, *Le Comus de John Milton: Masque Neptunien* (New York–London, 1964); D. Bush, *John Milton: A Sketch of His Life and Writings* (New York, 1964); R. D. Emma, *Milton & Grammar* (The Hague, 1964); P. Hagin, *The Epic Hero and the Decline of Epic Poetry* (Berne, 1964); A. E. Barker, ed., *Milton: Modern Essays in Criticism* (New York–London, 1965); M. Y. Hughes, ed., *Ten Perspectives on Milton* (New Haven, 1965); J. Thorpe, ed., *Milton Criticism: Selections from Four Centuries* (London, 1965); N. Frye, *The Return of Eden: Five Essays on Milton's Epics* (Toronto–London, 1965); I. Williamson, *Milton and Others* (Chicago–London, 1965); J. H. Summers, ed., *The Lyric and Dramatic Milton* (New York–London, 1965); H. Gardner, *A Reading of Paradise Lost* (Oxford, 1966), the Alexander lectures, delivered at the University of Toronto, 1962; L. L. Marle, ed., *Milton: A Collection of Critical Essays* (Englewood Cliffs, N.J., 1966); B. K. Lewalski, *Milton's Brief Epic: The Genre, Meaning and Art of Paradise Regained* (Providence, R.I.–London, 1966); A. Rudrum, *Milton: Paradise Lost* (London, 1966); K. W. Gransden, *Paradise Lost and the Aeneid*, in *Essays in Criticism*, 17 (1967); P. Murray, *Milton: The Modern Phase. A Study of Twentieth-Century Criticism* (London, 1967), C. A. Patrides, *Milton and the Christian Tradition* (Oxford, 1967); C. A. Patrides, ed., *Milton's Epic Poetry: Essays on Paradise Lost and Paradise Regained* (Harmondsworth, 1967), contains a useful bibliography; A. Rudrum, *Comus, and Shorter Poems* (London, 1967); I. Samuel, *Dante and Milton: The Commedia and Paradise Lost* (London, 1967); J. M. Steadman, *Milton and the Renaissance Hero* (London, 1967); S. E. Fish, *Surprised by Sin: The Reader in Paradise Lost* (London–New York, 1967); J. Arthos, *Milton and the Italian Cities* (London, 1968); J. G. Demaray, *Milton and the Masque Tradition . . .* (Cambridge, Mass.–London, 1968); W. G. Madsen, *From Shadowy Types to Truth: Studies in Milton's Symbolism* (New Haven–London, 1968); H. Reesing, *Milton's Poetic Art: A Mask, Lycidas and Paradise Lost* (Cambridge, Mass.–London, 1968); A. Rudrum, *Milton, Modern Judgments* (London, 1968); E. L. Marilla, *Milton and Modern Man* (University, Ala., 1968); C. A. Patrides, ed., *Approaches to Paradise Lost* (London, 1968); John Carey, *Milton* (London, 1969); *Critical Essays from E. L. H.* (Baltimore, 1969), reprints articles from *Journal of English Literary History*; J. B. Leishman, *Milton's Minor Poems*, G. Tillotson, ed. (London, 1969); B. Rajan, ed., *Paradise Lost: A Tercentenary Tribute* (Toronto–Buffalo–London, 1969); J. D. Simmonds, *Milton Studies*, vol. I (Pittsburgh, 1969), vol. II (Pittsburgh, 1970); C. V. Wedgwood, *Milton and His World* (London, 1969).

Works of the 1970's include J. Halkett, *Milton and the Idea of Matrimony* (New Haven, 1970); J. H. Hanford, *A Milton Handbook*, 5th ed. rev. by J. H. Hanford and J. G. Taaffe (New York, 1970); J. T. Shawcross, ed., *Milton: The Critical Heritage* (London, 1970); *A Variorum Commentary on the Poems of John Milton* (London, 1970–   ), vol. I: "The Latin and Greek Poems" by E. Bush, and "The Italian Poems" by J. E. Shaw and A. Bartlett Giamatti; L. Ryken, *The Apocalyptic Vision in Paradise Lost* (Ithaca, N.Y.–London, 1970); H. Blamires, *Milton's Creation: A Guide Through Paradise Lost* (London, 1971); J. P. Hardy, *Reinterpretations: Essays on Poems by Milton, Pope and Johnson* (London, 1971); L. Potter, *A Preface to Milton* (London, 1971); J. A. Wittreich, ed., *The Romantics on Milton* (Cleveland, 1971); B. R. Rees, *Aristotle's Theory and Milton's Practice: Samson Agonistes* (Birmingham, 1972); L. Brisman, *Milton's Poetry of Choice and His Romantic Heirs* (Ithaca, N.Y., 1973); C. Grose, *Milton's Epic Process: Paradise Lost and Its Miltonic Background* (New Haven, 1973); G. Bouchard, *Milton: A Structural Reading* (London, 1974); J. D. Simmons, ed., *Milton Studies* (London–Pittsburgh, 1975); G. M. Crump, *The Mystical Design of Paradise Lost* (Lewisburg, Pa., 1975); J. H. Steadman, *Epic and Tragic Structure in Paradise Lost* (London–Chicago, 1977); A. Stein, *The Art of Presence: The Poet and Paradise Lost* (London–Berkeley, 1977).

VI. MISCELLANEOUS. *Milton's Illustrators*: William Blake made 53 illustrations for Milton's poetry, including 2 sets of watercolor drawings for *Comus* (1801), 12 watercolor drawings for *Paradise Lost* (1807) and a second set of 9 drawings (1808), 6 watercolor drawings for the "Nativity Ode" (1809), 12 designs illustrating "L'Allegro" and "Il Penseroso" (*ca.* 1816), and 12 watercolor drawings for *Paradise Regained* (*ca.* 1816). See Geoffrey Keynes, ed., *John Milton, Poems in English with Illustrations by William Blake* (London, 1926). Other major illustrators of Milton were Jean-Henri Füssli (1802) and John Martin (1824–1826).

Milton's Poetry Set to Music: Henry Lawes composed the music for *Comus* in 1634. Milton's "Sonnet to Henry Lawes" was set to music by Henry and William Lawes and appeared in their *Choice Psalmes, Put into Musick for Three Voices* (London, 1648). In 1677 Dryden wrote a rhymed opera, *The State of Innocence*, based on *Paradise Lost*.

Portraits of Milton: G. C. Williamson, *Milton Tercentenary: The Portraits, Prints and Writings of John Milton, Exhibited at Christ's College, Cambridge, 1908* (Cambridge, 1908); R. S. Granniss, *The Beverley Chew Collection of Milton Portraits* (New York, 1926).

FOUR METAPHYSICAL POETS

Margaret Willy

RICHARD CRASHAW
(*ca.* 1613–1649)

Poet and *Saint*! to thee alone are given
The two most sacred *Names* of *Earth* and *Heaven*.

THUS, seven years after his friend's death, Abraham Cowley apostrophized Richard Crashaw. A writer in 1657 named Crashaw in the same breath as the "refined witts" of Francis Bacon, Sir Philip Sidney, Ben Jonson, John Donne, and William Shakespeare; and thirty years later another critic was acclaiming him as "the Darling of the Muses . . . charming the ear with a holy Rapture." During the next hundred years Crashaw's reputation suffered the inevitable decline. But the nineteenth century found Coleridge declaring: "Where he does combine richness of thought and diction nothing can excel." Lines 43–64 of Crashaw's "A Hymn to the Name and Honor of the Admirable Sainte Teresa" had, he added, been constantly with him while he was writing the second part of *Christabel*, "if indeed, by some subtle process of the mind they did not suggest the first thought of the whole poem." Today Crashaw has less general appeal than Donne and Herbert; although T. S. Eliot found him "sometimes more profound and less sectarian" than either Herbert or Henry Vaughan.

Born in London in 1612 or early in 1613, the poet was the only son of a then famous father, the Puritan preacher and controversialist William Crashaw. He was educated at the Charterhouse School, where he had a thorough grounding in the classical poets and in writing verse exercises in imitation of their style. To this, no doubt, he owed something of the ability attributed to him in the preface to his *Steps to the Temple*: of having, "under locke and key in readinesse, the richest treasures of the best Greeke and Latine Poets, some of which Authors hee had . . . at his command by heart."

In 1631 Crashaw went up to Pembroke College, Cambridge, and three years later took his degree; in the same year he published a volume of Latin epigrams on selected New Testament texts entitled *Epigrammatum Sacrorum Liber*. In 1635 he became a fellow of Peterhouse, then the center of Laudian High Churchmanship in Cambridge. For eight years Crashaw enjoyed the "little contentfull kingdom," as he called it, of his "beloved Patrimony in St. Peter." Although the date of his ordination is not known, he served, during this time, as curate in the adjoining church of Little St. Mary's. His earliest biographer refers in glowing terms to the eloquence of Crashaw's preaching there ("those thronged Sermons on each Sunday and Holiday, that ravished more like Poems . . . scattering not so much Sentences as Extasies"). None of these, unfortunately, has survived.

It was during his Cambridge years, too, that Crashaw became friendly with Nicholas Ferrar, founder of the Anglican community at Little Gidding, and he was a frequent visitor at the celebrated vigils there.

Like all his friends and colleagues, Crashaw was a staunch royalist; and two years after the outbreak of civil war he was ejected from his fellowship by the parliamentary commissioners. Thenceforth his biography is a history of rootlessness, frustration, and repeated disappointments. He was for a time in Holland, and later in Paris where, about 1646— according to the contemporary historian Anthony à Wood—Cowley found him, "being a meer Scholar and very shiftless . . . in a sorry condition." Crashaw had by now become converted to the Roman Catholic faith; and Henrietta Maria, exiled in Paris, addressed a dispatch to the pope recommending the poet and his edifying example (praise that is echoed by Cowley in his elegy: "His *Faith* perhaps in some nice Tenents might/Be wrong; his *Life*, I'm sure, was *in the right*."). The queen's influence had little effect. Although Crashaw went at once to Rome, he was still there, waiting, over a year later, and suffering from poverty and ill health. He obtained, for a time, some employment in the service of Cardinal Palotto. But by 1649, shortly after his appointment to a post at the Cathedral of Loreto, Crashaw was dead (according to Cowley, of a fever) at the early age of thirty-seven.

Steps to the Temple. Sacred Poems, With Other Delights of the Muses had been published in London in 1646, followed by a new edition including a number of fresh pieces in 1648. With its substantial recasting of poems from the earlier volume, this second edition offers interesting evidence of Crashaw's habit of polishing, revising, and amplifying his work: often pruning stylistic extravagances (as, for example, some of the alterations made in the final versions of "Sainte Mary Magdalene, or The Weeper" and "A Hymne of the Nativity") in favor of more concrete expression. The additional poems show, too, that three wretched years of exile nevertheless yielded a good deal of creative activity. To the time between 1648 and Crashaw's death belong the "divine" poems that came out for the first time in 1652 in *Carmen Deo Nostro, Te Decet Hymnus, Sacred Poems*, published posthumously in Paris. This book consisted largely of poems that had appeared in their revised versions in 1648 or were first printed there.

The anonymous writer of the preface to *Steps to the Temple* (possibly Crashaw's friend and fellow poet Joseph Beaumont, a Peterhouse colleague who after the Restoration became master of the college) speaks of Crashaw as being "excellent in five Languages . . . *vid*. Hebrew, Greek, Latine, Italian, Spanish, the two last whereof hee had little helpe in, they were of his owne acquisition." Crashaw's reading in other languages played an important part in the development of his work. As already mentioned, he had been trained as a schoolboy in the artificial rhetoric of the Latin and Greek epigram; and as an undergraduate, much influenced by the style and spirit of Ovid, he continued these exercises. Many of Crashaw's essays in religious epigram show his gift for the striking phrase and achieve a concentrated intensity of poetic impact. This mastery of epigram reveals itself in his longer poems in the single telling line: as in "Immortall Hony for the Hive of Loves" ("Sospetto d'Herode"); "Candidates of Blissefull Light" ("To the Name of Jesus"); or in the final line of his poem on the Circumcision, "This knife may be the speares *Praeludium*."

Still more potent in his evolution as a poet was Crashaw's self-acquired knowledge of Spanish and Italian. The life and work of St. Teresa of Avila, canonized in 1622, made a deep impression on his imagination. As he wrote of her:

> What soule soever in any Language can
> Speake heaven like hers, is my soules country-man.

Equally pervasive was the influence of the Neapolitan poet Marino. In Marino's relentless emphasis on literal detail and in the highly colored, flamboyant elements in his style, Crashaw found encouragement for a strain of sensationalism in his own temperament. To this Italian influence we owe much of Crashaw's habit of elaborating, for their own sake, merely decorative metaphors that neither advance the movement nor illuminate the inward truth of a poem. Some of his poetic lapses into banality and bad taste, exhibiting the worst excesses of the "metaphysical conceit" (see "The Weeper"), as well as his exercise of wit in arid surface ingenuities, derived largely from Marino.

The cult of the emblem, then so popular in England and on the Continent, also made a distinct contribution to the shaping of Crashaw's style. Originating in medieval fable and allegory, emblems were allusive, often highly ingenious drawings symbolizing some moral precept, with companion verses translating the picture into words. With that of the impresa or heroic symbol, which epitomized a character or life by means of a single abstract sign, the influence of the emblem is plain in Crashaw's pictorial representation of abstract ideas and in his constant blend of literal with figurative, of homely realistic image with symbolic sublime.

Crashaw's happiness in his "little contentfull kingdom" of Peterhouse shows that his was a nature well satisfied by a life of study and contemplation. The "soft silken Houres" envisaged with

> That not impossible shee
> That shall command my heart and mee;

in "Wishes to His (Supposed) Mistresse," never in fact became reality. Perhaps Crashaw's truer desire was expressed in his epigram "On Marriage":

> I would be married, but I'de have no Wife,
> I would be married to a single Life.

A college fellowship then imposed upon its holder the rule of celibacy; so when, sometime about 1645, Crashaw entered the Roman Catholic church, he merely exchanged one mode of monastic existence for another. Admiring the Lessian virtues of temperance and abstinence,[1] he had consciously chosen the contemplative way. Thomas Car says of him in his introductory verses to *Carmen Deo Nostro*,

> No care
> Had he of earthly trashe. What might suffice
> To fitt his soule to heavenly exercise,
> Sufficed him. . . .
> What he might eate or weare he tooke no thought.
> His needful foode he rather found than sought.

And yet as Joan Bennett points out in *Five Metaphysical Poets*, "The images of the ascetic Crashaw are far more predominantly sexual than those of Donne, who had known the pleasures of sensuality, or of Herbert, who never seems to have desired them." The needs of an enthusiastic and warmly emotional nature, disciplined by asceticism, found liberation both in the ritual of the church whose shelter Crashaw finally sought, and in poetic expression of his religious experience and belief; sometimes, in his poetry, betraying him into extravagance, a lush and cloying oversweetness. For him the sensuous is present in, and inextricable from, his conception of the most rarefied spiritual experience. The exalted mystical communion of the soul with God—of

> the divine embraces
> Of the deare spowse of spirits—

is communicated in terms of languorous physical sensation:

> Amorous Languishments, Luminous trances,
>   Sights which are not seen with eyes,
> Spirituall and soule peircing glances.
>   Whose pure and subtle lightning, flies
> Home to the heart, and setts the house on fire;
> And melts it downe in sweet desire. . . .
>
>   . . . Delicious deaths, soft exhalations
> Of soule; deare, and divine annihilations.

[1]Crashaw's commendatory poem "In Praise of Lessius His Rule of Health" had accompanied the 1634 Cambridge translation of Lessius' *Hygiasticon*.

> A thousand unknowne rites
> Of joyes, and rarifyed delights.

("On a Prayer Booke Sent to Mrs M. R.")

The poet goes on to invoke the joys of divine love, the experience of the soul who

>   shall discover,
>   What joy, what blisse,
> How many heavens at once it is,
> To have a God become her lover,

in symbols of the "pure inebriating pleasures" known to human sense.

Constantly Crashaw uses images of physical love—of "birth, milk and all the rest," as Gerard Manley Hopkins put it in a poem peculiarly reminiscent of Crashaw—to communicate his perceptions of its spiritual and divine counterpart. Mary Magdalene's eyes are "swolne wombes of sorrow"; the Easter sepulchre is "Natures new wombe, . . . faire Immortalities perfumed Nest"; while the day of Christ's name, coming to earth, is welcomed as the "Womb of Day" and exhorted to

> Unfold thy fair Conceptions; And display
> The Birth of our Bright Joyes.

There are, too, the many "nursing" images: "Two sister-Seas of Virgins Milke" in "A Hymne of the Nativity"; the infant martyrs' heaven, which will be "at the worst/Milke all the way"; or in "The Weeper," where heaven's bosom drinks the "gentle stream" of the Magdalene's tears:

> Where th' milky rivers creep,
> Thine floates above; & is the cream.

The nest, both as refuge sheltered by parental protection and the nourishing source of all love, is one of the most frequently recurring symbols in Crashaw's work.

From the same, sensuous source in his nature sprang Crashaw's characteristic—often, it must seem to us, morbid—preoccupation with experiences of physical agony in a religious context. His detailed, intensely literal attention to different aspects of Christ's body (as in the poem on the Circumcision and those on the Passion) owes much, of course, to Marino, and something to a European form of contemplative exercise that influenced other English religious verse of the time. Some of Crashaw's epigrams and lyrics on these subjects actually originate in lines by the Italian poet. Nevertheless, an obsessive compulsion to contemplate, even luxuriate in, bodily torment does seem to be an undoubted trait of Crashaw's poetic individuality. He speaks of Christ's torturers clothing him in the rich garment of his own blood, "Opening the purple wardrobe of thy side," and elsewhere declares that "Not a haire but payes his River/To this *Red Sea* of thy blood." In writing of the Christian martyrs Crashaw elaborates, almost voluptuously, the visual aspect of their sufferings. The weapons of their persecutors, he says,

> . . . sett wide the Doores
> For Thee: Fair, purple Doores, of love's devising;
> The Ruby windows which inrich't the EAST
> Of Thy so oft repeated Rising.
> Each wound of Theirs was Thy new Morning;
> And reinthron'd thee in thy Rosy Nest . . .

The poem "On the Wounds of Our Crucified Lord," with its conjunction of bleeding flesh with erotic imagery, implicitly identifies and fuses the anguish of crucifixion with sensations of love:

> O these wakefull wounds of thine!
>   Are they Mouthes? or are they eyes?
> Be they Mouthes, or be they eyne,
>   Each bleeding part some one supplies.
>
> Lo! a mouth, whose full-bloom'd lips
>   At too deare a rate are roses.
> Lo! a blood-shot eye! that weepes
>   And many a cruell teare discloses . . .
>
> This foot hath got a Mouth and lippes,
>   To pay the sweet summe of thy kisses . . .

Clearly the wounds of martyrdom symbolized for Crashaw the most complete and eloquent physical expression of spiritual love. As he says in one of his poems to St. Teresa:

> For in love's field was never found
> A nobler weapon than a WOUND.

Crashaw wrote three poems celebrating the life of this saint, and her martyrdom.[2] The first of them

(which was praised by Coleridge), "A Hymn to the Name and Honor of the Admirable Sainte Teresa," with its superb opening lines:

> Love, thou art Absolute sole lord
>   OF LIFE & DEATH,

is among Crashaw's finest and most fully realized poems. Here again we hear the note of pleasure in pain:

> O how oft shalt thou complain
> Of a sweet & subtle PAIN.
> Of intolerable JOYES;
> Of a DEATH, in which who dyes
> Loves his death, and dyes again.
> And would for ever so be slain.

It should be noted that the same idea, of an extremity of physical pain mounting to merge in spiritual bliss, occurs in the autobiographical *La Vida de la Santa Madre Teresa de Jesus*, an English translation of which appeared in 1642 and with which Crashaw was doubtless familiar.

The concluding invocation of his third St. Teresa poem, "The Flaming Heart Upon the Book and Picture of the Seraphicall Saint Teresa," rises to a height of lyrical rapture unsurpassed anywhere in Crashaw's work:

> O thou undaunted daughter of desires!
> By all thy dow'r of LIGHTS & FIRES;
> By all the eagle in thee, all the dove;
> By all thy lives & deaths of love;
> By thy large draughts of intellectuall day,
> And by thy thirsts of love more large than they;
> By all thy brim-fill'd Bowles of fierce desire
> By thy last Morning's draught of liquid fire;
> By the full kingdome of that finall kisse
> That seiz'd thy parting Soul, & seal'd thee his;
> By all the heav'ns thou hast in him
> (Fair sister of the SERAPHIM!)
> By all of HIM we have in THEE;
> Leave nothing of my SELF in me.
> Let me so read thy life, that I
> Unto all life of mine may dy.

Just as Crashaw seems to savor the pleasurable sensations of pain, he likewise invites and finds a similar sweetness in grief:

> Welcome my Griefe, my Joy; how deare's
> To me my Legacy of Teares!

---

[2] In fact St. Teresa died a natural death.

or, in "The Weeper":

> No where but here did ever meet
> Sweetnesse so sad, sadnesse so sweet.

Even allowing for the special fascination tears held for the seventeenth-century metaphysical poet (see, among other poems, Donne's "A Valediction: Of Weeping," Andrew Marvell's "Eyes and Tears," and Thomas Vaughan's "The Stone"), their attraction for Crashaw appears peculiarly compelling. The very thought of them at once conjures for him a multitude of affinities, with stars, diamonds, pearls, watery blossoms, liquid jewels and rain showers, streams and milky rivers, seas and floods. He writes an epigram on the tears of Lazarus, exhorts them from Pilate, and devotes a well-known poem, "The Teare," to those of the Virgin; while in his lines "Upon the Death of a Gentleman" he declares:

> Eyes are vocall, Teares have Tongues,
> And there be words not made with lungs;
> Sententious showers, ô let them fall,
> Their cadence is Rhetoricall.

Tears are the central, sustaining image of "The Weeper," a poem strongly influenced by Marino in subject, stanza form, and even specific phrases, although the intensity of religious emotion and of vision are Crashaw's own. Here the objects of contemplation, and starting point for elaborating the various ideas they suggest to him, are the weeping eyes of Mary Magdalene (" . . . sister springs!/ Parents of sylver-footed rills!"). The timelessness of her ever-falling tears, as well as the dignity and majesty of sorrow, are finely communicated in stanzas twenty-three ("Does the day-starre rise?") and twenty-six ("Not, so long she lived"). Among the exuberant fancies Crashaw's imagination calls up are that of a "brisk Cherub" sipping the Magdalene's tears, so that " . . . his song/Tasts of this Breakfast all day long"; and of a heavenly feast (with verbal echoes of Donne's "Twicknam Garden") at which

> Angels with crystall violls come
> And draw from these full eyes of thine
> Their master's Water: their own Wine.

But the lines most frequently quoted, in illustration of how precipitately the metaphysical conceit could plunge a poet into bathos, are Crashaw's description of Christ being

> . . . follow'd by two faithfull fountaines;
> Two walking baths; two weeping motions;
> Portable, & compendious oceans.

To the modern mind the whole visual suggestion is keenly ludicrous. Yet (as L. C. Martin points out in the commentary to his edition of Crashaw's poems) what seems to us the incongruity of mundane epithets like "portable" and "compendious" in such a context, and of the prosaically concrete "bath" metaphor, has in fact many parallels in both English and continental poetry of the time.

That element in his nature that sometimes led Crashaw into poetic excess was also the source of his greatest strength. The strong sensuous vein lends his work a special purity, warmth, and sweetness; a limpid flow of cadence whose music appeals to the ear as powerfully as its impressions of scent, light, and color entrance the other senses. Crashaw writes best when apparently with the most ease and simplicity, his utterance unclogged by lush imagery or artificial conceits. This can be seen in the extracts from his St. Teresa poems quoted above; in the melodious tenderness of the shepherds' "Hymne of the Nativity," full of such felicities as "Love's architecture is his own"; in the second stanza of "Easter Day":

> Of all the Gloryes Make Noone gay
> This is the Morne.
> This rocke buds forth the fountaine of the streames
> of Day.
>
> In joyes white Annals live this houre,
> When life was borne,
> No cloud scoule on his radiant lids, no tempest lowre,

or these from "Sospetto d'Herode":

> That the Great Angell-blinding light should shrinke
> His blaze, to shine in a poore Shepheards eye.
> That the unmeasur'd God so low should sinke,
> As Pris'ner in a few poore Rags to lye . . .
> . . . That a vile Manger his low Bed should prove,
> Who in a Throne of stars Thunders above.
>
> That hee whom the Sun serves, should faintly peepe
> Through clouds of Infant flesh: that hee the old
> Eternall Word should bee a Child, and weepe.
> That hee who made the fire, should feare the cold . . .

This poem, Crashaw's translation of the first canto of Marino's *La Strage degli Innocenti*, is far more striking in concreteness of imagery and atmospheric detail than its original. Here especially—in the mellifluous cadences, crowding personifications, and above all in the use of sensuous richness to communicate moral sentiment and spiritual meaning—Crashaw's debt to Spenser is plain. The pictorial and musical qualities of his verse may have owed something also to his natural talents for "Musicke, Drawing, Limning, Graving" mentioned in the preface to *Steps to the Temple*. (It is thought that at least two engravings in *Carmen Deo Nostro* are his own illustrations.) With his fragrant showers dropping "a delicious dew of spices," his perfumed and balmy air, his lambs in the "laughing meads" and sun-gilded fleece of grazing flocks, his April flowers and "pure streames of the springing day," Crashaw at his best has the vernal freshness, delicacy, and radiance of Botticelli.

HENRY VAUGHAN
(*ca.* 1622–1695)

PERHAPS through Nicholas Ferrar at Little Gidding, Crashaw knew, and much admired, the work of George Herbert. He sent to a friend, as an aid to prayer, a copy of Herbert's poems, and probably derived from Herbert's *The Temple* the title for his own first volume; while the writer of the preface to *Steps to the Temple* declared that "Here's Herbert's second, but equall, who hath retriv'd Poetry of late."

In Henry Vaughan, Herbert found a still more devout disciple. Vaughan's preface to *Silex Scintillans* refers to "the blessed man, *Mr George Herbert*, whose holy *life* and *verse* gained many pious *Converts*, (of whom I am the least)." In all his work after the first volume, the influence of Herbert is pervasive not only in subject and spirit, but in many obvious echoes of Herbert's titles, meters, and phrases.[3] That Vaughan was no mere imitator of the man who was his acknowledged master in both his poetry and his religious life can be seen in the finest poems in *Silex Scintillans*. In this volume Herbert's influence, though nowhere stronger, has been assimilated and transmuted by Vaughan's in-

dividual way of seeing. At his best, he speaks with the distinctive voice of a poet in his own right: one whose apprehension of reality is different from Herbert's (especially in their respective attitudes to nature); who is more lyrical in the soaring of his religious exaltation or grief; and who, at the moments of his most intense spiritual vision, "sees *Invisibles*" with a quality of mystical rapture quite outside Herbert's scope.

Henry Vaughan and his younger twin, Thomas, were born in 1621 or early in 1622 at Newton St. Bridget, Brecknockshire, by the river Usk. Vaughan spent most of his life in Wales; and on all his books after the first he called himself by the title "Silurist," after the ancient tribe of Silures, who had once inhabited that southeastern district of his native country. The boys were educated locally by Matthew Herbert, rector of a neighboring parish. In 1638 they went up to Jesus College, Oxford. Henry left without taking his degree and was sent to London sometime in 1640, being, he says, "designed by my father for the study of the Law."

Like that of Crashaw, though neither so permanently nor so disastrously, Vaughan's career suffered through the outbreak of hostilities in 1642. According to him, "our late civil warres wholie frustrated" the plans for his legal future. Like most Welshmen, Vaughan was strongly royalist and seems for a time to have served with the king's forces. His "Elegie on the Death of Mr R. W. Slain in the Late Unfortunate Differences at Rowton Heath, Neer Chester, 1645," contains what reads like an eyewitness account of his friend's prowess in the battle. Another, humorous, poem "Upon a Cloke Lent Him by Mr J. Ridsley" also refers to Vaughan's own presence on the scene of the "differences" at Rowton Heath, and to the time " . . . this Jugling fate/Of Souldierie first seiz'd me!"

It is not known when Vaughan began to practice medicine; but in 1673 he wrote from Brecon telling his cousin Aubrey, the antiquary, that he had been a physician "for many years with good successe . . . & a repute big enough for a person of greater parts than my selfe." He died in 1695, and was buried in his birthplace, where his grave in the churchyard may still be seen.

Vaughan's first book of poems was published the same year as Crashaw's *Steps to the Temple* appeared. *Poems, with the Tenth Satyre of Juvenal Englished* (1646) contains a number of love poems addressed to Amoret (sometimes identified with

---

[3]These are far too numerous to cite here. Readers interested in tracing the similarities and borrowings should see the Notes to L. C. Martin, *The Works of Henry Vaughan* (2nd ed., 1957), especially those to *Silex Scintillans*, pp. 727–751.

Vaughan's first wife, Catherine Wise). These are conventionally fashionable songs, of tears and sighs, a cruel fair one with "a Womans easie Faith," and a young man dying of love. Echoes, here, from Vaughan's contemporaries Habington and Randolph recur in his later secular volumes, with others from Cartwright and Owen Felltham's *Resolves.* Still more obvious is the borrowing from Donne, especially from "A Valediction: Forbidding Mourning." (Compare the fourth and fifth stanzas of that poem with the third and fourth of Vaughan's "To Amoret, of the Difference 'twixt Him, and Other Lovers, and What True Love Is," and also with the penultimate couplet of "To Amoret Gone from Him.")

Vaughan's second collection of secular verse, *Olor Iscanus,* followed in 1651. From the date of its dedication, only a year after the appearance of his first book, it seems that publication was postponed for some time and that much of what Vaughan originally intended to publish was withdrawn. The publisher's preface affirms that "The Author had long agoe condemn'd these Poems to Obscuritie." Vaughan's reticence, perhaps partly due to the political uncertainties of the later 1640's, possibly owed still more to the profound influence exerted on his whole habit of mind by his discovery of Herbert. This deepening seriousness led him, in his preface to *Silex Scintillans,* published the previous year, to deplore in vigorous terms his contemporaries' "inexcusable desertion of *pious sobriety*" in their taste for "*vicious verse,*" "*lascivious fictions,*" and "*idle books*" and to announce that he himself had "supprest [his] *greatest follies.*"

The title poem in *Olor Iscanus* celebrates the "*lov'd Arbours*" and "*green banks and streams*" of the Usk. The book contains verses to various friends, and in praise of the work of admired writers, including John Fletcher, William Cartwright, Sir William Davenant, and Katherine Philips, the "wittie fair one" known to her circle as "the matchless Orinda." There are verse translations from Ovid, Ausonius, Boethius, and the Polish poet Casimir, and some in prose from Plutarch and other writers. (Throughout the 1650's Vaughan published prose works such as *The Mount of Olives,* a manual of meditation and prayer free from the "fruitlesse curiosities of Schoole-Divinity"; or *Flores Solitudinis,* "collected in his Sicknesse and Retirement," which contained three translations and a biography of St. Paulinus of Nola.)

The third volume of Vaughan's secular poems, *Thalia Rediviva,* subtitled "The Pass-times and Diversions of a Countrey-Muse," was published in 1678 (although it contains work of much earlier date). Apart from further translations, and a group of not very remarkable love poems addressed to "Etesia," there are several religious pieces in the mood of *Silex Scintillans,* probably written after the second part of that collection appeared in 1655. Some of these, "Looking Back," "The Recovery," and the opening of "The World," depart from the eight- or ten-syllable couplets favored by Vaughan in his secular poems to share the greater metrical flexibility and variety of the work in *Silex Scintillans.* The last poem in *Thalia Rediviva,* entitled "Daphnis, an Elegiac Eclogue" between two shepherds, may have been written for the death of Vaughan's younger brother William in 1648, and afterward adapted for that of Thomas, his twin, in 1666.

According to their mutual friend Dr. Thomas Powell, Henry and Thomas Vaughan resembled each other as closely in spirit as in body. "Not only your *faces,*" he declared, "but your *wits* are *Twins.*" Certainly there are striking parallels between passages in the prose writings of Thomas Vaughan and such poems by his brother as "Regeneration," "Resurrection and Immortality," "Vanity of Spirit," "Corruption," and "Cock-crowing." After his eviction from his living in 1650, Thomas Vaughan studied alchemy; and he is described by Anthony à Wood as "a great chymist, a noted son of the fire, an experimental philosopher." Under the name of Eugenius Philalethes, he published a number of alchemical and mystical treatises that owe much to Hermeticism, the occult philosophy that originated in the Greek texts attributed to Hermes Trismegistus. Hermetic traditions, both philosophical and scientific, exercised a powerful attraction for the seventeenth-century mind. The poetry of Donne, for example, and the prose of Sir Thomas Browne abound in Hermetic allusions to elixirs, tinctures, essences, influences, and signatures, and in *Religio Medici,* Browne defines death in alchemical terms. This Hermetic interest is plainly recognizable in the work of Henry Vaughan: not only in his translations of two treatises by Nollius, published as *Hermetical Physick* (1655) and *The Chymist's Key* (1657), expounding the medical aspects of Hermetic doctrine, but also in images and ideas found in the symbolism of "Vanity of Spirit," "Cock-crowing,"

"The Night," "The World," "The Constellation," and "Resurrection and Immortality." On the whole, however, the imagery in *Silex Scintillans* carries many more echoes both of Herbert, and of biblical language and allusion, than of Hermetic ideas. Essentially Vaughan's are Christian poems that Hermetic terms and notions sometimes furnished with analogies, both apt for his purpose and familiar to contemporary readers, to illustrate the apprehensions of spiritual reality he sought to communicate.[4]

What is the nature of the experience embodied by *Silex Scintillans*? Despite the all-pervading influence of Herbert, this is the work (first published in 1650 and, in a new edition with a second part added, in 1655) that assures Vaughan his secure and permanent place among English religious poets. In it two contrasting themes are clearly defined. One is that of a desolating sense of separation from God through man's sin, which fills the poet with self-disgust and despair; the other, joy in the Presence that animates and illumines all creation, itself visible proof of his power and love.

In his vein of distaste for human life, Vaughan sees earthly existence as a

> . . . sad captivity,
> This leaden state, which men miscal
> Being and life, but is dead thrall.
>
> ("The Ass")

The imprisoned spirit "truly hates to be detained on earth"; and in "Love-sick" Vaughan complains that

> These narrow skies . . .
> So barre me in, that I am still at warre,
> At constant warre with them.

All through Vaughan's work recurs the desire to escape, "winged and free," into the "true liberty" of heaven. And not only is man a prisoner on earth, he is an exile, banished from home and forever pining for it:

> He knows he hath a home, but scarce knows where,
> He sayes it is so far
> That he hath quite forgot how to go there.
>
> ("Man")

[4] Ross Garner, in *Henry Vaughan: Experience and the Tradition* (1959), gives in chapter 3 a useful summary of the relative importance of Hermeticism in Vaughan's work.

The poem "Corruption" relates how "He came (condemned,) hither," and

> . . . sigh'd for *Eden*, and would often say
> *Ah! what bright days were those?*

In a world variously referred to as "wilde woods," parching desert, and wilderness, the spirit yearns with nostalgia:

> O how I long to travell back
> And tread again that ancient track!
>
> ("The Retreate")

The nature of the place from which man is shut out is memorably epitomized in "Peace":

> My Soul, there is a Countrie
> Far beyond the stars . . .
> If thou canst get but thither,
> There grows the flowre of peace,
> The Rose that cannot wither,
> Thy fortresse, and thy ease;

Much preoccupied with the cause of this exile from grace, Vaughan views with loathing "the mule, unruly man," whose body is a "quicken'd masse of sinne." Repeatedly the flesh is denounced in such terms as vile, foul, obscene: "impure, rebellious clay," "all filth, and spott." This uncleanness, which obscures the light and alienates man from God, evokes from Vaughan the impassioned cry:

> O that I were all Soul! that thou
> Wouldst make each part
> Of this poor, sinfull frame pure heart!
>
> ("Chearfulness")

But although in moods of world-weariness and self-disgust Vaughan aspired to an impossible ideal of "man all pure love, flesh a star," he did not share the Hermetic view of matter as intrinsically evil. Many poems make clear that, for him, the source of sin and separation lies not in the body itself but in the "dark Confusions" it houses, which "soyl thy Temple with a sinful rust" ("Dressing"). Vaughan blames the weakness and waywardness resulting from man's apostasy: his "black self-wil" and "sinfull ease," the peevish stubbornness, disobedience, and rebellion of his "hard, stonie heart."

Abundant proof that Vaughan did not despise

material substance as such lies in his frank and lyrical delight in the universe. He saw the wonders of nature as bodying forth the goodness of God, whose "glory through the world dost drive," and all creation actively proclaim him:

> There's not a *Spring*,
> Or *Leafe* but hath his *Morning-hymn*; Each *Bush*
> And *Oak* doth know *I AM*;
>
> ("Rules and Lessons")

and, in "The Morning-watch":

> In what Rings,
> And *Hymning Circulations* the quick world
> Awakes, and sings;
> The rising winds,
> And falling springs,
> Birds, beasts, all things
> Adore him in their kinds.
> Thus all is hurl'd
> In sacred *Hymnes*, and *Order*, The great *Chime*
> And *Symphony* of nature.

That "All things here shew [man] heaven . . . and point him the way home" is, to Vaughan, their ultimate justification. Visible, finite beauty is a bridge to the invisible, infinite, and transcendent one it symbolizes. The "Heraldrie/Of stones, and speechless Earth" shows us our "true descent" ("Retirement"); the "weaker glories" of "some *gilded Cloud*, or *flowre*" intimate to the gazing child "Some shadows of eternity" ("The Retreate"). God's "wondrous Method" in creating the universe is, in short, the outward proof and pledge of his omnipresence:

> Thou canst not misse his Praise; Each *tree, herb, flowre*
> Are shadows of his *wisdome*, and his Pow'r.
>
> ("Rules and Lessons")

It is here that Vaughan differs most from Herbert, in whose work nature is little more than a convenient source of telling metaphor; whereas Vaughan's conception of it is central to his religious belief. In the plan of creation he perceived a marvelous unity of design, in which the ordering of natural phenomena was echoed and repeated in the patterns of man's spiritual processes. In all of it, as he says in "The Book," Vaughan "lov'd and sought [God's] face."

"No one else among Donne's followers," affirms Joan Bennett, "watched the earth, sky and water, the birds and flowers with the same emotion, nor with the same delicacy of observation." This loving precision of eye and felicity of phrase may be seen in Vaughan's descriptions of a spring path "*Primros'd*, and hung with shade," of snow that "*Candies* our Countries wooddy brow," or of the "purling Corn"; in a glimpse of dawn:

> I see a Rose
> Bud in the bright East, and disclose
> The Pilgrim-Sunne . . .
>
> ("The Search")

or of stars that "nod and sleepe, / And through the dark aire spin a firie thread"; of "man [as] such a Marygold . . . That shuts, and hangs the head." One of Vaughan's favorite images for the soul is that of a flower or plant. "Surly winds," he says in "Regeneration," "Blasted my infant buds"; and, in "The Morning-watch":

> with what flowres,
> And shoots of glory, my soul breakes, and buds!

"True hearts," Vaughan believed, "spread, and heave/Unto their God, as flow'rs do to the Sun." Sometimes they send out "Bright *shootes* of everlastingnesse" (this image of shoots recurs in several poems); but at others, shaken by the storms of sin, the spirit is a "sully'd flowre," a "sapless Blossom" thirsting for dew and, at worst, a "frail" or "thankless" weed.

E. K. Chambers has said, in his preface to *The Poems of Henry Vaughan, Silurist* (1896), that Vaughan "is very much the poet of fine lines and stanzas, of imaginative intervals"; that in a number of poems he begins well and tails off, or else "some very flinty ground yields a quite unanticipated spark." The truth of this has to be admitted. Many of Vaughan's poems of conventional religious sentiment are as commonplace as the average hymn, unlit by any memorable flash of poetic insight or language. Vaughan can be—as in "Church Service," "The Passion," "Tears," "Holy Scriptures," "The Relapse," or the jogtrot jingle of "Thou that know'st for whom I mourne"—disconcertingly trite and sententious, even banal. He has, compared with Herbert, little sense of form or the disciplines of verbal economy. But there are whole poems—"The Retreate," "The Morning-watch," "Peace," "Affliction," "Man," "They Are All Gone Into the World of Light!"—that do sustain a high poetic level; and for the isolated splendors, where (in Vaughan's own image) the flint does strike off sparks, how luminous some of these are.

> I saw Eternity the other night
> Like a great *Ring* of pure and endless light,
>   All calm, as it was bright,
> And round beneath it, Time in hours, days, years
>   Driv'n by the spheres
> Like a vast shadow mov'd, in which the world
>   And all her train were hurl'd;
> ("The World")

or

> There is in God (some say)
> A deep, but dazling darkness . . .
> O for that night! where I in him
> Might live invisible and dim.
> ("The Night")

or his apostrophe in "They Are All Gone Into the World of Light!":

> Dear, beauteous death! the Jewel of the Just,
>   Shining nowhere, but in the dark;

and, from the same poem:

> It glows and glitters in my cloudy brest
> Like stars upon some gloomy grove . . .

All these lodge in the imagination with the unforgettable impact, the haunting inevitability, of pure poetry.

It will be noticed how many of these magical lines enshrine images of light. Present in many contexts, light glows through and permeates all Vaughan's work. His books are "Burning and shining Thoughts." Man before the fall was as "intimate with Heav'n, as light." The saints

> Like Candles, shed
> Their beams, and light
> Us into Bed,

while the dead walk

>   in an Air of glory,
> Whose light doth trample on my days.

Imploring "The beams, and brightness of thy face," the poet appeals to God to

> brush me with thy light, that I
> May shine unto a perfect day;

and aspires toward a state where he may

> Rove in that mighty, and eternall light
>   Where no rude shade, or night
> Shall dare approach us.

For Vaughan light is the primary symbol of spiritual illumination, of that clarity and purity of vision man possessed most fully when he "Shin'd in [his] Angell-infancy."

Two human conditions, Vaughan believed, enable the achievement of this illumination at its steadiest and most radiant. One (as already seen) is in man's attunement to natural beauty in constant awareness of its being divinely infused:

> . . . *rural shades* are the sweet fense
> Of piety and innocence . . .
> If Eden be on Earth at all,
> 'Tis that, which we the *Country* call.
> ("Retirement")

The other state of being which, in Vaughan's view, is the habitation of angels and reflects the image of Eden is our early years of innocence: that

>   first, happy age;
>   An age without distast and warrs,

as he sees it in "Looking Back"; and, in "Childe-hood," as the

> Dear, harmless age! the short, swift span,
> Where weeping virtue parts with man.

Leaving infancy behind, man finds that, amid the world's insistent claims and clamor, sin has "Like Clouds ecclips'd [his] mind":

> I find my selfe the lesse, the more I grow;
>   The world
> Is full of voices; Man is call'd, and hurl'd
>   By each, he answers all.
> ("Distraction")

The most complete embodiment of Vaughan's belief in the sanctity of childhood experience is "The

Retreate," a poem that has sometimes been regarded as one of the germinative influences on Wordsworth's *Ode on the Intimations of Immortality.* Although this is not established, the two poets certainly share the same nostalgic reverence for the vision of those years when, according to Wordsworth:

> trailing clouds of glory do we come
> From God, who is our home:
> Heaven lies about us in our infancy!

and, in the words of Vaughan:

> Happy those early dayes! when I
> Shin'd in my Angell-infancy.
> Before I understood this place
> Appointed for my second race,
> Or taught my soul to fancy ought
> But a white, Celestiall thought,
> When yet I had not walkt above
> A mile, or two, from my first love,
> And looking back (at that short space,)
> Could see a glimpse of his bright-face;
> When on some *gilded Cloud,* or *flowre*
> My gazing soul would dwell an houre,
> And in those weaker glories spy
> Some shadows of eternity;
> Before I taught my tongue to wound
> My Conscience with a sinfull sound,
> Or had the black art to dispence
> A sev'rall sinne to ev'ry sence,
> But felt through all this fleshly dresse
> Bright *shootes* of everlastingnesse.

The phrase "first love," or "early love," recurs with peculiar poignancy in different poems—"Corruption," "The Constellation," "The Seed Growing Secretly"—for man's relation with God. In the same way the idea of angels, walking and talking as man's familiars, is one of Vaughan's favorite symbols—as in "Religion," "Corruption," "The Jews," "Childe-hood," and "Retirement"—to convey his conception of our lost Eden. A return to the state of mind, heart, and spirit known in childhood is, Vaughan believed, the way back to that original fullness of communion between man and his Creator:

> Some men a forward motion love,
> But I by backward steps would move,
> And when this dust falls to the urn
> In that state I came return.

THOMAS TRAHERNE
(ca. 1637–1674)

IN 1895 two unsigned manuscript notebooks, one in prose, the other verse, were discovered on a London bookstall. First ascribed to Vaughan, because of certain resemblances to the style and spirit of his writing, they were finally established as the work of a contemporary, Thomas Traherne.

The original confusion of authorship was understandable. A strong vein of mysticism runs through the writing of both Vaughan and Traherne—one a Welshman, the other born in Herefordshire, near the Welsh border. There are similarities in vocabulary as well as in verse forms. But the most striking affinity lies in their common attitude toward childhood. Vaughan's thought in "The Retreate" is vividly paralleled by Traherne's writing, both in verse and prose, about early experience. Everything then, says Traherne, seemed to have "been made but to Day Morning," and was seen with the eyes of an angel or of the first man:

Certainly Adam in Paradise had not more sweet and curious apprehensions of the World, than I when I was a child.

I was Entertained like an Angel with the Works of GOD in their Splendour and Glory; I saw all in the Peace of Eden; Heaven and Earth did sing my Creators Praises and could not make more Melody to Adam, then to me.[5]

In the poem "Eden," Traherne recalls that

> Only what Adam in his first Estate,
>   Did I behold . . .

> Those things which first his Eden did adorn,
>   My Infancy
>   Did crown.

For Traherne, as for Vaughan, "The first Impressions are Immortal all" ("Dumnesse"); the purity of infant intuitions provides the key to life's most fundamental realities, a mystery "which the Books of the Learned never unfold":

Those Pure and Virgin Apprehensions I had from the Womb, and that Divine Light wherewith I was born are the Best unto this Day. . . . Verily they seem the Greatest

---

[5]*Centuries of Meditations.*

Gifts His Wisdom could bestow, for without them all other Gifts had been Dead and Vain.[6]

We see Vaughan, in the poem "Childe-hood," aspiring to recapture the unique quality of that early vision:

> I cannot reach it; and my striving eye
> Dazles at it, as at eternity,

and apostrophizing the "age of mysteries":

> How do I study now, and scan
> Thee, more then ere I studyed man.

In the same way Traherne, throughout his adult life, regarded it as the first duty of a man to regain that wisdom, "unattainable by Book," that informs our childhood apprehensions of a world beyond the visible one. The felicity possible for all human beings could, he believed, be achieved by deliberately and diligently cultivating the innocence of the "Infant-Ey," and "becom[ing] as it were a little Child again."[7]

The son of a shoemaker, Thomas Traherne was born about 1637, in Hereford. He was brought up by well-to-do relatives; and it was almost certainly through the provision of his uncle, Philip Traherne, a prosperous innkeeper and twice mayor of Hereford City, that Thomas, in his fifteenth year, went to Oxford—the first in a family of farmers and tradesmen to achieve the distinction of a university education. His zestful pursuit of his studies, which he describes in *Centuries of Meditations*, and his intellectual curiosity and eagerness to explore the individual mysteries and whole nature of the universe were typical of the spirit of his age.

Like Crashaw, Traherne made a deliberate choice of the "little contentfull kingdom" of celibacy and study. At the end of 1657, having resolved

to Spend [all my Time] whatever it cost me, in Search of Happiness . . . [choosing] rather to live upon 10 pounds a yeer, and to go in Lether Clothes, and feed upon Bread and Water, so that I might have all my time clearly to my self . . .

(Third Century:46)

he went as rector to the parish of Credenhill, near Hereford. There, with intervals of absence at Ox-

ford, Traherne lived the simple, but for him deeply satisfying, life of an obscure country parson. In 1667 he went to London as private chaplain to Sir Orlando Bridgeman, Charles II's lord keeper of the seal. He remained in Sir Orlando's service until his patron's death in 1674. But a few months later, at the same early age as Crashaw, Thaherne himself died. Opening up far wider horizons to one who was, on his own admission, "a sociable Creature . . . a lover of company," and thereby enlarging and enriching his terms of reference, the last seven years were of immense benefit to the vitality of his work.

Traherne's writings cannot be placed in any certain order of composition. The only book to be published in his lifetime was *Roman Forgeries*, which appeared in 1673, anonymously, but with a bold dedication to Traherne's patron, by now disgraced and deprived of office. This was one more installment in the ceaseless religious controversy between the Anglican church and Rome; and its author accused "the Pope's sworn Adjutants" of forging early church records. Its interest today is slight, but it does reveal something of Traherne's formidable intellectual capacity—both the scope of his scholarship and the clarity and incisiveness of his argument.

Christian Ethicks, dispatched to the publisher immediately before Traherne's death, appeared the following year. It is a treatise on human conduct, a discussion of morality with a difference; for, unlike many contemporary writers on ethics, Traherne was little concerned with castigating vice, being "entirely taken up with the Worth and Beauty of Virtue." A protest against the materialism of Hobbes's *Leviathan* (1651), the book is an impassioned and eloquent exposition both of the reality of spiritual values and of Traherne's personal creed of joy—what he called "Christian epicureanism." Structurally *Christian Ethicks* is rambling and uncoordinated; but as a record of inner adventure and discovery, written out of the knowledge its author "gained in the nature of *Felicity* by many years earnest and diligent study," it is an impressive piece of spiritual autobiography.

In 1699 there appeared, again anonymously, the book of devotions with a cumbersome title (probably not the author's own), which is generally known simply as *Thanksgivings*. These are a series of prose poems in gratitude for such benefits as "The Glory of God's Works" and "The Wisdom of his Word," carrying echoes of the *Devotions* of

---

[6]*Centuries of Meditations.*   [7]*Ibid.*

Lancelot Andrewes and, in their rhythms and reiterations, of the Psalms. In the exuberant outpouring of synonymous phrases, the incantatory piling up of images in freely flowing, flexible lines, and their sense of soaring, triumphant vitality, these "rapturous tumbling catalogue[s] of delights and interests" (as Sir Arthur Quiller-Couch described them) convey the impression that the writer can scarcely contain his exultation: being "in danger of bursting, till we can communicate all to some fit and amiable recipient, and more delight in Communication than we did in the Reception."[8] A sense of urgent, impetuous motion is as characteristic of Traherne's writing as its quality of radiance diffused through images of light ("Pure Primitive Virgin Light," "burning Ardent fire," "Glorious Rayes," "Shining Beams"), for which he has a fondness almost equaling Vaughan's.

A Collection of Meditations and Devotions in Three Parts, which appeared in 1717, also apparently belongs to Traherne's Credenhill years. The first part, "Hexameron," or "Meditations on the Six Days of Creation," has the same energy and sense of the wonderful diversity of life that characterizes the "Thanksgivings." The second, "Meditations and Devotions upon the Life of Christ," contains many incidental passages of self-revelation: in particular, misgivings about personal faults and failures, fluctuations of mood and faith, and, above all, concerning that desolation of spiritual banishment the writer calls "the dark dismal Destitutions of all Light."

Traherne's poems were not published until the early twentieth century, the first volume in 1903, and a second—which had been prepared by his brother Philip, with assiduous and often disastrous "revisions," under the title *Poems of Felicity*—in 1910. Traherne employed the heroic couplet or, more frequently, the long, elaborately patterned, irregular stanza. His exaltation of childhood innocence, and perception of its kinship with the mystic's awareness of harmony and happiness, produced some of his best poems, such as "The Salutation," or the opening of "Wonder":

> How like an Angel came I down!
> How Bright are all Things here!
> When first among his Works I did appear
> O how their GLORY me did Crown!

[8] *Christian Ethicks.*

> The World resembled his ETERNITIE,
> In which my Soul did Walk;
> And evry Thing that I did see
> Did with me talk.

In "News" he describes those intimations of immortality that are the child's memories of the place whence he came, their now "Absent Bliss" beckoning him to its rediscovery.

But Traherne's poetry is, on the whole, far inferior in quality to his prose. There are the scattered felicities, as

> I within did flow
> With Seas of Life like Wine;
> ("Wonder")

or

> Drown'd in their Customs, I became
> A Stranger to the Shining Skies,
> Lost as a dying Flame.
> ("The Apostasy")

But too often the long, cumulative lists of attributes or blessings sprawl, as in the third and fourth stanzas of "Desire," into trite and repetitive diffuseness. Traherne as a poet lacked the discipline to prune superfluous verbiage, to cut out the meaningless, redundant phrase used merely to achieve a rhyme; the rhyming itself is frequently facile and expected enough to result in a jingle.

Traherne's strength as a writer of prose lay in his equal mastery of two styles, employed according to the subject and purpose of the work in hand. In *Christian Ethicks*, and the energetic argument of *Roman Forgeries*, he rejected what a Royal Society writer of 1644 had impatiently dismissed as the current "luxury and redundance of speech . . . amplification, digressions, and swellings of style," in favor of short sentences and plain, straightforward exposition. The personal note of frank and easy address to his reader, which is so engaging a feature of nearly all Traherne's prose work, derived largely from Abraham Cowley (borrowing in his turn from Montaigne). These new trends in English prose were a reaction against pompous and bombastic "volubility of Tongue." But, when occasion demanded, Traherne could command all the dignity and sonorous splendor of the older manner, with its stately rhythms, reiterations, and antitheses. Indeed, it is through his successful blend of the vigorous simplicity of the new style and rhetorical grandeur of the old with a tone of friendly, familiar discourse that Traherne achieves so remarkable a range and richness of expression in *Centuries of Meditations.*

This book, which after the manuscript's chance discovery was published in 1908, places Traherne among the masters of English religious prose. Here, as nowhere else in his writing, he attained a harmonious fusion of form and content. To compare a passage from the *Centuries* with one from the *Thanksgivings* will at once show how his earlier stylistic exuberance has been disciplined by a new economy and restraint.

Centuries of Meditations was written, as a manual of instruction in the way of felicity, for a friend (almost certainly Mrs. Susanna Hopton of Kington, near Credenhill). This fact partly accounts for its note of intimacy and fullness of self-revelation. For his friend's spiritual guidance, Traherne filled the small leather notebook she had given him "with Profitable Wonders . . . Things Strange yet Common; Incredible, yet known; Most High, yet plain; infinitly Profitable, but not Esteemed" (*First Century*: 1 and 3). The manuscript consisted of four complete groups, and part of a fifth, of a hundred numbered prose sections. In these we find the inner history of their author's achievement of happiness: the most complete expression of his profound religious convictions and philosophy of dedicated joy. *Centuries of Meditations* is a testament of praise: those praises which, Traherne declared, are "the Marks and Symptoms of a Happy Life . . . the very End for which the World was created" (*Third Century*: 82).

Nowhere, perhaps, have the feel and flavor of childhood experience been more vividly recaptured. In his infancy, Traherne affirms in the second section of the *Third Century* (and also in the poem "Wonder"), he was oblivious of adult cares:

I Knew not that there were any Sins, or Complaints, or Laws. I dreamed not of Poverties Contentions or Vices. All Tears and Quarrels, were hidden from mine Eys. Evry Thing was at Rest, Free, and Immortal. I Knew Nothing of Sickness or Death, or Exaction.

Later, "the first Light which shined in my Infancy in its Primitive and Innocent Clarity was totally ecclypsed." Yet before that inevitable loss, and the conflicts of adolescence so convincingly described in poems like "Dissatisfaction" and "Solitude"—

despite, too, an early inclination "secretly to Expostulate with GOD for not giving me Riches" (*Third Century*: 14)—the picture of childhood felicity shines bright and unflawed. In the magic circle of the self-enclosed, yet limitless, world the child inhabits

All appeared New, and Strange at the first, inexpressibly rare, and Delightfull, and Beautifull. I was a little Stranger which at my Enterance into the World was Saluted and Surrounded with innumerable Joys.

(*Third Century*: 2)

It is not, of course, as mere straightforward autobiography that we should read Traherne's revelations of his childhood. The child's imaginative preoccupations, such as those of the poem "Shadows in the Water," or the speculations described in *Third Century*: 17 and 18, are intended always to symbolize the spirit's activity in a sphere beyond the everyday material one. "A man's life of any worth," said Keats, "is a continual allegory." It is as an allegory of the adventures of the spirit that Traherne's early life is to be interpreted; the *Centuries* and poems—like Shakespeare's works as envisaged in Keats's letter—are the comments on it.

The essence of Traherne's apprehension of the child's-eye view of the universe is concentrated in the famous third section of the *Third Century*, beginning:

The Corn was Orient and Immortal Wheat, which never should be reaped, nor was ever sown. I thought it had stood from everlasting to everlasting. The Dust and Stones of the Street were as Precious as GOLD. The Gates were at first the End of the World, The Green Trees when I saw them first through one of the Gates Transported and Ravished me; their Sweetness and unusual Beauty made my Heart to leap, and almost mad with Extasie, they were such strange and Wonderfull Things.

In the subtle shadings of sentence pattern and gradations of rhythm, which so skillfully communicate the pulse of mounting exultation, this is one of the sublime passages of English prose. Once heard, its majestic, reverberating cadences continue to haunt the imagination and the inward ear.

Three main aspects of Traherne's attitude to life are expressed here. First, there is his exaltation of the child's ignorance of the "Dirty Devices of this World." Then there is the sense of wonder that springs directly from that innocence: the freshness and luminous intensity of vision that can transmute the common dust and stones of the street into a substance as precious as gold, turn the tumbling playmates into "moving Jewels," and cause the very trees to ravish the beholder's eyes and make his heart leap, "almost mad with Extasie." Thirdly, and perhaps most potently of all, we are conscious of release into a state of boundlessness: of the illimitable horizons, unconfined by either time or space, that Traherne is looking back to praise as the purest of his early joys. For him, then, "All Time was Eternity, and a Perpetual Sabbath" (*Third Century:* 2). It was no ordinary corn but immortal wheat that waved in the harvest fields; human life was still unshadowed by mortality ("I knew not that they were Born or should Die"). There was neither beginning nor end in this region where "Eternity was Manifest in the Light of the Day, and som thing infinit Behind evry thing appeared." It is in his communication of these world-without-end intimations that Traherne comes nearest to Blake, for whom also it was an "augury of innocence" to

Hold Infinity in the palm of your hand
And Eternity in an hour.

No child is ever actively conscious of being happy: indeed it is that very freedom from awareness of self, oblivious of the rarity of his state, that is a condition of the child's wonder and freshness of vision. Yet Traherne's pursuit of felicity, in *Centuries of Meditations*, depends largely on an enriching *consciousness* of happiness:

You never Enjoy the World aright, till you so love the Beauty of Enjoying it, that you are Covetous and Earnest to Persuade others to Enjoy it.

(*First Century:* 31)

Striving to recapture and perpetuate in maturity the timeless joys of infancy, Traherne the man was consciously practicing what, as a child, he had unconsciously possessed.

"Enjoy" and "enjoyment" are among the most frequently used words in *Centuries of Meditations*. It could be said that Traherne was one of the world's great "enjoyers"; and nowhere does this emerge more triumphantly than in the twenty-ninth and thirtieth sections of the *First Century*. These express the passionate conviction of a man who could never have been so joyous a servant of God if he had not first loved the earth's beauty to his fullest capacity as a human being:

You never Enjoy the World aright, till the Sea it self floweth in your Veins, till you are Clothed with the Heavens, and Crowned with the Stars: and Perceiv your self to be the Sole Heir of the whole World: and more then so, becaus Men are in it who are evry one Sole Heirs, as well as you. Till you can Sing and Rejoyce and Delight in GOD, as Misers do in Gold, and Kings in Scepters, you never Enjoy the World.

Till your Spirit filleth the Whole World, and the Stars are your Jewels, till you are as Familiar with the Ways of God in all Ages as with your Walk and Table . . . you never Enjoy the World.

And it was not only the immensities of sea, sky, and stars that were Traherne's objects of enjoyment and, therefore, of worship. We are reminded of Blake's grain of sand in the opening of the twenty-seventh section of the *First Century:*

You never Enjoy the World aright, till you see how a Sand Exhibiteth the Wisdom and Power of God.

Nothing was too small or insignificant to minister to this man's delight and call forth his praise; from such familiar daily blessings as the "lovly lively air," the "Precious Jewel" of a waterdrop, and "evry Spire of Grass," to the diverse personalities of men and women, who are, he affirms in *Third Century:* 22, "when well understood a Principal Part of our True felicity." Traherne rejoiced in everything from the simple fulfillment of his material needs—bread, meat and drink, his clothes, fuel, and "Household stuff, Books, Utensils, Furniture"—to the intricate mechanism of the human body (*First Century:* 66) and the treasures of art.

If, in brief, Traherne's eyes were for the most part fixed on things beyond this earth, his feet were always firmly planted upon it. His appetite for enjoyment was wonderfully comprehensive. He saw the gift of human existence so constituted that man might taste both the sensuous pleasure of the animals and the spiritual ecstasy of the angels. To be satisfied as God is, he declares in the *First Century*, men must first want like gods: for "Infinit Want is the very Ground and Caus of infinit Treasure."

To despise and dismiss the divinely planned pattern of the earth seemed to Traherne a sin against man's potentialities for praise; an "abominable corruption" of his nature that denied that "heavenly Avarice" implanted in him as positive proof of his immortal soul and its destination. And so the universe became for him the "Book from Heaven" he had demanded in adolescence, a book in whose pages he constantly read the power and love of its Author. Traherne did, however, perceive the necessity for disciplining sensuous enjoyment through dedicating it. The senses could never, to him, be more than—in the metaphor of "News"—ambassadors bringing tidings from a foreign country that housed his true treasure. Men are spiritual, Traherne believed, according to the degree in which they esteem and enjoy their temporal gifts:

> Wine by its Moysture quencheth my Thirst, whether I consider it or no: but to see it flowing from his Lov who gav it unto Man Quencheth the Thirst even of the Holy Angels. To consider it, is to Drink it Spiritualy.

In that last sentence lies the core of Traherne's philosophy. To "consider," and in doing so, to praise: thus, for the contemplative man, could the everyday pleasures of sense be perpetually sanctified.

It was this capacity for enjoying the world on two planes, natural and transcendental—for extracting, here and now, the essence from temporal delight while simultaneously viewing it sub specie aeternitatis—that made Thomas Traherne "Felicity's perfect lover." For him indeed

> Life! Life [was] all: in its most full extent
> Stretcht out to all things, and with all Content!

ABRAHAM COWLEY
(1618–1667)

ABRAHAM COWLEY has already been mentioned as a Cambridge friend and admirer of Crashaw. Six years his junior, he too was born in London, in 1618, the son of a wealthy stationer and bookseller, and was educated at Westminster School. His early reading of Spenser's *Faerie Queene* inspired a precocious poetic talent, and between the ages of ten and twelve Cowley composed two epic romances. Both appeared in his *Poetical Blossomes*,

published in 1633; and while he was still a schoolboy he also wrote a pastoral comedy, *Love's Riddle*, published in 1638 with a Latin comedy entitled *Naufragium Joculare*, two years after he had gone up to Trinity College, Cambridge. He took his degree in 1639 and was elected a fellow of his college the following year. His literary activities at Cambridge included a play called *The Guardian*—later published in 1650, then revised and reissued in 1663 under the title *Cutter of Coleman-Street*—which was acted at the college before Prince Charles.

Cowley's fortunes, like those of Crashaw, were adversely affected by the Civil War. Because of his royalist sympathies, he too—with, as he says in a characteristic passage, his "heart wholly set upon Letters"—was "torn" from the university by "that violent Publick storm which would suffer nothing to stand where it did, but rooted up every Plant, even from the Princely Cedars to Me, the Hyssop." In 1643 he joined Charles I at Oxford; and in the following year he went to Paris as secretary to Lord Jermyn and cipher secretary to Queen Henrietta Maria, decoding the correspondence that passed between her and the king. He was also employed on various diplomatic missions. In his absence abroad there appeared in 1647, without his authority, a volume of love poems, *The Mistress*, which immediately earned him a high reputation.

During the next decade Cowley returned to England; and in 1655 he was arrested and imprisoned as a royalist spy. Though later released on bail, he thereafter was viewed suspiciously by both sides. The first verse of "Destinie" was interpreted by his own side as a reference to royalist mistakes, while a passage in the 1656 preface to his *Poems* seemed even more conciliatory in its submission to the Commonwealth. This undoubtedly contributed to Cowley's disappointment at the Restoration in his expectations of certain promised preferments for his services to the royalist cause. He was, however, restored to his Cambridge fellowship in 1661; and his patrons secured him a lease of lands that afforded a sufficient income and leisure at last to enjoy the kind of life he had always desired.

Cowley's later withdrawal from the political arena recalls the attitude during the Civil War of another eminent royalist gentleman of similar tastes and temperament: John Evelyn, to whom he dedicated his essay "The Garden." Like Evelyn's, it was probably dictated less by caution than the natural bent of his inclinations and studious, retiring nature. Even as a boy, he tells us in his engaging essay "Of My Self," he preferred solitude in the fields with a book to playing with his companions. In a poem published as early as 1647, "The Wish," he plainly perceived that "This busie world and I shall ne're agree"; and recoiling from "The *Crowd*, and *Buz*, and *Murmurings*/Of this great *Hive*, the *City*," unequivocally voiced his modest ambition to be "The happy *Tenant*" of "a *small House*, and *large Garden*" in company with "a *few Friends*, and *many Books*, both true," and "A *Mistress* moderately fair." In "Destinie" he sees himself preordained not for public life but a secluded one, as a poet in the line of "all thy great *Forefathers* . . . from *Homer* down to *Ben*"; while in his 1656 preface he expressed still more uncompromisingly his wish "to forsake this world for ever, with all the *vanities* and *Vexations* of it, and to bury my self . . . in some obscure retreat." In England, before the Restoration, he had turned from politics to botany and lived in the country, collecting plants (and composing in Latin verse six books on herbs, flowers, and trees) as part of the medical studies for which in 1657 he received the degree of doctor of physic, at Oxford. After his final retirement he was able to devote his time to rural pursuits and to writing the *Essays in Verse and Prose*, reflective in the manner and spirit of Montaigne and colored by the thought of the ancients he so copiously quotes, which were posthumously published in the 1668 edition of his *Works*. Their style of "smooth and placid equability," as Samuel Johnson described it, and their very titles—"Of Greatness," "Of Obscurity," "The Dangers of an Honest Man in Much Company," "Of Solitude"—mirror the mind "courtly though retired,/ . . . and finding rich amends/For a lost world in solitude and verse" later celebrated by William Cowper in *The Task*.

The reality did not quite match the imagined idyll, and Cowley ruefully admitted to "many little encumbrances and impediments" in his country life. "His Solitude from the very beginning," said his earliest editor and biographer, Thomas Sprat, "had never agreed so well with the constitution of his Body, as of his Mind"; and Cowley suffered much ill health before dying, in 1667, at Chertsey, in Surrey, at the age of forty-nine. Evelyn gives an eyewitness account of his funeral—"near one hundred coaches of noblemen and persons of quality following, among them all the wits of the town,

divers bishops and clergymen"; and he was buried near Chaucer and Spenser in Westminster Abbey. Sprat paid tribute to his friend's "unaffected modesty . . . always content with moderate things," to his "great integrity, and plainness of Manners"; and a contemporary obituary hailed him as a "great ornament of our nation, as well by the candour of his life as the excellency of his writings." Charles II himself, on receiving news of his death, was moved to declare "That Mr. Cowley *had not left a better Man behind him in England*."

Cowley was the most popular poet of his day: praised by Clarendon and revered by Dryden as an "authority . . . almost sacred to me," while Milton ranked him with Spenser and Shakespeare. The impact of his influence on his contemporaries, and later, may be traced in clear echoes of his images and cadences in poets as diverse as Milton, Marvell, Dryden, and Pope.

In the perspective of literary history it is not difficult to understand the reasons for what must today seem such extravagantly high esteem. Cowley was a writer of wide-ranging interests, active enterprise, and versatile accomplishment—and one, as Johnson says, "replete with learning." He epitomized the Restoration mind, at once elegant and inquiring, expressed the prevailing temper of his time, and satisfied its tastes. Coming at the end of the age of Donne, he could write in the still fashionable manner of metaphysical wit, while making none of the emotional and imaginative demands of his predecessors. This cooling of passion could only commend him to readers tired of the intensities and turmoil of the "rough and troubled" times, as he described them, earlier in the century. They welcomed his concept of poetry as (like God's creation of the world in *Davideis*) a "*Storehouse* of all *Proportions*"; of order, and a harmony "without *Discord* or *Confusion*," imposed upon the "ungovern'd" chaos of contrarieties. The restraint of "Unruly *Phansie* with strong *Judgment*" commended in "The Muse," the "well-worded *dress*" of a poetry in which Reason must "the *Inferior Powers* controul," was equally congenial to the spirit of the succeeding Augustan Age, which it anticipated. Johnson found Cowley "undoubtedly the best" of the metaphysicals, and nearly thirty years after the poet's death Addison declared that he possessed "as much true wit as any Author that ever writ; and indeed all other Talents of an extraordinary Genius."

Moreover, Cowley shared a lively interest in

science, the "new philosophy," with eminent contemporaries like Evelyn and Samuel Pepys. His name appeared with theirs (as, appropriately, Dr. Cowley) among the founder members of the Royal Society; and in 1661 he published a pamphlet entitled *A Proposition for the Advancement of Experimental Philosophy*, which set forth the aims of the institution that received its royal charter the following year. Sprat's *History of the Royal Society of London* in 1667 included an ode by Cowley (probably the last poem he wrote) in honor of these "few exalted Spirits" active in encouraging discovery in the natural sciences. Cowley had earlier seen his vocation in the "god-like *Poets* fertile *Mind*"; but here he values "The Riches which doe hoorded for [Man] lie/In Natures endless Treasurie," and "the plain Magick of true Reasons Light," above "painted Scenes, and Pageants of the Brain." His emphasis has shifted "From Words, which are but Pictures of the Thought . . ./To things, the Minds right Object," much as in his praise of Sir William Davenant's *Gondibert* he preferred the new world of "*Men* and *Manners*" to the former "fantastick *Fairy Land*" of heroic poetry. Impatiently dismissing the subtleties of the medieval Scholasticism—"all the cobwebs of the schoolmen's trade"—that had so richly nourished the imagination of Donne, he declared in his ode "To Mr. Hobs" that the "*Living Soul*" of philosophy "in the *School-mens* hands . . . perisht quite at last." It was to thinkers like Thomas Hobbes and to Bacon—hailed in "To the Royal Society" as the "mighty Man" who "like *Moses*, led us forth at last" into the light of knowledge from the wilderness of ignorance and superstition—that Cowley's "bright dry intellect" (as Grierson well describes it) was irresistibly attracted. In "To Mr. Hobs" he expresses unbounded admiration for this "great *Columbus* of the *Golden Lands* of *new Philosophies*"; and celebrates in another ode, "Upon Dr. Harvey," the achievement of the physician whose treatise on the circulation of the blood had been published in 1628. Cowley's images—of star and meteor, "multiplying" glass, his comparison of nature to the "springs and smallest wheels" of a "well-set clock," and many more—are likewise vividly expressive of his scientific enthusiasm.

Yet this topical appeal, which was responsible for his astonishing contemporary success, likewise accounted for the later, and no less striking, decline of Cowley's reputation. A century after his death his wit was no longer in fashion: Johnson was using its more "fantastic" flights to castigate the whole metaphysical school, and Cowper was lamenting its "erroneous taste." Still earlier Pope, another opponent of the metaphysicals' "glittering thoughts," demanded in his *Epistle to Augustus* (1737), "Who now reads Cowley?" The question has had a continuing relevance. In the nineteenth century, Coleridge contrasted Milton's "highly *imaginative*" mind with Cowley's "very *fanciful*" one, and his poetry was largely neglected; while in the modern revival of interest in Donne and his fellows, Cowley's work alone has seemed frigid and artificial.

Generally regarded as the last considerable poet in the metaphysical manner, he does indeed in this context exhibit what Eliot called "a kind of emotional drought, and a verbal ingenuity" that has "no great depth of feeling to work upon." The concept of wit expounded in Cowley's ode of that title is radically opposed to the fusion of feeling with thought described by Herbert Grierson as "passionate ratiocination," through which Donne and Marvell achieved such intensity and illumination of their imaginative insights. "Judgement begets the strength and structure," pronounced Hobbes, "and Fancy begets the ornaments of a Poem"; and Cowley, his disciple, echoes in both theory and practice this view of the conceit as a mere decorative embellishment rather than as a fundamental of poetic meaning.

This essential difference from his metaphysical predecessors is most apparent in Cowley's love poems. In itself the imagery is substantially similar: lovers' exchange of hearts, the broken heart, eyes and tears, sighs associated with winds, and so on. Cowley shared Donne's and Marvell's delight in metaphors of voyages to new worlds and in the resonance of exotic place names: Egypt as an analogy for the man parched by love ("Sleep"); travel in "uncivilis'd" countries of the heart, "Either by savages possest,/Or wild, and uninhabited," with lust in some as "the scorching dog-star," in others "Pride, the rugged Northern Bear" ("The Welcome"); or the "Vain weak-built isthmus" of man's life "o'erwhelm'd" by "the endless oceans" ("Life and Fame"). But there the resemblance ends. We have only to place the idea of the heart sighed out in the lover's breath, in the last line of Cowley's "The Concealment," beside Donne's similar closing conceit in "A Valediction: Of Weeping"; to contrast his expression of the feminine ideal opposed to its reality, in "Against Fruition," with Donne's in the first verses of "Aire and Angels" and "The Good-Morrow"; or to compare the alchemical images of the reconstituted heart, and of metal and alloy, in Cowley's "The Given Heart" with those used by Donne in "A Valediction: Forbidding Mourning" and "The Exstasie," to see how far and how fatally the pressure and urgency of passion have been drained from conceit. In "Platonic Love," presenting a reasoned consideration of the relative roles of body and soul, Cowley reduces the charged argument in "The Exstasie," with its magnificent culminating image of their complementary necessity, "Else a great Prince in prison lies," to flat prose statement:

> When souls mix 'tis an happiness;
> But not complete till bodies too combine,
> And closely as our minds together join . . .
> That souls do beauty know,
> 'Tis to the bodies help they owe . . .

Another characteristic difference in the treatment of a similar idea may be seen by comparing the cool classicism of Cowley's "The Spring" (one of his most gracefully accomplished love lyrics) with Donne's address to the countess of Bedford ("Madame, You have refin'd mee").

But more than anywhere we may detect the lowering of poetic and emotional temperature when three poems by Cowley are juxtaposed with Marvell's "To His Coy Mistress," whose opening "geographical" images echo those of Cowley's "The Account":

> I have not yet my *Persian* told,
> Nor yet my *Syrian Loves* enroll'd

nor the Indian, Arabian, African, and the rest. Cowley's illustration of the central conceit of his mistress as "Th' *Arithmetician* of my *Love*" provides still more striking parallels with Marvell:

> An hundred Loves at *Athens* score,
> At *Corinth* write an hundred more . . .
> Write me at Lesbos ninety down,
> Full ninety *Loves*, and half a One . . .
> Three hundred more at *Rhodes* and *Crete* . . .

The figure is sustained with a humorous dexterity that pleases on its intended level. But this mood, persisting to the end of the poem, makes it a charm-ing ingenuity and no more: on a different plane from Marvell, whose whimsical introduction is only a starting point for moving on into somber meditation on the themes of change, mortality, and dissolution. Again, the last verse of Cowley's "My Dyet" anticipates some of the initial conceits in Marvell's poem:

> On' a *Sigh* of Pity I a year can live,
> One *Tear* will keep me twenty 'at least,
> Fifty a gentle *Look* will give;
> An hundred years on one *kind word* I'll feast:
> A thousand more will added be,
> If you an *Inclination* have for me;
> And all beyond is vast *Eternity*.

Marvell's idea of time as relative to the lover's experience is also foreshadowed by Cowley in "Love and Life":

> Now sure, within this twelve-month past,
> I'have *lov'd* at least some twenty years or more:
> The account of *Love* runs much more fast
> Than that, with which our *Life* does score . . .

> . . . the self same *Sun*,
> At once does slow and swiftly run . . .

> When *Soul* does to *my self* refer,
> 'Tis then my *Life*, and does but slowly move;
> But when it does relate to her,
> It swiftly flies, and then is *Love* . . .

Yet nowhere here has Cowley's thought finally "modified his sensibility" (as Eliot so memorably observed of Donne) to transcend the merely clever cerebral exercise of wit.

Nevertheless the impressive diversity of Cowley's literary achievement, from metaphysical ingenuity to Jonsonian classical elegance, commands respect. His spirit of enterprise made him a pioneer in both religious epic and the ode form. In days of slavishly literal translation, his ventures in this field earned Johnson's approval for having "freed translation from servility, and, instead of following his author at a distance, walked by his side." Johnson likewise admired Cowley's critical acumen, whose influence on Pope may be seen in passages in the *Essay on Criticism*; while his remarks in the preface to *Pindarique Odes* about viewing poets in the context of their time anticipate the "historical" attitude in later criticism. As a poet he ranged over love lyrics, elegies, and Latin verse; and his polished philosophical prose has continued to give pleasure through succeeding centuries.

The greater part of *Davideis*, a "*Heroical Poem* of the *Troubles of David*," of which only four books were completed of a projected twelve, was, according to Sprat, written while Cowley was still an undergraduate, although it was not published until 1656. Little regarded in its day, this ambitious undertaking essayed, for the first time in English poetry, the composition of an original sacred epic rather than mere paraphrase of biblical narrative. Modestly disclaiming success for his "weak and imperfect attempt," Cowley expressed the hope that it might open "a way to the courage and industry of some other persons, who may be better able to perform it." This was fulfilled eleven years later, with the publication of Milton's epic handling of a scriptural theme in the classical manner, *Paradise Lost*; and also in having provided for Dryden an invaluable model and inspiration for the development of the heroic couplet.

Among Cowley's formal elegies, "On the Death of Sir Henry Wootton" dutifully eulogizes the knowledge and industry of a diplomat now "gone to *Heav'n* on his *Fourth Embassie*." More personal in feeling, his ode "On the Death of Mr. William Hervey" mourns a Cambridge contemporary who died there in 1642. Although Johnson found "very little passion" in this elegy, it communicates with genuine poignancy a young man's grief for his "truest *Friend* on earth . . ./My sweet *Companion*, and my gentle *Peere*," with whom he had walked in the fields sharing such talk of "deep *Philosophy*,/ *Wit, Eloquence*, and *Poetry*":

> Henceforth, ye gentle *Trees*, for ever fade;
> Or your sad branches thicker joyn,
> And into darksome shades combine,
> *Dark* as the *Grave* wherein my *Friend* is laid.

"On the Death of Mr. Crashaw," with its self-contained couplets and alexandrines, is by contrast metrically less flexible and more rhetorical—but still a sincere and memorable tribute to a venerated fellow poet.

These elegies appeared in 1656 among Cowley's *Miscellanies*, which display a great variety of manner and mood. The "familiar and festive" vein approved by Johnson in *Anacreontiques* celebrates amorous and convivial delights ("Let me alive my pleasures have:/All are Stoics in the grave") in deft and graceful pieces like "The Swallow," "Drinking," and "The Epicure." Johnson also applauded as an "airy frolic of genius" the "gaiety of fancy" and "dance of words" in "The Chronicle," a lighthearted account of the virtues and "politick Arts" of a succession of imaginary mistresses. He did not extend such unqualified enthusiasm to the love poems in *The Mistress*, finding outrageously "far-fetched" such amorous conceits as that of a lover's heart which, tormented by his "stubborn" mistress, will "tear and blow up all within,/Like a grenado shot into a magazine." In his preface to the *Poems*, Cowley had observed "that *Poets* are scarce thought *Free-men* of their *Company*, without paying some duties, and obliging themselves to be true to *Love*"; and Johnson commented tartly upon this attitude of conventional "obligation to amorous ditties." The justice of this complaint that Cowley's mistress "has no power of seduction: 'she plays round the head, but reaches not the heart,'" her attributes producing "no correspondence of emotion," has already been acknowledged. In his witty lip service to love, that imagined "one dear *She*" of "The Wish" is nowhere more than a generalized abstraction envisaged by an ingenious but ultimately uninvolved spectator.

Yet Marvell's indebtedness to Cowley is plain: "To His Coy Mistress" did not appear until 1681, while "My Dyet" and "Love and Life" were published in *The Mistress* as early as 1647, and "The Account" included among the 1656 *Anacreontiques*. And in fact not only many of his contemporaries, but later poetic generations down to the great nineteenth-century romantics, owed much to Cowley's active, alert, and adventurous mind. The influence of the classical poets in whom he was from schooldays so deeply versed is pervasive throughout his work: from his books on plants in imitation of their style, and his meditative Horatian essays, to the *Anacreontiques* paraphrasing the manner of the Greek poet Anacreon. He aspired to literary immortality through emulation of the "mighty *Three*," Aristotle, Cicero, and Virgil. But it was the triumphal and processional odes of Pindar that inspired Cowley's important legacy to posterity. Many of his addresses to persons—"To Mr. Hobs," "Ode upon Dr. Harvey," "To the Royal Society"—and to abstractions "Of Liberty," "Destinie," "Hymn. To Light"—were written in Pindaric stanzas, irregularly rhymed and varying in both the length and number of their lines, to afford greater technical scope and freedom than the familiar formal pattern of such Horatian odes as Marvell's *Upon Cromwell's Return from Ireland*.

Two main classical models have served as inspiration for the English ode: the Greek poet Pindar (*ca.* 518–*ca.* 438 B.C.), who composed ceremonial songs in honor of the victorious athletes and their families in the annual national festivals; and the Roman poet Horace (65–8 B.C.), who wrote not to celebrate great occasions but in an altogether more intimate, thoughtful, and sometimes ironical vein. Pindar's festal poems were designed for performance by choir and orchestra, and this is reflected in the exuberant lyrical surge of their rhythms and irregular lengths of line, the darting, impulsive thought that often follows no logical sequence, and an intense imaginative energy infectiously communicating the excitement of communal rejoicing. Their sentence structure and verse patterns are governed by the pulse beat and breathing pauses in the music and dancing that accompanied them; so Cowley was right to insist, in his preface to *Pindarique Odes*, upon the importance of relating Pindar's work to the time and purpose for which it was written.

The great difference between Pindar and Horace is that between the public and the private poet. Horace wrote in carefully molded, precisely ordered stanzas usually of four lines, with few variations on this traditional form. This "calm, restrained, elegant, enlightened Epicurean," as Gilbert Highet describes him,[9] warned later poets of the dangers of trying to imitate or emulate what seemed to him the torrential, undisciplined power of his great predecessor. Highet admirably sums up the distinguishing characteristics of the two, and of their poetic successors:

The Pindarics admire passion, daring, and extravagance. Horace's followers prefer reflection, moderation, economy. Pindaric odes follow no pre-established routine, but soar and dive and veer as the wind catches their wing. Horatian lyrics work on quiet, short, well-balanced systems. . . . Pindar loves the choir, the festival, and the many-footed dance. Horace is a solo singer, sitting in a pleasant room or quiet garden with his lyre.

[9]In *The Classical Tradition: Greek and Roman Influences on Western Literature* (Oxford, 1949). See chapter 12 for a detailed and illuminating discussion of the respective influences of Pindar and Horace upon English poetry.

Horace had been familiar to European readers in the Middle Ages, and in England his odes were taught and quoted in schools before poets began to imitate him. Mindful that the word *ode* means "song," Horatian writers in the Renaissance and baroque periods often set their odes to music, or attempted to reproduce the effect of music in the movement and harmony of the words; but any accompaniment was envisaged for the solo singer, or at most a small group, by contrast with the bold choric and orchestral sweep of Pindar. The odes of the Greek master were known in Europe only through Horace's qualified admiration, until they were printed at Venice in 1513. They were thus still something of a poetic novelty to the seventeenth-century reader when Milton wrote, in 1629, the first great Pindaric poem in English, his hymn "On the Morning of Christ's Nativity," shortly after he had bought a copy of Pindar (now in Harvard University Library); and Ben Jonson in the same year composed his "Ode on the Death of Sir H. Morison," a poem more characteristically Horatian in thought and tempo, but Pindaric in its verse patterns.

Cowley was in fact the first to direct the attention of English readers to the odes of Pindar, to offer any detailed and sympathetic scrutiny of his spirit and technique, and to attempt to translate his poetic principles into his own practice. It was a conscious and carefully considered innovation, which aimed not at slavish imitation but set out to recreate the manner in which Pindar might have written in contemporary English. Discussing his methods at length in the preface to his *Poems*, he expressed doubt that this unfamiliar form would be understood by many of his readers; for, as he said:

The digressions are many, and sudden, and sometimes long . . . . The *Figures* are unusual and *bold*, even to *Temeritie*, and such as I durst not have to do withal in any other kind of *Poetry*: The *Numbers* are various and irregular, and sometimes (especially some of the long ones) seem harsh and uncouth, if the just measures and cadencies be not observed in the *Pronunciation*.

Anticipating Samuel Johnson's complaint of the "lax and lawless versification" licensed by the removal of traditional restraints, he concluded by affirming that "though the *Liberty* of them may incline a man to believe them easie to be composed, yet the undertaker will find it otherwise."

Cowley's enthusiasm for his model is given full

rein in "The Praise of Pindar," written in imitation of the Second Ode of Horace: extolling—in Horace's own image—"The *Theban Swan*" and the "rich embroidered *Line*" of "his *Nimble, Artful, Vigorous* Song," with its

> impetuous *Dithyrambique Tide,*
> Which in no *Channel* deigns t'abide,
> Which neither *Banks* nor *Dikes* controul.

"The Resurrection," an ode that Cowley himself called "truly *Pindarical*, falling from one thing into another, after his *Enthusiastical manner*," also characterizes the nature of the *"Pindarique Pegasus"*:

> an unruly, and a *hard-Mouth'd Horse,*
> Fierce, and unbroken yet,
> Impatient of the *Spur* or *Bit*.
> Now *praunces* stately, and anon flies o're the place,
> Disdains the *servile Law* of any settled *pace*,
> *Conscious* and *proud* of his own *natural force*

which will fling *"Writer* and *Reader* too that *sits* not *sure*." "The Muse" further elaborates, in the Pindaric manner, Cowley's characteristic ideas about the nature and function of poetry.

The widespread influence of Cowley's Pindaric odes was responsible for many pompously pretentious effusions for more than a century to come. Yet his was—in his own phrase—"no *unskilful Touch*"; and, as Sprat contended, the very irregularity of the form made "that kind of Poesie fit for all manner of subjects . . . the frequent alteration of the Rhythm and Feet, affects the mind with a more various delight, while it is soon apt to be tyr'd by the setled pace of any one constant measure." In Cowley's hands, he concluded, "this loose, and unconfin'd measure has all the Grace, and Harmony of the most confin'd." Addison too praised Cowley's felicitous adaptation of "the deep-mouth'd *Pindar*":

> whom others in a labour'd strain,
> And forc'd expression, imitate in vain.
> Well-pleas'd in thee he soars with new delight;

and even Johnson had to admit "great fertility of fancy," and that "no man but Cowley could have written" his Pindarics.

If for us today Cowley's Pindaric experiments are neither wholly successful as free imitations of their original, nor vividly memorable as poems, his pioneering exploitation of the flexible possibilities of a form comparatively new then in England proved a liberating force for generations of poets to come. Its impact may be traced from Dryden's "Alexander's Feast" and his great public odes, through Gray's "Progress of Poesy," to the powerful ebb and flow of alternating joy and regret evoked by the irregular verse forms of William Wordsworth's "Immortality" ode; and is to be detected even as late as Alfred Lord Tennyson's "Ode on the Death of the Duke of Wellington." Percy Bysshe Shelley was another of the great romantics notably indebted to the freedom of Pindaric improvisation in poems such as his "Ode to Naples," and even more clearly in the mounting, impetuous urgency of image and emotion in "Ode to the West Wind"; and Grierson points a parallel between lines 45–48 of Cowley's "Hymn. To Light" and the third stanza of Shelley's "Hymn of Apollo." John Keats, like William Collins, was more Horatian in mood, yet the contemplative solitude of his great odes generates an intensity that soars to Pindaric peaks of spiritual exaltation. In fact, small distinction between the two classical influences was made by many English nineteenth-century poets; and in their work the solitary serenity of Horace often blends effortlessly with the passionate imagination and transcendental visionary quality of the Greek poet made generally familiar by Cowley nearly two centuries earlier. Whatever his shortcomings when viewed as the last major representative of metaphysical poetry, in the sphere of the Pindaric ode Cowley did indeed, in his own words about Davenant, "leave bright *Tracks* for following Pens to take."

SELECTED BIBLIOGRAPHY

RICHARD CRASHAW

I. BIBLIOGRAPHY. See L. C. Martin, ed., *The Poems, English, Latin and Greek*, and R. C. Wallerstein, *Crashaw: A Study in Style and Poetic Development*, below.

II. COLLECTED WORKS. A. B. Grosart, ed., *Complete Works*, 2 vols. (London, 1872–1873; with suppl., 1887–1888), in the Fuller Worthies' Library; A. R. Waller, ed., *Poems* (Cambridge, 1904); J. R. Tutin, ed., *Poems*

(London, 1905); L. C. Martin, ed., *The Poems, English, Latin and Greek* (Oxford, 1927; 2nd ed., 1957), the definitive ed., with notes on the MSS and early eds.

III. SEPARATE WORKS. *Epigrammatum Sacrorum Liber* (London, 1634); *Steps to the Temple. Sacred Poems, With Other Delights of the Muses* (London, 1646), 2nd ed., 1648, added new pieces; *Carmen Deo Nostro, Te Decet Hymnus, Sacred Poems, Collected, Corrected, Augmented* (Paris, 1652), reprinted with the 1646 ed. of *Steps to the Temple* (1670); *Poemata et Epigrammata, Editio Secunda, Auctior et Emendatior* (Cambridge, 1670).

IV. SOME BIOGRAPHICAL AND CRITICAL STUDIES. K. M. Loudon, *Two Mystic Poets* (London, 1922), treats Crashaw and Vaughan; J. Bennett, *Four Metaphysical Poets* (Cambridge, 1934; rev. ed., 1953), treats Donne, Herbert, Vaughan, and Crashaw, 2nd rev. ed. titled *Five Metaphysical Poets* (London, 1964), adds a chapter on Marvell; R. C. Wallerstein, *Crashaw: A Study in Style and Poetic Development* (Madison, Wisc., 1935), includes full bibliography of Crashaw's sources and of work by Crashaw scholars; A. Warren, *Crashaw: A Study in Baroque Sensibility* (Baton Rouge, 1939); M. Praz, *Crashaw* (Brescia, 1946); B. Willey, *Crashaw* (London, 1949), a perceptive and illuminating memorial lecture delivered at Peterhouse, Cambridge; G. W. Williams, *Image and Symbol in the Sacred Poetry of Richard Crashaw* (Columbia, S.C., 1963).

HENRY VAUGHAN

I. BIBLIOGRAPHY. For the early eds. see L. C. Martin, ed., *The Works*, below. The work of Vaughan scholars through the end of 1945 is listed in E. L. Marilla, *A Comprehensive Bibliography of Henry Vaughan* (University, Ala., 1948).

II. COLLECTED WORKS. *The Sacred Poems and Private Ejaculations* (London, 1847), with a memoir by H. F. Lyte; A. B. Grosart, ed., *The Works in Verse and Prose Complete* (London, 1870–1871), in the Fuller Worthies' Library; E. K. Chambers, ed., *The Poems of Henry Vaughan, Silurist*, 2 vols. (London, 1896); L. C. Martin, ed., *The Works* (Oxford, 1914; rev. ed., 1957), the definitive ed.; E. L. Marilla, ed., *The Secular Poems* (Cambridge, Mass., 1958); L. C. Martin, ed., *Poetry and Selected Prose of Henry Vaughan* (London, 1963), Oxford Standard Authors ed., based on Oxford English Texts ed. (London, 1957), above, contains all the poetry and *The Mount of Olives, Man in Darkness*, and *Primitive Holiness*.

III. SEPARATE WORKS. *Poems, With the Tenth Satyre of Juvenal Englished* (London, 1646); *Silex Scintillans: Sacred Poems and Private Ejaculations* (London, 1650), so-called "Second Edition," consisting of a reiss. of the first with a second "Book," 1655, and W. A. L. Bettany, ed. (London, 1905); *Olor Iscanus: Select Poems, and*

Translations (London, 1651; reiss. 1679); *The Mount of Olives: or Solitary Devotions . . .* (London, 1652); *Flores Solitudinis: Collected in His Sickness and Retirement* (London, 1654), a translation of four Latin prose works; *Hermetical Physick . . . Englished* (London, 1655), a translation of Nollius' *Systema Medicinae Hermeticae Generale*, 1613; *The Chymist's Key* (London, 1657); *Thalia Rediviva* (London, 1678).

IV. SOME BIOGRAPHICAL AND CRITICAL STUDIES. G. E. Hodgson, *A Study in Illumination* (London, 1914); K. M. Loudon, *Two Mystic Poets* (London, 1922); E. Holmes, *Henry Vaughan and the Hermetic Philosophy* (Oxford, 1932); J. Bennett, *Four Metaphysical Poets* (Cambridge, 1934; rev. ed., 1953), and *Five Metaphysical Poets* (London, 1964); J. B. Leishman, *The Metaphysical Poets* (Oxford, 1934), treats Donne, Herbert, Vaughan, and Traherne; L. C. Martin, "Henry Vaughan and the Theme of Infancy," in *Seventeenth-Century Studies, presented to Sir Herbert Grierson* (Oxford, 1938); F. E. Hutchinson, *Henry Vaughan: A Life and Interpretation* (Oxford, 1947), the standard biography; R. Garner, *Henry Vaughan: Experience and the Tradition* (Chicago, 1959); E. C. Pettet, *On Paradise and Light* (London, 1961), a study of Vaughan's *Silex Scintillans*; R. A. Durr, *On the Mystical Poetry of Henry Vaughan* (Harvard, 1963).

THOMAS TRAHERNE

I. BIBLIOGRAPHY. G. I. Wade, *Traherne: A Critical Biography* (Princeton, 1944), contains a bibliography; "The Manuscripts of Traherne" in *Bodleian Library Record* III (1951).

II. COLLECTED WORKS. G. I. Wade, ed., *The Poetical Works* (London, 1932); A. Quiller-Couch, ed., *Felicities of Thomas Traherne* (London, 1934); H. M. Margoliouth, ed., *Thomas Traherne: Centuries, Poems and Thanksgivings*, 2 vols. (Oxford, 1958), the definitive ed.; A. Ridler, ed., *Thomas Traherne: Poems, Centuries, and Three Thanksgivings* (London, 1966), Oxford Standard Authors ed., based on the Oxford English Texts ed. (London, 1958), above, a fresh collation of texts with manuscripts, includes all the poems, *Centuries of Meditations* in entirety, three *Thanksgivings*, and short extracts from *Christian Ethicks*.

III. SEPARATE WORKS. *Roman Forgeries, By A Faithful Son of the Church of England* (London, 1673); *Christian Ethicks* (London, 1675), contains eight of the eleven poems printed in the poet's lifetime; [G. Hickes, ed.], *A Serious and Pathetical Contemplation of the Mercies of God, In Several Most Devout and Sublime Thanksgivings for the Same* (London, 1699), R. Daniells, ed. (Toronto, 1941); *A Collection of Meditations and Devotions in Three Parts* (London, 1717); B. Dobell, ed., *The Poetical Works, Now First Published, From the Original Manu-*

scripts (London, 1903); B. Dobell, ed., *Centuries of Meditations, Now First Printed from the Author's Manuscript* (London, 1908; rev. ed., 1928); H. I. Bell, ed., *Poems of Felicity* (London, 1910), text from the MS in the British Museum, contains thirty-nine poems not in the Dobell MSS in the Bodleian Library; J. R. Slater, ed., *Of Magnanimity and Chastity* (New York, 1942).

IV. BIOGRAPHICAL AND CRITICAL STUDIES. J. B. Leishman, *The Metaphysical Poets* (Oxford, 1934); Q. Needale, *Traherne* (Oxford, 1935); G. I. Wade, *Thomas Traherne* (Princeton, 1944), contains the fullest biography and a detailed examination of the individual writings; K. W. Salter, *Thomas Traherne: Mystic and Poet* (London, 1964).

ABRAHAM COWLEY

I. COLLECTED WORKS. T. Sprat, ed., *Works* (London, 1668), with the earliest biography of Cowley, the 2nd part appeared in 1681, and the 2nd and 3rd parts together in 1689; A. B. Grosart, ed., *The Complete Works in Verse and Prose*, 2 vols. (London, 1881); J. R. Lumby, ed., *Prose Works* (London, 1887), revision by A. Tilley, ed. (London, 1923); A. R. Waller, ed., *The English Writings*, 2 vols. (London, 1905–1906); A. B. Gough, ed., *Essays and Other Prose Writings* (London, 1915); J. Sparrow, ed., *The Mistress with Other Select Poems* (London, 1926); L. C. Martin, ed., *Poetry and Prose* (Oxford, 1949), a representative selection, including Sprat's *Life* and comments on the work by critics from Dryden to Grierson.

II. SEPARATE WORKS. *Poetical Blossomes* (London, 1633; 2nd ed., 1636), second ed. includes *Sylva*; *Love's Riddle and Naufragium Joculare* (London, 1638); *The Puritan and the Papist* (London, 1643); *The Mistress* (London, 1647), published without Cowley's authority during his absence from England; *The Guardian* (London, 1650; rev. ed., 1663), revision entitled *Cutter of Coleman-Street*; *Poems* (London, 1656), comprised *Miscellanies*, *The Mistress, Pindarique Odes*, and *Davideis*, Cowley's critical preface to this first authorized ed. of his mature poems is highly illuminating in its comments on his own work, his political attitude, and his views on poetry as a whole; *A Proposition for the Advancement of Experimental Philosophy and A Vision* (London, 1661), the former a pamphlet to promote the institution of the Royal Society; *A. Couleii Plantarum Libri Duo* (London, 1662); *Verses Lately Written upon Several Occasions* (London, 1663); *A Poem on the Late Civil War* (London, 1679).

III. SOME BIOGRAPHICAL AND CRITICAL STUDIES. S. Johnson, "Abraham Cowley," in *Lives of the Poets* (London, 1779), in World's Classics ed. and Everyman's

Library ed., important for its typical Augustan view not only of Cowley but of the metaphysical school in general; A. H. Nethercot, *Abraham Cowley, the Muse's Hannibal* (Oxford, 1931); J. Loiseau, *Abraham Cowley, sa vie, son oeuvre* (Paris, 1931); R. Wallerstein, "Cowley as a Man of Letters," *Transactions of the Wisconsin Academy of Sciences, Arts, and Letters*, 27 (1932); F. R. Leavis, "The Line of Wit," *Revaluation* (1936); R. B. Hinman, *Cowley's World of Order* (Cambridge, Mass., 1960).

ANTHOLOGIES

H. J. C. Grierson, ed., *Metaphysical Lyrics and Poems of the Seventeenth Century* (Oxford, 1921), with a prefatory essay that constitutes the best critical intro. to seventeenth-century metaphysical poetry; N. Ault, ed., *Seventeenth-Century Lyrics* (London, 1925); H. J. C. Grierson and G. Bullough, eds., *The Oxford Book of Seventeenth-Century Verse* (Oxford, 1934); H. Gardner, ed., *The Metaphysical Poets* (London, 1957), contains an illuminating critical intro.; L. L. Martz, ed., *The Meditative Poems* (New York, 1963).

GENERAL CRITICISM

T. S. Eliot, "The Metaphysical Poets," in the *Times Literary Supplement* (London, 1921), reprinted in *Selected Essays*, 1932; J. B. Leishman, *The Metaphysical Poets* (Oxford, 1934); J. Bennett, *Four Metaphysical Poets* (Cambridge, 1934; rev. ed., 1953), and *Five Metaphysical Poets* (London, 1964); H. C. White, *The Metaphysical Poets: A Study in Religious Experience* (New York, 1936); M. Praz, *Studies in Seventeenth-Century Imagery* (London, 1939); D. Bush, *English Literature in the Earlier Seventeenth Century* (Oxford, 1945); R. Tuve, *Elizabethan and Metaphysical Imagery* (Chicago, 1947); R. Freeman, *English Emblem Books* (London, 1948); R. C. Wallerstein, *Studies in Seventeenth-Century Poetic* (Madison, Wisc., 1950); R. F. Jones et al., *The Seventeenth Century* (Stanford, 1951), studies in the history of English thought and literature from Bacon to Pope; L. L. Martz, *The Poetry of Meditation: A Study in English Religious Literature of the Seventeenth Century* (New Haven, 1954); B. Ford, ed., *From Donne to Marvell* (London, 1956), The Pelican Guide to English Literature, III; A. Alvarez, *The School of Donne* (London, 1961); G. Williamson, *Seventeenth-Century Contexts* (London, 1961); G. Williamson, *The Proper Wit of Poetry* (London, 1962); W. R. Keast, ed., *Seventeenth-Century*

English Poetry: Modern Essays in Criticism (New York, 1962); K. G. Hamilton, *The Two Harmonies: Poetry and Prose in the Seventeenth Century* (London, 1963); R. Nevo, *The Dial of Virtue: A Study of Poems on the Affairs of State in the Seventeenth Century* (Princeton, 1963); L. L. Martz, *The Paradise Within: Studies in Vaughan, Traherne and Milton* (New Haven, 1964); G. Williamson, *Milton and Others* (London, 1965).

SOCIAL AND LITERARY BACKGROUND

H. J. C. Grierson, *The First Half of the Seventeenth Century* (London, 1906); H. J. C. Grierson, *Cross Currents in English Literature of the Seventeenth Century* (London, 1929); B. Willey, *The Seventeenth-Century Background* (London, 1934); C. V. Wedgwood, *Seventeenth-Century English Literature* (London, 1950).

ANDREW MARVELL

(1621-1678)

John Press

I

WHEN Andrew Marvell died in 1678 his admirers mourned him as a verse satirist and pamphleteer whose attacks on the court and on the pretensions of the Anglican episcopate had made him obnoxious to the government of Charles II. Nowadays he is admired chiefly for a few poems (none of which was published in his lifetime), whose peculiar distinction has been celebrated by T. S. Eliot and by many lesser critics of the past fifty years. We may find it strange that one man should have acquired two such divergent reputations—the first depicting him as a violent, audacious satirist, the second emphasizing the fineness of his lyrical sensibility and the urban, civilized quality of his metaphysical wit.

All modern commentators agree that in Marvell's finest poems there is a sense of underlying conflict and tension, although it is not easy to explain its origin. The Civil War and the general political uncertainties of the time may lie at the root of the matter, or it may be that Marvell was profoundly affected by a conflict that was not, in the narrow sense of the word, political—a conflict engendered by the rival claims upon his nature of sensuous Renaissance mysticism, scientific rationalism, and thoughtful, strenuous Puritanism. A study of his life and of his works may illustrate the ways in which Marvell responded to the pressure of public events and to the promptings of his temperament.

II

ANDREW MARVELL's father, also named Andrew, was an Anglican clergyman strongly influenced by Calvinist doctrine, who in 1624 became lecturer of Holy Trinity Church, Hull, and master of the charterhouse. The family home was in the rural parts just outside the bustle of the town, so younger Andrew, who was born at Winestead in Holderness, near Hull, on 31 March 1621, grew up among the sounds and sights and smells of the countryside. Despite Parker's gibe half a century later that Marvell was reared "among Boatswains and Cabin-boys," it seems probable that he was educated at Hull grammar school, from which, in 1633, he went up to Cambridge as a sizar of Trinity College. He was admitted as a scholar in April 1638, and took his bachelor of arts degree that same year. After going down from Cambridge some time before September 1641, without taking his master of arts degree, Marvell spent four years traveling on the Continent (probably 1642–1646), acquiring in the process a knowledge of foreign languages to which Milton testified in 1653.

The elegies of 1648 and 1649 on Francis Villiers, Lord Hastings, and Richard Lovelace suggest that until then Marvell favored the royalists, although he seems to have taken no active part in the Civil War. Nor can we tell why or even when he became converted to the Puritan cause. He may have been repelled by the raffish elements in the Cavalier party and have come to admire the exhilarating virtues of Puritanism, the moral strength and probity that it fostered, its concern for spiritual values, and its contempt for worldliness. Yet the stages of his conversion remain a matter of conjecture for, however we may interpret "An Horatian Ode," there is no satisfactory explanation of the poem he composed on Tom May's death. May was a former royalist poet whose desertion to the other side was regarded by his old colleagues as the act of a renegade. We can account for Marvell's hostile references to May by supposing that he personally disliked the dead man; but we can put no such gloss upon his insulting references to the Parliamentary commanders. May died on 13 November 1650: late in 1650 or early in 1651 Marvell was installed at Nun

Appleton House, Yorkshire, as tutor to Mary Fairfax, daughter of a leading Cromwellian general who had resigned from the army after disagreeing with Cromwell's aggressive policy toward the Scots.

He left Nun Appleton late in 1652 or early in 1653, as we know from a letter written by Milton on 21 February 1653 to Bradshaw, president of the council of state, recommending Marvell's employment as an assistant Latin secretary. Although he was not appointed, Marvell was chosen to write the Latin verses that were sent with Cromwell's portrait to Queen Christina of Sweden in April 1654. Having failed to get an official post, Marvell again became a tutor, this time to William Dutton, a ward of Oliver Cromwell's, who lived in John Oxenbridge's household at Eton. In the summer of 1656, William Dutton was in Saumur, accompanied by his tutor, whom J. Scudamore in a letter to Sir Richard Browne, dated 15 August 1656, described as "one Mervill, a notable English Italo-Machavillian." Milton's letter to Oldenburg, of 1 August 1657, mentions a learned friend who in the summer of 1656 had lent a copy of Milton's pamphlet against Morus to various scholars in Saumur. The chances are that the learned friend was Andrew Marvell and that he remained at Eton until 2 September 1657, when he obtained the post in the civil service for which he had applied some years previously. Although in 1673 Marvell claimed that he had "not the remotest relation to publick matters, nor correspondence with the persons then predominant, until the year 1657," and that he had accepted his appointment with reluctance, the evidence suggests that he welcomed the chance of serving Cromwell, whom he had come to revere as the sole guarantor of peace at home and prestige abroad. His "Poem Upon the Death of O.C.," which was not printed until 1681, is more than a eulogy of a dead statesman: the mark of personal grief is stamped upon those lines where Marvell describes how he gazed at Cromwell's body:

> I saw him dead, a leaden slumber lyes,
> And mortal sleep over those wakefull eyes:
> Those gentle rays under the lids were fled,
> Which through his looks that piercing sweetnesse shed;
> That port which so majestique was and strong,
> Loose and depriv'd of vigour, stretch'd along.
>
> (247–252)

In the period of uncertainty after Cromwell's death on 3 September 1658, Marvell began to play an active part in political life, being elected in 1659 as a member of Parliament for Kingston-upon-Hull, which he continued to represent in the House of Commons until his death in 1678. He probably frequented Harrington's Rota, or political debating club, whose members included the most daring revolutionary thinkers of the time. General Monk's brief dictatorship, followed by the Restoration of Charles II to the throne, compelled the Rota to disperse and marked the end of Harrington's visionary republicanism.

Unlike his fellow servants of the Commonwealth, John Dryden and Edmund Waller, Marvell did not write an effusive poem in honor of Charles II, yet despite his obdurate silence and his past record he was not only unpunished but even sent on diplomatic missions to Holland, Russia, Sweden, and Denmark. His mounting hostility to the policy of Charles II; his speeches in the Commons; his suspected authorship of satires against the government; the belief that he acted as secretary to Opposition groups who met in coffeehouses (rather as the Rota had once met): all these factors brought him into official disfavor. By 1673, when both parts of *The Rehearsal Transpros'd* had appeared, Marvell was recognized as perhaps the most formidable pamphleteer and satirist of the Opposition, and from 1672 to 1674 he may have worked with Peter Du Moulin, who, as an agent of William of Orange, was trying to break Charles II's alliance with Louis XIV against the Dutch. In the last few years of his life his detestation of the court became so violent and bitter that he grew increasingly savage and even fanatical in his onslaughts upon his political foes. It is not surprising that he was both dreaded and hated, nor that popular rumor attributed his death to poison, although it is highly probable that he died of tertian fever through lack of proper medical care. He was buried on 18 August 1678, in St. Giles in the Fields, London.

III

FRIENDS and enemies of Marvell have left us vivid, though all too brief, accounts of his character, which we can supplement by fragments of his biography. John Aubrey says of him:

> He was a great master of the Latin tongue; an excellent poet in Latin or English: for Latin verses there was no man

could come into competition with him. . . . He was of a middling stature, pretty strong sett, roundish faced, cherry-cheek't, hazell eie, browne haire. He was in his conversation very modest, and of very few words: and though he loved wine he would never drinke hard in company, and was wont to say that, *he would not play the good-fellow in any man's company in whose hands he would not trust his life.* He kept bottles of wine at his lodgeing, and many times he would drinke liberally by himselfe to refresh his spirits, and exalt his muse.

Aubrey remarks that Marvell "had not a generall acquaintance," but he chose his friends with a discriminating care. Among them were numbered John Pell, a mathematician and a friend of Thomas Hobbes; the poet Richard Lovelace; religious and political thinkers such as John Hales and James Harrington. His admiration for the satires of the earl of Rochester and for Samuel Butler's *Hudibras* is a sign that his Puritanism was in no way fanatical or narrow. It was John Milton whom Marvell revered above all his contemporaries. Having, with characteristic loyalty and courage, protected Milton in 1660 from the attacks of his enemies, he continued to defend his conduct and to extol his memory. In the lines "On Mr. Milton's Paradise Lost," printed in the second edition of Milton's poem (1674), he celebrated the genius of his dead friend:

> At once delight and horrour on us seize,
> Thou singst with so much gravity and ease;
> And above humane flight dost soar aloft,
> With Plume so strong, so equal, and so soft.
> The *Bird* nam'd from that *Paradise* you sing
> So never Flags, but alwaies keeps on Wing
> (35–40)

Yet if Marvell was a loyal friend he was also a fierce hater, as the virulence of his satirical writings may suggest. He was also a quick-tempered man: we know of three instances in which he began a quarrel that ended in blows, although one of them may have been a playful scuffle. His satires gained him a number of bitter enemies, who jeered at his fashionable manners, his full-bottomed wig, his fondness for larding his conversation with Gallic phrases, and his frequenting of coffeehouses. Not content with these minor insults, they descended to the most scurrilous and extravagant libels, accusing Marvell of having committed homosexual acts with Milton, and suggesting that he had grown virtuous of late only because he had become impotent. The

anonymous *A Letter from Amsterdam to a Friend in England* (1678) gets in one or two jabs at Marvell:

. . . make sure of Andrew; he's a shrewd man against popery, though for his religion you may place him, as Pasquin at Rome placed Henry the Eighth, betwixt Moses, the Messiah and Mahomet, with his motto in his mouth *Quo me vertam nescio.* It is well he is now transposed into politicks; they say he had much ado to live upon poetry.

The last sentence may remind us that, with the publication of *The Rehearsal Transpros'd* (parts I and II) in 1672 and 1673, Marvell had become famous as a deadly pamphleteer. Samuel Parker had, in his youth, been a Puritan, but, on becoming an orthodox Anglican soon after the Restoration, he did not hesitate to attack and to ridicule his old friends. By 1672, when he was archdeacon of Canterbury, he had acquired a reputation as a controversialist skilled in defending the Anglican church against the doctrines of Hobbes and the errors of Protestant Dissenters. He objected to Charles II's Declaration of Indulgence on the grounds that it was unsafe to grant toleration to Roman Catholics or to Protestant rebels against the Anglican hierarchy. In his answer to Parker, Marvell christens his adversary Mr. Bayes. The duke of Buckingham's play, *The Rehearsal*, contains a character named Bayes, who is a malicious caricature of Dryden; Marvell's borrowing from Buckingham enables him both to ridicule Parker and to show his contempt for Dryden. We cannot hope to summarize Marvell's arguments, but we can show why, in Bishop Burnett's words, he had "all the *laughers* of his side."

Marvell raises a number of laughs by what present-day readers would regard as dirty abuse, and by sly innuendoes about Parker's keeping a mistress whom Marvell nicknames his "comfortable Importance." Even Parker's wife, whom he had married in the interval between the publication of parts I and II, becomes a target for these indecent jokes. More justifiably, Marvell emphasizes his contempt for a man who had changed sides in order to gain preferment, and who had purged himself of all puritanical taint by imitating the vices of fashionable society:

In order to do this he daily enlarged, not only his conversation, but his conscience, and was made free of some of the town-vices; imagining, like Muleasses King of

Tunis . . . that by hiding himself among the onions, he should escape being traced by his perfumes.

Having drawn attention to Parker's timeserving, Marvell proceeds to expose the weakness of his arguments. Like all dutiful Anglicans, Parker was bound to acknowledge the authority of the king as a temporal sovereign and also as supreme governor of the Church of England, yet here he was trying to compel Charles II to persecute the Dissenters. Marvell takes a malicious delight in showing that Anglican loyalty to the crown will last only as long as the crown humors the Church's itch to harry its religious opponents:

Is this at last all the business why he hath been building up all this while the Necessary, Universal, Uncontroulable, Indispensible, Unlimited, Absolute Power of Governors; only to gratifie the humour and arrogance of an Unnecessary, Universal, Uncontroulable, Dispensible, Unlimited and Absolute, Archdeacon? Still must, must, must: But what if the Supream Magistrate won't?

Parker's narrowness and distortion of all sane values invite Marvell's ironical commendation: "The Church of England is much obliged to Mr. Bayes for having proved that Nonconformity is the Sin against the Holy Ghost." He strikes a deeper note when he proclaims the sanctity of the individual conscience, a theme dear to him. Believing that "the Supreme Magistrate hath some power, but not all Power in matters of Religion," Marvell judges it good morals and sound policy that the ruler should not peer too closely into men's souls, but allow decent, quiet citizens to worship God as they think fit. Parker, who argued that in religious matters a subject should be obedient, even against his conscience, was rash enough to advise the subject to say "My Obedience will hallow, or at least excuse my Action." Marvell, with his unfailing verbal dexterity, seizes on this unhappy choice of words:

If ever our Author come for his merits in election to be a Bishop, a man might almost adventure instead of Consecrated to say that he was Excused.

Marvell's prophecy was fulfilled. Parker was consecrated (or excused) bishop of Oxford in 1686 and in 1687 characteristically allowed James II to install him as president of Magdalen College, Oxford, in the course of the king's attempt to coerce the university. He lived to enjoy the fruits of his servility and of his bishopric until 1688.

No other prose work brought Marvell such renown as *The Rehearsal Transpros'd*, although *An Account of the Growth of Popery and Arbitrary Government* (1677), in which he unblushingly attacks Charles II for having issued the Declaration of Indulgence, devastatingly analyzes the government's misdeeds. The *Mock Speech from the Throne* (1675), a masterpiece of cool, bantering irony, has not been proved to be by him, but it is hard not to accept the view of the leading Marvell scholar, Pierre Legouis, that it comes from Marvell's pen. Modern readers, discerning in this pasquinade those qualities of wit, poise, and elegance that they prize in Marvell's verse, will probably value it more highly than all the long political and religious tracts on which he lavished his talents in the closing years of his life.

IV

THE *Miscellaneous Poems* of Andrew Marvell appeared in 1681, with a preface by Mary Marvell, assuring the reader that the poems "are Printed according to the exact copies of my late Dear Husband." Mary Palmer, for many years Marvell's housekeeper, asserted in the course of the long, sordid lawsuit that followed his death that he had secretly married her on or about 13 May 1667 in the Church of the Holy Trinity in the Little Minories, a statement that is hard to disprove since, although all the other church records are intact, the registers of marriage for the years 1662–1683 are missing. It seems likely that she arranged for the publication of Marvell's poems to bolster up her extremely shaky claim, and that many purchasers of this volume bought it for the sake of his portrait, which has been torn out of a large number of the surviving copies. Marvell was admired by his contemporaries almost exclusively for his prose, and his poetry remained largely unknown throughout the eighteenth century, despite the publication in 1776 of Thompson's splendid three-volume edition, which seems to have been welcomed chiefly by the Whigs as a weapon in their campaign against George III. In his *Account of the Growth of Popery* (1677) Marvell had used the phrase "the Country Party" in a sense that, according to the New English Dictionary, it did not acquire until 1735–1738. The Whigs of George III's reign, who liked to imagine themselves as the true heirs of the Opposition to Charles II, admired Marvell for what they held to be his republican zeal and for his Cromwellian enthusiasm rather than for his poetic gifts. Even as late as 1807 Wordsworth's sonnet "Great men have been among us" links Marvell not only with Milton but also with Harrington, Algernon Sidney, and Sir Henry Vane, upholders of strict republican virtue and patriotism.

Soon after the turn of the century Marvell's reputation as a lyrical poet began to rise, Bowles praising him for his precise delineation of nature in a passage from "Upon Appleton House":

> Then as I carless on the Bed
> Of gelid *Straw-berryes* do tread,
> And through the Hazles thick espy
> The hatching *Thrastles* shining Eye . . .
> (529–532)

As the nineteenth century wore on, such diverse critics as Campbell, Hazlitt, Lamb, Mitford, Emerson, Poe, and FitzGerald recognized the rare quality of Marvell's verse. Palgrave, doubtless prompted by Tennyson, his friend and mentor, paid Marvell the tribute of including three of his poems in *The Golden Treasury*—"An Horatian Ode," "The Garden," and "Bermudas." He did not print "To His Coy Mistress," confessedly out of deference to the prudery of his age, although Tennyson, with his characteristic admiration for vigorous magnificence,[1] regarded it as a sublime poem. T. S. Eliot's famous essay of 1921 summed up and intensified the admiration for Marvell's verse that was expressed by a number of critics during the preceding twenty years, although in a review published in the *Nation and Athenaeum* of 29 September 1923, Eliot referred to Bishop Henry King as "greater than Marvell." Since 1921 Marvell's reputation as a poet has continued to rise almost as high as the floods of books and articles that sometimes threaten to overwhelm with scholastic ingenuity the poetry that they purport to interpret and to praise. The Victorians admired Marvell as a lyrical poet who celebrated nature with a remarkable purity and in-

sight, whereas for the past sixty years the revival of interest in the seventeenth-century metaphysicals has directed our attention to qualities in Marvell's verse that our grandfathers ignored or undervalued, above all to the irony and wit that lie coiled beneath the surface of his poetry. Indeed, some of the recent scholarship and critical ingenuity lavished upon his poems appear to be misplaced; for, while it is undeniable that he was a highly subtle writer, certain critics have attributed to him philosophical implications and verbal ambiguities of which he himself was unaware. Marvell's poetry displays and fuses into a harmonious whole a rich metaphysical subtlety, a moral seriousness, and a sensuous lyricism, part of its fascination residing in the ordered interplay of these varied elements. Before passing on to examine individual poems, we must first consider the operation and the relative importance of these elements in his verse.

Metaphysical poetry habitually displays certain qualities that, though closely interrelated, are yet distinct from one another. It is primarily concerned with problems deriving from or akin to the ancient problem of the One and the Many, body and soul, mind and body, transience and permanence, mortality and immortality, unity-in-duality. Because it is preoccupied with such teasing perplexities, it will tend either to reveal a sense of strain or, at the best, to attain only a momentary poise after which the mind will again pursue the ramifications and apparent contradictions of truth. There must be in a good metaphysical poem a ceaseless tension and also an intellectual control, which can be achieved only by use of the metaphysical conceit. The conceit is not designed to be a fanciful hyperbole, an extravagant adornment, or an exuberant manifestation of baroque energy, although it may sink into being no more than these things. Its true purpose is to fuse the warring elements of the poem into a unity that will intensify the vitality of each element and yet enable them to cohere.

Marvell's poetry fully answers to this description of metaphysical poetry. The mere titles of some poems—"A Dialogue Between the Soul and Body," "A Dialogue Between the Resolved Soul, and Created Pleasure"—hint at his obsession with the central problem that metaphysical poetry attempts to solve. In the garden poems the various light of the created world is contrasted with the unchanging radiance of eternity, and the two great love poems, "The Definition of Love" and "To His Coy

---

[1]Tennyson also spoke in the highest terms of Rochester's "A Satyr Against Mankind."

Mistress," convey with a vibrant intensity the poet's awareness of paradox and of man's perpetually thwarted desire to transcend his ordained limitations.

The poise and balance that metaphysical poetry demands are everywhere visible in Marvell's verse, even in the slightest of his poems such as "Mourning" or "The Mower to the Glo-Worms," and notably in his finest and most ambitious poems such as "An Horatian Ode," where the divergent elements are kept under perfect control.

Moreover, one can find in Marvell every type of metaphysical conceit, ranging from the ingenious pun to the highly serious and even tragic conceit that resolves all contradictions in a flash. Legouis remarked that Marvell was indebted in his satirical poems to John Cleveland (1613–1658), a notorious exponent of the witty conceit, and in his amorous poems to John Donne. In part II of *The Rehearsal Transpros'd*, he quotes from Donne's "The Progress of the Soul" a singularly inapposite passage coupling Luther with Mahomet, as if he wishes to pay tribute to a writer whom he had loved in his youth, and who had long been out of fashion.

It must be confessed that many of Marvell's conceits, however charming, are fanciful and even at times a shade ludicrous, though one suspects that Marvell cherished an affection for some of his more outrageous inventions. The most famous example of a deliberate indulgence in Clevelandism occurs in the last stanza of "Upon Appleton House":

> But now the *Salmon-Fishers moist,*
> Their *Leathern Boats* begin to hoist;
> And, like *Antipodes* in Shoes,
> Have shod their *Heads* in their *Canoos.*
> How *Tortoise like,* but not so slow,
> These rational *Amphibii* go?
> (769–774)

Yet the best of Marvell's conceits are free of such flaws, and reveal the fineness of his perceptions no less than the elegance of his wit:

> What in the World most fair appears,
> Yea even Laughter, turns to Tears:
> And all the Jewels which we prize,
> Melt in these Pendants of the Eyes.
> ("Eyes and Tears," 13–16)

> And, while vain Pomp does her restrain
> Within her solitary Bowr,

> She courts her self in am'rous Rain;
> Her self both *Danae* and the Showr.
> ("Mourning," 17–20)

> Gentler times for Love are ment.
> Who for parting pleasure strain
> Gather Roses in the rain,
> Wet themselves and spoil their Sent.
> ("Daphnis and Chloe," 85–88)

It is proof of Marvell's candor and suppleness of mind that when drawing upon his recollection of solemn biblical passages he should have still employed the same witty tone, even where to us it may appear incongruous, as in "Daphnis and Chloe" where, immediately after a reference to the ravishment of a warm corpse, there occurs a biblical allusion to the death that overtook the Jews in the wilderness while the manna and quail remained unchewed in their mouths. Happier examples may be found in "Upon Appleton House," stanza 47, where Marvell recalls a passage from Numbers 13 : 33 about the sons of Anak:

> And now to the Abbyss I pass
> Of that unfathomable Grass,
> Where Men like Grashoppers appear,
> But Grashoppers are Gyants there:
> They, in their squeking Laugh, contemn
> Us as we walk more low then them:
> And, from the Precipices tall
> Of the green spir's, to us do call.

Two stanzas later he refers to the crossing of the Red Sea by the Israelites:

> The tawny Mowers enter next;
> Who seem like *Israelites* to be,
> Walking on foot through a green Sea.
> To them the Grassy Deeps divide,
> And crowd a Lane to either side.

Marvell also employs with supreme art the serious and tragic pun. His grief at the ravages of the Civil War was deep and lasting, yet in "Upon Appleton House" he chooses to express this sense of loss by an almost lighthearted wordplay:

> Unhappy! shall we never more
> That sweet *Militia* restore,
> When Gardens only had their Towrs,
> And all the Garrisons were Flowrs,
> When Roses only Arms might bear,

And Men did rosie Garlands wear?
Tulips, in several Colours barr'd,
Were then the *Switzers* of our *Guard.*
(329-336)

In the description of Charles I on the scaffold in "An Horatian Ode":

But with his keener Eye
The Axes edge did try
(59-60)

the Latin word *acies* means both eyesight and blade, and, in Neoplatonism, denotes the intent inward gaze of the mind. The lines that depict Cromwell living, in his early days, reserved and austere,

As if his highest plot
To plant the Bergamot
(31-32)

probably contain not only a pun on the word plot, but a suggestion that faint inklings of a royal destiny may even then have flickered through Cromwell's mind, for the bergamot was known as "the pear of Kings." As a last example of this device we may take the passage from "The First Anniversary" in which Cromwell is compared with Amphion, who raised cities by the power of his lute:

Such was that wondrous Order and Consent,
When *Cromwell* tun'd the ruling Instrument.
(67-68)

The Platonic musical symbolism is grounded in the historical fact that in 1653 the Instrument of Government established Cromwell's Protectorate.

The moral seriousness that is the second noteworthy element in Marvell's poetry pervades almost everything he wrote. We can discern it most clearly in the poems where he overtly rejects the pleasures of the senses and even of the arts, but it informs so apparently slight a poem as "Clorinda and Damon," in which Damon thrusts aside the temptations proffered by Clorinda:

C. Near this, a Fountaines liquid Bell
Tinkles within the concave Shell.
D. Might a Soul bath there and be clean,
Or slake its Drought?
(13-16)

Moreover, his concern for social order, his feeling for the unspoiled life of the countryside, and his admiration for the values fostered by great country houses rooted in local tradition give his poetry a fine, mature dignity. A humble gratitude for God's bounty informs his sense of nature as a divine theater alive with symbols and hieroglyphs, a sense that is implicit in the garden poems and explicit in "Bermudas" where, after enumerating the luxuriant fruits and trees, Marvell proclaims the true glory of the islands:

He cast (of which we rather boast)
The Gospels Pearl upon our Coast.
And in these Rocks for us did frame
A Temple, where to sound his Name.
Oh let our Voice his Praise exalt,
Till it arrive at Heavens Vault:
Which thence (perhaps) rebounding, may
Eccho beyond the *Mexique Bay.*
Thus sung they, in the *English* boat,
An holy and a chearful Note,
And all the way to guide their Chime,
With falling Oars they kept the time.
(29-40)

The adjectives "holy" and "chearful" suggest the distinctive blend and quality of Marvell's Puritanism.

His inner harmony and balance are reflected in the tone of his voice. Like Ben Jonson, whose influence, coupled with that of Spenser, came, if not to supplant, at least to temper, the extravagance of his early Clevelandism, Marvell speaks with the unaffected ease of a man sure of his place in society talking to his equals. We find in him a courtly elegance, a poised, alert wit, an urbane irony that never degenerates into cheap cynicism, a fierce passion far removed from the licentious insolence of the Restoration songwriters, and an assured sense of values that frees him to relish the small joys of life without guilt because he has made his peace with things of great account.

Finally, we must consider the element of lyrical delight, without which metaphysical wit becomes frigid, and moral strength mere wooden didacticism. The Victorians prized Marvell for the freshness and the intensity of his lyricism, Francis Turner Palgrave compared him with Shelley and held "The Garden" to be "a test of any reader's insight into the most poetical aspects of poetry." Modern critics have become shy of praising a poet for his music, though they pride themselves on analyzing his tonal modality, and it is more rewarding to demonstrate than to define the exquisite cadences and sensuous delicacy that we find in Marvell's poetry:

> He hangs in shades the Orange bright,
> Like golden Lamps in a green Night.
> And does in the Pomgranates close,
> Jewels more rich than *Ormus* shows.
> He makes the Figs our mouths to meet;
> And throws the Melons at our feet.
> ("Bermudas," 17–22)

> See how it weeps. The Tears do come
> Sad, slowly dropping like a Gumme.
> So weeps the wounded Balsome: so
> The holy Frankincense doth flow.
> The brotherless *Heliades*
> Melt in such Amber Tears as these.
> ("The Nymph Complaining for the
>   Death of Her Faun," 95–100)

> How wide they dream! The *Indian* Slaves
> That sink for Pearl through Seas profound,
> Would find her Tears yet deeper Waves
> And not of one the bottom sound.
> ("Mourning," 29–32)

> When we have run our Passions heat,
> Love hither makes his best retreat.
> The *Gods*, that mortal Beauty chase,
> Still in a Tree did end their race.
> *Apollo* hunted *Daphne* so,
> Only that She might Laurel grow.
> And *Pan* did after *Syrinx* speed,
> Not as a Nymph, but for a Reed.
> ("The Garden," 25–32)

> Where you may lye as chast in Bed,
> As Pearls together billeted.
> All Night embracing Arm in Arm,
> Like Chrystal pure with Cotton warm.
> ("Upon Appleton House," 189–192)

Unlike two other great metaphysical poets, Donne and George Herbert, Marvell was not a resourceful inventor of stanzaic forms. In certainty of touch, felicitous graduation of tone, sensitivity of texture, and melodic smoothness he is at least their equal; and it was doubtless of these gifts that George Saintsbury was thinking when he said, with pardonable exaggeration, that in "fingering"—the power "of getting the utmost possible out of metres borrowed or invented—not the greatest poet in English or in literature is Marvell's superior."

V

WE cannot date more than a handful of Marvell's poems with any precision, and since even the most learned critics disagree about their order of composition it may be more helpful to group them roughly according to theme and tone, even if in doing so we are obliged to make certain assumptions about their chronological order. Bearing in mind our ignorance of dates, we may suggest the following crude and tentative grouping:

1. Verse tributes to Villiers, Hastings, and Lovelace; elegant and witty poems on love and on women, such as "Mourning," "Eyes and Tears," "The Match," "The Fair Singer," "Daphnis and Chloe," "The Gallery," "The Unfortunate Lover"; love poems in the pastoral convention, such as "Ametas and Thestylis Making Hay-Ropes," "Clorinda and Damon," "A Dialogue Between Thyrsis and Dorinda." "Fleckno, an English Priest at Rome" is probably an early poem, since the incidents related in it belong to 1645 or 1646.

2. Poems of retreat, contemplation, and solitude, including those in which appear the Mower and Juliana; the finest poems in this group are "The Garden" and "Upon Appleton House."

3. Poems of Marvell's full maturity on themes of love and death. "To His Coy Mistress" and "The Definition of Love" are the outstanding poems in this group, to which we may add "The Picture of Little T.C. in a Prospect of Flowers" and possibly "The Nymph Complaining for the Death of Her Faun."

4. Philosophical and religious poems, strongly tinged with a Puritan renunciation of worldly vanity. The outstanding poems in this group are "On a Drop of Dew," "A Dialogue Between the Resolved Soul, and Created Pleasure," "A Dialogue Between the Soul and Body," and "The Coronet."

5. Poems celebrating Oliver Cromwell and the Protectorate, notably "An Horatian Ode," "The First Anniversary of the Government under O.C.," "A Poem upon the Death of O.C.," "The Character of Holland," "On the Victory Obtained by Blake," and "Bermudas."

6. Satires on the reign of Charles II.

VI

THE early poems of Marvell are occasionally spoiled by a conscious self-indulgence in witty but frigid conceits, yet even in these slight, elegant lyrics one notices the assurance of the poet's control and the delicacy of his touch. In "Mourning," for example, the poem moves through a succession of faintly cynical reflections upon Chlora's tears, rises to the beautiful penultimate stanza about the Indian slaves diving for pearls, and ends with a gravely ironical judgment by the poet:

> I yet my silent Judgment keep,
> Disputing not what they believe:
> But sure as oft as Women weep,
> It is to be suppos'd they grieve.
> (33–36)

The gradation of tone is managed with even more subtlety in "Daphnis and Chloe," where the lover resists the importunities of his mistress who, too late, is bent upon giving herself to him at the very moment of parting. He breaks away from her in anguish, and then suddenly Marvell reverts to a cool speculation about masculine inconstancy and feminine coyness in the game of love:

> At these words away he broke;
> As who long has praying ly'n,
> To his Heads-man makes the Sign,
> And receives the parting stroke.
>
> But hence Virgins all beware.
> Last night he with *Phlogis* slept;
> This night for *Dorinda* kept;
> And but rid to take the Air.
>
> Yet he does himself excuse;
> Nor indeed without a Cause.
> For, according to the Lawes,
> Why did *Chloe* once refuse?
> (97–108)

The pastoral poems also occasionally take an unexpected twist, for though Ametas and Thestylis end their duel of wits in the traditional country manner:

> Then let's both lay by our Rope,
> And go kiss within the Hay
> (15–16)

Clorinda and Damon turn from love to sing the praise of Pan, and Thyrsis and Dorinda prepare wine steeped in poppies that they may more speedily find Elizium.

VII

MARVELL'S retreat into the solitude of Appleton House seems to have inspired deeper, more reflective poetry than any he had composed previously. The poems in which the Mower and Juliana appear, though partly love poems, and partly poems about the countryside, contain darker and more serious undertones. Death is present and with his scythe mimics the destruction wrought upon the grass by the Mower and upon the Mower by Juliana:

> For *Juliana* comes, and She
> What I do to the Grass, does to my Thoughts and Me.
> (23–24)

Marvell reflects also upon man's relationship with nature, and upon the way in which his ordering of the countryside is both a perfecting and yet a perversion of nature:

> His green *Seraglio* has its Eunuchs too;
> Lest any Tyrant him out-doe.
> And in the Cherry he does Nature vex,
> To procreate without a Sex.²
> ("The Mower Against Gardens,"
> 26–29)

The world of nature held for Marvell a profound moral and spiritual import. Unlike Randolph and the French libertine poets, who used the garden as a symbol to inculcate a naturalist glorification of sensual indulgence, Marvell depicts it as the *hortus conclusus*, the enclosed garden of *The Song of Songs*, where the withdrawn and solitary intellect may pass beyond the senses and contemplate the Divine. We need not pause to investigate the precise debt (if any) that Marvell owed to Bonaventura, Hugh of St. Victor, Richard of St. Victor, Plotinus, Ficino, Hermes Trismegistus, Lipsius, the Divine Casimire, or any other candidates advanced by ingenious commentators and source hunters. Such refinements of scholarship may serve to strengthen our understanding of "The Garden" and "Upon Appleton House"; but our first task must be to respond, by an exercise of imaginative sympathy, to the images and symbols that he employs in these poems of contemplative ecstasy.

"Upon Appleton House," for all its brilliance and variety, has seemed to many readers a muddled and uneven poem, because in it Marvell is trying to

---

²The reference is probably to the stoneless cherry.

counterpoint a number of complex and diverse themes. He desires to pay a courtly, reasoned compliment to the Fairfaxes, and in the process to convey his admiration of the secure, harmonious life that a country house guarantees. This leads him to survey the history of the house, in the course of which he attacks the Catholic technique of sensual sublimation, contrasting it with the Puritan ideal personified in Mary Fairfax, a child soon to become a woman. Fairfax's retirement from politics is lamented, because he might have saved England from the desolation that threatens it, the notion of England as a garden inspiring Marvell to a characteristically poignant, yet witty, stanza:

> Oh Thou, that dear and happy Isle
> The Garden of the World ere while,
> Thou *Paradise* of four Seas,
> Which *Heaven* planted us to please,
> But, to exclude the World, did guard
> With watry if not flaming Sword;
> What luckless Apple did we tast,
> To make us Mortal, and The Wast?
> (321–328)

Marvell then passes to the central portion of the poem, his retreat into the countryside surrounding the house. The precise and loving description of the creatures thronging the woods, meadows, and pools; an evocation of nature's teeming, elaborate richness; the play of a shimmering wit upon the objects of the poet's contemplation; a quaint humor, a steady piety, and a soaring ecstasy are entwined by Marvell in this poem with consummate artifice. He draws from the sight of the birds, insects, trees, and plants the certainty reserved for those who find a pattern behind the fluctuations of the visible world, and rejoices in the strength that comes from rural solitude:

> Already I begin to call
> In their most learned Original:
> And where I Language want, my Signs
> The Bird upon the Bough divines;
> And more attentive there doth sit
> Then if She were with Lime-twigs knit.
> No Leaf does tremble in the Wind
> Which I returning cannot find.
>
> Out of these scatter'd *Sibyls* Leaves
> Strange *Prophecies* my Phancy weaves:
> And in one History consumes,
> Like *Mexique Paintings*, all the *Plumes*.

> What *Rome, Greece, Palestine*, ere said
> I in this light *Mosaick* read.
> Thrice happy he who, not mistook,
> Hath read in *Natures mystick Book*.
>   . . .
> How safe, methinks, and strong, behind
> These Trees have I incamp'd my Mind;
> Where Beauty, aiming at the Heart,
> Bends in some Tree its useless Dart;
> And where the World no certain Shot
> Can make, or me it toucheth not.
> But I on it securely play,
> And gaul its Horsemen all the Day.
> (569–584; 601–608)

There follow stanzas that combine a formal compliment to Mary Fairfax with a description of nightfall.

> The modest *Halcyon* comes in sight
> Flying betwixt the Day and Night;
> And such an horror calm and dumb,
> *Admiring Nature* does benum.
>
> The viscous Air, wheres' ere She fly,
> Follows and sucks her Azure dy;
> The gellying Stream compacts below,
> If it might fix her shadow so;
> The stupid Fishes hang, as plain
> As *Flies* in *Chrystal* overt'ane;
> And Men the silent *Scene* assist,
> Charm'd with the *Saphir-winged Mist*.
>
> *Maria* such, and so doth hush
> *The World*, and through the *Ev'ning* rush
> (669–682)

After the praise of Mary Fairfax is concluded, this brilliant poem draws to its close with the conceit about the salmon fishers, and with a final couplet that reinforces our sense of having traversed a world of rich sensual experience, now subject to the dark:

> Let's in: for the dark *Hemisphere*
> Does now like one of them appear.
> (775–776)

"The Garden," though it is shorter and less widely ranging than "Upon Appleton House," is at once the most sensuous and the most philosophical of all Marvell's poems. Its concealed puns, tantalizing ambiguities, and metaphysical complexity have given rise in recent years to many learned commentaries. Scholars have minutely investigated the sources and the precise connotation of the images that Marvell employs with such certainty and lyrical resonance—the bird waving its plumes, the melon, the garden itself; while the single word "green" (a favorite of Marvell's) has been interpreted by reference to Renaissance color symbolism, hermetic speculation, and medieval Neoplatonism, though in this context it is almost certainly meant to conjure up associations of freshness and innocence. Yet for all the latent word-play and subtle undertones that mold and color the poem, its central theme is clearly defined.

After deprecating human ambition, Marvell launches into the praise of woodland solitude, contrasting the green of plants and trees with the emblematic colors of female beauty, white and red:

> No white nor red was ever seen
> So am'rous as this lovely green.
> (17–18)

Even the god's pursuit of Daphne and Syrinx has as its true end their metamorphosis into laurel and reed.

Then follow three stanzas, which bring together the poem's leading motifs:

> What wond'rous Life in this I lead!
> Ripe Apples drop about my head;
> The Luscious Clusters of the Vine
> Upon my Mouth do crush their Wine;
> The Nectaren, and curious Peach,
> Into my hands themselves do reach;
> Stumbling on Melons, as I pass,
> Insnar'd with Flow'rs, I fall on Grass.
>
> Mean while the Mind, from pleasure less,
> Withdraws into its happiness;
> The Mind, that Ocean where each kind
> Does streight its own resemblance find;
> Yet it creates, transcending these,
> Far other Worlds, and other Seas;
> Annihilating all that's made
> To a green Thought in a green Shade.[3]
>
> Here at the Fountains sliding foot,
> Or at some Fruit-trees mossy-root,
> Casting the Bodies Vest aside,
> My Soul into the boughs does glide:

> There like a Bird it sits, and sings,
> Then whets, and combs its silver Wings;
> And, till prepar'd for longer flight,
> Waves in its Plumes the various Light.
> (33–48)

In this paradisal garden, Woman being absent, even the Fall is innocent, as the contemplative soul prepares for its flight toward God.

Finally, after the rapt vision of these stanzas, Marvell returns again to the garden where Woman is excluded but where the industrious bee, symbol of social order, computes Time, which is itself dependent on the living flowers woven into that sophisticated invention of man, the floral sundial:

> How well the skilful Gardner drew
> Of flow'rs and herbes this Dial new;
> Where from above the milder Sun
> Does through a fragrant Zodiack run;
> And, as it works, th' industrious Bee
> Computes its time as well as we.
> How could such sweet and wholsome Hours
> Be reckon'd but with herbs and flow'rs!
> (65–72)

Less brilliant and ingenious than "Upon Appleton House," "The Garden" has a sustained piety and gravity, a perfectly controlled sensuous melody and a profound yet delicate wit that Marvell never surpassed. If indeed "The Garden" was composed at Appleton House and was the last poem he wrote before quitting the Fairfax household for the "uncessant labours" of public life, it was a worthy farewell.

VIII

ALTHOUGH Marvell insisted that there was no place for Woman in the garden, he wrote two love poems of the highest quality, one of which celebrates with passionate conviction the power and ardor of physical desire. Yet even in "To His Coy Mistress," Marvell's customary wit and intellectual control do not desert him, the poem unfolding with the rigorous exactitude of a medieval syllogism. It opens with a quiet, conversational remark:

> Had we but World enough, and Time,
> This coyness Lady were no crime.

[3]Margoliouth's note brings out the ambiguity of this couplet: "either 'reducing the whole material world to nothing material, i.e. to a green thought,' or 'considering the whole material world as of no value compared to a green thought.'"

In a series of extravagant conceits the lover assures his mistress that he would prolong his courtship indefinitely,

> And you should if you please refuse
> Till the Conversion of the *Jews*
>
> (9–10)

which, according to ancient tradition, would take place immediately before the end of the world. Then follows the second movement of the poem which, though logically inevitable, achieves a sharp surprise by its change of tone:

> But at my back I alwaies hear
> Times winged Charriot hurrying near:
> And yonder all before us lye
> Desarts of vast Eternity.
> Thy Beauty shall no more be found;
> Nor, in thy marble Vault, shall sound
> My ecchoing Song: then Worms shall try
> That long preserv'd Virginity:
> And your quaint Honour turn to dust;
> And into ashes all my Lust.
> The Grave's a fine and private place,
> But none I think do there embrace.
>
> (21–32)

Finally, the lover demands that he and his mistress should enjoy what John Donne calls "the right true end of love"; yet despite the uncompromising sexuality of the lines quoted above and of the imagery in the poem's concluding lines, Marvell has invested the old classical commonplace of carpe diem with an intensity and a nobility that seem to affirm the triumph of love over time, in the teeth of the evidence:

> Let us roll all our Strength, and all
> Our sweetness, up into one Ball:
> And tear our Pleasures with rough strife,
> Through the Iron gates of Life.
> Thus, though we cannot make our Sun
> Stand still, yet we will make him run.
>
> (41–46)

"The Definition of Love," though far less sensuous than "To His Coy Mistress," conveys with equal force the longing of two lovers to be united:

> And yet I quickly might arrive
> Where my extended Soul is fixt,

> But Fate does Iron wedges drive,
> And alwaies crouds it self betwixt.
>
> (9–12)

By means of geometrical and astronomical images Marvell develops the paradox that the lovers' separation is a proof of their spiritual correspondence, and a guarantee of their spiritual union:

> As Lines so Loves *oblique* may well
> Themselves in every Angle greet:
> But ours so truly *Paralel*,
> Though infinite can never meet.
>
> Therefore the Love which us doth bind,
> But Fate so enviously debarrs,
> Is the Conjunction of the Mind,
> And Opposition of the Stars.
>
> (25–32)

"The Picture of Little T. C. in a Prospect of Flowers," differing as it does in theme and tone from the love poems, reminds us that fate and death shatter the most innocent dreams of youthful love. Little T. C., "this Darling of the Gods," plays among the flowers, courted by nature, aware only of life. In the third stanza Marvell introduces the image of the shade:

> Let me be laid,
> Where I may see thy Glories from some shade
>
> (23–24)

as though to prepare for the sudden turn of the poem in the final stanza, where the shadow of death falls upon this Arcady:

> But O young beauty of the Woods,
> Whom Nature courts with fruits and flow'rs,
> Gather the Flow'rs, but spare the Buds;
> Lest *Flora* angry at thy crime,
> To kill her Infants in their prime,
> Do quickly make th' Example Yours;
>   And, ere we see,
> Nip in the blossome all our hopes and Thee.[4]
>
> (33–40)

There is still much controversy about the significance of "The Nymph Complaining for the

---

[4]If T. C. is Theophila Cornewall, these lines take on an added poignancy, for she was named after an elder sister who died in infancy.

Death of Her Faun." To regard it as the lament of an Anglican for his stricken church, or as a conscious allegory of the church's love for Christ crucified, borders on the improbable: this is not to deny that there are in it unmistakable references to *The Song of Songs* or that Marvell allowed these symbolic overtones to deepen the poem's imaginative richness and to enlarge its range. Overtly and primarily, it remains the lament of a young girl for a fawn given to her by a faithless lover. The rhythm, the diction, and the imagery are so dramatically appropriate that many readers will be content to accept the poem at its face value or, if they feel compelled to probe for a hidden meaning, may find in it a lamentation for love destroyed, not by time, fate, or death, but by the sinful inconstancy of man.

IX

MARVELL, though a sensual and religious man, did not, like Crashaw, explore the relation between divine and erotic love, for such a procedure would have been repugnant to his fastidious temperament even if it had not run counter to his doctrinal beliefs. He was indeed acutely aware of the conflicts between the warring impulses within himself, two of his dialogues being variations on this theme. In one of them, "A Dialogue Between the Resolved Soul, and Created Pleasure," the soul wins the battle a shade too easily, the Chorus celebrating the victory with an operatic flourish:

> *Triumph, triumph, victorious Soul;*
> *The World has not one Pleasure more:*
> *The rest does lie beyond the Pole,*
> *And is thine everlasting Store.*
>
> (75–78)

The scales are poised more evenly in "A Dialogue Between the Soul and Body," which opens with the complaint of the soul:

> O who shall, from this Dungeon, raise
> A Soul inslav'd so many wayes?
> With bolts of Bones, that fetter'd stands
> In Feet; and manacled in Hands.
> Here blinded with an Eye; and there
> Deaf with the drumming of an Ear.
>
> (1–6)

Yet the body, which rebels against the even more insidious tyranny of the soul, is granted the last word:

> What but a Soul could have the wit
> To build me up for Sin so fit?
> So Architects do square and hew,
> Green Trees that in the Forest grew.
>
> (41–44)

One commentator on this poem has challenged the conventional view that it is deeply rooted in Christian theology, and has accused Marvell of displaying a callous, vicious cynicism and a "deliberate indifferentism" to the problems of existence.[5] There can be no disputing the fact that in the most moving of all his religious poems Marvell unequivocally renounces the subtlest lures of the world, sacrificing even the long cherished illusion that his poems are garlands woven for Christ's head, and acknowledging that the Serpent lies hidden there. "The Coronet" invites comparison with George Herbert's "The Collar" in the exactitude with which its fluctuating rhythm mirrors the twists and turns of the recalcitrant spirit, in the harmonious progression of its imagery, and in the unaffected humility and grace of the poet's final surrender to God:

> But thou who only could'st the Serpent tame,
> Either his slipp'ry Knots at once untie,
> And disentangle all his winding Snare:
> Or shatter too with him my curious frame:
> And let these wither, so that he may die,
> Though set with Skill, and chosen out with Care.
> That they, while Thou on both their Spoils dost tread,
> May crown thy Feet, that could not crown thy Head.
>
> (19–26)

X

"An Horatian Ode upon Cromwel's Return from Ireland," presumably written in the early summer of 1650, was one of the three Cromwell poems that have been canceled by the printer in all but two surviving copies of the 1681 edition of the *Miscellaneous Poems*. This alone casts grave doubts upon the modern supposition that it is a royalist poem, though the mere fact that reputable scholars can put

[5]A. Birrell in *The Downside Review*, 73 (1952), p. 232.

forward this hypothesis is a tribute to the extraordinary balance that Marvell preserved in the greatest of his political verses.

In 1672 Marvell wrote of the Civil War:

I think the cause was too good to have been fought for. . . . For men may spare their pains where nature is at work, and the world will not go the faster for our driving. Even as his present Majestie's happy Restoration did it self, so all things else happen in their best and proper time, without any need of our officiousness.

A similar recognition of historical necessity informs the "Ode," enabling Marvell to pay tribute to Charles I's serene courage upon the scaffold, and yet to acknowledge that his blood had to flow before new order could be created out of chaotic violence:

> He nothing common did or mean
> Upon that memorable Scene:
>   But with his keener Eye
>   The Axes edge did try:
> Nor call'd the *Gods* with vulgar spight
> To vindicate his helpless Right,
>   But bow'd his comely Head,
>   Down as upon a Bed.
> This was that memorable Hour
> Which first assur'd the forced Pow'r.
>   So when they did design
>   The *Capitols* first Line,
> A bleeding Head where they begun,
> Did fright the Architects to run;
>   And yet in that the *State*
> Foresaw it's happy Fate.
>   (57–72)

Marvell speaks of Cromwell with a kind of horrified awe, as if he were a destructive aspect of nature, like three-forked lightning:

> Then burning through the Air he went,
> And Pallaces and Temples rent.
>   (21–22)

So, in Marvell's eyes, all the ruthless, destructive acts of Cromwell—the trapping of Charles at Carisbrooke, the massacre of the Irish, the coming subjugation of the Scots—are justified, because he is the product of fate:

> But thou the Wars and Fortunes Son
> March indefatigably on;
>   (113–114)

and because, like a falcon, he remains obedient to England, the falconer.

The puns, ironies, and ambiguities that give this ode its peculiar tension cease to be puzzling once we understand how deeply all are imbued with Marvell's exultant sense of religious destiny that finds so perfect an expression in the weighty grandeur of the poem's meter and language.

Of the remaining poems written during the Commonwealth only "Bermudas" recaptures the impassioned vision of a divinely ordered society living in harmony with itself.[6] The other two Cromwell poems, for all their energy and formal splendor, reveal a sense of strain, even of desperation, as if Marvell were aware that between England and chaos there stood only Cromwell, depicted as a cross between a Hebrew warrior-statesman and a Neoplatonic mythological hero. By 1658 Marvell was moving away from the beautifully poised assurance of the earlier poems to the reiterated bludgeoning violence of the post-Restoration satires.

XI

Scholars still disagree about which of the satires attributed to Marvell are in fact by him, and it is unwise to be dogmatic about their authorship. Opinions also differ about the merits of those satires that are probably authentic: it is possible to argue that they do not represent a sad decline in Marvell's genius; but once we have allowed that they possess the rollicking vigor of good street ballads and a certain rough effectiveness we have said almost all there is to be said in their favor. The lines on young Douglas' death, and the setpiece on the vision of England that appears to Charles II (both in "The Last Instructions to a Painter") glow with something of Marvell's former ardor:

> Like a glad Lover, the fierce Flames he meets,
> And tries his first embraces in their Sheets.
> His shape exact, which the bright flames infold,
> Like the Sun's Statue stands of burnish'd Gold.
> Round the transparent Fire about him glows,
> As the clear Amber on the Bee does close:
> And, as on Angels Heads their Glories shine,
> His burning Locks adorn his Face Divine.
>   (677–684)

---

[6]It had taken a Cromwellian fleet in 1651 to convert the colony to the Puritan cause.

Paint last the King, and a dead shade of Night,
Only dispers'd by a weak Tapers light;
And those bright gleams that dart along and glare
From his clear Eyes, yet these too dark with Care.
There, as in the calm horrour all alone,
He wakes and Muses of th' uneasie Throne:
Raise up a sudden Shape with Virgins Face,
Though ill agree her Posture, Hour, or Place:
Naked as born, and her round Arms behind,
With her own Tresses interwove and twin'd:
Her mouth lock't up, a blind before her Eyes,
Yet from beneath the Veil her blushes rise;
And silent tears her secret anguish speak,
Her heart throbs, and with very shame would break.

(885–898)

More typical of the satires are the following passages, one taken from "The Statue in Stocks-Market," describing Sir Robert Viner's statue of Charles II, and one from "A Dialogue Between the Two Horses":

But Sir Robert affirms we do him much wrong;
For the graver's at work to reform him thus long.
But alas! he will never arrive at his end,
For 'tis such a king as no chisel can mend.

(53–56)

More Tolerable are the Lion Kings Slaughters
Than the Goats making whores of our wives and
    our daughters.
The Debauch'd and the Bloody since they Equally Gall us,
I had rather Bare Nero than Sardanapalus,

(131–134)

The satires are, like *The Rehearsal Transpros'd*, larded with crude jokes about vomiting, bodily functions, and venereal disease; and spiced with wild accusations of secret crimes and unnatural vice. Unlike Dryden and Pope, who are equally obscene but who contrive by sheer energy and artifice to transcend their dirtiness, Marvell all too frequently gets stuck in his own filth. The fact seems to be that as he grew older Marvell, for reasons that we can only conjecture, suffered an emotional or even a physiological coarsening that betrays itself in the very rhythms of his later poetry.

Yet Marvell himself might have believed the price worth paying in order to safeguard the liberties of England. All the poems published in his lifetime sprang from a desire to celebrate a public occasion, pay tribute to a friend, or attack a specific evil, the later satires conforming precisely to Marvell's con-ception of the poet's task as defined in "Tom May's Death":

When the Sword glitters ore the Judges head,
And fear has Coward Churchmen silencèd,
Then is the Poets time, 'tis then he drawes,
And single fights forsaken Vertues cause.
He, when the wheel of Empire, whirleth back,
And though the World's disjointed Axel crack,
Sings still of ancient Rights and better Times,
Seeks wretched good, arraigns successful Crimes.

(63–70)

Marvell's lonely and perilous opposition to Charles II's government matches in faith and courage the defiant gesture of the cavalier Sir Robert Shirley, whose epitaph in Staunton Harold Church records that

in the year 1653, when all things sacred were throughout the nation either demollisht or profaned, Sir Robert Shirley baronet founded this church, whose singular praise it is to have done the best things in the worst times, and hoped them in the most calamitous.

Even if it is true that Marvell's place in English literature is secure only because he wrote a handful of lyrics that display an intuitive moral and aesthetic certainty as rare as the perfection of their phrasing, to concentrate on them alone would be to distort Marvell's true image. The dusty political and religious causes for which he labored in the last twenty years of his life, although to us they may seem not worth the devotion he gave them, were to Marvell of supreme importance. Had he cared less passionately for things other than poetry, his verse might have lacked the urgency, the gravity, and the resolute dignity that lend it so fine a distinction. Little as we may concern ourselves with the quarrels of seventeenth-century Englishmen, and with the part that Marvell played in them, we shall find that a lively sympathy for the aspirations of the Puritan and the patriot will help us to understand more fully the achievement and the stature of the poet.

SELECTED BIBLIOGRAPHY

I. BIBLIOGRAPHY. P. Legouis, *André Marvell: poète, puritain, patriote, 1621–1678* (Paris—London, 1928), contains a full, annotated bibliography including a list of prose works attributed to Marvell; D. G. Donovan, *An-*

drew Marvell, 1927–1967 (London, 1969), one of the Elizabethan Bibliographies Supplements; G. R. Guffey, *A Concordance to the English Poems of Andrew Marvell* (Chapel Hill, N. C., 1974); H. Kelliher, comp., *Andrew Marvell: Poet and Politician, 1621–1678* (London, 1978), the catalog of the exhibition at the British Library in 1978 to mark the three-hundredth anniversary of Marvell's death, an excellent survey of his career.

II. Collected and Selected Works. *Miscellaneous Poems* (London, 1681), in all but two recorded copies the three Cromwell poems have been canceled; one of these copies, preserved in the British Museum, contains "An Horatian Ode," "The First Anniversary," and "A Poem upon the Death of O.C.," lines 1–184; a reprint of the British Museum copy was published in a limited ed. by the Nonesuch Press (London, 1923); T. Cooke, ed., *The Works*, 2 vols. (London, 1726; reiss. 1772), contains the 1681 poems, State Poems, the Greek and the Latin poems in honor of Princess Anne's birth, a short life of Marvell, and a few letters; E. Thompson, ed., *The Works*, 3 vols. (London, 1776), contains all the letters and poems of Cooke's ed., some new poems and satires, a life, the bulk of the *Corporation Letters*, and a few private letters—a completely uncritical ed., containing poems that are certainly not by Marvell; A. B. Grosart, ed., *The Works*, 4 vols. (Blackburn, 1872–1875), vols. I and II (*Poems* and *Letters*) have been superseded by Margoliouth, but vols. III and IV are the only available collection of Marvell's prose writings, in the Fuller Worthies' Library; E. Wright, ed., *Poems and Satires* (London, 1904); H. M. Margoliouth, ed., *Poems and Letters*, 2 vols. (Oxford, 1927; 2nd ed., 1952), vol. I: *Poems*, vol. II: *Letters*, the definitive ed., in the Oxford English Texts series, second ed. contains additional notes; D. Davison, ed., *Selected Poetry and Prose* (London, 1952), contains most of the poetry and a little of the prose, a valuable intro. by Davison; H. Macdonald, ed., *The Poems* (London, 1952), a reprint of the unique British Museum copy of the 1681 ed., with some additional poems, in the Muses' Library, superseding the original Muses' Library ed. in 2 vols., edited by H. Aitken (London, 1892); W. A. McQueen and K. A. Rockwell, *The Latin Poetry of Andrew Marvell* (Chapel Hill, N. C., 1964); F. Kermode, ed., *Selected Poetry* (New York, 1967); G. de F. Lord, ed., *Complete Poetry* (New York, 1968); D. I. B. Smith, ed., *The Rehearsal Transpros'd and The Rehearsal Transpros'd, the Second Part* (Oxford, 1971); E. S. Donno, ed., *The Complete Poems* (Harmondsworth, 1972), reissued as *The Complete English Poems* (London, 1974).

III. Separate Works. *An Elegy upon the Death of My Lord Francis Villiers* (London, 1648), verse, undated and unique copy is at Worcester College, Oxford; see Margoliouth, vol. I, pp. 432–436, for reasons for believing it to be by Marvell; *The Character of Holland* (London, 1665), verse, appeared anonymously; *The Rehearsal Transpros'd . . .* (London, 1672), prose, appeared anonymously, probably printed in London; *The Rehearsal Transpros'd: The Second Part . . .* (London, 1673), prose; *Mr. Smirke: or, The Divine in Mode . . .* (London, 1677), prose, appeared anonymously; *A Short Historical Essay . . .* (London, 1677), prose; *An Account of the Growth of Popery and Arbitrary Government in England . . .* (Amsterdam, 1677), prose, appeared anonymously; *Remarks Upon a Late Disingenuous Discourse . . .* (London, 1678), prose, appeared anonymously.

IV. Some Biographical and Critical Studies. J. Dove, *The Life of Andrew Marvell . . .* (London, 1832); A. Birrell, *Andrew Marvell* (London, 1905), in the English Men of Letters series; P. Legouis, *André Marvell: poète, puritain, patriote, 1621–1678* (Paris—London, 1928), a masterly biographical and critical survey, abridged English version (London, 1965); V. Sackville-West, *Andrew Marvell* (London, 1929).

G. Williamson, *The Donne Tradition* (Oxford, 1930); W. Empson, *Seven Types of Ambiguity* (London, 1930); T. S. Eliot, *Selected Essays* (London, 1932), contains "The Metaphysical Poets" and "Andrew Marvell"; F. R. Leavis, ed., *Determinations* (London, 1934), contains W. Empson, "Marvell's Garden," and J. Smith, "On Metaphysical Poetry"; W. Empson, *Some Versions of Pastoral* (London, 1935); F. R. Leavis, *Revaluation* (London, 1936), contains an important essay, "The Line of Wit."

R. L. Sharp, *From Donne to Dryden: The Revolt Against Metaphysical Poetry* (Chapel Hill, N.C., 1940); M. C. Bradbrook and M. G. Lloyd Thomas, *Andrew Marvell* (Cambridge, 1940; repr. with corrections, 1961), a scholarly and original study full of stimulating critical observations, an excellent suppl. to Legouis; D. Bush, *English Literature in the Earlier Seventeenth Century, 1600–1660* (Oxford, 1945; 2nd ed., 1962).

R. Wallerstein, *Studies in Seventeenth-Century Poetic* (Madison, Wisc., 1950), a learned and authoritative study of the seventeenth-century philosophical background, contains discussion of Marvell's poetry and elaborate analyses of individual poems, a work of great importance; P. Cruttwell, *The Shakespearean Moment* (London, 1954); G. Walton, *Metaphysical to Augustan* (Cambridge, 1955); J. Wain, ed., *Interpretations* (London, 1955), contains L. D. Lerner's "Andrew Marvell: 'An Horation Ode upon Cromwel's Return from Ireland'"; C. Hill, *Puritanism and Revolution: Studies in Interpretation of the English Revolution of the 17th Century* (London, 1958), contains "Society and Andrew Marvell," which first appeared in *Modern Quarterly*, I, no. 4 (1946).

J. V. Cunningham, *Tradition and Poetic Structure* (Denver, 1960), contains a chapter on Marvell; C. V. Wedgwood, *Poetry and Politics under the Stuarts* (Cambridge, 1960); A. Alvarez, *The School of Donne* (London, 1961), contains a chapter on Marvell; J. Hollander, *The Untuning of the Sky: Ideas of Music in English Poetry,*

1500–1700 (London, 1961); J. A. Mazzeo, ed., *Reason and the Imagination* (London, 1962), contains Mazzeo's essay "Cromwell as Davidic King"; M-S. Røstvig, *The Happy Man: Studies in the Metamorphosis of a Classical Ideal, 1600–1700* (Oslo, 1962), a revised ed. of a work first published in 1954; H. R. Swardson, *Poetry and the Fountain of Light* (London, 1962), contains a chapter on Marvell; J. B. Leishman, *Some Themes and Variations in the Poetry of Andrew Marvell* (London, 1963), the British Academy Warton lecture, 1961; J. Bennett, *Five Metaphysical Poets* (Cambridge, 1964), a revised ed. of *Four Metaphysical Poets* (1934) with an additional chapter on Marvell; D. Davison, *The Poetry of Andrew Marvell* (London, 1964), a brief but admirable discussion of the poetry; L. W. Hyman, *Andrew Marvell* (New York, 1964); P. Legouis, *Andrew Marvell: Poet, Puritan, Patriot, 1621–1678* (Oxford, 1965), an abridged version in English by Legouis of his great work of 1928, incorporates and gives references for the large mass of Marvell scholarship produced since the mid-1920's; K. M. Scoular, *Natural Magic: Studies in the Presentation of Nature in English Poetry from Spenser to Marvell* (Oxford, 1965), contains the chapter "Upon Appleton House"; H. E. Toliver, *Marvell's Ironic Vision* (New Haven, 1965); J. B. Leishman, *The Art of Marvell's Poetry* (London, 1966; 2nd ed., 1968), an erudite study of Marvell's nonsatirical poems; J. M. Wallace, *Destiny His Choice: The Loyalism of Andrew Marvell* (Cambridge, 1968), an analysis of Marvell's political attitudes; G. de F. Lord, ed., *Andrew Marvell: A Collection of Critical Essays* (Englewood Cliffs, N. J., 1968); J. Carey, ed., *Andrew Marvell: A Critical Anthology* (Harmondsworth, 1969), an excellent collection that reprints important articles in full or in part, and extracts from full-length studies, intros., and other editorial material are admirable; M. Wilding, *Marvell: Modern Judgements* (London, 1969), a collection of recent critical essays.

A. E. Berthoff, *The Resolved Soul: A Study of Marvell's Major Poems* (Princeton, 1970); R. L. Colie, *"My Ecchoing Song": Andrew Marvell's Poetry of Criticism* (Princeton, 1970); P. Cullen, *Spenser, Marvell, and Renaissance Pastoral* (Cambridge, Mass., 1970); D. M. Friedman, *Marvell's Pastoral Art* (London, 1970); C. Ricks, ed., *English Poetry and Prose, 1540–1674* (London, 1970), vol. II of the Sphere *History of Literature in the English Language*, contains M-S. Røstvig's "Andrew Marvell and the Caroline Poets"; E. Duncan-Jones, *A Great Master of Words: Some Aspects of Marvell's Poems of Praise and Blame* (London, 1976), the British Academy Warton lecture, 1975, by a fine Marvell scholar; B. King, *Marvell's Allegorical Poetry* (Cambridge, 1977); A. M. Patterson, *Marvell and the Civic Crown* (Guildford, 1978); E. S. Donno, ed., *Andrew Marvell: The Critical Heritage* (London, 1978), the intro. surveys the development of Marvell's reputation down to the present day, the main body of the book is devoted to the reprinting of critical judgments on Marvell, starting with those of his contemporaries and ending with T. S. Eliot's; R. I. Hodge, *Foreshortened Time: Andrew Marvell and Seventeenth-Century Revolutions* (Ipswich, 1978); J. D. Hunt, *Andrew Marvell: His Life and Writings* (London, 1978), a biographical study of Marvell, with many illustrations; K. Friedenreich, ed., *Tercentenary Essays in Honor of Andrew Marvell* (Hamden, Conn., 1978); C. A. Patrides, ed., *Approaches to Marvell: The York Tercentenary Lectures* (London, 1978), contributors include distinguished scholars from Britain, continental Europe, the United States, and Canada.

THE CAVALIER POETS

Robin Skelton

INTRODUCTION

THE lyrical poet in the reign of Elizabeth I was not very much concerned with actuality. His job was to make delightful verbal patterns filled with ideal sentiments, and, very frequently, addressed to some impossibly chaste and beautiful lady. She, turning a deaf ear to all his protestations, could be relied upon to accept some suitable gift from time to time, or to rouse him to ecstasies of happiness by a word of encouragement, or plunge him into despair with a frown. Of course this caricature is hardly fair; the better poets saw that there was more in lyrical poetry than this. Shakespeare rebelled in one sonnet to the extent of admitting that "My Mistress's eyes are nothing like the sun," and even Sir Philip Sidney went so far as to end one mellifluous complaint with an accusation of ingratitude. Sir Walter Ralegh, Ben Jonson, and others, too, made vital poetry from the Petrarchan convention, and managed to give their readers an impression that something of real importance was going on. Nevertheless, even their poetry often had an air of existing largely because they enjoyed being ingenious in compliment, witty in description, and musical in speech.

There can be no objection to this. It is a poor heart that never rejoiceth, and it would be stupidly puritanical to object to a poem because it was beautiful and ingenious but little else. Still, once the poetry of an age becomes simply an exercise in the purely decorative use of language, trouble is bound to occur. Someone is going to try to go further.

John Donne was not alone in trying to make lyrical poetry have a more direct impact, but he was the most successful of the rebels. He could rebel because he, unlike many of the previous generation, did not think of lyrical poetry as being either in a formal Petrarchan sonnet tradition, or as being accompanied by music. Donne was philosophical, but it isn't his introduction of rugged thinking into the lyrical tradition that must delay us now so much as his introduction of a new tone of voice. He threw aside the implication of "high poetic style" that a poet is a special kind of person with a special vocabulary and sensitivity, and wrote with colloquial directness. By so doing he gave his lyrics a highly personal tone; you could feel that it was not the representative of an aesthetic master race but a quite ordinary, though obviously intelligent, man who cried "For God's sake hold your tongue, and let me love," or who said, simply and directly, "Sweetest love I do not go, For weariness of thee." It could be said now that the poem became moving and pleasing largely because of the reader's or hearer's sense of an individual personality behind it.

This personality was, in Donne's case and in the case of George Herbert, Henry Vaughan, Henry King, and the other metaphysicals, just as ingenious as the more corporate personality of the contributors to the Elizabethan song books, but it was ingenious with a difference. Instead of feeling that the surprising comparisons and the bizarre metaphors are purely decorative, we feel that they have arisen naturally from the pressure of the poet's passionate intelligence. Obsessed with his situation, his ideas become as powerful and disturbed as his feelings; the passionate heart and the formidable intelligence cannot be divorced from one another. We hear, indeed, the accents of the complete man, concerned to explore, by way of his poetry, all that most interests and disturbs him. When Herbert writes of a "rope of sands" we know that this perception is at the heart of him. When Donne writes:

> Only our love hath no decay:
> This no to-morrow hath nor yesterday;
> Running, it never runs from us away,
> But truly keeps his first, last, everlasting day,

we feel that the riddling complexity is born of intense personal feeling.

It is a far cry from the exquisite prosody of Thomas Campion, the elegance of Sidney, or even that of Jonson, who, though tolerably ingenious at times and even crudely forthright, so often gives us the impression that his lyrics are a leisure activity, like writing letters or taking a sketch pad out on Sundays. Indeed, Jonson has several verse letters to his friends which have just that air of happy improvisation and enjoyment of ingenuity which one might expect. Donne wrote verse letters too, and many of his poems also seem casual products, but he can never avoid a passionate statement. Every conversation is a manifesto with Donne, even if it is one about the general advantages of having more than one mistress. There is none of that affectionate ease of speech, that elegance, of which Jonson is a master.

Though the cavalier poets only occasionally imitated the strenuous intellectual conceits of Donne and his followers, and were fervent admirers of Jonson's elegance, they took care to learn from both parties. In fact, reading the work of Thomas Carew, Sir John Suckling, Richard Lovelace, Lord Herbert of Cherbury (elder brother of George), Aurelian Townsend, William Cartwright, Thomas Randolph, William Habington, Sir Richard Fanshawe, Edmund Waller, and the marquess of Montrose, it is easy to see that they each owe something to both styles. The common factor that binds the cavaliers together is their use of direct and colloquial language, expressive of a highly individual personality, and their enjoyment of the casual, the amateur, the affectionate poem written by the way. They are cavalier in the sense not only of being royalists (though Waller changed sides twice) but in the sense that they distrust the overearnest, the too intense. They accept the ideal of the Renaissance gentleman, who is at once lover, soldier, wit, man of affairs, musician, and poet, but abandon the notion of his also being a pattern of Christian chivalry. They avoid the subject of religion, apart from making one or two graceful speeches. They attempt no plumbing of the depths of the soul. They treat life cavalierly, indeed, and sometimes they treat poetic conventions cavalierly too. For them life is far too enjoyable for much of it to be spent sweating over verse in a study. Their poems must be written in the intervals of living, and are celebratory of things that are much livelier than mere philosophy or art. A mistress is no longer an impossibly chaste goddess to be wooed with sighs, but a woman who may be spoken to in a forthright fashion. Though the poems written to her may be more important to the writer than she is herself, there is no pretense that this is not the case. Poetry need not be a matter of earnest emotion or public concern. Dick might like to have a ballad, so Dick gets one. Lady X gave an admirable party, and so here is a thank-you poem. On the other hand, a wedding or a funeral deserves a line or two. And why not upbraid a girl for her coldness or point out to a young man that the world won't end simply because he has been jilted?

It may all sound rather trivial, and much of it no doubt is; but the cavaliers made one great contribution to the English lyrical tradition. They showed us that it was possible for poetry to celebrate the minor pleasures and sadnesses of life in such a way as to impress us with a sense of ordinary day-to-day humanity, busy about its affairs, and, on the whole, enjoying them very much.

THOMAS CAREW
(ca. 1595–1639)

THOMAS CAREW was the son of Sir Matthew Carew. He was educated at Merton College, Oxford, and received his bachelor of arts in 1611. For about a year he studied law in the Middle Temple, and from 1613 to 1615 he acted as secretary to Sir Dudley Carleton, the ambassador to Italy. Carew was a favorite of Charles I and was notorious for his dissipation. His masque, *Coelum Britannicum*, was performed in the banquet hall at Whitehall in February 1634. He died in 1639.

Carew's life is not untypical of the cavaliers. He was a courtier, a wit, a rake, in casual employment as an aide to traveling diplomats. His masque, *Coelum Britannicum*, appeared in 1634, but otherwise only ten of his poems reached print during his lifetime, and all were commendatory verses attached to someone else's book. This is not an infrequent situation in the seventeenth century, but it indicates that the poet could not be very much concerned with the public value or reception of his works. Manuscripts were, of course, circulated; the poet's friends and patrons read them and commented upon them; reputations were made in the small literary and court circles, where verses were always a social asset, indicating that the man concerned had a certain intelligence, education, and wit. Carew was very highly valued. His wit was loved by Aurelian Townsend and by Thomas Randolph; Lord Herbert called him "that excellent wit," and "my witty Carew"; Sir William Davenant concurred, finding his verses "smooth." Others wagged a minatory finger at his loose living, but did not fail to admit his excellence as a lyricist.

Carew himself was clearly aware of his own poetic character. Suckling tells us that he wrote with great care, and, indeed, with some pain. Carew reveals his interest in his craft in his "Elegie upon the Death of . . . Dr. John Donne," in which he praised his "deepe knowledge of dark truth," his "Giant phansie," and "imperious wit," and said:

> Thou hast redeem'd and open'd Us a Mine
> Of rich and pregnant phansie, drawne a line
> Of masculine expression. . . .

One can see traces of Donne in his poems. The elaborate conceits are now a mere decorative grace rather than a passionate thought. Nevertheless the masculine note is striking. Where earlier poets implied an abandonment to sensual pleasure that was almost entirely passive—the receiving of a divine sanction and an overwhelming sacrament—Carew describes sexual "rapture" in active and impulsive terms. He does not adopt the rough accents of the young Donne, however, but the classical vocabulary of the learned Jonson, for Jonson, whose "terser Poems" he admires, is another of his masters.

> I will enjoy thee now my *Celia*, come
> And flye with me to Loves Elizium:
> That Gyant, Honour, that keepes cowards out,
> Is but a Masquer.
>
> ("A Rapture")

The ensuing lines with their high spirits and witty use of sexual imagery retain the masculine fervor, without losing the fanciful dexterity. The consequence is that we feel Carew is greatly enjoying his poem and kicking over the moral traces; but we are not convinced that a real Celia is in question. Such poems are exercises in wit, which contrive, if not to sound sincere as expressions of emotion, to amuse us as accurate portrayals of masculine sexuality. They are vigorous, sensual, witty, and objective.

There is a sharp eye glinting from the carnival mask.

It is this sense of controlled and contrived passion which gives the poems their urbanity and poise. Indeed, passion is always to be suspected as a disguise for the less high-flown, but more intelligible, emotion of lust; the passionate statement is a lure or an amusement; affection is a more serious, because more balanced, emotion. Friendship and hospitality are as important to Carew as to Jonson, and the younger poet's "To Saxham" celebrates the "inward happiness" of the country house, with its good cheer and simplicity, with as sure a touch as his elder's "To Penshurst." The most important things in life are not hectic or hysterical, but based firmly upon old and well-tried values. It is not really as odd as one might at first suppose that Carew should write metrical versions of the psalms as well as amusing and wanton songs: the divine and the secular moods have each their place. There is no place, however, for pretentious affectation, and thus, when Carew imitates the pastoral eclogue, writes a complaint to his mistress for denying him her favors, or enjoys himself with a hyperbolic compliment, absurdity is never far away.

In "The Complement" he piles epithet upon epithet, each one more inventive than the last, in an effort to describe the beauty of his mistress, and then, just as we are beginning to believe that such a creature could hardly be expected to love in any earthly fashion, he introduces a sly double-entendre, an admission that all his words have only one purpose. The high rhetoric crumples. It is as much as to say "Fine words butter no parsnips; let us admit that a good deal of this is simply an elaborate disguise for a simple lust." Yet the poem ends with a curiously tender verse—a compound of conventional compliment, admitted as simply a tactic in the sex conflict, and an honest indication of affectionate admiration. The catalog of his mistress' attractions has become perfunctory and reveals itself as simply a device toward an end, but the dropping of the mask also gives us a hint of the real and tender smile behind the painted and professionally seductive one.

> I love not for those eyes, nor haire,
> Nor cheekes, nor lips, nor teeth so rare;
> Nor for thy speech, thy necke, nor breast,
> Nor for thy belly, nor the rest:
> Nor for thy hand, nor foote so small,
> But wouldst thou know (deere sweet) for all.

The last line, the culmination of so many verses, places the reader at last in a real human relationship. The poet has been teasing her, and now the joke is done.

This is an instance of the true cavalier tone—the careless ease, the humor, the subtle inflections of the voice. Carew is a master in this manner. "Epitaph on the Lady Mary Villers" makes use again of the revelatory last line. Here, after a series of conventional, though delicately balanced lines, in which direct address to the reader gives an effect of the poet's friendly intimacy, the final statement has an ambiguous ring:

> The Lady *Mary Villers* lyes
> Under this stone; with weeping eyes
> The Parents that first gave her birth,
> And their sad Friends, lay'd her in earth:
> If any of them (Reader) were
> Knowne unto thee, shed a teare,
> Or if thyselfe possesse a gemme,
> As deare to thee, as this to them,
> Though a stranger to this place,
> Bewayle in theirs, thine owne hard case;
> For thou perhaps at thy returne
> Mayest find thy Darling in an Urne.

The intimacy is broken. The wry humor is too obvious for the mask of pretended concern to conceal it. The friend that buttonholed you at the graveside is a damned odd fellow, insolent almost, if one could put one's finger on it.

Sometimes one can identify the insolence as a deliberate breaking of the rules of nice conduct, a controlled unexpectedness, which alters the mood of the poem completely. More frequently, however, it appears only as a part of Carew's general presentation of casual wit. In "Good Counsel to a Young Maid" two adjacent verses read:

> Love, that in those smooth streames lyes,
> Under pitties faire disguise,
> Will thy melting heart surprize.
>
> Netts, of passions finest thred,
> Snaring Poems, will be spred,
> All, to catch thy maiden-head.

This element of unexpectedness is, of course, a powerful aid to the giving of an impression of spontaneity; the surprise remark has the air of having just occurred to the mind of the speaker while he was in full flow. Nevertheless, few if any of Carew's poems lack an air of delighted contrivance which, at first sight, might seem to rule out any impression of spontaneity. We must distinguish, perhaps, between the artless spontaneity of the emotional, outpouring, overflowing heart and the sudden lucky "inspiration" of the quick intelligence. The romantics, generally speaking, aimed at moving us with the former; the cavaliers entertain us with the latter. Thus, while we accept the literary flavor and the self-conscious and self-mocking wit as evidence of a witty personality engaged in contriving something for his own (and incidentally our) entertainment, we also accept, in the same breath, the colloquial directness, the casual parentheses, and the sudden alterations of tone, as evidence that this adroit person is, after all, a man among men and inclined to be properly suspicious of too much formal attitudinizing. Sometimes he lets a careless arrogance, a take-it-or-leave-it attitude, appear just when we are expecting some sample of high seriousness. In other words, we are presented with an interesting, complex character and with a sense of insecurity.

Carew does his best to make us feel insecure. "To A. L." is a flawless specimen of aesthetic skating on thin ice. The poem's job is the traditional one of persuasion to love. We can expect the usual arguments derived from nature and classical mythology in favor of fruition. We can also expect from Carew a touch of impudence, possibly even a risqué joke or two. In fact we get a poem written in firm, colloquial octosyllabic couplets that begins with a direct and racy appeal to reason and self-interest.

> Thinke not cause men flatt'ring say,
> Y'are fresh as Aprill, sweet as May,
> Bright as is the morning starre,
> That you are so, or though you are
> Be not therefore proud, and deeme
> All men unworthy your esteeme.
> For being so, you loose the pleasure
> Of being faire. . . .
>   ("To A. L.")

The raciness and directness, however, do not increase as the poem gathers momentum. The illustrations of the argument are formal devices, and their conventional status is clearly admitted by the use of words that remind us of the no-nonsense beginning of the poem. For example:

For that lovely face will faile,
Beautie's sweet, but beautie's fraile;
'Tis sooner past, 'tis sooner done
Than Summers raine, or winters Sun:
Most fleeting when it is most deare,
'Tis gone while wee but say 'tis here.
These curious locks so aptly twined,
Whose every haire a soule doth bind,
Will change their abroun hue, and grow
White, and cold, as winters snow.
That eye which now is *Cupids* nest
Will proue his grave, and all the rest
Will follow; in the cheeke, chin, nose
Nor lilly shall be found nor rose.

Here the commonplace "cheeke, chin, nose" not only contrast with the "curious locks," and "lilly" and the "rose," in order to emphasize the idea of the fading of the poetically beautiful young lady into the plain woman, but also indicate the shrewd, matter-of-fact observation that lies behind the strategic verbal gestures. One might say, indeed, that Carew is the poet of normality. He suspects the overelaborate and the exaggerated expression of emotion as being no more than a game on the part of the speaker. Admittedly, he himself could play the game, and play it well, but hardly ever without an ironic half-smile, a quiet glee. He presents his sense of values to us clearly enough in "Disdaine Returned":

Hee that loves a Rosie cheeke,
  Or a corall lip admires,
Or from star-like eyes doth seeke
  Fuell to maintaine his fires;
As old *Time* makes these decay,
So his flames must waste away.

But a smooth and stedfast mind,
  Gentle thoughts, and calme desires,
Hearts, with equall love combind,
  Kindle never dying fires.
Where these are not, I despise
Lovely cheekes, or lips, or eyes.

Behind the mockery, the gaiety, the enjoyment of ingenious description, the erotic trivialities, and the light, casual songs lies the firm belief in honesty, sympathy, steadfastness, and affection. This is the driving force behind the delicate description of spring, at once elaborate and tender.

Now that the winter's gone, the earth hath lost
Her snow-white robes, and now no more the frost

Candies the grasse, or castes an ycie creame
Upon the silver Lake or Chrystall streame:
But the warm Sunne thawes the benummed Earth,
And makes it tender, gives a sacred birth
To the dead Swallow; wakes in hollow tree
The drowzie Cuckow, and the Humble-Bee. . . .
                              ("The Spring")

The speaker of these lines may not be possessed by any great imaginative vision, but he is simply and movingly affected by natural beauty. Such a man will never really lose his emotional balance; he may pretend passion in order to tease or amuse, or to gain his masculine ends, but he is perfectly prepared to admit and ridicule his own duplicity. If he ever loses his temperate voice, it will be because he is angry and, probably, because his normal male vanity has been disturbed.

When thou, poore excommunicate
From all the joyes of love, shalt see
The full reward, and glorious fate,
Which my strong faith shall purchase me,
Then curse thine owne inconstancie.

A fayrer hand than thine, shall cure
That heart, which thy false oathes did wound;
And to my soule, a soule more pure
Than thine, shall by Loves hand be bound,
And both with equall glory crown'd.

Then shalt thou weepe, entreat, complaine
To Love, as I did once to thee;
When all thy teares shall be as vaine
As mine were then, for thou shalt bee
Damn'd for thy false Apostasie.
                    ("To My Inconstant Mistris")

It is not a cry de profundis. It is not even very original, for it reminds us immediately of Donne's "The Curse." It has, however, the immense virtue of vitality and ease, and in these cavalier lines we can easily perceive the presence of a man feeling as most men feel at one time or another, and putting it down in language most men will accept. The perception is not an extraordinary one, but it is absolutely faithful to the psychology of the male animal. It is this fidelity to the emotional and intellectual perceptions of ordinary masculinity which makes Carew so rewarding a writer. Unlike so many of our greater poets he is no more, and no less, than a man.

THE CAVALIER POETS

SIR JOHN SUCKLING
(1609–1642)

SIR JOHN SUCKLING was born at Whitton, in Twickenham, Middlesex. He attended Trinity College, Cambridge, but did not take a degree. As a young man, he traveled on the Continent and fought in the Thirty Years' War under Gustavus II. Upon his return to England in 1632, he joined the court, where he became known as a wit and a rake. He took part in the expedition against Scotland in 1639. In 1641 he played a part in the conspiracy to free the earl of Strafford, but fled to France when the plot was discovered. He died in Paris in 1642.

Sir John Suckling was, like his friend Carew, very much a man about town. A royalist, a rake, a part-time soldier more attracted, John Aubrey suggests, by the panoply of war than by any love of action, he treated literature lightly. His plays, *Aglaura*, *The Goblins*, *The Tragedy of Brennoralt*, and *The Sad One* (unfinished), are carelessly put together and slackly written. The characters are stock puppets from the playbox of the period, and only occasionally does a passage of blank verse or, more frequently, a passage of prose surprise us with its vigor, if not with its sense. The language is at once pedestrian and pretentious, as if the intention to write a play had arisen from motives other than those of creative excitement and had been carried out simply as an exercise in the fashionable arts.

It is this quality of careless pastiche which spoils a great deal of Suckling's writings. He has not the ability of Carew to imitate an accepted manner or form in such a way as to present an ironic comment upon it, and so extend its range. The self-consciousness is that of the lazily ingenious amateur rather than that of the professional who is aware of the tricks of the trade.

It is, however, the amateur's zest that accounts for Suckling's successes. There is a wholehearted vigor of movement in those of his lyrics that are not crippled by any pretense of literary style. He is able to throw aside all decorum and achieve a bold and direct colloquialism, both cruder and more jovial than that of Carew.

Why so pale and wan, fond lover?
  Prithee, why so pale?
Will, when looking well can't move her,

Looking ill prevail?
  Prithee, why so pale?

Why so dull and mute, young sinner?
  Prithee, why so mute?
Will, when speaking well can't win her,
  Saying nothing do't?
  Prithee, why so mute?

Quit, quit, for shame, this will not move:
  This cannot take her.
If of herself she will not love,
  Nothing can make her:
  The devil take her!
        (Song from Act IV of *Aglaura*)

This song is even more in opposition to the Petrarchan attitude than are the songs of Donne, for the language is that of the street, not the study. The affair does not even, it appears, merit that passionate thinking which derives from intensity of feeling. It has a backslapping heartiness, a brusque common sense.

Donne is, however, one of Suckling's masters, and echoes of his work appear frequently. Sometimes the whole method of the poem derives from Donne in its ingenious working out of an extended metaphor.

'Tis now, since I sat down before
  That foolish fort, a heart,
(Time strangely spent), a year and more,
  And still I did my part,

Made my approaches, from her hand
  Unto her lip did rise,
And did already understand
  The language of her eyes;

Proceeded on with no less art—
  My tongue was engineer:
I thought to undermine the heart
  By whispering in the ear.

When this did nothing, I brought down
  Great cannon-oaths, and shot
A thousand thousand to the town;
  And still it yielded not. . . .

The poem goes on to describe the siege, but as we read it we feel that the speaker is far more interested in his own wit than in anything else. This wit, however, does little to engage our emotions; the deliberately contrived imagery does not imply

226

either a passionately ironic detachment from a deeply felt experience of bodily attraction, or an intelligence wrought to a new intensity and complexity by the operations of emotion. It is a game. Nevertheless, the siege called off, and the retreat begun, the speaker appears to be forced by a momentary burst of feeling into a savage directness of expression.

> To such a place our camp remove,
>   As will no siege abide:
> I hate a fool that starves her love
>   Only to feed her pride.
>   ["Love's Siege"]

This epigrammatic element takes the place of the metaphysical conceit in the poems of several of the cavaliers, in that it is a sudden passionate perception, in terms of the intelligence, of an emotional attitude or truth. It is, usually, however, the climax of the poem, and stands almost apart from it, being the resolution of the problem, rather than its motive center.

Suckling's poems often end with a pseudodidactic moral statement:

> Spare diet is the cause love lasts;
> For surfeits sooner kill than fasts,

ends the poem "Against Absence."

> They who know all the wealth they have, are poor,
> He's only rich that cannot tell his store

sums up the argument of "Against Fruition."

> As good stuff under flannel lies, as under silken clothes

is the conclusion of "Love and Debt Alike Troublesome."

This last-named poem, with its jocose and swinging meter, reveals clearly where Suckling's strength lies:

> This one request I make to him that sits the clouds above,
> That I were freely out of debt, as I am out of love.
> Then for to dance, to drink and sing, I should be very
>   willing,
> I should not owe one lass a kiss, nor ne'er a knave a
>   shilling. . . .

It would be an exaggeration to suggest that the language and attitude of this poem are those of the common people, but they are certainly not those of the court and gentry alone. The words are commonplace, and the rhythm is that of many a street ballad, while the view of the man-woman relationship is free of any literary brand of elaboration. In another poem "The Careless Lover" sings:

> When I am hungry, I do eat,
> And cut no fingers 'stead of meat;
> Not with much gazing on her face
> Do e'er rise hungry from the place:
> She's fair, she's wondrous fair,
> But I care not who know it,
> Ere I'll die for love, I'll fairly forego it.

This view of the sexual relationship is unashamedly predatory and selfish and extremely refreshing and lively. In "Proferred Love Rejected" the tone is more cynical and almost brutal.

> It is not four years ago,
>   I offered forty crowns
> To lie with her a night or so:
>   She answered me in frowns.
>
> Not two years since, she meeting me
>   Did whisper in my ear,
> That she would at my service be,
>   If I contented were.
>
> I told her I was cold as snow
>   And had no great desire;
> But should be well content to go
>   To twenty, but no higher.

This presentation of the economics of lust springs from the same source as the jibe on "T(homas) C(arew) having the P(ox)," the obscene verse upon the functions of the candle for the "female crew," and the lines on "The Deformed Mistress," in which the speaker gloats over the nauseating and the decayed. There is a dark strand in Suckling's imagination. It appears also in "Against Fruition," where he speaks with the voice of dissolute satiety:

> Fruition adds no new wealth, but destroys,
> And while it pleaseth much the palate, cloys;
> Who thinks he shall be happier for that,
> As reasonably might hope he might grow fat
> By eating to a surfeit; this one past,
> What relishes? even kisses lose their taste.

The skepticism and the disillusionment expressed in these lines add a certain strength to many of the sweeter love lyrics, in that, because of the frequent use of down-to-earth words and commonplace locutions, we sense behind the delighted anticipation the shadow of futility and emptiness. Not that this despair is in any way cosmic; there is no Swiftian melancholy here; it is rather the half-comic, half-bitter knowingness of the experienced male.

> Out upon it! I have lov'd
> Three whole days together;
> And am like to love three more,
> If it prove fair weather.
>
> Time shall moult away his wings
> Ere he shall discover
> In the whole wide world again
> Such a constant lover.
>
> But the spite on't is, no praise
> Is due at all to me:
> Love with me had made no stays,
> Had it any been but she.
>
> Had it any been but she,
> And that very face,
> There had been at least ere this
> A dozen dozen in her place.
> ("A Poem with the Answer")

Here Suckling has rejected the use of obvious ingenuity in order to present an apparent straightforwardness that is much more subtle in its effect. The use of common expressions such as "whole wide world" and "the spite on't" and the deliberate avoidance of unusual and highly emotive adjectives in such phrases as "constant lover" and "that very face" make us feel that the speaker is using no contrivance, but is more concerned with his feelings than his art. Yet, because of the very simplicity of the expression, we also feel slightly superior to the speaker, recognizing the "unliterary" quality of his verse. In the case of this song our superiority leads us towards affectionate amusement at the speaker's frank self-revelation; and in every case in which this method is used we find ourselves observing the speaker's ideas and feelings rather than becoming ourselves involved in them.

Suckling clearly knew what he was about in writing in this way, for, though he was often tempted to be fashionably elaborate, in "A Ballad upon a Wedding" he not only uses a commonplace vocab-

ulary and a naive style once again but places the poem in the mouth of a fictional character, who speaks in near-dialect and in a conversational tone:

> I tell thee, Dick, where I have been;
> Where I the rarest things have seen,
> O, things without compare!
> Such sights again cannot be found
> In any place on English ground,
> Be it at wake or fair.
>
> At Charing Cross, hard by the way
> Where we (thou knows't) do sell our hay,
> There is a house with stairs;
> And there did I see coming down
> Such folk as are not in our town,
> Forty at least, in pairs.
>
> Amongst the rest, one pest'lent fine
> (His beard no bigger though than thine)
> Walkt on before the rest:
> Our landlord looks like nothing to him:
> The King (God bless him!), 'twould undo him,
> Should he go still so dressed.

We smile amusedly at a man who prizes wakes and fairs so highly and who is not used to seeing houses with stairs in them, even while we enjoy (and envy perhaps) his capacity for simple wonder and his unself-consciousness. Once we have been led into this attitude towards the speaker, we read on with an affectionate discernment that allows Suckling to vary the direction of the narrative in several ways. We feel just sufficiently superior to the speaker to accept simple jokes as part of the poem's portrayal of character, and yet we envy his innocent wonderment so much that we want to accept his description of beauty as more than a tribute to his own impressionability. The images and phrases used continually remind us of the character of the speaker also, so that we are never in danger of changing our relationship with him. Thus, the bride is described in homely terms:

> Her finger was so small, the ring
> Would not stay on, which they did bring;
> It was too wide a peck:
> And to say truth (for out it must)
> It lookt like the great collar (just)
> About our young colt's neck.
>
> Her feet beneath her petticoat,
> Like little mice, stole in and out,

As if they fear'd the light:
But O, she dances such a way!
No sun upon an Easter-day
   Is half so fine a sight.

He would have kist her once or twice;
But she would not, she was so nice,
   She would not do't in sight:
And then she lookt as who should say,
"I will do what I list to-day,
   And you shall do't at night."

Even the occasional forced rhyme, and the sometimes subtly lame, sometimes aggressively jog-trot, rhythm are appropriate to the character of the narrator, who interrupts his own story every now and then with an aside:

Now hats fly off, and youths carouse,
Healths first go round, and then the house:
   The bride's came thick and thick;
And, when 'twas nam'd another's health,
Perhaps he made it hers by stealth;
   (And who could help it, Dick?)

Suckling's talents were perfectly adapted to this poem, for in it his merely fanciful (rather than imaginative) mind, and his amateur's careless vigor can be seen as part of the poem's "personality." Suckling's real contribution to English poetry was, indeed, this outspoken zest and this adoption of the language as well as the attitude of everyday masculinity. He is nowhere near as important a poet as Carew, but he developed one aspect of Carew's concern with the presentation of masculine attitudes in a startlingly vigorous manner. Much of his work is merely fashionable, much quite simply bad, but in his best work he followed his own prescription in "A Session of the Poets" that "A laureat muse should be easy and free," and his ease and freedom three hundred years later are still immensely enjoyable.

RICHARD LOVELACE
(ca. 1618–1657)

RICHARD LOVELACE was born at his father's house in Woolwich. He was educated at Charterhouse and Gloucester Hall, Oxford, where he took his master of arts in 1636. He took part in the Scottish expedition of 1639 and was imprisoned for supporting the Kentish Petition in 1642. But he joined Charles I at Oxford, in 1645, to fight for the royalist cause. After fighting in the siege of Dunkirk in 1646, he was again imprisoned by Parliament in 1648 and released the following year. After having exhausted his patrimony, mostly through various attempts to serve the crown, he died in poverty in 1657.

The tone of the elegies on the death of Richard Lovelace is very different from the tone of those upon Suckling and Carew. The two older poets are praised as "wittie"; but Lovelace is regarded as "honourable," and the "beauty" of his soul is referred to, not infrequently. It all reminds one rather of Sir Philip Sidney. Lovelace was, clearly, much more than either Suckling or Carew, the model of a Renaissance gentleman, being a soldier, lover, wit, and pattern of chivalry. Nevertheless, as one reads his poems, one notices that something is missing. The expected "careless ease" is there, and something of the expected vigor, but the poems are much less personal. Though the superbly balanced love songs are neatly passionate, and appropriately conversational, they do not put us into a familiar relationship with the speaker:

Tell me not (Sweet) I am unkinde
   That from the Nunnerie
Of thy chaste breast, and quiet minde,
   To Warre and Armes I flie.

True a new Mistresse now I chase,
   The first Foe in the Field;
And with a stronger Faith embrace
   A Sword, a Horse, a Shield.

Yet this Inconstancy is such,
   As you too shall adore;
I could not love thee (Deare) so much,
   Lov'd I not Honour more.
   ("To Lucasta, Going to the Warres")

The statements are lucid, grave, and temperate. It is a sweetly reasonable poem that manages to avoid smugness because of the tender note in the personal appeal to his "Sweet" and "Deare." There is a love of symmetry here, however, which seems almost to be stronger than the love of the mistress. This is perhaps the real difference between Lovelace and his predecessors. Both Carew and Suckling have a good conceit of themselves. They prize their wit above their honesty, maybe, but, at their best, one feels this wit is a part of the animal spirit, which makes the pursuit of a mistress desirable. Lovelace's wit has a more withdrawn, impersonal, almost abstract air about it. Moreover, his moralizing is earnest rather than gay, and sometimes he finds it necessary to give dignity to his verses by the inclusion of a good deal of classical drapery. "Gratiana Dancing and Singing" has as its last verse:

> So did she move; so did she sing
> Like the Harmonious spheres that bring
>   Unto their Rounds their musick's ayd;
> Which she performed such a way
> As all th'inamoured world will say
>   The *Graces* daunced, and *Apollo* play'd.

This is pleasant and tuneful. It is at once relaxed and entertaining, and no irony is allowed to prevent our accepting the ideal description. Lovelace is, indeed, an enemy to irony. His strong suit is the lucid and dignified presentation of sentiment in lines of restrained rhythm which are given force by the use of parallelism, antithesis, and paradox. Thus his "An Elegie. Princesse Katherine" opens with a beautifully controlled set of balanced opposites:

> You that can aptly mixe your joyes with cries,
> And weave white Ios with black Elegies,
> Can Caroll out a Dirge, and in one breath
> Sing to the Tune, either of life or death;
> You that can weepe the gladnesse of the spheres,
> And pen a Hymne in stead of Inke with teares,
> Here, here, your unproportion'd wit let fall
> To celebrate this new-borne Funerall,
> And greete that little Greatnesse, which from th' wombe
> Dropt both a load to th' Cradle and the Tombe.

This is the poetry of ceremony rather than spontaneity, and in Lovelace one feels continually that sense of the inner dignity of humanity which is so lacking in Carew and Suckling. Even when lighthearted, his humor leads him toward gentle absurdity rather than raillery, and his slightest and most casual lines have an air of sweetness about them. His is not a questioning mind. He accepts the fashionably elaborate compliment at its face value, and continually praises his mistress in high-sounding terms, using vast cosmic similitudes or pastoral and idyllic language. As a result of this we feel the poetry to be "amateur" in a fashion very different from that of Suckling or Carew. With them one feels that their amateur status existed in their vigor and careless ease; their impertinence, their air of not really minding very much if the poem, as a

literary object, were not in the best taste, or flawlessly made. Lovelace, however, gives the impression that he wishes his verse always to be in the best of taste and beautifully contrived, but is not really involved emotionally in his subject matter. His verse only occasionally appears to be anything more than a well-mannered and graceful diversion for the cultured reader. These diversions can, however, have a musical purity, a formal elegance that the wilder poems of Carew or Suckling never have.

> Amarantha sweet and faire,
>   Ah brade no more that shining haire!
>   As my curious hand or eye,
>   Hovering round thee let it flye.
>
> Let it flye as unconfined
> As it's calme Ravisher, the winde;
>   Who hath left his darling th'East,
> To wanton o're that spicie Neast.
>
>   Ev'ry Tresse must be confest
> But neatly tangled at the best;
>   Like a Clue of golden thread,
> Most excellently ravelled.
>
> Doe not then winde up that light
> In Ribands, and o're-cloud in Night;
>   Like the Sun in's early ray,
> But shake your head and scatter day.
>   ("To Amarantha, That She Would
>   Dishevell Her Haire")

This is a poem of the ideal, and the ideal and the idyllic are Lovelace's pet themes. He adopts the pastoral manner more than once, and in his long pastoral, "Aramantha," moves completely away from any sense of actuality into a world of dream.

> Into the neighbring Wood she's gone,
> Whose roofe defies the tell-tale Sunne,
> And locks out ev'ry prying beame;
> Close by the Lips of a cleare streame
> She sits and entertaines her Eye
> With the moist Chrystall, and the frye
> With burnisht-silver mal'd, whose Oares
> Amazed still make to the shoares;
> What need she other bait or charm
> But look? or Angle, but her arm?
> The happy Captive gladly ta'n,
> Sues ever to be slave in vaine,
> Who instantly (confirm'd in's feares)
> Hasts to his Element of teares.

THE CAVALIER POETS

Poetry becomes, in such lines, simply a matter of charm, good humor, and pretty fancy. The poet's status is reduced to that of the drawing room entertainer, who takes great care not to offend the ladies by any too brutal reference to life's coarser realities. Nevertheless, it would be unfair to dismiss such work as entirely valueless, for as we read we are impressed by the delicacy of the sentiment and the description, and appreciate the writer's simple enjoyment of whatever is ingenious, musical, and well made. Moreover, behind the facade of fashionable artifice we suspect the presence of a strong sensibility and a sturdy common sense. These qualities emerge clearly in others of Lovelace's poems. His good-humored portrait of "The Ant," with its mock heroic reverence and deliberate use of familiar and commonplace images, is in the great tradition of good-humored and sensible fables:

> Forbear thou great good Husband, little Ant;
>   A little respite from thy flood of sweat;
> Thou, thine owne Horse and Cart, under this Plant
>   Thy spacious tent, fan thy prodigious heat;
> Down with thy double load of that one grain;
>   It is a Granarie for all thy Train.

> Cease large example of wise thrift a while,
>   (For thy example is become our Law)
> And teach thy frowns a seasonable smile:
>   So *Cato* sometimes the nak'd Florals saw.
> And thou almighty foe, lay by thy sting,
> Whilst thy unpay'd Musicians, Crickets, sing.

Later in the poem he refers, delightfully, to the Ant's enemies:

> Hovering above thee, Madam, *Margaret Pie*,
>   And her fierce Servant, Meagre, *Sir John Daw*

and the same touch of absurdity and humor appears in his two poems on "The Snayl," where it is addressed as "Compendious Snayl," and told that

> . . . in thy wreathed Cloister thou
> Walkest thine own Gray fryer too;
> Strickt, and lock'd up, th'art Hood all ore
> And ne'r Eliminat'st thy Dore.

In these poems Lovelace comes closer to Suckling and Carew than in most others, for here his use of the mock heroic implies a degree of detached amusement at the earnestly inflated solemnities of so much conventional verse. We can recognize that the speaker is a complex human being, caught between sheer enjoyment of fine-sounding words and the suspicion that the splendor of these may be a little pretentious and artificial. We can detect, too, the moralist, intent upon teaching, who is sufficiently aware of his audience to poke a little quiet fun at his own earnestness. Once we contrast these fables with "Aramantha," or with such tangled and highfalutin expressions of serious passion as "To Night," which begin by being pretentious and end by becoming absurd: once we compare the Lovelace of the charming and decorative poems of good taste with the Lovelace of "The Vintage to the Dungeon," or "To Althea from Prison," we can see clearly that all his work expresses a dichotomy. He doesn't know whether the poet in him is an aesthetic decorator with a penchant for complicated cornices, or merely one aspect of a civilized gentleman who enjoys good food, wine, laughter, music, and women, but who also has a serious moral side to his make up. Is the poet in fact a pose or a person, a couturier or a character?

This is really the question that all the cavalier poets had to face. Insofar as they enjoyed Jonsonian elegance and the ingenuity of Donne, they saw themselves as entertainers, but insomuch as they reverenced the strong masculine quality and the satirical bent of Jonson, and Donne's tremendously effective projection of a passionate personality, they felt they should be more critical, idiosyncratic, and personal. Careless ease must always be characteristic of their work, but must this lead toward a smooth and polished expression, devoid of dramatic vitality, or toward an almost insolent flouting of good taste and a carefully contrived freedom of meter?

In both Suckling and Lovelace the dilemma is obvious, but whereas Suckling's best poems come down successfully on the side of vigor and abandon, Lovelace's successes are, generally, of the other party. True, he can, every now and then, adopt a careless and lighthearted tone:

> For Cherries plenty, and for Coran's[1]
> Enough for fifty, were there more 'on's;
> For Elles of Beere,[2] Flutes of Canary

[1]Currants.
[2]A linear measure slightly greater than a yard; portions of beer and wine were sometimes described in such terms since they were often served in tall glasses resembling flutes.

That well did wash downe pasties-mary;[3]
For Peason,[4] Chickens, Sawces high,
Pig, and the Widdow-Venson-pye; . . .
Whether all of, or more behind-a
Thanks freest, freshest, Faire *Ellinda*:
  ("Being Treated, to Ellinda")

He can also retain the strong masculine note, even when his poems are elaborate and artificial:

Ah me! the little Tyrant Theefe!
 As once my heart was playing,
He snatch it up and flew away,
 Laughing at all my praying.

Proud of his purchase he surveyes,
 And curiously sounds it,
And though he sees it full of wounds,
 Cruell still on he wounds it.

And now this heart is all his sport,
 Which as a ball he boundeth
From hand to breast, from breast to lip,
 And all it's rest confoundeth.
  ("A Loose Saraband")

It is, however, when he contrives a gracefully tender poem, full of gentle ceremony and musical balance, and when he allows his fancy free play within the confines of a decorously rigid meter that he is most himself. Indeed, his most "cavalier" poems are his least typical ones. We do not often get work with the controlled strength, the strong personal touch, and the gaiety and courage of "To Althea from Prison":

When Love with unconfined wings
 Hovers within my Gates;
And my divine *Althea* brings
 To whisper at the Grates:
When I lye tangled in her haire,
 And fettered to her eye;
The *Gods* that wanton in the Aire,
 Know no such Liberty.

When flowing Cups run swiftly round
 With no allaying *Thames*,
Our carelesse heads with Roses bound,
 Our hearts with Loyall Flames;
When thirsty griefe in Wine we steepe,
 When healths and draughts go free,
Fishes that tipple in the Deepe,
 Know no such Liberty.

When (like committed Linnets) I
 With shriller throat shall sing
The sweetness, Mercy, Majesty,
 And glories of my KING;
When I shall voyce aloud, how Good
 He is, how Great should be;
Inlarged Winds that curle the Flood,
 Know no such Liberty.

Stone Walls doe not a Prison make,
 Nor Iron bars a Cage;
Mindes innocent and quiet take
 That for an Hermitage;
If I gave freedome in my Love,
 And in my soule am free;
Angels alone that sore above,
 Injoy such Liberty.

The last verse is perhaps Lovelace's finest achievement in poetry. In it we do sense a degree of personal feeling, and suspect that, at this point, the writer felt poetry alone could say what had to be said. That is, after all, the justification of poetry; it must appear to be a compulsion rather than a choice of a pleasing mode of expression.

Lovelace's sheer enjoyment of words and music is often sufficient to make us feel he had a general compulsion to play with words, ideas, and sounds, but it is rare for us to feel that any particular poem was a necessity, even if only a necessity of the moment. Nevertheless, Lovelace added poems to the language that we would not willingly miss, and if his soul is not aflame with the brightest genius, it does possess its own gentle radiance.

EDMUND WALLER
(1606–1687)

EDMUND WALLER was born on 3 March 1606, the eldest son of Robert and Anne Waller. He received his education at Eton and King's College, Cambridge, though there is no record of his taking a degree. He became a member of Parliament in 1621 and was a favorite of the king. In 1643 Waller was arrested and imprisoned for conspiracy by Parliament, and he narrowly escaped hanging. He toured Italy with John Evelyn in 1646. He wrote a panegyric on Oliver Cromwell in 1655 and, later, a poem of praise for Charles II on his Restoration in

[3]Meat pies. [4]Peas.

1660; and he became a member of Parliament again in 1661. He died on 21 October 1687.

There was never any doubt in Edmund Waller's mind as to the poetry he wished to write. Aubrey has a story that "When he was a briske young sparke, and first studyed poetry, 'Me thought,' said he, 'I never sawe a good copie of English verses; they want smoothness; then I began to essay.'" Aubrey's stories may not always be factually correct, but they are often psychologically illuminating, and this particular anecdote hits off Waller perfectly. We may, in reading Lovelace, feel occasionally that the stylist has got the better of the artist in him; with Waller we only rarely feel otherwise. His thoughts are commonplace, without having the extenuating characteristic of being expressed with force. His epithets are pleasingly conventional. His verses are smooth to the point of being soporific. Moreover, while he can be regarded as a cavalier in that his work always has the air of having been written "by the way," and his verses flow with "ease," he certainly does not appear to be careless of his audience, or in any way inclined to flout the gods of social usage. It might be said that whereas Carew, Suckling, and Lovelace celebrated whatever took their fancy or aroused their passions, Waller wrote of whatever he could possibly fit a verse to, being more interested in displaying his craftsmanship and flattering the influential than in exploring his perceptions.

This is a harsh judgment, but one forced upon any reader of the collected poems who becomes dazed with the multitude of such titles as "To Vandyk," "To the King," "On a Brede of Divers Colours Woven by Four Ladies," "On the Head of a Stag," "On the Discovery of a Lady's Painting," "To My Lord Northumberland upon the Death of His Lady." One title at least reminds one more of the vast canvases of the nineteenth-century academicians, with their acres upon acres of deftly anecdotal oil paint, than of anything else. This is his "Instructions to a Painter for the Drawing of the Posture and Progress of His Majesty's Forces at Sea, under the Command of His Highness-Royal: Together with the Battle and Victory Obtained over the Dutch, June 3, 1665." There are 310 lines, beginning:

> First draw the sea, that portion which between
> The greater world and this of ours is seen;
> Here place the British, there the Holland fleet,
> Vast floating armies! both prepared to meet.

It is perhaps unfair to mock Waller for the thunderous banality of his failures, but such poems as the "Advice to a Painter" do reveal a difference between him and the other cavaliers. A kind of professionalism has replaced the zest of the amateur; the poet considers it to be a part of his job to comment upon matters of national importance and to offer his poems to the public, not as amusing and ingenious expressions of personal feeling, which his readers may, perhaps, enjoy, but as public statements of which his readers should approve.

He could express, or perhaps imply, a nation's grief in a series of deft lines "Upon Our Late Loss of the Duke of Cambridge," and he could, as a good politician, representative of the "top people," present His Majesty, as a birthday present, with "A Presage of the Ruin of the Turkish Empire." The elegant rectitude of the style is, in fact, as worthy of praise as the moral and social propriety of the statements.

We are nowadays so conscious of the notion that a poet writes "for posterity" that it is hard for us to believe that Waller wrote ephemeral poetry from choice rather than by accident. Yet in his lines "Of English Verse," he clearly tells us that English is inferior to Latin or Greek for the expression of important matters, and is only suitable as an aid to the seduction of a mistress, or for the making of a poem that will retain its vitality as long as the poet retains his:

> Poets that lasting marble seek,
> Must carve in Latin, or in Greek;
> We write in sand, our language grows,
> And, like the tide, our work o'erflows.
>
> Chaucer his sense can only boast;
> The glory of his numbers lost!
> Years have defaced his matchless strain;
> And yet he did not sing in vain.
>
> The beauties which adorned that age,
> The shining subjects of his rage,
> Hoping they should immortal prove,
> Rewarded with success his love.
>
> This was the generous poet's scope;
> And all an English pen can hope,
> To make the fair approve his flame,
> That can so far extend their fame.
>
> Verse, thus designed, has no ill fate,
> If it arrive but at the date

Of fading beauty; if it prove
But as long-lived as present love.

This is, of course, a not uncommon opinion of the period, but while these verses faithfully express the cavalier's view that Latin and Greek poetry were important and could usefully serve as models for writers in English, and to some extent explain their passion for translation, they also explain Waller's own deliberate pursuit of the flawlessly made heroic couplet, for this, to him, was the English equivalent of the Latin discipline he so admired. In his lines "Upon the Earl of Roscommon's Translation of Horace," he reveals more of his views:

> Though poets may of inspiration boast,
> Their rage, ill-governed, in the clouds is lost.
> He that proportioned wonders can disclose,
> At once his fancy and his judgement shows.
> Chaste moral writing we may learn from hence,
> Neglect of which no wit can recompence. . . .

It is worth commenting upon the emphasis upon judgment and morality in these lines. The poet is no gay dog, but a conscientious corrector of public taste:

> The Muses' friend, unto himself severe,
> With silent pity looks on all that err;
> For where a brave, a public action shines,
> That he rewards with his immortal lines.
> Whether it be in council or in fight,
> His country's honour is his chief delight;
> Praise of great acts he scatters as a seed,
> Which may the like in coming ages breed.

Such a picture of the poet is one we expect rather of the eighteenth than the late seventeenth century. It is with something of a shock that one turns to his lyrics and reads:

> Go, lovely Rose!
> Tell her that wastes her time and me
> That now she knows,
> When I resemble her to thee,
> How sweet and fair she seems to be.
>
> Tell her that's young,
> And shuns to have her graces spied,
> That hadst thou sprung
> In deserts, where no men abide,
> Thou must have uncommended died.

> Small is the worth
> Of beauty from the light retired;
> Bid her come forth,
> Suffer herself to be desired
> And not blush so to be admired.
>
> Then die! that she
> The common fate of all things rare
> May read in thee;
> How small a part of time they share
> That are so wondrous sweet and fair!
>   ("Go, Lovely Rose!")

This possesses that direct and personal vitality which we have come to expect of the cavaliers, and while its language has a touch of the ceremonious about it, largely because of its inversions, this adds dignified restraint to the straightforward appeal to the lady in question. There is also a carefully delicate touch of pathos in the closing lines immediately following the sudden dramatic injunction "Then die!" As with Lovelace, however, one feels that a certain kind of vigor is missing, though it is perhaps compensated for by the superb balance of the phrases and the strong economy of the language. "Go, Lovely Rose!" is, of course, Waller's most anthologized poem, and it is untypical. Waller's forte is neat charm rather than controlled passion. His "Written in My Lady Speke's Singing Book" runs:

> Her fair eyes, if they could see
> What themselves have wrought in me,
> Would at least with pardon look
> On this scribbling in her book:
> If that she the writer scorn
> This may from the rest be torn,
> With the ruin of a part,
> But the image of her graces
> Fills my heart and leaves no spaces.

These lines are suitable for any young lady's autograph album, and if their wit totters upon the edge of the bathetic, this is one of the risks a poet must take who is determined never to offend by originality, but always to give pleasure with a neat version of an expected and acceptable compliment. An occasional liveliness of speech adds vigor to some of Waller's trivia, as when he writes "Under a Lady's Picture":

> Some ages hence, for it must not decay,
> The doubtful wonderers at this piece, will say

Such Helen was! and who can blame the boy
That in so bright a flame consumed his Troy?
But had like virtue shined in that fair Greek,
The amorous shepherd had not dared to seek
Or hope for pity; but with silent moan,
And better fate, had perished alone.

The colloquial vitality of "who can blame the boy," added to the concise force of the following line, with its suggestion of heroic passion, succeeds in giving the whole poem a certain degree of intensity. Though the thought of the following lines may be conventional, the craftsmanship holds our attention. The verbs "shined" and "had" occur precisely at the centerpoint of the lines in which they appear, as do the pauses in the two concluding lines. It is Waller's strength that he could almost always make an acceptable conventionality appear pleasingly ingenious and original by obtruding his craftsmanship upon us. This craftsmanship was most often employed in arranging a smooth metrical regularity, given a restricted degree of variety by the careful use of pauses and occasional abrupt statements. These abrupt statements never have the take-it-or-leave-it brusqueness of Suckling or Carew; they only momentarily alter the speed with which the poem runs, and never quite reach that note of real vigor that we can hear in the splendidly disciplined lines of Dryden:

He that alone would wise and mighty be,
Commands that others love as well as he.
Love as he loved!—How can we soar so high?—
He can add wings, when he commands to fly.
Nor should we be with this command dismayed;
He that examples gives, will give his aid;

This fragment from "Of Divine Love" is a clear indication of Waller's transitional position as a poet. His heroic couplets look forward to those of the eighteenth century. Like many poets from Dryden to Samuel Johnson, he is fond of the epigrammatic moral statement:

Man's boundless avarice his want exceeds,
And on his neighbours round about him feeds.

Though justice death, as satisfaction, craves,
Love finds a way to pluck us from our graves.

Waller's lyrics, too, remind one more of later than of earlier poets. Though there is immense charm, and sometimes liveliness, there is no highly personal idiosyncrasy to give them any real human immediacy. Carew and Suckling may have written their songs as games, but it is impossible to mistake the one's style of play for the other's. This is no longer true with the Restoration wits. It is possible to mistake a Dryden song for one by Sir Charles Sedley, Sir George Etherege, or even (sometimes) the incomparable Rochester. The song is no longer part of the perception of an individual singer, but an exercise in a conventional genre. The examples are often delightful, but they are basically anonymous.

Waller must be held as to some extent responsible for the anonymous style. He took over the highly personalized careless ease of the cavaliers, and, with great care, gave it more ease, and less personality. The strong masculine tone of Suckling, Carew, and Lovelace, and of so many of the minor figures—Randolph, Townsend, Montrose, and others—is replaced by a mild decisiveness of style. Even at the close of one of his most successful lyrics, where there is an attempt at the passionate exuberance of the lover, Waller only achieves a hollow gesture:

That which her slender waist confined,
Shall now my joyful temples bind;
No monarch but would give his crown
His arms might do what this has done.

It was my heaven's extremest sphere,
The pale which held that lovely deer.
My joy, my grief, my hope, my love,
Did all within this circle move!

A narrow compass! and yet there
Dwelt all that's good, and all that's fair;
Give me but what this ribband bound,
Take all the rest the sun goes round.
                                    ("On a Girdle")

It is charming, it is not without vigor, but it pales beside the cry of Donne, whom Carew thought so worthy of reverence. The period of the aggressively individual style and of the highly personal tone is over. Egos are out of favor, and will remain out of favor in any real sense until the romantics give the eccentric wheel another twist. Only Swift in the eighteenth century really employs the carelessly and insolently idiosyncratic style which is so enlivening in Carew and Suckling. Dryden and

Pope and their followers (not forgetting Dr. Johnson, who occasionally out-Wallers Waller) went on a different tack. There is still zest, but it is of a different kind. One no longer quite expects the colonel of the cavalry to be a poet of the first rank. The complete gentleman, once a soldier, statesman, courtier, and sportsman, effortlessly accomplished in versifying and playwriting, and casually brilliant as a musician, architect, and philosopher, is becoming more of a specialist. The ideal man of the Renaissance, universally gifted, and educated in all branches of knowledge, who could lead a battle, design a mansion, dispute with bishops, compose a song, govern a province, and win a mistress, all with an equally careless dexterity and poise, is dying. In 1711 Alexander Pope wrote of Crashaw:

> I take this Poet to have writ like a Gentleman, that is, at leisure hours, and more to keep out of idleness, than to establish a reputation; so that nothing regular or just can be expected from him . . . no man can be a true Poet, who writes for diversion only.

It is the judgment of a later generation than Waller's, but it is in Waller's poetry that we can see the amateur being edged off the stage by the busy professional, the man of letters with a reputation to earn, and matters of public concern to talk about.

CONCLUSION

ALTHOUGH the poetry of the cavaliers is only a part of the poetry written in England between the death of Shakespeare and the Restoration, it combines almost all the poetic characteristics of the period. The so-called metaphysical poets (George Herbert, Vaughan, King, Crashaw) may have been more thorough in their allegiance to Donne and his strong personal exploration of emotional and intellectual states of mind in terms of elaborate conceits, and poets like William Strode, Thomas Stanley, Sir William Davenant, and James Shirley may have adopted a more completely Jonsonian manner, but the cavaliers partook of both schools. Even the minor religious moralists, with their penchant for biblical paraphrases and their love of didactic epigrams, are like the cavaliers in being fond of translations and direct colloquial language. The great Milton, moreover, shows in his earlier work a truly cavalier sensuality and wit (though the careless ease is missing), and Cowley's "The Mistress," though often described as metaphysical, has more in common with Carew and Lovelace than with Herbert, Vaughan, and their fellows.

Just as the cavalier poets stand at the center of the poetic sensibility of the time, so do they show us the way in which poetry was changing generally throughout the period, from an expression of personal attitudes to a statement of public truth. When the cavalier considers an affair of public importance he considers his own personal reaction to it. This is even the case with Waller and with Sir John Denham, who ranks alongside Waller in establishing the smooth heroic couplet as the main medium of poetic expression for the years to come. The poet of the Restoration, however, is more obviously moved by a sense of social responsibility, and his satirical verses are as likely to be the result of political conviction as of personal spleen or amusement. Perhaps the most striking example of the cavaliers' attitude in this respect is the marquess of Montrose's "An Excellent New Ballad." Here the political viewpoint is used to illuminate the private emotions of the lover, and the references to royalism and Puritanism are deliberately frivolous. It is as much as if to say (as Yeats said in one of his poems), "What is the value of these political notions compared with the value of human relationships?"

> My dear and only love, I pray
> That little world of thee
> Be governed by no other sway
> Than purest monarchy;
> For if confusion have a part,
> (Which virtuous souls abhor,)
> And hold a *synod* in thine heart,
> I'll never love thee more.
>
> Like Alexander I will reign,
> And I will reign alone;
> My thoughts did evermore disdain
> A rival on my throne.
> He either fears his fate too much
> Or his deserts are small,
> That dares not put it to the touch
> To gain or lose it all.
>
> And in the empire of thine heart,
> Where I should solely be,
> If others do pretend a part,
> Or dare to view with me,
> Of if *committees* thou erect,

And go on such a score,
I'll laugh and sing at thy neglect,
And never love thee more.

But if thou wilt prove faithful then,
And constant of thy word,
I'll make thee glorious by my pen,
And famous by my sword;
I'll serve thee in such noble ways
Was never heard before;
I'll crown and deck thee all with bays,
And love thee more and more.

James Graham, marquess of Montrose, typifies the cavalier spirit. He was a dedicated statesman and a brilliant military tactician, who spent all his maturity in war and the planning of war. He helped the Scottish covenanters to free themselves from the domination of the bishops, and then, when the covenanters threatened to rebel against the crown, he led the wild Gordons and Macdonalds of the Highlands into battle for the king's cause. He was captured at last, during the Commonwealth, leading another army for the royalists, and was hanged before he was forty. His poems all have that careless brilliance which the age expected of the verses of its "compleat gentlemen," and this song illustrates particularly clearly the way in which the cavalier lyric combines casual ease and forceful expression in such a way as to give an impression of real and vital humanity. The poem is always more than the sum of its parts, but this is particularly true of the work of the cavaliers. From even the most trivial verses of Lord Herbert, William Cartwright, William Habington, Aurelian Townsend, Thomas Randolph, Sidney Godolphin, Sir Richard Fanshawe, and their fellows we derive a far from trivial impression of intense curiosity, zest, and sensitivity. The poems may or may not indulge in some philosophical or moral statement, but their general effect is always to impress upon us the importance of honest skepticism, uninhibited enjoyment, freedom of thought, and moral candor. Life should be enjoyed on many levels. There is a place for the merely fanciful, as for the deeply imaginative. One should not make a fool of oneself by being over pretentious, or pretending always to be devoted to the profoundest moral problems. On the other hand, one should not be afraid of making a fool of oneself by confessing one's own enjoyment of the trivial or one's occasional spasms of simple masculine animality. Life, viewed through the thick lens of philosophy, may appear to be in the service of God or Truth, but looked at with the eyes of everyday it seems at once less important and more amusing. Life was made for man to use, not man for life to discipline into some creature of a narrow dogma.

Whether or not this attitude is just, it is certainly invigorating, for it throws the Muse's doors wide open to all comers. Nothing that is experienced can be inappropriate to poetry. The cavaliers, indeed, released poetry from the various bondages of previous fashions and, as a consequence, the writers of the eighteenth century were able to develop new techniques and explore new subjects. The value of the cavaliers is not only historical, however. They gave us something that no one else has given us since—a strong masculine poetry that is continually life-enhancing, and always courageous, vigorous, and charming. The style is debased in Waller's work, admittedly, but in that of Carew, Suckling, Lovelace, and a host of others it provides us with tremendous pleasure and much wise instruction, and as we shut the book we cannot help recalling the words of a much later poet who was, in some ways, a cavalier at heart. "A man's a man for a' that," said Robert Burns, and it might well have been said by his fellow countryman Montrose.

SELECTED BIBLIOGRAPHY

A list of the separate works of the poets discussed in this essay is given in the Grolier Club's *A Catalogue of . . . English Writers from Wither to Prior*, 3 vols. (New York, 1905).

THOMAS CAREW

I. BIBLIOGRAPHY. A list of all the manuscripts printed and sources for the establishment of the authoritative text is printed in *The Poems of Thomas Carew* (Oxford, 1949).

II. COLLECTED WORKS. [T. Maitland], ed., *The Works* (Edinburgh, 1824); W. C. Hazlitt, ed., *The Poems* (London, 1870); J. W. Ebsworth, ed., *The Poems and Masque* (London, 1893); A. Vincent, ed., *The Poems* (London, 1899), in the Muses' Library; G. Saintsbury, ed., *Minor Poets of the Caroline Period*, 3 vols. (Oxford, 1905–1921); R. G. Howarth, ed., *Introduction to Minor Poets of the Seventeenth Century* (London, 1931; repr., 1953), an anthology containing the work of Carew, Lovelace, Suckling, and Lord Herbert of Cherbury, in Everyman's

Library; R. Dunlap, ed., *The Poems with His Masque "Coelum Britannicum"* (Oxford, 1949), the definitive ed., intro. includes a biography of Carew.

III. SEPARATE WORKS. *Coelum Britannicum. A Masque at Whitehall in the Banquetting-House, on Shrove-Tuesday-Night, the 18 of February, 1633* (London, 1634); *Poems* (London, 1640; other eds., 1651, 1653, 1671), additional poems in the later eds.

IV. SOME CRITICAL STUDIES. A. T. Quiller-Couch, *Adventures in Criticism* (London, 1896); C. L. Powell, "New Material on Thomas Carew," *Modern Language Review*, 11 (1916); E. E. Duncan-Jones, "Carew and Guez de Balzac," *Modern Language Review*, 46 (1951).

SIR JOHN SUCKLING

I. COLLECTED WORKS. *The Works* (London, 1676; repr., 1696); W. C. Hazlitt, ed., *The Poems, Plays and Other Remains*, 2 vols. (London, 1874; rev. ed., 1892); A. H. Thompson, ed., *The Works* (London, 1910; reiss., 1965); H. Berry, ed., *Sir John Suckling's Poems and Letters from Manuscript* (London—Ontario, 1960).

II. SEPARATE WORKS. *Aglaura* (London, 1638); *The Discontented Colonel* [London, 1640], retitled *Brennoralt* in *Fragmenta Aurea* (London, 1646); *A Coppy of a Letter Written to the Lower House of Parliament* (London, 1641); *Fragmenta Aurea. A Collection of All the Incomparable Peeces Written by Sir John Suckling* (London, 1646; 2nd ed., 1648; 3rd ed., 1658), 3rd ed. included for the first time *Letters to Several Persons of Honor* and *The Sad One, A Tragedy.*

RICHARD LOVELACE

I. BIBLIOGRAPHY. A list of all the manuscripts printed and sources for the establishment of the authoritative text is printed in *The Poems* (Oxford, 1925).

II. COLLECTED WORKS. S. W. S[inger], ed., *Lucasta: in Two Parts* (London, 1817–1818); W. C. Hazlitt, ed., *Lucasta* (London, 1864; rev. ed., 1897), also in H. Child, ed. (London, 1904) and W. L. Phelps, ed., 2 vols. (Chicago, 1921); C. H. Wilkinson, ed., *The Poems* (Oxford, 1930), the definitive ed., intro. includes a biography of Lovelace, also in a limited, deluxe ed., 2 vols. (London, 1925).

III. SEPARATE WORKS. *Lucasta: Epodes, Odes, Sonnets, Songs, &c., To Which Is Added Amarantha, A Pastorall* (London, 1649); *Lucasta: Posthume Poems* (London, 1659).

EDMUND WALLER

I. COLLECTED WORKS. E. Fenton, ed., *The Works in Verse and Prose* (London, 1729; repr., 1730, 1758); *The Works in Verse and Prose, with Life* (London, 1772); G.

Thorn-Drury, ed., *The Poems* (London, 1893), the best ed., in the Muses' Library; *The Poems* (London, 1977), the Scolar Press ed.

II. SEPARATE WORKS. *Speech Against Prelates Innovations* (London, 1641); *Mr. Waller's Speech in the Painted Chamber* (London, 1641); *Speech. 4 July 1643* (London, 1643); *The Workes of Edmund Waller in This Parliament* (London, 1645); *Poems* (London, 1645; repr., 1664, 1668, 1682, etc.); *A Panegyrick to My Lord Protector* (London, 1655); *Upon the Late Storme, and of the Death of His Highnesse* (London, 1658); *To the King, upon His . . . Happy Return* (London, 1660); *To My Lady Morton* (London, 1661); *A Poem in St. James's Park* (London, 1661); *To the Queen, upon Her . . . Birthday* (London, 1663); *Upon Her Majesty's New Buildings* (London, 1665); *Of the Lady Mary* (London, 1679); *Divine Poems* (London, 1685); *The Maid's Tragedy, Alter'd* (London, 1690); *The Second Part of Mr. Waller's Poems* (London, 1690; repr., 1705, 1711, etc.), with anonymous biography.

III. SOME BIBLIOGRAPHICAL AND CRITICAL STUDIES. P. Stockdale, *Life of Waller* (London, 1772); S. Johnson, *Lives of the Poets* (London, 1791), later in G. B. Hill, ed. (Oxford, 1905); J. Cartwright, *Sacharissa* (London, 1893); C. Lloyd, "Waller as a Member of the Royal Society," *PMLA*, 43 (1928); A. W. Allison, *Towards an Augustan Poetic: Edmund Waller's "Reform" of English Poetry* (Lexington, Ky., 1962); W. L. Cherniak, *The Poetry of Limitation* (New Haven, 1968).

OTHER CAVALIER POETS

WILLIAM HABINGTON (1605–1654). H. C. Combs, ed., *Castara* (Evanston, Ill., 1939); K. Allott, ed., *The Poems* (Liverpool, 1948).

THOMAS RANDOLPH (1605–1635). W. C. Hazlitt, ed., *Poetical and Dramatic Works*, 2 vols. (London, 1875); G. Thorn-Drury, ed., *Poems* (London, 1929).

LORD HERBERT OF CHERBURY (1583–1648). G. C. Moore Smith, ed., *Poems* (Oxford, 1923); C. H. Herford, *Autobiography* (London, 1928); H. R. Hutcheson, trans. and ed., *Religio laici* (New Haven, 1944); M. M. Rossi, *La vita, le opere, i tempi . . .* , 3 vols. (Florence, 1947).

SIDNEY GODOLPHIN (1610–1643). W. Dighton, ed., *The Poems* (Oxford, 1931).

SIR JOHN DENHAM (1615–1669). T. H. Banks, ed., *The Poetical Works* (New Haven, 1928).

JAMES GRAHAM, MARQUESS OF MONTROSE (1612–1650). J. L. Weir, ed., *Poems* (London, 1938).

WILLIAM CARTWRIGHT (1611–1643). G. B. Evans, ed., *The Plays and Poems* (Madison, Wisc., 1951).

GENERAL CRITICISM

J. B. Emperor, "The Catullan Influence in English Lyric Poetry, 1600–90," *University Studies*, 3 (1928); K. A. McEuen, *Classical Influence upon the Tribe of Ben* (Cedar

Rapids, Ia., 1939); J. Miles, *The Primary Language of Poetry in the 1640's* (Berkeley, 1948); G. Walton, *Metaphysical to Augustan* (Cambridge, 1935); B. Ford, ed., *From Donne to Marvell*, Pelican Guide to English Literature, vol. III (London, 1956), contains G. Walton, "The Cavalier Poets."

SOCIAL AND LITERARY BACKGROUND

G. M. Trevelyan, *England under the Stuarts* (London, 1904); H. J. C. Grierson, *The First Half of the Seventeenth Century* (London, 1906); M. Coate, *Social Life in Stuart England* (London, 1924); H. J. C. Grierson, *Cross Currents in English Literature of the Seventeenth Century* (London, 1929); B. Willey, *The Seventeenth-Century Background* (London, 1934; reiss., 1963); M. B. Pickel, *Charles I as Patron of Poetry and Drama* (London, 1936); J. A. K. Thompson, *The Classical Background of English Literature* (London, 1948); J. Morpurgo, *Life under the Stuarts* (London, 1950); C. V. Wedgwood, *Seventeenth-Century English Literature* (London, 1950); S. L. Bethell, *The Cultural Revolution of the Seventeenth Century* (London, 1951); D. Bush, *English Literature in the Early Seventeenth Century, 1600–1660* (London, 1962).

JOHN BUNYAN

(1628-1688)

Henri A. Talon

I

John Bunyan, man of the people, village tinker, had no other ambition in his writing than to serve his faith and to help his fellows; he had no idea of producing a masterpiece that would outlast the passage of centuries. Yet today we can hardly imagine the nonexistence of *Grace Abounding* and *The Pilgrim's Progress*, so important a place have they won in our cultural heritage.

Nevertheless, Bunyan has not met with undiluted praise. Though Jonathan Swift, Samuel Johnson, William Cowper, Thomas Macaulay, and many others rendered him homage, he has had violent detractors. All down the ages, the critical spirit endeavors to find new perspectives and to suggest fresh evaluations; but once an author has become part of history, he is entitled to expect a certain objectivity from his readers, and Bunyan seems to have reached the point where he may enjoy this privilege. One can have more or less liking for him, read him for pleasure or merely as a duty, but his name cannot be ignored.

He owes his position primarily to his talent as a writer, but some of his fame is also due to the virile personality that made him share intensely the fervor of his time, and even to the very lowliness of his social status: Bunyan speaks with the voice of the seventeenth-century working man; his work is the expression of popular culture. And because he combines dramatic genius with a vigorous faith, he helps us more than any other writer to understand Puritanism both as an intellectual movement and as a way of life.

Bunyan was born in the pretty village of Elstow, near Bedford, in 1628, probably in November, as he was baptized on the thirtieth of that month.

In his will his father described himself as a "braseyer," and his grandfather as a "pettie chapman." They were humble folk, but were of old stock: for three hundred years Bunyans had owned land in Bedfordshire, and in better days they had been yeoman farmers. The family seems to have been degenerating when John brought it fresh vigor.

Despite the humble circumstances of his parents, "it pleased God," John says, "to put it into their hearts to put me to school." Whether he attended school at Elstow, or Bedford, or Houghton Conquest, a neighboring parish that boasted a grammar school, Bunyan can only have received a rudimentary education that was soon forgotten, if we are to believe his own words. In the workman's cottage, bread-eaters must soon become bread-winners, and John must certainly have begun his apprenticeship to his father's craft at a very early age. But in his autobiography, *Grace Abounding*, he is sparing of details about the first nineteen years of his life, and he does little to satisfy the modern reader's curiosity about those decisive influences that are received in childhood.

His father, Thomas Bunyan, belonged to the Established Church, but he does not seem to have been a deeply religious man or to have possessed great delicacy of feeling. In June 1644 he lost his second wife, in July he lost a daughter; and yet he remarried in August. It is not unlikely that his father's unseemly haste wounded John's oversensitive nature, and that he was not displeased to be called to arms in the autumn of the same year.

In the war between king and Parliament, Bedfordshire had taken sides with the latter, and John was sent to Newport Pagnell in accordance with a parliamentary edict demanding 225 recruits from the town of Bedford. The garrison was commanded by Sir Samuel Luke, a figure immortalized by Samuel Butler in his amusing though unfair satire, *Hudibras*.

Though Bunyan could have regained his freedom in 1645, he preferred to join another regiment, which was destined for Ireland. What lay behind his choice? A taste for adventure? The desire to fight and to see fresh horizons? We do not know, but whatever John's hopes may have been, they were disappointed. He did not reach Ireland, he never saw active service, and in July 1647 he was back in civilian life.

Twenty-one months in the army at an age when one is so impressionable, so full of ardor and of dreams, could only strengthen the influences of Bunyan's early life; for in those days religious fervor was in the very air men breathed. In his book *Cromwell's Army*, Sir Charles Firth has shown how the army abounded with visionaries; every leader, almost every soldier, was also a preacher and a theologian; and battles opened and closed with prayer.

So at Newport Pagnell as at Elstow, Bunyan lived in a Puritan atmosphere. But what is Puritanism? Broadly speaking, it is an austere disciplining of life in the service of a fervid religious faith. It has been asserted that the Bible constituted the whole of religion for the Protestants, and certainly its authority was accepted by the Puritans with the utmost rigor. Bunyan speaks for almost all Puritans when he writes, with reference to the Scriptures, "all our words are truth, one of as much force as another." For them the Bible is "school of all wisdom, sole food of our spirits," as John Calvin says; it is all knowledge, according to Bunyan; it is a model for government, according to Thomas Cartwright, Lady Margaret professor of divinity at Cambridge, who in 1571 gave so great an impetus to Puritanism.

Puritanism rejected reliance on reason and tradition as sources of authority. Consequently the individual was thrown back on his own subjective relationship with God. By the seventeenth century Calvinism had become the dominant theological influence on the Puritans, and at the heart of Calvinism there lies the notion that God, through foreknowing those who will persevere in faith to the end, compels before the beginning of the world a very small number of persons to salvation. These are known as the elect. The remainder of mankind are damned: neither good works nor holiness of life can save them. Only faith, the grace of God freely given to the few who are chosen, can save. The elect have a strong assurance of their own salvation, but inevitably doubts arise. Without the doctrine of election we can understand nothing of Bunyan's restlessness, his habit of introspection, his spiritual torment, and his intense inner life.

The stern exigencies of such a creed could not fail to leave their mark upon private and public life,

and Macaulay went so far as to say that Puritanism "threw over all life a more than monastic gloom." But the great historian left out of account the depths of gloom that shrouded some of the medieval monasteries, and he gave altogether too somber a picture of Puritan England. Under Cromwell, people did not stop laughing or singing or even dancing. Even without wider historical investigation, the reading of *The Pilgrim's Progress* would be enough to give a truer idea of the atmosphere of the time, and of the kind of spiritual nourishment Bunyan received in the army and in the village to which he returned in 1647.

He married soon after his return, perhaps during the following year, but the exact date is unknown. There is no mention of the marriage in the registers at Elstow, and no precise information is given in *Grace Abounding*. Though he describes carefully his spiritual life and the variations of light and shade that played upon his consciousness, in his autobiography his marriage is barely mentioned; for, occasionally, Bunyan shows little understanding of external influence.

Yet his young wife brought him more than the feminine tenderness of which his mother's death had all too soon deprived him, more than the two books that were to make a profound impression upon him: Arthur Dent's *The Plaine Mans Path-Way to Heaven*, and Lewis Bayly's *The Practice of Piety*. Her greatest gift was the example of her own piety. Bunyan's marriage ushered in the true springtime of his spiritual life. The seeds sown ever since childhood burst forth, and that painful process began that was to transform the restless youth into a strong man who had won the mastery of his soul.

This growth, which Bunyan calls his conversion, cannot be summarized; it must be read entire in *Grace Abounding*. Here it only need be said that Bunyan began to frequent the village church, to read the Bible feverishly, and to give up innocent amusements that seemed to him sinful. Torn by doubts and remorse, he went through a period of storm and stress that was not immediately ended by his joining the Baptist Church at Bedford in 1653. But membership of a group where his talents as a preacher were called upon helped Bunyan to regain his balance and to reflect the radiancy of the peace he had won.

In 1660 his faith was put to the test by the return of the Stuarts, who were the enemies of Puritanism. He was arrested on 12 November 1660. He might have regained his physical liberty at the price of spiritual servitude: if he gave up preaching, he was told, he would be allowed to go back to his family. But Bunyan was not the man to do this. He knew that actions speak louder than words:

Besides, I thought, that seeing God of his mercy should choose me to go upon the forlorn hope in this country, that is, to be the first that should be opposed, for the Gospel; if I should fly, it might be a discouragement to the whole body that might follow after.

And again,

I was not altogether without hopes but that my imprisonment might be an awakening to the saints in the Country.

So he chose prison; and he remained there for twelve years.

It must be stressed that Bunyan did not embrace this sacrifice out of that yearning for martyrdom that is perhaps the subtlest form of pride; he resolved to let himself be thrown into the county jail at Bedford because he could not do otherwise without betraying both his faith and his brethren. But for one so full of warm human tenderness the choice was not easy:

I found myself a man, and compassed with infirmities. The parting with my wife and poor children hath oft been to me in this place as the pulling the flesh from my bones; and that not only because I am somewhat too fond of these great Mercies, but also because I should have often brought to my mind the many hardships, miseries and wants that my poor family was like to meet with, should I be taken from them, especially my poor blind child, who lay nearer my heart than all I had besides.

At the very moment when he was risking his life, Bunyan was assailed again by the classic doubt of the Calvinist: am I really among the elect? Will death bring me eternal bliss or eternal torment? This, the crucial moment of his existence, culminated in that decision to venture all for his faith that was for him like a leap in the dark:

Wherefore, thought I, the point being thus, I am for going on, and venturing my eternal state with Christ, whether I have comfort here or no. If God doth not come in, thought I, I will leap off the ladder even blindfold into eternity, sink or swim, come Heaven, come Hell, Lord Jesus, if Thou wilt catch me, do; if not, I will venture for thy name.

But this courageous gesture enabled him to accomplish one of the tasks that, according to him, God has entrusted to man: "To find what we are." His supreme act of will was the supreme revelation of himself to himself. And if, as Ben Jonson, Milton, and many others have thought, it is the high moral quality and the virility of a man that give distinction to his writing, the most creative experience in Bunyan's life was his imprisonment and total renunciation.

In jail he was by no means idle, "making many hundred grosse of long-tagged thread laces" to keep his family, teaching his fellow prisoners, giving guidance to those who came to him for advice, and continuing the writing he had begun as far back as 1656, during a controversy with the Quakers.

Of the sixty works that Bunyan left, fifty-six are now almost forgotten. These pamphlets, sermons, and treatises contain forceful and lively pages, but they belong to old quarrels, and the theology that they express has become foreign to most of us. Anyone interested in the seventeenth century can still find useful material in *The Life and Death of Mr. Badman* (1680); and the student of English literature cannot dispense with reading *The Pilgrim's Progress* (1678), a work fraught with spiritual significance. But it must be acknowledged that today, especially on the Continent, *Grace Abounding* (1666) is read with more interest than any other of Bunyan's works.

The theological drama that is unfolded in *The Pilgrim's Progress* awakens less response among modern readers than the forthright account of a spiritual conflict given in the autobiographical work. The former has lost for us some of its meaning and much of its urgency; but the introspective analysis of the latter has a universal quality. Even if our faith is not Bunyan's, we are at once aware of the fervor of his exacting conscience and of his unquiet heart. Our doubts and difficulties may not be his, our hopes may have other goals, our sufferings other springs, but how well we recognize the rhythm of the inner life, those accounts of despair and of joy that Bunyan has evoked with such forceful and yet such subtle truth.

After 1668 Bunyan's imprisonment was much less strict. From time to time he was allowed to attend meetings of his sect, as the *Church Book* bears witness. In January 1672, "after much seeking God by prayer," his brethren chose him as their minister. In March, Charles II signed the Declaration of Indulgence; in May, Bunyan obtained a license to preach; and on 13 September the royal pardon was officially granted him.

It was therefore with an increased sense of authority that Bunyan resumed his battle for Christ, preaching in the surrounding villages and even going as far as Reading and London. According to his friend Charles Doe, his success was so great that the Londoners flocked to hear him. And the nickname of Bishop Bunyan given him by his enemies also bears witness to the reputation and influence of the preaching tinker.

Under the Stuarts the liberty of Dissenters was never sure. In 1673 Charles II was constrained to repeal the Declaration of Indulgence, Parliament refusing to admit, as Macaulay puts it, "an act so liberal done in a manner so despotic." And when the king called to office the earl of Danby, who was hostile to the Puritans—and also, may it be said, to the Roman Catholics—religious persecution began again.

On 4 March 1675 a warrant for arrest was issued against Bunyan, but it is doubtful whether he was actually imprisoned again in the county jail in that year. Joyce Godber has discovered a bond dated 21 June 1677, in which two Londoners were sureties for the release of Bunyan, and she therefore thinks that he was not imprisoned earlier than December 1676. This surmise is worth noting because, as we shall see, another question depends upon it—that of the date of composition of *The Pilgrim's Progress*. This book extended Bunyan's reputation over the whole of the British Isles, to the Continent, and even as far as America, and earned for him the title "Anglus egregius," given him in 1708 by a specialist in religious and mystical literature.

In August 1688 Bunyan was called to Reading to settle a quarrel between a father and son. He went there on horseback instead of by coach, which, as David Ogg tells us, was considered a sign of effeminacy in the seventeenth century. As a result of a journey of forty miles in the rain, he caught a chill and was obliged to take to bed in a friend's house in London. Worn out by his life of labor, he sank rapidly, and died on the last day of the month.

II

It was in Bedford Jail, in 1666, that Bunyan wrote his spiritual autobiography, with the aim of edify-

ing the brethren from whom he was separated. This type of writing belongs to a strong tradition among Dissenters, though it is stronger among Quakers than Baptists. But Bunyan was obeying an inner urge rather than conforming to a tradition.

Protestantism, particularly in its Puritan form, prompts a man to examine his conscience, and even, as John Henry Newman asserted, to contemplate himself:

I do not mean to say that Christ is not mentioned as the Author of all good, but that stress is laid rather on the believing than on the object of belief, on the comfort and persuasiveness of the doctrine rather than on the doctrine itself. And in this way religion is made to consist in contemplating ourselves, instead of Christ; not simply in looking to Christ, but in *seeing* that we look to Christ.[1]

In the spiritual life of every Christian, and of the Puritan more especially, two movements can be discerned: the first, born of penitence and humiliation before the face of God, turns inward to examine the self; the second is the contrary movement, drawing away from introspection toward the contemplation of the goals to be attained. And one of the most important of these is the work of evangelization. *Grace Abounding*, it would seem, was created out of these two movements; in it are to be found their ebb and flow, their currents now rushing ahead, now being checked and losing themselves in eddies and backwaters.

Bunyan's need of unburdening himself is turned into a means of edification, and he derives from it a sober pleasure. To tell his life story is to deepen his awareness of the richness of his own spiritual drama. As Kierkegaard remarked, if life is lived forward, it is only understood backward. So memory is the soul of Bunyan's work as it is the center of his thought. And in endeavoring, in one book after another and especially in his autobiography, to convert others, Bunyan never ceases to deepen his own faith.

Grace Abounding offers, firstly, a psychological interest. The book sheds light upon Puritan thought and feeling, and it is a remarkable account of the conversion of a religious spirit tinged with mysticism.

It would be impossible here to enter into the question of Bunyan's sincerity; but it must at least be pointed out that the resemblances often noted be-

[1]*Lectures on Justification* (London, 1838).

tween *Grace Abounding* and other Puritan autobiographies by no means prove that Bunyan was mechanically conforming to the laws of a literary genre.

True, he does imitate. Nobody today would claim for him a kind of intellectual virginity. But this is a secondary matter in literary creation, though it is of prime importance in the formation of a mind. If the confessions of the "mechanic preachers" offer certain similarities, it is first and foremost because their authors lived at the same period, in the same environment, and passed through similar experiences. Their works bear a family likeness because they themselves shared the same faith. It is a question of souls imitating souls, not of books imitating books.

But *Grace Abounding* is more than a psychological document: it is a literary masterpiece. Though it is too much to say, with Renan, that "what one says of oneself is always poetry," yet personal confession does at times become great art. It is enough to recall Rousseau's *Confessions*, Goethe's *Dichtung und Wahrheit*, Newman's *Apologia*, Gide's *Et nunc manet in Te*.

The first quality that marks *Grace Abounding* as a work of art is the creative tension communicated to it by the exceptionally vigorous temperament of the author. The second is a kind of impersonality that, paradoxically, is achieved within the very omnipresence of the author. For Bunyan sees in his own story an example—or, as we should say today, a case—which goes beyond himself and attains a general value. Even as he expresses himself in the personal manner, his personality is being effaced. He is already on the way to that dramatic transposition of his experience that is to be fully realized in *The Pilgrim's Progress*.

A comparison of sections 37 and 38 of his autobiography with sections 53 and 54, where he makes use of the same incident, should make this clear. In the former, we see Bunyan going about his work in the little town of Bedford. It is fine. A few housewives stand talking at their doors. Their remarks reflect their Calvinist faith, and they are radiant with peace and joy. In the later paragraphs, the street in Bedford has disappeared. The scene is laid on a hill, everywhere and nowhere at the same time. The spring sun has become a symbolic sun, splendid and almost divine. The little group of pious women has become a chosen people set apart by their faith from the corrupt, doomed world:

About this time, the state and happiness of these poor people at Bedford was thus, in a *dream*, or *vision*, presented to me. I saw, as if they were set on the sunny side of some high mountain, there refreshing themselves with the pleasant beams of the sun, while I was shivering and shrinking in the cold, afflicted with frost, snow, and dark clouds. Methought, also, betwixt me and them, I saw a wall that did compass about this mountain.

Bunyan then describes his attempt to break a way through the wall, and his joy at having succeeded:

Then was I exceeding glad, and went and sat down in the midst of them, and so was comforted with the light and heat of their sun.

This passage contains the keyword dream, or vision. Dreams, which were daily fare for Bunyan, allow him here, as later in *The Pilgrim's Progress*, to widen his own horizon, and to absorb without effort the lesson that every artist must learn: that to express oneself, one must know how to efface oneself.

A reflection of Pascal's is applicable to Bunyan's self-portrait: "a portrait comprises both absence and presence." It comprises the presence of the particular individual represented; and it comprises absence insofar as it goes beyond this individual and offers an image of humankind.

Bunyan tells the story of his life with tact, without ever raising his voice:

I could also have stepped into a style much higher . . . and could have adorned all things more . . . but I dare not. God did not play in convincing of me; the Devil did not play in tempting of me . . . wherefore I may not play in my relating of them . . .

The familiar style is not sought after or cultivated; it comes naturally to the pen of this man of the people:

Yea, my heart . . . would now continually hang back . . . and was as a clog on the leg of a bird to hinder her from flying.

The vocabulary is rendered expressive by its rustic flavor, and often by a kind of concrete solidity:

This, for that instant, did benumb the sinews of my best delights . . . This sentence stood like a mill post at my back . . . I have found my unbelief to set, as it were, the shoulder to the door to keep him out.

The words Bunyan uses reproduce felicitously the phenomena of automatism and the hallucinations that he experienced:

That sentence fell with weight upon my spirit . . . a voice did suddenly dart from Heaven into my soul . . . bolted upon me.

Whether the sentences grip the thought, or give way to the flow of feeling, they are always vigorous. At times there is a slight breathlessness, a hesitation, but this is soon followed by an eager springing forward toward those personal events that for Bunyan remained forever marvellous: his visions and the miracles that he believed had been worked upon him.

Frequently there are sentences composed almost entirely of monosyllabic Anglo-Saxon words that seem rather harsh:

Peace now, and before I could go a furlong as full of fear and guilt as ever heart could hold; and this was not only now and then, but my whole seven weeks' experience.

But with Bunyan even awkwardness may become beautiful; the lack of polish, the rugged rhythm, the homeliness and roughness of the words succeed in convincing us that the mode of expression is perfectly adapted to the thought and feeling. Bunyan's style is part of himself, and it vibrates with him in his struggles and his ecstasies:

Oh! the mount Sion, the heavenly Jerusalem, the innumerable company of angels, and God the judge of all, and the spirits of just men made perfect, and Jesus, have been sweet unto me in this place. I have seen that there, that I am persuaded I shall never, while in this world, be able to express.

One catches in this passage a note of nostalgia for those invisible realms that Bunyan had contemplated. The final vision in *The Pilgrim's Progress* is anticipated here, and we have a foreshadowing of the closing sentence of that work, with its melancholy restraint:

And after that, they [the angels] shut up the gates: which when I had seen, I wished myself among them.

For Bunyan, as for St. Augustine, this realm is not an object of contemplation, but a home.

Biblical reminiscences mingle with personal recollections to give a grave resonance to the style. Sometimes Bunyan uses an actual biblical quotation in the text, sometimes he merely takes a suggestion from the Bible and his imagination transmutes it.

The imagination that enables Bunyan to give a general value to his own life story also elevates his style. For style, as Proust said, is not made from a recipe, it is a matter of vision. It is because of its style, and the abiding interest of the experiences it describes, that *Grace Abounding* remains a living work.

III

THE first part of *The Pilgrim's Progress* was entered in the Stationers' Register on 22 December 1677; it was licensed in February 1678, and published in London the same year. These, the known facts, are not sufficient to satisfy the curiosity of Bunyan scholars. With that regard for precision that does honor to specialists, even when they are playing with a speculation, they want to know when the book was written.

Internal evidence and the interpretation of the facts may lead to various possibilities.

Two-thirds of the way through the book, the story is needlessly interrupted.[2] "So I awoke from my dream," says the narrator, as if he were going to end his story. And then he carelessly picks up the thread again and begins a new paragraph: "And I slept and dreamed again."

What inference may be drawn from this? John Brown, the great biographer of Bunyan, thought that the book was begun during the author's last imprisonment, broken off on his release (I awoke), and taken up again later (I dreamed again).

But when was Bunyan imprisoned for the second time? We have noted the existence of two documents: a warrant of arrest dated 4 March 1675 and a bond for Bunyan's release dated 21 June 1677. Did he then spend another period, of over two years, in Bedford Jail? According to his friend Charles Doe, the second period of captivity did not last for more than six months. It is therefore possible that Bunyan was not after all imprisoned in 1675; but that hav-

---

[2]Mr. James F. Forrest has now convinced me that the break is artistically justifiable. See his interesting article: "Bunyan's Ignorance and the Flatterer: A Study in the Literary Art of Damnation," *Studies in Philology*, 60, no. 1 (January 1963).

ing failed to appear before the Archdeacon's Court in 1676 for nonattendance at the parish church, he was only then sent to jail.

Vera Brittain and Roger Sharrock conclude from this that *The Pilgrim's Progress* was begun during the first term of imprisonment and continued during the second, four or five years later. I cannot believe this. This vigorous book, in which one feels the pressure of creative force and creative joy, and the need to press forward as quickly as possible to the end of the road that lies ahead, could not possibly have been laid aside for four years.

In the verse apology that serves as a preface to *The Pilgrim's Progress*, Bunyan tells us that the subject came to him suddenly, while he was writing another book (probably *The Heavenly Foot-man*), which he at once abandoned in order to follow this new inspiration. Ideas came to him "Like sparks that from the coals of fire do fly." Writing had never seemed to him so sweet: "Thus I set pen to paper with delight." If, as has been said, works of art can be divided into two groups, those that are "obtained" and those that are "given," *The Pilgrim's Progress* must surely be placed in the second group.

Some timorous friends objected that the reader would find in this book only a pleasant tale and be content to enjoy the "outside" of Bunyan's dream, without seeking its meaning. Bunyan took no notice of them: "I print it will; and so the case decided."[3] To our delight, in his haste he even forgot to reread what he had written. In the first edition the grammar is faulty, but this gives the language all the more relish. Later Bunyan corrected his text, and in 1679 he published a third edition, which was revised and considerably expanded.

The allegory had scarcely appeared before the author was being accused of plagiarism: "Some say the Pilgrim's Progress is not mine." Modern scholars, given to making finer distinctions, speak only of influences. Since the Middle Ages, the spiritual life of man had often been likened to a pilgrimage or a battle; there are recurring images that suggest themselves naturally to Christians brought up on the Bible; they are common property. Originality consists, in part, in the art of using the ideas of others and of appropriating anything

that may be turned to good account, wherever it may be found.

Bunyan can hardly have failed to know some of his forerunners. If he had not read Guillaume de Deguileville's *Le Pélerinage de l'homme*, even though there was a seventeenth-century English version, he had probably come across other allegorical tales inspired by the work of Deguileville. It is certain that he had made use of Richard Bernard's *The Isle of Man* (1627). Bernard provided him with actual suggestions for one of his books, *The Holy War* (1682), and also, in a more diffused and subtle way, was one of those who encouraged him "In handling figure, or similitude" and who emboldened him to indulge in "fancies [that] will stick like burs."

The Pilgrim's Progress stands at the meeting point of various currents of religious and popular literature. Bunyan owes much to the literary convention of "emblems," or a few lines of verse serving as a commentary on a picture. In the seventeenth century, one of the authors of such emblems, Francis Quarles, was called "the darling of our plebeian judgements." Bunyan, true plebeian, had a taste for this concrete poetical form of teaching, and he made use of it. He is also indebted to the books of "characters" that were fashionable in his day; and he confesses to a liking for sermons written "dialogue wise." He owes a particularly heavy debt to Arthur Dent, whose *The Plaine Mans Path-Way to Heaven* (1601), which Bunyan's first wife made him read, is a masterpiece of this type of literature. Dent's concrete, sinewy language heralds Bunyan's, which it certainly helped to form.

Finally, before his conversion, Bunyan had been a great reader of stories and romances:

Give me a ballad, a news-book, *George on horseback*, or *Bevis of Southampton*; give me some book that teaches curious arts, that tells of old fables.

He had of course given up this profane reading, but he had not forgotten it. As he was writing *The Pilgrim's Progress*, his memory was flooded with it. So the pious allegory is not without its giants, its fierce animals, and its monsters; and what glorious fights there are. The spirit of childhood lives on in the mature man.

No author ever followed the development of his own stories with greater interest than Bunyan. If he assumes an air of detachment in the narrative, he

[3]See Bunyan, *The Author's Apology*, lines 39–49. It is Bunyan's answer to his friends: "Since you are thus divided/I print it will; and so the case decided." *The Pilgrim's Progress* is, of course, "it."

makes up for this in the margin. There he bare-facedly gives way to his feelings: "O good riddance," "O brave talkative," "Christian snibbeth his fellow." But the initial enthusiasm passed and Bunyan realized that he must appear more serious; so, with charming hypocrisy, he removed from the second edition the exclamations that had added relish to the first.

Recollections of romances mingle therefore with biblical reminiscences in *The Pilgrim's Progress*. Strange bedfellows indeed. Yet, on reflection, this union of fiction and Scripture is not surprising, for the Bible was for Bunyan not only the authentic record of the word of God, but also a collection of marvellous adventure stories.

No more surprising is Bunyan's sturdy denial of any debt toward his predecessors: "It [the *Pilgrim*] came from mine own heart, so to my head. Manner and matter too was all mine own." When one has carried memories about since childhood, one honestly forgets that they came from outside; and with the help of a little vanity, it is easy to believe oneself more original than one is.

There is no doubt that Bunyan had carried *The Pilgrim's Progress* about with him for a long time. A reading of the books that preceded his greatest work shows how the allegory slowly formed itself and how it was seeking to be born. Here and there, in the sermons and treatises, one comes across the germs of ideas that are to be developed in *The Pilgrim's Progress*, and there are foreshadowings of some of the characters. If the book was conceived suddenly, bearing its author along with it irresistibly, it was preceded by a long, secret preparation.

And after all, when it is reduced to its elements, the pilgrimage of the chief character, Christian, is the story of a conversion, that is to say of an experience so intensely felt by the author as to be ever present in his heart and mind, so that he could not think or write anything without drawing upon it. Invisible, and yet pervading the work with his presence, Bunyan could claim in good faith, if not without pride: "Manner and matter too was all mine own."

Only a prolonged study of the text can do justice to its rich symbolism. Every specific episode assumes a spiritual value and has moral implications. The more one understands Puritanism, the better one can appreciate the significance a particular detail had for Bunyan and his fellow believers. But *The Pilgrim's Progress* is not wrapped up in the history of its time like a larva in its cocoon. Like every work of art, it has an autonomous existence and lives on independently of the life of its author. A work of art, Lascelles Abercrombie once said, does not exist in what it may have meant to someone else, but in what it means to me: that is the only way it can exist.

To read this old book with delight, one must achieve the same freshness of response as before a primitive picture or a medieval illumination; one must look at certain scenes through Bunyan's eyes, which have been likened to those of the artists who dressed biblical characters in the costume of fifteenth-century Italy. But then, having done this, one must venture to read *The Pilgrim's Progress* in the light of present-day thoughts and cares.

One of the first episodes gives the tone of the whole work. The author, sleeping by a cave, sees in a dream a man clothed in rags, headed away from his own house, with a book in his hand and a great burden upon his back. To everyone's amazement he is preparing to leave his own town, for he knows it to be threatened by the wrath divine. His family and friends refuse to follow him, so he sets out alone.

Who is this man? We are not told: it is simply "he," a vague pronoun. His identity is not disclosed until after a swamp has been crossed with great difficulty. Whatever may have been the exact value given it by Bunyan, this detail is full of meaning for us, irrespective of the author's intentions. To escape from the accursed city, to lift oneself out of the anonymity of the common herd, one must struggle without ceasing. In the crowd where everyone behaves like everyone else, nobody really exists. Man is degraded and lost in the indefinite. To be worthy of a distinguishing name, one must be capable of making difficult decisions, of accepting suffering and conflict.

Before Kingsley, Bunyan offered an example of muscular Christianity. Before Kierkegaard, *The Pilgrim's Progress* taught that the man who fully exists is a man on the march, stumbling but picking himself up again, always there and always elsewhere, because his gaze is fixed upon far horizons that are forever extending.

Bunyan would perhaps have been surprised by certain details of this commentary, but surely not by its general lines. For the whole book affirms that the Christian life—and indeed any life—must be the expression of a dynamic will. Through his personal experience, Bunyan knows and demonstrates that spiritual man is not a simple product of natural man, but the result and the reward of a persevering struggle.

Christian's path is strewn with obstacles: a door to be opened, a hill to be climbed, a dark valley to be crossed in the fear of death, and a fair, rank with the corruption of a world hostile to pure hearts, which it imprisons, tortures, and slays.

But the road also has its pleasant resting places: the Palace Beautiful, the Delectable Mountains, the Country of Beulah; these rare moments of repose offer the traveller the encouragement of a vision rather than the sweetness of rest. From the Palace Beautiful the Delectable Mountains can be seen, and from their summit, Heaven. In *The Pilgrim's Progress*, as in Browning's *Paracelsus*, the pilgrim's way is continually being shortened by the revelation of future truth.

The success of the book called forth a "sequel." But Bunyan did not understand the nature of the popular demand. Instead of continuing *The Pilgrim's Progress*, he produced a companion to the portrait of Christian in the portrait of a damned soul: the pilgrimage toward the celestial city is followed by the race down to hell. In 1680 *The Life and Death of Mr. Badman* appeared. It was not at all the sort of book the public was looking for. This was the signal for the publication by a certain T.S. of *The Second Part of Pilgrim's Progress* (1682). T.S. was not a common forger, but a pious man even more serious-minded than Bunyan. Far from seeking to pass himself off as Bunyan, he was endeavoring to correct the latter's errors. His chief aim was to suppress the laughter raised by the story "in some vain and frothy minds."

After receiving this lesson about the wishes of his readers, Bunyan went back to his dream, and, at the beginning of 1684, he published the true continuation of his allegory.

IV

THE first part of *The Pilgrim's Progress* described a conversion. It was a solitary journey; Christian's two companions, Faithful and Hopeful, are really only two other aspects of himself. Writing from his own intimate experience, Bunyan showed that on the mystical pilgrimage, "one cannot possibly have company," as Kierkegaard says.

The second part is not the projection of a personal drama, but a transposition of pastoral experience. Bunyan's human horizon has broadened and lost its hardness of line. The author has learned that one can be a good Christian without having a heroic soul, and that among the elect there are weak people like Mr. Fearing, Mr. Ready-to-Halt, Mr. Much-Afraid, Mr. Feeble-Mind. So the progress of a group is substituted for that of a solitary man. After the grandeur of lone battles comes the warmth of fighting shoulder to shoulder and the sweetness of friendship.

The doctrinal responsibility of the pastor is shown in details that interested the first readers. As for the presence of women, it can be explained, as Sharrock says, by the growing place they occupied in the church at Bedford.

As in the first part, the atmosphere is created from the outset, and its quality is sustained throughout. Christian's wife and her friend Mercy set out one "sunshine morning." Bunyan has learned that, as another Puritan, Richard Baxter, says, the signs of a soul reborn are not sorrowing and tears but love and joy. His dealings with others have taught him this, and also, and above all, his personal experience, which is not recorded completely in *Grace Abounding*. To say, as has sometimes been said, that Bunyan's religion is that of a sick soul is to ignore the second part of *The Pilgrim's Progress*. On the contrary, his religion is that of a healthy mind.

Christiana's route is the same as her husband's, but where for him darkness broods, for her there is light. In the journey of the soul throughout the world, it is not the places that change but the traveller.

Christiana is accompanied by friends whereas Christian journeys alone, so introspection gives way to the observation of others by a man who smiles at life and allows himself innocent mischief. The tense, swift-moving spiritual drama is succeeded by a sort of middle-class novel. Above all, a less narrow ideal of life is manifested—a friendliness toward the good things of the earth, a compassion and a love for mankind that are Bunyan's finest moral and religious messages.

A book so richly nourished by self-knowledge and knowledge of others could be no ordinary allegory. Usually, allegory only dresses up phantoms duly labeled Avarice, Lust, Faith, Charity, and so on. To every action and every character is attached a precise meaning and one meaning only, which is guessed once and for all. Allegory belongs to the realm of convention. But *The Pilgrim's Progress* belongs to the realm of nature and of life; its pilgrims are not deprived of flesh and blood. Bunyan has even stressed this concrete quality through one of his heroes: "Not *Honesty* in the abstract, but *Honest* is my name."

We are not asked to watch capital-letter Vices and Virtues, but, as Coleridge so aptly put it, villagers whose neighbors have given them nicknames. This is another way of saying that one of the first merits of the book is its realism, its twofold realism: the psychological realism of the characters and the descriptive realism of the setting, which owes much to Bedfordshire.

The mystic path of the pilgrims is also an old Roman way, in poor repair, passing by dangerous swamps, resounding to the wheels of coaches, frequented by thieves as well as by honest folk, skirting an orchard enclosed by high walls or a meadow bounded by hedges. Now it climbs a hill, now it descends into a valley that echoes with a shepherd's song.

Bunyan's love of nature is expressed with that vigor that he put into all his feelings and all his actions:

Here he would lie down, embrace the ground and kiss the very flowers that grew in this valley. He would now be up every morning by break of day.

He borrowed many details from the life of his time, and his Vanity Fair, that microcosm of a corrupt world, resembles the fairs at Elstow, at Stourbridge near Cambridge, or even St. Bartholomew Fair, immortalized by Ben Jonson.

At times the observation is enlivened by a touch of satire, as in the description of the tribunal before which the pilgrims appeared. To depict this scene, a sorry farce showing only a parody of justice, Bunyan had only to remember his own trial or that of many another Puritan.

The historian can even detect in *The Pilgrim's Progress* the reflection of the author's doctrinal and other quarrels, as well as of his pastoral duties. For it must be remembered that to Bunyan's contemporaries this tale was also, and perhaps even primarily, a tract, of which Coleridge could say, "It

is in my conviction, incomparably the best *summa theologiae evangelicae* ever produced by a writer not miraculously inspired"; but a theology, may it be noted, upon which Coleridge was too much inclined to exaggerate Luther's influence at the expense of Calvin's.

The modern reader who is unable to discern what is polemic and propaganda and strict Calvinism in the book must lose part of its primary meaning. But our unawareness of some of the original implications of the allegory does not necessarily lead to a weakening of its human significance and its reduction to "a pleasant narrative of devils and angels," to quote a critic of the historical school. In any case, in the second part these devils and angels are almost entirely superseded by familiar figures, who are grouped together in numerous scenes where the dignity of the Puritan home is charmingly depicted.

Bunyan's creative talent is displayed even more in the character studies than in the painting of the background. Naturally the most detailed portrait is that of Christian, in whom the author has fused imaginatively the good and bad qualities that he has found and analyzed in himself. Yet how flat this character is beside its model. How much richer is the real living figure captured in *Grace Abounding*. How much less strange are the battles fought by Christian against the monster Apollyon than the tinker's own demons and inner conflicts.

Bunyan has intentionally imposed a rather systematic order upon what is in real life tumult and chaos. He has apportioned out his experience and his being, giving a little of himself to several characters, allowing each one life and vitality, but not endowing any with all of his own complexity.

This is in no way surprising, for Bunyan's intention was only to use intelligently the various traditions upon which he was drawing. His chosen literary form had its own requirements and limits, but within these limits the author has succeeded in giving life to a world whose bold contours give vigorous expression to the truth of his observation.

It is a world that has the variety of life itself, where homeliness mingles with grandeur and heightens it by contrast; a world where reality is peopled by the creatures of dreams, and where the marvellous is revealed to the creatures of earth; a world in which Bunyan believes because he sees it with intense clarity during the whole process of creation.

With what sure movements he leads us into this

little universe. The first scene in the book affords a perfect example of this:

As I walk'd through the wilderness of this world, I lighted on a certain place, where was a den; and I laid me down in that place to sleep; and as I slept I dreamed a dream. I dreamed and behold I saw a man cloathed with rags standing in a certain place, with his face from his own house, a Book in his hand, and a great burden upon his back. I looked and saw him open the Book, and read therein; and as he read, he wept and trembled: and not being able longer to contain, he brake out with a lamentable cry, saying, what shall I do?

Bunyan presents things in the bareness of their outlines; he does not clog his meaning by using adjectives. He multiplies the verbs, rejecting the imperfect form in favor of the aorist, and furnishes his sentences with short words, whose pure clearsounding vowels are carried vigorously along by the firm compact consonants.

The ragged pilgrim, so forcefully portrayed at the very outset, throws his shadow over the whole book. The unity of the story is created around its symbolic hero.

Bunyan always links narrative and dialogue together very naturally. The dialogue is brisk, sprinkled with colloquialisms and racy proverbs:

His house is as empty of religion as the white of an egg is of savour. . . . Will a man give a penny to fill his belly with hay? . . .

And always everywhere there is that simplicity that Coleridge considered necessary to works of imagination because only through simplicity can the reader enter fully into the fiction.

Bunyan commands a variety of tone. The familiar tone often becomes grave. The rather rugged phrasing of the dialogue follows a more musical and flowing passage of narrative. And if the good homely words used by the mystic pilgrims bind them to the earth, the biblical expressions and metaphors give to their horizon perspectives of infinity:

Now as they walked in this land, they had more rejoicing than in parts more remote from the Kingdom to which they were bound; and drawing near to the City they had yet a more perfect view thereof. It was builded of pearls and precious stones, also the street thereof was paved with gold, so that by reason of the natural glory of the City, and the reflection of the sunbeams upon it, Christian, with desire fell sick. . . . If you see my Beloved, tell him that I am sick of love.

Of course, the second part of *The Pilgrim's Progress* differs from the first in form as well as in content. The first book, being the story of a conversion, a man's spiritual biography, possesses a dramatic unity that the second lacks. What tension there is in the book resides in the life of the hero and is only a softened reflection of the vital tension of the author. The first book is a forerunner of those novels in which the passage of time reveals growth of character. The second book, on the other hand, heralds those in which the characters are static and remain unchanged in all circumstances. But both will stand the test of prolonged and detailed study better than many works that at first sight appear more brilliant.

The Pilgrim's Progress grows upon one as one becomes more familiar with it. It may disappoint at first, but it wins over every reader who gives it a friendly trial. It brings the riches of a strong personality, of thought, and of an ancient and deeply-rooted popular culture. It is both an individual and a collective work. Q. D. Leavis is right in saying: "It is not fantastic to assert that it was the puritan culture as much as Bunyan that produced *The Pilgrim's Progress*."

V

Grace Abounding and *The Pilgrim's Progress* reveal Bunyan at his best, but in order to measure his stature accurately, at least two more of his works must be considered: *The Life and Death of Mr. Badman* and *The Holy War*.

On the whole, Bunyan specialists agree in admiring *The Pilgrim's Progress*, but as regards *Badman* they agree to differ—a point worth noting because it is significant: a book that provokes controversy is a live book. In a valuable article Maurice Hussey speaks unreservedly of the greatness of the work. Sharrock, in an excellent study, also expresses much admiration, though with a certain reserve. But both critics affirm the literary value of *Badman* rather than analyze it. They both, rightly, stress the historical interest of this work, but in so doing they defeat their own intention of taking it away from the student of history to offer it to a wider public. *Badman* certainly deserves more readers, precisely because social history is too rich a field to be turned into a private preserve for specialists only.

The work is at one and the same time a manual of personal, family, and social behavior, and a record of the habits of the middle class at the time of the Restoration. This record is not without pleasing sketches; but the central figure, who promises to overflow with life, for his rascality is of an extremely vigorous kind, is stifled by the didactic purpose of the author. He ceases to be a man and becomes a scarecrow, or, as Bunyan says in a moment of unconscious self-criticism, "one massy body of sins," of all the vices in their very often picturesque seventeenth-century costumes.

Badman is not a person, he is an example intended to warn the reader by frightening him. He has his ancestor in the exempla of the medieval sermons and of various other books that Bunyan was fond of, such as Samuel Clarke's *A Mirrour or Looking-Glasse Both for Saints and Sinners* (1646).

Since Badman is Christian's counterpart, it is permissible to compare them. Christian is a truly symbolic personage, that is to say he is rich in potentialities. He is not squeezed into an allegorical garment that paralyzes him. Badman has none of the suppleness and diversity that are qualities of the true symbol as they are qualities of life. He does not come before us as a creature of flesh and blood in whom we can believe; nor has he the power of one of those great conventional literary creations that in spite of everything are endued with something of the mystery of life.

Every work of art possesses an internal coherence; every great work of literature is a universe with its own atmosphere and its own being, which belong so completely to it that they appear unreal, or ridiculous, or lifeless outside of it. *Badman* does not fulfill either of these criteria. It is the biography, tortuous yet void of surprise, of a model scoundrel who becomes more and more wicked in obedience to a determinism as pitiless as Calvin's predestination. Nowhere do I feel the author's creative imagination at work, either in the portrait of the principal figure or in the pictures of social life.

It is usual to praise the book's realism, but is there any value in the realism that is no more than a reproduction of ordinary life? True realism is a creation, not a copy. Bunyan has failed to recreate the society that he has observed; all he has done is to provide laborious illustrations of its customs and its spirit.

These illustrations are nevertheless always interesting. The observation is precise, picturesque, plentiful. The strokes of the drawing are rather thick, rather heavy, but they are not blurred. Even if Bunyan has lost the creative joy that bore him along on an irresistible wave in the wake of the heavenly pilgrims, he has lost none of his force and none of his good workmanship.

True, the dialogue is sometimes wearisome. We hear the Bunyan of the meetinghouse instead of the Bunyan of Parnassus. But at their best the sentences are sinewy, the vocabulary keeps its concrete and evocative solidity. And the student of literary history will find in *Badman* a notable landmark on the way leading to the flowering of the novel in the eighteenth century.

Like *Badman*, *The Holy War* is a work "obtained" rather than a work "given," but nowhere are Bunyan's subtlety and the extent of his knowledge more marked.

It is another allegory, in which it may be said that, among other things, Bunyan proposes to justify the ways of God to man, according to his own ideas. The work has its epic moments, such as the account of the fall of the angels and their attack upon the human soul. But the author is not content with that. He returns to the story of his conversion and of his inner conflicts, enlarging his scope still further. After the journey of Christian, we now have the struggle of an entire city. Moreover, secondary themes are associated with the main theme of conversion. A political and social theme based upon contemporary events runs through the book; and a sectarian theme also appears occasionally, connected with belief in the millennium, or what was then called the Fifth Monarchy.

For these themes to have been fused into a coherent story, they would have had to respond to one another like the melodies of a fugue, to have been represented by the same symbols, and to have mingled without either losing themselves or conflicting. But no amount of skill in literary counterpoint could have succeeded, or could ever succeed, in harmonizing such discordant strains.

The Holy War provides an interesting example of the failure of a man who goes against his own genius. Bunyan, a spontaneous writer, is never more felicitous than when he is driven on by his passion and the fervor of his inspiration and lets his pen run away with him; yet he spent two years in contriving and arranging the meanings of his allegory according to architectural plans that, despite their admirable boldness, are totally lacking in harmony and clarity.

The Holy War is a failure, but it is the superb failure of a great ambition, the failure of a vigorous and courageous intelligence.

VI

BUNYAN's strong personality united and harmonized opposing qualities. A manual worker, he was essentially an intellectual in the only sense the word ought to bear: he was not only a man who loved books (Bunyan may have read little but he thought deeply about what he read), but a man whose thought directed and governed his life.

But he was an intellectual who became a writer less from a taste for writing—however pronounced that taste may have been—than from a sense of duty and the need to act; for with him, writing was primarily a form of action. And this action found its meaning and its spring in his religious and moral fervor, as his great allegories found their inspiration in his dreams and mystical visions.

Though Bunyan felt the potency of words, he never yielded to it without disciplining his pleasure and submitting it to a purpose. Without the genius that so often raised him above commonplace didacticism, he would only have been an energetic preacher, gifted with great verbal facility. Of course a work of art teaches also, but it is by offering a vision of order and not by enunciating precepts.

Having suffered, struggled, meditated—in short, having lived fully—Bunyan could pour into his work the riches of an authentic existence: his difficult growth, the conflicts of his divided mind, the unifying force of a faith deepened by action, then the fruit of it all—gravity and dignity without inflexibility, wider human understanding, warm sympathy toward people, and a tranquil attitude toward things.

As he said himself in so many words, the solemn music of the bass gave way to the joyful chords of the high notes. To achieve maturity, to conquer his own soul, was for him to reach the clear harmonies of the trumpet and the harp:

The first string that the musician usually touches is the bass, when he intends to put all in tune. God also plays upon this string first . . . [but] in the Book of the Revela-

tions, the Saved are compared to a company of Musicians that play upon their trumpets and harps, and sing their songs before the Throne.

Bunyan presents at one and the same time the true aspect of Puritanism—which is not the fanaticism with which it has often been willfully confused—and the spectacle of a type of humanity that transcends the doctrine and the age that formed it.

His work has gained in power and in profundity from having been born in hours of oppression and sorrow rather than in the exaltation of the short-lived triumph of Puritanism. This late birth brought it the twofold benefit of the author's broader human experience and of a closer agreement with the nation as a whole. Puritanism would hardly have understood its own nature so well if it had sought to express itself in the fever of action. In its time for remembering, it was fortunate in having an artist for whom memory was the soul of thought.

SELECTED BIBLIOGRAPHY

I. BIBLIOGRAPHY. E. Venables, *Life of John Bunyan* (London, 1888), contains a bibliography by J. P. Anderson of Bunyan's works and of critical and biographical studies; J. B. Wharey, ed., *The Pilgrim's Progress* (Oxford, 1928), 2nd ed. rev. by R. Sharrock (Oxford, 1960) contains bibliography of the first eds. of *The Pilgrim's Progress*; F. M. Harrison, *A Bibliography of the Works of John Bunyan*, Supplement to the Bibliographical Society's Transactions, no. 6 (Oxford, 1932); F. M. Harrison, *Catalogue of the John Bunyan Library* (Bedford, 1938), describes the Frank Mott Harrison Collection at Bedford Public Library; F. M. Harrison, *A Handlist of Editions of the First Part of The Pilgrim's Progress* (lim. ed., Hove, 1941); F. M. Harrison, "Notes on the Early Editions of *Grace Abounding*," *Baptist Quarterly*, vol. 11 (1943); D. E. Smith, "Publication of John Bunyan's Works in America," *Bulletin of the New York Public Library* (December 1962); R. Sharrock, "John Bunyan," in A. E. Dyson, ed., *The English Novel: Select Bibliographical Guides* (London, 1974), an excellent critical and bibliographical guide.

II. COLLECTED WORKS. *The Works of That Eminent Servant of Christ, Mr. John Bunyan . . . Together with a Large Alphabetical Table [by C. Doe. With a Prefatory Epistle by E. Chandler and J. Wilson]*, 1 vol. fol. (London, 1692); *The Second Edition [with additions]*, 2 vols. (London, 1736–1737); *The Third Edition [with new addi-*

tions, and a preface by the Rev. G. Whitefield], 2 vols. (London, 1767–1768); G. Offor, ed., *The Works of John Bunyan*, 3 vols. (Glasgow, 1853; repr. New York, 1973), contains an intro. to each treatise, notes, and a sketch of his life, times, and contemporaries; H. Stebbing, ed., *The Entire Works of John Bunyan*, 4 vols. (London, 1859–1860; repr. Hildesheim—New York, 1970), with original intro., notes, and a memoir of the author.

III. SEPARATE WORKS. *Some Gospel-Truths Opened according to the Scriptures* (London, 1656); *A Vindication of . . . Some Gospel-Truths* (London, 1657); *A Few Sighs from Hell* (London, 1658); *The Doctrine of the Law and Grace Unfolded* (London, 1659); *Profitable Meditations, Fitted to Mans Different Condition* (London, 1661); *Christian Behaviour; or, The Fruits of True Christianity* (London, 1663); *I Will Pray with the Spirit* (2nd ed., London, 1663); *A Mapp Shewing the Order and Causes of Salvation and Damnation* (London, ca. 1664), no copy known of 1st ed., repr. in Doe's folio ed. of 1692; *One Thing Is Needful* (London, ca. 1665); *The Holy City; or, The New Jerusalem* (London, 1665); *The Resurrection of the Dead, and Eternal Judgement* (London, 1665); *Grace Abounding to the Chief of Sinners* (London, 1666); *A Christian Dialogue*, probably printed between 1666 and 1672, no copy known; *A New and Useful Concordance* (London, ca. 1672); *A Confession of My Faith, and a Reason of My Practice* (London, 1672); *A Defence of the Doctrine of Justification, by Faith in Jesus Christ* (London, 1672); *The Barren Fig Tree: or, The Doom and Downfal of the Fruitless Professor* (London, 1673); *Differences in Judgement about Water Baptism, No Bar to Communion* (London, 1673); *Peaceable Principles and True* (London, 1674), no copy known of 1st ed.; *Instruction for the Ignorant* (London, 1675); *Light for Them That Sit in Darkness; or, A Discourse of Jesus Christ* (London, 1675); *Saved By Grace* (London, 1676), no copy known of 1st ed., repr. in Doe's folio ed. of 1692; *The Strait Gate; or, Great Difficulty of Going to Heaven* (London, 1676); *Come and Welcome, to Jesus Christ* (London, 1678); *The Pilgrim's Progress, Part I* (London, 1678); *A Treatise of the Fear of God* (London, 1679); *The Life and Death of Mr. Badman* (London, 1680); *The Holy War: Made by Shaddai upon Diabolus, for the Regaining of the Metropolis of the World* (London, 1682); *A Case of Conscience Resolved* (London, 1683); *The Greatness of the Soul, and Unspeakableness of the Loss Thereof* (London, 1683); *A Caution to Stir Up to Watch Against Sin* (London, 1684); *A Holy Life, the Beauty of Christianity* (London, 1684); *The Pilgrim's Progress, Part II* (London, 1684); *Seasonable Counsel: or, Advice to Sufferers* (London, 1684); *A Discourse upon the Pharisee and the Publicane* (London, 1685); *Questions about the Nature and Perpetuity of the Seventh-Day Sabbath* (London, 1685); *A Book for Boys and Girls: or, Country Rhimes for Children* (London, 1686); *The Advocateship of Jesus Christ* (London, 1688); *A Discourse of the Building of the House of God* (London, 1688); *Good News for the Vilest of Men: or, A Help for Despairing Souls* (London, 1688), 2nd ed. entitled *The Jerusalem Sinner Saved; or Good News for Despairing Souls* (London, 1689); *Solomon's Temple Spiritualized* (London, 1688); *The Water of Life* (London, 1688).

IV. POSTHUMOUSLY PUBLISHED WORKS. (*Note*: Posthumous works dated 1692 were first printed in Doe's one-vol. folio ed. of *The Works*. Those dated 1736 first appeared in vol. I of Doe's 2nd ed.) *Mr. John Bunyan's Last Sermon* (London, 1689); *The Acceptable Sacrifice: or, The Excellency of a Broken Heart* (London, 1689); *A Description of Antichrist and His Ruin* (London, 1692); *Christ a Compleat Saviour in His Intercession* (London, 1692); *The Desires of the Righteous Granted* (London, 1692); *An Exposition of the First Ten Chapters of Genesis* (London, 1692); *Of the House of the Forest of Lebanon* (London, 1692); *Israel's Hope Encouraged* (London, 1692); *Of Justification by Imputed Righteousness* (London, 1692); *Paul's Departure and Crown* (London, 1692); *The Saint's Knowledge of Christ's Love* (London, 1692); *The Saint's Privilege and Profit* (London, 1692); *The Heavenly Foot-Man* (London, 1698), printed for Charles Doe, date of composition unknown but was begun before *The Pilgrim's Progress*; *Of the Law and a Christian* (London, 1736); *Of the Trinity and a Christian* (London, 1736); *A Relation of the Imprisonment of Mr. John Bunyan* (London, 1765).

V. SELECTED FACSIMILE AND ANNOTATED EDITIONS. *The Pilgrim's Progress* (London, 1847), printed from 1st ed., with notices of all subsequent additions made by the author, with intro. by G. Offor; *The Pilgrim's Progress* (London, 1875, 1877, 1895, 1930), repro. of the 1st ed., facs. of 2nd ed. of Pt. I (London, 1970); E. Venables, ed., *The Pilgrim's Progress, Grace Abounding, and A Relation of His Imprisonment* (Oxford, 1879; 2nd ed., rev., 1900), revision by M. Peacock; Rev. J. Brown, ed., *The Pilgrim's Progress* (London, 1887), with intro. and notes; J. B. Wharey, ed., *The Pilgrim's Progress* (Oxford, 1928; 2nd ed., rev., Oxford, 1960, corr., 1968), revision by R. Sharrock; *The Pilgrim's Progress and The Life and Death of Mr. Badman* (London, 1928), intro. by G. B. Harrison; G. B. Harrison, ed., *Grace Abounding and The Life and Death of Mr. Badman* (London, 1928); *The Life and Death of Mr. Badman* (London, 1929), with an intro. by B. Dobrée; H. A. Talon, ed., *God's Knotty Log* (New York, 1961), contains intro. and *The Heavenly Foot-Man* and *The Pilgrim's Progress*; R. Sharrock, ed., *Grace Abounding* (Oxford, 1962); R. Sharrock, ed., *The Pilgrim's Progress* (Harmondsworth, 1965); R. Sharrock, ed., *Grace Abounding and The Pilgrim's Progress* (London, 1966), in the Oxford Standard Authors series; J. F. Forrest, ed., *The Holy War* (New York, 1967); J. Thorpe, ed., *The Pilgrim's Progress* (Boston, 1969); *Grace Abounding* (Menston, 1970); R. Sharrock, gen. ed., *The Miscellaneous Works of John Bunyan*, 13 vols. (Oxford,

1976), vol. II: *The Doctrine of the Law and Grace Unfolded and I Will Pray with the Spirit*, edited by R. L. Greaves; the series will include all of Bunyan's works except *Grace Abounding, The Pilgrim's Progress, The Life and Death of Mr. Badman*, and *The Holy War*.

VI. SOME CRITICAL AND BIOGRAPHICAL STUDIES. T. B. Macaulay, *Critical and Historical Essays*, 3 vols. (London, 1843), vol. I contains the essay "John Bunyan," which was published separately (Cambridge, 1898; Oxford, 1914); J. B. Grier, *Studies in the English of Bunyan* (Philadelphia, 1872); J. A. Froude, *Bunyan* (London, 1880); Rev. J. Brown, *John Bunyan, His Life, Times and Work* (London, 1885), revised by F. M. Harrison (London, 1928; repr. New York, 1969).

J. B. Wharey, *A Study of the Sources of Bunyan's Allegories* (Baltimore, 1904), with special reference to de Deguileville's *Le Pélerinage de l'homme*; W. H. White [Mark Rutherford], *John Bunyan* (London, 1905); G. B. Shaw, *Dramatic Opinions and Essays*, 2 vols. (London, 1907), contains an essay on Bunyan; C. H. Firth, *John Bunyan*, English Association leaflet no. 19 (London, 1911), reprinted in his *Essays, Historical and Literary* (Oxford, 1938); G. O. Griffith, *John Bunyan* (London, 1927); G. B. Harrison, *John Bunyan: A Study in Personality* (London, 1928); F. M. Harrison, *John Bunyan: A Story of His Life* (London, 1928; repr. 1964).

W. Y. Tindall, *John Bunyan, Mechanick Preacher* (New York, 1934; repr. New York, 1967); M. P. Willcocks, *Bunyan Calling: A Voice from the Seventeenth Century* (London, 1943); R. Sharrock, "Bunyan and the English Emblem Writers," *Review of English Studies*, 21 (April 1945); R. Sharrock, "Spiritual Autobiography in *The Pilgrim's Progress*," *Review of English Studies*, 24 (April 1948); H. A. Talon, *John Bunyan: L'Homme et l'oeuvre* (Paris, 1948), translated by B. Wall as *John Bunyan: The Man and His Work* (London, 1951); J. Godber, "The Imprisonments of John Bunyan," *Transactions of the Congregational Historical Society*, 16 (1949); M. Hussey, "Bunyan's Mr. Ignorance," *Modern Language Review*, 44 (October 1949); M. Hussey, "Bunyan's *The Life and Death of Mr. Badman*," *Congregational Quarterly*, 28 (November 1950); F. R. Leavis, *The Common Pursuit* (London, 1952), contains the essay "Bunyan Through Modern Eyes"; D. Van Ghent, *The English Novel: Form and Function* (New York, 1953), contains the chapter "On *The Pilgrim's Progress*"; R. Sharrock, *John Bunyan* (London, 1954; rev. ed., 1968); L. D. Lerner, "Bunyan and the Puritan Culture," *Cambridge Journal*, 7 (January 1954); J. Blondel, *Allégorie et réalisme dans "The Pilgrim's Progress,"* Archives des Lettres Modernes, no. 28 (Paris, 1959).

O. E. Winslow, *John Bunyan* (New York, 1961); H. A. Talon, "Space and the Hero in *The Pilgrim's Progress*," *Études anglaises*, 14 (April 1961); J. F. Forrest, "Bunyan's Ignorance and the Flatterer: A Study in the Literary Art of Damnation," *Studies in Philology*, 60 (January 1963); J. F. Forrest, "Mercy with Her Mirror," *Philological Quarterly*, 62 (January 1963); L. L. Schücking, *Die Puritanische Familie in Literarsoziologischer Sicht* (Berne–Munich, 1964), translated by B. Battershaw as *The Puritan Family: A Social Study from Literary Sources* (London, 1969), originally published as *Die Familie im Puritanismus: Studien uber Familie und Literatur im England im 16., 17. und 18. Jahrhundert* (Leipzig–Berlin, 1929); R. Pascal, "The Present Tense in *The Pilgrim's Progress*," *Modern Language Review*, 60 (January 1965); M. R. Watson, "The Drama of *Grace Abounding*," *English Studies*, 46 (December 1965); R. Sharrock, *John Bunyan: The Pilgrim's Progress*, Studies in English Literature, 27 (London, 1966); J. N. Morris, *Version of the Self: Studies in English Autobiographies from John Bunyan to John Stuart Mill* (New York, 1966); D. J. Alpaugh, "Emblem and Interpretation in *The Pilgrim's Progress*," *English Literary History*, 33 (September 1966); D. E. Smith, *John Bunyan in America* (Bloomington, Ind., 1966); U. M. Kaufmann, *"The Pilgrim's Progress" and Traditions in Puritan Meditation*, Yale Studies in English, no. 163 (New Haven, 1966); B. J. Mandel, "Bunyan and the Autobiographer's Artistic Purpose," *Criticism*, 10 (Summer 1968); R. L. Greaves, *John Bunyan* (Appleford—Abingdon, 1969), a study of Bunyan's theology.

D. Ebner, *Autobiography in Seventeenth-Century England* (The Hague, 1971); S. E. Fish, "Progress in *The Pilgrim's Progress*," *English Literary Renaissance*, 1 (Autumn 1971), reprinted and expanded in *Self-Consuming Artifacts* (Berkeley—Los Angeles—London, 1972); R. F. Hardin, "Bunyan, Mr. Ignorance, and the Quakers," *Studies in Philology*, 69 (1972); O. C. Watkins, *The Puritan Experience* (London, 1972); J. R. Knott, Jr., "Bunyan's Gospel Day: A Reading of *The Pilgrim's Progress*," *English Literary Renaissance*, 3 (Autumn 1973); W. Iser, "Bunyan's *Pilgrim's Progress*: The Doctrine of Predestination and the Shaping of the Novel," in *The Implied Reader: Patterns of Communication in Prose Fiction from Bunyan to Beckett* (Baltimore—London, 1974), earlier ed. published in German (Munich, 1972), the essay on Bunyan originally published in German (1960); M. Furlong, *Puritan's Progress: A Study of John Bunyan* (London, 1975); E. W. Bruss, *Autobiographical Acts: The Changing Situation of a Literary Genre* (Baltimore, 1976); R. Sharrock, ed., *Bunyan: The Pilgrim's Progress* (London, 1976).

THE RESTORATION COURT POETS

Vivian de Sola Pinto

INTRODUCTION

THE last group of English courtier poets belonged to a set of lively young people in whose company Charles II spent much of his time after the Restoration. In 1661 James Butler, duke of Ormonde, described them to the lord chancellor, Edward Hyde, earl of Clarendon, as "confident young men who abhorred all discourse that was serious, and, in the liberty they assumed in drollery and raillery, preserved no reverence towards God or man, but laughed at all sober men, and even at religion itself." The historian Gilbert Burnet gives us the names of some of these "confident young men": "the three most eminent wits of that time . . . the earls of Dorset and Rochester and Sir Charles Sidley." A brilliant addition to the group was George Etherege, who became acquainted with Lord Buckhurst (later earl of Dorset) as a result of the success of his first play, *The Comical Revenge*, in March 1664. These young men, together with the slightly older and immensely rich George Villiers, duke of Buckingham, and a number of less distinguished figures, formed the circle known as the court wits, described by Andrew Marvell as "the merry gang," who led a gay, dissipated life in the 1660's and 1670's, the period called by Dryden "A very Merry Dancing, Drinking, Laughing, Quaffing, and unthinking Time." Legends clustered round the personalities of the court wits, and they were built up into figures of diabolical wickedness in the age of the new puritanism that followed the Glorious Revolution. Thomas Macaulay in the second chapter of volume I of his *History of England* speaks in horrified tones of "the open profligacy of the court and Cavaliers" after the Restoration and "the outrageous profaneness and licentiousness of the Buckinghams and the Sedleys." Unfortunately criticism of their writings was for long colored by this moralistic condemnation of their lives. Now that the great flood of English puritanism has sub-

sided, it is possible to see the court wits and their writings in a truer perspective.

They were certainly no mere idle profligates. Their diversions included music, the theater, reading and translating the classics, and literary discussion as well as women and drinking. Both Rochester and Buckhurst fought as volunteers at sea in the second Dutch war. Rochester, surprisingly, seems to have been an affectionate, if not a faithful, husband and a good landlord. Dorset (Buckhurst) was a generous and discerning patron of poets and dramatists. Sedley, after a riotous youth, became a useful member of the House of Commons, and Etherege was a successful dramatist and later, by seventeenth-century standards, an efficient diplomat. They were men living between two worlds, on the one hand the old hierarchical universe mirrored in the traditional life of the court, and on the other, the new materialistic philosophy and science and the atomized society of free individuals. They now can be seen not, as they have been traditionally pictured, as a set of young royalists indulging in wild orgies as a reaction against the austerity of the Rule of the Saints, but as a postwar generation reacting as much against the stiff formality of the old cavaliers as against the narrow religiosity of the Puritans. They were intellectuals as well as gay young men about town. Both Rochester and Sedley received part of their education at Wadham College, Oxford, one of the cradles of the new experimental science; and they all read and admired the works of Thomas Hobbes, the first English philosopher to propound a purely materialistic and utilitarian system. Hobbes was to them something very much like what Karl Marx was to the young English poets of the 1930's, a symbol of liberation from antique inhibitions and outworn ideas. Sedley, addressing a typical court wit, wrote:

Thou art an Atheist, *Quintus*, and a Wit,
Thinkst all was of self-moving Attoms made.

If Hobbes was right and the universe consisted merely of atoms governed by mathematical laws, it surely was only sensible to enjoy the good things of this world and ignore the croakings of killjoys, whether they were Anglican parsons, Puritan preachers, or old-fashioned cavaliers. The age was one of experiment, and the court wits tried the experiment of living in a little pagan paradise of sensual, aesthetic, and intellectual pleasure. Behind the experiment lay a vision and a theory. The vision was well described by Charles Lamb as "the Utopia of gallantry, where pleasure is duty and the manners perfect freedom." The theory was what was known in seventeenth-century Europe as "libertinism,"[1] a term that implied a revolt against traditional morality and institutions, and a way of life based on the satisfaction of natural passions and appetites. Rochester, who had the most philosophical mind of the group, summed up the libertine theory in the following lines:

> Thus, whilst 'gainst false reas'ning I inveigh,
> I own right *Reason*, which I wou'd obey;
> That *Reason*, which distinguishes by sense,
> And gives us *Rules* of good and ill from thence:
>
> Your *Reason* hinders, mine helps t' enjoy,
> Renewing Appetites, yours wou'd destroy.
> ("A Satyr Against Mankind," 98–101; 104–105)

The attempt to live in accordance with these principles was bound to fail in the face of the realities of the human condition; but the vision that lay behind it, as well as the contradictions that it involved, provided material for the best comedies of the period and for the poetry of the courtiers.

The court wits must not be judged as professional poets. Like their predecessors, the cavalier poets of the court of Charles I, they were gentlemen amateurs and their verses, which were mostly "occasional," were written not for publication in the modern sense of the word but for circulation in manuscript among their friends. This does not mean that they were mere *dilettanti*, for whom the writing of verse was simply an elegant game. This was, doubtless, true of the minor figures in the court circle, but for the leading wits poetry was an art and a vital expression of a truly creative culture founded on a knowledge of books and experience of life. They aimed at what they called "ease" or colloquial naturalness in poetry, and were well aware that this could be achieved only by craftsmanship, even though their practice was sometimes marred by gentlemanly carelessness. Their poetry belongs to the courtly-classical or polite tradition, which descends from Ben Jonson through the cavalier poets of the reign of Charles I. This tradition underwent a change somewhere about the middle of the century, when it began to acquire the character that is called Augustan. The change is apparent in the poetry of Edmund Waller and Abraham Cowley, two poets of the midcentury whose work was greatly admired by the wits.

Hobbes, who was influential both as a literary critic and as a philosopher, had close connections with both these poets; and in their best work they are trying to carry into effect his demand for a new "perspicuity," worldliness, and realism in poetry.[2] They saw themselves as new Augustans renovating English poetry after the English Civil War, as Virgil and Horace renovated Latin poetry after the civil wars of Rome. This new "Augustan" movement could tend either toward a greater actuality and realism, in accordance with the spirit of the new science and the new philosophy, or toward an elegant, rococo neoclassicism, not without charm but always in danger of becoming pompous and insipid. Both tendencies are apparent in the poetry of the court wits. At its worst it is not very far removed from Etherege's parody of the fashionable love lyric in *The Man of Mode* (1676):

> How Charming Phillis is, how fair!
> Ah that she were as willing,
> To ease my wounded heart of Care
> And make her Eyes less killing.

But in their best poetry they were saved from this kind of thing by their good sense, their wit, and their irony. They were helped, too, by their contact with a tradition that is commonly ignored by the literary historians. This was the tradition of the street ballad and popular song, that lusty growth of English vernacular poetry found in innumerable broadsides sold in the streets and taverns, and in the popular verse miscellanies such as the *Drolleries*

---

[1] It is well described by Dale Underwood in *Etherege and the Seventeenth-Century Comedy of Manners* (1957), pp. 10–36.

[2] See his "Answer to Davenant" (1650) in J. E. Spingarn, ed., *Critical Essays of the Seventeenth Century*, II, p.63.

and *Academies of Compliments*, which were best-sellers in the Restoration bookshops.

The two chief kinds of poetry the court wits practiced were the love lyric and the satire or "libel." They often tend to shade into each other, of which one of the distinguishing marks is the combination of the singing voice of the lyric with the critical and ironic spirit of satire. They were the last English poets successfully to use the pastoral convention as part of the courtly love game. This convention had lost the imaginative grandeur with which it was invested in the High Renaissance, but it remained a symbol for a nonmoral dream world of delicate charm and grace. At the end of the century it had become absurd when Lady Wishfort, in Congreve's *The Way of the World* (1700), proposed to "retire to deserts and solitudes, and feed harmless sheep by groves and purling streams." The court wits in their best lyrics avoid this sort of silly escapism by disinfecting the pastoral with what Ezra Pound called "a dash of bitters." With them reality, like cheerfulness in the philosophy of Dr. Johnson's friend, kept breaking in. At times, too, their realistic temper enabled them to use the convention to express a human situation when it became clear that Thirsis or Strephon was a real man feeling a genuine affection for his Celia or Phillis. The "libel," lampoon, or satire was a feature of Restoration court life as common as the love song. It could be simply a string of witty and usually bawdy insults in verse, but, in the hands of its ablest practitioners, notably Rochester, it became a vehicle for genuine social criticism based on a perception of the glaring contradictions between the smooth exterior of court life and the sordid actualities that lay behind it.

The court wits were a small, rather closely knit community. Professor J. H. Wilson has estimated that about fourteen persons can be reckoned as belonging to the inner circle. As far as is known, they never authorized the printing of any of their works; and a large quantity of their songs, "libels," and other verses have survived in manuscript miscellanies, printed broadsides, contemporary anthologies, and editions, often of doubtful authenticity, published after their deaths. The result has been that it is extremely difficult for modern editors to establish either a reliable text or an authentic canon of the writings even of the leading figures.

As with the circle of Thomas Wyatt and Henry Howard, earl of Surrey, in the early sixteenth century and that of the "Sons of Ben Jonson" in the early seventeenth, there is a kind of basic poetic voice common to all the Restoration wits who wrote verse. One can hear it in the opening lines of a poem ascribed rather doubtfully to Dorset:

> Though, Phillis, your prevailing charms
> Have forc'd me from my Celia's arms,
> That kind defence against all powers,
> But those resistless eyes of yours:
> Think not your conquest to maintain
> By rigour and unjust disdain;
> In vain, fair Nymph, in vain you strive,
> For love does seldom hope survive . . .

This sort of rather thin, graceful poetry of conventional gallantry, strongly influenced by Waller and the slightly earlier French poetry of writers like Voiture and Sarrazin, could be written by almost any member of the circle, including such minor poetasters as Lord Mulgrave and Wentworth Dillon, earl of Roscommon, Sir Car Scroop, or Sir Fleetwood Shepherd. The "most eminent wits," to use Gilbert Burnet's expression, all sometimes use this "basic" poetic voice, but they are distinguished from their fellow courtiers by their power of speaking (or singing) in other voices covering wider and more interesting areas of experience.

JOHN WILMOT, EARL OF ROCHESTER
(1647–1680)

JOHN WILMOT, second earl of Rochester, was the son of a cavalier general. Born in 1647, he was educated at Wadham College, Oxford, where he took the M.A. in 1660. He then traveled in France and Italy, returning to England in 1664, when he appeared at court and earned a reputation for wit and dissipation. He served at sea in the Dutch war in 1665–1666. Charles II enjoyed his company, but he was banished from court more than once for his outspoken satires on the king. His health declined in the late 1670's. In 1679 he made the acquaintance of Gilbert Burnet, later bishop of Salisbury, with whom he had a series of conversations on religion in the winter of 1679–1680. After a dramatic conversion to Christianity, he died on 26 July 1680.

Rochester had by far the most powerful and original mind of all the court wits. His distinguishing characteristics are an unusual capacity for intellectual and sensual experience, a profound skepticism, and a share in that quality of "terrifying honesty" that T. S. Eliot ascribed to William Blake. He began his career as a wholehearted disciple of Hobbes, but this was only the starting point for an intellectual voyage that ended with his deathbed conversion to Christianity and his total rejection of what he then described as "the absurd and foolish philosophy that the world so much admired, propagated by Mr. Hobbes and others." In a letter to his wife he writes of "so great a disproportion 'twixt our desires and what it has ordained to content them" and of those who are "soe intirely satisfyed with theire shares in this world, that theire wishes nor theire thoughts have not a farther prospect of felicity & glory." One of his admirers called him an "Enthusiast in Wit," and if this is interpreted as meaning that he combined intellectual toughness with a passionate aspiration to "felicity and glory," the description is apt.

In the lyric he can play the game of the courtly pastoral and can also enjoy the fun of deflating its sentiment by substituting for the languishing swain and the chaste nymph a pair of cynical sensualists:

> How perfect, Cloris, and how free
> Would these enjoyments prove,
> But you with formal jealousy
> Are still tormenting Love.
>
> Let us (since Wit instructs us how)
> Raise pleasure to the top,
> If Rival bottle you'll allow,
> I'll suffer rival fop.
>
> There's not a brisk insipid spark
> That flutters in the Town
> But with your wanton eyes you mark
> Him out to be your own . . . .
> ("To a Lady in a Letter," 1–12)

Such a poem as this is obviously a deliberate "shocker." One can hear in it the voice of the hardboiled "confident young men" who made people like the duke of Ormonde shudder. J. M. Synge wrote in 1908 that "before verse can become human again it must learn to be brutal." These words can be applied to the age when seventeenth-century romanticism was dying, as well as to that which saw the collapse of Victorian romanticism.

Rochester is writing from a far deeper level of experience in the following poem, in which he gives a philosophic dimension to a favorite theme of the court wits, inconstancy:

> All my past Life is mine no more,
> The flying hours are gone:
> Like transitory Dreams giv'n o'er,
> Whose Images are kept in store
> By Memory alone.
>
> The Time that is to come is not;
> How can it then be mine?
> The present Moment's all my Lot;
> And that, as fast as it is got,
> *Phillis*, is only thine.
>
> Then talk not of Inconstancy,
> False Hearts, and broken Vows;
> If I, by Miracle, can be
> This live-long Minute true to thee,
> 'Tis all that Heav'n allows.
> ("Love and Life," 1–15)

This attitude is very different from that of the thoughtless pleasure-seeker. The plangent cadences of the opening lines convey a sense of the mystery of the time process, and the whole poem is suffused with melancholy for the precariousness of the artificial paradise that the lover finds in the arms of his Phillis.

Rochester's breakthrough to reality in the lyric can take the form of passionate tenderness as well as of brutality. This is found in a handful of lyrics that F. R. Leavis has well described as "peculiarly individual utterances" and that were aptly compared by Sir Herbert Grierson with the songs of Robert Burns:

> My dear Mistress has a Heart
> Soft as those kind looks she gave me;
> When, with Love's resistless Art,
> And her Eyes, she did enslave me;
> But her Constancy's so weak,
> She's so wild, and apt to wander;
> That my jealous Heart wou'd break,
> Should we live one day asunder.
>
> Melting Joys about her move,
> Killing Pleasures, wounding Blisses;
> She can dress her Eyes in Love,
> And her Lips can arm with Kisses;
> Angels listen when she speaks,
> She's my delight, all Mankind's wonder;
> But my jealous Heart would break,
> Should we live one day asunder.
> ("A Song," 1–16)

Here the "ease" and unaffected naturalness that the court wits prized are combined with a note of rapture and a crystalline perfection of phrase and form of which Rochester alone among them knew the secret.

His satiric poems are of two kinds. Some, like his attacks on Lord Mulgrave and Sir Car Scroop, are simply "libels" in the fashion of the day, and distinguished from the numerous other contemporary squibs only by their greater pungency and literary force. His lampoons on the king deserve special mention. The character of Charles II seems to have fascinated him, perhaps because, like his own, it was full of paradoxes. The contrast between the traditional view of the monarch hedged by divinity and the actual person of the "sauntering," informal Charles Stuart was a never-failing source of ironic amusement to the poet. It is neatly embodied in his celebrated extempore epigram:

> We have a pritty witty king
>   And whose word no man relys on:
> He never said a foolish thing,
>   And never did a wise one.

Charles's good-humored reply is said to have been that what Rochester observed was easily explained. He was responsible for his words; his ministers, for his actions. This epigram, though, is mild compared with some of the longer lampoons on the king ascribed to Rochester. What seemed to him especially despicable in the king was not that he took his pleasure with his mistresses, but that he allowed himself to be governed by them:

> Restless he rolls about from Whore to Whore,
> A merry Monarch, scandalous and poor.

Rochester's more serious work in satire deserves to be called philosophic; it can be seen as reflecting the dialectical process that transformed the gay young spark of the 1660's into the dying penitent of 1680. One characteristic of these poems is his intense and vivid perception of the "waste land" of the world revealed by the new materialistic philosophy and the sordidness of a society vulgarized by the growth of the money power. The other is the creative use of his reading. He was the first poet to use the Augustan method of "imitation," later brilliantly exploited by John Oldham, Pope, and Johnson. Not only his fine "Allusion to the Tenth Satire of the Second Book of Horace" but also each of his major satiric works is at once a criticism of contemporary life and in some measure an "imitation" or recreation of a work of ancient or contemporary poetry, often with a touch of parody. His famous "Upon Nothing" is a kind of inversion of Cowley's "Hymn to Light," and at the same time he makes use of the conception of Nothing as an active force found in the Renaissance Latin poems quoted by Johnson in his account of Rochester in *The Lives of the Poets*; behind the poem, too, lie still more august antecedents: the book of Genesis, the first verses of the Fourth Gospel, and the Aristotelian doctrine of form and matter.

> Nothing! thou Elder Brother ev'n to Shade,
> That hadst a Being ere the World was made,
> And (well fixt) art alone, of ending not afraid.
>   (1–3)

In the last stanzas the irony is transferred from metaphysics to contemporary society:

> Nothing who dwell'st with Fools in grave Disguise,
> For whom they rev'rend Shapes, and Forms devise,
> Lawn Sleeves, and Furs, and Gowns, when they like thee
>   look wise.
>
> The great Man's Gratitude to his best Friend,
> King's Promises, Whore's Vows, tow'rds thee they bend,
> Flow swiftly into thee, and in thee ever end.
>   (43–45; 49–51)

The emptiness that lies behind the facade of human institutions and social life is visualized here as a kind of evil abstract deity (Blake's "Nobodaddy"), and Swift's doctrine of man as a "micro-coat" (see *A Tale of a Tub*) is clearly foreshadowed. Pope must have studied this poem carefully, for he wrote a clever imitation of it in his youth, and the triumph of Dullness at the end of *The Dunciad* probably owes much to Rochester's triumph of Nothing.

"The Maim'd Debauchee," described by Charles Whibley as a "masterpiece of heroic irony," recalls William Davenant's epic *Gondibert* as "Upon Nothing" recalls Cowley's "Hymn to Light." The stately meter and diction of Davenant's "heroic" poem are used to exhibit the old age of a gentlemanly rake, who is ironically equated with a superannuated admiral watching a naval battle from a safe position on shore. Like all of Rochester's best satiric

259

work, this poem is not a statement but a vision. We are made to see the absurdly ferocious old sailor:

> From his fierce Eyes flashes of Rage he throws
>   As from black Clouds when Lightning breaks away,
> Transported thinks himself amidst his Foes,
>   And absent, yet enjoys the bloody Day.
>
> (9–12)

This image is, as it were, superimposed upon that of the old roué inciting his young friends to the life of pleasure:

> My pains at last some respite shall afford,
>   While I behold the Battels you maintain:
> When Fleets of Glasses sail around the Board,
>   From whose Broad-Sides Volleys of Wit shall rain.
>
> (17–20)

Is one looking at a riotous banquet or a naval battle? It is impossible to say; the two images are fused into a simple whole.

In his most powerful social satire, "A Letter from Artemiza in the Town to Chloë in the Country," Rochester shows us the obverse of the utopia of gallantry in which the court wits and ladies of Whitehall spent their time. In this poem the horror of the life of a prostitute in Restoration London is etched with the mordant realism of a Hogarth or a Goya:

> That wretched thing *Corinna*, who has run
> Through all the sev'ral ways of being undone:
> Cozen'd at first by Love, and living then
> By turning the too-dear-bought-cheat on Men:
> Gay were the hours, and wing'd with joy they flew,
> When first the Town her early Beauties knew:
> Courted, admir'd, and lov'd, with Presents fed;
> Youth in her Looks, and Pleasure in her bed:
>
> . . .
>
> Now scorn'd of all forsaken and opprest,
> She's a *Memento Mori* to the rest:
> Diseas'd, decay'd, to take up half a Crown
> Must Morgage her Long Scarf, and Manto Gown;
> Poor Creature, who unheard of, as a Flie,
> In some dark hole must all the Winter lye:
> And want, and dirt, endure a whole half year,
> That, for one month, she Tawdry may appear.
>
> (189–196; 201–208)

This is a glimpse of the hell over which the heaven of the Strephons and Chloës of Whitehall was precariously constructed.

The culmination of contemporary society is seen in Rochester's "Satyr Against Mankind," in which the revolt is extended to an attack on the human condition itself. The poem was suggested by the eighth satire of Nicolas Boileau, reinforced by hints from Montaigne and La Rochefoucauld. Nevertheless, it is a profoundly original work, for Rochester, like Pope, is never so original as when he is making full use of his reading. The poem is stamped with the peculiar strength of his personality in every line, and expresses with an almost frightening intensity his mood of indignation and disillusionment. He never created a more striking image than that at the opening of the poem, of mankind as the Lost Traveller, who, deceived by Reason, "an *Ignis fatuus* of the Mind,"

> Stumbling from Thought to Thought, falls headlong down
> Into Doubt's boundless Sea, where like to drown,
> Books bear him up awhile, and make him try
> To swim with Bladders of Philosophy,
>
> Then old Age, and Experience, hand in hand,
> Lead him to Death, and make him understand,
> After a Search so painful, and so long,
> That all his Life he has been in the wrong.
> Hudled in dirt, the reas'ning Engine lyes,
> Who was so proud, so witty, and so wise.
>
> (18–21; 25–30)

Nowhere in the English poetry of the seventeenth century is the moral crisis of the age expressed with such force and precision; in the new mechanical-materialist universe of Descartes, Hobbes, and the scientists, man is only a "reas'ning Engine" (the phrase was probably suggested by an expression of Robert Boyle, the great contemporary chemist), yet the pitiful creature has the presumption to call himself witty and wise, and to seek an explanation of a universe in which he seems to be little better than an irrelevant accident. The central passage of the poem, containing a comparison between man and the beasts, is one of the most searching pieces of moral realism in English poetry:

> Be Judge yourself, I'le bring it to the test,
> Which is the basest Creature Man or Beast?
> Birds feed on Birds, Beasts on each other prey;
> But Savage Man alone does Man betray:
> Prest by necessity, they Kill for Food,
> Man undoes Man to do himself no good.
> With Teeth and Claws by Nature arm'd they hunt,

Nature's allowances, to supply their want;
But Man with smiles, embraces, Friendships, praise,
Unhumanely his Fellows life betrays;
With voluntary pains works his distress,
Not through necessity, but wantonness.
For hunger, or for Love, they fight or tear,
Whilst wretched Man is still in Arms for fear;
For fear he arms, and is of Arms afraid,
By fear, to fear, successively betray'd,
Base fear, the source whence his best passions came,
His boasted Honor, and his dear bought Fame.
That lust of Pow'r, to which he's such a Slave,
And for the which alone he dares be brave . . .

                                                (127–146)

Rochester is here piercing the defenses of his aristocratic readers and showing the real passions that lay behind their high-flown talk of honor and fame. It is a passage that communicates forward to the Swift of *Gulliver's Travels*: the king of Brobdingnag's denunciation of the Europeans and the superiority of those wise and humane quadrupeds, the Houyhnhnms, to the filthy, cowardly Yahoos.

Rochester's reputation, like Byron's, has suffered from the blaze of notoriety that surrounded his life and personality. Andrew Marvell, no mean judge, declared that he was "the best English satyrist and had the right veine"; Voltaire went further and called him "a man of genius and a great poet." As a craftsman in verse, compared with his contemporary John Dryden, he is a brilliant amateur. His place is among the daring thought-adventurers of English poetry, whose work lives by the intensity of their passion, the forthrightness of their speech, and the searching clarity of their vision.

CHARLES SACKVILLE, EARL OF DORSET
(1643–1706)

CHARLES SACKVILLE, sixth earl of Dorset, born in 1643, became Lord Buckhurst in 1652, when his father inherited the title of earl of Dorset. After spending a year at Westminster School, he traveled on the Continent, returning to England soon after the Restoration. He collaborated with Sedley and others in a translation of a tragedy by Corneille, which was produced in 1663, and in June of that year took part with Sedley in a wild frolic at the Cock Tavern in Covent Garden. He served at sea against the Dutch in 1665, and in 1677 inherited the earldom of Dorset. In the House of Lords, in 1689 he voted in favor of offering the throne to William and Mary, and he became lord chamberlain to the new monarchs. A generous patron to many men of letters, he died in January 1706.

Dorset (known throughout the early part of his career as Lord Buckhurst) was the least productive, though by no means the least gifted, of the Restoration wits. The works that can be certainly attributed to him are a translation of one act of a tragedy by Corneille; a few lampoons, prologues, and epilogues; a ribald parody; the well-known ballad "Song Written at Sea, in the first Dutch War"; and a small sheaf of lyrics. He was rich and indolent, and delighted in the company of men of letters, to whom he was a munificent host and patron. The condition of such a wealthy and universally flattered nobleman, "fed," like Pope's Bufo, "with soft dedication all day long," was perhaps even worse for a creative artist than the poverty and obscurity of an Oldham or a Thomas Otway. When Dryden couples his name with those of Virgil, Shakespeare, and Donne, and Matthew Prior states that "There is a Lustre in his Verses, like that of a Sun in Claude Loraine's Landskips," we are listening to the courtly hyperboles of the grateful recipients of his bounty. Pope, though, who was under no obligation to him, rated his poetry very highly, and if one can trust Joseph Spence's *Anecdotes*, surprisingly preferred it even to Rochester's. His own work shows that he studied it carefully.

Dorset's celebrated ballad deserves its reputation. An excellent example of the benefit that the court wits derived from their contact with the vernacular tradition, it is a true street ballad written to be sung to the traditional tune of "Shackerley Hay." We know from the Stationer's Register and from Pepys's diary (2 Jan. 1665) that it was actually published under the title of "The Noble Seaman's Complaint" as a broadside, and was a popular hit. In this poem, as can be judged from the following quotation of the three opening stanzas, the rhythmic vitality of vernacular poetry is happily combined with the sophisticated wit and irony of the courtier, producing an effect that remains fresh and sparkling after more than three centuries:

            To all you Ladies now at Land
              We Men at Sea indite;
            But first wou'd have you understand

How hard it is to write;
The Muses now, and Neptune too,
We must implore to write to you.

For tho' the Muses should prove kind,
    And fill our empty Brain;
Yet if rough Neptune rouze the Wind,
    To wave the azure Main,
Our Paper, Pen, and Ink, and we,
Roll up and down our Ships at Sea.

Then if we write not by each Post,
    Think not we are unkind;
Nor yet conclude our Ships are lost
    By Dutchmen, or by Wind:
Our Tears we'll send a speedier way,
The Tide shall bring 'em twice a day.
                                    (1–18)

Another lyric in the ballad style and meter has a touch of the sturdy vulgarity and sensuality of popular art:

Methinks the poor Town has been troubled too long,
With Phillis and Chloris in every Song;
By Fools, who at once can both love and despair,
And will never leave calling 'em cruel and fair;
Which justly provokes me in Rhime to express
The Truth that I know of bonny black Bess.

This Bess of my Heart, this Bess of my Soul,
Has a Skin white as Milk and Hair black as Coal,
She's plump, yet with ease you may span her round Waste,
But her round swelling Thighs can scarce be embrac'd:
Her Belly is soft, not a word of the rest;
But I know what I think when I drink to the best.

The Plowman and 'Squire, the arranter Clown,
At home she subdu'd in her Paragon Gown;
But now she adorns the Boxes and Pit,
And the proudest Town-gallants are forc'd to submit;
All hearts fall a-leaping wherever she comes,
And beat Day and Night, like my Lord Craven's Drums.

Perhaps Dorset's most original and distinctive work is seen in the sequence of his four little poems on Katherine Sedley, the daughter of his friend Sir Charles Sedley. The character of this bold, witty young woman, who became the mistress of the duke of York, later James II, seems to have fascinated him. In these verses Dorset is creating a new kind of poem, in which lyrical movement is combined with satiric force. It was, doubtless, of them that Rochester was thinking when he called

Dorset "the best good Man, with the worst natur'd Muse." The following poem has an economy of language and a classic perfection of form unrivaled in English poetry outside the works of Walter Landor:

Dorinda's sparkling Wit, and Eyes,
United, cast too fierce a Light,
Which blazes high, but quickly dies,
Pains not the Heart, but hurts the Sight.

Love is a calmer, gentler Joy,
Smooth are his Looks, and soft his Pace;
Her Cupid is a black-guard Boy,
That runs his Link full in your Face.

The metaphor of a painfully dazzling fire links the two stanzas with admirable art, and the sudden transition in the last two lines from the rococo cupid to the "black-guard Boy" with his flaming "Link" (torch) takes one with a pleasurable shock from the dream world of the pastoral convention to the actuality of night in the murky streets of Restoration London, where there were no street lamps and the only illumination was provided by the torches of link-boys.

In another poem on Katherine Sedley, the same verbal economy and felicity of imagery give force to a penetrating piece of social satire:

Tell me, Dorinda, why so gay,
    Why such embroid'ry, fringe and lace?
Can any Dresses find a way,
To stop th' approaches of decay,
    And mend a ruin'd Face.

Wilt thou still sparkle in the Box,
    Still ogle in the Ring?
Canst thou forget thy Age and Pox?
Can all that shines on Shells and Rocks
    Make thee a fine young Thing?

So have I seen in Larder dark
    Of Veal a lucid Loin
Replete with many a brilliant Spark,
As wise Philosophers remark,
    At once both stink and shine.

This is not merely an attack on Katherine Sedley. It is a dramatization of a true social criticism that sees all the glittering apparatus of court life ("embroid'ry, fringe and lace" and "all that shines on Shells and Rocks") as a mockery masking the hideous realities of venereal disease and decaying flesh. There is a sharp visualization of ugly and sordid images in this poem, revealing a new kind of poetic sensibility that was to be exploited with remarkable results by Pope and Swift. A similar quality is found in one of Dorset's lampoons on the Hon. Edward Howard, a contemporary dramatist who was one of the favorite butts of the court wits:

> Thou damn'd Antipodes to Common sense,
> Thou Foil to Flecknoe, pry'thee tell from whence
> Does all this mighty Stock of Dullness spring?
> Is it thy own, or hast it from Snow-Hill,
> Assisted by some Ballad-making Quill?
> No, they fly higher yet, thy Plays are such
> I'd swear they were translated out of Dutch,
> Fain wou'd I know what Diet thou dost keep,
> If thou dost always, or dost never sleep?
> Sure hasty-pudding is thy chiefest Dish,
> With Bullock's Liver, or some stinking Fish;
> Garbage, Ox-cheeks, and Tripes, do feast thy Brain
> Which nobly pays this tribute back again,
> With Daisy roots thy dwarfish Muse is fed,
> A Giant's body with a Pygmy's head.
>
> . . .
>
> Think on't a while, and thou wilt quickly find
> Thy Body made for Labour, not thy Mind.
> No other use of Paper thou should'st make,
> Than carrying Loads and Reams upon thy Back.
> Carry vast Burdens till thy Shoulders shrink,
> But curst be he that gives thee Pen and Ink:
> Such dang'rous Weapons shou'd be kept from Fools,
> As Nurses from their children keep Edg'd-Tools:
> For thy dull Fancy a Muckinder[3] is fit
> To wipe the slabberings of thy snotty Wit.

Dr. Johnson rightly saw in these lines evidence of "great fertility of mind." They show a strength and a freedom of imagination that make one think of *The Dunciad* and regret that Dorset's birth and fortune prevented him from developing his considerable literary potential.

SIR CHARLES SEDLEY
(1639–1701)

SIR CHARLES SEDLEY (or Sidley), born in 1639, was the son of a Kentish baronet. He was educated at

[3]Handkerchief.

Wadham College, Oxford, and inherited the baronetcy on the death of his brother in 1656. After the Restoration he became a lively member of the "merry gang" at court. His comedy *The Mulberry Garden* was staged in 1668, his tragedy *Antony and Cleopatra* in 1677, and a second comedy, *Bellamira*, in 1687. He was member of Parliament for New Romney, and was a frequent and vigorous speaker in the House of Commons after the Glorious Revolution. He died in August 1701.

Pope described Sedley as "a very insipid writer; except in some few of his little love-verses." This is not quite fair to Sedley, who wrote some good poetry besides his "little love-verses," but it is possible to understand what Pope meant. Sedley's poetry has neither Rochester's passionate intensity and intellectual energy nor the satiric bite and sensuality of Dorset's best work. He uses the old stereotypes of the courtly pastoral convention with grace and wit, sometimes with tenderness, but rarely with passion. His attitude to the sexual relationship is rational and humorous:

> Phillis, let's shun the common Fate
> And let our Love ne'r turn to Hate.
> I'll dote no longer than I can
> Without being call'd a faithless Man.
> When we begin to want Discourse
> And Kindness seems to taste of Force,
> As freely as we met we'll part
> Each one possest of his own Heart.

In two poems he uses the theme of the address to a very young girl, already treated with imaginative richness by Marvell and with courtly grace by Waller. The following are the opening stanzas of the song to Cloris in Sedley's comedy *The Mulberry Garden*:

> Ah Cloris! that I now could sit
>   As unconcern'd, as when
> Your Infant Beauty cou'd beget
>   No pleasure, nor no pain.
>
> When I the Dawn us'd to admire,
>   And prais'd the coming Day;
> I little thought the growing fire
>   Must take my Rest away.
>
> Your Charms in harmless Childhood lay,
>   Like metals in the mine,
> Age from no face took more away,
>   Than Youth conceal'd in thine.

But as your Charms insensibly
   To their perfection prest,
Fond Love as unperceiv'd did flye,
   And in my Bosom rest.

My Passion with your Beauty grew,
   And Cupid at my heart,
Still as his mother favour'd you,
   Threw a new flaming Dart.

This is, perhaps, a little too pretty. It might be described as boudoir poetry, recalling some erotic French eighteenth-century painting of the school of Boucher. More astringent and satisfying to a modern taste in its delicate, playful humor is the poem addressed "To a Devout Young Gentlewoman":

Phillis, this early Zeal asswage,
   You over-act your part;
The Martyrs, at your tender Age,
   Gave Heaven but half their Heart.

Old Men (till past the Pleasure) ne're
   Declaim against the Sin;
'Tis early to begin to fear
   The Devil at Fifteen.

The World to Youth is too severe,
   And, like a treacherous Light,
Beauty, the Actions of the Fair,
   Exposes to their sight.

And yet the World, as old as 'tis,
   Is oft deceiv'd by't too;
Kind Combinations seldom miss,
   Let's try what we can do.

The first two stanzas of this poem are nearly flawless, but the last two are marred by both banality of thought and verbal clumsiness, seen in the awkward inversions and the slipshod grammar of the penultimate stanza. A similar failure of inspiration mars the lyric beginning with the following often-praised and beautiful lines:

Love still has something of the Sea,
   From whence his Mother rose . . .

The expectation aroused by this rich opening is immediately damped by the next two lines, with their hackneyed imagery and inversion for the sake of the rhyme:

No time his Slaves from Doubt can free,
   Nor give their Thoughts repose: . . .

After a series of stanzas filled with frigid allegory, the poem ends with lines almost worthy of its superb opening:

And if I gaz'd a thousand Years
   I could no deeper love.

None of the weaknesses noted in these poems is found in two of Sedley's songs that long retained their popularity through the contemporary musical settings. In the following poem the courtly convention is most happily wedded to the appreciation of an exquisite moment of actual experience:

Hears not my Phillis, how the Birds
   Their feather'd Mates salute?
They tell their Passion in their Words;
   Must I alone be mute?
Phillis, without Frown or Smile,
Sat and knotted all the while.

The God of Love in thy bright Eyes
   Does like a Tyrant reign;
But in thy Heart a Child he lyes,
   Without his Dart or Flame.
Phillis, without Frown or Smile,
Sat and knotted all the while.

So many Months in Silence past,
   And yet in raging Love,
Might well deserve one Word at last
   My Passion shou'd approve.
Phillis, without Frown or Smile,
Sat and knotted all the while.

Must then your faithful Swain expire,
   And not one look obtain,
Which he to sooth his fond Desire,
   Might pleasingly explain?
Phillis, without Frown or Smile,
Sat and knotted all the while.

This lyric must be heard sung to Henry Purcell's exquisite setting if its full effect is to be realized, but even on the printed page it succeeds in conveying the poet's delight in the balletlike situation, in the movement of the verse and the conventional images, which his emotion endows with a surprising freshness and vitality. Equally successful is an even more famous song that shows an originality of metrical invention unusual in Sedley's work and is due, doubtless, in some measure to the music:

Phillis is my only Joy,
   Faithless as the Winds or Seas;
Sometimes coming, sometimes coy,
   Yet she never fails to please;
     If with a Frown
     I am cast down,
     Phillis smiling,
     And beguiling,
Makes me happier than before.

Tho', alas, too late I find,
   Nothing can her Fancy fix;
Yet the Moment she is kind,
   I forgive her all her Tricks;
     Which, tho' I see,
     I can't get free;
     She deceiving,
     I believing;
What need Lovers wish for more?

In one lyric Sedley achieves the expression of tender feeling in language of diaphanous simplicity that almost equals that of Rochester's best songs, though, as so often in his poetry, the magnificent promise of the opening lines is hardly sustained:

Not Celia, that I juster am
   Or better than the rest,
For I would change each Hour like them,
   Were not my Heart at rest.

But I am ty'd to very thee,
   By every Thought I have,
Thy Face I only care to see,
   Thy Heart I only crave.

All that in Woman is ador'd,
   In thy dear self I find,
For the whole Sex can but afford,
   The Handsome and the Kind.

Why then should I seek farther Store,
   And still make Love anew;
When Change itself can give no more,
   'Tis easie to be true.

Sedley is not exclusively what Ben Jonson calls "a woman's poet." There is a more masculine quality in some of the poems probably written in the later part of his life. This quality is found especially in his translations and imitations of Latin poetry. Matthew Prior, with true critical insight, described him as "Sir Charles that can write and better Translate." His version of the eighth ode of the Second Book of

Horace is one of the finest verse translations of the seventeenth century. It is one of those rare translations that reads like an original poem. Horace's dangerous old harlot is transmuted into one of the glittering, rapacious courtesans of the court of Charles II, and the poem is as vivid, incisive, and carefully controlled as the Latin original:

Did any Punishment attend
   Thy former Perjuries
I should believe a second time
   Thy charming Flatteries:
Did but one Wrinkle mark this Face,
Or hadst thou lost one single Grace.

No sooner hast thou, with false Vows,
   Provok'd the Powers above;
But thou art fairer than before
   And we are more in love,
Thus Heaven and Earth seem to declare,
They pardon Falshood in the Fair.

Sure 'tis no Crime vainly to swear,
   By ev'ry Power on high,
And call our bury'd Mother's Ghost
   A witness to the Lye:
Heaven at such Perjuries connives,
And *Venus* with a Smile forgives.

The Nymphs and cruel *Cupid* too,
   Sharp'ning his pointed Dart
On an old hone besmear'd with Blood,
   Forbear thy perjur'd Heart.
Fresh Youth grows up, to wear thy Chains,
And the Old Slave no Freedom gains.

Thee, Mothers for their eldest Sons,
   Thee, wretched Misers fear,
Lest thy prevailing Beauty should
   Seduce the hopeful Heir.
New-marry'd Virgins fear thy Charms
Should keep their Bridegroom from their Arms.

A similar strength is found in a series of adaptations of epigrams by Martial, one of the best of which is cast in the form of a Shakespearian sonnet and must be one of the very few poems in this form written between the early seventeenth and early nineteenth centuries:

Thou art an Atheist, *Quintus*, and a Wit,
   Thinkst all was of self-moving Attoms made,
Religion only for the Vulgar fit,
   Priests Rogues, and Preaching their deceitful Trade;

Wilt drink, whore, fight, blaspheme, damn, curse and swear:
  Why wilt thou swear by God, if there be none?
And if there be, thou shouldst his Vengeance fear:
  Methinks this Huffing might be let alone;
'Tis thou art free, Mankind besides a Slave,
  And yet a Whore can lead thee by the Nose,
A drunken Bottle, and a flatt'ring Knave,
  A mighty Prince, Slave to thy dear Soul's Foes,
Thy Lust, thy Rage, Ambition and thy Pride;
He that serves God, need nothing serve beside.

This poem shows that Sedley was capable not only of living in the libertine "Utopia of Gallantry" but also of outgrowing it and criticizing it, though his criticism lacks the philosophic depth and fierce irony of Rochester's.

At the end of his life he wrote a long poem on marriage called *The Happy Pair*. In spite of some rather banal theorizing, the passages denouncing mercenary and loveless marriages have a note of actuality due, no doubt, to the poet's own bitter experience; he was married at the age of seventeen to a woman who became a paranoiac. The conclusion of the poem, with its praise of quiet domesticity, shows that the wild gallant of the 1660's had by the end of the century developed into an Augustan "man of feeling." In the following lines there is a sensuous perception of "images of external nature" that foreshadows the rural-sentimental poetry of the eighteenth century:

Love, like a cautious fearful Bird ne'er builds,
But where the Place Silence and Calmness yields:
He slily flies to Copses, where he finds
The snugging Woods secure from Blasts and Winds,
Shuns the huge Boughs of a more Stately Form,
And laughs at Trees torn up with ev'ry Storm.

SIR GEORGE ETHEREGE
(1635–1692)

SIR GEORGE ETHEREGE, born in 1635, probably spent part of his early life in France, where his father died in 1649. He was apprenticed to a London attorney in 1653, and made the acquaintance of Buckhurst (Dorset) through the success of his play *The Comical Revenge* in March 1664. His second comedy, *She Wou'd if She Cou'd*, was staged in February 1668, and in August 1668 he went to Constantinople as secretary to the British ambassador. He was in London in 1671, and his best comedy, *The Man of Mode*, was produced with great success in 1676. In 1679 he was knighted, and in 1685 he went to Ratisbon (Regensburg) as British envoy to the Diet of the Empire. At the Glorious Revolution he relinquished his post at Ratisbon and went to Paris, where he died in May 1692.

Unlike the other members of the court circle, Etherege did not come from a wealthy, aristocratic background. His grandfather was a "vintner," or publican, at Maidenhead; his father, after spending some time in Bermuda, held a small appointment at the court of Charles I and died in exile in France after the royalist defeat. The only certain fact about the young George Etherege is that he was apprenticed by his grandfather to a London attorney at the age of eighteen. Eleven years later his first play was produced with great success at the Duke's Theatre; he dedicated it to Lord Buckhurst (Dorset), and there is no doubt that it was through his friendship with that nobleman that he was accepted as a member of the "merry gang." This experience was the central fact of his life. Like Oscar Wilde two centuries later, he was a wit and an artist in comedy who was admitted into aristocratic circles, and was enchanted by the ideal of the man of fashion and leisure who was master of the art of living. In each of his three comedies one finds this figure, beginning with the sketch of the gay and charming Sir Frederick Frollick in *The Comical Revenge*, proceeding to the two attractive young sparks, Courtall and Freeman in *She Wou'd if She Cou'd*, and culminating in the finished portrait of Dorimant in *The Man of Mode*, said to be based on the character of Rochester. Contrasted with Dorimant in this play is Sir Fopling Flutter, that "eminent Coxcomb," who embodies all that is absurd in the fashionable ideal.

Etherege himself was probably something halfway between Dorimant and Sir Fopling. Just as Wilde called himself a poseur, so Etherege called himself a fop. In one of his letters he writes, "I confess I am a fop in my heart; ill customs influence my senses, and I have been so used to affection [affectation] that without the air of the Court nothing can touch me." Unlike the other members of the "merry gang," he never outgrew the courtly-libertine ideal of the 1660's. Like Wilde he was never so much himself as when he was acting a part, and the part of the fop or perfect aesthetic hero became second nature to him. It might be imagined that such a man, when he wrote verse, would speak only in the "basic voice" of the court poet. Actually, in Etherege's poetry, slight as it is in quantity, one can hear other and more individual voices. John Palmer acutely ascribed to him "a worldly simplicity captivating from its entire lack of self-consciousness," and this describes very well the quality of his best lyrics. His poem addressed "To a Very Young Lady" has none of the playfulness and boudoir eroticism of Sedley's "Song to Cloris," but a kind of innocent freshness that brings him nearer to Marvell or even Henry Vaughan than to Waller or Sedley:

> Sweetest bud of beauty, may
> No untimely frost decay
> The early glories that we trace,
> Blooming in thy matchless face;
> But kindly opening, like the rose,
> Fresh beauties every day disclose,
> Such as by nature are not shown
> In all the blossoms she has blown—
> And then what conquest shall you make
> Who hearts already daily take?
> Scorched in the morning with thy beams,
> How shall we bear those sad extremes
> Which must attend thy threatening eyes
> When thou shalt to thy noon arise.

The following lyric is more characteristic. Here the voice is that of a persona, the "shepherd" or ideal poet of the court pastoral, a fairy-tale or tapestry world. The attitude of the "shepherd," one may notice, is highly ambiguous. Ostensibly he is issuing a warning against the love of women, but the reader is told that love's "chain" is "imperial" and its "pain" "enchanting." It seems obvious that the loss of "quiet" by those who gaze on "beauteous eyes" is a not unenviable condition:

> Ye happy youths, whose hearts are free
> From Love's imperial chain,
> Henceforth be warned and taught by me
> T'avoid the enchanting pain.
> Fatal the wolves to trembling flocks,
> Sharp winds to blossoms prove,
> To careless seamen hidden rocks,
> To human quiet Love.
>
> Fly the fair sex if bliss you prize,
> The snake's beneath the flower;
> Whoever gazed on beauteous eyes
> That tasted quiet more?

> How faithless is the lover's joy!
> How constant is his care!
> The kind with falsehood do destroy,
> The cruel with despair.

The craftsmanship of this poem is remarkable. The common ballad quatrain is enlivened by a subtle pattern of alliteration and assonance, and the cadences ("human quiet Love," "gazed on beauteous eyes," "tasted quiet more") are the work of a fine artist in verbal music. He is equally successful with flowing anapaests in the song called "Silvia." Here the feeling is genuine, but it is of the kind that can be called operatic, like that of Tom Moore's best songs, the manner of which is remarkably foreshadowed in this poem. It is interesting to find that it was immensely popular as "words for music," and was set by no fewer than four different contemporary composers:

> The Nymph that undoes me is fair and unkind,
> No less than a wonder by Nature design'd;
> She's the grief of my heart, the joy of my eye,
> And the cause of a flame that never can die.
>
> Her mouth, from whence wit still obligingly flows
> Has the beautiful blush and the smell of the rose;
> Love and destiny both attend on her will,
> She wounds with a look, with a frown she can kill.
>
> The desperate Lover can hope no redress
> Where beauty and rigour are both in excess:
> In *Silvia* they meet, so unhappy am I,
> Who sees her must love and who loves her must die.

Etherege can speak in other voices besides that of the courtly gallant. In some of the lyrics in his plays, one can hear the voice of the man of the street, the tavern, and the coffeehouse, using the idiom of the popular song, catch, and street ballad. The following lines, trolled by the sharper Palmer in the tavern scene in *The Comical Revenge* (II. 2), have the salty tang of vernacular speech and the hearty sensuality of popular poetry:

> If she be not kind as fair
> But peevish and unhandy,
> Leave her—she's only worth the care
> Of some spruce Jack-a-dandy.
>
> I would not have thee such an ass,
> Hadst thou ne'er so much leisure
> To sigh and whine for such a lass
> Whose pride's above her pleasure.

Make much of every buxom girl
  Which needs but little courting;
Her value is above the pearl,
  That takes delight in sporting.

The song sung by the "wanton" Gatty in the first scene of the fifth act of *She Wou'd if She Cou'd* is a genuine street ballad that was reprinted in two broadsides. It is poetry that springs as directly from the life of Restoration London as an entry in Pepys's diary:

To little or no purpose I spent many days,
In ranging the Park, the Exchange, and the Plays;
For ne'er in my rambles till now did I prove
So lucky to meet with the man I could love.
Oh! how I am pleased when I think on this man,
That I find I must love, let me do what I can!

How long I shall love him, I can no more tell
Than had I a fever when I should be well.
My passion shall kill me before I will show it,
And yet I would give all the world he did know it;
But oh how I sigh when I think he would woo me,
I cannot deny what I know would undo me.

As a poet Etherege is seen at his best in his lyrics; his few complimentary and erotic poems in the heroic couplet are polished but undistinguished. His lines to the marchioness of Newcastle "After the Reading of Her Incomparable Poems" might have been written by any competent imitator of Waller:

Those graces nature did till now divide
(Your sex's glory and our sex's pride)
Are joined in you, and all to you submit,
The brightest beauty and the sharpest wit.
No faction here or fiercer envy sways,
They give you myrtle, while we offer bays.
What mortal dares dispute this wreath with you,
Armed thus with lightning and with thunder too.

He is said to have written lampoons railing at women, but no "libel" can be certainly ascribed to him. If he is the author of "Mrs. Nelly's Complaint," a satire on Nell Gwynn attributed to him in *The Miscellaneous Works of the Duke of Buckingham*, he cannot be credited with a satiric talent beyond that of those whom Dryden calls "our common libellers." The best passage in the poem gives an amusing glimpse of the strangely variegated company that was to be found in the royal presence at Whitehall in the reign of Charles II:

Let mountebanks make market houses ring
Of what great feats they've done before the King,
Let learned Sir *Sam* his *Windsor* Engine try,
Before great Charles let quacks and seamen lie.
He ne'er heard swearers till *Moll Knight* and I,
Never heard oaths less valued, or less true
(And yet 'tis said, he has paid for swearing too)
Loudlier we swore than plundering dragoons,
'Sblood followed 'Sblood, and Zoons succeeded Zoons.

A more individual note is heard in a series of verse epistles written by Etherege to his friends in the tumbling, four-accent "Hudibrastic" meter popularized by Butler's famous poem. In this meter he conducted a witty but obscene correspondence with Buckhurst and, later, when he was British envoy at Ratisbon, wrote verse epistles to his friend and official superior Lord Middleton. One of these epistles contains a description of one of "rough Danube's beauties" that combines the picturesque with the comic in a manner that Byron would not have despised:

How would the ogling sparks despise
The darling damsel of my eyes,
Did they behold her at a play,
As she's tricked up on holiday,
When the whole family combine
For public pride to make her shine.
Her hair which long before lay matted
Are on this day combed out and platted
A diamond bodkin in each tress
The badges of her nobleness;
For every stone as well as she
Can boast an ancient pedigree

. . .

No serpent breaking in the air
Can with her starry head compare
Such ropes of pearls her hands encumber
She scarce can deal the cards at ombre;
So many rings each finger freight,
They tremble with the mighty weight:
The like in England ne'er was seen
Since Holbein drew Hal and his Queen.
But after these fantastic sights
The lustre's meaner than the lights
She that bears this glittering pomp
Is but a tawdry ill-bred ramp
Whose brawny limbs and martial face
Proclaim her of the Gothic race,
More than the painted pageantry
Of all her father's heraldry . . .

Unlike the other "eminent wits," Etherege never goes beneath the surface in his poetry. It is all light verse but, at the same time, it is the work of a true artist and succeeds in transmitting his gaiety, insouciance, and attractive mixture of innocence and sophistication.

CONCLUSION

THE pattern of life and writing of the "merry gang" arose from a particular phase of society and culture, and could not be repeated. Men like George Granville, Lord Lansdowne, and William Walsh, who tried to reproduce it after the Glorious Revolution, appear now as Young Pretenders, mere pale and colorless imitations. By the end of the century the character of the libertine court wits had become the absurd anachronism that Swift caricatures in *A Tale of a Tub* when he describes the activities of the three brothers in high society: "they writ and rallied, and rhymed and sung and said, and said nothing: they drank and fought, and slept, and swore, and took snuff: they went to new plays on the first night, haunted the chocolate houses, beat the watch, lay on bulks, and got claps: they bilked hackney-coachmen, ran in debt with shopkeepers, and lay with their wives: they killed bailiffs, kicked fidlers downstairs, eat at Will's, loitered at Lockets . . . ." The men who did these things in Swift's time were, to use his own expression, mere micro-coats, imitators of the externals of what had once been a life of gaiety, poetry, and adventure. Alone among men of the post-Revolution generation William Congreve caught the authentic note of the Restoration wits in a few poems such as the following lyric, the first stanza of which, at least, Rochester would not have disowned:

> False though she be to me and love,
>   I'll ne'er pursue revenge;
> For still the charmer I approve
>   Though I deplore her change.
>
> In hours of bliss we oft have met,
>   They could not always last;
> For though the present I regret,
>   I'm grateful for the past.

The best of the poetry of the court wits lives today by virtue of its youthfulness, insouciance, direct and unaffected speech, irreverence, and sensuality. These qualities are, perhaps, more acceptable now than at any time since the latter part of the seventeenth century. For long the aura of scandal surrounding the personalities of the wits obscured the historical significance of their writings. They rendered two great services to English poetry. One was to keep the singing voice of the lyric alive in an age of mathematics and scientific positivism. Boileau said that Descartes had cut the throat of poetry. It was to a large extent due to the "merry gang" that the positive spirit of Descartes, Hobbes, and the scientists failed to cut the throat of the English lyric. Their other memorable achievement was to diversify and invigorate the Augustan tradition by preserving the happy freedom of colloquial, informal English poetry, a heritage they handed on to the Queen Anne wits, Swift, Pope, Prior, and Gay, and through them to the Byron of *Beppo, The Vision of Judgment,* and *Don Juan.*

SELECTED BIBLIOGRAPHY

JOHN WILMOT, EARL OF ROCHESTER

I. BIBLIOGRAPHY. J. Prinz, *John Wilmot, Earl of Rochester: His Life and Writings* (Leipzig, 1927), contains a full descriptive bibliography of Rochester's writings; J. Thorpe, ed., *Rochester's Poems on Several Occasions* (Princeton, 1950), deals with the complex status and order of the "Antwerp" eds. (see below)—it and Vieth (below) contain valuable bibliographical information not in Prinz; D. M. Vieth, *Attribution in Restoration Poetry: A Study of Rochester's Poems of 1680.* (London, 1963).

II. COLLECTED WORKS. *Poems on Several Occasions* ("Antwerp," 1680), includes a number of poems not by Rochester and an Antwerp imprint that is almost certainly spurious—at least ten eds. (fewer than twenty copies of which survive) were surreptitiously printed from 1680 on, dated or antedated that year, or without date (a facsimile of the Huntington Library copy, J. Thorpe, ed. [Princeton, 1950], contains a valuable intro. and notes); *Poems on Several Occasions* (London, 1685; repr. 1701, 1712), omits nine poems that appeared in the 1680 collection but adds five others; *Poems &c. on Several Occasions, with Valentinian, a Tragedy* (London, 1691; repr. 1696, 1705), published by Jacob Tonson, with preface by Thomas Rymer, is an expurgated text that contains additional authentic poems; *The Miscellaneous Works* (London, 1707), printed and sold by B. Bragge, pirated by Edmund Curll (London, 1707, 1709), contains poems by other authors besides Rochester (the "Life of Rochester" is not, as stated in the title, by Charles de Saint-Évremond); *The Works* (London, 1714), a reprint of Tonson's ed. of 1705, including a number of Rochester's letters (for later eds., notably the 2-vol. collection of poems by Rochester, Roscommon, Dorset, and others [London, 1714], reprinted many times during the eighteenth century with or without "The Cabinet of Love" appendix, see Prinz's bibliography); J. Hayward, ed., *The Collected Works* (London, 1926), a Nonesuch lim. ed., contains almost everything that has been attributed to Rochester, including a number of spurious poems; V. de S. Pinto, ed., *Poems* (London, 1953; rev. ed., 1964), in the Muses' Library, the first attempt to establish a reliable canon (though not a definitive text) of the poems, includes an appendix of poems attributed to Rochester on doubtful authority; D. M. Vieth, ed., *The Complete Poems* (New Haven–London, 1968).

III. Separate Works. "A Satyr Against Mankind Written by a Person of Honour" (London, *ca.* 1679), a folio poem published, according to Anthony à Wood, in June 1679; "Upon Nothing by a Person of Honour" (London, *ca.* 1679), two undated folios published about 1679, repr. by E. Curll (London, 1711) and by R. H. Griffiths (Austin, Tex., 1946); "A Letter from Artemizia in the Town to Chloë in the Country" (London, n.d. [1670]), of which two eds. exist in folio; *Valentinian: A Tragedy as 'Tis Alter'd by the Late Earl of Rochester* (London, 1685), twice issued in 1685, contains an important preface by Robert Wolseley and was repr. in J. E. Spingarn, ed., *Critical Essays of the Seventeenth Century*, III (London, 1909); *Familiar Letters*, 2 vols. (London, 1697; repr. 1699, 1705); J. H. Wilson, ed., *The Rochester-Savile Letters, 1671–1680* (Columbus, Ohio, 1941), a modern ed. of the letters to Henry Savile in *Familiar Letters*, together with Savile's extant letters to Rochester; V. de S. Pinto, ed., "The Famous Pathologist or the Noble Mountebank," (Nottingham, 1961), Rochester's "Mountebank Bill," printed from the MS of his servant Thomas Alcock, with Alcock's preface telling how he masqueraded as the Italian quack doctor "Bendo" (a contemporary, possibly the original, printed edition of Alexander Bendo's advertisement—without place, printer, or date—has survived in an apparently unique copy).

IV. Some Biographical and Critical Studies. R. Parsons, *A Sermon Preached at the Funeral of the Right Honourable John Earl of Rochester* (Oxford, 1680); G. Burnet, *Some Passages of the Life and Death of the Right Honourable John Earl of Rochester* (London, 1680), repr. in many eighteenth-century eds. and in V. de S. Pinto, ed., *English Biography of the Seventeenth Century* (London, 1951), and the basis of many hortatory tracts and pious pamphlets issued as religious propaganda until the end of the nineteenth century; S. Johnson, *The Lives of the Most Eminent English Poets* (London, 1781), includes Johnson's "Life of Rochester"; E. D. Forgues, "John Wilmot comte de Rochester," in *Revue des deux mondes*

(Aug.–Sept. 1857); J. Prinz, ed. and comp., *Rochesteriana* (Leipzig, 1926); J. Prinz, *John Wilmot, Earl of Rochester: His Life and Writings* (Leipzig, 1927); C. Williams, *Rochester* (London, 1935); F. Whitfield, *Beast in View: A Study of the Earl of Rochester's Poetry* (Cambridge, Mass., 1939); V. de S. Pinto, "Rochester and the Right Veine of Satire," in *Essays and Studies by Members of the English Association*, n.s. 5 (London, 1953); D. M. Vieth, "Rochester's 'Scepter Lampoon' on Charles II," *Philological Quarterly*, 37 (1958); V. de S. Pinto, "Rochester and Dryden," in *Renaissance and Modern Studies*, 5 (1961); V. de S. Pinto, *Enthusiast in Wit: A Portrait of John Wilmot Earl of Rochester* (London, 1962), a rev. and enl. ed. of his *Rochester: Portrait of a Restoration Poet* (London, 1935); R. Berman, "Rochester and the Defeat of the Senses," *Kenyon Review*, 26 (Spring 1964); G. R. Hibbard, G. A. Panichas, and A. Rodway, eds., *Renaissance and Modern Essays: Presented to V. de Sola Pinto in Celebration of His Seventieth Birthday* (London, 1966), includes H. Erskine-Hill's essay "Rochester: Augustan or Explorer?"

CHARLES SACKVILLE, EARL OF DORSET

I. Bibliography. H. A. Bagley, "A Check-List of Dorset's Poems," *Modern Language Notes*, 47 (Nov. 1932), 454–461; R. G. Howarth, "Some Additions to the Poems of Lord Dorset," *Modern Language Notes*, 50 (Nov. 1935), 457.

II. Collected Works. *The Works of the Earls of Rochester, Roscommon, Dorset &c.*, 2 vols. (London, 1714), vol. II of which contains the earliest known collection of "Poems by the Earl of Dorset"; *The Works of the Most Celebrated Minor Poets*, 2 vols. (London, 1749; repr. Dublin, 1751), vol. I of which contains "Poems by the Earl of Dorset"; *A Supplement to the Works of the Minor Poets, Part I* (London, n.d.), contains additional poems by Dorset.

III. Separate Works. *Pompey the Great* (London, 1664), translation of Corneille's *La mort de Pompée* (see below, under Sedley); "The Noble Seamans Complaint to the Ladies at Land to ye Tune of Schackerley Hay," a broadside ballad, entered in the Stationers' Register on 30 Dec. 1664, of which no copy is known to survive—usually known as "Song Written at Sea in the First Dutch War": the earliest extant printed version is in *Wit and Mirth or Pills to Purge Melancholy*, V (London, 1714), pp. 168–170, under the title "A Ballad by the Late Lord Dorset When at Sea"; an early MS version of the poem is in Br. Mus. Harl. MS 3991, printed by N. Ault in his *Seventeenth Century Lyrics* (London, 1928), p. 333; *A Collection of Poems Written Upon Several Occasions by Several Persons* (London, 1672), printed for Hobart Kemp, contains three poems probably by Buckhurst

(Dorset), and was the predecessor of a number of other Restoration miscellanies containing a few poems by him; *Poems on Affairs of State* (London, 1697) contains Dorset's "The Duel of the Crabs," a parody of Sir Robert Howard's "The Duel of the Stags."

IV. SOME BIOGRAPHICAL AND CRITICAL STUDIES. S. Johnson, *The Lives of the Most Eminent English Poets* (London, 1781), includes his "Life of Dorset"; B. Harris, *Charles Sackville, Sixth Earl of Dorset: Patron and Poet of the Restoration* (Urbana, Ill., 1940).

SIR CHARLES SEDLEY

I. BIBLIOGRAPHY. V. de S. Pinto, ed., *The Poetical and Dramatic Works*, 2 vols. (London, 1928), contains a bibliography of Sedley's writings.

II. COLLECTED WORKS. Capt. Ayloffe, ed., *The Miscellaneous Works* (London, 1702), repr. with additional material, not all of which is by Sedley (London, 1707, 1710); *The Works*, 2 vols. (London, 1722; repr. 1776, 1778), contains an account of the life of Sedley, possibly by Defoe; V. de S. Pinto, ed., *The Poetical and Dramatic Works*, 2 vols. (London, 1928).

III. SEPARATE WORKS. *Pompey the Great* (London, 1664), a translation of Corneille's *La mort de Pompée* by Waller, Buckhurst, Sedley, Godolphin, and Filmer (act III possibly by Sedley); *The Mulberry Garden: A Comedy* (London, 1668; repr. 1675, 1688); *A Collection of Poems Written Upon Several Occasions by Several Persons* (London, 1672), printed for Hobart Kemp, contains about thirty poems by Sedley—repr. with some additional matter for T. Collins and J. Ford (London, 1673), and with further additional matter and some alterations for F. Saunders (London, 1693); *Antony and Cleopatra: A Tragedy* (London, 1677; repr. 1696); *Bellamira or the Mistress: A Comedy* (London, 1687); *The Happy Pair, or, A Poem on Matrimony* (London, 1702).

IV. SOME BIOGRAPHICAL AND CRITICAL STUDIES. V. de S. Pinto, *Sir Charles Sedley* (London, 1927); H. N. Davies, "Dryden's *All for Love* and Sedley's *Antony and Cleopatra,*" *Notes and Queries* (June 1967).

SIR GEORGE ETHEREGE

I. BIBLIOGRAPHY. H. F. B. Brett Smith, ed., *The Dramatic Works*, 2 vols. (Oxford, 1927), contains a bibliography of the plays; J. Thorpe, ed., *The Poems* (Princeton, 1963), contains valuable bibliographical information about the poems.

II. COLLECTED WORKS. *The Works* (London, 1704); A. W. Verity, ed., *The Works* (London, 1888); H. F. B. Brett Smith, ed., *The Dramatic Works*, 2 vols. (Oxford,

1927; repr. 1971); J. Thorpe, ed., *The Poems* (Princeton, 1963).

III. SEPARATE WORKS. *The Comical Revenge, or, Love in a Tub* (London, 1664; repr. 1667, 1669, 1689, 1697); *She Wou'd if She Cou'd: A Comedy* (London, 1668; repr. 1671, 1693, 1710), also in C. M. Taylor, ed., Regents Restoration Drama series (Lincoln, Nebr., 1972); *The Man of Mode, or, Sir Fopling Flutter* (London, 1676; repr. 1684, 1693, 1711), also in W. B. Carnochan, ed., Regents Restoration Drama series (Lincoln, Nebr., 1972); S. Rosenfeld, ed., *The Letterbook of Sir George Etherege* (Oxford, 1928).

IV. SOME BIOGRAPHICAL AND CRITICAL STUDIES. E. Gosse, *Seventeenth Century Studies* (London, 1883); J. Palmer, *The Comedy of Manners* (London, 1913); B. Dobrée, *Essays in Biography* (London, 1925); Dorothy Foster, contributions to *Notes and Queries*, 153 (1927) and 154 (1928), and to *Review of English Studies*, 8 (1932); J. Dennis, "A Defense of Sir Fopling Flutter" (London, 1722), repr. in E. N. Hooker, ed., *The Critical Works of John Dennis*, 2 vols. (Baltimore, 1939–1943); D. Underwood, *Etherege and the Seventeenth Century Comedy of Manners* (New Haven, 1957), vol. 135 of Yale Studies in English; P. E. Boyette, "Songs of George Etherege," in *Studies in English Literature, 1500–1900*, VI (Houston, Tex., 1966).

GENERAL WORKS

I. BIBLIOGRAPHY. A. E. Case, *A Bibliography of English Poetical Miscellanies, 1521–1750* (London, 1935); C. L. Day and E. Boswell, *English Song Books, 1651–1702, a Bibliography* (London, 1940).

II. SOME BIOGRAPHICAL AND CRITICAL STUDIES. Anthony à Wood, *Athenae Oxonienses*, 2 vols. (London, 1691–1692), also in P. Bliss, ed., 4 vols. (London, 1813–1820); S. Johnson, *The Lives of the Most Eminent English Poets*, 4 vols. (London, 1781), rev. ed. of 1783 by G. B. Hill, ed., 3 vols. (Oxford, 1905); J. Spence, *Anecdotes, Observations and Characters of Books and Men Collected From the Conversation of Mr. Pope and Other Eminent Persons of His Time*, S. W. Singer, ed. (London, 1820), a def. ed. by J. M. Osborn, ed. (London, 1966); J. Aubrey, *Brief Lives*, A. Clark, ed., 2 vols. (Oxford, 1898), also in A. Powell, ed. (London, 1949); J. E. Spingarn, ed., *Critical Essays of the Seventeenth Century*, 3 vols. (Oxford, 1908); *Cambridge History of English Literature*, VIII (London, 1912), contains C. Whibley, "The Court Poets"; F. R. Leavis, *Revaluation* (London, 1936); J. H. Wilson, *The Court Wits of the Restoration* (Princeton, 1948); V. de S. Pinto, *Restoration Carnival* (London, 1954), a Folio Society lim. ed.; J. R. Sutherland, *English Literature in the Late Seventeenth Century* (Oxford, 1969).

III. HISTORICAL AND SOCIAL BACKGROUND. A. Hamilton, *Mémoires du Chevalier de Gramont* (Cologne, 1713), also by Peter Quennell, trans. (London, 1930), and in C. Engel, ed. (Monaco, 1958); G. Burnet, *The History of My Own Time*, 2 vols. (London, 1724–1734), in O. Airy, ed., 2 vols. (Oxford, 1897–1900); *The Life of Edward Earl of Clarendon Written by Himself* (Oxford, 1759; 2nd ed., 2 vols., Oxford, 1857); H. B. Wheatley, ed., *The Diary of Samuel Pepys*, 10 vols. (London, 1893–1899); A. Bryant, *King Charles II* (London, 1931); E. S. de Beer, ed., *The Diary of John Evelyn*, 6 vols. (Oxford, 1955); D. Ogg, *England in the Reign of Charles II*, 2 vols. (Oxford, 1956); C. V. Wedgwood, *Poetry and Politics Under the Stuarts* (London, 1960); G. de F. Lord, ed., *Poems on Affairs of State*, vol. I, *1660–1678* (New Haven–London, 1963).

JOHN EVELYN

(1620-1706)

SAMUEL PEPYS

(1633-1703)

Margaret Willy

INTRODUCTION

WHAT is the impulse that prompts men and women to keep diaries? History shows that the practice may spring from a variety of motives. John Wesley's aim in recording his missionary journeys and spectacular conversions was mainly evangelical. Henry Fielding kept a journal of a voyage taken to Lisbon during his last illness in the hope that its publication might help provide for his family after his death. Noting with delicate precision every detail of the seasons' and weather's changes in Somerset and at Grasmere, Dorothy Wordsworth confessed that she wrote her journals "to please William." Robert Falcon Scott's account of his last journey, found beside the bodies in his tent on the ice barrier, was written in the growing certainty that none of the explorers would survive to tell his tale.

Yet these are the exceptions. The inveterate diarist has no such practical purpose, nor indeed an eye on any kind of public. That the essence of this impulse is self-expression rather than self-exposure is nicely illustrated by Fanny Burney's addressing her juvenile journal to "a Certain Miss Nobody." Committing self and life to the pages of a private notebook for purely personal satisfaction, the habitual writer of a diary sets out not to communicate experience but to record it. Translating the ephemeral stuff of everyday existence into words lends an illusion of permanence to what is passing, of completeness to the inconclusive. It both intensifies and imposes a satisfying sense of order upon the fragmentary business of living, so that in the pattern that seems to emerge, even trifles may

appear altogether more vivid, interesting, and significant.

It is noteworthy that most English diaries that have survived for our pleasure have been kept not by creative writers but by men and women busy in other spheres of activity. The observant and reflective person, with a need of expression and a gift for words, but little inventive talent or impulse to shape and transmute material into more imaginative forms, will often turn to this medium. Thus the diary is frequently the outlet of the creative writer manqué. Dorothy Wordsworth once said that she was "more than half a poet." Fanny Burney seemed to possess all the natural capacity, as well as the material advantages, of a considerable novelist. Lacking the discipline to develop her talents, she instead poured her zestful sense of life into the journal for which she is chiefly remembered.

The reader of most diaries may be said to eavesdrop on one who is talking to oneself without suspecting the presence of an audience, and who is therefore not posing for a picture in full regalia, but lounging in a dressing gown in the privacy of one's own room. This self-portrait of someone completely off guard, and thus divested of customary disguises, is one of the diary addict's main rewards. A human being is revealed in all the frailties and foibles the reader recognizes as his own, which make the diarist not less but more human. Our knowledge of the total personality of Jonathan Swift would be incomplete if we saw only the satirist of *Gulliver's Travels* and *A Tale of a Tub* and missed the doting, sometimes fatuous, lover of Stella revealed in his journal to her. We should be immeasurably poorer for knowing only the worthy public Mr. Pepys, diligent and dependable, and not the victim of ignominious impulses and passions so often laid bare by his *Diary*. The tantrums and the avarice, the furtive amours and petty anxieties, consort strangely with the persona of that respectable and respected higher civil servant. It is because a man's diary, the language of his most private self, will frequently contradict rather than confirm the conduct of his public life—or, at any rate, reveal unsuspected, apparently inconsistent facets of his character—that it affords us this special sense of privileged intimacy.

Diaries also feed our perennial love of gossip: the appetite for glimpses of the great when off-duty, for entertaining oddities of character and anecdote, and for those comfortable trivia that make up the texture of every day, now as then—the dearness of coal, the price of a theater seat, a dining room table, or the weekly housekeeping. In October 1660, Pepys wrote of his new household furnishings ("green serge hanging and gilt leather") in the same breath as he recorded the execution of two traitors. The serene domestic commonplace, set beside violent death and the distant reverberations of civil war, lends a new dimension of reality to the familiar facts of the history books. Such juxtapositions of the humdrum or homely private circumstance with the public catastrophes of war, revolution, or plague are constantly to be found in diaries, animating scene after scene with a sharp and present actuality. For the re-creation of a past age the diarists are perhaps our richest source of detail: not only in the major historical events and personalities they depict, but also in their social background of manners and morals, contemporary tastes and fashions in recreation, food, and dress.

Although there were earlier diarists, like the boy king, Edward VI, or Dr. John Dee, the Elizabethan astrologer, the form did not begin to flourish until the seventeenth century, the heyday of the English diary. Sir William Dugdale, a Warwickshire gentleman who fought for Charles I, kept a journal during the latter half of his life. For the most part it consists of rather dull, fragmentary jottings about his domestic affairs, but now and then some such entry rewards us as that for 30 January 1649:

The King beheaded at the gate of Whitehalle. . . . His head was thrown downe by him yt tooke it up; bruised ye face. His haire cut of. Souldiers dipped their swords in his blood. Base language uppon his dead body.

Another diarist of the day, Dr. Edward Lake, recalled how Charles I had caused a diversion in church by striking "his present majesty" on the head with his staff when he observed him laughing at some ladies during the sermon. In the 1670's, the Reverend Henry Teonge went to sea as chaplain on a man-of-war, and kept a journal of his voyages; a little earlier a Lancashire apprentice, Roger Lowe, was recording in his diary his birds'-nesting, shooting, and fishing expeditions. But for most readers the seventeenth-century diary begins with those two incomparable chroniclers of their time, John Evelyn and Samuel Pepys.

JOHN EVELYN

Son of a prosperous country gentleman, Evelyn was born on 31 October 1620 at Wotton, near Dorking in Surrey: a place that he describes in the early pages of his *Diary* as "so sweetely environ'd with . . . delicious streames and venerable Woods" that "it may be compared to one of the most tempting and pleasant seates in the Nation." Having successfully resisted his father's intention to send him to Eton—being, he says, "unreasonably terrified with the report of the severe discipline there"—he was educated at Lewes in Sussex, until he went up to Oxford; and afterward, without enthusiasm for that "impolish'd study," he read law in London. When the Civil War broke out, young Evelyn prepared himself to fight for the king. He arrived on a scene of royalist defeat. Realizing that if he joined Prince Rupert's troop his estates would be forfeit, and that nothing was known of his intention anyway, he prudently withdrew to Wotton, to build "a little study over a Cascade, to passe my Melancholy houres shaded there with Trees," and await the outcome. After the decisive victory of Parliament, he managed to evade taking the oath of loyalty, and in November 1643 he went abroad, where he stayed—apart from an eighteen-month interval—until February 1652. He then returned to England to settle at Sayes Court, Deptford, his home for the next forty years.

After the Restoration, for which he had actively worked, Evelyn occupied himself in a variety of useful employments. At the end of 1660 he was one of the founder-members of that group of men interested in science, and "the Improvement of naturall knowledge by Experiment," which became the Royal Society. He sat on a number of commissions, such as those for examining the work of the Royal Mint, for the care of sick and wounded seamen during the war with the Dutch, which began in 1664, and for reporting on proposals for the repair of St. Paul's Cathedral. Under William III, he acted as treasurer of Greenwich Hospital, the royal palace converted into a home for naval pensioners. The end of Evelyn's life was spent between his London house and his "Sweete & native aire at *Wotton*" (he had inherited his childhood home in 1699, after his brother's death). He died in London on 27 February 1706, at the ripe age of eighty-five, commemorated by his wife in her will as a faithful and affectionate husband and acclaimed by his contemporaries for his courtesy and accomplishment in many fields. "Certainly the *inquisitive* World is much indebted to this *generous* Gentleman for his very *ingenious* Performances," declared Dr. Joseph Glanvill, "as . . . of *Sculpture, Picture, Architecture*, and the like *practical, useful* things with which he hath inrich'd it."

Evelyn is an excellent example of the cultured, intelligent, and talented amateur of the arts and sciences produced by that age. As a boy, he says, he took an "extraordinary . . . fansy to drawing, and designing," and architecture remained one of his great absorptions. At Oxford he "began to looke upon the rudiments of Musick, in which I afterwards ariv'd to some formal knowledge"—a delight richly shared later with his friend Samuel Pepys. Throughout his life he wrote prolifically on many topics. In the cause of "cultivating the *Sciences*, and . . . the most polite and useful *Arts*," he was diligent in the self-confessed "*drudgery* of *Translating* of *Books*." His translations include part of Lucretius' *De rerum natura*, with a commentary linking its ideas to the discoveries of modern science; *The Golden Book of St. John Chrysostom, Concerning the Education of Children*, from the Greek; and various French works on gardening, painting, and architecture, and the building of a library. His original work ranged over subjects as diverse as engraving, the collecting of medals, the tyranny of foreign fashions in dress, and political and religious argument; while his *Life* of his friend Mrs. Godolphin was animated by an admiring affection that made it, although not intended for publication, one of the best things he wrote. In his lifetime Evelyn's most celebrated book, which ran into many edi-

tions and established his reputation as an authority on forestry, was *Sylva, or A Discourse of Forest-Trees*, published in 1664.

Among his contemporaries' tributes are lines by Abraham Cowley praising Evelyn's "prudence, how to choose the best," his rejection of the "empty shows and senceless noys;/And all which rank Ambition breeds" for the "soft, yet solid joys" of books and gardens. Throughout his *Diary* the word "discreet" recurs as one of Evelyn's most frequent terms of approbation. Prudence, and a discretion that often proved the better part of valor, were in fact the guiding principles of Evelyn's life. They emerge in his statement, after the battle of Brentford, that active allegiance to the royalist cause would have "left both me and my Brothers expos'd to ruine, without any advantage to his Majestie" (a ruin that countless others risked and suffered for their convictions without calculating the cost). His caution may again be observed in Evelyn's ambivalent attitude during the Protectorate: in the words of William Bray, his first editor, "he had personal friends in the Court of Cromwell at the same time that he was corresponding with his father-in-law, Sir Richard Browne, the ambassador of King Charles II at Paris . . . though he remained a decided Royalist he managed so well as to have intimate friends even amongst those nearly connected with Cromwell." Various other incidents in Evelyn's career—his response to religious persecution under the Puritans is an honorable exception—illustrate this capacity for the convenient compromise. Standing in a time of dissensions and violence for the refinements, graces, and order of the civilized life, he was reluctant to disrupt its even tenor or jeopardize his interests by courting unwise antagonisms. Yet despite his policy of prudent evasion in place of participation or positive protest, Evelyn was in many ways one of the ornaments of his age. Soberly observing its follies, holding aloof from what he called the "gilded toys" of worldly preoccupations (he repeatedly declined both the presidency of the Royal Society and the honor of a knighthood), he was typical of the seventeenth century's eager and wide-ranging spirit of inquiry, its love of learning, and its ideals of public service.

His *Diary* (whose main manuscript the author entitled *Kalendarium*) opens in 1641, when Evelyn was twenty-one, with a retrospective summary of his parentage, birthplace, and boyhood; and the story of all he saw and did in a long and busy life is continued until within a month of his death, nearly sixty-five years later. At the early age of ten or eleven he had formed the habit of making autobiographical jottings; and he kept his *Diary* mainly for his own satisfaction—not only as a record of prosaic daily experience but also, in the manner of other devout Christians of that century, as an aid to spiritual progress. Later, when recasting the section on his early years in the fragment he called *De Vita Propria*, he seems to have had the idea of writing for the pleasure and benefit of his descendants; especially in the meticulous account of his travels, which would serve them as a practical private guidebook to places worth visiting abroad.

From his frequent references to events later than those he is recording it is evident that Evelyn did not follow the method of day-by-day entries, and that much of the *Diary* was written up long afterward from notes made at the time. Also, it emerges, from many similarities between his phrasing and that of contemporary descriptions of places and events, that he often supplemented personal observation with generous borrowings from the guidebooks, topographical works, and newspapers of the day.[1]

Edited by the antiquary William Bray, the *Diary* was first published in 1818. The success it enjoyed was instant and immense, for apart from its intrinsic interest as a social and historical document, Evelyn's dignified, pious character made a special appeal. Sir Walter Scott voiced nineteenth-century opinion in his pronouncement that Evelyn's "life, manners, and principles, as illustrated in his Memoirs, ought . . . to be the manual of English gentlemen."

As a record of many facets of life at home and abroad in the latter part of the seventeenth century, Evelyn's *Diary* is one of our fullest available sources of information. He lived mostly out of England in the 1640's—taking a trip to Holland before the Civil War, and during his period of voluntary exile in the early years of the Protectorate wandering extensively in France and Italy. Never did any sightseer perform his duties more conscientiously (he stayed out all night, for instance, to watch the Christmas Eve ceremonies in various churches in Rome, and more

than once recorded "being pretty weary of my continual walkings").

Like other seventeenth-century travellers, Evelyn believed in the educational benefits of exploring foreign countries. Thus his primary purpose in setting down details of where he went and what he saw was to provide the fullest possible objective information about the buildings, monuments, and art collections of the towns and cities he visited, rather than to give his own impressions. Yet it is in fact these—the personal encounter or incident slipped in between solid blocks of architectural description incorporated from accounts by other travelers and topographers—that enliven this part of the *Diary*. Evelyn is most readable where his observations are original and the phraseology, as well as the experience, his own: as when he exclaims at the sight of dogs harnessed like coach horses to carts, in the streets of Brussels; meets a shepherd in Normandy who tells the travellers that only yesterday his companion was killed in the midst of his flock by a wolf; or records how fireflies near Ferrara were so bright that "beating some of them downe & applying them to a book, I could read in the darke, by the light they afforded." Some of Evelyn's word pictures have a directness that conjures a scene clearly before the mind's eye, as that of the Luxembourg Gardens:

You shall meete some Walkes & Retirements full of Gallants and Ladys; in others, melancholy Lovers, Friars & studious Scholars: In others Jolly Citizens, some sitting & Lying on the Grasse, others running & jumping: Some at Bowles & Ball, others Dauncing & Singing; and all this without the least disturbance, by reason of the amplitude of the Place.

There is a vivid eyewitness account of the ceremonial celebrations in Rome of the newly crowned Pope Innocent X taking possession of the Lateran, the ancient episcopal seat of the popes; and another of Venice:

The innumerable cages of Nightingals, which they keepe . . . entertaines you with their melody from shop to shop, so as shutting your Eyes, you would imagine your selfe in the Country, where indeede you are in the middle of the Sea: besides there being neither rattling of Coaches nor trampling of horses, tis almost as silent as the field.

Appreciation of natural scenery was not common in Evelyn's day, but his genuine feeling for it emerges both in the sketches he often made and in

[1] Evelyn's borrowings are given in the footnotes to E. S. de Beer, ed., *The Diary of John Evelyn: Vol.II, Kalendarium, 1620-1649* (see bibliography), and in the "General Bibliographical Notes on Evelyn's Sources for His Accounts of His Travels," on pp. 569-579 of that volume.

descriptions like his telling evocation of the mountain landscape at Radicofani:

We seemed to be rather in the Sea than the Clowdes, till we having pierc'd quite through, came into a most serene heaven, as if we had been above all human Conversation, the Mountaine appearing more like a great Iland, than joynd to any other hills; for we could perceive nothing but a Sea of thick Clowds rowling under our feete like huge Waves, ever now & then suffering the top of some other mountaine to peepe through, which we could discover many miles off, and betweene some breaches of the Clowds, Landskips and Villages of the subjacent Country.

Or there is the graphic recital of the travellers' adventures while returning home over the Simplon Pass, unable to "see above a pistol shoote before us," deafened and drenched by the roaring cataracts, "freezing in the Snow, & anon frying by the reverberation of the Sun against the Cliffs as we descend lower."

Evelyn's particular preoccupations abroad—interesting as an index to the tastes of the traveller of his time—were artistic and architectural rather than human. Nevertheless, there are occasional lively glimpses of people: of the formidable fury of a Genoese waterman bilked of his fare; of prostitutes in Naples; of the "merry, Witty and genial" Neapolitan peasant; of curious fashions in dress among Venetian ladies; and of the character and appearance of the Swiss. Especially memorable is Evelyn's description of the galley slaves he saw at Marseilles:

The miserable wretches close shaved & stark naked, all save their Canvase Drawers, & red Capps, was a new, & cruel spectacle: Some had double Chaines about their midles & Legs; & so Coupl'd with his fellow, & made fast to the Banks of the *Gallys*. . . . I was astonish'd at the manner of their Lying in the Gally, Considering how they were Crowded & Chained together: Yet was there hardly one but had some Occupation or other; by which as leasure in great Calmes & other times [permits], they are permitted to exercise their Trades, & gaine a little mony, some knitting stockings, making Gloves, Carving, Turning &c: So as some after many yeares servitude have scrap'd-up enough to purchase their liberty. . . . They are also ruled & unmercifully Drub'd on their feete & chastized, upon the least displeasur of their Captaines & Officers: for all which they are full of Jollity & knavery.

Evelyn's relish for travel was all part of the—to us, sometimes naive—appetite he shared with Pepys and most men of his age for the novel and marvellous: whether these took the form of freaks at the London fairs or the private entertainment, when dining out, of a fire-eater who "devoured *Brimston* on glowing coales, chewing and swallowing them downe; he also mealted a beere glasse & eate it quite up." It was the same instinctive curiosity that made him one of the prominent figures in the Royal Society from its inception. For many years Evelyn regularly attended discourses on topics from the manufacture of woolen cloth or tinting of glass to aspects of anatomy and medicine; the demonstration of inventions like Boyle's vacuum machine or Newton's burning glass, and innumerable experiments, including some of the first in blood transfusion. As his references to these in the *Diary* are confined to brief mentions, they are useful as a record of the diversity of scientific interests then, rather than for particulars of method and procedure (better reported in the published minutes of the Royal Society).

Far more detailed than his scientific jottings are Evelyn's accounts of some of the happenings in a lifetime that spanned a crowded and exciting period of English history ("an age of extraordinary events, & revolutions," as his epitaph puts it). His *Diary* stretches from "that blessed Halcyon tyme in England" before 1642, through years of civil strife, plague and fire, foreign wars, and plots at home that ended in the execution of traitors, to the comparative serenity of the reigns of William III and Queen Anne. Living on the edge of London, frequently at court, and knowing distinguished men in various spheres of activity, Evelyn was in the thick of the national life and admirably placed to observe its momentous events. He refused to attend the "execrable wickednesse" of Charles I's execution, but witnessed without sorrow Cromwell's funeral procession, drily commenting:

It was the joyfullest funerall that ever I saw, for there was none that Cried, but dogs, which the souldiers hooted away with a barbarous noise; drinking, & taking Tabacco in the streetes as they went.

This staunch royalist was, of course, present at the triumphal return of Charles II on his birthday in May 1660, and at his coronation the following spring, and gives a detailed account of the king's last illness, and death, twenty-four years later. Evelyn's description of the coronation procession, taken from a newspaper, is not nearly as vivid as in Pepys (who also includes colorful glimpses of the feast in Westminster Hall, which Evelyn barely mentions). Similarly, it is to Pepys that we owe the more comprehensive picture of the Great Plague of 1665. Evelyn stayed in London all through those harrowing weeks, performing his duties as a commissioner for sick and wounded seamen with a devotion that earned from the king "many thanks for [his] Care, & faithfullnesse in his service, in a time of that greate danger, when every body fled their Employments"; but his information about it is disappointingly sparse. His account of the Great Fire, which broke out in London in September 1666, is altogether more satisfying, and remains, with Pepys's, the best-known contemporary description that has come down to us.

All the skie were of a fiery aspect, like the top of a burning Oven, & the light seene above 40 miles round about for many nights: God grant mine eyes may never behold the like, who now saw above ten thousand houses all in one flame, the noise & crackling & thunder of the impetuous flames, the shreeking of Women & children, the hurry of people, the fall of towers, houses & churches was like an hideous storme, & the aire all about so hot & inflam'd that at the last one was not able to approch it. . . . Thus I left it this afternoone burning, a resemblance of Sodome, or the last day.

After the flames were finally extinguished, Evelyn walked through the devastated city:

clambring over mountaines of yet smoking rubbish, & frequently mistaking where I was, the ground under my feete so hott, as made me not onely Sweate, but even burnt the soles of my shoes. . . . I did not see one loade of timber unconsum'd, nor many stones but what were calcind white as snow, so as the people who now walked about the ruines, appeard like men in some dismal desart, or rather in some greate Citty, lay'd wast by an impetuous & cruel Enemy.

Particularly interesting are his details of the ruin inside St. Paul's, where the stones had flown out "like grenades" and the lead melted in a stream down the streets. Later, Evelyn submitted various proposals for rebuilding the destroyed areas of "the most august Cittie in the world." Intensely concerned with the welfare of the capital, and full of plans for the improvement of its streets and buildings, for purifying its air of factory smoke,

and so on, he adds substantially to our knowledge of London at that time. The *Diary* contains some pictorial passages describing the city during the severe winter of 1683–1684, when the Thames was frozen over for about six weeks:

I went crosse the *Thames* upon the Ice (which was now become so incredibly thick, as to beare not onely whole streetes of boothes in which they roasted meate, & had divers shops of wares . . . but Coaches & carts & horses passed over) . . . also on sleds, sliding with skeetes; There was likewise Bull-baiting, Horse & Coach races, Pupetplays & interludes, Cookes & Tipling, & lewder places; so as it seem'd to be a bacchanalia, Triumph or Carnoval on the Water.

In its representation of the religious life of the period Evelyn's *Diary* is probably unparalleled. It provides, for one thing, rare firsthand glimpses of worship among the royalist exiles in Paris during the early years of the Protectorate. The experience, later, of the Anglicans under Cromwell has been nowhere more effectively communicated. Soon after his return from France, Evelyn began to attend Anglican services in London; and he continued after their prohibition in November 1655, when the faithful met in private houses and chapels and were, in this time of persecution, "generaly much more devout & religious, than in our greatest prosperity." At the end of an illicit service on Christmas Day 1657, "The Chapell was surrounded with Souldiers. . . . These wretched miscreants held their muskets against us as we came up to receive the Sacred Elements, as if they would have shot us at the Altar." Evelyn was detained, and that afternoon asked "frivolous & insnaring questions, with much threatning," before being finally dismissed. His note for 27 December laconically records: "Our Viccar proceeded." Such passages form a plain and moving tribute to those who, undeterred by insecurity and danger, remained loyal to the forbidden church.

The influence of religion upon everyday life then pervades the pages of Evelyn's *Diary*: not only in the importance of religious observances, but in the intensity of conviction among many individuals, even at court. One such person was Margaret Blagge (later Mrs. Godolphin), a maid of honor to the queen: an "incomparable Creature . . . a rare example of so much piety, & Virtue in so great a Witt, beauty & perfection; This Miracle of a young Lady in a licentious Court & so deprav'd an age."

Evelyn made a compact of friendship with her, in 1672, that was rooted in the shared prayers and spiritual discussion of a mutually valued devotional life, and declared, on her tragically early death: "We were but one Soule." Other exemplary lives praised by Evelyn in his *Diary* include those of the "plaine honest Carpenter" Jonas Shish, an old master shipwright in the parish, and of a young woman in the village of Swallowfield, in Berkshire. "A Maiden of primitive life," Evelyn called her, "a *Saint* of an extraordinary sort" whose "strange humility and contentednesse" voluntarily embraced poverty, celibacy, and prayer, giving alms and visiting the sick. Among Evelyn's personal friends were some of the great divines of his day—men like Jeremy Taylor and Thomas Tenison, later archbishop of Canterbury; and the central place of religion in his own life is everywhere apparent. In his earliest pages, before the Civil War, he records each occasion on which he received the Sacrament; and the *Diary* abounds in prayers for his preservation from temptation or physical danger and thanksgivings for his delivery, and in notices of the sermons he heard—gradually expanding from brief jottings of text, theme, and preacher to detailed reports of their content. He describes services held not only in London churches and at Wotton but also in the private oratory of the palace. The sight of Roman Catholics prominent at the court of James II, of the elaborate embellishment of the new chapel at Whitehall and of Jesuits officiating at the altar, filled this loyal Anglican with a distress quite as acute as he experienced during the years of Puritan persecution. Evelyn came away from one of these occasions "not believing I should ever have lived to see such things in the King of Englands palace, after it had pleas'd God to inlighten this nation," and praying for his "threatened church" as fervently as he had voiced his unshakable faith in it on hearing Pepys's news that Charles II had died a Catholic.

Evelyn's natural interests, as well as his natural prudence, did not dispose him to involve himself in politics, and many of the political notices in the *Diary* are taken from newspapers. But in the ten years preceding the Glorious Revolution of 1689 he does reflect, as plainly as he represents the convinced Anglican's reactions to religious matters under James II, the trend of public opinion about the government and state of the country and the progress of "the universal discontent." Others may have been more outspoken and active in their increasing resentment of the regime; Evelyn nevertheless epitomizes the disillusion and estrangement from the Stuarts, during that decade, of those men of principle who had been their strongest supporters. If he did not help to bring about the fall of the king, he was certainly never inclined to oppose it; and he was among the crowd that flocked to St. James's to see the newly arrived William of Orange, whom he records as being "very stately, serious & reserved."

For all his political detachment, Evelyn was on friendly terms with many of the leading statesmen of the time; and the *Diary* contains revealing portraits of Lord Sandwich (Pepys's cousin and patron), Lord Arlington, secretary of state and afterward lord chamberlain, Sir Thomas Clifford, lord high treasurer, and of both Stuart kings, who held Evelyn in high regard. (There is an engaging glimpse of the recently restored Charles II posing for a portrait head for the new coins, while Evelyn held the candle for the artist and chatted to the royal sitter about painting and engraving.) Of special biographical interest is what Evelyn records of his discovery and encouragement of an obscure young woodcarver named Grinling Gibbons, to whose later fame he substantially contributed by introducing his work to the king and to influential men like Pepys and Wren. Evelyn's studies of scientists include an excellent appreciation of the gifted and versatile Sir William Petty, a fellow member of the Royal Society. But his brief biographies are not confined to the eminent. We are introduced to such affectionately delineated personalities as his parents, the small son Richard he lost at the age of five ("a prodigie for Witt, & understanding; for beauty of body a very Angel, & for endowments of mind, of incredible & rare hopes"), and his daughter Mary, a girl of "greate innocency & integrity," who also died young.

Evelyn was, on the whole, more interested in human activities than in the complexities of character, which he seldom depicts in any depth. It is perhaps because of this, and because things—buildings, pictures, landscapes, scientific phenomena—attracted him more than the enigmas of personality, that his *Diary* is relatively scant in the information it gives about himself, apart from the manifold employments that engrossed him from youth to old age. Only rarely does he provide such a direct autobiographical statement as that, at the time of his father's death in 1641, he was "of a raw, vaine, uncertaine and very unwary inclination," thinking "of nothing, but the pursuite of Vanity, and the confus'd imaginations of Young men." Inevitably there is a certain amount of indirect self-revelation. Where, for instance, he is revolted by the vivisection of a dog or the baiting to death of a horse, writes indignantly of the "butcherly Sports, or rather barbarous cruelties," of cockfighting, dogfighting, and bear- and bullbaiting, and is filled with horrified pity at the stoical suffering of a seaman whose leg he sees amputated, Evelyn emerges as a humane and compassionate man. But we miss in his *Diary* the frailties, the passions, and with them the warmth of ordinary humanity; and it is left to his friend Pepys to provide glimpses of Evelyn more vivid than any he gives us himself.

He appears on one occasion in Pepys's *Diary* in high good humor at dinner, "inspired into . . . such a spirit of mirth" on hearing the news of Lord Sandwich's capture of some Dutch vessels that he launched into impromptu versifying, "so aptly . . . and so fast" that he made the company "die almost with laughing." A certain strain of complacency sometimes to be detected in Evelyn is confirmed by Pepys's tale of his friend reading him "part of a play or two of his own making, very good, but not as he conceits them, I think, to be"; and also, "with too much gusto, some little poems of his own, that were not transcendant." But, Pepys adds, "a most excellent person he is, and must be allowed a little for a little conceitedness . . . being a man so much above others." The more he knew of Evelyn, declared Pepys, the more he loved him. It was a mutual regard, which began through official contacts and the discovery of many off-duty tastes in common, and survived the fortunes and vicissitudes of forty years. Often the friends walked together in Evelyn's garden at Deptford with "mighty pleasure," having "most excellent discourse touching all manner of learning" or shaking their heads over the iniquities of the government, the vanity and vices of the court, and the country's imminent ruin. When Pepys died three years before him, Evelyn paid tribute to his "particular Friend . . . a very worthy, Industrious & curious person, none in England exceeding him in the Knowledge of the Navy . . . universaly beloved, Hospitable, Generous, Learned in many things, skill'd in Musick, a very greate Cherisher of Learned men, of whom he had the Conversation."

SAMUEL PEPYS

SAMUEL PEPYS was born at St. Bride's, London, in 1633, educated at St. Paul's School, and went up on a scholarship to Cambridge. His father was a tailor (a good, gentle man of whom Pepys speaks throughout his *Diary* with unfailing affection); but if this branch of the prolific Pepys family was a modest one, it had more exalted connections. Pepys's cousin, Edward Montagu (later Lord Sandwich), was in 1655 appointed joint commander of the English battle fleet about to set sail for Spain; and in his absence he left Samuel, recently married and very poor, installed in his household to look after his affairs. In 1658, Pepys became a clerk of the exchequer. He had grown up a Cromwellian, but the trend of events after the Protector's death converted both him and Montagu to royalist sympathies. In March 1660 he went to sea as secretary to his cousin the admiral, returning two months later on the flagship carrying the king home. This voyage, affording many useful contacts with important and influential persons, gave the ambitious young man his first real taste of what the future might hold for him. Evelyn's social position, as a gentleman of the comfortably privileged class, freed him from the obligation of putting a price on his abilities. Pepys, on the other hand, lacking those advantages of birth, breeding, and fortune, was forced constantly into the exhausting competitive scramble for office: astute to smell out changes of favor and "unwilling to mix [his] fortune with him that is going down the wind," always busily maneuvering for advancement. Much anxious canvassing and campaigning, with Montagu's backing, secured him the fiercely contested place of clerk of the acts of the navy, followed by the clerkship of the Privy Seal; and in 1665 Pepys was appointed surveyor general of victualing for the navy.

Thus his *Diary*, beginning on the eve of the Restoration, records the hopes, fears, and gratifications of an obscure, impecunious clerk possessing little but a capacity for hard work and an immense determination to get on. Because the struggle for success is invariably so much more interesting than the picture of ambition attained, the nine years covered by the diarist are those in his life we would most wish to read about. Already the *Diary's* later pages are overburdened—at any rate for the ordinary reader—with a weight of pedestrian detail about the cares of office.

By the time increasing eye trouble, combined with the press of affairs, had forced Pepys to abandon his closely written entries, he had entered the years of fame: of his secretaryship of the admiralty, his election as a member of Parliament, his presidency of the Royal Society, and many other public distinctions. These inevitably brought the dangers and disasters that then threatened all eminent men. In 1679, Pepys was accused by his enemies of implication in the Popish Plot and of selling naval information to France, and was committed to the Tower. No case was proved against him, but after his discharge he remained for four years out of office before being reappointed secretary of the admiralty in 1684. This marked the beginning of Pepys's great campaign of naval reform, which established him as an administrator of integrity and genius. In 1690, in retirement, he published his *Memoirs of the Navy*, and died at Clapham, London, in 1703.

Pepys's *Diary* was written in a current system of shorthand and a cipher of his own invention, consisting of odd contractions and a smattering of foreign words and phrases, which he employed mainly in the passages describing his amorous escapades. Calculated to resist the efforts of the most persistent decoder, these confessions were clearly not intended for any scrutiny but the writer's own. The publication of Evelyn's *Diary* aroused interest in the friend mentioned in it so often; and Pepys's manuscript, bequeathed with his library to his old Cambridge college, Magdalene, was patiently deciphered between 1819 and 1822 by a graduate named John Smith. Part of it was published under the editorship of Lord Braybrooke in 1825, followed by fuller editions later in the century. If it was Pepys's misfortune to have the secrets of the self, so assiduously hidden from his neighbors, displayed for all the world to see more than a century after his death, it was posterity's great gain. Never has any writer presented us with a self-portrait more relentlessly honest, freer from shame and self-respect alike, and from the average autobiographer's temptation to dramatize his defects and polish up his virtues.

While the attraction of Evelyn's *Diary* lies predominantly in its panorama of an age, the reader of Pepys is equally delighted by his delineation of the contemporary scene and his candid revelation, uncensored by the habitual conventions and decencies, of one man's character, tastes, preoccupations,

and pleasures. Like Evelyn, Pepys was keenly interested in the graphic arts, especially painting. He was an eager reader, up at four in the morning with his copy of Cicero, spending hours browsing at his booksellers, and buying so lavishly that—books "now growing numerous and lying one upon another on my chairs"—new shelves had to be erected. Above all, he enjoyed music—"the thing of the world," he says, "that I love most." He refers frequently to airs of his own composition, including his song "Beauty Retire," and to his singing lessons. Whenever a few friends and Samuel Pepys gathered together, it was an occasion for music—four-part psalms, a "variety of brave Italian and Spanish songs," or "barber's music" with a cittern and a pair of candlesticks "with money in them, for cymbals." Diligently he piped on his flageolet or practiced on his lute, and was gratified to "have the neighbors come forth into the yard to hear me." The musical instruments mentioned in the course of Pepys's *Diary*, from the dulcimer to trumpets and kettledrums, merit a study to themselves.

Another of Pepys's great enthusiasms was the theater, which too often for his conscience tempted him to play truant from work, emptied his pockets, and led to repeated solemn vows of renunciation foredoomed to be broken. The *Diary* affords innumerable glimpses of plays and players of the time, and also of the behavior of fashionable audiences, such as the "two talking ladies" and their escort whose "mighty witty" comments spoiled the play, of Pepys's neighbor at *Othello* who cried out in alarm when Desdemona was smothered, or the lady who spat on him by mistake in the dark (but observing that she was very pretty, he forgave her). This avid theatergoer was an exacting—if not always discriminating—critic, given to such tart comment as "the most insipid, ridiculous play that ever I saw in my life" (of *A Midsummer Night's Dream*). That Pepys far preferred Ben Jonson to Shakespeare may have been partly due to bad acting or current methods of Shakespearean production. *Romeo and Juliet*, for instance, was "the worst acted that ever I saw these people do," while *Macbeth* was warmly applauded for its "variety of dancing and music"!

True to the habit of his Puritan upbringing, if not to its spirit—for the pious avowals in Pepys's *Diary*, unlike Evelyn's, never sound a more than perfunctory note—Pepys was an indefatigable churchgoer and sermon fancier. Nothing daunted by the varying quality of the preachers, he would spend all Sunday "till churches were done . . . going from one church to another, and hearing a bit here and a bit there." Often, indeed, the performance in the pulpit proved less entertaining than the week's theatrical pleasures, and the listener was lulled into slumber. "I slept, God forgive me!" is a reiterated refrain; although it should in fairness be added that the devout Evelyn also succumbed on many occasions to the soporific of those lengthy homilies ("Exceedingly drowsy: The Lord pardon my infirmitie").

The zest that Pepys brought to his play- and church-going also emerges in the *Diary* in his prowess at table. There is a great deal here about food: eel pie or lamprey pie, swan, lobsters, chines of beef, and barrels of oysters, "two dozen of larks all in a dish," and on one occasion a venison pasty that proved, alas, to be "palpable mutton, which was not handsome." It is not only the relish with which they are recorded, but also the monumental size of these feasts that amazes. No wonder so prodigious an eater frequently paid the penalty of overindulgence: ill all night after an orgy of wine and anchovies, or over his share of two hundred walnuts consumed at a sitting.

Almost as numerous in the *Diary* as the bon vivant's gastronomical feats and recitals are the details of dress. About his clothes Pepys was something of a peacock, paying scrupulous attention to what he wore. This innocent vanity was perhaps due partly to his father's trade, which made him more conscious than most people of cut and texture, and partly to memories of earlier poverty "when, for want of clothes, I was forced to sneak like a beggar." For public occasions now Pepys took care to make himself "as fine as [he] could," and often describes with disarming self-congratulation how this effect was achieved. One Easter Day he went to church in the finery of a "close-kneed coloured suit, which with new stockings of the same colour, with belt and new gilt-handled sword, is very handsome"; more sober attire for an ordinary Sabbath consisted of his "best black cloth suit, trimmed with scarlet ribbon, very neat, with my cloak lined with velvet, and a new beaver." There is mention of a white suit with silver lace coat, of green watered silk for a morning waistcoat, and of ordering a cloak with gold buttons and a silk suit ("the first that ever I wore in my life"), which prompts the hope that its wearer can pay the bill.

Samuel was not the only member of the Pepys household extravagant over self-adornment. Many a time did he go to bed "in a discontent," or even "mighty troubled," over reckless spending on a petticoat with rich lace or a new gown. (It is interesting to note, however, that once when Pepys found himself badly out of pocket, the sum spent on his wife's attire had been £12, and on his own, £55.)

But proprietary pride in Mrs. Pepys's elegance and beauty generally outweighed the qualms and quarrels over clothes. At a fashionable wedding the complacent husband remarked that "among all the beauties there, my wife was thought the greatest"; and that standing near Princess Henrietta, his Elizabeth, "with two or three black patches on and well dressed, did seem to me much handsomer than she." Pepys had married her when she was fifteen (three years older than Evelyn's wife on their marriage), and she died soon after the *Diary* ends. Its pages are filled with their wranglings over money, the servants, her neglect of the house, or his infidelities; and bickering or tiff flares every so often into an undignified scene where he blacks her eye or she threatens him with red-hot tongs. Yet almost as soon as Pepys had flown into a rage over some trifle—flinging the trenchers about the room when he found the tablecloth crumpled, kicking and breaking a basket he had brought his wife from Holland, or tearing up his love letters to her—he was repenting of his quick temper, making amends to the "poor wretch," and they were "friends again." Reading aloud to her and taking her to the theater, teaching her astronomy and arithmetic and encouraging her painting, he acknowledged Elizabeth on the whole "a very good companion"; he only regretted she had not more ear for music, one of the two diversions that, he confessed, "I cannot but give way to, whatever my business is."

The other irresistible addiction, on his own admission and amply illustrated in the *Diary*, was women. It was in fact his ungovernable and apparently incurable susceptibility that provoked much of Pepys's marital unhappiness. Repeatedly avowing his guilt and begging forgiveness for his follies—the furtive fondlings in coaches, the assignations in taverns and cheap lodgings, or even with his wife's maid in their own room—he seems to have been constitutionally incapable of the fidelity he promised. Eye and hand continued to rove after feminine attractions, not only at the theater and in friends' houses, but even in church. There his attempts at hand holding were nicely thwarted by the pretty, modest maid of his choice, who produced pins from her pocket; but with her friendlier and more obliging neighbor the undaunted philanderer had better luck.

Yet even the record of his promiscuities is pervaded by that quality that makes Pepys as lively a companion for the present-day reader as he was for his contemporaries: a cheerful exuberance of spirits impossible to cast down for long. Only occasionally do we find him going to bed "very sad": most days ended for him with "much mirth" or "good sport," and nights of making "mighty merry" into the small hours with music, drinking, and kissing of ladies resulted in an aching head and mornings "mighty sleepy." His taste in the theater was generally for plays with plenty of music and dancing; he did not enjoy those that were "too sad and melancholy." Like a schoolboy he savored teasing and practical jokes, or a furious coach race against a friend; he had a keen sense of the ridiculous (as when he chuckles at a prayer heard in Westminster Abbey that the Almighty would "imprint His word on the thumbs of our right hands and on the great toes of our right feet"). Joking with workmen in his house, he remarked that he seemed to have the luck "to meet with a sort of drolling workmen on all occasions," apparently unaware that it was his own genial and infectious good humor that was, like Falstaff's, the cause of it in other men.

With equal clarity, however, the *Diary* reveals a very different strain in Pepys's nature: that of the moderation and shrewd, sober good sense that characterized his public career. His reaction to the excessive—from licentiousness at court or the extravagance of some church ceremonies ("they do so overdo them") to actresses overpainting their faces—was invariably impatience or distaste. King's man as he was, the sight of people at the Restoration drinking Charles II's health on their knees in the streets seemed "a little too much." However imperfect was Pepys's judgment in his private risks and indiscretions, on public matters it emerges as considered, discriminating, and scrupulously fair.

Another tough fiber running through all the frivolities recorded in the *Diary* is that of its writer's ambition to attain wealth and high office. Meticulously each month the minor government official set down details of his household accounts and—from the day he found himself worth the modest sum of £40—the progress of his steadily mounting savings. Lamenting when he had spent too much on theaters or clothes, he piously offered up thanks for the Almighty's especial attention to his finances ("My heart was glad and blessed God") when he could record a rising total. Only when the diarist had consolidated his fortune and position in the world did the anxious accounting disappear from his pages. Yet Pepys's concern over money remained—possibly ingrained by memories of humble beginnings and the determination never again to be poor. Throughout the *Diary* pieces of gold continue to be a "pleasant sight" to cheer his heart. Restless with fears of being robbed, he often lost sleep through noises in the night, which threw him into a panic over the safety of his savings. Prowling about the house, thinking "every running of a mouse really a thief," caused him to sympathize with the fears of rich men and to reflect "how painful it is sometimes to keep money as well as to get it."

But the lucrative gains of office, and his rewards for favors solicited or received—for a word at the right moment in the ear of the great, or the price of a promotion —were not the sole source of Pepys's pleasure in his rise to success. Quite as gratifying as being promised "a rapier . . . a vessel of wine, or a gun, and one offered me his silver hatband to do him a courtesy," was the fact of his growing influence and importance in the eyes of his equals. Even more satisfactory was the esteem of his superiors, when he found himself "made a fellow to the best commanders in the fleet" or invited to dine out among fine company at the Tower, the duke of York's calling him Pepys by name, and the king personally acknowledging his services. "As I do take pains," exulted the flattered young clerk, "so God blesses me, and hath sent me masters that do observe that I take pains." Pepys marvels too consciously at his own good fortune, in having become "no mean fellow, but can live in the world and have something," entertain more lavishly than his neighbors, and even contemplate buying enough ground to build a coach house and stable, ever to seem merely complacent. Although temporarily "put into a despair" or "quite pulled down" when a rival seemed about to cheat him of some coveted office, Pepys's nature had little of that restless discontent that so often accompanies ambition. He was a man who counted his blessings: not only his accumulating capital and the respect of his betters, but also his health (he annually celebrated an operation he had successfully undergone a few years earlier). "If I have a heart to be contented," he declared, "I think I may reckon myself as happy a man as any is in the world. . . . The Lord be blessed, and make us thankful."

This gratitude and ingenuous satisfaction endear Pepys to his readers as warmly as do all those other engagingly human minutiae that quicken the pages of his *Diary*. The man who flings his clean collars on the floor in a pet when he finds them not ironed to his liking, is vexed at having to walk slowly when his wife's new shoes pinch or at seeing clerks from the office in more expensive seats at the theater, and whose fascination with a new watch makes him carry it in his hand to see "what o'clock it is one hundred times," is no remote historical figure dim with distance, but a personality peculiarly real and close to us today.

On one occasion Pepys records being "very merry . . . at our gossips' dinner"; indeed, his pages abound in that gossip so delightful to the reader of diaries. Early on, there are some engrossing passages in which Charles II, aboard the ship carrying him to England, describes his experiences after his escape from Worcester—tales that, said Pepys, "made me ready to weep." Later the *Diary* keeps us primed with talk of the town picked up in coffeehouse or tavern, at the office or dining out: of who is in favor and who on the wane, of the latest duel and precipitate flight into hiding, or the most up-to-date scandalous rumor about the "amours and mad doings" of fashionable society. (The spectacle of the king disporting himself with his different mistresses provokes the comment that "there is nothing almost but bawdry at Court from top to bottom.")

Another kind of gossip eagerly relished by Pepys took the form of the—often tall—tales related by merchants or travellers returned from abroad. With wondering curiosity he sets down apocryphal stories of the king and court of Portugal, of Ivan the Terrible in Russia, and of the horrible punishment of malefactors by the king of Siam; or marvels at the longevity of natives in recently colonized West Africa, at the winter rigors, bears, and wolves of Prussia, and at an explorer's account of mountain travels in Asia and the strange beauty of a world above the clouds. He was as enthralled as a child by the travellers' trophies—goldfish from China, a baboon from Guinea, the seahorse teeth brought to Whitehall by Russian ambassadors, or the strange

bird from the East Indies that "talks many things and neighs like the horse."

Alert as he was for the telling detail, the color and movement of a scene, the small humors and pathos of incident that serve to humanize history, Pepys is even more absorbing in his various eyewitness descriptions of stirring contemporary events. Early in the *Diary* comes his account of London's Restoration rejoicings—the "burning, and roasting, and drinking for rumps . . . tied upon sticks and carried up and down," the butchers at the maypole in the Strand ringing "a peal with their knives when they were going to sacrifice their rump." The following year the king's coronation ride from the Tower to Whitehall was "so glorious . . . with gold and silver, that we were not able to look at it, our eyes at last being so much overcome"; and the next night, after the feasting and music in Westminster Hall, the city had "a light like a glory round about it, with bonfires." Dazzled, Pepys declared that he would not in future trouble "to see things of state and show, as being sure never to see the like again in this world."

As spectacular in the scale of its miseries as the coronation in its splendors, the Plague has had no chronicler more graphic than Pepys. It was at the beginning of June 1665 that he first noticed what was to become an all too common sight: "houses marked with a red cross upon the doors, and 'Lord have mercy upon us!' writ there." By the end of the month the court had fled to the country, and Pepys was sending his mother, and later his wife, out of town. The tolling bells and daylight burials in open fields, the grisly rumors and anecdotes, such individual tragedies as the two women Pepys passed in the street crying and carrying a man's coffin between them, the disappearance of so many familiar figures—his grocer, the waterman of his barge, the publican and waiter at his alehouse—all grimly drove home the horror, prompting Pepys to make his will. Commenting on the callousness bred of panic, he observed "this disease making us more cruel to one another than . . . to dogs." After weeks at his post in a city "distressed and forsaken," with grass growing in Whitehall and the river and quays deserted, Pepys reported it "a delightful thing" to see London gradually repopulating as the menace abated, and shops and taverns beginning to open their doors.

A year later Pepys, like Evelyn, survived unscathed the second great catastrophe of the 1660's, which he re-creates with equal realism. It was he who carried firsthand news of the Great Fire to the king at Whitehall, and took back to the lord mayor in the city the royal instructions to pull down all houses in the path of the flames. But the fire could not be checked; and soon Pepys, too, was packing up his belongings, carrying them out into the garden by moonlight, and later riding with them, in his nightgown in a cart, to various places of safe deposit until the danger was over. The scenes of destruction and distress—people running hither and thither trying to save their possessions, piling them into churches, friends' houses still intact, and into boats on the river; the sick carried out in their beds, the poor refusing to leave their homes until the flames had reached them—are conjured by Pepys's packed, vigorous narrative with all the urgent actuality of a modern running commentary. Nowhere do they touch the imagination more poignantly than in those small, particular details in which Pepys excels (and far surpasses Evelyn): a cat burned in a chimney, pigeons falling with singed wings from the balconies, and one out of every three boats of household goods drifting on the water containing a pair of virginals. Pepys watched the city burn by night in "one entire arch of fire" with "a most horrid, malicious, bloody flame"; and afterward he walked through the smoldering ruins, where he picked up a piece of glass from a burned-out chapel "melted and buckled with the heat of the fire like parchment." No wonder that for many weeks to come this vigilant observer was to suffer from insomnia and nightmares—"mightily troubled in my sleep, with fire and houses pulling down."

Not only for its brilliantly pictorial accounts of domestic rejoicing or calamity is Pepys's *Diary* so valuable. As an official increasingly involved in national affairs, he was able to depict the inside story of England's sea war with the Dutch during that decade. From his privileged vantage point he provides, beyond the ordinary news of public jubilation over victories and alarm and despondency at setbacks, many less familiar details of the preoccupations of those then in office, and particularly of his own responsibilities in the discipline of the fleet, and of the general state of the navy at that time.

But it is perhaps less the pomp of pageantry or horrors of large-scale disaster than the everyday occurrences Pepys records that bring Restoration England most vividly to life: such incidents as that, seen from his coach, of two gallants and their footmen dragging off by force a pretty seller of ribbons and gloves on Ludgate Hill. Violence and sudden death are unsurprising commonplaces of Pepys's pages. An actor is set upon and murdered; a well-known surgeon is killed by a Frenchman in a drunken quarrel; an earl's son stabs his brother to death in a tavern; a Scottish knight dies in Covent Garden, "where there had been a great many formerly killed"; and there are constant bloody frays between butchers and weavers or Thames watermen. Disease was a still greater enemy of life. Deaths among Pepys's family, friends, and acquaintances recur with a frequency less appalling than his matter-of-course acceptance of them. In one place he records that of children born to relations of his within a single month of 1660, all five died. Inured to these stark facts of existence, Pepys was seldom shocked by the brutalities of his age. He shared, for instance, its taste for attending executions as a free form of entertainment, and mentions these casually in the same entry as the purchase of a new hat. He paid a shilling to stand on the wheel of a cart and see a thief hanged ("there was at least 12 to 14,000 people in the street"), climbed a turret to get a good view of two traitors' heads, and with ghoulish inquisitiveness touched with his bare hand the body of a seaman hanged for robbery. He was no more than typical of his time in beating his young maidservant with a broom and shutting her all night in the cellar, or whipping his serving boy for a lie until his arm ached.

Yet—so curious are the contradictions and inconsistencies that a human being comprises—Pepys could condemn as "very barbarous" the public indifference to a body drifting in full view for four days in the Thames, and be moved by the sight of people arrested for attending illegal religious meetings (wishing "to God they would either conform, or be very wise and not be catched!"). His repeated censures of "a sad, vicious, negligent Court," with its amours, drunkenness, debts, sycophancy, and contempt of the Church, are matched by many feeling comments on the plight of the poor. Especially were his indignation and helpless pity aroused by the grief of wives whose husbands had been seized by the press gang. "To see poor, patient, labouring men and housekeepers, leaving poor wives and families, taken up on a sudden by strangers" was, he declared, "very hard." His compassion again emerges when he records a conversation he had with a boy he met picking up rags by lantern light, who told him how "he could get sometimes three or four bushels of rags in a day, and got 3d. a bushel for them . . . and how many ways there are for poor children to get their livings honestly." If ambition early determined Pepys on wealth and success for himself, his sympathies remained with the privations of the people.

Side by side with more serious affairs, the *Diary* portrays most of the popular pastimes of the day. We see Pepys at leisure, watching the newly introduced sport of ice skating in St. James's Park, or the monkeys, Italian ropedancers, and "women that do strange tumbling tricks" at Bartholomew Fair; walking in Vauxhall Gardens (where "the wenches gathered pinks" and his boy crept through the hedge and stole roses), at the wrestling at Moorfields, or the bear garden ("a very rude and nasty pleasure"). For the first time in a gaming house, he concluded that "a gamester's life . . . is very miserable, and poor, and unmanly." On another first visit, to the cockpit, he admired the gallantry of the fighting cocks, savored the diversity of spectators ranging from a member of Parliament to "the poorest 'prentices, beggars, brewers, butchers, draymen and what not," and marveled how much they would bet and lose, even when they "look[ed] as if they had not bread to put in their mouths."

Though Pepys had soon had enough of the novelties of the cockpit, he "would not," he says, "but have seen it once." The remark is characteristic. Never was any man endowed with a keener, more tireless spirit of inquiry about the life going on around him. He describes a visit to the mint to watch money being made, and another backstage at the King's Playhouse to see the dressing rooms and stage machinery, his attendances at the Royal Society experiments, or chatting about building with a laborer sawing marble for the new Somerset House (and giving him the price of a drink). He owned a telescope, and looked at the moon and stars from the top of his house. He was indeed, as he says, "with child to see any strange thing"—or to try any new one: sampling his first cup of tea, heartily approving of the innovation of actresses on the stage, and with self-conscious daring embarking on the recent masculine fashion of the periwig.

This busy curiosity also embraced the human beings Pepys encountered. He had an appreciative eye for character, and can make a personality spring piquantly alive in a phrase or two. There is the garrulous one-eyed Frenchman who shared his coach and insisted on telling Pepys his life story; the "deaf

and most amorous melancholy gentleman, who is under a despair in love"; or the good old shepherd at Epsom, with his dog and a little boy reading to him from the Bible, who was "the most like one of the old patriarchs that ever I saw in my life." The *Diary* is also abundant in the kind of odd or bizarre incident that never failed to catch the writer's interest—such as the doctor's dog said to have killed and buried more than a hundred cats, or the stolen horse disguised with black cloth ears and a false mane.

No aspect of the pageant of life in his time was too small or unimportant to be worth noting by this man so "infinite of business that [his] heart and head were full"; and he paints it in the precise and prodigal, animated detail of a scene by Brueghel. Direct, impulsive, so plainly unpremeditated, Pepys's style runs on with the artless spontaneity of thought association; it communicates the often fragmentary quality of life itself. In the psychological truth of this great *Diary* we recognize the fundamental and reassuring sameness of human nature through the centuries. In the immediacy of its many fresh and evocative glimpses of ordinary moments—

I stayed up till the bell-man came by with his bell just under my window as I was writing of this very line, and cried, "Past one of the clock, and a cold, frosty, windy morning"—

we recapture the very essence of the age that produced it.

SELECTED BIBLIOGRAPHY

JOHN EVELYN

I. Bibliography. G. Keynes, *John Evelyn: A Study in Bibliophily and a Bibliography of His Writings* (London, 1937; 2nd ed., 1968), the MSS of Evelyn's *Diary* and of much else are deposited in the library of Christ Church, Oxford.

II. Collected Works. W. Upcott, ed., *The Miscellaneous Writings of John Evelyn, Esq., F. R. S.* (London, 1825).

III. Editions of the Diary. W. Bray, ed., *Memoirs, Illustrative of the Life and Writings of John Evelyn, Esq., F.R.S. Comprising His Diary, from the Year 1641 to 1705-6, and a Selection of His Familiar Letters*, 2 vols. (London, 1818), various further revised and enlarged eds. were published throughout the nineteenth century, including the 4-vol. ed. revised by W. Upcott and edited by J. Forster (London, 1850–1852) and that of 1879 with a biographical intro. by H. B. Wheatley; a revision of the Everyman's Library ed. (London, 1907) was published in 2 vols. (London, 1952; 1-vol. repr., 1966); A. Dobson, ed., *The Diary of John Evelyn*, 3 vols. (London, 1906), excludes the correspondence, reprinted in Globe ed. (1908, etc.); E. S. de Beer, ed., *The Diary of John Evelyn, Now First Printed in Full from the Manuscripts Belonging to Mr. John Evelyn*, 6 vols. (Oxford, 1955), the definitive Oxford English Texts ed., with a biographical sketch of Evelyn's life and character, a detailed textual and critical consideration of the *Diary*, and the full text of Evelyn's MSS annotated and indexed with great thoroughness; E. S. de Beer, ed., *The Diary of John Evelyn*, 1 vol. (London, 1959), in the Oxford Standard Authors series, uses the text of the above ed., contains the whole of the principal manuscript of the *Diary*, called "Kalendarium" by Evelyn (but omitting his reports of the contents of sermons he heard), and some extracts from his later recension of the *Diary*, entitled *De Vita Propria*.

IV. SEPARATE WORKS. (For an exhaustive list of Evelyn's many published writings, of which the following is a representative selection, see Keynes above.) *Of Liberty and Servitude* (London, 1649), translated from F. de la Mothe le Vayer; *The State of France, As It Stood in the IXth Year of This Present Monarch, Lewis XIII* (London, 1652), "Written to a Friend by J.E."; *An Essay on the First Book of T. Lucretius Carus de Rerum Natura* (London, 1656), "Interpreted and Made English verse"; *The French Gardiner: Instructing How to Cultivate All Sorts of Fruit-Trees, and Herbs for the Garden* (London, 1658), translated from N. de Bonnefons by "Philocepos" and several times reprinted during Evelyn's lifetime; *The Golden Book of St. John Chrysostom, Concerning the Education of Children* (London, 1659), "Translated out of the Greek by J. E. Esq."; *A Character of England, As It Was Lately Presented in a Letter to a Noble Man of France* (London, 1659), three editions appeared within the year; *An Apologie for the Royal Party: Written in a Letter to a Person of the Late Council of State. By a Lover of Peace and of His Country* (London, 1659); *A Panegyric to Charles the Second, Presented to His Majestie the XXIII of April, Being the Day of His Coronation MDCLXI* (London, 1661); *Fumifugium: or The Inconveniencie of the Aer and Smoak of London Dissipated* (London, 1661; facs. repr., Exeter, 1976), the first treatise on "smokeless zones"; *Instructions Concerning Erecting of a Library* (London, 1661), a translation from Gabriel Naudé; *Sculptura: or The History and Art of Chalcography and Engraving in Copper* (London, 1662); *Sylva, or A Discourse of Forest-Trees, and the Propagation of Timber in His Majesties Dominions* (London, 1664), published with *Pomona*, a treatise on fruit-growing for cider, and *Kalendarium Hortense*, a garden almanac; Evelyn's most famous work in his day and many times reprinted during his lifetime and in the early eighteenth century; *A Parallel of the Antient Architecture with the Modern* (London, 1664), translated from R. Fréart de Chambray, ran into several eds. during the first half of the eighteenth century; *The Pernicious Consequences of the New Heresie of the Jesuites Against the King and the State* (London, 1666), translated from P. Nicole; *Publick Employment and an Active Life Prefer'd to Solitude* (London, 1667); *An Idea of the Perfection of Painting* (London, 1668), translated from R. Fréart de Chambray; *Navigation and Commerce* (London, 1674); *A Philosophical Discourse of Earth, Relating to the Culture and Improvement of It for Vegetation, and the Propagation of Plants, &c.* (London, 1676); *Mundus Muliebris: or, The Ladies Dressing-Room Unlock'd* (London, 1690), in part by Evelyn's daughter Mary; *The Compleat Gard'ner: or, Directions for Cultivating and Right Ordering of Fruit-Gardens and Kitchen-Gardens: With Divers Reflections on Several Parts of Husbandry*, 2 vols. (London, 1693), translated from J. de la Quintinye, a 1-vol. abridgement appeared in 1699 and was reprinted three times from 1701–1710; *Numismata, A Discourse of Medals, Antient and Modern* (London, 1697); S. Wilberforce, ed., *The Life of Mrs. Godolphin* (London, 1847), published posthumously, the best ed., from a variant MS, was H. Sampson, ed. (Oxford, 1939); E. S. de Beer, ed., *Londinium Redivivum* (Oxford, 1938), Evelyn's views on the rebuilding of London after the Great Fire in 1666.

V. SOME BIOGRAPHICAL AND CRITICAL STUDIES. C. G. S. Foljambe, *Evelyn's Pedigree and Memoranda* (London, 1893); F. E. R. Heygate, ed., *Seven Letters of John Evelyn, 1665–1703* (London, 1914); H. M. Smith, ed., *John Evelyn in Naples 1645* (Oxford, 1914); H. Evelyn, *History of the Evelyn Family* (London, 1915); H. C. Levis, *Extracts from the Diaries and Correspondence of John Evelyn and Samuel Pepys Relating to Engraving* (London, 1915); H. M. Smith, ed., *The Early Life and Education of John Evelyn* (Oxford, 1920), this, like *John Evelyn in Naples 1645*, is a short extract from the *Diary* with detailed and enlightening commentary; V. Woolf, "Rambling Round Evelyn," in *The Common Reader*, 1st ser. (London, 1925); E. G. Craig, "John Evelyn and the Theatre," in his *Books and Theatres* (London, 1925); W. B. Squire, "Evelyn and Music" (1924–1926), a series of articles published in *The Times Literary Supplement*; Lord Ponsonby, *John Evelyn* (London, 1933); W. G. Hiscock, *Evelyn and Mrs. Godolphin* (London, 1951); W. G. Hiscock, *Evelyn and His Family Circle* (London, 1955).

SAMUEL PEPYS

I. BIBLIOGRAPHIES. E. K. Purnell, ed., *Report of the Historical MSS Commission on the Pepys MSS Preserved* at *Magdalene College, Cambridge* (London, 1911); *Bibliotheca Pepysiana: A Descriptive Catalogue of the Library of Samuel Pepys*, J. R. Tanner, ed., Part I: *Sea MSS* (London, 1914); E. G. Duff, ed., Part II: *Early Printed Books to 1558* (London, 1914); M. R. James, ed., Part III: *Medieval MSS* (London, 1923); W. J. Carlton, ed., Part IV: *Shorthand Books* (London, 1940); the Pepysiana Library at Magdalene College, Cambridge, has been entirely recataloged, the revised catalog will be published under the general editorship of Robert Latham, in 8 vols. comprising, respectively: Printed Books, Prints and Drawings, Portraits, MSS, Music and Maps, Ballads, Bindings, and a facsimile of Pepys's own catalog, vol. I: *Printed Books* (Ipswich, 1978); H. E. Rollins, ed., *The Pepys Ballads*, 8 vols. (Cambridge, Mass., 1929–1932), an exemplary ed. of the valuable collection of black letter ballads (1595–1639) in the Pepysian Library; a selection by the same editor, *A Pepysian Garland*, was published (London, 1922); E. Chappell, *Bibliographia Pepysiana* (London, 1933), privately printed.

II. EDITIONS OF THE DIARY. (The printed texts of the *Diary* up to 1970 are neither complete nor even correct transcriptions of the shorthand original.) Lord Braybrooke, ed., *Memoirs of Samuel Pepys, Comprising His Diary from 1659 to 1669, Deciphered by the Rev. J. Smith from the Original Short-Hand MS. in the Pepysian Library, and a Selection from His Private Correspondence*, 2 vols. (London, 1825; 5 vols., 1828), enlarged and retitled *The Diary of Samuel Pepys*, 5 vols. (London, 1848–1851) and subsequent 4-vol. eds. (1854; 1858); Rev. J. Smith, *The Life, Journals and Correspondence of Samuel Pepys* (London, 1841); Rev. M. Bright, ed., *Diary and Correspondence of Samuel Pepys, with Life and Notes by Richard Lord Braybrooke*, 6 vols. (London, 1875–1879), deciphered with additional notes from the shorthand MS in the Pepysian Library, Magdalene College, Cambridge, edited and enlarged by H. B. Wheatley, 10 vols. (1893–1899); G. G. Smith, ed., *Diary of Samuel Pepys* (London, 1905), the Globe ed.; J. Warrington, ed., *Diary of Samuel Pepys*, 3 vols. (London, 1953), in Everyman's Library; J. P. Kenyon, ed., *Diary of Samuel Pepys* (rev. ed., London, 1963); R. Latham and W. Matthews, eds., *Diary of Samuel Pepys*, 9 vols. (London, 1970–1976), a new transcription that presents the first complete and authoritative text, the definitive ed. of the *Diary*, companion and index vols. will complete the 11-vol. project; R. Latham, ed., *The Illustrated Pepys* (London, 1978), admirably selected extracts from the *Diary* by the coeditor of the complete text, supplemented with a discriminating and illuminating choice of illustrations.

III. SEPARATE WORKS. *The Portugal History, or A Relation of the Troubles That Happened in the Court of Portugal in the Years 1667 and 1668* (London, 1677); *Memoirs Relating to the State of the Royal Navy of England for Ten Years Determined December 1688* (London, 1690); J. R. Tanner, ed., *Samuel Pepys's Naval Minutes* (London, 1926); E. Chappell, ed., *The Tangier Papers of Samuel Pepys* (London, 1935); W. Rees-Mogg, ed., *His Majesty Preserved: An Account of King Charles II's Escape after the Battle of Worcester Dictated to Samuel Pepys by the King Himself* (London, 1954), first published by Sir D. Dalrymple in 1766 and often reprinted, an ed. published with other documents and narratives assembled by Pepys was made in 1967 by W. Matthews; R. Thompson, sel. and ed., *Samuel Pepys's "Penny Merriments": Being a Collection of Chapbooks, Full of Histories, Jests, Magic, Amorous Tales of Courtship, Marriage and Infidelity, Accounts [of] Rogues and Fools, Together with Comments on the Times* (London, 1976).

IV. CORRESPONDENCE. J. R. Tanner, ed., *Private Correspondence and Miscellaneous Papers of Samuel Pepys, 1679–1703*, 2 vols. (London, 1926); J. R. Tanner, ed., *Further Correspondence of Samuel Pepys, 1622–1679* (London, 1929); R. G. Howarth, *Letters and the Second Diary of Samuel Pepys* (London, 1932); E. Chappell, ed., *Shorthand Letters of Samuel Pepys* (Cambridge, 1933); H. T. Heath, ed., *The Letters of Samuel Pepys and His Family Circle* (Oxford, 1955), contains 162 new letters.

V. SOME CRITICAL AND BIOGRAPHICAL STUDIES. J. E. Bailey, *On the Cipher of Pepys's Diary* (London, 1875); W. C. Pepys, comp., *Genealogy of the Pepys Family, 1273–1887* (London, 1887; new ed., 1952); H. B. Wheatley, *Pepysiana: or, Additional Notes on the Particulars of Pepys's Life and on Some Passages in the Diary* (London, 1899); F. Bridge, *Samuel Pepys, Lover of Musique* (London, 1903); J. H. Boardman, *Notes on Pepys's Diary* (London, 1905); P. Lubbock, *Samuel Pepys* (London, 1909); J. R. Tanner, *Samuel Pepys and the Royal Navy* (Cambridge, 1920); J. R. Tanner, *Mr. Pepys: An Introduction to the Diary, Together with a Sketch of His Later Life* (London, 1925); *Occasional Papers Read by Members at Meetings of the Samuel Pepys Club*, vol. I (London, 1917), vol. II (London, 1925); W. H. Whitear, *More Pepysiana* (London, 1927); Lord Ponsonby, *Samuel Pepys* (London, 1928), in the English Men of Letters series; Sir A. Bryant, *Samuel Pepys: The Saviour of the Navy* (London, 1932); Sir A. Bryant, *Samuel Pepys: The Man in the Making* (London, 1933); Sir A. Bryant, *Samuel Pepys: The Years of Peril* (London, 1935), the standard biography of Pepys, the three vols. by Bryant form the most complete available picture of Pepys's life, achievement, and times; C. Marburg, *Mr. Pepys and Mr. Evelyn* (Philadelphia, 1935), contains six unpublished letters to Evelyn; P. Hunt, *Samuel Pepys in the Diary* (Pittsburgh, 1959); C. S. Emden, *Pepys Himself* (London, 1963); M. H. Nicolson, *Pepys's Diary and the New Science* (London, 1965); R. L. Ollard, *Pepys: A Biography* (London, 1974).

JOHN DRYDEN
(1631-1700)

Bonamy Dobrée

THE DEVOTED LIFE

WITHIN a very few days of John Dryden's death on 1 May 1700, his last written work, "The Secular Masque," was performed as part of Sir John Vanbrugh's version of *The Pilgrim*. In it he sketched a picture of the preceding hundred years—the reign of James I with his love of hunting, the Civil Wars, the voluptuous court of Charles II, symbolized in turn by Diana, Mars, and Venus. It ended:

> Momus.　All, all of a piece throughout:
> 　　　　　*Pointing to Diana.*
> 　　　　Thy chase had a beast in view;
> 　　　　　*To Mars.*
> 　　　　Thy wars brought nothing about;
> 　　　　　*To Venus.*
> 　　　　Thy lovers were all untrue.
> Janus.　'Tis well an old age is out.
> Chronos.　And time to begin a new.
> 　　　　　　　　　　　　　(86–91)

the chorus rechanting the lines as a grand finale. The vigorous conclusion might serve as an epitome of the man; his admirable craftsmanship, his ironic vision of the social enthusiasms of his century, but himself no prey to disillusion, holding, as he seemed to do, that a new age really did mean a new beginning, to which his own unfailing vigor might contribute. Copiousness, energy, vitality are the key words for Dryden; not profundity, not subtlety, not exquisite delicacy, nor, except rarely, by implication alone, deep conflict—but the energy of intellect flowing like sunlight over a wide landscape, the vitality of being inspiring a passion for his craft. These never abated. He was, as William Congreve said, "an improving writer to the last"; and as he quite justly said of himself in his last great preface of 1700: "I think myself as vigorous as ever in the faculties of my soul . . . . What judgement I had, increases rather than diminishes; and thoughts, such as they are, come crowding in so fast upon me, that my only difficulty is to choose or to reject; to run them into verse, or to give them the other harmony of prose."

It has been said that "reading him we are aware of a character as solid as Dr. Johnson; but look for him, and he is not there: the lines of the human figure dissolve as you turn, into those of the literature of his own age." Such embracing statements are never wholly true, but this one is not far off the mark. For since literature was the overriding interest of Dryden's life, becoming a fervor to "purify the language of the tribe," all his endeavors, apart from the domestic ones, revolve about his own writings or those of others. Yet, picking up a hint here, reading between the lines there, one can see what the temperament was that made this passion the thing by which he lived. Involved by the nature of things in the affairs of his time, he to some extent shared its moral and intellectual fashions; but within him there lay a deep-rooted skepticism as to the value, even the virtue, of human effort, a sense that the gratification of ordinary, everyday impulses, ambitions, or desires was hardly worthwhile. The very animals, even the birds, are better adjusted:

> Man only clogs with cares his happiness:
> And, while he should enjoy his part of bliss,
> With thoughts of what may be, destroys what is.

A juvenile fancy, if you will (it occurs in an early play), an adolescent groping toward the commonplace that *le mieux est l'ennemi du bien*; but later one finds a passage that seems to come, rather, from experience, as an achieved Stoicism:

> In wishing nothing, we enjoy still most;
> For even our wish is, in possession, lost:
> Restless we wander to a new desire,
> And burn ourselves by blowing up the fire:

We toss and turn about our fev'rish will,
When all our ease must come by lying still:
For all the happiness mankind can gain,
Is not in pleasure, but in rest from pain.

At the end of Satan's first speech in *The State of Innocence* one finds a terrible heightening, a black vision of man's worst fate:

In liquid burnings, or on dry to dwell,
Is all the sad variety of hell.

So much, then, for the ordinary human strivings after happiness. Not that Dryden dwelt in unvaried gloom, or lacked joyousness. Far from it. His songs alone, his odes, some of which are paeans in praise of life, by their very radiance attest this. But where was the ultimate satisfaction? Not here, surely.

Was the life of affairs any better? Born at Aldwinkle All Saints, Northamptonshire, in August 1631, Dryden passed his boyhood in the uneasy period of the Civil Wars; grown to manhood, he was employed in the service of the Commonwealth (as were Milton and Marvell), had a glimpse behind the scenes of the wranglings and dissensions of the chief participants, and witnessed the collapse of what to the Puritans was "the good old cause." What, after all, had been the result of the clash, the reward for all the bloodshed, and the expense of spirit? As he was to say in *"The Secular Masque"*:

The fools are only thinner,
With all our cost and care;
But neither side a winner,
For things are as they were.
(67-70)

Then, after the Restoration in 1660, the ups and downs of politics, the intrigues, the shoddy ambitions, the cupidities and treacheries, the brutality inseparable from government: the whole business disgusted him. In one of his few, perhaps his only, public outbursts of temper, Dryden declared: "No government has ever been, or ever can be, wherein time servers and blockheads will not be uppermost. The persons only are chang'd, but the same jugglings in state, the same hypocrisy in religion, the same self-interest and mismanagement, will remain for ever" (dedication of *Examen Poeticum*, 1693). No; the satisfaction was not to be found there. In this realm Dryden's skepticism reaches its extreme point; it hardens into cynicism. There are better things to do than to bother about politics, let alone

meddle in them. He came to be, he confessed in the dedication of the *Aeneis* (1697), "of Montaigne's principles, that an honest man ought to be contented with that form of government, and with those fundamental constitutions of it, which he receiv'd from his ancestors, and under which he himself was born." It was a deep need for quiet, which implies order, that made him conservative, a Tory in politics, and a classicist in literature.

It was his mingled skepticism and love of order that, more than anything, brought about his change of faith, from near Dissent to Catholicism, by way of the Church of England. Nevertheless, in the field of religion one comes to something deeply interesting in Dryden's makeup. It was a constant preoccupation with him, as one can tell from the religious arguments that occur again and again in his plays. His primary skepticism was expressed clearly enough in *The Indian Emperour* (1665), where Montezuma declares to the contending Indian and Christian priest:

In seeking happiness you both agree;
But in the search the paths so different be,
That all religions with each other fight,
While only one can lead us in the right.
But till that one hath some more certain mark,
Poor human kind must wander in the dark.
(V. ii. 53-58)

Dryden's first reaction against the grimmer forms of dissent seems to have been—to judge from that curious quasi-mystical play *Tyrannick Love*— almost an exalted vision of God as Light, not very different, superficially at least, from Milton's. Here Damilcar, who occupies a state midway between man and the angels, appeals to a being higher than himself:

Mercy, bright spirit; I already feel
The piercing edge of thy immortal steel:
Thou, Prince of day, from elements art free:
And I all body when compar'd to thee.
Thou tread'st the Abyss of light!
And where it streams with open eyes can'st go:
We wander in the fields of air below;
Chang'lings and fools of Heav'n: and thence shut out,
Wildly we roam in discontent about:
Gross-heavy-fed, next Man in ignorance and sin,
And spotted all without, and dusky all within,
Without thy sword I perish by thy sight
I reel, and stagger, and am drunk with light.
(IV. i. 175-187)

If he lacked, as one is told, the transcendental qualities that distinguish the greatest poets, Dryden was certainly not unaware of them; yet one feels that when he touches upon them, they are descriptions from outside, rather than accounts of inner experience.

And no doubt the impulse of his religious change was partly political; for, wearied with the incessant and violent controversies, the wildness of "enthusiasm" that embraced the most fantastic religious deviations and disturbed social tranquillity, he hankered after a creed with authority enough to appease the sectarian feuds that bedeviled politics:

> For points obscure are of small use to learn:
> But common quiet is mankind's concern.
> (449-450)

he concluded in *Religio Laici* (1682). Dryden's path to Rome, in any event no easy one, was all the more difficult since it led away from his political loyalties. Moreover, in an age where politics and religion were so closely interwoven, to embrace a faith proscribed by government can have meant no half-conviction, in view of all that was involved by way of civil disabilities and the loss of any hope of preferment. For by nature Dryden was a proud man, conscious of unusual powers, impatient of having thoughts or ideas dictated to him, with a good deal of the hubris proper to youth. As he says in that strange ratiocinative poem, *The Hind and the Panther* (1687):

> My thoughtless youth was wing'd with vain desires,
> My manhood, long misled by wand'ring fires,
> Follow'd false lights; and when their glimpse was gone,
> My pride struck out new sparkles of her own.
> Such was I, such by nature still I am,
> Be thine the glory, and be mine the shame!
> (I. 72-77)

That, of course, is intellectual humility before the mysteries of religion, a result, perhaps, of profound skepticism of the validity of the reason beyond definite limits. But later one finds something far more personal—connected, it is true, with religious submission, but revelatory of the struggle Dryden felt in giving up worldly position, not for that in itself alone, but for the cramping of his poetic mission:

> If joys hereafter must be purchas'd here
> With loss of all that mortals hold so dear,
> Then welcome infamy and public shame,
> And, last, a long farewell to worldly fame.
> 'Tis said with ease, but, O, how hardly tried
> By haughty souls to human honour tied!
> O sharp convulsive pangs of agonising pride!
> (III. 281-287)

Clearly he could not have stayed in the Anglican position so well argued in *Religio Laici*; persuaded from the first of the inefficacy of reason in this realm, he craved for a position based on something more secure than private judgment, one where he could say in all relief:

> Rest then, my soul, from endless anguish freed.
> (I. 146)

Given, then, these attitudes to life—not, of course, established from the first, but arrived at—what was Dryden to do? Born into an age of new and daring intellectual adventure, the age of Bacon, Descartes, and Newton, and of religious questioning with Port Royal and Pascal, the Cambridge Platonists, and other more extravagant adventurers in thought, he was very much alive to what was going on. Unequal to philosophy, having an aversion to the world of affairs, he decided, though he matured late, to become a writer; and, aware of his power and his great ability, he aimed at achieving fame. "For what other reason," he was to ask rhetorically in the dedication of *Examen Poeticum* (1693),

. . . have I spent my life in so unprofitable a study? why am I grown old, in seeking so barren a reward as fame? The same parts and application which have made me a poet might have raised me to any honours of the gown, which are often given to men of as little learning and less honesty than myself.

In application, in unceasing labor, he found his satisfaction. And more than satisfaction: the shining reward accorded to those who lead the life of devotion.

FINDING THE WAY

To what precise end his talents were to be shaped did not at once seem plain. It was no easy time for men of letters, though Dryden had, to be sure, certain initial advantages. Both his parents came of estated gentlefolk with responsibilities to the community and some power in it—such people, in fact, by whom and between whom the Civil War was fought. From the first he must have come in touch with the political violence of his day, his family being ardently engaged in the struggle on the Puritan side; but he was too young to do more than see the conflict as a schoolboy in London might be expected to see it. As a pupil at Westminster School he already showed poetic leanings, not only in a prize translation from Persius but also in a lament on his schoolfellow Lord Hastings, a piece in couplets with some good lines, but made horrific with dire metaphysical conceits on the more loathsome manifestations of the smallpox from which Lord Hastings had died. In 1650 he was elected a Westminster scholar at Trinity College, Cambridge, where he wrote two innocuous poems. He took his degree in 1654, the year his father died; and, finding himself with a small estate, and his head "too roving and active" for college life, he took himself to London, where his father's cousin, Sir Gilbert Pickering, whom Cromwell had appointed his lord chamberlain, obtained him a post in the civil service. Nothing came from his pen until the death in 1658 of the Protector, to whose "glorious memory" he "consecrated" his "Heroic Stanzas," a series of quatrains in which Cromwell's character is praised but his politics silently shelved. At this time he seems to have begun his literary career by doing hackwork for the publisher Henry Herringman, and by mixing with literary figures, such as Sir Robert Howard, whose sister, Lady Elizabeth, he married in 1663. At the Restoration in 1660 he wrote *Astraea Redux*, to welcome Charles II, in which are the significant lines:

> At home the hateful names of Parties cease
> And factious Souls are weary'd into peace.
> (312–313)

Apart from other occasional verses in couplets, Dryden printed no poem until 1667, when, ushered in by one of his discursive prefaces, he published *Annus Mirabilis*, a patchily brilliant poem of 304 quatrains, celebrating the triumphant issue of London from the calamities of unsuccessful war, the plague, and the Great Fire.

But by 1663, Dryden had embarked on the period of playwriting that was to absorb most of his literary energies for nearly twenty years; and from the beginning one is increasingly aware of where Dryden's passionate interest in literature lay: to improve, clarify, and enrich the language; also to "reform its numbers," that is, to bring order, grace, and expressiveness into verse writing. No mere study philologist, no armchair prosodist, he was always the eager craftsman, molding as he went the instrument he wished to use. Finding as he progressed that he had no particular vision of life to impart, except for his always constructive view of order, Dryden was content to do what came to his hand to effect. He did not appear to mind what he wrote about, so long as in writing he could continue his great chosen mission. After all, what is subject matter "before it is modelled by the art of him who writes it"? Almost the only poem that "was neither impos'd upon [him], nor so much as the subject given [him] by any man" was *The Hind and the Panther*. He had naturally an eye to what enabled him to live as one of the many struggling authors whose livelihood depended largely on the favor of the court, the denizens of which, the aristocrats, the politicians, were themselves often no mean literary figures and capable of informed criticism.

Being made poet laureate and historiographer royal in 1670 gave Dryden status and a small, irregularly paid income; thus when he tired of the theater in the late 1670's it was natural for him to turn to polemical writing. In 1681 he produced the greatest political poem in the language, *Absalom and Achitophel*, followed by the two lengthy poems of religious argument; and always what he wrote was accompanied by an enriching critical preface, or epistle dedicatory. But after the Glorious Revolution of 1688, losing his official posts, he returned intermittently to the theater to buttress up his failing finances, but more and more fell back upon translations of large extracts from Lucretius, Juvenal, Ovid, Horace, and the whole of Virgil. His last volume, the *Fables* (1699), consists of stories freely rendered from Ovid, Boccaccio, and Chaucer, always—at least this was part of his intention—with the purpose of seeing what he could make the language do and what he himself could accomplish in perfecting the instrument. As he told his cousin, Mrs. Stewart, in 1699, he would wish people to "consider [him] as a man who has done [his] best to improve the language, especially the poetry."

One does not, of course, read the works of a creative writer merely for the sake of what he did for the language, but rather for what he did with it. Nevertheless, with Dryden the two interests are inseparable, since his precepts seem to arise so spontaneously from what his practice as an artist impelled him to do. All the time he was trying to make the language, which was at that time in a state of confusion, into a valid, flexible instrument. Dissatisfied with the muddle, glorious though it sometimes is, of, say, Abraham Cowley and Richard Crashaw in verse, and the loaded style of Sir Thomas Browne in prose, he was anxious for directness. But not to excess. Dryden was a member of the Royal Society committee, the results of whose cogitations, taken to their logical conclusion, led to the Projectors in book 3 of *Gulliver's Travels*, who carried about sackfuls of objects to which they pointed instead of using their tongues. Dryden saw that what the Royal Society was aiming at simply would not do. Words are not merely signs for objects; among other things they are, as Walter Bagehot said, good to eat.

As early as his first critical essay, the epistle dedicatory of *The Rival Ladies* (1664), Dryden threw in casually: "I wish we might at length leave to borrow words from other nations, which is now a wantonness in us, not a necessity," a point of view markedly at variance with his later judgment; but then Dryden was always ready to allow experience, the findings of the artificer, to qualify and alter his conclusions. He is the least dogmatic of theorizers because he is always close to the creative impulse, aware that "technique" is not an absolute, but on each occasion the solution of a particular artistic problem. Thus he moved to another position in regard to words. In 1679, in the preface to his *Troilus and Cressida*, he says that the English language was "full of monosyllables, and those clogg'd with consonants," and he wished to make it one worthy of English minds, which foreigners would not disdain to learn. In the dedication of the *Aeneis* (1697), he is ready to borrow words, not indiscriminately, for fashion's sake, as Melantha did in his comedy *Marriage A-la-Mode*, picking from a list that began *en sottises* and ended *en ridicule*, but judiciously, with attention to weight and fine shades of meaning.

'Tis true that, when I find an English word significant and sounding, I neither borrow from the Latin nor any other language; but when I want at home, I must seek abroad.

If sounding words are not of our growth and manufacture, who shall hinder me to import them from a foreign country? I carry not out the treasure of the nation, which is never to return; but what I bring from Italy I spend in England . . . I trade both with the living and the dead, for the enrichment of our native language.

His final pronouncement comes in the preface to the *Fables:*

When an ancient word for its sound and significancy deserves to be reviv'd, I have that reasonable veneration for antiquity to restore it. All beyond this is superstition. Words are not like landmarks, so sacred as never to be remov'd.

Dr. Johnson perhaps used a somewhat clumsy metaphor when he said that Dryden "found the language brick and left it marble," but one can see the force of the remark. In the middle of the seventeenth century, the language was something like a magnificent heap of rubble; he left it shapely and habitable; or, if one prefers an organic metaphor, he found it a tangled forest shrubbery and left it a grove of flowering trees. We have his beautifully modulated flow, the variation of phrase from the long, supple sentence to the epigrammatic thrust, and the vigor, the incisive stress where he wants it, the clarification of meaning. "He is always shrewd and penetrating," Walter Landor commented, "explicit and perspicuous, concise where conciseness is desirable, and copious where copiousness can yield delight." And though Landor was speaking of Dryden's poetry, the judgment is as true of his prose, which, when he is in a gay, confident mood, is as full of lively imagery as his verse.

THE PLAYS

THE heroic drama of the Restoration period was a glorious extravaganza written for a special audience; to enjoy it today—and this is true to a lesser extent of the comedies—is perhaps to indulge an acquired vice. Largely outside the tradition of the English theater, it contains both the loose Shakespearean method and the French neoclassical form, to which the courtiers exiled during the Commonwealth had become accustomed. Emotions and states of mind (that are, to the final degree, romantic) are tailored into, or at least partly wear, severe classical garb. It is, in short, baroque—dynamic, sometimes fantastic ornament being added to a formalized structure. As Dryden himself remarked, "'tis unjust that they who have not the least notion of heroic writing, should therefore condemn the pleasure which others receive from it, because they cannot comprehend it." He was careful to add that he would not "dispute the preference of Tragedy; let every man enjoy his taste." Certainly, to read these plays or to go to see them, in the expectation of being plunged into the abundant life of the Elizabethan theater or of meeting the realism of a later period, is to court disappointment. One may even find them grotesque, susceptible to rollicking parody, as the duke of Buckingham, Thomas Sprat, and others found when they gleefully concocted *The Rehearsal*.

But accept the *données* of each play, be prepared to enter a world of absolute emotions—the heroism, the ideas of honor and of love, the Romanism, and so forth—these dramas can give a piquantly flavored pleasure, if only, and markedly with Dryden, from the sheer virtuosity of the performance, the flamboyance—the quality that so largely faded from English literature as it grew older. A play was a heroic poem, an epic in little; and its business, Hobbes had asserted, was "to raise admiration, principally for three virtues, valour, beauty, and love." Artificial? Of course. Why not? Heroic drama is consciously artificed; and with Dryden one often feels that he is standing aside, with a twinkle in his eye, watching himself perform. Thus, however bombastic the sentiments may be, Dryden's handling is firmly secure; he can even produce effects of prettiness, which, as he places them, are not at all destructive but, on the contrary, charmingly enhancing of the result. Moreover, inserted in the plays are the enormously varied songs, prosodically delightful, ranging from those breathing nostalgia, or the futility of human endeavor, to the frankly, and so harmlessly, erotic.

In *The Indian Emperour* (1667), one finds:

> Ah fading joy, how quickly art thou past!
> Yet we thy ruin haste.
> As if the cares of human life were few,
> We seek out new:
> And follow fate, which would too fast pursue . . .
>
> Hark, hark, the waters fall, fall, fall,
> And with a murmuring sound

> Dash, dash upon the ground
> To gentle slumbers call.
>
> (IV. iii. 1–5, 13–16)

In *Tyrannick Love* (1670), the song beginning:

> Ah how sweet it is to love!
> Ah how gay is young desire!
> (III. 1–2)

And in *King Arthur* (1691), the famous patriotic lyric disguised as a Song of Venus:

> Fairest isle, all isles excelling,
>   Seat of pleasures and of loves;
> Venus here will choose her dwelling,
>   And forsake her Cyprian groves.
>
> Cupid from his fav'rite nation
>   Care and envy will remove;
> Jealousy, that poisons passion,
>   And despair, that dies for love . . . .
>   (X. 61–68)

which Henry Purcell set to such dulcet, singable melody. With the plays go the equally varied prologues and epilogues, in which Dryden enters into an evidently friendly relation with his audiences, sometimes chaffing them, sometimes scolding, even a little scornfully upbraiding, now and again indulging in acute, pertinent criticism. There is a characteristic captivating vigor about them all, and, with the laughter they provoke, a dominant persuasiveness.

Yet the plays will be widely read only by devotees of the history of drama; not even all Dryden enthusiasts will tackle them wholesale, for they are not all easy to read, thanks to the sudden reversals of fortune in the tragedies and the intricacy of the plots in the comedies, which are apt to be bewildering in the study. They would clarify on the stage, certainly, for the playwrights of those days had a lively dramatic sense. Yet even in reading such a play as *The Conquest of Granada* (in two parts, 1672), the high point of the heroic bubbles with special interests. The same will be found with *The State of Innocence* (1674), the quite individual rendering in rhyme of *Paradise Lost*; the Shakespeare adaptations; or, to go to the other extreme, the purposefully blunt *The Kind Keeper* (1678). But there are two tragedies at least, and one comedy, of abundant general appeal, that serve to round off the canon. For all its slightly exotic flavor, its heroic sentiments, its too ingenious plot, *Aureng-Zebe* (1675), the last of the rhymed plays, is moving and actual, if only for the emotive quality of the speeches, of which the most famous, if not the deepest-reaching, is the haunting

> When I consider life, 'tis all a cheat;
> Yet, fool'd with hope, men favour the deceit;
> Trust on, and think to-morrow will repay:
> To-morrow's falser than the former day;
> Lies worse; and while it says, we shall be blest
> With some new joys, cuts off what we possess.
> Strange cozenage! none would live past years again,
> Yet all hope pleasure in what yet remain;
> And from the dregs of life, think to receive
> What the first sprightly running could not give.
> I'm tir'd with waiting for this Chymick gold,
> Which fools us young, and beggars us when old.
>
> (IV. i. 33–44)

There is the mastery of rhyme, never dictating the sense, never interfering with the run of the phrase.

But by now Dryden had satisfied his instinct to conquer the couplet for stage purposes. His prologue declares:

> Our author by experience, finds it true,
> 'Tis much more hard to please himself than you;
> And out of no feign'd modesty, this day,
> Damns his laborious trifle of a play;
> Not that it's worse than what before he writ,
> But he has now another taste of wit;
> And, to confess a truth, (tho' out of time,)
> Grows weary of his long-lov'd mistress, Rhyme.
>
> (Prologue, 1–8)

In his next great venture, *All for Love* (1678), in which he handled the story of Antony and Cleopatra in his own original way—one feels he is wholly involved; confessedly it was the one play he wrote to please himself—in his style he "professed to imitate the divine Shakespeare," that is, he "disencumbered himself from rhyme." The result is the best dramatic blank verse since Shakespeare, at once concise and rich, flexible, capable of grandeur and also of lightness. It can achieve

> While within your arms I lay
> The world fell mouldering from my hands each hour.
>
> (II. i. 294–295)

equally with

> O horror, horror!
> Egypt has been; our latest hour is come:
> The queen of nations from her ancient seat,
> Is sunk for ever in the dark abyss:
> Time has unroll'd her glories to the last,
> And now clos'd up the volume.
>
> (V. i. 70–75)

and the monosyllabic simplicity of

> Farewell! Ever my leader, ev'n in death!
> My queen and thou have got the start of me,
> And I'm the lag of honour.
>
> (V. i. 338–340)

In this proud and lovely masterpiece, this somber tragedy, as it has been called, one is held and swayed by the interplay of the emotions of all the characters, though more especially by the revulsions of feeling in Antony. Plunged into the depths of despair until roused by the goading urgency of Ventidius (in a scene Dryden thought the best he had written), he is later torn between his pride, his passion for Cleopatra, and his sense of duty toward Octavia; and the conduct of the play builds it up into an integrated whole, fused together by Antony's inner conflicts, the unities being "more exactly preserved, than, perhaps, the English theatre requires." The accents are always human, free of rant, with a minimum of high-flying imagery. Take, for example, the beautifully molded speech of Cleopatra struggling to maintain her hold of Antony:

> How shall I plead my cause, when you, my judge,
> Already have condemn'd me? Shall I bring
> The love you bore me for my advocate?
> That now is turn'd against me, that destroys me;
> For love, once past, is at the best forgotten;
> But oftener sours to hate: 'twill please my lord
> To ruin me, and therefore I'll be guilty.
> But, could I once have thought it would have pleas'd you,
> That you would pry, with narrow searching eyes
> Into my faults, severe to my destruction:
> And watching all advantages with care
> That serve to make me wretched? Speak, my lord,
> For I end here. Though I deserve this usage,
> Was it like you to give it?
>
> (II. i. 332–345)

Nor is the play lacking those *sententiae*, the great commonplaces, without which no seventeenth-century play was complete, though as the century progressed they became less and less Senecan. No one would claim that Dryden's phrases, however memorable, compare with the tremendous platitudes with which Shakespeare well-nigh sears one; nevertheless, they are a measure. This play has the once well-known "Men are but children of a larger growth . . ." and

> O that I less could fear to lose this being,
> Which, like a snow-ball, in my coward hand,
> The more 'tis grasp'd, the faster melts away.
> Poor reason! what a wretched aid art thou!
> For still, in spite of thee,
> These two long lovers, soul and body, dread
> Their final separation.
>
> (V. i. 132–138)

The play, to be sure, has echoes—but they are only echoes—from Shakespeare and Daniel, especially where Plutarch is invoked; but it exists in its own full-blooded right as an individual contribution to the corpus of English tragedy, and is still, from time to time, acted.

So is the most lively of Dryden's comedies, the yet sparkling *Marriage-A-la-Mode* (1673), embodying the quintessence of Restoration comedy, the antagonism between the sexes so delicately handled by Congreve. Many of the court and its hangers-on at that period were engaged in the desperate attempt to rationalize love, trying to conduct their lives on the assumption that sexual attraction was easily separable from affection, that jealousy was ridiculous, and that a husband was, almost by definition, a fool whose obvious destiny was to be cuckolded. A large part of the game of Restoration comedy was to show how disastrous, how contrary to common sense, the assumptions were; for this comedy was, in the main, classical "critical" comedy intent upon "curing excess." Far from being "artificial," as it is commonly dubbed, it was very nakedly down to earth, and had a direct bearing upon how life was lived. Dryden states the theme at once with the song:

> Why should a foolish Marriage Vow,
>   Which long ago was made,
> Oblige us to each other now,
>   When Passion is decay'd?
> We lov'd, and we lov'd, as long as we cou'd,
>   Till our love was lov'd out in us both:
> But our Marriage is dead, when the Pleasure is fled:
>   'Twas Pleasure first made it an Oath.

> If I have Pleasures for a Friend,
>   And farther Love in store,
> What wrong has he whose Joys did end,
>   And who could give no more?
> 'Tis a Madness that he
>   Shou'd be jealous of me,
> Or that I shou'd bar him of another:
>   For all we can gain,
> Is to give ourselves Pain,
>   When neither can hinder the other.
>
> (I. 1–18)

The play is conducted with a romping gaiety throughout, until, schooled by bitter, stark experience, the would-be erring couples agree to give over their frolics, and make a "firm league not to invade each other's property." The epilogue, full of delicious mockery, drives the point home. And parallel with the brisk comedy there runs a modulated, almost serene, heroic pastoral play that, a little sadly, treats the theme of constancy on another level. This different tinge of feeling gives an added depth to the pure critical comedy, the two plays not jarring with each other but making an emotionally coherent whole.

Dryden did not altogether abandon playwriting until 1694; but there was a large gap, which he did not regret. He never felt himself very fitted for the theater, least of all for comedy—because, he said, of the "sullenness" of his temper; indeed, most of his comedies tend to become uproarious farces of incident. As for his tragedies, at one moment he carelessly cast off the remark "They were bad enough to please." Yet in some ways his later work, in which he very considerably modified the heroic strain, is preferable to his earlier. In the comedies there is his version of *Amphytrion* (1690), in opera *King Arthur* (1691), and in tragedy, as opposed to heroic drama, the moving and often tense *Don Sebastian* (1690) and *Cleomenes* (1692). And, whatever he did, the vigor is always there, the amplitude of mind, and the confident versification.

THE POETRY

DRYDEN's poetry can roughly be classified in three groups: the occasional, comprising the greater odes, the epistles, elegies, and complimentary addresses; the politico-religious; and the translations, though the second group is also in the proper sense occasional. Though he wrote few direct satires (he translated several), a strong vein of satirical comment runs through the body of his verse, and indeed flickers intermittently in his plays. But apart from what he may have been writing about, his verse is always characteristic, molded partly by what he thought a poet ought to be and what he should accomplish. Regarding the former, he stated—to quote one of his passages on this theme:

Mere poets and mere musicians are as sottish as mere drunkards are, who live in a continual mist, without seeing or judging anything clearly.

A man should be learned in several sciences, and should have a reasonable, philosophic, and in some measure a mathematical head, to be a complete and excellent poet: and besides this, should have experience in all sorts of humours and manners of men, should be thoroughly skilled in conversation, and should have a great knowledge of mankind in general.

(*Notes and Observations on "The Empress of Morocco"*)

Elsewhere he says that he thinks little of a poet who cannot argue well. His poetry, then, deals with what is common experience—not, of course, omitting spiritual experience. There is none of the yearning of the Romantics, the reachings out for the impalpable, in the attempt to grasp the inapprehensible; his vivid, actual imagination plays around the actions and passions of men and women as they live out their lives, in soul as well as in body. He does not confront one with profound, searching sentiment, making one face the innermost nature of being; but he has a firm grasp over a wide field, handling at no despicable level the eternal religious issues and the scientific development of his age.

Dryden's diction is in tune with his ideas; he disciplines himself to use the precise word rather than the word with a vague aura of association, endeavoring always to express as clearly and firmly as possible what he means to say—in a way, moreover, that is pleasantly acceptable. "Would not Donne's *Satires*, which abound with so much wit, appear more charming, if he had taken care of his words, and of his numbers?" The musician in the poet was not to be ignored, as he might have seemed to suggest in the passage quoted above. For

. . . by the harmony of words we elevate the mind to a sense of devotion as our solemn music, which is inarticulate poesy, does in churches.

Here, of course, is the eternal question of pleasure and profit, of the aesthetic as against the moral. "Delight," he said in the "Defence of an Essay of 'Dramatick Poesie'" (1668), "is the chief, if not the only, end of poesy: instruction can be admitted but in the second place, for poesy only instructs as it delights"; a few pages later, though, he says that poetry must "resemble natural truth, but it must be ethical." He sums up his attitude best in his *Discourse on Satire* (1693):

They who will not grant me, that pleasure is one of the ends of poetry, but that it is only a means of compassing the only end, which is instruction, must yet allow, that, without the means of pleasure, the instruction is but bare and dry philosophy: a crude preparation of morals, which we may have from Aristotle or Epictetus, with more profit than from any poet.

But words, Dryden held, were only the coloring of the poem-picture; what was important was the idea, and the structure, though the coloring was what first struck the eye. So whatever words he uses, his is still the language that might be spoken by men to men. It is never, pejoratively speaking, "poetic." That is one of his great triumphs. Even in his most grandiose odes or addresses he keeps his colloquial phrasing; there is no tortuousness, none of the "exhausting nagging after effect" (as George Barker has called it) of the metaphysicals.

It was because he saw his main task as the redeeming of English verse from obfuscation that Dryden insisted so much upon rhyme, since this "bounds and circumscribes the fancy. For imagination in a poet is a faculty so wild and lawless, that, like an high-ranking spaniel, it must have clogs tied to it, lest it outrun the judgement." Fancy and judgment—those were the faculties a poet must ever try to balance, so as to bring out the richest and clearest thoughts, fancy being what is now called imagination, "moving the sleeping images of things towards the light." That was a view put forward in 1664 (dedication of the *Rival Ladies*) and maintained in 1697 (dedication of the *Aeneis*):

And whereas poems which are produced by the vigour of the imagination only have a gloss upon them at the first which time wears off, the works of judgment are like the diamond; the more they are polished, the more lustre they receive.

As for "numbers" (mellifluous prosody), Dryden considered John Denham and Edmund Waller to be the fathers of English poetry, with Spenser as a forebear, admiring their "smoothness" as opposed to the rugosities of Donne. Smoothness of course is not enough; it can be overdone, as critics a generation later were to find. Pope himself said in his "Imitations of Horace":

> Waller was smooth; but Dryden taught to join
> The varying verse, the full-resounding line,
> The long majestic march, and energy divine.
> (Epistles, II. i. 266–268)

Or, as Coleridge put it, "The wheels take fire from the mere rapidity of their motion." What one gets from Dryden, then, is an invigoration of being that tends to release the imagination.

His attack is always superb, plunging one straight into the sweeping movement of his theme, as, for instance, in the first of his three wide-embracing occasional pieces, *Absalom and Achitophel*. This, by him called simply "A Poem," and best described by Dr. Ian Jack as a "witty heroic poem," was written for the purpose of setting public feeling against Lord Shaftesbury, leader of the Whig faction scheming to exclude the Catholic duke of York from the succession, and perhaps put the king's natural son, the duke of Monmouth, on the throne. Dryden opens with a deliciously bland excuse for Charles II's virile manifestations:

> In pious times, ere priestcraft did begin,
> Before polygamy was made a sin;
> When man on many multiplied his kind,
> Ere one to one was cursedly confin'd: . . .
> Then Israel's monarch after Heaven's own heart,
> His vigorous warmth did, variously, impart
> To wives and slaves; and, wide as his command,
> Scatter'd his Maker's image thro' the land.
> (Part I, 1–10)

Then one is led into the story—or, rather, situation. Though the poem is not primarily a satire, the satirical element soon appears—in the biting description of the English, the Jews of the story:

> God's pamper'd people, whom, debauch'd with ease,
> No king could govern, nor no God could please;
> (Gods they had tried of every shape and size,
> That god-smiths could produce, or priests devise:
> (Part I, 47–50)

Only a modicum of historical knowledge is needed to enjoy the poem; the drama unrolls to culminate in the great temptation scene, where Achitophel (Shaftesbury) lures Absalom (Monmouth) to his doom, pricking him into saying:

> Why am I scanted by a niggard birth?
> My soul disclaims the kindred of her earth;
> And, made for empire, whispers me within,
> "Desire of greatness is a godlike sin."
> (Part I, 369–372)

Achitophel's reaction to his triumph is pressed home with deliberate Miltonism:

> Him staggering so when Hell's dire agent found,
> While fainting Virtue scarce maintain'd her ground,
> He pours fresh forces in, and thus replies . . .
> (Part I, 373–375)

The grip is never relaxed through the more than 1,000 lines.

Yet Dryden, always in control, orders the rise and fall, eases the tension as he will, partly by pace but largely by the "characters," who are, in the main, satirically drawn. The most famous is that of Achitophel, though he himself thought that of Zimri (Buckingham) "worth the whole poem," since it was "not bloody, but ridiculous enough"—in fact, more subtle by being raillery rather than bludgeoning. Yet that of Shaftesbury must always be the favorite, as it contains more poetic power:

> For close designs and crooked counsels fit,
> Sagacious, bold, and turbulent of wit,
> Restless, unfix'd in principles and place,
> In pow'r unpleas'd, impatient of disgrace;
> A fiery soul, which, working out its way,
> Fretted the pigmy body to decay:
> And o'er-inform'd the tenement of clay . . . .
> (Part I, 152–158)

The pressure continues for some fifty lines without a hint of monotony, the caesuras being brilliantly varied in depth and position as stroke follows devastating stroke. Other personages crowd upon the scene and are treated bitterly, scornfully, or disdainfully as occasion serves, sometimes with one or two deft shafts of ridicule —for instance, Shimei (Slingsby Bethell), who

> Did wisely from expensive sins refrain,
> And never broke the Sabbath, but for gain: . . .
> (Part I, 587–588)

The religious sects receive due buffeting, as do the petty political intriguers and the deluded populace. Not for a moment does the poem fail in pungency, and through it pierces Dryden's innate conservatism, summed up in one phrase, "For innovation is the blow of fate."

Very different is *The Medal*, again directed against Shaftesbury, in which Dryden achieved sheer Juvenalian satire; *MacFlecknoe*, on the other hand, is a gloriously comic mock heroic, the first in the language, in which Dryden lampooned Thomas Shadwell, who is treated with equal contempt in the second part of *Absalom and Achitophel*. The opening is delusively magniloquent:

> All human things are subject to decay,
> And when fate summons, monarchs must obey.

The account of the enthronement of Shadwell as successor to the throne of Nonsense proceeds with a gorgeous pomposity. The piece is variegated by parodied echoes of other poets while the low is exalted and fantastic absurdities are rocketed to dazzling heights. The poem is more poetically sensuous than Alessandro Tassoni's *La secchia rapita*, more wittily barbed than Nicolas Boileau's *Le lutrin*.

The first great debating poem, *Religio Laici*, is not difficult to follow, being mostly written in the plainest language, since "a man is to be cheated into passion, but to be reason'd into truth." It is an argument for adherence to the national religion; political stability demands a commonly held faith. And what, Dryden asks, is wrong with Anglicanism? No sublimity is demanded, since finite cannot reach infinity (a favorite phrase of his); the stress is again and again on *needful* faith. As always he is contemptuous of those who "barter solid quiet to obtain/The windy satisfactions of the brain." After all,

> Th' unletter'd Christian, who believes in gross,
> Plods on to Heav'n, and ne'er is at a loss.
>
> (322-323)

Too many men, though, itch to expound:

> . . . crowds unlearn'd, with rude devotion warm,
> About the sacred viands buzz and swarm;
> The fly-blown text creates a crawling brood,
> And turn to maggots what was meant for food.
>
> (417-420)

Satire, whetted by Dryden's stubborn dislike of priests, is never long absent, and makes the argument spin along briskly. And though "unpolish'd, rugged verse [he] chose,/As fittest for discourse and nearest prose," there are passages that sweep along with compelling poetic pulse. Take the opening:

> Dim as the borrow'd beams of moon and stars
> To lonely, weary, wand'ring travellers
> Is Reason to the soul: and, as on high
> Those rolling fires discover but the sky,
> Not light us here, so Reason's glimmering ray
> Was lent, not to assure our doubtful way,
> But guide us upward to a better day.
> And as those nightly tapers disappear
> When day's bright lord ascends our hemisphere,
> So pale grows Reason at Religion's sight,
> So dies, and so dissolves in supernatural light.
>
> (1-11)

Is man, after all, one asks, to be reasoned into truth?

Wholly to grasp *The Hind and the Panther*, essentially a plea for toleration, demands rather more background knowledge, both of the political situation, "when the nation was in a high ferment," and of the claims of the various religions and sects. Early in the poem, in one passage among many in these two poems that establish Dryden as a noteworthy religious poet, is the statement of Dryden's submission to the Roman communion:

> What weight of ancient witness can prevail,
> If private reason hold the public scale?
> But, gracious God, how well dost thou provide
> For erring judgments an unerring guide!
> Thy throne is darkness in th'abyss of light,
> A blaze of glory that forbids the sight.
>
> (Part I, 62-67)

And what had "the monster breed" of Protestants accomplished?

> Such wars, such waste, such fiery tracks of dearth
> Their zeal has left . . .
>
> (Part I, 227-228)

Bitter experience had shown that

> Of all the tyrannies on human kind
> The worst is that which persecutes the mind.
>
> (Part I, 239-240)

299

Every here and there occur memorable phrases, molded by the driving force of conviction, made aphoristic by great poetic power:

> Revenge, the bloody minister of ill,
> With all the lean tormentors of the will.
> (Part III, 74–75)

A great deal of nonsense has been uttered about the fable form being unsuitable; but if rats can talk about the virtue of dining peaceably, why should not nobler animals discuss religion? At all events, one soon accepts the framework of the fabular, which at least gives Dryden a chance of characterizing the religions. The milk-white Hind, immortal and unchanged, is, of course, Roman Catholicism; the Panther, fairest creature of the spotted kind, is the Anglican church; there are also the bloody Bear, the Independent beast; the buffoon Ape, who stands for the freethinkers; the Calvinistic Wolf, who pricks up his predestinating ears; the Anabaptist Boar, who "with fat pollutions fills the sacred place"; and so on. The conversation moves vigorously and has its dramatic moments, as when the Panther threatens the Hind with the gallows. The third part ensconces the two vivid fables within the fable, those of the swallows and of the doves, each a beautiful little poem in itself, apart from the political implications. The astonishing thing is that though now and then one encounters some tedious passages of outmoded argumentation, the total impact is poetic rather than philosophical.

The most triumphant of Dryden's other poems were written late in life: the elegy on John Oldham in 1684; that richly baroque picture frame, the Anne Killigrew ode, in 1686; the Saint Cecilia ode in 1687; *Alexander's Feast* in 1697. Though the poems differ enormously, the success of all is due partly to his making words not generally used in great numbers in ordinary speech sound perfectly natural even when densely packed. Take some of the lines I have quoted. In prose the words would become turgid, but in Dryden's verse they have wings:

> Sagacious, bold, and turbulent of wit.

or

> O sharp convulsive pangs of agonising pride.

Sometimes, the commonplace expression jostles the more ceremonious, as in his rendering of *Veni, Creator Spiritus*:

> Our frailties help, our vice control,
> Submit the senses to the soul;
> And when rebellious they are grown,
> Then lay thy hand, and hold 'em down.
> (22–25)

His words are just as forceful as Donne's, of whom he said that he gave us deep thoughts in common language.

The ideas were not necessarily startling. The lines on Oldham are composed of clichés, or references one might think outworn, and that in anybody else's hands would be jaded; but the result is an acknowledged gem, expressive of just so much emotion, of personal feeling, as the relationship between the two poets required. An altogether different matter is the second Saint Cecilia ode, *Alexander's Feast*. Outrageous, one might think, in conception, flaunting in its prosody, verging on the burlesque in its imagery—it has been called "immortal ragtime"—Dryden's contemporaries acclaimed it as his best poem. Perhaps its most unexpected feat is to bring the rushing, tumultuous movement to the quiet close of

> Let old Timotheus yield the prize,
>   Or both divide the crown:
> He rais'd a mortal to the skies;
>   She drew an angel down.
> (177–180)

Perhaps it was the unexpectedness of the poem, its imaginative originality, that captivated his contemporaries, familiar as they were with the ode of ten years earlier, which was far more normally conceived, graceful, sensuous, and conventionally religious in tone.

Of Dryden's translations there is little room to speak, though they form the great bulk of his work. His task, he felt, lay in "the maintaining the character of an author, which distinguishes him from all others." Yet his own distinctive quality is always there. In a sense, then, these "paraphrases" become original poems, as is inescapably felt when reading his Lucretius on the fear of death. A few of his versions—some of Horace, a good deal of Virgil—maintain their place as renderings that are still alive and actual; but translations must inevitably be for their own age, couched in the idiom of their day. The fashion changes, and they become outmoded, a fate that has inevitably overtaken Dryden's work in this field. But part of his purpose was to make great European literature familiar to the many, and here he succeeded within the limits he set himself. He may not be at the summit of Parnassus, but he is very near it. He was humble enough about it in all conscience. "I do not know," he is reported to have said, "if posterity will think me a great poet; they will not be able to deny that I was a good versifier."

CRITICISM

As with his poetry, most of Dryden's prose is occasional. The exception is his *Essay of Dramatick Poesy*, a dialogue Platonic in its framework and general conduct. Otherwise it is made up of dedications and prefaces, the former sometimes becoming critical essays, as the latter always are. The dedications tend to be regarded as fulsome; they are addressed for the most part to noble patrons, even to royalty, and may seem ludicrously, or shamefully, laudatory—but the dedication was a genre of its own, with its laws and traditions. Nobody—least of all, one imagines, the addressees—took them literally. Dryden's, beautifully phrased, always graceful, sometimes witty, invariably retain a perfect balance, the tribute paid never being wholly undeserved. But they need not detain us here. The prefaces are another matter. They are full of meat, lively, to the point, still of vital interest to any writer who takes his craft seriously. They are never stiff or pedantic; they border on looseness, for a preface, Dryden held, should be a rambling sort of affair, never wholly in the way, nor ever wholly out of it. No one, Dr. Johnson pronounced, ever found them tedious. Sometimes Dryden attacks; sometimes he defends himself; but for the greater part he is thinking aloud, as an artist handling his material.

Dryden, to quote Johnson again, "may properly be considered as the father of English criticism." There had, of course, been critics before him, but their approach was sectional, dealing either with philosophic ideas or with narrow technique. Dryden not only combined and broadened the two, but was the first critic to define, by practice rather than by precept, what were the important things to talk about. Take, for instance, the *Essay of Dramatick Poesy*. The important things to talk about, then, now, and always, are structure and diction, and his characters argued about them. One may not go hand in hand with the debaters there; today the matter is approached a little differently. But here, as everywhere, Dryden puts the issues squarely before us, not attempting to dragoon us into one opinion or another. He stimulates our thoughts to make up our own minds, for no two people think in quite the same way, and "our minds are perpetually wrought on by the temperament of our bodies." So long as he is writing plays, he discusses the drama; when he engages in other forms, he divagates upon those—for instance, upon satires in *The Original and Progress of Satire*—and when he comes to translation, he talks about that, especially when prefacing his *Aeneis*. But in his tremendous, easy discourses, those to the various miscellanies known as the preface to *Sylvae* (1685), the dedication of *Examen Poeticum* (1693), and the final preface to the *Fables*, and others, he tries to get at the heart of the writers he is criticizing.

This seems to come in incidentally, as when Dryden is explaining why he translates various authors in different ways, how he is striving to get at their being before deciding how they would have said in English in the late seventeenth century what they said in their own tongue in their own age. To choose a little at random:

> If I am not mistaken, the distinguishing character of Lucretius (I mean of his soul and genius) is a certain kind of noble pride, and positive assertion of his opinions. . . . From this sublime and daring genius of his, it must of necessity come to pass that his thoughts must be masculine, full of argumentation, and that sufficiently warm. From the same fiery temper proceeds the loftiness of his expressions and the perpetual torrent of his verse, where the barrenness of his subject does not too much constrain the quickness of his fancy. . . .

That is discriminating criticism; we understand Lucretius, and think also of the implications of Dryden's seemingly casual remarks. Or look at what he says about Chaucer, some of whose work he modernized from his desire to keep him in the tradition of English literature. In his day many judges, including Cowley, regarded Chaucer as "a dry, old-fashioned wit, not worth reviving," or, on the other hand, held him in such "veneration due to his old language . . . that it [was] little less than profanation and sacrilege to alter it." But Dryden wanted Chaucer to be read.

. . . as he is the father of English poetry, so I hold him in the same degree of veneration as the Grecians held Homer, or the Romans Virgil: he is a perpetual fountain of good sense; learn'd in all sciences; and therefore speaks properly on all subjects; as he knew what to say, so he knows also when to leave off, a continence which is practis'd by few writers . . . .

He must have been a man of a most wonderful comprehensive nature, because, as has been truly observ'd of him, he has taken into the compass of his *Canterbury Tales* the various manners and humours (as we now call them) of the whole English nation, in his age. . . . 'Tis sufficient to say, according to the proverb, that here is God's plenty.

Dryden was always eager to pay tribute to his giant predecessors, which is not only part of his humility toward those who have done superbly the task he assigned himself, but also proof of his extraordinary judgment. It is easy enough to regard Chaucer, Spenser, Shakespeare, Milton as towering figures; but it was Dryden who first declared they were so. As early as the *Essay of Dramatick Poesy* he could write:

To begin, then, with Shakespeare. He was the man who of all modern, and perhaps ancient poets, had the largest and most comprehensive soul. All the images of Nature were still present to him, and he drew them, not laboriously, but luckily; when he describes any thing, you more than see it, you feel it too. Those who accuse him to have wanted learning, give him the greater commendation: he was naturally learn'd; he needed not the spectacles of books to read Nature; he looked inwards, and found her there.

There is hardly anything more to be said; but Dryden said it at a time when Shakespeare was dubiously regarded, looked upon as a barbarous author, who did indeed want learning. That he needed trimming Dryden agreed with Ben Jonson in thinking. He also knew that for his plays to be popular, they must be infused a little with the sense of the new age; Dryden was the first to appreciate that different ages have different needs. What is more remarkable still for a practicing poet, he could pay homage to a near contemporary working toward different ends by methods other than his own; earliest among critical contemporaries he hailed *Paradise Lost* as "undoubtedly one of the greatest, most sublime poems which either this age or nation has produced."

For with his wide comprehensiveness Dryden regarded all literature as one, a gift given to creative writers but unavoidably a little foreign to the academic mind, which was intent upon separating, reluctant to believe with Dryden that "Mankind is ever the same, and nothing lost out of Nature, though every thing is alter'd." And throughout he reveals a superb common sense, in itself amounting to genius: he never allows an idea to rush him into extravagance; he merely sets forth his own at the time. "I have only laid down," he ends, "The Author's Apology for Heroic Poetry and Poetic Licence," "and that superficially enough, my present thoughts; and shall be glad to be taught better by those who pretend to reform our poetry." He does not presume to constrict anything so fluid, so *divers et ondoyant* as the great human activity of dividing literature into compartments, emaciating by definitions, strangling by categories. For after all—from the same essay—"they wholly mistake the nature of criticism who think its business is principally to find fault. Criticism . . . was meant a standard of judging well; the chiefest part of which is, to observe those excellencies which should delight a reasonable reader."

CONCLUSION

Iᴛ is perhaps natural that the picture most people have of Dryden should be that of the monarch of Will's Coffee House in Covent Garden, the old giant surrounded by the lesser fry and the young aspirants, for that is the best-documented. It escapes one too easily that he spent the larger proportion of his life in the country, to which he was devoted, especially where fishing was to be had, and that his most taking epistle is the Horatian one to his kinsman John Driden in praise of the rural pieties. One forgets earlier struggles, the squabbles with Howard and with Elkanah Settle, and, properly, the gossip, unsubstantiated as it is, about his private life. The best portrait is that sketched by his young friend Congreve, whom he praised, one may think, beyond his merit, as he certainly did Addison.

He was of a nature exceedingly humane and compassionate, ready to forgive injuries, and capable of a sincere reconciliation with those that had offended him. His friendship, where he professed it, went beyond his professions. He was of very pleasing access; but somewhat slow, and, as it were, diffident in his advances to others. . . . He was extremely ready and gentle in his correction of the errors of any writer who thought fit to consult him, and full as ready and patient to admit of the reprehension of others, in respect of his own oversights and mistakes.

But Dryden's last years were far from placid. Battered by political circumstance, without hope of quiet leisure, condemned to write more and more to sustain his mentally deranged wife and his ailing son, he felt impelled to write:

What Virgil wrote in the vigour of his age, in plenty and at ease, I have undertaken to translate in my declining years; struggling with wants, oppressed by sickness, curbed in my genius, liable to be misconstrued in all I write; and my judges, if they are not very equitable, already prejudiced against me by the lying character which has been given them of my morals. Yet steady to my principles, and not dispirited by my afflictions, I have by the blessing of God on my endeavours, overcome all difficulties, and, in some measure, acquitted myself of the debt which I owed the public when I undertook this work.

Sanity and balance marked him to the last, and the zest that enabled him, when nearly seventy, to brush off his forehead with a gesture of magnificent assurance such petty rivals as Luke Milbourne and Sir Richard Blackmore, while with splendid dignity firmly drawing the limit of his error in the matter of the obscenity with which Jeremy Collier had charged him. The nonjuring parson had attacked him in his notorious *Short View of the Stage*, and though Dryden pleads guilty to the use of certain expressions, he asserts that Collier has traduced him:

Besides that, he is too much given to horse-play in his raillery: and comes to battle, like a dictator from the plough. I will not say, the Zeal of God's House has eaten him up; but I am sure it has devour'd some part of his good manners and civility.

This might imply little were it not coupled with the homage he was always ready to pay to those who do things well, as good craftsmen, or good poets.

One of the engaging things about him is the absence of rancor against the younger generation that would tread him down.

In thinking of Dryden it is a sense of overall greatness that remains; he is the superb all-round man. His influence has been enormous, but this is always a difficult matter to assess. It does, though, seem to be undoubted that he made the ode live on as an English form, which he made shapely rather than formalized. It is certain that his Saint Cecilia odes, "Anne Killigrew," and perhaps others, prepared the ground for the odes of Collins and Gray, and made possible Wordsworth's "Immortality Ode" (which Dryden would have disliked for its imprecision) and his "Ode to Duty." By his example he sustained the variety of the lyric; and without him, for better or for worse, eighteenth-century poetry would have been very different from what it is: to begin with, one may say, "No Dryden, no Pope," with all that that involves. It may be noted further that poets have turned to him in their distress, as Keats began to do when he found that Milton failed him. Craftsmen in poetry—that is to say good poets—even now are not slow to salute him; and those who venture upon the other harmony find themselves echoing Matthew Arnold: "Here at last we have the true English prose, a prose such as we would all gladly use if only we knew how."

SELECTED BIBLIOGRAPHY

I. BIBLIOGRAPHY. P. J. Dobell, *Bibliographical Memoranda* (London, 1922); T. J. Wise, comp., *A Dryden Library* (priv. ptd., 1930), a bibliographical catalog of the extensive collection in the Ashley Library, now in the British Museum; H. Macdonald, *A Bibliography of Early Editions and of Drydeniana* (Oxford, 1939), an indispensable work for the student, elaborately annotated and with full particulars of the numerous works relating to the various controversies in which Dryden was involved; S. H. Monk, *John Dryden, a List of Critical Studies Published From 1895 to 1948* (Minneapolis, Minn., 1950). (Detailed bibliographical information can also be found in the appropriate volume of the *Cambridge Bibliography of English Literature*.)

II. COLLECTED WORKS. *The Works*, 4 vols. (London, 1691–1695), the first collected edition, was made up of separate editions of plays and poems with a general title page, variously dated; *The Comedies, Tragedies, and Operas. The Works*, 4 vols. (London, 1701), consists of two volumes of plays, one volume of poems, one volume of translations from Virgil (all in folio); *The Dramatic Works*, 6 vols. (London, 1717), edited mainly by Congreve; S. Derrick, ed., *The Miscellaneous Works*, 4 vols. (London, 1760); E. Malone, ed., *The Critical and Miscellaneous Works of Prose*, 3 vols. (London, 1800); Sir Walter Scott, ed., *The Works*, 18 vols. (Edinburgh, 1808), contains an important biographical and critical appreciation, rev. by G. Saintsbury (Edinburgh, 1882–1892); H. J. Todd, ed., *The Poetical Works*, 4 vols. (London, 1811), with notes by Joseph and John Warton; W. D. Christie, ed., *The Poetical Works* (London, 1870), the Globe ed., with a memoir, and revised text and notes, by Christie; J. C. Collins, ed., *The Satires* (London, 1905), with memoir, intro., and notes by Collins; G. R. Noyes, ed., *The Poetical Works* (Boston, 1908–1909; rev. edn., Cambridge, Mass., 1950), the most thorough ed. to date; T. Sargeant, ed., *The Poems* (London, 1910), the Oxford Standard Authors ed., unannotated; M. Summers, ed., *The Dramatic Works*, 6 vols. (London, 1930–1931), the Nonesuch Press limited ed., textually very unreliable; C. L. Day, ed., *The Songs* (Cambridge, Mass., 1932), with facsimiles of contemporary musical settings; W. B. Gardner, ed., *The Prologues and Epilogues* (New York, 1951), lacks much essential annotation; J. Kinsley, ed., *Poems*, 4 vols. (Oxford, 1958), the definitive text, in the Oxford English Texts series; J. Kinsley, ed., *The Poems and Fables* (London, 1962), the Oxford Standard Authors series; the University of California Press is preparing a complete edition—the following volumes have been published to date: E. N. Hooker and H. T. Swedenberg, eds., vol. I, *Poems, 1649–1680* (1956); J. H. Smith et al., eds., vol. VIII, *Plays: The Wild Gallant, The Rival Ladies, The Indian Queen* (1962); J. Loftis and V. A. Dearing, eds., vol. IX, *Plays: The Indian Emperor, Secret Love, Sir Martin Mar-All* (1966); E. Miner and V. A. Dearing, eds., vol. III, *Poems, 1685–1692* (1970); M. E. Novak and G. R. Guffey, eds., vol. X, *Plays: The Tempest, Tyrannick Love, An Evening's Love* (1970); S. H. Monk and A. E. Maurer, eds., vol. XVII, *Prose, 1668–1691* (1972); H. T. Swedenberg, ed., vol. II, *Poems, 1681–1684* (1973); A. B. Chambers et al., eds., vol. IV, *Poems, 1693–1696* (1974); A. Roper and V. A. Dearing, eds., vol. XVIII, *Prose: The History of the League, 1684* (1974); E. Miner, ed., vol. XV, *Plays: Albion and Albanius, Don Sebastian, Amphytrion* (1976).

III. SELECTED WORKS. W. P. Ker, ed. and comp., *Essays*, 2 vols. (Oxford, 1900); G. Saintsbury, ed., *Selected Plays* (London, 1904), contains eight plays; G. R. Noyes, ed., *Selected Dramas* (Chicago, 1910); W. D. Christie and C. H. Firth, eds., *Selected Poems* (Oxford, 1911); D. Nichol Smith, ed., *Poetry and Prose* (Oxford, 1925); L. I. Bredvold, ed., *The Best of Dryden* (New York, 1933); B. Dobrée, comp., *Poems* (London, 1934); D. Grant, comp., *Poetry, Prose, and Plays* (London, 1952), in the Reynard Library, the best selection available; D. Grant, comp., *Poetry and Prose* (London,

1955), in paperback; J. Kinsley, ed., *Selected Poems* (London, 1963).

IV. SEPARATE POEMS AND VERSE TRANSLATIONS. *Three Poems Upon the Death of His Late Highnesse Oliver, Lord Protector* (London, 1659), by Dryden, Waller, and Sprat (Dryden's poem was first printed separately in 1681 as *An Elegy on the Usurper O.C.*); *Astraea Redux. A Poem on the Happy Restoration . . . of . . . Charles the Second* (London, 1660); *To His Sacred Majesty, a Panegyrick on His Coronation* (London, 1661); *To My Lord Chancellor . . .* (London, 1662); *Annus Mirabilis: The Year of Wonders* (London, 1667); *Absalom and Achitophel* (London, 1681), in J. and H. Kinsley, eds. (London, 1961); *The Second Part of Absalom and Achitophel* (London, 1682); *The Medall: A Satyre Against Sedition* (London, 1682); *Mac Flecknoe or a Satyre Upon the True-Blew-Protestant Poet, T[homas]. S[hadwell]* (London, 1682); *Religio Laici or a Layman's Faith* (London, 1682); *Threnodia Augustalis: A Funeral Pindarique Poem Sacred to the Happy Memory of King Charles II* (London, 1685); *The Hind and the Panther* (London, 1687); *A Song for St. Cecilia's Day* (London, 1687); *Britannia Rediviva: A Poem on the Birth of the Prince* (London, 1688); *Eleonora: A Panegyrical Poem . . .* (London, 1692); *An Ode, on the Death of Mr. Henry Purcell* (London, 1696); *Alexander's Feast: Or the Power of Musique. A Song in Honour of St. Cecelia's Day* (London, 1697); *The Works of Virgil* (London, 1697), Dryden's masterpiece of translation (included in vol. IV of *The Works* in sets of the folio collected edition); *Fables Ancient and Modern &c.* (London, 1699), contains 19 paraphrases or translations from Homer, Ovid, Chaucer, and Boccaccio, with a few "original" poems; *The Primer, or Office of the B. Virgin Mary* (London, 1706), contains a number of hymns translated from the Latin and wrongly ascribed to Dryden (see Noyes and Potter, *Hymns Attributed to Dryden*, below).

Dryden contributed commendatory or memorial verses to the following works: *Lachrymae Musarum* (1650); John Hoddeson's *Sion and Parnassus* (1650); Howard's *Poems* (1660); *Chorea Gigantum* (1663); Nathaniel Lee's *The Rival Queens* (1677); W. D. Roscommon's *An Essay on Translated Verse* (1684); John Oldham's *Remains* (1684); John Northleigh's *The Triumph of Our Monarchy* (1685); Anne Killigrew's *Poems* (1686); Henry Higden's *Modern Essay* (1687); *Paradise Lost* (fol. 1688); Thomas Southern's *The Wives Excuse* (1692); William Congreve's *The Double Dealer* (1694); George Granville's *Heroick Love* (1698); Peter Motteux's *Beauty in Distress* (1698); and a number of contemporary miscellanies.

Verse translations by Dryden are included in Ovid's *Epistles* (1680); Boileau's *The Art of Poetry* (1683); *The Satires* [of Juvenal and Persius] (1693); Ovid's *Art of Love* (1709); and the important "Dryden-Tonson Miscellanies," which he compiled and edited: *Miscellany Poems* (London, 1684), *Sylvae* (London, 1685), *Examen*

Poeticum (London, 1693), *The Annual Miscellany* (London, 1694).

V. SEPARATE PLAYS, PROLOGUES, AND OTHER WORKS. *The Rival Ladies* (London, 1664), a tragicomedy; *The Indian Queen*, in Sir Robert Howard, *Four New Plays* (London, 1665), a tragedy written with Howard; *The Indian Emperour or the Conquest of Mexico by the Spaniards, Being the Sequel of the Indian Queen* (London, 1667), a tragedy, the 2nd ed. (1668) was prefaced by Dryden's "Defence of an Essay of 'Dramatick Poesie' "; *Secret Love, or the Maiden Queen* (London, 1668), a tragicomedy; *Sir Martin Mar-All or the Feign'd Innocence* (London, 1668), a comedy; *The Wild Gallant* (London, 1669), a comedy, the first of his plays to be performed; *The Tempest or the Enchanted Island* (London, 1670), a comedy; *Tyrannick Love, or the Royal Martyr* (London, 1670), a tragedy; *An Evening's Love, or the Mock Astrologer* (London, 1671); *The Conquest of Granada by the Spaniards* (London 1672), a tragedy; *Marriage A-la-Mode* (London, 1673), a comedy; *Amboyna* (London, 1673), a tragedy; *The Assignation, or Love in a Nunnery* (London, 1673), a comedy; *The State of Innocence, and Fall of Man* (London, 1674), an opera; *Aureng-Zebe* (London, 1676), a tragedy; *All for Love: or the World Well Lost* (London, 1678), a tragedy; *The Kind Keeper: Or, Mr. Limberham* (London, 1678), a comedy; *Oedipus* (London, 1679), a tragedy; *Troilus and Cressida, or Truth Found Too Late* (London, 1679), a tragedy; *The Spanish Fryar: Or, the Double Discovery* (London, 1682), a comedy; *The Duke of Guise* (London, 1683), a tragedy; *Albion and Albanius* (London, 1685), an opera; *Amphytrion: or, the Two Sosias* (London, 1690), a comedy; *Don Sebastian, King of Portugal* (London, 1690), a tragedy; *King Arthur; or, the British Worthy* (London, 1691), an opera; *Cleomenes, the Spartan Hero* (London, 1692), a tragedy; *Love Triumphant: Or, Nature Will Prevail* (London, 1694), a tragicomedy, to which Dryden contributed the prologue, the epilogue, and "The Secular Masque"; *The Pilgrim* (London, 1700), Vanbrugh's adaptation of Fletcher's play.

Dryden wrote a number of prologues and epilogues for his own plays, some of which were printed separately in folio half sheets. He contributed a prologue or an epilogue to the following plays by other dramatists: Sir George Etherege's *The Man of Mode* (1676); Charles Davenant's *Circe* (1677); Nathaniel Lee's *Mithridates* (1678); Thomas Shadwell's *The True Widow* (1678); Lee's *Caesar Borgia* (1680); Nahum Tate's *The Loyal General* (1680); Charles Saunders' *Tamburlaine* (1681); *Sophonisba* (1681); Thomas Southern's *The Loyal Brother* (1682); John Banks's *The Unhappy Favourite* (1682); Lee's *Constantine the Great* (1684); Southern's *The Disappointment* (1684); Mrs. Belin's *The Widow Ranter* (1690); Beaumont and Fletcher's *The Prophetess* (1690); Joseph Harris' *The Mistakes* (1691); John Bancroft's *Henry II* (1693); John Dryden the younger's *The Husband His Own Cuckold* (1696).

VI. SEPARATE PROSE WORKS. *Of Dramatick Poesie, An Essay* (London, 1668); *Notes and Observations on "The Empress of Morocco"* (London, 1677), in collaboration with Thomas Shadwell and John Crowne; *His Majesties Declaration Defended* (London, 1681), an anti-Whig pamphlet almost certainly by Dryden; *The Vindication &c.* (London, 1683), a defense of *The Duke of Guise* against a scurrilous attack; C. E. Ward, ed., *Letters* (Durham, N.C., 1946), contains Dryden's few surviving letters (62 in all) and 15 letters addressed to him.

Dryden translated *The History of the League* (London, 1684); *The Life of St. Francis Xavier* (London, 1688); and *De Arte Graphica* (London, 1695). In addition to the important prefaces to certain of his own works, he contributed essays to Plutarch's *Lives* (1683); *A Dialogue Concerning Women* (1691); Charles de St.-Évremond's *Essays* (1692); the *History* of Polybius (1693); and the *Annals* of Tacitus (1698).

VII. SOME BIOGRAPHICAL AND CRITICAL STUDIES. G. Langbaine, *An Account of the English Dramatic Poets* (Oxford, 1691); J. Dennis, *The Impartial Critick* (London, 1693); J. Dennis, *Miscellaneous Letters and Essays Addressed on Several Subjects Directed to John Dryden* (London, 1694); J. Downes, *Roscius Anglicanus, or an Historical Review of the Stage* (London, 1708); J. Dennis, *Remarks Upon Mr. Pope's Translation of Homer* (London, 1717); S. Johnson, *Lives of the Poets*, vol. I (London, 1781); J. Weston, "An Essay on the Superiority of Dryden's Versification Over That of Pope and the Moderns" in *Philotoxi Ardenae* (Birmingham, 1780); W. Hazlitt, *Lectures on the English Poets* (London, 1818); J. R. Lowell, *Among My Books* (London, 1870); G. Saintsbury, *Dryden* (London, 1881); G. S. B[owen], *A Study of the Prologue and Epilogue in English Literature, From Shakespeare to Dryden* (London, 1884); O. Shipley, *Annus Sanctus* (London, 1884); R. Garnett, *The Age of Dryden* (London, 1895); J. C. Collins, *Essays and Studies* (London, 1895); M. Sherwood, *Dryden's Dramatic Theory and Practice* (Boston, 1898).

L. N. Chase, *The English Heroic Play* (New York, 1903); A. W. Verrall, *Lectures on Dryden* (Cambridge, 1914); M. Van Doren, *The Poetry of John Dryden* (New York, 1920), English ed., with intro. by B. Dobrée (London, 1931); A. Nicoll, *Dryden as an Adapter of Shakespeare* (London, 1922), a Shakespeare Association pamphlet; A. Nicoll, *Dryden and His Poetry* (London, 1923); B. J. Pendlebury, *Dryden's Heroic Plays: A Study of the Origins* (London, 1923); B. Dobrée, *Restoration Comedy* (London, 1924), includes a chapter on Dryden; A. Lubbock, *The Character of John Dryden* (London, 1925), a pamphlet; T. S. Eliot, *Homage to John Dryden* (London, 1925), the title essay is a study of Dryden; K. M. Lynch, *The Social Mode of Restoration Comedy* (New York, 1926); B. Dobrée, ed., *Five Restoration Tragedies* (London, 1928), contains *All for Love* and an intro. on Restoration tragedy; D. D. Arundell, ed., *Dryden and*

Howard, *1664–68* (Cambridge, 1929), contains the *Essay on Dramatic Poesy*, *The Indian Emperour*, *The Duke of Lerma*, and other controversial matter; A. H. Thorndike, *English Comedy* (New York, 1929); H. J. C. Grierson, *Cross-Currents in English Literature of the XVIIth Century* (London, 1929); B. Dobrée, *Restoration Tragedy* (London, 1930), includes a chapter on Dryden; C. V. Deane, *Dramatic Theory and the Rhymed Heroic Play* (London, 1931); T. S. Eliot, *John Dryden: The Poet, the Dramatist, the Critic* (New York, 1932), a series of lectures; L. I. Bredvold, *The Intellectual Milieu of John Dryden* (Ann Arbor, Mich., 1934); B. Willey, *The Seventeenth Century Background* (London, 1934); R. B. Allen, *The Sources of John Dryden's Comedies* (Ann Arbor, Mich., 1935); A. O. Lovejoy, *The Great Chain of Being: A Study in the History of an Idea* (London–Cambridge, Mass., 1936); G. R. Noyes and G. R. Potter, *Hymns Attributed to John Dryden* (Berkeley, Calif., 1937); C. S. Lewis, *Rehabilitations, and Other Essays* (London, 1939), contains Shelley, Dryden, and T. S. Eliot; J. M. Osborn, *Some Biographical Facts and Problems* (New York, 1940; rev. ed., Gainesville, Fla., 1965); G. Tillotson, *Eighteenth Century Poetic Diction* in *Essays in Criticism and Research* (Cambridge, 1942); G. N. Clark, *The Seventeenth Century* (Oxford, 1945); J. H. Wilson, *The Court Wits of the Restoration* (Princeton, 1948); D. Nichol Smith, *John Dryden* (London, 1950), the Clark Lectures, 1948–1949; J. Butt, *The Augustan Age* (London, 1950); Allardyce Nichol, *A History of English Drama 1660–1900*: vol. I, *Restoration Drama, 1660–1700* (rev. ed., Cambridge, 1952); I. Jack, *Augustan Satire: Intention and Idiom in English Poetry, 1660–1750* (Oxford, 1952); E. M. W. Tillyard, *The English Epic and Its Background* (London, 1954); K. Young, *John Dryden* (London, 1954); W. Frost, *Dryden and the Art of Translation* (London, 1955); B. Ford, ed., *The Pelican Guide to English Literature*: vol. 4, *From Dryden to Johnson* (Harmondsworth–New York, 1957); B. Dobrée, *Five Heroic Plays* (London, 1960), contains *Aureng-Zebe* and an intro. on the heroic drama; R. N. Schilling, *Dryden and the Conservative Myth: A Reading of Absalom and Achitophel* (New Haven, 1961); C. E. Ward, *The Life of John Dryden* (Chapel Hill, N. C.–Oxford, 1961); A. W. Hoffmann, *John Dryden's Imagery* (Gainesville, Fla., 1962); R. Nevo, *The Dial of Virtue: A Study of Poems on Affairs of State in the Seventeenth Century* (Princeton, 1963); J. R. Sutherland, *John Dryden: The Poet as Orator* (W. P. Ker Memorial Lecture, Glasgow, 1963); R. M. Schilling, ed., *Dryden: A Collection of Critical Essays* (Englewood Cliffs, N.J., 1963); T. S. Eliot, *The Use of Poetry and the Use of Criticism* (2nd ed., London, 1964), contains *The Age of Dryden*; A. Roper, *Dryden's Poetic Kingdoms* (London–New York, 1965); J. Loftis, ed., *Restoration Drama* (London, 1966), contains two interesting essays on Dryden; H. T. Swedenberg, ed., *Essential Articles for the Study of John Dryden* (Hamden, Conn., 1966); E. Miner, *Dryden's Poetry* (Bloomington, Ind., 1967); J. R. Sutherland, *The Oxford History of English Literature*: vol. VI, *English Literature in the Late Seventeenth Century* (Oxford–New York, 1969); A. T. Barbeau, *The Intellectual Design of Dryden's Heroic Plays* (New Haven, 1970); R. D. Hume, *Dryden's Criticism* (Ithaca, N.Y., 1971); J. and H. Kinsley, eds., *Dryden, the Critical Heritage* (London, 1971); E. Miner, ed., *John Dryden* (London, 1972), in the Writers and Their Background series; R. McHenry and D. Lougee, eds., *Critics on Dryden* (London, 1973); E. Pechter, *Dryden's Classical Theory of Literature* (Cambridge, 1975); D. Wykes, *A Preface to Dryden* (London, 1975); S. J. Latt and S. A. Monk, eds., *A Survey and Bibliography of Critical Studies, 1895–1974* (Minneapolis, 1976); G. McFadden, *Dryden, the Public Writer* (Princeton, 1978).

WILLIAM WYCHERLEY

(1641-1716)

P. F. Vernon

LIFE

"WILLIAM WYCHERLEY A Shropshire Gentleman, who has excell'd all Writers in all Languages, in Comedy"—a partial view undoubtedly, yet by no means extraordinary in the dramatist's lifetime, when he was generally considered to be the greatest English comic writer since Ben Jonson. He lived in turbulent times, when social and moral attitudes were shifting rapidly; and after his death these changes began to undermine his reputation. In the second half of the eighteenth century the theaters accepted only tame adaptations of his comedies that had cut out the satiric bite. His work then disappeared completely from the stage. By the middle of the nineteenth century Restoration comedy was commonly regarded as a scandalous and barely mentionable chapter in the history of English literature. Wycherley was singled out as the most obnoxious offender. Thomas Macaulay compared his work to a skunk, protected from the critics because it was too filthy to handle. In the early part of the present century critics began to take a new and sympathetic interest in Restoration drama, but Wycherley's status remained somewhat ambiguous. The typical comedy of manners was now felt to be cynical, detached, and amoral, a view that probably helped to widen the popularity of Restoration comedy after World War I. But Wycherley, with his obvious fondness for moralizing, seemed something of a misfit; he had now become too moral. His comedies did not catch on as readily as those of William Congreve, the other major comic dramatist of the period. Many Restoration comedies have been successfully revived on the professional stage, but apart from *The Country-Wife*, Wycherley continues to be overlooked in favor of his younger contemporaries, Congreve, Sir John Vanbrugh, and George Farquhar. This neglect is odd, for, of all the comedies of the period, his seem the best fitted to sustain that concern with the social structure that has characterized some of the most important productions of Restoration comedies.

Although greatly admired by his contemporaries, Wycherley did not lead a particularly happy life. His father, Daniel, was born in the town of Clive, near Shrewsbury in Shropshire, where members of the family had lived comfortably for over two centuries. He became high steward in the marquess of Winchester's household at Basing House in Hampshire and married Bethia Shrimpton, lady-of-honor to the marchioness. William, the first of six children, was probably born on 28 May 1641; the date is not absolutely certain. Less than two years later civil war broke out. In 1645 Basing House was destroyed by parliamentary forces under Cromwell, the marquess was imprisoned, and his estates were confiscated. Daniel acted as his deputy until the Restoration of the monarchy in 1660 and during this time managed to set aside for himself a large sum of money with which he later bought substantial property in his native county. He eventually became a barrister, spending much of his time and the greater part of his fortune on lengthy lawsuits—a fact that helps to explain his son's lifelong contempt for the legal profession. When he was about fifteen years old, William was sent to study in France. While living in the Charente district he seems to have been deeply impressed by the conversation of the marchioness de Montausier, daughter and disciple of the celebrated Madame de Rambouillet, whose salons had fostered the cult of refined manners and "Platonic" love known as *préciosité*. Thus at an early age he came into direct contact with a literary movement that deeply influenced English drama both before and after the Restoration. He became a Roman Catholic; but on his return to England in 1660 he was sent to Oxford for a short while, and there reconverted to Protestantism. Toward the end of the same year he took up legal studies at the Inner Temple in London.

Nothing much is known of his activities during

his twenties. He may well have spent some time in Madrid in the household of the poet-ambassador, Sir Richard Fanshawe, and he probably took part in the naval battle of 1665 against the Dutch. In 1669 his first work was published anonymously, an irreverent verse burlesque of the Hero and Leander story. Feeble as they seem now, burlesques of this kind were popular when the Greek and Roman classics had almost the status of sacred texts in the educational syllabus. Two years later his first comedy, *Love in a Wood; or, St. James's Park*, was performed by the actors known as the King's Men at the Theatre Royal in Bridges Street. The London theaters at this time catered to an intimate and privileged social circle; so the success of Wycherley's first play did more than spread his name. It also secured his position among the select group of leading writers and wits who moved within the court circle; gained him the friendship of such important figures as John Wilmot, second earl of Rochester, and George Villiers, duke of Buckingham; and eventually led to the favor and patronage of King Charles II himself. His next work, *The Gentleman Dancing-Master*, was put on in 1672 by the rival company of actors at the new and splendid Dorset Garden Theatre, as the Theatre Royal had been burnt down earlier in the year. It was a comparative failure. But early in 1675, at the new Theatre Royal in Drury Lane, Wycherley scored a triumph with *The Country-Wife*, one of the most influential plays of the century. At the end of the following year *The Plain-Dealer* was produced at the same theater. The play apparently puzzled the first-night audience, and its fate seemed uncertain until the balance was tilted in its favor by the enthusiastic applause of Buckingham and his friends. It soon became the most admired of Wycherley's works and earned him the nicknames "Plain Dealer" and "Manly" from the name of the principal character. But those who knew him always insisted that the dramatist resembled the rude and surly Manly only in his truthfulness and courage, his own manner being courteous and charming.

Wycherley was to live some forty years longer, but he wrote nothing further for the theater. Already he was suffering from the ill health that was to trouble him for the rest of his life, and soon other problems were to occupy his mind. He had by now wholeheartedly adopted the habits and outlook of the wealthy gentlemen whose lives centered on the theaters, the coffeehouses, and the other places of wit and entertainment to be found in the capital. He despised the mercenary values of the business world and the unsophisticated life of the country, even though these had provided the means for his education. Yet the life led by a London gentleman demanded money, and Wycherley had no secure source of income. In an age when it was considered undignified to write for profit, he never escaped from the endless struggle to make ends meet. The king helped him to spend the winter of 1678–1679 in the healthier climate of France and, on Wycherley's return, proposed that he become tutor to the young duke of Richmond. This plan, which would have brought a permanent pension, came to nothing when it was discovered that in the autumn of 1679 Wycherley had secretly married the recently widowed countess of Drogheda. It was an unfortunate marriage from every point of view. His wife not only made him miserable by her violent jealousy while she lived, but failed to leave him, when she died, the fortune for which he had married her. At her death, a mere two years after the marriage, the legal disputes over her first husband's will, which were to last for more than fifteen years, had only just entered the preliminary stages. Meanwhile Wycherley's debts overwhelmed him. From 1682 to 1685 he was pursued by creditors, and eventually spent at least ten months in prison until, early in 1686, James II helped to clear his debts and promised him a pension after influential friends had arranged a performance of *The Plain-Dealer* at court. When James fled the country less than three years later, the dramatist was again left penniless.

After this he lived modestly, partly in London, partly in Shropshire, with occasional visits to Bath to improve his health. He did not lose contact with the literary world. When in London he was the accepted leader of the men of letters who gathered at Will's Coffee House. He had many friends and admirers among the younger writers, including the dramatist William Congreve and the critic John Dennis. He had been writing poems off and on throughout his life, and sometime before 1696 he decided to bring out a collection consisting mainly of new verse. The volume was ready by 1699 but, owing to difficulties with the publisher, did not appear until 1704. It was poorly received. Wycherley's memory was now failing, and many of the poems suffer from repetitiveness and appalling metrical lapses. At this time Wycherley met Alexander Pope, then only sixteen years old, and, impressed by the elegance of the young poet's early pieces, asked him to polish up some of his own poems. Pope at first welcomed the task as an honor but, finding it more and more troublesome, eventually told the dramatist to continue his revision himself. For a while the warm friendship between the two cooled, though Pope kept in touch with the dramatist until the latter's death.

At the age of seventy-four, Wycherley married again. The whole affair reads like the plot of one of his own comedies. In 1715, a cousin, Captain Thomas Shrimpton, suggested that Wycherley might marry a young woman who could offer a cash dowry large enough to pay off his debts. She would benefit in turn from the jointure provided by old Daniel's will should his eldest son remarry. The woman proposed by Shrimpton was in fact his own mistress. According to the servants, this unscrupulous fortune hunter used every possible kind of pressure to force the old dramatist's consent, from getting him drunk to threatening him with the debtors' prison. Seriously ill, Wycherley protested that he needed a panel of doctors rather than a wife. Sometime before this he had been reconverted to Catholicism and, his condition worsening, received the last sacrament. Shrimpton intensified his efforts. Worn out and indifferent, if fully conscious of what was happening, the old man eventually put his signature to the marriage contract. "Matrimony is plac'd after Extreme Unction in our Catechism, as a kind of Hint of the Order of Time in which they are to be taken"—Wycherley would have appreciated Pope's dry comment. Eleven days after the marriage, on 31 December 1715, he died. He was buried in St. Paul's Church, Covent Garden. Shortly afterward Shrimpton married the now wealthy widow.

SATIRE AND SOCIAL CRITICISM

A first glance at Wycherley's comedies reveals one striking characteristic: his fondness for maxims. The dialogue, particularly in his later comedies, is often made up entirely of an exchange of these terse moral generalizations. This suggests something of his whole approach to comedy. In the first place, he set out quite openly to teach his audience. On the title page of *The Gentleman Dancing-Master* he

placed a motto from Horace that begins, "It is not enough to make the listener laugh aloud." He took it for granted that the highest function of comedy was to instruct. Secondly, he shared the common concern of his age for the simple, general truths of experience. Like Descartes, Hobbes, and the other influential philosophers of his time, like the scientists and artists who founded the Royal Society after the Restoration, he felt confident that the universe contained an underlying order, a strictly determined pattern of cause and effect. His comedies try to reveal something of this order and to make clear some of the basic principles of human behavior. In their very structure they give the impression of careful design rather than of spontaneous, accidental growth. Most European comedy displays a classical regularity of this kind, but readers brought up on some of the less disciplined Elizabethan plays often feel that formal symmetry is bound to curb the imagination and lead to superficiality. In fact, the art of establishing connections offers plenty of scope for subtlety and imaginative depth.

As a satirist, for instance, Wycherley could not be content simply to judge the things he disliked according to some accepted moral standard. Antisocial behavior, he assumed, must arise from some confusion in thinking, from some simple inconsistency that people would avoid if only they could be made to think logically. Like Ben Jonson, a dramatist with whom he had a great deal in common, he had a clear, incisive mind, which enabled him to seek out the false premises underlying various social habits and to pursue them relentlessly in his comedies to an extreme conclusion, where everyone could see how absurd they were.

Wycherley differs from other Restoration dramatists both in his seriousness and in his artistic consistency. Sharp, pointed, bold, masculine, strong— these were the words his contemporaries chose when describing his work. They suggest both sound judgment and acute penetration. His dramatic method is exceptionally purposeful. He begins with a clear end in view and rarely loses sight of it. Consider these opening sentences: "Not a Husband to be had for money" (*Love in a Wood*); "To confine a Woman just in her rambling Age! take away her liberty at the very time she shou'd use it!" (*The Gentleman Dancing-Master*). These plunge the audience straight into the problems the plays are about to consider. Everything then turns upon the central themes. The characters are not rounded individuals: once introduced, they do not reveal new and surprising facets of personality. Rather they are illustrations in an argument, pruned of all irrelevant features. The audience knows exactly how they will behave; yet they do not seem to be mere puppets manipulated by their creator. This is because their actions follow logically from the attitudes they hold. In this sense the plots are plausible and "natural," even though they would often be impossible in real life. The dialogue, though it suggests colloquial speech, is quite unlike ordinary conversation. Crammed with imagery, witty aphorisms, similes, and double meanings, it is designed as an indirect commentary for the benefit of the audience rather than as an imitation of the way people really talk.

Despite their neatness and order, Wycherley's comedies retain something of the crowded vigor of earlier English comedy. He will combine in a single play incidents that his older French contemporary, Molière, found sufficient for two or even three separate comedies. But he always succeeded in fusing the separate strands of an action, so that they seemed only related aspects of a single problem. His young friend, John Dennis, one of the most perceptive commentators on his work, noted that he was "almost the only Man alive who has made Comedy instructive in its Fable; almost all the rest, being contented to instruct by their Characters." Indeed, although he borrowed the rough outlines of nearly all his plots from other writers, one of his chief excellences lay in his ability to construct a plot in which even the smallest detail had some significance.

Recent studies have abstracted from his work a body of ideas similar to much of the naturalistic and skeptical thinking of the period; but his comedies actually deal with particular social problems rather than with philosophy in the narrow sense. Their themes, generally speaking, concern the preservation of traditional ideals in a changing society. Capitalism at this time continued to develop at a rapid pace, despite the apparent setback of the Restoration. Wycherley regarded the loosening of rigid class divisions, the growing influence of the business community, and the spread of acquisitive values as a serious threat to the humane and civilized level of personal relationships achieved, or at least aimed at, by the most intelligent among the upper-class group for whom he wrote. What particularly worried him was the effect of mercenary competition on friendship and sexual relations. The breakdown of family ties, which disturbed the Elizabethan dramatists so much, left him unmoved. "FRIENDSHIP," he wrote, "is a greater Tye on Faith than Blood, and free Love than Marriage-Bonds."

Marriage was a favorite topic with the Restoration dramatists, and it is the main butt of Wycherley's satire. To understand why, it is necessary to remember what marriage involved in seventeenth-century England. Marriage was not then a private and wholly voluntary contract between two individuals. As in many parts of the world today, it was felt to be the concern of the family group. Matches were generally arranged by the heads of families, by fathers, or by elder brothers. An entry in Samuel Pepys's *Diary* concerning his brother's marriage illustrates the typical attitude fairly well:

My chiefest thought is now to get a good wife for Tom, there being one offered by the Joyces, a cozen of theirs, worth £200 in ready money.

(31 December 1661)

Among the wealthy classes such matters as fixing a dowry and jointure and preserving or enlarging family estates took priority. The wishes of those about to be married were not entirely ignored, but normally had to take second place. Women seldom had much say in the choice of their partners. Traditionally they were conceded the right to refuse a proposed husband, but, as Samuel Richardson's novel *Clarissa* in the mid-eighteenth century shows so vividly, refusal might well involve a more than average degree of heroism. Men were allowed greater freedom of choice, but would rarely risk offending relatives on whom they depended financially. Parents still occasionally arranged marriages between young children in this period; young women were sometimes coupled with middle-aged men, and Wycherley's personal experiences of marriage show that there were many other ways in which money could destroy the faintest chance of a happy married relationship.

This was, of course, no new state of affairs. For centuries European writers had been expressing their frustrated desire for a love free from the social ties of arranged marriage—nowhere more intensely than in the imaginary "Platonic" world of the French aristocratic romances and the closely related

English court drama under Charles I. But after the Restoration, plaintive escapism of this kind was stiffened with a good measure of down-to-earth thinking. The traditional code of family conduct had always been intimately linked with political theory and practice. The revolution and the execution of Charles I had forced all thinking men to make a thorough reassessment of the relations between ruler and subject, and now some of them felt the need to reexamine the bonds that held the miniature state of the family together. They began to question the right of a father to dictate to his adult sons and daughters; began to challenge the absolute sovereignty of husband over wife, and even to doubt the binding force of marriage vows that were not freely contracted. Reasoning of this kind lies behind many of the comic situations in Restoration drama; it is the very fabric of Wycherley's work. His attack on the contemporary marriage of convenience does not, therefore, necessarily imply a criticism of all marriage. For him "free love" did not have its modern meaning; it meant rather a freely chosen partnership based on mutual attraction and respect. In his comedies he always implied that this partnership could work within the framework of marriage.

Wycherley's emphasis on free choice in personal relationships is clearly related to the new individualism of the century. But he saw himself as a conservative, defending what he believed to be traditional values against the economic effects of individualism. Forced marriage, fortune hunting, jealousy, indifference, and inconstancy—all these he considered to be the evil results of treating people as if they were property; and he blamed them, not always fairly, on the rise of the middle class. But he was also interested in other aspects of social climbing. His comedies are crowded with fops and would-be wits, men who have bought titles or tried in other ways to edge themselves into the highest social circles. At first sight it may seem as though he is breaking butterflies upon a wheel, that his affected fools are too insignificant to deserve the ridicule he heaps upon them. But Wycherley sensed danger in their feeble and superficial attempts to imitate the culture of true gentlemen. It was not just that they lacked correct manners; Wycherley always connected their emphasis on display, on external accomplishments, with a crippling moral deficiency that led to selfishness and treachery in their relations with others. His defense of social and literary decorum forms part of that long tradition of satiric writings that includes Dryden's "MacFlecknoe" and reaches its highest point in Pope's *Dunciad* where it appears most clearly as a struggle for the survival of an entire way of life and thought.

Wycherley's comedies are also concerned with changes that were taking place in the lives of upperclass women. With the spread of capitalist methods of business organization, the longer periods spent by noblemen in London away from their country estates, and the greater number of servants, women who would formerly have held important responsibilities in the family were leading a life of increasing idleness. In London and the big spas an exclusive feminine social life was developing, trivial, affected, and inward-looking. Wycherley attacked this world of card games and scandal, with its false veneer of prudery, as yet another obstacle in the way of intelligent, open, and equal relationships between men and women.

These interests place Wycherley firmly in the mainstream of English satirists from Ben Jonson to Swift and Pope. Like all Restoration comedy, his work differs from the masterpieces of these great satirists in its narrower scope. It expresses the interests and the limited vision of a small social group. One soon becomes aware of an inability to reach out imaginatively to the motives and needs of other classes, even to see far beyond the limits of the court at Westminster and the fashionable districts of the capital. Wycherley was deeply affected by the major political and social changes of his time, but was able to judge them only by their effect on the personal lives of a privileged group. Yet the class he represented was in many respects enlightened, and its way of life contained qualities worth preserving: qualities that allowed him to see serious limitations in the forces that were altering society. One may miss in his work the breadth of vision revealed in any one of Jonson's finest comedies, or in the total output of Molière, but his analysis of a smaller field is remarkably acute.

LOVE IN A WOOD

WHEN the public theaters reopened at the Restoration, after a long period of enforced silence, it almost seems as though the dramatists consciously set out to search for some fruitful comic tradition they could build upon. As the taste for spiteful satires on the Puritans dwindled, they turned for inspiration to Molière in France, to the Spanish comedy of intrigue, to Francis Beaumont and John Fletcher, to Ben Jonson, and to other earlier English writers. Almost everything they handled was reduced to undistinguished farce. John Dryden and Sir George Etherege obtained the most promising results by developing elements in the comedies of Richard Brome and James Shirley, written before the Civil Wars. They combined in various ways satire on fops and false wits, the intrigues of cunning cheats, the trials and adventures of romantic heroes and heroines, and, most important, witty quarrels between upper-class lovers who, like Beatrice and Benedick in Shakespeare's *Much Ado About Nothing*, after a show of reluctance finally join together in marriage. Wycherley in his first play, *Love in a Wood*, grafted on to this loose comic form an adaptation of a Spanish cloak and sword drama[1] to produce a comedy that, though complicated, had greater unity and more serious meaning than any recent work for the stage.

It is fascinating to see Wycherley's clear mind forcing order out of apparent chaos. The play contains two quite distinct worlds. The first, presented satirically, contains fortune hunters, social climbers, and bawds who cheat one another in a series of intrigues and counterintrigues that remind one of Jonson's *Volpone* or *The Alchemist*. The second, more benevolent and urbane in manner, following the Spanish play, consists of true lovers from a higher social class. These two separate strands have at first sight so little in common that, despite the skillful weaving of the plot, they seem doomed to fall apart. But Wycherley cleverly turns this apparent weakness to advantage by making a moral contrast between the two a central part of his play's meaning. Every incident, every joke indeed, has some bearing on the main theme, which is the importance of trust and esteem in love, courtship, and marriage.

All the characters in the satiric intrigues are linked by a common weakness; they have all, in some way or another, allowed money to sully their approach to love. Unknown to one another, they are all manipulated by a cunning bawd and matchmaker, a fitting representative of the forces that

poison love by mixing it with greed for money. She alone prospers as interests clash, plots become entangled, and the biters themselves are bit.

The dialogue in these scenes, though vigorous and colloquial, is stuffed with meaningful images that form a continuous, indirect commentary. A succession of references to card-sharpers and confidence tricksters, for example, creates the atmosphere of an underworld of crooks. Whenever the Puritan miser, Gripe, appears, witty play with religious phrases underlines his hypocrisy. In the following episode he is visiting a mistress in her poor lodgings. The bawd, Mrs. Joyner, tries to force him to spend freely, while he invents pious excuses not to do so. Notice how, in his last speech, images connected with food suggest the coarseness of his real emotions:

> *Joyn.* What do you look for, Sir?
> *Gripe.* Walls have ears, Walls have ears; besides, I look for a private place to retire to, in time of need; oh here's one convenient.
> *[Turns up a Hanging, and discovers the slender provisions of the Family]*
> *Joyn.* But you see poor innocent Souls, to what use they put it, not to hide Gallants.
> *Gripe.* Temperance is the nurse of Chastity.
> *Joyn.* But your Worship may please to mend their fare; and when you come, may make them entertain you, better than, you see, they do themselves.
> *Gripe.* No, I am not dainty, as I told you; I abominate Entertainments; no Entertainments, pray, Mrs. Joyner.
> *Joyn.* No! *[Aside]*
> *Gripe.* There can be no entertainment to me, more Luscious and Savoury, than the communion with that little Gentlewoman; will you call her out, I fast till I see her.[2]

(III. iii. 15–28)

The two pairs of upper-class lovers, who put genuine feeling before financial interests, provide a decent alternative to fortune hunting and prostitution. But this is true only at the end of the play. At the start their relationships suffer from serious flaws that plunge them temporarily into the atmosphere of mistrust that surrounds the inferior group. One

---

[1]Pedro Calderón's *Mañanas de abril y mayo (April and May Mornings)*.

[2]Here the words "communion" and "fast" have both religious overtones and associations with food. Quotations from Wycherley's works follow the first editions, with slight alterations in spelling and punctuation where the originals might present difficulty. Act and scene references are according to the Mermaid edition.

of the gentlemen is a libertine, the other is absurdly jealous. Wycherley relates both faults to a lack of faith in the intelligence and integrity of their mistresses, which comes close to the view held by the other characters that women can be treated as a form of property. An entertaining sequence of comic disasters finally purges them of their mistaken attitudes.

It is in his use of the stage setting to bind the action together that Wycherley shows the most originality.[3] St. James's Park, which gives the play its subtitle and where many of the incidents take place, looms over the whole action. The main title is itself a pun, for the phrase "in a wood" at this time meant "in confusion," and in the play the wooded park at night becomes a symbol of the confusion caused by the various intrigues that take place within it. Wycherley makes the new fashion of rambling in the park stand for the latest patterns of sexual behavior. St. James's Park had only recently been opened to the public; previously it had been a royal game preserve. How typical of modern life, Wycherley suggests. Gone are the old deer hunts; and, instead, men and women are now chasing one another in the park. It is a racy idea, handled with wit and subtlety. Wycherley made excellent dramatic use of darkness in his three finest comedies; and here a group of words such as "see" and "blind," in the metaphorical senses of "realize" and "deceived," give added meaning to the imaginary blackness of the stage. The various characters, muttering about the lack of light, keep mistaking one another in the dark, and in this way the stage scene gradually comes to represent a deeper misunderstanding. The park thus links up all the different forms of deception in the play, including the self-deception of the true lovers. The final confusion in the darkness unravels their mistakes, leading them "out of the dark" and away from the winding alleys between the trees, the bypaths of love "where we are still way-lay'd, with Surprizes, Trapans,[4] Dangers, and Murdering disappointments"; leaving the rest to grope their way through the gloomy wood of mistrust.

As one might expect, the play shows signs of inexperience. The dialogue is stiff in places; there are too many set pieces that have not been worked smoothly into the action. Above all, the plot contains unnecessary duplication. Wycherley had a great deal to say and had not yet learned the importance of sacrificing detail for the sake of clarity. Yet *Love in a Wood* was a breakthrough: a fully integrated comedy with a consistent, serious purpose.

THE GENTLEMAN DANCING-MASTER

The Gentleman Dancing-Master did not fulfill this early promise. A gayer work, more full of laughter, it is also more superficial. Were it not for the attack on "senseless Plays" in the prologue, one might be tempted to dismiss it merely as pleasant farce. The basic ingredients of the simple plot come from the common Restoration stockpot; some of the flavoring again comes from Spain.[5] The daughter of a wealthy merchant thwarts his scheme to marry her to a rich fool and wins a gentleman of her own choosing. It is not hard to see why the familiar story appealed to Wycherley. He hammers the implied message home in the closing lines:

> When Children marry, Parents shou'd obey,
> Since Love claims more Obedience far than they.
> (V.i)

Though there is plenty of farce, the action does have point: the incidents bring out effectively the connection between the father's sternness, the proposed bridegroom's unworthiness, and the daughter's rebellion. Whenever he can, Wycherley darts in with a sharp satiric thrust, such as this reply by the heroine, Hippolita, to her guardian aunt, Mrs. Caution:

> *Mrs. Caut.* Well, Malapert! I know you hate me, because I have been the Guardian of your Reputation. But your Husband may thank me one day.
> *Hipp.* If he be not a Fool, he would rather be oblig'd to me for my vertue than to you, since, at long run he must whether he will or no.
> (I. i. 263–268)

The richest comedy springs from the supposed naiveté of Hippolita, who is underestimated by

---

[3]The Restoration stages, unlike those on which Shakespeare's plays were first acted, used painted scenery that could be changed during performance.
[4]Trapans: traps, tricks.

[5]Wycherley developed a hint he found in Calderón's *El maestro de danzar* (*The Dancing Master*).

every other character, including her lover, Gerrard. The love scenes show Wycherley at his most charming; the mood of tenderness is enhanced by gentle humor and good sense:

Ger. How's this? you surprise me as much as when first I found so much Beauty and Wit in Company with so much Innocency. But, Dearest, I would be assur'd of what you say, and yet dare not ask the question. You h—— do not abuse me again, you h—— will fool me no more sure.

Hipp. Yes, but I will sure.

Ger. How! nay, I was afraid on't.

Hipp. For I say you are to be my Husband, and you say Husbands must be Wittols[6] and some strange things to boot.

Ger. Well, I will take my Fortune.

Hipp. But have a care, rash man.

Ger. I will venture.

Hipp. At your peril, remember I wish'd you to have a care, fore-warn'd, fore-arm'd.

Pru. Indeed now that's fair; for most men are fore-arm'd before they are warn'd.

Hipp. Plain dealing is some kind of honesty however, and few women wou'd have said so much.

Ger. None but those who wou'd delight in a Husband's jealousie, as the proof of his love and her honour.

Hipp. Hold, Sir, let us have a good understanding betwixt one another at first, that we may be long Friends; I differ from you in the point, for a Husband's jealousie, which cunning men wou'd pass upon their Wives for a Compliment, is the worst can be made 'em, for indeed it is a Compliment to their Beauty, but an affront to their Honour.

Ger. But, madam ——

Hipp. So that upon the whole matter I conclude, jealousie in a Gallant is humble true Love, and the height of respect, and only an undervaluing of himself to overvalue her; but in a Husband 'tis arrant sawciness, cowardise, and ill-breeding, and not to be suffer'd.

Ger. I stand corrected gracious Miss.

(V. i. 196–231)

Hippolita's sophisticated wit may seem unlikely in a middle-class girl of fourteen, but Wycherley needed her youth to emphasize the naturalness of her disobedience, and in his eyes no woman could be really desirable without a mature intelligence.

Paris, the proposed bridegroom, is among the best of the many Frenchified fops in Restoration comedy. With less malice than most of Wycherley's fools, he gives plenty of scope for the pathetic

[6]Wittol: a contented cuckold, a man who willingly accepts his wife's infidelity.

brand of clowning. Colley Cibber, the actor-dramatist immortalized in Pope's *Dunciad*, has given a lively description of James Nokes, the actor who almost certainly played the part on the first night:

In the ludicrous distresses, which by the laws of comedy, folly is often involv'd in; he sunk into such a mixture of piteous pusillanimity, and a consternation so rufully ridiculous and inconsolable, that when he had shook you, to a fatigue of laughter, it became a moot point whether you ought not to have pity'd him. When he debated any matter by himself, he would shut up his mouth with a dumb studious powt, and roll his full eye into such a vacant amazement, such a palpable ignorance of what to think of it, that his silent perplexity (which would sometimes hold him several minutes) gave your imagination as full content as the most absurd thing he could say upon it.

Given this style of acting, one can imagine the effect of the scene where Paris, who has been ordered to change into Spanish clothes, enters wearing a fantastic mixture of French and Spanish costumes and then, struggling to stop himself from swearing in French, pleads to be allowed to keep just his favorite French cravat.

Wycherley learned some useful lessons in writing this play. He now knew how to keep his action clear and uncluttered. The dialogue, with its quick exchange of short speeches, shows a new lightness of touch. There is none of the stiffness that marred his first play. But the thinness of the plot gave little scope for the rich exposition of ideas at which he excelled.

THE COUNTRY-WIFE

In *The Country-Wife* Wycherley succeeded in combining the thoughtfulness of his first play with the high spirits of his second. He had now turned to comedies by Molière for his plot material, and the example of the great French dramatist seems to have helped him to clarify his own aims. Certainly in *The Country-Wife* he has absolute control over his medium. Built partly out of incidents in *L'École des maris* (*The School for Husbands*) and *L'École des femmes* (*The School for Wives*), it is a masterpiece of dramatic design. The plot is planned as a detailed demonstration of the play's main thesis: the failure of contemporary marriage arrangements. Wycher-

WILLIAM WYCHERLEY

ley begins by supposing two typical arranged marriages. These are, as it were, the agreed premises necessary before any argument can take place. Pinchwife, a middle-aged rake, has deliberately picked as his wife a naive country girl, on the assumption that ignorance will keep a woman submissive and faithful. Sir Jaspar Fidget, an old businessman too occupied with business affairs to spend any time with his young wife, imagines he can prevent her thinking about other men by confining her to a trivial social life among safe companions of his own choosing. Blown up into the exaggerated form usual in comedy, these two marriages represent assumptions commonly held by men at the time. Wycherley sets out to show that they contain the seeds of their own destruction, contradictions that can only lead to unhappiness and infidelity. It only needs the appearance on the scene of a determined libertine, Horner, to spark off the inevitable explosion. Having spread the rumor that an attack of venereal disease has left him impotent, Horner becomes tame enough in Sir Jaspar's eyes to join the circle of friends he allows Lady Fidget. Once the opportunity presents itself, she and other women of the town, similarly starved for love, come rushing into the welcoming arms of Horner. The hypocritical mask of prudery, demanded of women by husbands and parents, drops, while the simple country wife develops all the brilliant cunning of a sophisticated townswoman in her efforts to tear a way through to her lover. A third marriage is being arranged. Pinchwife plans to give his sister Alithea to the affected Sparkish, a fool who thinks of her only as a means of making money and as a beautiful possession to show off to his friends. Here again an agent appears, Horner's companion, Harcourt, who opens Alithea's eyes to Sparkish's real motives and himself offers the genuine respect and affection on which they can build together a sound alternative to the diseased marriages all about them.

The action illustrates perfectly Horner's maxim that "a foolish Rival and a jealous Husband assist their Rival's Designs; for they are sure to make their Women hate them, which is the first step to their love, for another Man." Once the catalyzing agents are introduced, the process of change sets in quite automatically; to use Wycherley's own image, the disease spreads like an epidemic. Sir Jaspar actually forces Horner on his wife, so that he can get away to his business; just as Sparkish forces Harcourt on

Alithea, so that he can run off to the playhouse. As for Pinchwife, every effort he makes to keep his wife in ignorance only helps to teach her what he wishes to conceal. The situation is rich in irony. The very simplicity of his wife, the quality for which he married her, leaves him completely helpless. Here he is explaining why he has forbidden her to go to the theater:

Mr. Pin. First, you like the Actors, and the Gallants may like you.
Mrs. Pin. What, a homely Country Girl? no, Bud, no body will like me.
Mr. Pin. I tell you, yes, they may.
Mrs. Pin. No, no, you jest—I won't believe you, I will go.
Mr. Pin. I tell you then, that one of the lewdest Fellows in Town, who saw you there, told me he was in love with you.
Mrs. Pin. Indeed! who, who, pray who wast?

(II. i. 99–105)

Every step Pinchwife takes to protect his wife brings her closer to her lover. As his treatment grows more cruel, she grows correspondingly more cunning. The humor involves continuous use of dramatic irony. The audience has been shown the logical fallacy in Pinchwife's method and knows that his disappointment is quite unavoidable, that all his efforts are as futile as King Lear's shouts against the wind and rain. No hint of tragedy creeps in, since Pinchwife has only himself to blame for his suffering. The country wife does not need our pity, since she remains imperturbable even with a knife thrust in her face. Here Pinchwife is forcing her to write a rude letter to Horner:

Mrs. Pin. Indeed, and indeed, but I won't, so I won't.
Mr. Pin. Why?
Mrs. Pin. Because he's in Town, you may send for him if you will.
Mr. Pin. Very well, you wou'd have him brought to you; is it come to this? I say take the pen and write, or you'll provoke me.
Mrs. Pin. Lord, what d'ye make a fool of me for? Don't I know that Letters are never writ, but from the Countrey to *London*, and from *London* into the Countrey; now he's in Town, and I am in Town too; therefore I can't write to him you know.
Mr. Pin. So I am glad it is no worse, she is innocent enough yet. *[Aside]*
Yes you may when your Husband bids you write Letters to people that are in Town.

315

Mrs. Pin. O may I so! Then I'm satisfied.

Mr. Pin. Come begin—Sir—   [*Dictates*]

Mrs. Pin. Shan't I say, Dear Sir? You know one says always something more than bare Sir.

Mr. Pin. Write as I bid you, or I will write Whore with this Penknife in your Face.

Mrs. Pin. Nay good Bud—Sir—   [*She writes*]

Mr. Pin. Though I suffer'd last night your nauseous, loath'd Kisses and Embraces—Write.

Mrs. Pin. Nay, why shou'd I say so, you know I told you, he had a sweet breath.

Mr. Pin. Write.

Mrs. Pin. Let me but put out, loath'd.

Mr. Pin. Write I say!

Mrs. Pin. Well then.   [*Writes*]

Mr. Pin. Let's see what have you writ?—[*Takes the paper and reads*]. Though I suffer'd last night your kisses and embraces—Thou impudent creature, where is nauseous and loath'd?

Mrs. Pin. I can't abide to write such filthy words.

(IV. ii. 72–103)

But having learned the use of the words, she is ready enough to apply them to her husband when the occasion arises. This splendid action leads up to a forceful dramatic symbol. His wife being heavily disguised, Pinchwife unwittingly takes her by the hand and leads her into the arms of her lover.

How fresh and unforced Wycherley's wit seems in these scenes! Yet all the time he is building up connections, searching out the root causes of the folly he is satirizing. Sir Jaspar, Sparkish, and Pinchwife seem, on the face of it, completely unlike one another. One is a businessman; one a dilettante; one a rake turned countryman. Pinchwife guards his wife like a jailer; Sir Jaspar and Sparkish cannot escape from their women quickly enough. Wycherley finds a common connection: a refusal to recognize that women have an intelligence equal to that of men. That "sweet, soft, gentle, tame, noble Creature Woman, made for Man's Companion"— Sir Jaspar's phrase captures exactly that mixture of reverence and contempt that, for more than two centuries, reduced women to the position of idolized slaves. Wycherley understood that there was really nothing to choose between the praise of a Sir Jaspar and the contempt of a Pinchwife who saw women as "dough-bak'd, senseless, indocile animals," or the scorn of a Sparkish who felt that "virtue makes a Woman as troublesome, as a little reading or learning." They all contained the assumption expressed so crudely in Pinchwife's

description of his wife as "my own Free-hold"; and they all led to tyranny, whether the physical imprisonment of Mrs. Pinchwife or the intellectual imprisonment of Lady Fidget.

Wycherley's satire on the affectation of Lady Fidget and her companions is a real tour de force. Words such as *honor, innocent, virtue, reputation, noble,* and *breeding* appear over and over again in situations that undercut their ordinary meaning, until Wycherley only has to introduce one of them to get a laugh. In the scene where Lady Fidget discovers Horner's virility, he slyly attacks the word *honor* until it becomes almost obscene. Lady Fidget has, as Wycherley puts it, so much honor in her mouth, that she has none elsewhere:

Lady Fid. But, poor Gentleman, cou'd you be so generous? so truly a Man of honour, as for the sakes of us Women of honour, to cause your self to be reported no Man? No Man! and to suffer your self the greatest shame that cou'd fall upon a Man, that none might fall upon us Women by your conversation; but indeed, Sir, as perfectly, perfectly, the same Man as before your going into *France*, Sir; as perfectly, perfectly, Sir?

Hor. As perfectly, perfectly, Madam; nay, I scorn you shou'd take my word; I desire to be try'd only, Madam.

Lady Fid. Well, that's spoken again like a Man of honour, all Men of honour desire to come to the test: But indeed, generally you Men report such things of your selves, one does not know how, or whom to believe; and it is come to that pass, we dare not take your words, no more than your Taylors, without some staid Servant of yours be bound with you; but I have so strong a faith in your honour, dear, dear, noble Sir, that I'd forfeit mine for yours at any time, dear Sir.

Hor. No, Madam, you shou'd not need to forfeit it for me, I have given you security already to save you harmless, my late reputation being so well known in the World, Madam.

Lady Fid. But if upon any future falling out, or upon a suspicion of my taking the trust out of your hands, to employ some other, you your self should betray your trust, dear Sir; I mean, if you'l give me leave to speak obscenely, you might tell, dear Sir.

Hor. If I did, nobody wou'd believe me; the reputation of impotency is as hardly recover'd again in the World, as that of cowardise, dear Madam.

Lady Fid. Nay then, as one may say, you may do your worst, dear, dear, Sir.

Sir Jas. Come, is your Ladyship reconciled to him yet? have you agreed on matters? for I must be gone to *Whitehall*.

(II. i. 522–553)

Although he ridicules the pretended virtue of society ladies like Lady Fidget, Wycherley is not wholly unsympathetic toward them. He shows that their deceitfulness develops naturally as a reaction to the cruelty and indifference of men. The progress of the country wife demonstrates exactly how craft grows in response to tyranny. The women are not ultimately responsible for their behavior, and so they are left unpunished at the end of the play. But they are not rewarded with the happiness at which the true lovers, Alithea and Harcourt, arrive. "Love," as Alithea remarks, "proceeds from esteem"; and esteem cannot exist side by side with hypocrisy.

Though he obviously believed passionately in what he was saying, Wycherley in this play never gives the impression that he is preaching. Mainly, of course, this is owing to his perpetual delight in the absurd; but another important reason is the remarkable fluency of his dialogue. In one sense the language is more artificial than anything he had written before. We have already seen something of his ingenious use of double meanings, and images of every kind abound. There can hardly be another comedy in English that contains so many similes. Nevertheless, the speeches seem tailored to fit the different characters. Take one of the many passages where Wycherley builds up the idea that sexual desire is spreading like a disease. Spoken by Margery Pinchwife, it involves an extremely elaborate play on words associated with illness. The organization of the sentences is actually highly sophisticated. Yet, with its simple words, mostly of one syllable only, and its tiny clauses, it has the very ring of a naive, childlike person talking to herself:

Well, 'tis e'en so, I have got the *London* disease, they call Love, I am sick of my Husband, and for my Gallant; I have heard this distemper, call'd a Feaver, but methinks 'tis liker an Ague, for when I think of my Husband, I tremble and am in a cold sweat, and have inclinations to vomit, but when I think of my Gallant, dear Mr. *Horner*, my hot fit comes, and I am all in a Feaver, indeed, & as in other Feavers my own Chamber is tedious to me, and I would fain be remov'd to his, and then methinks I shou'd be well.

(IV. iv. 1–9)

Compare this with the conversation between Pinchwife and Sparkish a little further on. They are carrying on with the same analogy, but Sparkish

appears foolish and affected, Pinchwife grave and pompous:

Spar. Lord, how shy you are of your Wife, but let me tell you Brother, we men of wit have amongst us a saying, that Cuckolding like the small Pox comes with a fear, and you may keep your Wife as much as you will out of danger of infection, but if her constitution incline her to't, she'l have it sooner or later by the world, say they.

Pin. What a thing is a Cuckold, that every fool can make him ridiculous— [*Aside*]
Well Sir—But let me advise you, now you are come to be concern'd, because you suspect the danger, not to neglect the means to prevent it, especially when the greatest share of the Malady will light upon your own head....

(IV. iv. 67–77)

In *The Country-Wife* Wycherley brought to perfection his system of writing in maxims. Here a warning may be necessary. One tends to assume that any finely expressed idea in a play carries with it the author's approval. Wycherley's maxims, however, take their place in the normal course of the dialogue. Each character is given witty sentiments appropriate to his special situation and peculiar cast of thought. These may well be the exact opposite of Wycherley's own beliefs. The main advantage of the method is that it allows the dramatist to draw out the general significance of a situation without interrupting the flow of the action. Examined closely, some scenes in *The Country-Wife* seem perilously near to formal and static debate, but, in fact, they are moving the plot forward at the same time. Consider the remarkable scene where Horner worms out of Pinchwife his real reasons for marrying a country wife. On the story level, Pinchwife is being teased about his marriage and his past life by the three young men, Horner, Harcourt, and Dorilant. It is part of the torture he has inflicted on himself, and the audience enjoys watching him squirm. But the teasing, an ingenious analogy with gambling spread over several speeches, takes the form of a series of general maxims. These raise the particular scene to a more abstract level, where Pinchwife becomes only one of thousands, and where Wycherley is able to establish a wider connection between licentiousness and jealousy:

Hor. But tell me, has Marriage cured thee of whoring, which it seldom does?

Har. 'Tis more than age can do.

Hor. No, the word is, I'll marry and live honest; but a Marriage vow is like a penitent Gamester's Oath, and en-tring into Bonds, and penalties to stint himself to such a particular small sum at play for the future, which makes him but the more eager, and not being able to hold out, loses his Money again, and his forfeit to boot.

Dor. Ay, ay, a Gamester will be a Gamester, whilst his Money lasts; and a Whoremaster, whilst his vigour.

Har. Nay, I have known 'em, when they are broke and can lose no more, keep a fumbling with the Box in their hands to fool with only, and hinder other Gamesters.

Dor. That had wherewithall to make lusty stakes.

Pin. Well, Gentlemen, you may laugh at me, but you shall never lye with my Wife, I know the Town.

Hor. But prithee, was not the way you were in better, is not keeping better than Marriage?

Pin. A Pox on't, the Jades wou'd jilt me, I cou'd never keep a Whore to my self.

Hor. So then you only marry'd to keep a Whore to your self; well, but let me tell you, Women, as you say, are like Souldiers made constant and loyal by good pay, rather than by Oaths and Covenants, therefore I'd advise my Friends to keep rather than marry; since too I find by your example, it does not serve one's turn, for I saw you yesterday in the eighteen penny place with a pretty Country-wench.

Pin. How the Divel, did he see my wife then? I sate there that she might not be seen; but she shall never go to a play again.　　　　　　　　　　　　　　　[*Aside*]

Horner's generalization here slides perfectly easily into the particular information that he has seen Mrs. Pinchwife. Pinchwife's embarrassment now leads back quite naturally to a further generalization:

Hor. What dost thou blush at nine-and-forty, for having been seen with a Wench?

Dor. No Faith, I warrant 'twas his Wife, which he seated there out of sight, for he's a cunning Rogue, and understands the Town.

Har. He blushes, then 'twas his Wife; for Men are now more ashamed to be seen with them in publick, than with a Wench.

(I. i. 410–439; 440–445)

It is difficult to imagine a finer medium for dramatic satire. Packed with meaning, the speeches can carry as much imagery as verse; yet they have all the speed and vigor of colloquial prose.

The Country-Wife is certainly one of the great English comedies. It has gusto, abundant wit, and perfect form. Moreover, its shapely structure is no mere embellishment of style; it is the instrument with which Wycherley probes social behavior to achieve that "studied insight into the springs of character" that Hazlitt admired so much.

THE PLAIN-DEALER

It was *The Plain-Dealer*, and not *The Country-Wife*, that made the deepest impression on fellow writers and critics. Wycherley's last comedy had a new earnestness: that unmistakable note of moral seriousness that critical theory insisted the best literature ought to have. It struck the literary world as the grandest, most worthy comedy of the age. But the general public does not always take the favorite of the critics to its heart. *The Plain-Dealer* did not arouse the spontaneous enthusiasm that had greeted *The Country-Wife*. The first-night audience had to be prodded into applauding by its betters, and, though the play remained in the repertory for a century, it was less popular than many other Restoration comedies. The instinct of the ordinary theatergoer in this instance proved sounder than the considered verdict of the critics. *The Plain-Dealer* is an interesting, in many ways an admirable, play, but it is less than a masterpiece.

For the first time Wycherley had difficulty in adapting his source material to his own purposes. The play is based on Molière's great comedy *Le Misanthrope*, which deals with an embittered man who, shocked at the hypocrisy and corruption around him, deliberately sets out to make a martyr of himself. The French play contains some satire on affectation and injustice, but its main purpose is to plead for compromise, for a sense of proportion; and its ridicule falls mostly on the central figure of the misanthropist. Wycherley had no more of the man-hater about him than Molière, but he was more intent on satirizing society in *The Plain-Dealer*. He decided that the figure of the misanthropist could be turned into an excellent satiric spokesman. Being a balanced and urbane man himself, however, he could not resist keeping something of Molière's ridicule of extremism. The result is confusing. Sometimes one is looking at society through the eyes of the misanthrope Manly; sometimes one is looking at him critically from the outside.

But the failure of the play goes deeper. Wycherley

was finally moving away from the analysis of a particular social problem to a more general indictment of society. This in itself deserves praise, for it is unique on the Restoration stage. Yet one is forced to ask whether Wycherley was really equipped to make a sweeping comment of this kind. Moving only in a small social circle, how could he be? He did what he could. He put more stress than ever before on treachery among friends and on the flattery of courtiers. He also brought in the one other field he knew well—the law. But he was unable to invent incidents strong enough to support the ambitious generalizations he wanted to make. He relied, instead, on the long tirades of his plain dealer, Manly:

... here you see a *Bishop* bowing low to a gaudy *Atheist*; a Judge to a Door-keeper; a great Lord, to a Fishmonger, or a Scrivener with a Jack-chain about his neck; a Lawyer, to a Serjeant at Arms; a velvet *Physician*, to a threadbare Chymist: and a supple Gentleman Usher, to a surly Beef-eater: and so tread round in a preposterous huddle of Ceremony to each other, whil'st they can hardly hold their solemn false countenances. . . .

... here thou wilt live to be cherish'd by Fortune and the great ones; for thou may'st easily come to out-flatter a dull Poet, out-lie a Coffee-house or Gazette-writer, out-swear a Knight of the Post,[7] out-watch a Pimp, out-fawn a Rook,[8] out-promise a Lover, out-rail a Wit, and out-brag a Sea-Captain.

(I. i. 323–330; 400–406)

Forceful all this may be, but it cries out for a plot of great range, the kind of plot Jonson could offer, sweeping through every corner of society from the palace to the gutter. In fact, *The Plain-Dealer* only tells the story of a man who is betrayed by his friend and jilted by his mistress. It is too flimsy to bear the weight of Wycherley's wholesale indictment.

This weakness helps to explain the unsatisfactory figure of Fidelia, a woman dressed in boy's clothes, who follows Manly through all his dangers and distresses with doglike devotion. Wycherley was an optimist at heart. He always included in his comedies characters who stood for the right way of doing things. In the earlier plays, the true lovers, who join in an intelligent, equal partnership, provide an effective and convincing contrast to the particular

[7]Knight of the post: a man hired to give false evidence in court.
[8]Rook: a swindler.

evil of mercenary marriage. Now, Wycherley obviously needed a more comprehensive good alternative. Fidelia was his answer, a character representing faithfulness, whose blank verse soliloquies were meant to arouse deep compassion. As an answer to social corruption she seems totally ineffective. One feels that Wycherley is asking decent personal relationships to solve weaknesses in the structure of society. Moreover, the solemnity with which he handles Fidelia strikes an utterly false note in the comedy.

"In Works of Wit and Fancy," Wycherley wrote, "everything that is not perfectly excellent displeases." Fortunately this is only a half truth, and there is much to please in *The Plain-Dealer*. On familiar ground he is as entertaining as ever. Manly's outspokenness gives rise to plenty of amusing satire. His effect on the polite world is rather like that of a nasty smell. This is how he receives the genteel Lord Plausible:

L. Plaus. What, will you be singular then, like no Body? follow, love, and esteem no Body?
Man. Rather than be general, like you; follow every Body, court and kiss every Body; though, perhaps at the same time, you hate every Body.
L. Plaus. Why, seriously with your pardon, my dear Friend—
Man. With your pardon, my no Friend, I will not, as you do whisper my hatred, or my scorn, call a man Fool or Knave, by signs, or mouths over his shoulder, whil'st you have him in your arms: for such as you, like common Whores and Pickpockets, are only dangerous to those you embrace.
L. Plaus. Such as I! Heavens defend me!—upon my Honour—
Man. Upon your Title, my Lord, if you'd have me believe you.

(I. i. 17–34)

When the marriage of Vernish and Olivia, Manly's false friend and mistress, falls apart, the results are riotously funny, with both husband and wife chasing lustfully after the epicene Fidelia. "Did you not hear my Husband say, he found me with a Woman in Man's clothes?" asks Olivia. "And d'ye think he does not know a Man from a Woman." "Not so well, I'm sure, as you do," her cousin replies. When Olivia receives her lover in the dark only to discover that the man in her arms is her husband, her reaction is unforgettable: "Ha! my Husband returned! and have I been throwing away so many kind Kisses on my Husband, and wrong'd my Lover already?"

The play also succeeds in capturing something of the robust spirit of earlier English comedy. With its sailors and lawyers and bailiffs, it shows a wider, rougher world than his other plays. Towering above the rest stands the forbidding figure of the Widow Blackacre, a woman eaten up by a passion for legal brawling, a mother who has crushed all the independence out of her miserable son, Jerry:

Go, save thy breath for the Cause; talk at the Bar, Mr. *Quaint*: You are so copiously fluent, you can weary any one's ears, sooner than your own tongue. Go, weary our Adversaries Counsel, and the Court: Go, thou art a fine-spoken person: Adad, I shall make thy wife jealous of me: if you can but court the Court into a Decree for us. Go, get you gone, and remember—[*Whispers*] [*Exit* Quaint].
Come, Mr. *Blunder*, pray bawl soundly for me, at the *Kings-Bench*; bluster, sputter, question, cavil; but be sure your Argument be intricate enough, to confound the Court; And then you do my business. Talk what you will, but be sure your tongue never stand still; for your own noise will secure your Sense from Censure: 'tis like coughing or heming when one has got the Belly-ake, which stifles the unmannerly noise. Go, dear Rogue, and succeed; and I'll invite thee, ere it be long, to more souz'd Venison.

(III. i. 199–215)

The Widow Blackacre has all that vigorous, abusive speech the Elizabethans delighted in, a gift for the absurdly mundane image. She is derived from characters like Ursula, the pig woman, in Jonson's *Bartholomew Fair*, and she looks forward to Congreve's Lady Wishfort. She is essentially English—with a coarseness French audiences would not have tolerated—but full of life. This is her reply to an old fellow who proposes marriage:

Wid. Thou sensless, impertinent, quibling, driveling, feeble, paralytic, impotent, fumbling, frigid Nincompoop!
Jerr. Hey, brave Mother, for calling of names, ifac!
Wid. Wou'dst thou make a Caudlemaker,[9] a Nurse of me? Can't you be Bed-rid without a Bed-fellow? Won't your Swan-skins, Furs, Flannels, and the scorch'd Trencher[10] keep you warm there? Wou'd you have me your Scotch warming-Pan,[11] with a Pox to you? Me!—

(II. i. 978–985)

[9]Caudle: gruel mixed with wine and spices.
[10]Scorched trencher: a wooden dish heated to warm a bed.
[11]Scotch warming pan: a slang phrase for a prostitute.

If the liveliness of *The Plain-Dealer* needs any further testimony, what more impressive than the enthusiasm of the great French satirist, Voltaire, who declared that he did not know a single comedy, ancient or modern, that contained so much wit.

POEMS AND MAXIMS

SOME twenty years later, Wycherley began to turn out verse in enormous quantity. His debts had forced him to pocket his pride, and he was now making a business of writing. He was no poet, and he knew it. In the errata list to the collection published during his lifetime, "that Damnd Miscellany of Madrigals of mine," as he called it, he disarmingly included "the Whole BOOK." The wits, who had long looked forward to a new work by their leader, had to agree. Wycherley had relied on his good sense and his genius for paradox to carry him through. But his readers demanded a certain minimum of grace and elegance. This Wycherley could not provide. His satires were rambling and shapeless, and even his songs could not be scanned. Senile decay must have been partly responsible, as he had once been able to write competent lyrics for his plays.

The satires shed further light on his beliefs, but there is little that cannot be deduced from the comedies. Once again he attacks misers, poor wits, fortune hunters, and flatterers. One poem proves that priests are worse than pimps, because marriage is more mercenary than prostitution; another shows that business is really idleness because the results of its activity are futile. Some of the lighthearted, risqué love songs might amuse the casual reader, though the titles are often as witty as the poems themselves, and sometimes almost as long: "To a *Fine Singer*, who had gotten a *Cold*; and, whose *Lover* endeavour'd to stop Her *Tongue* in Her *Mouth* with His, to save her *Honour*, (as He call'd it.)"; "To a fine Young *Woman*, who being ask'd by her Lover, *Why she kept so filthy a thing as a Snake in her Bosom*; answer'd, *'Twas to keep a filthier thing out of it, his Hand*; and, *that her Snake was to play with, and cool her in hot Weather*; which was his Aversion." One or two of the drinking songs come near to the gracious ease one expects from a good Restoration lyric:

Reason our Foe, let us destroy,
   Which still disturbs us, when we drink;
Which lets us not our selves enjoy,
   But puts us to the pains to think.

But even here the clumsiness of the third line intrudes.

In looking over the poems, Pope kept making the sensible suggestion that Wycherley turn some of the wittier paradoxes into prose maxims, after the manner of La Rochefoucauld and other French writers. Wycherley evidently took the proposal to heart, for the papers published after his death include a collection of over three hundred such maxims. With these he was far more at home:

MAY we not fairly say Marriage makes more Sinners than free Love, since it forces most of its Disciples, first or last, to Repentance?

Anyone who has admired the maxims George Bernard Shaw published with *Man and Superman* would appreciate Wycherley's collection. Not all are original, however. He kept a volume of maxims by various French writers in front of him, and halfway through he began translating, carefully taking one from each author in turn so that no one would notice the extent of his borrowing. One feels almost ashamed that modern scholarship should have found him out. But he had an excellent defense, for, as he insisted in the preface to his *Miscellany Poems*, necessity "is always an Excuse for all Thefts."

Wycherley would not have wanted to be remembered for his dotages, for works created in need. He had been the great dramatist of the 1670's, writing then for pleasure, not for business. He had seen his plays direct the course of English drama for thirty years. The best of the younger dramatists had all followed in his footsteps. Congreve had refined upon his wit; Vanbrugh had inherited something of his seriousness. But neither had launched out in strikingly new directions. Until the arrival of sentimental comedy at the turn of the century, his own *Plain-Dealer* had remained the most significant attempt to move away from the pattern set by *The Country-Wife*.

He can hardly affect us as deeply now as he did his contemporaries. The social problems in which he was most interested have lost their urgency, though there are many countries where his satire on arranged marriage would still seem relevant and challenging. But he has survived remarkably well the hazards that befall any writer who concentrates on the social scene. We do not have to learn outdated jargon to understand him. There are few of those topical details that make performance of Ben Jonson's comedies so difficult. If we have to rebuild in our imagination the conditions in which he lived, little effort is needed to understand his beliefs. The deep-rooted faith in the intellectual equality of women that runs through all his work and the importance he attached to sound personal relationships in a world crippled by self-interest compel our sympathy. Despite the cries that he is obscene, or morbid, or trivial, on his rare appearances in the theater he is still able to set audiences laughing in the same critical spirit that he intended.

SELECTED BIBLIOGRAPHY

I. COLLECTED WORKS. *Miscellany Poems* (London, 1704); *The Works* (London, 1713; repr., 1720, 1731, 1735; Dublin, 1733; etc.); L. Theobald, ed., *The Posthumous Works* (London, 1728), contains poems, a collection of maxims, and a memoir by R. Pack; A. Pope, ed., *The Posthumous Works*, II (London, 1729), not a continuation of the previous work but an attempt to prove Theobald's unreliability as an editor, contains different texts of some poems and the Wycherley-Pope correspondence; L. Hunt, ed., *The Dramatic Works of Wycherley, Congreve, Vanbrugh, and Farquhar* (London, 1840); W. C. Ward, ed., *Plays* (London, 1888), in the original Mermaid series; M. Summers, ed., *The Complete Works*, 4 vols. (lim. ed., London, 1924), amply annotated but textually unreliable; G. Weales, ed., *The Complete Plays* (New York, 1966), textually sound and fully annotated.

II. CORRESPONDENCE. J. Dennis, W. Wycherley et al., *Letters upon Several Occasions* (London, 1696); G. Sherburn, ed., *The Correspondence of Alexander Pope*, 5 vols. (Oxford, 1956), vol. I contains the Pope–Wycherley correspondence.

III. SEPARATE WORKS. *Hero and Leander, in Burlesque* (London, 1669), published anonymously; *Love in a Wood; or, St. James's Park* (London, 1672); *The Gentleman Dancing-Master* (London, 1673); *The Country-Wife* (London, 1675), also in T. H. Fujimura, ed. (Lincoln, Nebr., 1965), J. D. Hunt, ed. (London, 1973), and D. Cook and J. Swannell, eds. (London, 1975); adaptations by J. Lee, ed. (London, 1765), D. Garrick, ed. (London, 1766), appeared as *The Country Girl*, B. C. d'Arien, ed., *Das Landmaedchen oder Weiberlist geht uber Alles*

(Schwerin–Weimar, 1794); *The Plain-Dealer* (London, 1677), also in L. Hughes, ed. (Lincoln, Nebr., 1967), F. M. A. de Voltaire, *Oeuvres de M. de Voltaire*, III (Dresden, 1748), with adaptations and titled *La Prude ou la gardeuse de cassette*, I. Bickerstaffe, ed. (London, 1766; rev. ed., 1796), revised by J. P. Kemble; *Epistles to the King and Duke* (London, 1682), published anonymously; *The Folly of Industry* (London, 1704; reiss., 1705), reissued as *The Idleness of Business: A Satyr*; *On His Grace the Duke of Marlborough* (London, 1707), published anonymously. *Note*: Three short poems were first published in miscellaneous collections of verse by various authors: "The Answer" to "A Letter from Mr. *Shadwell*, to Mr. *Wicherly*" in *Poems on Affairs of State, Part III* (London, 1698); "To My Friend, Mr. *Pope*, on His Pastorals" in *Poetical Miscellanies: The Sixth Part* (London, 1709); "An Epistle to Mr. *Dryden*, from Mr. *Wycherley*. Occasion'd by His Proposal To Write a Comedy Together" in *Poems on Several Occasions* (London, 1717), Wycherley's prologue to C. Trotter's *Agnes de Castro* appeared in the 1st ed., 1696.

IV. Some Biographical and Critical Studies. A. Boyer, ed., *Letters of Wit, Politicks and Morality* (London, 1701), includes a memoir by G. Granville, Lord Lansdowne; Sir R. Steele, *The Tatler*, No. 3 (London, 1709); C. Gildon, *Memoirs of the Life of William Wycherley, Esq.* (London, 1718), published anonymously, includes Lansdowne's memoir; J. Dennis, "Letters on Milton and Wycherley" (London, 1722), reprinted with other works containing critical and biographical remarks on Wycherley in E. N. Hooker, ed., *The Critical Works of John Dennis*, 2 vols. (Baltimore, 1939–1943); F. M. A. de Voltaire, *Letters Concerning the English Nation* (London, 1733); W. C. Hazlitt, *Lectures on the English Comic Writers* (London, 1819), includes "On Wycherley, Congreve, Vanbrugh and Farquhar"; J. Spence, *Anecdotes, Observations, and Characters, of Books and Men* (London, 1820), contains Pope's reported comments on Wycherley; C. Lamb, *Elia* (London, 1823), includes "On the Artificial Comedy of the Last Century"; T. B. Macaulay, "The Dramatic Works of Wycherley, Congreve, Vanbrugh, and Farquhar" in *Edinburgh Review*, 22 (1841), a review of Hunt's ed., above; C. Cowden Clarke, "Wycherley and Congreve" in *The Gentleman's Magazine*, 7 (1871); J. Palmer, *The Comedy of Manners* (London,

1913); G. H. Nettleton, *English Drama of the Restoration and Eighteenth Century* (New York, 1914); C. Perromat, *William Wycherley, Sa vie—son oeuvre* (Paris, 1921); A. Nicoll, *A History of Restoration Drama, 1660–1700* (Cambridge, 1923), revised as *A History of English Drama 1660–1900*, I (Cambridge, 1952); B. Dobrée, *Restoration Comedy* (Oxford, 1924); J. W. Krutch, *Comedy and Conscience After the Restoration* (New York, 1924); H. T. E. Perry, *The Comic Spirit in Restoration Drama* (New York, 1925); K. M. Lynch, *The Social Mode of Restoration Comedy* (New York, 1926); W. Archer, *The Old Drama and the New* (London, 1929); W. Connely, *Brawny Wycherley: First Master in English Modern Comedy* (London, 1930); H. Granville-Barker, *On Dramatic Method* (London, 1931), includes "Wycherley and Dryden"; G. Sherburn, *The Early Career of Alexander Pope* (Oxford, 1934), gives the best account of Wycherley's relations with Pope; J. Wilcox, *The Relation of Molière to Restoration Comedy* (New York, 1938); L. C. Knights, *Explorations* (London, 1946), includes "Restoration Comedy: The Reality and the Myth"; J. H. Smith, *The Gay Couple in Restoration Comedy* (Cambridge, Mass., 1948); J. H. Wilson, *The Court Wits of the Restoration* (Princeton, 1948); W. Empson, *The Structure of Complex Words* (London, 1951); L. Kronenberger, *The Thread of Laughter* (New York, 1952); T. H. Fujimura, *The Restoration Comedy of Wit* (Princeton, 1952); N. N. Holland, *The First Modern Comedies* (Cambridge, Mass., 1959); W. Van Lennep, ed., *The London Stage, 1660–1800. Part I, 1660–1700* (Carbondale, Ill., 1965); J. R. Brown and B. Harris, eds., *Restoration Theatre*, Stratford-upon-Avon Studies 6 (London, 1965); R. Zimbardo, *Wycherley's Drama* (New Haven, 1965); J. Loftis, ed., *Restoration Drama* (New York, 1966); E. Miner, ed., *Restoration Dramatists* (Englewood Cliffs, N.J., 1966); J. H. Wilson, *A Preface to Restoration Drama* (Cambridge, Mass., 1968); J. R. Sutherland, *English Literature of the Late Seventeenth Century* (Oxford, 1969); I. Donaldson, *The World Upside Down* (Oxford, 1970); K. Muir, *The Comedy of Manners* (London, 1970); B. R. Schneider, Jr., *The Ethos of Restoration Comedy* (Urbana, Ill., 1971); K. M. Rogers, *William Wycherley* (New York, 1972); D. Bruce, *Topics of Restoration Comedy* (London, 1974); W. R. Chadwick, *The Four Plays of William Wycherley* (The Hague–Paris, 1975).

SIR JOHN VANBRUGH
(1664-1726)

Bernard Harris

THE MODEL OF THE MIND

IN 1703, during the absence abroad of Jacob Tonson, printer and founder of the Kit-Cat Club, John Vanbrugh fitted up a room in Tonson's house, Barn Elms, Surrey, for future meetings of the club, and Sir Godfrey Kneller undertook to adorn its walls with portraits of their fellow members. Both affairs were in a radiant muddle by the middle of June, when Vanbrugh wrote to Tonson in Amsterdam:[1]

Sr Godfrey has been most in fault. The fool has got a country house near Hampton Court, and is so busy about fitting it up (to receive nobody), that there is no getting him to work. Carpenter Johns, too is almost as bad. I went up yesterday under a tylt (as everybody has done that has gone by water these three weeks, for the Devils in the sky); there's all in disorder still; every room is chips—up to your chin!

The disorder within was matched by nature's disarray:

Neighbour Burgess has been too honest; the pease and beans ly all languishing upon the earth; not a cod has been gathered. There will be a hundred thousand apricocks ripe in ten days; they are now fairer and forwarder than what I saw at the Queens table at Windsor on Sunday —and such strawberrys as never were tasted: currants red as blood to; and gooseberrys, peaches, pairs, apples, and plumbs to gripe the gutts of a nation.

The vivid phrasing of this plea for Tonson to come home is part of the special appeal of Vanbrugh's world, that paradise running to seed, where evil manifested itself most obviously in the English weather, and punishment was consequent upon an appetite for fruit; it was a world of convivial human energy and prodigal bounty, and possessed, in a Shakespearean expression, "double vigour, art and nature."

Kneller's pictures no longer hang in "Jovial Jacob's academic room," but in the National Portrait Gallery. Here it is still possible

> by turns in breathing paint to trace
> The Wit's gay Air, or Poet's genial face.[2]

Vanbrugh, Sir Samuel Garth, and William Congreve—Pope's "three most honest-hearted, real good men of the poetical members of the Kit Cat Club"—kept company with Addison and Steele. Yet the club's atmosphere was scarcely literary, despite Tonson's inspiration, and in the first years of the eighteenth century it was a meeting place for Whigs of diverse character and power. Devoted to tippling, mutton pies, toastings, and light verse, the Kit-Cats shared a determination to preserve the Protestant cause and secure the Hanoverian succession. Among them were the earl of Halifax, sometime chancellor of the exchequer; the earl of Carlisle, twice first lord of the treasury; the dukes of Manchester and Newcastle; Viscount Cobham; Robert Walpole, the ascendant politician of that era; and John Churchill, duke of Marlborough, its military hero.

Halifax and Manchester were patrons of Vanbrugh's theatrical career, and his name as an architect is inseparable from such great houses as Castle Howard, built for Carlisle, Kimbolton, Claremont, and Stowe, where Manchester, Newcastle, and Cobham employed him respectively. Blenheim Palace, the nation's tribute to Marlborough, became Vanbrugh's most celebrated en-

---

[1]Quotations from letters and plays are taken from B. Dobrée and G. Webb, eds., *The Works of Sir John Vanbrugh*, 4 vols. (London, 1927).

[2]William Collins, *Drafts and Fragments of Verse*, edited by J. S. Cunningham (Oxford, 1956), p.21.

deavor, and only through Walpole's intervention was he paid for it. But Vanbrugh's relationships with patrons and clients were fuller than such terms imply, and were neatly expressed in Rowe's verses on "The Reconcilement between Jacob Tonson and Mr. Congreve":

I'm in with captain Vanburgh at the present,
A most *sweet-natur'd* gentleman, and pleasant;
He writes your comedies, draws schemes, and models,
And builds dukes' houses upon very odd hills:
For him, so much I dote on him, that I
If I were sure to go to heaven, would die.

Vanbrugh made his way to fame in that brilliant society—whether as Captain Vanbrugh, the soldier playwright, along with Captain Steele and Captain Farquhar; as Brother Van, the clubman and wit; or as Sir John Vanbrugh, architect of genius—because his nature proved so eminently capable of entertaining, evoking, and exhibiting the tastes of the period for both comedy and grandeur.

John Vanbrugh was christened on 24 January 1664 at his father's house in the parish of St. Nicolas Acons. To this area of merchant activity his grandfather, Gillis van Brugg of Ghent, had fled from Alva's persecution, changed nationality, married an Englishwoman, and set about recreating a dynasty whose ancestors had included a praetor of Ypres in 1383. Giles, their second son, married Elizabeth Barker, daughter of Sir Dudley Carleton, and John was the first surviving son of their nineteen children.

By 1667, Giles Vanbrugh had set up as a sugar baker in Chester, where he developed a sound business, kept company with religious dissenters, and concocted an unstable plan for the sack of Rome and the theft of the Vatican Library. John seems to have inherited something of this ambitious spirit, but he displayed a lifelong contempt for churchmen and for the provident virtues of tradesmen.

Nothing is known of his education and early life, until he was commissioned in the earl of Huntingdon's foot regiment on 30 January 1686, only to resign in August. At his father's death, in July 1689, John received a competence.

In the summer of 1690 Vanbrugh was arrested at Calais, was kept there nine months until his health suffered, and was transferred at his own cost to Vincennes, near Paris, in May 1691; early in 1692 he was imprisoned, with two other Englishmen, in the Bastille on the orders of Louis XIV. It was variously reported that he had been spying out the fortifications of Calais and that he had been informed against by a woman in Paris for attempting to leave France in wartime without a passport. Vanbrugh hinted to Tonson years later that his own stay in Paris had had a romantic origin. Whatever the true cause, it is clear that Vanbrugh and his companions were used in the complicated game of bartering prisoners; he was paroled in November 1692 and went home.

After a spell as an auditor for the Southern Division of Lancaster, Vanbrugh was next commissioned in Lord Berkeley's marine regiment of foot in 1696, served until it was disbanded in 1698, and was still petitioning for pay arrears in 1702 when he became a captain in a new regiment raised by his first commander, the earl of Huntingdon.

While in the Bastille, Vanbrugh drafted part of a comedy, and at some period in his military life when, according to Colley Cibber, "he was but an ensign, and had a heart above his income," he was helped by Sir Thomas Skipwith, a patentee of the Theatre Royal, Drury Lane. The theatrical conditions of the time soon enabled Vanbrugh to repay debts he incurred as a soldier with his talents as a playwright.

The decade 1695–1705, in which all of Vanbrugh's plays appeared, was a time of theater disputes involving the breakup and reuniting of companies. In 1695, after a quarrel over the management ethics of Christopher Rich (Skipwith's fellow patentee), Thomas Betterton, the greatest actor of the day, withdrew from the Theatre Royal, together with most of the experienced players, and opened the new theater in Lincoln's Inn Fields with Congreve's *Love for Love*. To assist the embarrassed Theatre Royal company, Colley Cibber turned playwright with *Love's Last Shift* in 1696, for which Vanbrugh supplied a sequel, *The Relapse; or, Virtue in Danger*. Written in six weeks, it became the success of the following season. During the intervening months Vanbrugh made a free adaptation of Boursault's *Les Fables d'Ésope* as a two-part *Aesop*, produced in 1697; but despite a topical scene about the current theater quarrel the play was unsuccessful. Vanbrugh surrendered his profits on these plays and presumably met his obligation to Skipwith.

He next completed his Bastille comedy as *The Provok'd Wife* and gave it to Lincoln's Inn Fields, where its first performance in May 1697, with Betterton as Sir John Brute and Mrs. Barry as Lady Brute, brought Vanbrugh immediate triumph and notoriety. It was in the following year that Jeremy Collier's vehement indictment of the contemporary theater, *A Short View of the Immorality and Profaneness of the English Stage*, made the works of Vanbrugh and Congreve major exhibits. The controversy did not impede Vanbrugh's engagement in theatrical affairs, for he adapted Carton Dancourt's farce *La Maison de campagne* as *The Country House*, in 1698, and welcomed the new century with a version of Fletcher's *The Pilgrim*, to which Dryden contributed a prologue, epilogue, and *A Secular Masque*, whose theme of resolute farewell to the past age was made poignant by Dryden's death.

In 1701, although commenced as an architect, Vanbrugh expediently adapted Dancourt's version of Le Sage's adaptation of Francisco de Rojas Zorilla's *La Traicion busca el castigo* as *The False Friend*, for Drury Lane, and in 1704 he joined with Congreve and William Walsh in writing *Squire Trelooby*, a translation of Molière's *Monsieur de Pourceaugnac*, for Lincoln's Inn Fields.

Vanbrugh sought to unite his skills in architecture and drama. He reported to Tonson in 1703 that he had given £2,000 for "the second Stable Yard going up the Haymarket," as a site for a new theater to be managed by Congreve and himself as a house for Betterton's company. When Queen Anne approved the enterprise as part of a policy for improving the moral tone of the stage, the Society for the Reformation of Manners vainly petitioned the bishop of London against the prospect of Vanbrugh as manager of the new morality. Nevertheless, the Queen's Theatre, or Italian Opera House, opened on Easter Monday 1705 with Giacomo Greber's *The Loves of Ergasto*, for which Garth supplied a prologue containing an ironic prophecy, "When marble fails, the muses' structures live." The occasion was greeted with hostility by opponents of the political establishment. Defoe's *Review* of 3 May 1705 sarcastically compared "the Ornament and Magnificence of its Building" with the "Great Zeal of our Nobility and Gentry, to the Encouragement of Learning, and the Suppressing of Vice and Immorality." *The Rehearsal of Observator* of 5 May 1705 was minatory:

The Kit-Cat Club is now grown Notorious all over the Kingdom. And they have built a Temple for their Dagon, the new Play-House in the Hay-Market.

Little is actually known of the temple that Cibber called a "vast triumphal Piece of Architecture," and of whose majestic features he pertinently asked:

what could their vast columns, their gilded cornices, their immoderate high roofs avail, where scarce one word in ten could be distinctly heard in it?

Vanbrugh was unsuccessful as a theater designer and premature, as a theater manager, in his interest in Italian opera. He fared no better as a property developer, for though he had confided to Tonson that he expected to be "reimburs'd every penny for it, by the Spare ground," the purchase of the Haymarket site proved a financial burden to Vanbrugh for years. When Congreve sensibly withdrew from the venture, Vanbrugh could no longer sustain the double task: despite the success of *The Confederacy*, adapted from Dancourt's *Les Bourgeoises à la mode* in 1705, Vanbrugh ended his practical theater career with a version of Molière's *Le Dépit Amoureux*, aptly titled *The Mistake*, in the same year.

A verse squib in Defoe's *Review* had already asked a difficult question:

> thus have their first Essays
> *Reform'd* their *Buildings*, not *Reform'd* their *Plays*.
> The Donor's Bounty may be well Design'd,
> But who can Guess the Model of the Mind?

Marlborough's victory at Blenheim in 1704 had determined Vanbrugh's future; he was appointed surveyor for the building of Blenheim Palace in 1705. Strong in political favor, he went in the capacity of Garter King-at-Arms to Hanover, in 1706, to invest the future King George I with that order: Vanbrugh was the first knight created on George's accession in 1714. He resigned from the surveyorship in 1716, after years of delay, frustration, political dissension, and the enduring hostility of the duchess of Marlborough. It was Vanbrugh's final humiliation to be shut out from the gates of Blenheim and to know that his Tory enemies rejoiced that the "Dutchman may not visit his own child." The occasion was the more bitter in that Vanbrugh had brought along his wife to see his grandest work, but ended in her sharing his greatest snub.

Vanbrugh's marriage was a late, yet characteristic, remodeling of his mind. On the day after Christmas 1718 he wrote from Castle Howard:

There has now fallen a Snow up to ones Neck. . . . In short, 'tis so bloody Cold, I have almost a mind to Marry to keep myself warm.

On 14 January 1719 he married Henrietta Maria, eldest child of James Yarburgh of Heslington Hall, York, a former lieutenant colonel of horse and aide-de-camp to Marlborough. Vanbrugh was fifty-five, Henrietta twenty-six. His courtship attracted notice, and his marriage speculation, for in a celebrated letter Lady Mary Wortley Montagu mentioned:

our York lovers (strange monsters, you'll think, love being as much forced up here as melons). In the first form of these creatures is even Mr. Vanbrugh. Heaven, no doubt, compassionating our dulnes, has inspired him with a passion that makes us all ready to die with laughing: 'tis credibly reported that he is endeavouring at the honourable state of matrimony, and vows to lead a single life no more. . . . his inclinations to ruins has given him a fancy for Mrs. Yarborough: he sighs and ogles so, that it would do your heart good to see him.[3]

The registers of St. Lawrence's Church, York, record on one page Vanbrugh's marriage entry, the burial of Anne, James Yarburgh's wife, on 20 April 1718, and the baptism of Anne, Yarburgh's daughter, on 10 May 1718. It seems unlikely that even Vanbrugh courted the pregnant wife of his future father-in-law; probably Lady Mary, once the infant toast of the Kit-Cats, was an avid spectator of a military exercise in diversion.

Vanbrugh feared the loss of bachelorhood like a gallant in a play, and six months after "this great Leap in the Dark, Marriage," as he quoted his own line to Tonson, held that marriage "was fitter to end Our Life, than begin it." He kept up a bluff defense against domesticity:

I am now two Boys Strong in the Nursery but am forbid getting any more this Season for fear of killing my Wife. A Reason; that in Kit Cat days, wou'd have been stronger for it, than against it: But let her live, for she's Special good, as far as I know of the Matter.

[3]*Letters and Works of Lady Mary Wortley Montagu* (1837), vol. I, p.155.

The robust confidence was misplaced. Only one of their three children survived infancy—Carlisle's godson Charles, who was killed at Fontenoy in 1745 and buried at Ath in his ancestors' country. But the pious wish was granted, for Henrietta outlived her husband by fifty years. Among her papers is part of a letter by Vanbrugh, describing a stay at Castle Howard in 1721, doubtless returned to her because of a passage about Charles's popularity with Carlisle's daughters, Lady Irwin and Lady Mary Howard, who

was as fond of him as she, going twenty times a day into the Nursery, and sitting an hour together by her self, at the Cradle feet, to see him sleep; then carrying him about in her arms as long as she was able, from whence he was handed from one to an other round the family of all Degrees, and a Favourite every where, because he never cry'd.[4]

Vanbrugh died, choked by a quinsy, in his Whitehall house on 26 March 1726, and was buried in the family vault at Sir Christopher Wren's church of St. Stephen, Walbrook. He left an unfinished play, *A Journey to London*, which Cibber completed as *The Provok'd Husband*: thus, a compliment was returned, and comedy extinguished.

A MATCHLESS SPIRIT OF IMPUDENCE

CIBBER's *Love's Last Shift; or, The Fool in Fashion*, dominated by his own performance as Sir Novelty Fashion, had been a comedy of manners that turned into a drama of sentiment. In it the dissolute Loveless, a wife-deserter and debt-evader, returned from overseas to find his loyal wife Amanda conveniently an heiress, and virtue unexpectedly profitable.

Vanbrugh's sequel raised Sir Novelty to the peerage as Lord Foppington, but introduced fresh perspectives by means of the subplot that takes the action out of London and describes the pursuit by Lord Foppington's younger brother of the heiress Miss Hoyden, daughter of Sir Tunbelly Clumsey.

The theme of the rake reformed was not one that

[4]Unpublished letter, quoted by permission of Mrs. Norah Gurney, archivist, Borthwick Institute of Historical Research, York.

SIR JOHN VANBRUGH

Vanbrugh endorsed, and the first scene of *The Relapse* shows Loveless proposing to Amanda a test of his newly acquired virtue. He intends to return to town. The risks are clear to her and to us, and Amanda's prudence in refraining from pressing her anxieties overbearingly upon Loveless makes us sympathize with this study of precarious love.

Vanbrugh's attitude to love is perhaps close to Loveless' ideal:

The largest Boons that Heaven thinks fit to grant
To Things it has decreed shall crawl on Earth,
Are in the Gift of Women form'd like you.
Perhaps, when Time shall be no more,
When the aspiring Soul shall take its flight,
And drop this pond'rous Lump of Clay behind it,
It may have Appetites we know not of,
And pleasures as refin'd as its Desires . . .
But till that Day of Knowledge shall instruct me,
The utmost Blessing that my Thought can reach,
           (Taking her in his arms)
Is folded in my Arms, and rooted in my Heart.

       (I.i)

"There let it grow for ever," replies Amanda. It is a modest acceptance of a realistic view of love, whose fears and raptures are devotedly human. Vanbrugh's ear for both is sensitive, without false artifice. Loveless cruelly persuades Amanda to force him to tantalize her with an anecdote revealing both his confidence in his relationship with her and his longing to talk about another woman:

Loveless.   Know then, I happen'd in the Play to find my very Character, only with the Addition of a *Relapse*; which struck me so, I put a suddain stop to a most harmless Entertainment, which till then, diverted me between the Acts. 'Twas to admire the workmanship of Nature, in the Face of a young Lady, that sat some distance from me, she was so exquisitely handsome.
Amanda.   So exquisitely handsome!
Loveless.   Why do you repeat my words, my Dear?
Amanda.   Because you seem'd to speak 'em with such pleasure, I thought I might oblige you with their Eccho.
Loveless.   Then you are allarmed, *Amanda*?
Amanda.   It is my Duty to be so, when you are in danger.
Loveless.   You are too quick in apprehending for me; all will be well when you have heard me out.

       (II.i)

Such easy words accomplish more in the theater than on the page. The audience is drawn into a rela-

tionship, familiarly comic yet tense. Amanda is both disturbed and sophisticated enough to engage in a game that offers no consolation to its losers. That she might lose becomes clear when the distracting theatergoer turns out to be her smart, widowed cousin, Berinthia, who complacently accepts Loveless' ardor and diagnoses his malady, "'Tis the Plague, and we shall all be infected." When Worthy stumbles upon their association, the infection spreads rapidly, for he persuades Berinthia, his former mistress, to help him corrupt Amanda. Vanbrugh is sufficiently unsentimental to let one attack succeed; and sufficiently idealistic to contain the other. In Act IV, scene iii, Loveless seduces Berinthia, who cries, "Help, help, I'm Ravish'd, ruin'd, undone. O Lord, I shall never be able to bear it. (*Very softly*)."

The quiet outrage sweeps us along with something of Berinthia's composure, because Vanbrugh never allows gratuitous moral instruction to hinder the progress of physical desire or the comic presentation of appetite.

Lord Foppington is a character richly gathered up from some of the follies of social attitudes of the time. He finds it "an unspeakable pleasure to be a Man of Quality—Strike me dumb," and that "the Ladies were ready to pewke at me, whilst I had nothing but Sir Navelty to recommend me to 'em—Sure whilst I was but a Knight, I was a very nauseous Fellow." Behind Foppington's acceptance of his pose as a beau is a shrewd determination to exploit his ten-thousand-pound inheritance, and a self-sufficiency that belies his decorous inanity. He courts Amanda as an exercise in the town's games and affects dismay at her pretense to literary culture:

Far to mind the inside of a Book, is to entertain ones self with the forc'd Product of another Man's Brain. Naw I think a Man of Quality and Breeding may be much diverted with the Natural Sprauts of his own.

But for all his privileged confidence he becomes a butt. His suit to Amanda ends disastrously, pricked by his own sword. His pride is humiliated when his younger brother impersonates him at Sir Tunbelly's house, secretly marries the heiress, and has him put in a dog kennel.

In the matching of Young Fashion with Miss Hoyden, Vanbrugh unites the comic themes of cynical fortune hunting and self-gratification.

Fashion does not mind whom he marries, so long as he acquires money; Miss Hoyden is equally indifferent about her husband, so long as he enables her to reach the haven of social freedom and individual liberation. The wish is not empty-headed, but full-bodied:

It's well I have a Husband a coming, or Icod, I'd marry the Baker, I wou'd so. No body can knock at the Gate, but presently I must be lockt up; and here's the young Greyhound Bitch can run loose about the House all the day long, she can; 'tis very well.

(III.iv)

The longing for an unconstrained life, which so many of Vanbrugh's characters display, is a state that the author sportingly approves and sometimes releases, with a spirited and licentious abandon. Young Fashion, charmed by Miss Hoyden's eager acceptance of him, soliloquizes, in affectionate but wide-eyed indulgence, about their future life:

I shall have a fine time on't with her in *London*; I'm much mistaken, if she don't prove a *March* Hare all the year round. What a scamp'ring Chace will she make on't when she finds the whole Kennel of Beaux at her Tail!

(IV.i)

When the golden prospect is threatened, the counsel of Coupler (the professional matchmaker) is effective because, whereas Fashion thinks of the Chaplain and the Nurse as "The Devil and the Witch," the older man knows that "we must find what stuff they are made of." By playing upon the Chaplain's real material needs, holding out a rich living and the added benefit of enforced marriage to the Nurse as a means of satisfying his conscience over the concealed marriage, Coupler and Young Fashion enable the clergyman to submit to providence and reconcile flesh and spirit.

In Vanbrugh's comedy, animal demands continually assail human feeling. The relationship between the Nurse and Miss Hoyden has none of the bawdy tenderness of Shakespeare's Nurse for Juliet; the earliest memory of Miss Hoyden, which her Nurse confides to Fashion, is unadorned:

alas, all I can boast of is, I gave her pure good Milk, and so your Honour wou'd have said, an you had seen how the poor thing suck't it—Eh, God's Blessing on the sweet Face on't; how it us'd to hang at this poor Tett, and suck and squeeze, and kick and sprawl it wou'd, till the Belly on't was so full, it wou'd drop off like a Leech.

(IV.i)

Miss Hoyden, humiliated by "a fiddlecome Tale of a draggle-tail'd Girl," urges "don't tell him what one did then, tell him what one can do now." Equally frankly, Berinthia tries to persuade Amanda that "In matters of Love, Men's Eyes are always bigger than their Bellies. They have violent Appetites, 'tis true; But they have soon din'd." When Amanda is appalled by men's inconstancy, Berinthia shrewdly distinguishes between the consequences of love for men and women by means of the usage of "baby" for "doll":

Now there's nothing upon Earth astonishes me less, when I consider what they and we are compos'd of. For Nature has made them Children, and us Babies. Now, Amanda, how we us'd our Babies, you may remember. We were mad to have 'em, as soon as we saw 'em; kist 'em to pieces, as soon as we got 'em; then pull'd off their Cloaths, saw 'em naked, and so threw 'em away.

(V.ii)

Vanbrugh's consistent comic cynicism makes us skeptical about Worthy's ability, when repulsed by Amanda, to find that "the vile, the gross desires of Flesh and Blood" have been "in a moment turn'd to Adoration." The facility of the phrasing matches the shallowness of the emotions. Whether promiscuously loveless or ashamedly worthy, Vanbrugh's weak characters share a self-deception about their basic natures. Against them the dramatist opposes a natural virtue, idealized in the goodness of women, made complete here in Amanda, maliciously self-betrayed in Berinthia, and wantonly rejected by Miss Hoyden. There is also a compensating comic virtue in the abused ignorance of Sir Tunbelly Clumsey.

Deputy lieutenant of his country and a county justice with £1,500 a year, Sir Tunbelly seeks social advancement by marrying his daughter to a peer. When Young Fashion comes awooing in disguise, his servant, Lory, senses behind the facade of the country house the strength of Sir Tunbelly's position:

Igad, Sir, this will prove some Inchanted Castle; we shall have the Gyant come out by and by with his Club, and beat our Brains out.

(III.iii)

And though Sir Tunbelly's welcome to the supposed lord is meticulously detailed in terms of the social necessity to meet rank by ostentation, the true giant comes out like the rampant spirit of the English squirearchy in arms to bar the door against the real Foppington. Just how doomed such rural weapons are against the urbane invasion is conveyed by Foppington:

A Pax of these Bumkinly People, will they open the Gate, or do they desire I should grow at their Moat-side like a Willow?

(IV.v)

The bumpkin triumphs temporarily over the foppish nobility, but the risks of sentimental comedy are skillfully avoided when both squire and noble are outwitted by youthful deceit and aged expediency.

The scene of the wedding celebration in Lord Foppington's London home builds by swift maneuvers to an explosive climax. Miss Hoyden looks forward to her debut among hostesses who will "laugh till they crack again, to see me slip my Collar, and run away from my Husband." Sir Tunbelly gets drunk before supper and ogles the ladies with gleeful violence: "Udsookers, they set my old Blood a-fire; I shall cuckold some body before Morning." The guests listen to a masque of the contention between Cupid and Hymen, the chorus of which chants for change:

> Constancy's an empty sound.
> Heaven, and Earth, and all go round,
> All the Works of Nature move,
> And the Joys of Life and Love
>   Are in Variety.

The change comes more rapidly than even these guests predict. Young Fashion claims his wife, supported by the sacred testimony of Parson Bull and the Nurse. Sir Tunbelly stumps off in rage. Lord Foppington decides to "put on a serene Countenance, for a Philosophical Air is the most becoming thing in the World to the face of a Person of Quality."

But Vanbrugh's play does not end with any delight in the moral conformity of this marriage. Fashion informs his bride that his brother will be at hand and "ready to come to" should their partnership fail, and Foppington swears devoutly, "Her Ladyship shall stap my Vitals, if I do."

Relapse is the condition of this changeful world, and what invites our laughter remains the spectacle of unregenerate nature. For Miss Hoyden, silent at last, stands ready to draw on the hounds like the tame hare her father so well nurtured.

The Provok'd Wife, Vanbrugh's only other completed original play, usually considered his masterpiece, has a long theatrical history. It owes its popularity mainly to the opportunities that the part of Sir John Brute has given to a long succession of actors, from Thomas Betterton to Sir Donald Wolfit.

Brute opens the play with a stunning assault upon the tedium of a two-year-old marriage that has "debaucht my five senses." His wife-cursing hatred generates an immediate quarrel and establishes a basic cross purpose. "You married me for Love," says Lady Brute. "And you me for Money," he retorts.

Lady Brute is efficient at self-analysis. She had married against advice because "I thought I had Charms enough to govern him; and that where there was an Estate, a Woman must needs be happy": it is a short paragraph from this observation to meditation upon revenge, and the persuasion that "a good part of what I suffer from my Husband may be a Judgment upon me for my Cruelty to my Lover"; and it is a shorter step, by way of comparison between the matrimonial vow and the easy covenant of a sovereign with his people, to dramatic decision:

if I argue the matter a little longer with my self, I shan't find so many Bug-bears in the way, as I thought I shou'd. Lord what fine notions of Virtue do we Women take up upon the Credit of old foolish Philosophers. Virtue's its own reward, Virtue's this, Virtue's that—Virtue's an Ass, and a Gallant's worth forty on't.

(I.i)

The direction that Lady Brute's thoughts take prepares us for the subsequent course of events in the play, which draws its dramatic tensions from the antagonisms of an incompatible marriage between characters who typify brutalized masculine conceit and natural feminine virtue. Sir John is addicted to gambling, drunkenness, and the company of roistering friends with a military swagger only equaled by their cowardice. Lady Brute is companioned by a niece, Bellinda, who is inexperienced enough to think she can sum up her aunt's feelings toward the loyal gallant Constant:

In a Word; never was poor Creature so spurr'd on by desire, and so rein'd in with fear.

Lady Brute's problem is more complex. She has common sense enough to admit that "Coquettry is one of the main ingredients in the natural Composition of a woman," and social sense enough to laugh at the vanity of her neighbor, Lady Fancyfull, a desperate flirt. But when Bellinda turns to a related subject, the jealousy of husbands, Lady Brute has to confess that Sir John "do's not love me well enough for that":

Lord how wrong Men's Maxims are. They are seldom jealous of their Wives, unless they are very fond of 'em; whereas they ought to consider the Woman's Inclinations, for there depends their Fate.

(I.i)

It is a light preface to an innocent intrigue, but it masks a strength of purpose and a power of feeling that the play's devices constantly arouse and subdue. Lady Brute's character enables Vanbrugh to explore the familiar men's maxim later expressed in D. H. Lawrence's contention that women have "the logic of emotion, men have the logic of reason. The two are complementary and mostly in opposition."

The drama of the provoked wife springs from the fact that this "woman's logic"—whether of Lady Brute, Lady Fancyfull, or Mademoiselle her maid —is "no less real and inexorable than the man's logic of reason":

She may spend years living up to a masculine pattern. But in the end, the strange and terrible logic of emotion will work out the smashing of that pattern, if it has not been emotionally satisfactory. This is the partial explanation of the astonishing changes in women. For years they go on being chaste Beatrices or child-wives. Then on a sudden—bash! The chaste Beatrice becomes a roaring lioness! The pattern didn't suffice, emotionally.[5]

The temptation of Lady Brute arises at once from her own inclinations and from the exceptional willingness of her society to provide her with a feminine pattern. Vanbrugh's dramatic instinct shares the

[5]D. H. Lawrence, "Give Her a Pattern," *Selected Essays* (1950), p.22.

social impulse toward that final "bash!" but his sense of comic irony contains it.

Lady Brute's feelings for Constant are intensified when she assists his friend Heartfree to court Bellinda, and they are complicated by the treacherous intriguing of Lady Fancyfull to gain Heartfree for herself, in which she is aided by her enterprising strumpet of a French maid and the enslaved Razor, Sir John's valet.

Vanbrugh's inventiveness of stage incident is at its strongest in *The Provok'd Wife*, and the effective surprises of action continually reinforce the play's overmastering irony. Thus the innocent assignation of Lady Brute and Bellinda with Constant and Heartfree in Spring Garden derives its piquancy initially from the fact that all four are being spied upon by Lady Fancyfull and her maid. But this episode of conventional intrigue is alarmingly transformed by the arrival of Sir John Brute, who has been freshly released from detention, after impersonating a parson and scandalizing the constabulary, and is seeking a whore. He seizes his wife and Bellinda in disguise; they are forced to reveal themselves to their suitors so that Lady Brute may escape from her husband's ravishing attention. The exposure removes the present danger, but promotes a greater one. Heartfree and Constant renew their demands, strengthened by the women's duplicity, and Lady Brute, crying, "Ah! I am lost," and forced by Constant toward a convenient arbor, is only recovered because Lady Fancyfull and her maid are driven out of the same refuge. It is a revelation that finally saves Lady Brute; her hair "stands on end," and she and Bellinda flee.

The irony of the play is constantly illustrated in terms of physical experience. Thus, Sir John's own salvation is accomplished by an appropriate crudity of behavior. Having arrived home drunk and displayed insulting affection for his wife, he momentarily abandons the warmth of sexual desire for a cup of her cold tea and opens the cupboard to discover Constant and Heartfree. The anticipated savagery is skillfully dissipated by his very inebriation. "All dirt and bloody" from his previous street scuffle, he is soon overcome by fatigue and falls asleep in his chair. He is thus preserved by this surrender to his body's gross appetite from a more despicable attempt to defend a fraudulent honor by provoking a duel that he is too cowardly to fight. The denouement finds him suitably chastened.

Vanbrugh's ear in *The Provok'd Wife* is as

responsive as his hand to the dramatic needs. He perfectly catches the confident masculine tone of the discussions between Heartfree and Constant, the delicacy of the exchanges between Constant and Lady Brute, or the intimacy of her talks with Bellinda. For instance, Lady Brute catechizes Constant upon his attitude to "That Phantome of Honour," testing their opposing logic:

Lady Brute. If it be a thing of so little Value, why do you so earnestly recommend it to your Wives and Daughters?

Constant. We recommend it to our Wives, Madam, because we wou'd keep 'em to our selves. And to our Daughters, because we wou'd dispose of 'em to others.

Lady Brute. 'Tis, then, of some Importance, it seems, since you can't dispose of 'em without it.

Constant. That importance, Madam, lies in the humour of the Country, not in the nature of the thing.

Lady Brute. How do you prove that, Sir?

Constant. From the Wisdom of a neighb'ring Nation in a contrary Practice. In Monarchies things go by Whimsies, but Commonwealths weigh all things in the Scale of Reason.

Lady Brute. I hope we are not so very light a People to bring up fashions without some ground.

Constant. Pray what do's your Ladiship think of a powder'd Coat for Deep Mourning?

Lady Brute. I think, Sir, your Sophistry has all the effect that you can reasonably expect it should have: it puzzles, but don't convince.

Constant. I'm sorry for it.

Lady Brute. I'm sorry to hear you say so.

Constant. Pray why?

Lady Brute. Because if you expected more from it, you have a worse opinion of my understanding than I desire you shou'd have.

Constant (aside). I comprehend her: She would have me set a value upon her Chastity, that I may think my self the more oblig'd to her, when she makes me a Present of it.

(III.i)

Such discourse has no trace of the combat of wits of lovers in the comedy of manners, and the reputation of Vanbrugh's style has suffered both from his own admission that he wrote as he spoke and from Cibber's report that actors found "the style of no author whatsoever gave their memory less trouble." Yet both statements deserve to be taken as compliments to Vanbrugh's skill in language, which is particularly effective in dealing with affectation and cant. For instance, the social hypocrisy of men and women is glanced at by Lady Brute and Bellinda, who practices before her mirror "both how to speak myself, and how to look when others speak":

Bellinda. But my Glass and I cou'd never yet agree what Face I shou'd make, when they come blurt out with a nasty thing in a Play: For all the Men presently look upon the Women, that's certain; so laugh we must not, tho' our Stays burst for't, because that's telling Truth, and owning we understand the Jest. And to look serious is so dull, when the whole House is a laughing.

Lady Brute. Besides, that looking serious do's really betray our Knowledge: For if we did not understand the thing, we shou'd naturally do like other People.

Bellinda. For my part I always use that occasion to blow my Nose.

Lady Brute. You must blow your Nose half off then at some Plays.

(III.iii)

Bellinda asks, "Why don't some Reformer or other beat the Poet for 't?" and Lady Brute shrewdly counters, "Because he is not so sure of our private Approbation, as of our publick Thanks."

Vanbrugh cleverly uses the traditional French complaint against English hypocrisy when Mademoiselle mimics with phrase and posture the encounter between Lady Brute and Constant in Spring Garden, inciting the wretched Razor to lustful complicity in lovemaking. He pleads, "But why wilt thou make me such a Rogue, my Dear?" and is taunted with "*Voilà un vrai Anglois! il est amoureux, et cependant il veut raisonner. Vet en au Diable.*" The desperate Razor surrenders to her plot: "In hopes thou'lt give me up thy Body, I resign thee up my Soul." Such comic inflation in no way diminishes the strength of their immoral defiance. Indeed, the defeat of Lady Fancyfull's schemes involves more than a mechanical return to respectability. When her mask is stripped off, and her pretensions harshly exposed, she struggles to regain some human dignity. She was more deeply committed to her amorous desire than Foppington was to his proposed marriage, and she is correspondingly less successful in putting on a social face. Bellinda, seeing "what a Passion she's in," forgives her with something of Olivia's pity for the abused Malvolio.

The Provok'd Wife concludes in mutual pardon and acknowledgment of faults. A similar tactful recognition seems required on the part of criticism, for Vanbrugh's immorality was attacked by just such a reformer as Bellinda mentioned, when Collier's *Short View* satirically and judiciously arraigned his plays for profanity, bawdy, and the scurrilous treatment of clergy and sacred script. Vanbrugh's retort, *A Short Vindication*, could scarcely hope to counter these charges and ought not to have so attempted. Vanbrugh's best defense lay in fresh attack, and the brief polemic that introduced the text of *The Relapse* is a pungent expression of his artistic aims. Apologizing for offenses given to "any honest Gentleman of the Town, whose Friendship or good Worth is worth the having," Vanbrugh admits that he had no other design "in running a very great Risk, than to divert (if possible) some part of their Spleen, in spite of their Wives and their Taxes," but adds "One more word about the Bawdy":

I own the first Night this thing was acted, some Indecencies had like to have happen'd, but 'Twas not my Fault.

The fine Gentleman of the Play, drinking his Mistress's Health in *Nants* Brandy, from six in the Morning to the time he waddled on upon the Stage, had toasted himself up to such a pitch of vigour, I confess I once gave *Amanda* for gone, and am since (with all due respect to Mrs. *Rogers*) very sorry she 'scapt; for I am confident a certain Lady (let no one take it to herself that's handsome) who highly blames the Play, for the Barrenness of the Conclusion, would then have allow'd it a very natural Close.

Vanbrugh's plays offer more inherent offense than might be given through the insobriety of Powell or any actor, and it is typical that his proposed apology should erupt into fresh insult. For the risks Vanbrugh accepted are inseparable from his comic force and directness. Leigh Hunt passed over *The Provok'd Wife* as a play "more true than pleasant," and though Vanbrugh prudently replaced the scene of Sir John Brute in a priest's gown by one in which he wears his wife's clothes, the substituted version has held the stage since, not only because it affords more continuous opportunities for topical satire but because it strengthens the element of sexual antagonism in Brute.[6]

The play was defended in its own time against the charge of "a loose Performance" when Giles Jacob discovered in its design a utilitarian morality that "teaches Husbands how they are to expect their Wives Should shew a Resentment, if they use them as Sir *John Brute* did his" (*The Poetical Register*, 1719). It seems wiser now to content ourselves with the position that W. C. Hazlitt adopted in "On Wit and Humour":

You cannot force people to laugh, you cannot give a reason why they should laugh;—they must laugh of themselves, or not at all. As we laugh from a spontaneous impulse, we laugh the more at any restraint upon this impulse. We laugh at a thing merely because we ought not.

Vanbrugh's only designedly didactic play, *Aesop*, had its origin in Boursault's Parisian success, which Vanbrugh did not expect would gain "so great a victory here, since 'tis possible by fooling with his Sword, I may have turn'd the Edge on't." The play is an interesting failure, if only because of Farquhar's remark in *A Discourse upon Comedy* (1702) that Aesop was "the first and original author" of comedy, and that "Comedy is no more at present than a well-framed tale handsomely told as an agreeable vehicle for counsel or reproof." It is a traditional enough argument—indeed Hazlitt, the best critic of Vanbrugh and his comic sensibility, makes Aesop central in his own exposition—and the subject ought to have occasioned good comedy. The reproving fables themselves are admirably done and are Vanbrugh's best verse. Pope praised them:

Prior is called the English Fontaine for his tales, nothing is more unlike. But your *Fables* have the very spirit of this celebrated French poet.[7]

Vanbrugh's "I protest to you I never read Fontaine's *Fables*," suggests the modest attention he sometimes gave to his art. The play remains an undramatic medley, enlivened by some admirable portraits: Jacob Quaint, a herald from Wales ("a Country in the World's backside, where every Man is born a Gentleman, and a Genealogist"); Mrs. Forge-Will, a scrivener's widow; and, among Vanbrugh's additions, a characteristically eccentric country gentleman, Sir Polydorus Hogstye of Beast-Hall, in Swine-County.

---

[6]Garrick, who made Sir John Brute one of his greatest roles, once satirized contemporary fashion in a hat laden with vegetables and decorated with a pendant carrot.

[7]See Austin Warren, *Alexander Pope as Critic and Humanist* (London, 1963) for the full context of this and other references to Vanbrugh.

Of Vanbrugh's other adaptations from French drama, *The Country House*, a two-act farce long popular as an afterpiece, now reads like a rumbustious prophecy of the fate of a stately home. It exploits the situation of Monsieur Barnard, a country squire so beset by visitors, neighbors, huntsmen, and relatives that he hangs an old rusty sword at his gate for an inn sign; eventually he marries off his children, gets rid of his house, and is willing to dispose of his wife too.

The headlong impetus of such a plot exuberantly displays that quality in Vanbrugh that Allardyce Nicoll terms "buoyant with a sort of uproariousness, upheld by wine." This is notably lacking in the two comic romances of *The False Friend* and *The Mistake*. Here intricate intrigues, though skillfully controlled, inhibit those generous tendencies of Vanbrugh's stage handling to issue into ribaldry and riot. Occasional comic moments, such as the bedroom scene in *The False Friend*, or the buffoonery with love tokens in *The Mistake*, and the energetic, pert dialogue of maids and manservants, insufficiently compensate for stock dramatic situations and a decline in linguistic vitality.

By contrast, *The Confederacy* is a play of strong characters that displays Vanbrugh's customary gusto. Clarissa and Araminta, wives of two scriveners, Gripe and Moneytrap, join in a conspiracy against their husbands. But though the play was long popular as *The City Wives' Confederacy*, its strength lies equally in the counterplot of Dick Amlet's pursuit of Gripe's daughter Corinna, aided by his friend Brass and the maid Flippanta, and involving the suppression of Dick's relationship with his mother, Mrs. Amlet, "a Seller of all Sorts of private Affairs to the Ladies." The play makes a comic analysis of bourgeois greed and idleness, a shrewd revelation of the false innocence of the sixteen-year-old Corinna, and a sharp caricature of snobbery in action—as Brass says to his pretended master, "You soared up to adultery with the mistress, while I was at humble fornication with the maid."

Yet, though the play fully deserves Hazlitt's commendation as "a comedy of infinite contrivance and intrigue, with a matchless spirit of impudence," and as "a fine, careless *exposé* of heartless want of principle," it has the stricter virtues of French realistic comedy rather than the broader capacities of Vanbrugh's original plays. The play is necessarily concerned more with avaricious than with amorous gratification, and there is a correspondingly reduced sense of that competition of the ideal with the materialistic, the ignorant with the sophisticated, that gives a fuller life to *The Relapse* and *The Provok'd Wife*.

In the three acts and one scene that Vanbrugh completed of *A Journey to London*, he returned to those enduring preoccupations of his art. The dilemma of Monsieur Barnard is reversed. Now, in his London house, Uncle Richard awaits the arrival of his nephew Sir Francis Headpiece and his family, who are to take possession of the metropolis:

> Forty years and two is the Age of him; in which it is computed by his Butler, his own person has drank two and thirty Ton of Ale. The rest of his Time has been employ'd in persecuting all the poor four-legg'd Creatures round, that wou'd but run away fast enough from him, to give him the high-mettled pleasure of running after them. In this noble Employ, he has broke his right Arm, his left Leg, and both his Collarbones—Once he broke his Neck, but that did him no harm; a nimble Hedge-leaper, a Brother of the Stirrup that was by, whipt off his Horse and mended it.
>
> (I.i)

This endearing fool, married to "a profuse young Housewife for Love, with never a Penny of Money," and finding that "Children and Interest-Money make such a bawling about his Ears," has set off for London to be a "Parliament-Man," and his wife "to play off a hundred Pounds at Dice with Ladies of Quality, before breakfast." Uncle Richard's man, James, gives a profusely detailed account of the hazards of their undertakings. The vanity of Lady Headpiece has "added two Cart-Horses to the four old Geldings" to impress the town with her coach and six, and "heavy *George* the Plowman rides Postillion." The coach is "cruelly loaden" with people, trunks, boxes, and the preposterous accoutrements of their ambitious journey:

> for fear of a Famine, before they shou'd get to the Baiting-place, there was such Baskets of Plumbcake, Dutch-Gingerbread, Cheshire-Cheese, Naples-Biscuits, Maccaroons, Neats-Tongues, and cold boyl'd Beef—and in case of Sickness, such Bottles of Usquebaugh, Black-cherry Brandy, Cinamon-water, Sack, Tent, and Strong beer, as made the old Coach crack again. . . . for Defence of this Good Cheer, and my Lady's little Pearl Necklace, there was the Family Basket-hilt Sword, the great Turkish Cimiter, the old Blunderbuss, a good Bag of Bullets, and a great Horn of Gunpowder. . . . Then for Band-boxes,

they were so bepiled up, to Sir *Francis's* Nose, that he cou'd only peep out at a chance Hole with one Eye, as if he were viewing the Country thro' a Perspective-Glass.

This clearly was the task that Vanbrugh set himself as dramatist, his perspective reaching across a range of contemporary social circumstances and attitudes. His observation takes in a series of disintegrating personal and social partnerships. The innocent Sir Francis is drawn to London, only to be disillusioned by the true nature of parliamentary patronage; the scheming Lady Headpiece is seduced by the world of Colonel Courtly and the gaming table fraternity.

Lord and Lady Loverule, neighbors and relatives of Sir Charles, provide Vanbrugh with his finest marital quarrel, unquotable because its entirety is needed to demonstrate its compulsive rhythmic growth, in which Lady Arabella Loverule's spirited claim for personal freedom grows uncontrollably toward the condition of total irresponsibility. (Cibber opened his version of the play with this scene, but could not match Vanbrugh's pace and attack.) And in the conversation of Lord Loverule and Sir Charles on the subject of divorce Vanbrugh finds a vocabulary for a previously inarticulate sensibility. They look back upon their idealized adoration of women and contemplate the prospect of reversal:

Lord Loverule. And what Relief?
Sir Charles. A short one; leave it, and return to that you left, if you can't find a better.
Lord Loverule. He says right—that's the Remedy, and a just one—for if I sell my Liberty for Gold, and I am foully paid in Brass, shall I be held to keep the Bargain? (*Aside*)
Sir Charles. What are you thinking of?
Lord Loverule. Of what you have said.
Sir Charles. And was it well said?
Lord Loverule. I begin to think it might.
Sir Charles. Think on, 'twill give you Ease—the Man who has courage enough to part with a Wife, need not much dread the having one; and he that has not ought to tremble at being a Husband.

(II.i)

Lord Loverule believes that "(tho' the Misfortune's great) he'll make a better Figure in the World, who keeps an ill Wife out of Doors, than he that keeps her within." Colley Cibber reported that what Vanbrugh "intended in the *Catastrophe*, was, that the Conduct of his Imaginary Fine Lady had so provok'd him, that he design'd actually to have made her Husband turn her out of his Doors." But when Cibber completed the play, he transformed this intention in the interest of reconciliation and the terms of sentimental comedy, just as Richard Brinsley Sheridan was to dilute the ribald energy of *The Relapse* in *A Trip to Scarborough*. Vanbrugh himself could not accomplish his design, and his unfinished masterpiece of *A Journey to London* ends, as his own life did, in an apoplectic hiatus:

Lady Headpiece. What do you mean, Sir *Francis*, to disturb the Company, and abuse the Gentleman thus?
Sir Francis. I mean to be in a Passion.
Lady Headpiece. And why will you be in a Passion, Sir *Francis*?
Sir Francis. Because I came here to Breakfast with my Lady there, before I went down to the House, expecting to find my Family set round a civil Table with her, upon some Plumb Cake, hot Roles, and a cup of Strong Beer; instead of which, I find these good Women staying their Stomachs with a Box and Dice, and that Man there, with the strange Perriwig, making a good hearty Meal upon my Wife and Daughter—

It is a revealing moment for Vanbrugh's art to have faltered, and eventually to have fallen silent. He possessed neither the passionate ferocity of Wycherley nor the satirical intelligence of Congreve, either of whom would have accomplished a dramatic solution for Vanbrugh's dilemma. Vanbrugh seems to have remained undecided between the resources of natural wit and cheerful violence, which would have led him to a characteristically explosive denouement and a new seriousness of mind, represented here in the conversation of Sir Charles and Lord Loverule, and owed perhaps to the example of Farquhar's *The Beaux' Stratagem*.

Vanbrugh and Farquhar are certainly near to each other in time, dramatic themes, and theatrical techniques, and their plays have more in common than the work of any other two dramatists of the Restoration period. Neither is much concerned with earlier preoccupations of Restoration comedy, such as witty heroines, gay couples, and the strict delineation of fashion; both manage to balance town sophistication with provincial vitality, and find the center of dramatic interest in marriage as much as in courtship. But there remains an important dissimilarity. Whereas *The Beaux' Stratagem* refines upon *The Provok'd Wife* and seeks for a change in the social attitude toward divorce, Vanbrugh's play reaches a conclusion in terms of personal freedom beyond the law. Farquhar, had he lived, might have managed the transition between the attitudes of the Restoration dramatists and those of the sentimentalists who succeeded them; he might indeed have given some of his strength and vivacity to their often maudlin morality.

Vanbrugh's art was created in response to the tendency toward sentimentalism that he discerned in Colley Cibber, and thrived in a decade dominated by farce. But Vanbrugh was not so much incapable of refinement—the frequent idealization of women indicate the possibility—as he was manfully resistant to it. Indeed, his qualities seem curiously inseparable from his weaknesses. His best plays survive and are still powerfully effective, because their basic themes appeal to common sense and to the common senses alike. In the eighteenth century, his plays often suffered adaptation and false refinement; in the nineteenth century, they were frequently reduced to their farcical elements and performed episodically; in the twentieth century, *The Relapse* has been adapted as a popular musical comedy. Yet Vanbrugh's honesty of viewpoint remains. If he had sustained his gaze upon human behavior, it would have proved essentially disconcerting. Indeed, had he completed *A Journey to London*, Vanbrugh might have exemplified Coleridge's maxim that "Farce is nearer Tragedy in its Essence than Comedy is."

A POET AS WELL AS AN ARCHITECT

Under this stone, reader, survey
Dead Sir John Vanbrugh's house of clay.
Lie heavy on him, earth! for he
Laid many heavy loads on thee.

Abel Evans' epitaph is fitter to begin a comment upon Vanbrugh's architecture than to end it; for, though he would have been the first to appreciate its wit, we ought to be the last to endorse it. It is the activity, not the inertness, of Vanbrugh's buildings that most imposes itself upon the spectator's eye, whether trained or untrained, devout or derisive.

Vanbrugh's amateur status as an architect and his professional reputation as a wit made him a fair target for others' witticisms. His Whitehall home was mocked by Jonathan Swift as "A thing resembling a Goose-pie," and the progress of his art was described from the time when

Van's genius, without thought or lecture,
Is hugely turn'd to architecture:

with passing reference to its inspiration in children's mud games, until

From such deep rudiments as these,
Van is become, by due degrees,
For building famed, and justly reckon'd,
At court Vitruvius the second.
(*The History of Van's House*, 1708)

The jest rankled. Swift reported in his *Journal to Stella* on 7 November 1710 that Vanbrugh "had a long quarrel with me about those Verses on his House; but we were very civil and cold. Lady Marlborough used to teaze with him, which made him angry, though he be a good-natured fellow."

Vanbrugh could expect such sallies from his political opponents, particularly in view of Alexander Pope's friendship with Lady Marlborough and his own creation of Eastbury Park for Pope's victim Bubb Doddington.

At Vanbrugh's death Swift and Pope repented in a joint preface to their *Miscellanies* of 1727:

In Regard to Two Persons only we wish our Railery, though ever so tender, or Resentment, though ever so just, had not been indulged. We speak of Sir John Vanbrugh, who was a Man of Wit, and of Honour, and of Mr. Addison, whose Name deserves all Respect from every Lover of Learning.

The company he keeps in this epitaph would have pleased the gregarious Vanbrugh, whom Pope depicted as "the most easy, careless writer and companion in the world . . . who wrote and built just as his fancy led him, or as those he built for and wrote for directed him."

There is a sense, however, in which, literally, Pope and Swift did not know what they were talking about. Vanbrugh was no Vitruvius. But he was, with Sir Christopher Wren and Nicholas Hawksmoor, the architect of the school of English Baroque that lasted for little more than a generation in England and had to wait for Horace Walpole before it received aesthetic admiration, and for Sir Joshua Reynolds' thirteenth discourse (11 December 1786) for any authoritative discernment of critical principles.

Vanbrugh's reputation can no longer stand apart from Hawksmoor's; Sir John Summerson sums up a continuing scholarly inquiry as follows:

The truth can only be that *both* Hawksmoor *and* Vanbrugh were very exceptional men; that they exploited the same sources in continuous mutual discussion, and shared, more fully, perhaps, then either knew, each other's treasuries of knowledge and invention.[8]

With this qualification prominently stated, it is still possible to find in Sir Joshua Reynolds' eulogy some of the terms still valuable for the appreciation of an architecture both heroic and human, grandly placed and intimately detailed.

Reynolds paid tribute to Vanbrugh "in the language of a Painter," as an architect who perfectly "understood in his Art what is the most difficult in ours, the conduct of the background":

What the background is in Painting, in Architecture is the real ground on which the building is erected; and no Architect took greater care than he that his work should not appear crude and hard; that is, it did not start abruptly out of the ground without expectation of preparation.

Reynolds understood Vanbrugh's concern with light and shadow, exemplified in his treatment of exterior and interior arcades, and his spectacular development of emphasis in approach. He admired, above all, those poetic towers and battlements that painters and poets "make a part of the composition of their ideal landscape":

it is from hence in a great degree, that in the buildings of Vanbrugh, who was a Poet as well as an Architect, there is a greater display of imagination, than we shall find perhaps in any other.

SELECTED BIBLIOGRAPHY

I. Bibliography. G. L. Woodward and J. G. McManaway, *A Check List of English Plays, 1641–1700* (Chicago, 1945); W. Van Lennep et al., *The London Stage 1660–1800* (Carbondale, Ill., 1960–1969).

II. Collected Works. *Plays, Written by Sir John Vanbrugh,* 2 vols. (London, 1719), the first collected ed., lacks *The Country House* and predates *A Journey to London,* which was added in 1730 and 1734; *Plays, Written by Sir John Vanbrugh,* 2 vols. (London, 1735); L. Hunt, ed., *The Dramatic Works of Wycherley, Congreve, Vanbrugh and Farquhar* (London, 1840), omits Cibber's *The Provok'd Husband;* W. C. Ward, ed., *The Plays of Sir John Vanbrugh,* 2 vols. (London, 1893), omits Cibber's *The Provok'd Husband;* B. Dobrée and G. Webb, eds., *The Complete Works of Sir John Vanbrugh,* 4 vols. (London, 1927–1928), the standard, limited ed.; vols. I–III, edited by Dobrée, contain all of the plays except the dubious *Squire Trelooby,* also includes *A Short Vindication;* vol. IV, edited by Webb from transcripts, contains majority of the letters and certain documents relating to Blenheim. *Note: The Pilgrim* is omitted from all eighteenth- and nineteenth-century collected eds.

III. Selected Works. A. E. H. Swaen, ed., *Sir John Vanbrugh* (London, 1896), contains *The Relapse, The Provok'd Wife, The Confederacy,* and *A Journey to London; Restoration Plays from Dryden to Farquhar* (London, 1912), includes *The Provok'd Wife.*

IV. Separate Works. *The Relapse; or, Virtue in Danger* (London, 1696), title page dated 1697, frequently reprinted and collected, appears in D. MacMillan and M. H. Jones, eds., *Plays of the Restoration and Eighteenth Century* (London, 1931), also in C. Zimansky, ed., Regents Restoration Drama series (Lincoln, Nebr., 1970), B. A. Harris, ed., New Mermaids series (London, 1971), adapted by J. Lee as *A Man of Quality* (London, 1776) and by R. B. Sheridan as *A Trip to Scarborough* (London, 1781); *Aesop* (London, 1697), parts 1 and 2 published both separately and in combined ed. (1697); *The Provok'd Wife* (London, 1697), frequently reprinted, the 1743 (Dublin) text contains Act IV, scenes i and iii as Vanbrugh rewrote them for performance in 1706; also in C. Zimansky, ed., Regents Restoration Drama series (Lincoln, Nebr., 1970), J. L. Smith, ed., New Mermaids series (London, 1974); *A Short Vindication of The Relapse and The Provok'd Wife, from Immorality and Profaneness, by the Author* (London, 1698); *The Pilgrim* (London, 1700); *The False Friend* (London, 1702), adapted as *Friendship à la mode* (Dublin, 1766); *To a Lady More Cruel Than Fair* (London, 1704), verses first printed in Tonson's *Dryden's Miscellany* (London, 1704); *The Confederacy* (London, 1705), adapted from Dancourt's *Les Bourgeoises à la mode,* often acted as *The City Wives' Confederacy; The Mistake* (London, 1706), a version of Molière's *Le Dépit Amoureux,* included in *Plays from Molière* (London, 1891), adapted by T. King as *Lovers' Quarrels; or, Like Master Like Man* (Dublin, 1770); *The Country House* (London, 1715), reprinted as *La Maison Rustique; or, The Country House* (London, 1740); *Sir John Vanbrugh's Justification of What He Depos'd in the Duke of Marlborough's Late Tryal* (London, 1721); *A Journey to London* (London, 1728), unfinished play,

[8]*Architecture in Britain: 1530–1830* (London, 1963), p.168.

afterward completed by Cibber as *The Provok'd Husband*; Sir John Vanbrugh and C. Cibber, *The Provok'd Husband; or, A Journey to London* (London, 1728); *Squire Trelooby* (London, 1704), an adaptation by Congreve, Vanbrugh, and Walsh of Molière's *Monsieur de Pourceaugnac*, unprinted or no copies preserved, translations by J. Ozell (London, 1704) and J. Ralph (London, 1734) may have been influenced by it, see J. C. Hodges, "The Authorship of *Squire Trelooby*," *Review of English Studies*, 4 (1928); *The Cuckold in Conceit*, adaptation from Molière, performed in 1707, presumed unprinted, see J. B. Shipley, "The Authorship of *The Cornish Squire*," *Philological Quarterly*, 47 (1968).

V. BIOGRAPHICAL STUDIES. B. Dobrée, *Essays in Biography* (London, 1925), the main materials for Vanbrugh's life are here and in the same author's intro. to the *Complete Works*; L. Whistler, *Sir John Vanbrugh, Architect and Dramatist, 1664–1726* (London, 1938), a brilliant, sympathetic, and full appraisal; L. Whistler, *The Imagination of Vanbrugh and His Fellow Artists* (London, 1954), additional letters; A. Rosenberg, "New Light on Vanbrugh," *Philological Quarterly*, 45 (1966), additional letters.

VI. SOME CRITICAL STUDIES. J. Collier, *A Short View of the Immorality and Profaneness of the Stage* (London, 1698); C. Cibber, *An Apology for the Life of Mr. Colley Cibber, by Himself* (London, 1740), standard ed., also in R. W. Lowe, ed., 2 vols. (London, 1889); W. Hazlitt, *Lectures on the English Comic Writers*, no. 4 (London, 1819); J. Palmer, *The Comedy of Manners* (London, 1913); A. Nicoll, *A History of English Drama, 1660–1900*, vols. I and II (London, 1923; 1925), the standard critical history, with supplementary checklists and stage documents, vol. I (4th ed., rev., 1961) and vol. II (3rd ed., rev., 1952); J. W. Krutch, *Comedy and Conscience After the Restoration* (New York, 1924; enl. ed., 1949), a useful wide-ranging account, including a discussion of the controversy between the companies; B. Dobrée, *Restoration Comedy, 1660–1720* (London, 1924); H. T. E. Perry, *The Comic Spirit in the Restoration Drama* (New Haven, 1925), still one of the most effective and attractive criticisms of Vanbrugh and his contemporaries; A. C. Sprague, *Beaumont and Fletcher on the Restoration Stage* (London, 1926), contains an analysis of Vanbrugh's handling of Fletcher's *The Pilgrim*; F. W. Bateson, *English Comic Drama* (London, 1929), valuable for Cibber and post-Vanbrugh drama; P. Mueschke and J. Fleisher, "A Re-evaluation of Vanbrugh" in *PMLA*, 49 (1934), a detailed study deserving particular attention; S. Rosenfeld, *Strolling Players and Drama in the Provinces, 1660–1765* (Cambridge, 1939); L. Hughes, *A Century of English Farce* (London, 1956), especially relevant reading for the decade 1696–1706, the period of Vanbrugh's dramatic activity; J. Loftis, *Comedy and Society from Congreve to Fielding* (Stanford, 1959), contains useful historical and comparative reference; K. A. Burnim, *David Garrick: Director* (Pittsburgh, 1961), reconstructs the stage business of Garrick's *The Provok'd Wife*; J. R. Brown and B. Harris, eds., *Restoration Theatre*, Stratford-upon-Avon Studies 6 (London, 1965); F. W. Patterson, "The Revised Scenes of *The Provok'd Wife*," *English Language Notes*, 4 (1966); J. Loftis, ed., *Restoration Drama: Modern Essays in Criticism* (London, 1966); K. Muir, *The Comedy of Manners* (London, 1970).

VII. ARCHITECTURAL STUDIES. A. T. Bolton and H. D. Hendry, eds., *The Wren Society*, vols. I–XX (London, 1924–1944); H. A. Tipping, *The Works of Sir John Vanbrugh and His School, 1699–1736* (London, 1928), vol. II in *English Homes, Period IV*; H. M. Colvin, *A Biographical Dictionary of English Architects, 1660–1840* (London, 1945), contains a concise checklist of Vanbrugh's buildings; J. Summerson, *Architecture in Britain: 1530–1830* (London, 1953; 4th ed., rev. and enl., 1963); L. Whistler, *The Imagination of Vanbrugh and His Fellow Artists* (London, 1954), a nearly definitive account, superbly illustrated and documented; K. Downes, *Hawksmoor* (London, 1959); F. H. W. Sheppard, gen. ed., *Survey of London*, vols. XXIX and XXX (London, 1960), important account of Vanbrugh's Haymarket Opera House; K. Downes, *Vanbrugh* (London, 1977), valuable for biography, detailed study of accounts, and the whole artistic achievement of Vanbrugh.

WILLIAM CONGREVE

(1670-1729)

Bonamy Dobrée

LIFE

WILLIAM CONGREVE was born at Bardsey, a village near Leeds, in January 1670. Four years later his father was commissioned to command the garrison at Youghal in Ireland, but was later transferred to Carrickfergus. From there, in 1681, Congreve attended the famous school at Kilkenny, proceeding in 1686 to Trinity College, Dublin, where he was again with his older schoolfellow Jonathan Swift. In 1688, probably because of the Revolution, the family moved to their home at Stretton, in Staffordshire, where Congreve wrote the first draft of *The Old Batchelour* to relieve, he said, the tedium of convalescence from an illness. In 1691 he went to study at the Middle Temple, in London, but he never worked seriously at the law, preferring to write; and in the next year he had printed, over the pen name Cleophil, *Incognita*, his novel, if it can be so called. He soon mixed among men of letters, and had some verses printed in the popular anthology of the day, Gildon's *Miscellany*. He was immediately noticed by John Dryden, who was always ready to encourage young men and so invited him to contribute to his translation of Persius, which the publishers issued headed by Congreve's complimentary lines "To Mr. Dryden."

By this time, then, he was already a coming young man, and the next year he "arrived" splendidly when *The Old Batchelour* opened on 9 March 1693 at the Theatre Royal, Drury Lane, generously overseen by Dryden. It was tremendously popular and ran for a fortnight, longer than any play had before. But his next play, *The Double-Dealer*, acted in October at the same theater, did not meet with popular approval. Eighteen months went by; there were great battles in the theater world, and a new company hived off to set up its standard at Lincoln's Inn Fields, where Congreve's next play—

and perhaps his best for performing—*Love for Love*, opened on 30 April 1695. This restored his reputation, putting him firmly in the front rank of dramatists. He became one of the managers of the new theater, promising to write a play for it every year, a promise he did not succeed in carrying out.

Being now established, Congreve was very much part of the literary scene, contributing his quota of odes and public verses, mourning the death of Queen Mary in a pastoral, celebrating the taking of Namur by William III, and so on. He also wrote, at the request of John Dennis, a rising young critic, for his collection of critical essays published as *Letters on Several Occasions* (1696), the essay "Concerning Humour in Comedy," which showed the way his mind was working in these matters. At this time he began to enjoy the benefits of a society in which men of some importance in the government could reward men of letters with minor posts, which, if not exactly sinecures, did not involve much labor. Thus in due course Congreve became one of the commissioners for licensing hackney coaches, occupied a post in the customs, and finally, in 1714, was made secretary of the island of Jamaica. Thus, having a small patrimony, and collecting something from the theater and from his royalties, he was, though never rich, always very comfortably off.

Early in 1697, as an earnest redeeming his promise to Lincoln's Inn Fields, he gave for acting his one tragedy, *The Mourning Bride*, which, strange though it may seem to us, was immensely popular and enormously enhanced his reputation. But in 1698 he was involved in the tedious business of trying to answer the attack on the theater made by Jeremy Collier, a nonjuring parson, who in April published his notorious *A Short View of the Immorality and Profaneness of the English Stage etc.*, which appealed both to the still strong, puritanical antitheater feeling and to the not unnatural dislike the citizenry of London felt at the way the comic dramatists had treated them. There was nothing new in this sort of attack: even Sir Philip Sidney, in 1595, could complain of theatrical "scurrility, unworthy of any chaste ears"; and William Prynne had delivered a violent diatribe against the theater in *Histriomastix* (1632). Such voices are not altogether stilled today. Many answered, and, somewhat against his will, Congreve was persuaded to join in the battle. Thus, arguing purely on his own account and leaving the larger issues aside, he produced his *Amendments of Mr. Collier's False and Imperfect Citations*, a not altogether feeble but not very convincing defense of certain of his expressions. But he was not the man to take an effective part in this sort of literary fisticuffs.

Congreve's real answer was *The Way of the World*, which has come to be regarded as his masterpiece. In its early days, however, it did not meet with much applause; and it may be for this reason that he ceased to write for the stage, though it is just as reasonable to suppose that he felt he had said all he had to say. He did not altogether cease his connection with the theater. He still continued as manager at Lincoln's Inn Fields, collaborated with Sir John Vanbrugh and William Walsh on *Monsieur de Pourceaugnac, or Squire Trelooby* in 1704, and took an interest in Vanbrugh's Queen's Theatre, or Italian Opera House, in 1705, writing a prologue for the first performance. His only other theatrical work was the writing of two opera libretti.

Otherwise he lived a quiet social life among his friends, Swift, Pope, and their circle, coming in contact also with Steele, for whom he wrote *Tatler* No. 292, and amusing himself as others did with a squib on the popular astrologer, Dr. John Partridge. As for his affairs of the heart, he had a tender affection for Mrs. Bracegirdle, the actress who brilliantly acted the leading parts in his plays, including the tragedy, but whether they were lovers in the full sense of the term is very doubtful. In his later years he became deeply attached to the second duchess of Marlborough, who had married the son of the lord treasurer, Sidney Godolphin. He lived largely in the Godolphin home, and it is hardly questioned now that he was the father of the duchess' younger daughter, Lady Mary, who became duchess of Leeds. At all events, when he died in 1729, he left the larger part of his fortune to the duchess of Marlborough, who spent most of it on a diamond necklace for her daughter. All that we know is that he spent the last few years of his life out of the limelight, quiet, and happy so far as gout and failing eyesight would allow.

THE COMEDY OF MANNERS

THE English form of this type of comedy flourished during the Restoration period, as it has never done since. Other types were being written at the same time, such as the comedy of humors by Thomas Shadwell, romantic comedy by Thomas Southerne, semipolitical comedy by Thomas Otway. By the comedy of manners, at this period, is meant that particular brand that mainly held the stage from Sir George Etherege's first play in 1664; was explored by William Wycherley, Sir John Vanbrugh, and George Farquhar until about 1710; and of which the chief glory are the plays of Congreve. It has been called the comedy of manners, to distinguish it from the comedy of humors, of which the great exponent was Ben Jonson: that is, it does not deal so much with ingrained character as with the way people behave in society. Men and women are treated according to the characteristics they adopt as clothing in which to face the world. These are often absurd and distorted, and become the "acquired follies" that the comic dramatists of the Restoration were bent upon having laughed out of social life. And since the social life of that time was the result of unusual circumstances, this comedy has a tang of its own, butts that no other comedy has in the same degree, purposes forced upon the writers of the time by the exaggerations peculiar to the period. It has been called "clique" drama; but then plays are always written for those who will go to see them. The London of those days was still largely puritanically theater-fearing, so the stage had to appeal to the court and all its ramifications, and in realistic drama treat of the people familiar to it. This is by no means to say that it belongs to that age alone. It is not only that human nature does not change very much through the centuries, but that the outstanding dramatists of the period were great enough to pierce through the temporary to what is permanent in the passions of men and women, so that what they have to say is in many respects relevant now, and is likely to be so long as any semblance of civilized society exists.

The butts of the comedy of manners were to a large extent those that have always attracted the comic spirit, with the peculiar flavor of the time, that was natural to a group of vital people returned from a period of exile, of which the court was largely composed. We therefore meet the Frenchified fop, the would-be wit with his eternal attempts at repartee and his straining after a new simile, the conceited gallant who thought himself irresistible to the ladies, the pompous man-of-affairs. We get also the pretentious amateur scientist, the hanger-on of the newly formed Royal Society, as well as the old-fashioned astrologer and the mystery-monger. There are also the old oppositions, youth and age, town and country, the gay life and the solemn. And if this society was bent on remaining secure, it was also determined to lead a joyous life.

The main theme of this comedy was that of sexual relations, of sex-antagonism, a struggle that was one of wit rather than of emotion, a matter that the less understanding moralists have always laid hold of as a handle against it. There was, certainly, a loosening of the old moral restraints, as always occurs after times of upheaval—and is especially noticeable at the present day. The men and women of those days attempted to "rationalize" sex, as we would say. The rake of either sex was an accepted figure; it was taken for granted that a married man would, as likely as not, have mistresses, and a married woman lovers; but that a couple should quarrel about it was absurd. Thus jealousy became a barbaric emotion of which a civilized man should rid himself. The amusing element of this comedy largely consists in watching people pretending to tame the untameable in themselves.

This comedy was basically realistic, constructed out of the people of the time and the urgent problems. Sometimes these problems were fantastically garbed, but they by no means were "sports of a witty fancy," as Charles Lamb, intent on defeating the Puritan, tried to argue, going on to say, "It is altogether a speculative scene of things, which has no reference whatever to the world that is." It was not, as he asserted, a land of cuckoldry, a Utopia of gallantry. For this comedy is essentially "critical comedy": its object was to "cure excess." So just as the comic dramatists of the time jibed at the fop, the virtuoso, the pretender to knowledge, the prude or false prude, so they subjected to trenchant criticism the assumptions about sexual behavior that fashionable London tried to live by. They said, in effect, "Here is life lived on these assumptions of yours: is it comfortable? Can you really go on like this?" In short, they wielded what Meredith called "the sword of common sense," and tried to laugh people back to a rational philosophy of social living.

It was at one time accepted that this comedy was an offshoot of the French variety, to please courtiers who while exiled in Paris had seen Molière's plays and those of his contemporaries. But this is a false view. It had its roots in the later Jacobean and Caroline theater, in plays such as John Marston's *Dutch Courtesan* (1605), and many plays by James Shirley, Philip Massinger, and Richard Brome, to mention only a few. The themes are all to be met with in these, and not always altogether in embryo. What the Restoration writers got from abroad was a better, tighter construction, a greater rapidity of phrase. There was nothing new even in the free treatment of sex. Ben Jonson himself complained about the bawdiness of much of the playwriting of his day; Dryden pointed out that John Fletcher's *The Custom of the Country* contained more bawdry than any play of his own time. So when in 1698 Jeremy Collier launched his *Short View of the Immorality and Profaneness of the English Stage*, following a lead given him by George Meriton in his *Immorality, Debauchery and Prophaneness*, earlier in the year, he caused great flurry in theatrical circles. It is a wild, extravagant, extraordinarily confused piece of writing so far as reasoning goes. Yet it is vigorous and clever; a good deal of what he said was cogent, and though he spoiled his case by overstatement, it came as a godsend to the morality-mongers. Although it did not much affect what was actually presented at the theaters, it caused great heart-searchings among the playwrights, who certainly became a little more careful. Some of them answered Collier, all somewhat ineffectually, for Collier was always shifting his ground; "he runs a-muck at all," as Vanbrugh said. There was, as Dryden remarked, too much horseplay in his raillery. Only Dennis answered him on a general enough level to be at all an adequate retort, but Congreve's *Amendments* made its own points.

CONGREVE'S COMEDIES

WHEN Dryden saw the manuscript of *The Old Batchelour* he declared that it was the most brilliant first play he had ever read. It needed, perhaps, a little adapting to the fashion of the moment, but that was all. It is undoubtedly a remarkable performance; the mechanism is close and complicated, but it works smoothly, with a rapidity of movement Congreve was not always able to maintain. Though it is a little baffling when read, one can see that it would spin along dancingly in the theater: the phrasing is extraordinarily skillful, incisive, well-modeled, and easy for an actor to speak effectively. It is easy to see why the play was at once immensely popular. It gave the audiences exactly what they were accustomed to, but done a great deal better than usual. The scenes and situations were familiar, with variations, and there were the usual characters, colored in a slightly different way: the immoral young woman, the false prude, the ridiculous old alderman and his charming young wife, who is ripe for seduction; the gay sparks, the young man who regards the pursuit of women as the grandest of games but shies off at the last moment; the cheat, the silly knight with his attendant coward who pretends to be tremendously brave, the miles gloriosus of classical comedy. It was all very laughable.

But though one can sense an individual mind at work, and feel that the writer is someone of more than common possibilities, little of the distinctive Congreve emerges. We feel that the writer has no special, no critical attitude toward the kind of life depicted. He seems to accept it, offering no criticism: but then, after all, he was very young indeed when he wrote it. How could he by then have formulated an attitude? We feel that he was intent not on commenting on life but on writing a well-made play, on mastering the technique. He may have felt a certain distaste for the material tradition seemed to offer him, as he wrote in his letter *Concerning Humour in Comedy*:

Is anything more common, than to have a pretended Comedy, stuff'd with such Grotesques, Figures, and Farce Fools? . . . I can never care for seeing things, that force me to entertain low thoughts of my Nature . . . I confess freely to you, I could never look upon a Monkey, without very Mortifying Reflections.

And the modest dedication that was added to the printed text, in which he says that he could find a great many more faults in it than his critics had, would seem to bear this out.

The Double-Dealer is almost startlingly different,

and the dedication is revealing. There Congreve says:[1]

I design'd the Moral first, and to that Moral I invented the Fable . . . I made the Plot as strong as I could, because it was single, and I made it single, because I would avoid Confusion, and was resolved to preserve the three Unities of the Drama.

And certainly the plot is clear, though intricate enough to keep the mind alert. But it is plain that in talking about "the Moral," Congreve felt that he had something to say, and one feels at the same time that he is dealing not with stage puppets but with people observed in the society that he moved in. To some extent, to be sure, they are types: the would-be wit, the amorous old woman, the false prude; but there is also the decent man—not so much the hero Mellefont as his friend Careless—and the charming, unspoiled young woman. And there is, as the title implies, the traitorous friend, the double-dealer, Maskwell. The moral is not so easy to define. Perhaps it is a little to overstate it in using John Keats's phrase, "the holiness of the heart's affections"; more certainly it is the necessity to guard against disillusion, a theme that was to come out more and more strongly as Congreve progressed. Here is Mellefont talking with Cynthia, his betrothed, after listening to some delightful absurdities exchanged between Lord and Lady Froth:

Mel. You're thoughtful, *Cynthia?*
Cynt. I'm thinking, tho' Marriage makes Man and Wife one Flesh, it leaves 'em still two Fools; and they become more conspicuous by setting off one another.
Mel. That's only when two Fools meet, and their Follies are oppos'd.
Cynt. Nay, I have known two Wits meet, and by the Opposition of their Wit, render themselves as ridiculous as Fools. 'Tis an odd Game we're going to Play at: What think you of drawing Stakes, and giving over in time?
Mel. No, hang't, that's not endeavouring to win, because it's possible we may lose; since we have shuffled and cut, let's e'en turn up Trump now.
Cynt. Then I find it's like Cards, if either of us have a good Hand it is an Accident of Fortune.

(II. iii)

That wistful note creeps in, while all the while the scathing, pretension-stripping comedy goes on.

[1]All the quotations from Congreve's dramatic works are taken from the World's Classics edition, 2 vols. (Oxford, 1925–1928).

Compare the above passage with one in which the self-deluded Lady Plyant thinks that Mellefont wishes to marry her stepdaughter Cynthia merely to have intimate access to herself. Mellefont is trying to explain to Lady Plyant (who denies her husband conjugal favors) that she is quite mistaken:

Mel. Nay, Madam, hear me; I mean—
Lady P. Hear you, no, no; I'll deny you first, and hear you afterwards. For one does not know how one's Mind may change upon hearing—Hearing is one of the Senses, and all the Senses are fallible; I won't trust my Honour, I assure you; my Honour is infallible and uncompatible.
Mel. For Heav'n's sake, Madam—
Lady P. O name it no more—Bless me, how can you talk of Heav'n! and have so much Wickedness in your Heart? May be you don't think it a Sin,—They say some of you Gentlemen don't think it a Sin—May be it is no Sin to them that don't think it is so; indeed if I did not think it a Sin—But still my Honour, if it were no Sin,—But then, to marry my Daughter for the Conveniency of frequent Opportunities,—I'll never consent to that, as sure as can be, I'll break the Match.
Mel. Death and Amazement,—Madam, upon my Knees—

(II. v)

But she refuses to be convinced, and she bubbles on for a minute or two of what is to us delicious absurdity. And here with great certainty Congreve is, as George Meredith said, "at once precise and voluble. If you have ever thought upon style you will acknowledge it to be a signal accomplishment. In this he is a classic, and is worthy of treading a measure with Molière." Yet the play was not well liked; it was a comparative failure: it is hard to understand why, seeing that it is so much better than *The Old Batchelour*. Perhaps it was an element of unfamiliarity that puzzled the audience.

But they seem to have been prepared for Congreve's next play, *Love for Love*, which was a success in spite of being rather too long, as he confesses in the dedication, giving as an excuse that, with so many characters, to have shortened the play would have meant doing some of them an injustice. For in this play he was to some extent returning to the tradition of the Jonsonian comedy of humors, especially in the characters of Foresight, the astrologer—a type familiar in those days, for astrology still retained some prestige, and Dryden himself was not altogether skeptical of it—and of

Sir Sampson Legend, the heavy father, of will-shaking propensities. Yet it is mainly the comedy of manners, with its foolish gallants, its flighty ladies, its age-youth opposition. And this part is done with a delightful precision of thought as well as of language. The sailor, Ben Legend, has a commonsense honesty, a sea-breeze freshness about him; and Prue is an innocent young girl, full of vitality, whom one can laugh at without despising. It is all extremely deft, as when the two sisters, Mrs. Foresight and Mrs. Frail, strip from each other their pretensions to virtue. They are quarreling:

Mrs. Fore. I suppose you would not go alone to the *World's-End* [a notorious resort].
Mrs. Frail. The *World's-End*! What, do you mean to banter me?
Mrs. Fore. Poor Innocent! You don't know that there's a Place call'd the *World's-End?* I'll swear you can keep your countenance purely, you'd make an admirable Player.
Mrs. Frail. I'll swear you have a great deal of Confidence, and in my Mind too much for the Stage.
Mrs. Fore. Very well, that will appear who has most: you were never at the *World's-End?*
Mrs. Frail. No.
Mrs. Fore. You deny it positively to my Face.
Mrs. Frail. Your Face, what's your Face?
Mrs. Fore. No matter for that, it's as good a Face as yours.
Mrs. Frail. Not by a Dozen Years wearing.—But I do deny it positively to your Face then.
Mrs. Fore. I'll allow you now to find Fault with my Face;—for I'll swear your Impudence has put me out of Countenance:—But look you here now,—where did you lose this Gold Bodkin?—Oh, Sister, Sister!
Mrs. Frail. My Bodkin!
Mrs. Fore. Nay, 'tis yours, look at it.
Mrs. Frail. Well, if you go to that, where did you find this Bodkin?—Oh Sister, Sister!—Sister every way.
Mrs. Fore. (Aside). O Devil on't, that I cou'd not discover her, without betraying myself.
Mrs. Frail. I have heard Gentlemen say, Sister; that one shou'd take great Care, when one makes a Thrust in Fencing, not to lye open one's self.
Mrs. Fore. It's very true, Sister: Well, since all's out, and as you say, since we are both wounded, let us do what is often done in Duels, take care of one another, and grow better Friends than before.
Mrs. Frail. With all my Heart, ours are but slight flesh Wounds, and if we keep 'em from Air, not at all dangerous: Well, give me your Hand in Token of Sisterly Secresie and Affection.

(II. ix)

They are witty and clever enough, these fine ladies, but their essential vulgarity is revealed when they descend to Billingsgate word slinging about each other's faces.

There is enough there to tickle an audience hugely. And, moreover, as Congreve said in his prologue:

> We've something, too, to gratifie ill Nature,
> (If there be any here) and that is Satire . . .[2]
> Since *The Plain-Dealer's* Scenes of Manly Rage,
> Not one had dar'd to lash this Crying Age.
> This time, the Poet owns the bold Essay,
> Yet hopes there's no Ill-manners in his Play. . . .

But lashing satire was not Congreve's talent; he could not hope, and would not try, to emulate Wycherley's scathing indictment, which was based on a deep revulsion against a society toward which he felt himself only too much drawn, and which comes out most hammeringly in *The Plain Dealer*. Congreve was made of gentler material; there might be scorn in him, but there was no hatred, and the satire in this play is rather more affectionate, if severe, chiding than the application of the lash, and it tends to disappear in the whirl of well-controlled movement.

But amid all the flurry and pother and intrigue, the especial thing that Congreve has to say comes out a little more clearly than it did in *The Double-Dealer*. The love affair between Valentine and Angelica brings out his fear of disillusion, his insistence that the precious thing in life—affection in human relations—must be preserved at all costs. Valentine is no good young man; he has had his fling, dissipated a fortune on mistresses and gaudy living; Angelica has the affectations of the witty, fine lady caricatured in Prue. But that they really love each other comes out in the scenes in which Valentine pretends to be mad. Valentine says to Angelica, "You are not leaving me in this uncertainty?" and she answers:

Wou'd any thing, but a Madman, complain of Uncertainty? Uncertainty and Expectation are the Joys of Life. Security is an insipid thing, and the overtaking and possessing of a Wish, discovers the Folly of the Chase. Never let us know one another better; for the Pleasure of the Masquerade is done, when we come to shew our

[2] In those days a perfectly good rhyme—pronounced "naytur," and "saytur."

Faces; but I'll tell you two things before I leave you; I am not the Fool you take me for: and you are mad, and don't know it.

(IV. xx)

Not only the need to guard against disillusion is here, but also the realization that human beings are savages—angels, perhaps, but lodged in the bodies of beasts. Fling off the masks of civilization and we are done for. And in the last speech of the play Angelica rounds upon men, always complaining of the inconstancy and flightiness of women:

'Tis an unreasonable Accusation, that you lay upon our Sex: You tax us with Injustice, only to cover your own want of Merit. You would all have the Reward of Love; but few have the Constancy to stay 'till it becomes your due. Men are generally Hypocrites and Infidels, they pretend to Worship, but have neither Zeal nor Faith: How few, like *Valentine*, would persevere even to Martyrdom, and sacrifice their Interest to their Constancy!

But perhaps the note was too gently played to be much noticed.

This is not so in *The Way of the World*, which brings out the delicacies of the spirit against the dark murk of the way of the fashionable world —and not the fashionable world alone. Hazlitt says: "It is an essence almost too fine; and the sense of pleasure evaporates, in an aspiration after something too exquisite ever to have been realised." It was not a success when first acted, for reasons clear enough to Congreve when he wrote his dedication:

That it succeeded on the Stage, was almost beyond my Expectation; for but little of it was prepar'd for that general Taste which seems now to be predominant in the Pallats of our Audience.
Those Characters which are meant to be ridicul'd in most of our Comedies, are of Fools so gross, that in my humble Opinion, they shou'd rather disturb than divert the well-natur'd and reflecting Part of an Audience; they are rather Objects of Charity than Contempt; and instead of moving our Mirth, they ought very often to excite our Compassion.

The play had been acted two or three days, he says later, before hasty judges "cou'd find the leisure to distinguish betwixt the Character of a *Witwoud* and a *Truewit*." In this last matter Congreve had been too subtle. His Witwoud is indeed a coxcomb, a jackass, but he is enough aware of his own continued affectation to prevent its becoming reality; a man who can say "A Wit shou'd no more be sincere, than a Woman constant; one argues a Decay of Parts, as t'other of Beauty" may be an unpleasant fellow, but he is no idiot, and it is not surprising that many years later Alexander Pope should ask: "Tell me if Congreve's fools are fools indeed?"

Another thing that militated against the success of the play, and to some extent still does, is not so much the villainy of the plot as the abrupt and unlikely way in which it is resolved. This masterpiece has to be appreciated for other reasons: the depth and sympathy of its characterization, together with the general sense of what is precious in life, and the magnificent handling of language— "purity of style" as he phrased it. Moreover, as in all excellent comic work, there is a hint of tragedy underlying the whole ethos, especially in the treatment of Lady Wishfort, who, in every respect fully fifty-five years of age, hankers after a marriage based upon her charms. She remains a comic figure, but there is nothing comic about Mrs. Marwood, whose baffled love renders her a traitress, and little to laugh at in Mrs. Fainall. And beneath the whole Mirabell–Millamant story there is a deep seriousness that conveys the moral of the play. For Congreve had that sound and capacious mind, always a grave one, which Landor makes Alfieri say is required for genuine humor and true wit.

Millamant, on the surface a flippant, shallow young woman, is basically serious. She has thought a great deal on the values that make a genuinely happy life for a woman of her class and culture. At her first entrance, which does not occur until well into the second act, she is overbrimming with gaiety, as she comes "full Sail, with her Fan spread and Streamers out, and a Shoal of Fools for Tenders." She is late because, as her maid Mincing reminds her, she stayed to peruse a packet of letters:

Milla. O ay, Letters—I had Letters—I am persecuted with Letters—I hate Letters—No Body knows how to write Letters; and yet one has 'em, one does not know why—They serve to pin up one's Hair.
Witwoud. Is that the way? Pray, Madam, do you pin up your Hair with all your Letters; I find I must keep Copies.
Milla. Only with those in Verse, Mr. *Witwoud.* I never pin up my Hair with Prose. I think I try'd once, *Mincing.*
Minc. O Mem, I shall never forget it.

Milla. Ay, poor *Mincing* tift and tift all the Morning.
(II. iv)

She turns to talk with Mirabell, having been a little ashamed of the silly company he had found her in the evening before. There is some slight sparring, during which Mirabell reminds her of the saying that beauty is the lover's gift:

Milla. O the Vanity of these Men! . . . Beauty the Lover's Gift—Lord, what is a Lover, that it can give? Why one makes Lovers as fast as one pleases, and they live as long as one pleases, and they die as soon as one pleases. And then if one pleases one makes more.
(II. iv)

It is beautifully phrased, the words shuttling about the lightly stressed "pleases" until the weight comes down heavily upon it the last time it is used. And she will not submit to portentously solemn reproaches from Mirabell:

Milla. Sententious Mirabell! Prithee don't look with that violent and inflexible wise Face, like *Solomon* at the dividing of the Child in an old Tapestry Hanging.
(II.v)

When she has gone, Mirabell can think only of a whirlwind.

Her real nature comes out in the famous "bargaining" scene with Mirabell, where they exchange the conditions on which they will marry each other. Millamant, who likes to quote the verses of Sir John Suckling—"gentle, easy Suckling"—a poet given to voicing the fear of disillusion, knows that life cannot be treated too roughly, that happiness can be preserved only if each party shows the greatest delicacy toward the other.

Milla. . . . And d'ye hear, I won't be call'd Names after I'm Marry'd; positively I won't be call'd Names.
Mira. Names!
Milla. Ay, as Wife, Spouse, my Dear, Joy, Jewel, Love, Sweet-heart, and the rest of that nauseous Cant, in which Men and their Wives are so fulsomly familiar,—I shall never bear that—Good *Mirabell* don't let us be familiar or fond, nor kiss before Folks, like my Lady *Fadler* and Sir *Francis*: Nor go to *Hide-Park* together the first *Sunday* in a new Chariot, to provoke Eyes and Whispers; And then never be seen there together again; as if we were proud of one another the first Week, and asham'd of one another ever after. Let us never Visit together, not go to a Play together, but let us be very strange and well bred: Let us be as strange as if we had

been marry'd a great while; and as well bred as if we were not marry'd at all.

(IV. v)

Mirabell finds her demands so far "pretty reasonable," and though he regards as "something advanc'd" her further conditions guarding her privacy before she will consent to "dwindle into a Wife," he proposes his own measures, all eminently sensible, lest he should beyond measure be "enlarg'd to a husband." It is all very lightly done, but we know that they both have sound and grave minds enabling them to indulge in humor and wit.

There are some grimy elements in this comedy, such as the bitter scene between Mrs. Marwood and Fainall (II. iii), and some rather cruel intriguing on the part of Mirabell himself, all to remind us that the way of the world is not altogether a pretty one. But the fools have redeeming qualities; there is some kindness in Witwoud; and his half-brother, Sir Wilful, though he incurs all the ridicule of the country lout, is crude, yet good-hearted and generous. The great comic character—though to look at her is to be touched with pity—is Lady Wishfort, in a sense Congreve's greatest invention. What endears her to us is her magnificent gift of language. Listen to her dismissing her traitorous maid:

Out of my House, out of my House, thou *Viper*, thou *Serpent*, that I have foster'd; thou bosom Traitress, that I rais'd from nothing—Begone, begone, begone, go, go—That I took from washing of old Gause and weaving of dead Hair, with a bleak blue Nose, over a Chafing-dish of starv'd Embers, and Dining behind a Traverse Rag, in a shop no bigger than a Bird-Cage,—go, starve again, do, do.

(V. i)

"The flow of boudoir Billingsgate in Lady Wishfort," Meredith said, "is unmatched for the vigour and pointedness of the tongue. It spins along with a final ring, like the voice of Nature in a fury"; and he might have added that her choice of vowel sounds reveals the genius of a born writer of prose. Listen to the sequence: bleak—blue—nose; or, go—starve again—do, do.

Here, of course, she is only the comic termagant; but she is pathetic when she is preparing to meet her proposed husband, the fake Sir Rowland, who is really Mirabell's servant Waitwell, who in turn is married to Foible:

Lady W. Will he be Importunate, *Foible*, and push? For if he shou'd not be importunate—I shall never break Decorums—I shall die with Confusion, if I am forc'd to advance—Oh no, I can never advance—I shall swoon if he should expect Advances. No, I hope Sir *Rowland* is better bred, than to put a Lady to the Necessity of breaking her Forms. I won't be too coy neither.—I won't give him Despair—But a little Disdain is not amiss; a little Scorn is alluring.

Foible. A little Scorn becomes your Ladyship.

Lady W. Yes, but Tenderness becomes me best—A sort of Dyingness—You see that Picture has a sort of a—Ha *Foible?* A Swimmingness in the Eyes—Yes, I'll look so—My Niece affects it; but she wants Features. Is Sir *Rowland* handsome? . . . Don't answer me. I won't know: I'll be surpriz'd. I'll be taken by Surprize.

Foib. By Storm, Madam. Sir *Rowland's* a brisk Man.

Lady W. Is he! O then he'll importune, if he's a brisk Man. I shall save Decorums if Sir *Rowland* importunes. I have a mortal Terror at the Apprehension of offending against Decorums.

(III. v)

This kind of exquisite absurdity is repeated before we get to the climax, when she accepts the advances of the supposed Sir Rowland. Her language is marvelous, her attitude painfully ridiculous:

Lady W. Well, Sir *Rowland*, you have the way,—You are no Novice in the Labyrinth of Love—You have the Clue—But as I am a Person, Sir *Rowland*, you must not attribute my yielding to any sinister Appetite, or Indigestion of Widowhood; nor impute my Complacency to any Lethargy of Continence—I hope you do not think me prone to any Iteration of Nuptials.—

Wait. Far be it from me—

Lady W. If you do, I protest I must recede—or think that I have made a Prostitution of Decorums, but in the Vehemence of Compassion, and to save the life of a Person of so much Importance—

Wait. I esteem it so—

Lady W. Or else you wrong my Condescension—

Wait. I do not, I do not—

Lady W. Indeed you do.

Wait. I do not, fair Shrine of Virtue.

Lady W. If you think the least Scruple of Carnality was an Ingredient—

Wait. Dear Madam, no. You are all *Camphire*[3] and *Frankincense*, all *Chastity* and *Odour*.

(IV. xiii)

[3]*Camphire.* That "causeth impotency unto Venery": Sir Thomas Browne, *Pseudodoxia Epidemica* (1646), known as *Vulgar Errors.*

345

She is equally voluble, laughingly comic, heart-rendingly pathetic when, after the cheat has been revealed to her, she suggests to Mrs. Marwood that she "would retire to Desarts and Solitudes; and feed harmless Sheep by Groves and purling Streams."

Congreve's place in English comedy, in the pure comedy of manners, is supreme. No one can touch him for sheer artistry, for exquisite use of language—though here Shaw runs him close, in the vigor and grace of his phrase—for delicate apprehension of the human issues involved. As Hazlitt wrote, "His style is inimitable, nay perfect. It is the highest model of comic dialogue. Every sentence is replete with sense and satire, conveyed in the most brilliant and polished terms. . . . His works are a singular treat to those who have cultivated a taste for the niceties of English style; there is a peculiar flavour in the very words, which is to be found in hardly any other writer." It has been complained that the Restoration comedy of manners is dull and trivial. If you cannot translate the idiom of a past time—the idiom of behavior as well as of language—into that of your own, it may seem dull; if you can do so it appears highly relevant. Trivial? Only if you cannot see through to the universality that underlies every phase of the social mask. It is sometimes complained that Congreve's fine gentlemen are no gentlemen; they often behave as cads. If they were really gentlemen, perfect in behavior, they would hardly be targets for the imps of comedy. He may not be among the really great writers of comedy, but not to like him is to confess yourself unworthy to admire Molière.

OTHER WORK

It is doubtful whether if Congreve had not written his comedies we would concern ourselves with his other work. Not that it is altogether negligible; and, though very minor, it tolerably represents what was being done in that age. Moreover, it has distinct qualities of its own and serves to fill out the picture of Congreve, not so much as a creator but as a man of letters.

His first publication, written when he was hardly more than a boy, and before he had ventured on a play, was *Incognita; or, Love and Duty Reconcil'd*, a delicious little skit on the popular romance of the time, utterly unrelated to life, and performed with a gaiety and a delight in words combined with a sense of structure, which makes it still readable. It is all deliberate nonsense, a sheer game that the reader is intended to enjoy. Here, for example, is a small part of the description of Leonora:

She had danced much, which together with her being close masked, gave her a tincture of Carnation more than ordinary. But *Aurelian* (from whom I had every tittle of her Description) fancy'd he saw a little Nest of Cupids break from the Tresses of her Hair, and every one officiously betake himself to his task. Some fann'd with their downy Wings, her glowing Cheeks, while others brushed the balmy Dew from off her Face, leaving alone a heavenly Moisture bulbing on her Lips, on which they drank and revell'd for their pains. . . .

and so on. It is sheer tomfoolery, but done with such extraordinary skill as to make it popular. Originally published over the name of Cleophil, in the next edition Congreve owned up to it.

Apart from the few "occasional" poems, Congreve's next extratheatrical publication was the letter to Dennis, already referred to, *Concerning Humour in Comedy* (1695), published early in the next year. Humor is to be understood in the Jonsonian sense; it is, as Congreve defined it, "from Nature . . . [it] shews us as we are." What he is in the main concerned with is to distinguish between humor, habit, and affectation; and wit also comes into the discussion. The whole thing now seems a little academic, especially as ideas about psychology have so radically changed; it does show something of what the playwrights of the time thought about the material they were handling, and serves a little to explain Congreve's treatment of some of his characters. His only other critical work, which we may deal with here, was *A Discourse on the Pindarique Ode*, which accompanied an ode written to the queen in 1706. As he remarked of the odes with that title that had for some years flooded the press:

The Character of these late Pindariques, is, a Bundle of rambling incoherent Thoughts, express'd in a like Parcel of irregular Stanzas, which also consist of such another Complication of disproportion'd, uncertain and perplex'd Verses and Rhimes.

Congreve pointed out that the true Pindaric ode was regular in form, with strophe, antistrophe, and epode following in regular succession, each conforming to the pattern set by the original three. This had already been pointed out by Milton's nephew, Edward Phillips, in his *Theatrum Poetarum* (1675), but it had been completely ignored, just as Jonson's example had been. Abraham Cowley was the greatest sinner, but Congreve conceded that "the Beauty of his Verses, are an Attonement for the Irregularity of his Stanzas," and at least he often happily copied Pindar in "the Force of his Figures, the Sublimity of his Stile and Sentiments."

It is almost unbelievable to us that Congreve's tragedy, *The Mourning Bride* (1697), should have been greeted with acclamation, and sent soaring Congreve's reputation as a dramatist. Even as an example of "heroic drama," or the type of tragedy current at the time, it is weak; the episodes, intrigues, and disguises seem to be more suitable to comedy than to tragedy, except that they end in murder rather than in marriage. Yet the play had an enormous vogue, possibly because there is a quality about the language and the conduct of the verse that makes it palatable in the theater. That Dr. Johnson, while condemning the tragedy as such, could yet say: "If I were required to select from the whole mass of English poetry the most poetical paragraph, I know not what I should prefer to an exclamation in *The Mourning Bride*," and he proceeds to quote the passage (II. iii) containing the speech that begins "How reverend is the Face of this tall Pile." And though today we may despise the tragedy as such, it has at least provided the language with two popular quotations, namely, the opening line "Music has Charms to sooth a savage Breast" and the lines that conclude Act III:

> Heav'n has no Rage, like Love to Hatred turn'd,
> Nor Hell a Fury, like a Woman scorn'd.

though that is an adaptation from Brome. Moreover, the play does contain some thoughtful speeches, reminiscent of the intellectual passages to be found in Chapman's dramas.

Whether because of the cold reception for *The Way of the World* or because Congreve felt he had no more to say, and was already, though barely thirty years old, feeling that his powers were unequal to any great effort—after all the output of the last ten years had been amazing—Congreve did little more for the theater beyond assisting in the launching and management of Vanbrugh's venture with the Opera House in the Haymarket and writing the libretti for the operas *The Judgement of Paris* (1701), performed to the music of Eccles, and *Semele* (1710), later rendered popular by Handel's setting. They render faithfully enough, and in lively fashion, the two classical myths, and, moreover, the words are admirably adapted for setting to music. Congreve was not concerned here to write striking poetry that could stand on its own merits, but to compose words that could easily be sung. These libretti are competent pieces of craftsmanship and, read as such, are agreeable enough.

Congreve's contribution to *Squire Trelooby*, an adaptation of Molière's *Monsieur de Pourceaugnac*, can hardly be considered his work. He wrote to his friend Joseph Keally, 20 May 1704:

> The translation you speak of is not altogether mine; for Vanbrugh and Walsh had a part in it. Each did one act of a French farce. Mine, and I believe theirs, was done in two mornings; so there can be no great matter in it.

Congreve's poetry is no more than at a fair average level of the verse being written at the period. It consists to a great extent of translations, from Homer, Ovid, Horace, and Juvenal, more scholarly than most, but not very vigorous or exciting. His complimentary addresses or official laments, such as the ones to William III on the taking of Namur, those on the deaths of Queen Mary and the marquess of Blandford (the only son of the duke of Marlborough), the ode to Queen Anne, and so on, are indistinguishable from the common run of such things. Where his individual note can be heard is in the shorter lyrics, not unlike those of Matthew Prior, but quieter, with a sense of the acceptance of things. Perhaps the best of them all is the well-known "Song":

> False, though she be to me and Love,
>   I'll ne'er pursue Revenge;
> For still the Charmer I approve,
>   Tho I deplore her Change.
>
> In hours of Bliss we oft have met,
>   They could not always last;
> And though the present I regret,
>   I'm grateful for the past.

Another at the same level of conciseness, of saying much in short space, is this lyric, also called "Song":

347

Pious *Selinda* goes to Pray'rs
  If I but ask the Favour;
And yet the tender Fool's in Tears,
  When she believes I'll leave her.

Wou'd I were free from this Restraint,
  Or else had hopes to win her;
Wou'd she cou'd make of me a Saint,
  Or I of her a Sinner.

Nevertheless, there is great variety in Congreve's verses, which exhibit a wide range of mastery over various forms, as well as covering a considerable range of emotions, none very deep, perhaps, but all sensitive. There are, for instance, his "Ode on Mrs. Arabella Hunt Singing" and the epigram on her death, the epistles, the translations from Juvenal, and so on, which are worth more than just a perusal.

CONCLUSION

CONGREVE published his *Works* in 1710, and virtually retired from the literary scene, at least as an active participant, unless the edition of Dryden's *Works*, which he produced in 1717 as an act of piety, is considered such. But he was very much in the literary scene, being the friend of most of the great writers of his time, such as Swift, Pope, who dedicated his *Iliad* to him in 1720, and Steele, who dedicated to him his edition of Joseph Addison's *The Drummer*, in 1722. John Gay, in *Mr. Pope's Welcome from Greece*, written to celebrate Pope's finishing of the *Iliad*, referred to him as "friendly Congreve, unreproachful man." He seems to have lacked the energy to write, suffering from obesity, gout, and an ever-increasing loss of sight. But he was apparently able to discharge the not very onerous duties of his civil service posts.

Giles Jacob, in the second volume of his *Poetical Register* (1720), a kind of literary *Who's Who*, said of him:

Mr. Congreve, notwithstanding he has justly acquir'd the greatest Reputation in Dramatick Writings, is so far from being puff'd up with Vanity (a Failing in most Authors of Excellency), that he abounds with Humility and good Nature. He does not shew so much the Poet as the Gentleman: he is ambitious of few Praises, tho' he deserves numerous Encomiums; he is genteel and regular in his Oeconomy, unaffected in Behaviour, pleasing and informing in his Conversation, and respectful to all.

But he did not want to be bothered with discussing his own work with eager young tuft hunters, such as Voltaire, who visited him in 1726. He had, after all, come to the verge of life, as Voltaire admitted; he really couldn't discuss his almost forgotten comedies with him. He passed them off as trifles, and said that he would be delighted to talk to Voltaire on general matters—what he called receiving a visit on the footing of a gentleman—but not, oh not, about *The Way of the World*. This led Voltaire to think that Congreve despised letters and was a social snob of the worst kind, an error absurdly emphasized by Macaulay, who surely knew that noblemen in those days themselves aspired to be recognized as men of letters, and should have realized the justice of Lamb's comment that "the little Frenchman was well answered." Congreve was quite ready to talk generally about literature, as is evidenced by the words of another foreigner, Luigi Riccoboni, who reported in *An Historical Account of the Theatre in Europe* (1744):

Among the Crowd of *English* Poets, Mr. *Congreve* is most esteemed for Comedy. He was perfectly acquainted with Nature; and was living in 1727, when I was in London. I conversed with him more than once, and found his Taste joined with great Learning. It is rare to find many Dramatic Poets of his Stamp.

For Congreve was no snob, but he wanted to be withdrawn from the bustle and contention of the literary life, which at that time presented no very edifying spectacle—witness the scurrilous attacks on Pope. If he had friends among the great, those whom he most loved to cultivate were of no eminence, such as Joseph Kneally, to whom he wrote frequently. Congreve was no great letter writer; his missives are friendly signals rather than revealing or informative documents, but they tell us much about him. For instance, he informs Kneally on 14 October 1704: "I am grown fat; but you know I was born with somewhat of a round belly. . . . However, think of me as I am, nothing extenuate." On 8 June 1706, he writes: "I am sure you know me well enough to know I feel very sensibly and silently for those whom I love." And already by 29 November 1708, "Ease and quiet is what I hunt after. If I have not ambition, I have other passions more easily gratified. Believe me, I find none more pleasing to me than my friendship for you." Perhaps what best sums up his character is the verse letter he wrote in 1728 to his old friend Viscount Cobham, to whom he had some years earlier, while the recipient was Sir Richard Temple, addressed the poem "Of Pleasing," a witty attack upon bad critics. In this final exercise, which begins "Sincerest Critick of my Prose, or Rhime," he first praises Cobham for the work he is doing in beautifying the estate of Stowe, which has been famous ever since, but concludes:

> Come, see thy Friend, retir'd without Regret,
> Forgetting Care, or striving to forget;
> In easy Contemplation soothing Time
> With Morals much, and now and then with Rhime,
> Not so robust in Body as in Mind,
> And always undejected, tho' declin'd;
> Not wondering at the World's new wicked Ways,
> Compar'd with those of our Fore-fathers Days,
> For Virtue now is neither more nor less,
> And Vice is only varied in the Dress;
> Believe it, Men have ever been the same,
> And all the Golden Age is but a Dream.

All may not agree with that philosophy, and some will combat it fiercely; yet it is wisdom of a kind and evinces a degree of serenity based upon an understanding knowledge of the past, and it might be expected of a man who had a good deal pondered and experienced the way of the world.

SELECTED BIBLIOGRAPHY

I. General Background on Restoration Comedy. W. Hazlitt, *Lectures on the English Comic Writers* (London, 1819), repr. in P. P. Howe, ed., *Complete Works*, vol. 6 (London, 1931); T. B. Macaulay, *Critical and Historical Essays* (London, 1843), includes "The Comic Dramatists of the Restoration"; J. Palmer, *The Comedy of Manners* (London, 1913); A. Nicoll, *History of the English Drama 1660–1900*, vol. 1: *Restoration Drama 1660–1700* (Cambridge, 1923; 4th ed., rev., 1952); B. Dobrée, *Restoration Comedy* (Oxford, 1924); J. W. Krutch, *Comedy and Conscience After the Restoration* (New York, 1929; rev. ed., 1949); H. T. E. Perry, *The Comic Spirit in Restoration Drama* (New Haven, 1925); J. H. Wilson, *The Influence of Beaumont and Fletcher on Restoration Drama* (Columbus, Ohio, 1928); L. C. Knights, *Explorations* (London, 1937), contains "Restoration Comedy: The Reality and the Myth"; J. Wilcox, *The Relation of Molière to Restoration Comedy* (New York, 1938); E. Mignon, *Crabbed Age and Youth: The Old Men and Women in the Restoration Comedy of Manners* (Durham, N. C., 1947); J. H. Smith, *The Gay Couple in Restoration Comedy* (Cambridge, Mass., 1948); T. Fujimura, *The Restoration Comedy of Wit* (Princeton, 1952; repr. London, 1968); J. E. Gagen, *The New Woman: Her Emergence in English Drama 1600–1730* (New York, 1954); B. Ford, ed., *The Pelican Guide to English Literature*, vol. 4: *From Dryden to Johnson* (Harmondsworth, 1957; rev. 1965), contains P. A. W. Collins' "Restoration Comedy"; J. Wain, *Preliminary Essays* (London, 1957), contains "Restoration Comedy and Its Modern Critics"; N. Holland, *The First Modern Comedies: The Significance of Etherege, Wycherley and Congreve* (Cambridge, Mass., 1959); D. Wilkinson, *The Comedy of Habit: An Essay on the Use of Courtesy Literature in a Study of Restoration Comic Drama* (Leyden, 1964); J. R. Brown and B. Harris, eds., *Restoration Theatre*, Stratford-upon-Avon Studies 6 (London, 1965); J. H. Wilson, *A Preface to Restoration Drama* (Cambridge, Mass., 1965); J. Loftis, ed., *Restoration Drama: Modern Essays in Criticism* (New York, 1966); E. Miner, ed., *Restoration Dramatists: A Collection of Critical Essays* (Englewood Cliffs, N. J., 1967); J. R. Sutherland, *The Oxford History of English Literature*, vol. 6: *English Literature of the Late 17th Century* (London, 1969); V. O. Birdsall, *Wild Civility: The English Comic Spirit on the Restoration Stage* (Bloomington, Ind., 1970); I. Donaldson, *The World Upside Down: Comedy from Jonson to Fielding* (Oxford, 1970); K. Muir, *The Comedy of Manners* (London, 1970); B. R. Schneider, *The Ethics of Restoration Comedy* (Urbana, Ill., 1971); C. Ricks, ed., *The Sphere History of Literature in the English Language* (London, 1971), contains J. Barnard's "Drama from the Restoration to 1710"; H. Hawkins, *Likenesses of Truth in Elizabethan and Restoration Drama* (Oxford, 1972).

II. Bibliographies. J. C. Hodges, ed., *The Library of William Congreve* (New York, 1955); A. M. Lyles and J. Dobson, *The John C. Hodges Collection of William Congreve: A Bibliographical Catalogue* (Knoxville, Tenn., 1970).

III. Collected Editions. *The Works*, 3 vols. (London, 1710), many eds. throughout the eighteenth century, including the Baskerville ed. (London, 1761; 2 vols., 1773 and 1774); A. C. Ewald, ed., *William Congreve* (London, 1887; repr. New York, 1956), in the Mermaid series; M. Summers, ed., *The Complete Works*, 4 vols. (London, 1923); B. Dobrée, ed., *The Comedies, The Mourning Bride, Poems and Miscellanies*, 2 vols. (Oxford, 1925–1928), in the World's Classics series; J. W. Krutch, ed., *The Comedies of William Congreve* (New York, 1927); F. W. Bateson, ed., *The Works* (London, 1930); J. C. Hodges, ed., *William Congreve. Letters and Documents* (New York—London, 1964); H. J. Davis, ed., *The Complete Plays* (Chicago, 1967).

IV. Separate Works. *Plays: The Old Batchelour* (London, 1693); *The Double-Dealer* (London, 1694), and in A. Barton, ed. (London, 1973); *Love for Love* (London, 1695), and in E. L. Avery, ed., Regents Restoration Drama series (Lincoln, Nebr., 1966), in A. N. Jeffares, ed. (London, 1967), and in M. Kelsall, ed., New Mermaids series (London, 1969); *The Mourning Bride* (London, 1697); *The Way of the World* (London, 1700), also in K. Lynch, ed., Regents Restoration Drama series (Lincoln, Nebr.—London, 1965), in A. N. Jeffares, ed. (London, 1966), in B. Gibbons, ed., New Mermaids series (London, 1971), and in J. Barnard, ed., Fountainwell Drama series (Edinburgh, 1972); *Squire Trelooby* (London, 1704), an adaptation by Congreve, Vanbrugh, and Walsh of Molière's *Monsieur de Pourceaugnac* (see Vanbrugh bibliography).

Fiction: Incognita; or, Love and Duty Reconcil'd: A Novel (London, 1692), also in H. Brett-Smith, ed. (Oxford, 1922); *An Impossible Thing: A Tale* (London, 1720).

Verse: The Mourning Muse of Alexis: A Pastoral (London, 1695); *A Pindaric Ode, Humbly Offer'd to the King on His Taking Namur* (London, 1695); *The Judgement of Paris. A Masque* (London, 1701); *A Hymn to Harmony* (London, 1703); *The Tears of Amaryllis for Amyntas: A Pastoral* (London, 1703); *A Pindarique Ode on the Victorious Progress of Her Majesties Arms* (London, 1706); *A Letter to Viscount Cobham* (London, 1729).

Other Prose: "An Essay Concerning Humour in Comedy," in J. Dennis, ed., *Letters upon Several Occasions* (London, 1696); *Amendments to Mr. Collier's False and Imperfect Citations* (London, 1698); W. Congreve, ed., *Preface to the Dramatic Works of Dryden* (London, 1717).

V. SOME CRITICAL AND BIOGRAPHICAL STUDIES. J. Dryden, *The Double-Dealer* (London, 1694), contains Dryden's preface "To My Dear Friend Mr. Congreve"; J. Collier, *A Short View of the Immorality and Profaneness of the English Stage* (London, 1698); [Charles Wilson], *Memoirs of Congreve* (London, 1730); W. C. Hazlitt, *Lectures on the English Comic Writers* (London, 1819); C. Lamb, *The Essays of Elia* (London, 1822), contains "The Artificial Comedy of the Last Century"; T. B. Macaulay,

"Comic Dramatists of the Restoration" in *Edinburgh Review* (January 1841); W. M. Thackeray, *The English Humourists of the Eighteenth Century* (London, 1853); E. Gosse, *Life of William Congreve* (London, 1888; rev. ed., 1924); A. Bennewitz, *Congreve and Molière* (Leipzig, 1890); D. Schmid, *Congreve, sein Leben und Werke* (Vienna, 1897); S. Johnson, *Lives of the Poets*, II, edited by G. B. Hill (Oxford, 1905); J. Palmer, *The Comedy of Manners* (London, 1913); C. F. Armstrong, *Shakespeare to Shaw: Studies in the Life's Work of Six Dramatists of the English Stage* (London, 1913); D. Protopopescu, *Un Classique moderne: William Congreve, sa vie, son oeuvre* (Paris, 1924); B. Dobrée, *Restoration Comedy* (Oxford, 1924); H. T. E. Perry, *The Comic Spirit in Restoration Drama* (New Haven, 1925); K. M. Lynch, *The Social Mode of Restoration Comedy* (New York, 1926); B. Dobrée, *Restoration Tragedy* (Oxford, 1929); D. C. Taylor, *William Congreve* (Oxford, 1931); B. Dobrée, *A Variety of Ways* (Oxford, 1932), includes "William Congreve"; H. T. E. Perry, *Masters of Dramatic Comedy* (Cambridge, Mass., 1939); J. C. Hodges, ed., *William Congreve the Man: A Biography from New Sources* (New York, 1941); K. M. Lynch, *A Congreve Gallery* (Cambridge, Mass., 1951); E. L. Avery, *Congreve's Plays on the Nineteenth-Century Stage* (New York, 1951); E. L. Avery, *Congreve's Plays on the Eighteenth-Century Stage* (New York, 1951); P. and M. Mueschke, *A New View of Congreve's Way of the World* (Ann Arbor, Mich., 1958); N. Holland, *The First Modern Comedies: The Significance of Etherege, Wycherley and Congreve* (Cambridge, Mass., 1959); J. Loftis, *Comedy and Society from Congreve to Fielding* (Stanford, 1959); W. H. Van Voris, *The Cultivated Stance of Congreve's Plays* (Dublin, 1965); R. C. Sharma, *Themes and Conventions in the Comedy of Manners* (London, 1965); J. R. Brown and B. Harris, eds., *Restoration Theatre*, Stratford-upon-Avon Studies 6 (London, 1965); M. Novak, *William Congreve* (New York, 1971), an outstanding critical intro.; B. Morris, ed., *William Congreve* (London, 1972), Mermaid Critical Commentaries, an important collection including essays by G. L. Evans, R. A. Foakes, and W. Myers.

GEORGE FARQUHAR

(1678-1707)

A. J. Farmer

LIFE

GEORGE FARQUHAR, the last of the Restoration dramatists, is an engaging figure about whom we should like to know more than we do. There is no contemporary account of his life. Most of our information is drawn from the memoir prefixed to the 1775 Irish edition of his work by Thomas Wilkes, of Dublin. Wilkes was writing nearly seventy years after Farquhar's death; most of those connected with the dramatist had disappeared, and he was obliged to draw largely upon the stock of anecdotes and traditions that had grown up around the personality and work of his fellow countryman. Modern scholarship has brought to light some new facts, but much remains uncertain or obscure.

Farquhar was born in 1678 at Londonderry, in northern Ireland. His father, a clergyman probably of Scottish extraction, occupied a small living in the neighboring countryside. The family seems to have been well connected, but not well off. The boy began his studies at the Londonderry Free School, no doubt at the age of seven or eight. The master, Ellis Walker, had acquired more than local fame; he liked to have his pupils perform not only the comedies of Terence but also Shakespeare, and it is tempting to imagine that Farquhar's vocation was awakened in this way. The siege of Londonderry must have been the great event of his school life. Later, his widow declared that her husband's family had lost everything during the siege, their house having been burned down by marauding troops, and that his father had died of grief shortly after. She also claimed, with less likelihood, that Farquhar had taken part in the subsequent battle of the Boyne, at the age of twelve. At any rate, his earliest known work, a Pindaric ode entitled "On the Death of General Schomberg, Kill'd at the Boyne," possibly dates from this period.

When, at seventeen, Farquhar entered Trinity College, Dublin, it was presumably with the intention of studying for the church. He was registered as a sizar—that is, he received his food or commons free and, in return, served at the table of the fellows. In May 1695, a little less than a year after his admission, he was awarded an exhibition amounting to £4 a year. This was almost immediately suspended, Farquhar having been involved, with other students, in riotous behavior at the neighboring Donnybrook Fair. But his case seems to have been less serious than that of his companions, for the exhibition was restored in February 1696. This is all we can learn from the college records concerning him. His studies appear to have come to an abrupt end. Was he expelled, as one tradition has it, for answering with unbecoming levity an examination question on a religious theme? Or had the attraction of the theater already become too strong to resist? All we know is that he left Trinity sometime after February 1696, without taking a degree.

Predictably, perhaps, it is not very long before we find him on the stage of the Smock Alley Theatre, the only one in Dublin at the time, where the actor Robert Wilks was the leading figure. Born, like Farquhar, in Ireland, Wilks was then a little over thirty, and had already laid the foundation of a brilliant career. He was to play a considerable part in Farquhar's life. Thanks to his friendly encouragement, Farquhar made his debut, if tradition is to be trusted, in the role of Othello, but his acting career was destined to be short and not particularly successful. He is said to have appeared as Young Bellair in Sir George Etherege's *The Man of Mode*, as Careless in Robert Howard's *The Committee*, as Young Loveless in Beaumont and Fletcher's *The Scornful Lady*; he was also seen in one or two tragic parts, the last being that of Guyomar in John Dryden's *The Indian Emperor*, which he played with such conviction that he seriously wounded a fellow actor in the duel scene of the last act. This was in the spring of 1697, and marks the end of his career as a player. Though we are assured that "He never met with the least repulse from the audience," he may have conceived some doubts as to his ability as an actor, and may already have started work on a play. At all events, on the advice and with the financial assistance of Wilks, he decided to try his luck as an author in London.

Farquhar arrived there probably in the latter part of 1697, furnished, no doubt, with a recommendation from Wilks for Christopher Rich, the manager of the Theatre Royal in Drury Lane, who had given Wilks his first engagement. Rich, not always so accommodating, gave the budding playwright his chance; and Farquhar's first comedy, *Love and a Bottle*, was successfully produced in December 1698. It ran for nine nights in the first season. Almost simultaneously there appeared a short novel, *The Adventures of Covent Garden*, which though anonymous, can be attributed with certainty to Farquhar: one of the love poems figuring in the text is reproduced in a later work, this time signed; and two lines of it are utilized in Farquhar's second play, in which, moreover, one of the central incidents of the story is taken up again and developed. Perhaps the young author had thought of story writing as an alternative, in case his play failed.

The Constant Couple, or, A Trip to the Jubilee was performed about a year later, on 28 November 1699, at Drury Lane. The jubilee year in Rome, beginning in December 1699, was the theme of all conversations at the time, and Farquhar had counted on this topical element. But what brought the play its unprecedented success—it ran for more than fifty nights—was the character of Sir Harry Wildair, played by Wilks, who had come over from Dublin some months before, probably at Farquhar's urging. The part was suited to his talent, and was to remain associated with him.

At twenty-one, Farquhar was fairly launched. He appeared at the fashionable coffeehouses and taverns, and he was one of those who gathered with the wits at Will's. His status as a playwright is illustrated by the anecdote concerning his discovery of Anne Oldfield, who was to become one of the outstanding actresses of the century. Dining at the Mitre Tavern, he heard the landlady's sixteen-year-old niece reading to her aunt a scene from Fletcher's

The Scornful Lady, in which he himself had played, and was so struck by her voice and delivery that he recommended her to Sir John Vanbrugh, who sent her to Rich. Rich engaged her for Drury Lane, and she later became Farquhar's leading lady. He is reported to have been in love with her, but she does not seem to have returned his feelings.

Another tribute to the position Farquhar had obtained in the theater is seen in the fact that several dramatists of the time—John Oldmixon, the future historian, in particular—asked him to give them a prologue or an epilogue for their plays. Abel Boyer invited him to contribute some letters to his volume *Familiar and Courtly Letters Written by Monsieur Voiture* (1700), a miscellany, of a kind popular at the period, containing letters not only by the French poet but also by Dryden, William Wycherley, and William Congreve. Farquhar figures, too, in a similar production, *Letters of Wit, Politicks and Morality* (1701); and in *Love and Business* (1702) he holds the field alone.

But, before this last work appeared, his luck had changed. In the autumn of 1700 he had made a trip to Holland, presumably on the proceeds of *The Constant Couple*. He seems to have enjoyed this visit to the Continent, marred only by a serious attack of illness concerning which he gives no details in his account of the journey. During this period Farquhar is supposed to have begun his third play, *Sir Harry Wildair, Being the Sequel of "The Trip to the Jubilee."* Staged at Drury Lane in early April 1701, it proved a complete failure, though the cast was substantially the same as had triumphed in the preceding play.

The unexpected setback seems to have disconcerted Farquhar. Mistrusting his own inspiration, he now turned to the old dramatist Fletcher, whose popularity had continued on the Restoration stage; and from *The Wild-Goose Chase* (1621), acted with great success in Fletcher's time, he took the essential elements of a new comedy, *The Inconstant, or, The Way to Win Him*, which appeared at Drury Lane in the first months of 1702. It was preceded by a prologue from the lively pen of Pierre Motteux, a French refugee who had made a name for himself as editor of *The Gentleman's Journal* and as translator of Rabelais and Cervantes. But it failed to please. Perhaps, as Farquhar suggested later, the competition of French dancers at a neighboring theater was too strong. Whatever the reason, the play was taken off after only six performances. A similar fate befell *The Twin Rivals*, performed at the end of 1702. Possibly the theme was too serious for the Drury Lane audience. There were only thirteen performances before the play was withdrawn.

Though other dramatists continued to apply to him for prologues and epilogues—Charles Gildon, Francis Manning, and Charles Boyle, now earl of Orrery, among them—Farquhar's position in the theatrical world must have been shaken by this series of failures. He depended on the theater for his livelihood and, though he does not seem to have been the young spendthrift he liked to portray in his plays, he found himself facing serious material problems. To add to them, he embarked on marriage. The tradition is that he wedded a young woman who had represented herself as an heiress, knowing Farquhar to be in need of money. What we know for certain is that he married, probably in 1703, Margaret Pemell, the widow of an army officer and already mother of three children. The marriage does not seem to have been a happy one.

But once again events took a new turn. With Motteux, Farquhar adapted from the French a short farce, *The Stage Coach*, which was played, not at Drury Lane, but at Lincoln's Inn Fields, in February 1704. It was well received, and delivered the author from some of his financial anxieties. Almost immediately afterward he made a trip to Dublin, where the play was published. He also gave there a performance of *The Constant Couple* at which the duke of Ormonde, newly appointed lord lieutenant of Ireland, was present. Farquhar appeared as Sir Harry Wildair, the audience was indulgent, and he found himself £100 in pocket as a result.

It was probably about this time that he was granted a commission in the army. We learn from the army lists and commission registers that Farquhar was a lieutenant in the infantry regiment raised by the earl of Orrery in March 1704. The commission assured him of a small but regular income—about £50 annually. But he was not destined, in these warlike times, for military glory. He spent the year of Marlborough's victories in England. Perhaps family responsibilities kept him at home: his first daughter, Anne Marguerite, was born toward the end of 1704, and his second daughter, Mary, a year later.

Meanwhile, the taking of Barcelona in 1705 inspired Farquhar to compose an epic poem, *Barcel-lona: or, The Spanish Expedition Under the Command of Charles, Earl of Peterborough*, published by his widow after his death. More important, he was sent on a recruiting campaign into the West of England. In 1705 he is reported to have visited Lichfield, then Shrewsbury. Henry Brett, to whom he had dedicated *The Twin Rivals*, was member of Parliament for the nearby town of Bishop's Castle, and also lieutenant colonel of a newly raised regiment. A friend of Joseph Addison, he was interested in the theater, and it was no doubt through him that Farquhar was introduced into Shropshire society, where, judging from his preface to *The Recruiting Officer*, he was warmly received. His new experience of provincial life is everywhere visible in this play, composed, if tradition is to be believed, during his stay at the Raven Inn in Shrewsbury. It triumphed at Drury Lane in April 1706, was played at Dorset Garden Theatre a few months later, and appeared at the new Queen's Theatre in the Haymarket in November.

But Farquhar seems to have gotten into deep water. To pay his debts, he is reported to have sold his commission, though this is by no means certain. At any rate, he seems to have disappeared from his home in York Buildings in early December 1706. Perhaps he was taking refuge from his creditors, and it is very possible that he had become completely estranged from his wife. The faithful Wilks finally discovered his friend in St. Martin's Lane, "in a most miserable situation, lodged in a back garret, and under the greatest agitation of mind." Wilks gave him 20 guineas and urged him to write a new play. Comforted and encouraged, Farquhar settled down to what was to be his last work, *The Beaux' Stratagem*, which he is said to have composed in six weeks. During those weeks he was constantly ill, writing most of the time in his bed, and, adds Thomas Wilkes, to whom we owe these details, "before he had finished the second act, he perceived the approaches of death." The play was completed, put into rehearsal, and finally produced on 8 March 1707, at the Queen's Theatre in the Haymarket, with Wilks, Anne Oldfield, and most of the Drury Lane company. It was greeted enthusiastically.

But Farquhar was too far gone for this success to change much. He died, according to Wilkes, who has been followed by most biographers, in the last week of April. But J. Hamard has pointed out that the date is not compatible with that of his funeral, which took place, as the register of St. Martin's in the Fields attests, on 23 May 1707. His death must have occurred about 20 May. No member of the family, not even his wife, seems to have come forward. The funeral was ordered and paid for by Wilks, for whom Farquhar had left this note:

> Dear Bob,
>   I have not anything to leave thee to perpetuate my memory but two helpless girls. Look upon them sometimes, and think on him that was, to the last moment of his life, thine.
>   George Farquhar

We have no clear indication of the malady that carried him off. It has been generally supposed that he was a victim of tuberculosis. He was only in his thirtieth year.

The two extant portraits of Farquhar show us, beneath a curled wig, a conventionally pleasant face, with well-shaped but hardly distinctive features. In one of his published letters in which, under the name of Damon, he may be speaking of himself—though this is doubtful—he describes his temperament as melancholy and retiring, and adds that his usual dress is black. This scarcely calls to mind the dashing young gallants, full of high spirits, whom he depicts in his comedies and in whom his biographers have seen a projection of himself. The truth is that we know next to nothing of the man. Of his contemporaries, none has left us any personal record of Farquhar: there is no mention of him in the letters of Wycherley, Congreve, or Vanbrugh; and Sir Richard Steele, who spoke in *The Tatler* of Farquhar's plays, does not allude to the author in his correspondence. Perhaps the fact that he wrote for a living placed him outside certain circles. It is substantially because of the type of hero he constantly paints that we are wont to imagine him, with William Hazlitt, as a "warm-hearted, rattle-brained, thoughtless, high-spirited young fellow" or, with Edmund Gosse, as a "sentimental soldier, garrulous and tender, contrasting in a good-natured way with the hard and cynical types of satirist who preceded him." It may be that he resembled his ebullient creations, as traditional accounts imply, but we are on surer ground if we see him as a sadly harassed young playwright, struggling hard to keep his head above water and, in the last years of his short life, dogged by ill health and ill fortune. In this respect, as in others, he stands apart from the "mob of gentlemen who wrote with ease."

NOVEL, POEMS, AND LETTERS

FARQUHAR is essentially a man of the theater. The poems, letters, and miscellaneous writings he has left belong only on the margin of his dramatic work; but they do shed some light on his outlook and on the nature of his talent.

The Adventures of Covent Garden, which appeared almost at the same time as Farquhar's first play, is a short novel professedly written "in imitation of Scarron's City Romance," but this latter work, as it was published in England in 1671, is not by Paul Scarron at all; it is Antoine Furetière's *Le roman bourgeois*, which had been printed in Paris five years before. Farquhar's novel owes little, in any case, to the French text, which unfolds its story against the dusty background of the world of Parisian notaries. We meet Farquhar's hero at Drury Lane, and we follow him through a series of amatory adventures that take us to the Rose Tavern, to Bartholomew Fair, and even to the Old Bailey. Peregrine, like his creator, is an impecunious young Irishman who has come to London to repair his fortune after Emilia, the young heiress he had hoped to wed, has been married off by her family to a richer suitor. In London he meets her again, but he is already courting a new love, Selina. Caught between the two women, duped by one and forced by the other into a duel, which fortunately does not materialize, he finally loses both. The background, the characters, the incidents, and even the dialogue might very well come from any Restoration comedy. In Peregrine, Farquhar created the type of young scapegrace he reproduced more or less in his plays; Roebuck, Wildair, Captain Plume, Archer, and Aimwell all have something of his careless good humor.

The letters are, for the most part, contributions to the miscellany volumes in vogue at the time. Those addressed to the bookseller Samuel Briscoe and signed by Farquhar in his own name contain some autobiographical details. The description of Dryden's funeral, seen with a disparaging eye, ends on an ironic note:

And so much for Mr. Dryden, whose burial was the same with his life: variety and not of a piece; the quality and mob, farce and heroics; the sublime and ridicule mixt in a piece; great Cleopatra in a hackney-coach.

The account of Farquhar's trip to Holland, addressed to the same correspondent, is written with color and vivacity. But, in general, the letters are stylistic exercises, designed to show the author's virtuosity. Sometimes they are grouped in the form of a narrative, recounting a love affair; at other times they discuss the problems figuring in most of the similar collections of letters at the time: feminine conduct, the nature of love, the ideal lover. Usually the characters concerned are designated by names drawn from conventional sources. Celadon or Damon writes to Astrea or Penelope with more or less fervor, evoking incidents or feelings that may, or may not, have a basis in reality. How far can Farquhar be identified with his epistolary heroes? Has he any connection with Celadon, who is finally rejected by Astrea, after a long siege, and who, when he sees another is preferred to him, concludes philosophically that he will be interested to meet the man for whose sake he was refused? Or is he the diffident young Damon, who courts Penelope in the sedatest of terms, protesting that he is seeking not superficial beauty, but beauty of character and intelligence? We know that Astrea is Susanna Carroll, the future Mrs. Centlivre, already launched on her career as a playwright: a literary courtship was for her in the order of things. Biographers have hastened to see in Penelope, Anne Oldfield; but Penelope is described as "a little lady in a half-mourning mantua," which hardly calls up the tall, strikingly beautiful actress. The poems that sometimes accompany the letters contain all the well-worn ornaments of love poetry: sighs are like winds, tears like waves, and so on. One can agree with Leigh Hunt that Farquhar's letters are "lively, good-humoured and sensible," but they are far from satisfying our curiosity concerning their writer.

Love and Business, which groups the most interesting letters, also contains *A Discourse Upon Comedy*, which represents Farquhar's contribution to the contemporary discussion on the nature and function of the stage. In the main it is concerned with the classic "rules." Aristotle and his followers, maintains Farquhar, were not practical men of the theater, and so were hardly qualified to lay down laws for the stage. In any case, principles that may have applied in ancient Greece are not necessarily valid for a Drury Lane audience in the present. The English playgoer demands above all change and variety. As for the improbabilities that may arise from the neglect of the "rules," they are of minor importance since, by its very nature, the theater is a place of illusion.

Turning to comedy, Farquhar considers it can claim as its province all that is not included in tragedy. Its purpose is to chastise vice, to rouse laughter at folly and weakness, to see that virtue is rewarded. The real source of comedy, he asserts, goes back to the mythology of the ancients, as it is seen in Aesop, who uses the fable essentially to teach a moral lesson in an amusing way. Comedy is really "a well fram'd tale, handsomely told, as an agreeable vehicle for counsel and reproof." Farquhar's defense of liberty against the "rules" is in accordance with the ideas of the time: it follows Dryden, John Dennis, Gildon. The linking of comedy with the Aesopic fable is ingenious, even if it has no foundation in fact. The insistence on the moral lesson is perhaps a sign of the changing atmosphere of the period. On the whole, the *Discourse* brings no strikingly new ideas, but it is presented with a relative ease and lightness that make it more readable than most similar works of the period.

Outside the short love poems to which allusion has been made, Farquhar is the author of two works in verse. His Pindaric ode relates "How the Great, Martial, Godlike Schomberg Fell" at the battle of the Boyne. The glorious commander is compared to Moses, Alcides, and Samson: like Samson, his fall brings down disaster on his enemies, after which he begins a triumphal march to the Styx. The poem is no doubt a youthful production, which may be an excuse. More ambitious is the epic *Barcellona*, the six cantos of which recount the expedition against the town and the capture of the citadel. All the trappings and devices of the classical epic are used—exaltation of the heroes, discussions of the generals in each camp, premonitory dreams, deliberations of the gods—and the storehouse of mythological imagery is plundered. But the verse, at its best, is plodding. As a poet, whether lyric, Pindaric, or Homeric, Farquhar can be passed over without injustice. A few agreeable songs scattered through the plays can scarcely modify this judgment.

PLAYS

It is on his work as a dramatist that Farquhar's reputation rests. He was active at a time when the Restoration theater had almost run its course. The type of play that had so long diverted the fashionable audiences of the two London playhouses was already finding less favor in the eyes of a public whose outlook had changed since the period of Etherege and Wycherley. The attack launched by Jeremy Collier in his pamphlet *A Short View of the Immorality and Profaneness of the English Stage* (1698) was a sign of the new social and moral conditions of the closing century, and the cool reception accorded to Congreve's *The Way of the World* (1700) pointed in the same direction.

The Collier controversy was in full swing when Farquhar wrote his first play, *Love and a Bottle*, but the latter shows very little of Collier's influence. The hero, Roebuck, is an impoverished Irish gentleman who, like Peregrine in the *Adventures of Covent Garden*, hopes to find in London the chance of a rich marriage. His riotous adventures, amatory for the most part, end only when a pretty heiress and an estate fall into his arms—most undeservedly, one is tempted to add, for the young man is not overburdened with scruples. By Roebuck's side Farquhar has placed Lovewell, "sober and modest," who will also wed a lady of considerable fortune, Lucinda. His sister Leanthe will be Roebuck's bride: like Wycherley's Fidelia, she has followed her hero, disguised as a page. Around these central characters are grouped typical comedy types—the would-be wit, the country squire anxious to acquire town graces, a bookseller, a poet, a stupid valet, a pert maid, and a London landlady—all sketched amusingly. The best scenes are perhaps those in which the country squire is instructed in the arts of town life by his dancing master and his fencing master, in the manner of Molière's *Le bourgeois gentilhomme*. The dialogue is animated enough, but is certainly not of a high order of refinement.

Altogether, there would be little to distinguish *Love and a Bottle* from the traditional Restoration comedy if it were not, first, that Roebuck is devoid of the cool, polished effrontery characteristic of the Restoration hero: his "wild and roving temper" is presented as a youthful trait that, like his careless indifference to moral considerations, does not involve a deliberate flouting of principles. Fundamentally, he is good-natured and generous; he can, on occasion, be ashamed of his impudent conduct. Leanthe sums him up thus:

Wild as winds, and unconfined as air!—Yet I may reclaim him. His follies are weakly founded, upon the principles of honour, where the very foundation helps to undermine the structure. How charming would virtue look in him, whose behaviour can add a grace to the unseemliness of vice!

(III. i)

A second difference lies in the general atmosphere surrounding the comedy. The cynical hardness of Wycherley and Congreve has given place to something warmer and more human; the pursuit of wit is less apparent. Already, while keeping the framework of Restoration comedy, Farquhar shows a certain originality.

The Constant Couple, or, A Trip to the Jubilee reveals similar characteristics. Sir Harry Wildair is also a rake, but endowed with a constant flow of high spirits and a laughing carelessness that, to some extent, attenuate his lack of principle. Like Roebuck, he is kindhearted. His foppery—he has just come back from Paris with all the latest fashions—is harmless enough. He is a new and gayer version of Etherege's Lord Frederick Frolick; and the fact that Wilks, who had come over from Dublin to play the part, had won outstanding success in his portrayal of Etherege's young beau may have influenced Farquhar in his conception of the character. The "constant couple" is composed of Lady Lurewell, "a lady of jilting temper, from a resentment of her wrongs from man," and Colonel Standard, a disbanded officer who turns out to be her first lover, separated from her in the past by a misunderstanding, but still faithful to her. Needless to say, the comedy ends not only with the reconciliation of Lurewell and Standard, but also with the betrothal of Sir Harry to a young heiress, Angelica. The various suitors of Lurewell—the hypocrite Vizard, the wily old merchant Smuggler, "Beau" Clincher, a former apprentice who has come into an inheritance and is determined to cut a figure—provide amusement by their efforts to outmaneuver each other. The scenes inspired from *The Adventures of Covent Garden*, in which "Beau" Clincher, after a hurried change of clothes imposed by Lady Lurewell, is thought to have been murdered and is, on his reappearance, arrested as a murderer himself, bear witness to a gift for farce.

356

Again the framework is that of Restoration comedy, but again the cynicism dissolves in a flow of rollicking fun. Sir Harry is a memorable creation, and his popularity on the stage is attested by the many revivals of the play in the course of the century.

Sir Harry Wildair, the sequel to *The Constant Couple*, hardly bears comparison. The principal characters are the same, but they have lost their gaiety. The "constant couple" have fallen out: Lurewell has become the stereotyped "fine lady" —vain, capricious, eager to make new conquests—while Standard has degenerated into a violently jealous husband. Sir Harry has made the trip to the jubilee but, when traveling far from Angelica, has been informed of the death of his young wife in France. Apparently he has taken up his old roistering life again. Alone the new characters—Captain Fireball, Standard's explosive sailor-brother, and Banter, the foppish younger brother of Sir Harry—(really Angelica, in disguise) —cannot make up for the weakness of the main figures. When at the end of the play, after masquerading as her own phantom, Angelica reveals herself, the rickety plot collapses. The last speeches are conventional homilies on the theme of good husbands and good wives. Nevertheless, even in this inferior work, Sir Harry remains, in the words of Leigh Hunt, "a kind of epitome of youthful spirits and freedom from care, let loose upon the world."

These first three plays have in common the type of character about which they are constructed—the young reprobate with saving qualities—and the boisterous good humor that gives them their particular atmosphere. Written between 1698 and 1701, they mark the emergence in the theater of the time of a new personality. The next three plays, composed in the two following years, show a certain hesitation on Farquhar's part, after the unexpected failure of *Sir Harry Wildair*.

The Inconstant, taken from Fletcher's *The Wild-Goose Chase* (1621), shows some independence in the remodeling of the old play. In the original comedy, the "wild goose" is Mirabel, a young Don Juan with an aversion to marriage, and constantly on the wing. He is chased by his betrothed, Oriana, who tries various wiles to bring him to the altar. This plot Farquhar keeps, but, if he remains close to Fletcher in the first three acts, he builds the last two on his own lines. In a general way he simplifies and

clarifies. In a subplot the older dramatist had two companions of Mirabel carrying on the parallel wooing of two pert young ladies; Farquhar is content with one pair of lovers, Captain Duretete and the temperamental Bisarre, whose stormy courtship ends, of course, happily. Mirabel, as Farquhar presents him, has something of Roebuck and Sir Harry Wildair, and he yields finally to Oriana because she has found a way to touch his heart. Fletcher's play has poetic moments that are lost, to some extent, in Farquhar's adaptation, but we observe considerable progress in construction, a greater skill in the handling of the characters. The dialogue is full of vivacity, as in this exchange between Mirabel and Oriana:

> *Mir.* . . . You shall have your liberty; here, take your contract and give me mine.
> *Ori.* No, I won't.
> *Mir.* Eh! what, is the girl a fool?
> *Ori.* No, sir, you shall find me cunning enough to do myself justice; and since I must not depend upon your love, I'll be revenged and force you to marry me out of spite.
> *Mir.* Then I'll beat thee out of spite; make a most confounded husband.
> *Ori.* O, sir, I shall match ye! a good husband makes a good wife at any time.
> *Mir.* I'll rattle down your china about your ears.
> *Ori.* And I'll rattle about the city to run you in debt for more.
> *Mir.* Your face-mending toilet shall fly out of the window.
> *Ori.* And your face-mending periwig shall fly after it . . .
> *Mir.* But, sweet madam, there is such a thing as a divorce.
> *Ori.* But, sweet sir, there is such a thing as alimony: so divorce on, and spare not.
>
> (II. i)

Coldly received on its first production, *The Inconstant* found more favor later in the century, and was successfully revived on several occasions.

Such was not the case with *The Twin Rivals*, in many ways a disconcerting play. Clearly Farquhar had set out to make his audience laugh, but he had devised a plot for his comedy that was not particularly laughable. The rivals are twin brothers battling for a legacy and a title. The younger, Benjamin Wouldbe, has seized both in the absence of the rightful heir, Hermes, and on his return tries, with the help of the unscrupulous lawyer Subtleman and the procuress Mandrake, to brazen it out. Right triumphs in the end, thanks largely to Teague, the elder brother's comic Irish servant, but only after scenes of perhaps misplaced dramatic intensity. Farquhar himself realized that his theme was not really suited to comedy, but he defended it, in his preface to the printed edition, in terms recalling his *Discourse*:

The most material objection against this play is the importance of the subject, which necessarily leads into sentiments too grave for diversion, and supposes vices too great for comedy to punish. 'Tis said, I must own, that the business of comedy is chiefly to ridicule folly; and that the punishment of vice falls rather into the province of tragedy; but if there be a middle sort of wickedness too high for the sock, and too low for the buskin, is there any reason that it should go unpunished? What are more obnoxious to human society than the villainies exposed in this play, the frauds, plots and contrivances upon the fortunes of men, and the virtue of women? But the persons are too mean for the heroic; then what must we do with them? Why, they must of necessity drop into comedy.

The plea is ingenious, and perhaps later in the century, with the advent of "bourgeois" drama, would have been heard. For the moment the public was not prepared for "serious" comedy, particularly from the author of *Love and a Bottle*. It was unfortunate, for, as William Archer points out, the play is well built and the characters are firmly drawn. The two brothers are well contrasted, and Subtleman is a sometimes amusing villain as Mandrake is a sometimes diverting bawd. The character of Teague was obviously inspired by the Teague of Robert Howard's comedy *The Committee, or, The Faithful Irishman* (1662), in which Farquhar had played in his early days as an actor. But Howard's Teague is a pale figure compared with Farquhar's full-blooded creation, who, in other circumstances, would have made the success of the play. He remains one of the most amusing of stage Irishmen.

The Stage Coach, Farquhar's only farce, is adapted from *Les carrosses d'Orleáns* (1680), by Jean de La Chapelle, long a favorite with French audiences. Farquhar keeps the essentials of the plot, changing only the names of the characters, who all become English, and modifying a few details of the outcome. All the events take place at an inn on the London Road, in which two young lovers, Captain Basil and Isabella, are brought together in time to thwart the plans of a domineering uncle and guard-

ian. Micher, who has designed to marry off his niece, for reasons of interest, to a wealthy Mr. Somebody. The last scene shows Micher outwitted, and the two young people married, with Isabella's fortune, which Micher had hoped to retain, safely in the captain's hands. Much of the play takes place at night, and the darkness favors a general confusion in which all the characters are at odds. Altogether, *The Stage Coach* is a lively production that, to some extent, marks a new departure, in that Farquhar has moved away from the London scene. The country inn becomes a meeting place for new character types—the innkeeper, the coachman, the hostler, the chambermaid—and Farquhar has introduced, in place of a Dutchman in the original play, another Irishman, Macahone, who brings gaiety with his brogue and incessant invocations to St. Patrick. The atmosphere is already that of the inn scenes of *The Beaux' Stratagem*.

Farquhar's last two plays show a remarkable advance on all his preceding work. It is already evident in *The Recruiting Officer*, directly inspired by his experiences when recruiting in the West of England. Dedicated "To All Friends Round the Wrekin,"[1] the comedy was born, says Farquhar in his preface, "from some little turns of humour that I met with almost within the shade of that ancient hill," and he goes on to admit that some of his characters were painted from life. Needless to say, this admission has brought forth any number of speculations as to the originals, and a number of identifications with local notables have been proposed, without it being possible to substantiate the claims. In any case, the interest of the work lies elsewhere. The play is characterized by a light-hearted gaiety that is already apparent in the opening scene, where we see the astute Sergeant Kite beginning his recruiting campaign in the market-place of the country town, and meditating his stratagems to bring the rustics into the queen's army. This gaiety runs through all the love scenes, in which the sprightly Captain Plume, one more version of the familiar Farquhar hero, with the added prestige of a uniform, is engaged with the no less sprightly Silvia, daughter of Justice Balance, who has disguised herself as a young man to be near her too adventurous lover. The episode in which Kite, made up as an astrologer, arranges his own affairs,

[1]The Wrekin is the hill north of the Severn River, overlooking Shrewsbury.

and those involving the countryman Bullock and his pretty sister Rose, with skillful impudence, are highly amusing. The appearance of the rustic recruits before the court presided over by the local justices, in accordance with the impressment laws of the time, gives rise to laughable dialogue. Predictably, it is on this aspect of the play that Bertolt Brecht based his adaptation, transforming the comedy into a mocking indictment of militarism, which was certainly not Farquhar's intention. Captain Brazen, Plume's fellow officer, is an original remaking of the stock character of the miles gloriosus: he has been everywhere, seen everything, knows everybody, and is ready, on the slightest pretext, to enlarge on his adventures, which are always, of course, unique.

In this comedy there are no displeasing characters, no conflicts other than those of young love. The provincial world Farquhar evokes is free of all care, delightful in every way: Leigh Hunt defines it well when he notes that "we seem to breathe the clear, fresh, ruddy-making air of a remote country-town, neighboured by hospitable elegancies." Critics have been quick to point out analogies between *The Recruiting Officer* and plays in which soldiers appear, like Fletcher's *The Humorous Lieutenant* (1647), Thomas Shadwell's *The Woman-Captain* (1680), and even Steele's *The Funeral* (1701); the only one to present a real similarity is Shadwell's, in which Mrs. Gripe, the woman captain, enlists, like Silvia, in the army—but in order to get away from her husband. Otherwise, the characters and situations are Farquhar's own. The constant high spirits, and the brisk lightheartedness with which the play moves along, testify to a newly found assurance, after the uncertainty and hesitation of the preceding works.

The same gay and confident atmosphere envelops the last and best of Farquhar's comedies, *The Beaux' Stratagem*. It takes place in Lichfield, and tradition has it that Farquhar visited this little country town first on his recruiting campaign; at the old George Inn there, the room in which he is supposed to have stayed is still displayed. We are at the inn when the curtain rises, in company with the eccentric landlord, Bonniface, and his pretty daughter, Cherry. The arrival of the two "beaux" from London, Aimwell and Archer, sets the action moving. The two young men hope to repair their sadly compromised fortunes by a rich marriage in the country. Their introduction into local society, Aimwell

in the role of his titled elder brother and Archer masquerading as his servant, will be followed by rapid consequences: Aimwell will win the heart of the heiress Dorinda, while Archer will have found his way into the good graces of Mrs. Sullen, the wife of the local squire, and will presumably marry her—and her £10,000—once she has obtained a divorce from her impossible spouse. In the meantime, we have been carried through a series of diverting scenes at the inn, and in the manor house, the home of Dorinda as well as of her brother, Squire Sullen, and his wife. At the inn we have met Gibbet, the affable highwayman, and his acolytes; Foigard, who gives himself out as a Flemish priest and is revealed as an Irishman, a "Teague"; and Count Bellair, a French officer on parole[2] who has begun to court Mrs. Sullen. At the manor house the squire's man, Scrub, and the maid, Gipsey, provide the comedy; and a late arrival on the scene, Sir Charles Freeman, Mrs. Sullen's brother, will bring about, in the last act, the peaceful separation of the warring couple.

All these characters are deftly presented, each with his or her marked and picturesque individuality, but it is naturally toward the principal figures that we look. Farquhar has differentiated his two "beaux": Aimwell has about him a touch of the romantic, Archer is closer to the witty Dorimants and Mirabels of Restoration tradition; Aimwell will be smitten with remorse before Dorinda's trustfulness and will confess his imposture, whereas Archer will refuse to forgo the advantages gained with Mrs. Sullen by his transparent disguise as a servant. Squire Sullen, in his perpetual ill temper, has his moments of humor; Dorinda is wholly charming, romantic yet sensible; and Mrs. Sullen has more depth than most stage wives: she is, in reality, the most interesting character, full of wit, vivacity, and intelligence. Here are the two women talking of their admirers:

Mrs. Sul. How a little love and good company improves a woman! Why, child, you begin to live—you never spoke before.

Dor. Because I was never spoke to.—My lord has told me that I have more wit and beauty than any of my sex; and truly I begin to think the man is sincere.

Mrs. Sul. You're in the right, Dorinda; pride is the life of a woman, and flattery is our daily bread; and she's a fool

[2]Captured in the war that had begun in 1702.

that won't believe a man there, as much as she that believes him in anything else. But I'll lay you a guinea that I had finer things said to me than you had.

Dor. Done! What did your fellow say to ye?
Mrs. Sul. My fellow took the picture of Venus for mine.
Dor. But my lover took me for Venus herself.
Mrs. Sul. Common cant! Had my spark called me a Venus directly, I should have believed him a footman in good earnest.
Dor. But my lover was upon his knees to me.
Mrs. Sul. And mine was upon his tiptoes to me.
Dor. Mine vowed to die for me.
Mrs. Sul. Mine swore to die with me.

But a moment later the banter has ceased; a sudden melancholy falls on Mrs. Sullen as she realizes that hers is perhaps an empty dream:

Mrs. Sul. Happy, happy sister! your angel has been watchful for your happiness, whilst mine has slept, regardless of his charge. Long smiling years of circling joys for you, but not one hour for me! (*Weeps*)
Dor. Come, my dear, we'll talk of something else.
(IV. i)

The scene, with its mingling of light raillery and emotion, illustrates the sureness with which Farquhar now handles character and dialogue. In a droller vein, the conversation between Archer and Cherry, the scenes in which, in turn, Bonniface, Gibbet, and Scrub try to penetrate the secret of Archer's identity, and the final debate between Mrs. Sullen and her husband are marked by an ease, a spontaneity, and a flow of humor that go beyond anything to be found in the earlier comedies.

The play has another particularity: it presents the picture of an ill-assorted couple constantly at strife. The theme was not a new one, for Restoration comedy is full of such couples. But Farquhar sees their situation differently than his fellow dramatists did. For them the normal solution was that the dissatisfied partner, usually the wife, should seek consolation elsewhere. Wycherley's *The Country Wife* (1675), to take perhaps the most striking example, shows us a series of discontented wives hastening to throw themselves into the arms of lovers. Closer to Farquhar, Vanbrugh's *The Provok'd Wife* (1697) paints a couple whose position is almost identical with that of Squire Sullen and his wife. Lady Brute, unhappily married, has long resisted the temptation to turn for solace to her faithful admirer Constant; but the end of the play will see her ready to yield, for such is, in her eyes, the only redress for the un-

just treatment she receives at the hands of her husband. In part the divorce laws were to blame: separation could be granted only by the ecclesiastical courts, and in rare cases; incompatibility of temperament was not an admitted ground. With smiling gravity Farquhar pleads for a more humane view:

Dor. But how can you shake off the yoke? Your divisions don't come within the reach of the law for a divorce.
Mrs. Sul. Law! What law can search into the remote abyss of nature? What evidence can prove the unaccountable disaffections of wedlock? Can a jury sum up the endless aversions that are rooted in our souls, or can a bench give judgment upon antipathies?
(III. iii)

Marriage, as Squire Sullen hears to his stupefaction, is not merely a union of bodies, but of minds:

Sir Ch. You and your wife, Mr. Guts, may be one flesh, because ye are nothing else: but rational creatures have minds that must unite.
Sq. Sul. Minds!
(V. i)

What Farquhar would wish for in such cases is separation by mutual consent; and the final scene, in which the squire and his wife, at last in accord, join hands, pictures amusingly, but with an underlying gravity, the solution he proposes:

Sq. Sul. These hands joined us, these shall part us—away!
(V. v)

It has been noted that his ideas on marriage and divorce echo those set out by Milton in a famous series of pamphlets more than half a century before, and it is certain that Farquhar had read these works carefully. This alone suffices to indicate the difference of his outlook from that of the other playwrights of the time. There is thus a serious note in this lighthearted comedy, where Farquhar's gifts find their best expression.

Highly popular in their century, both *The Recruiting Officer* and *The Beaux' Stratagem* have met with considerable success in revivals on the London stage.

CONCLUSION

FARQUHAR's career was a short one—some eight or nine years in all—but it shows a constant evolution.

GEORGE FARQUHAR

His early plays, close to the Restoration model, are licentious in tone; and it is largely because of them that his morality has been brought into question. But, even in these works, the licentiousness is in the language rather than in the thought. The time was not overly nice in expression, as is evident in the work of his fellow playwrights, Vanbrugh in particular, who is his direct contemporary. The later plays show a gradual improvement, due in part, no doubt, to the new standards that, in the opening eighteenth century, made for more refinement and decency in speech. If, in *The Recruiting Officer*, the dialogue has still that "pert, low" touch that Pope stigmatized, there is little to offend, and much to please, the taste of the modern reader or playgoer in the verbal exchanges of *The Beaux' Stratagem*. It is true that, down to the end, Farquhar keeps a certain liberty of expression; but the frank outspokenness does not cover, as with so many of his predecessors, a fundamental indifference to morality. "Farquhar," writes Edmund Gosse, "succeeds in being wholesome, even when he cannot persuade himself to be decent."

More important, the characters themselves have moved away from the stock figures of the older theater. Out of the Restoration rake, the fickle and heartless libertine of Etherege and Wycherley, he has made a new type. Roebuck and Wildair—gay, vivacious, open, if wild and unpredictable in their behavior—have a good deal in common with Fielding's Tom Jones: together with his heedless flightiness, they have his warm heart. More restrained, Mirabel the inconstant and Captain Plume are of the same complexion; they can be moved by a sincere sentiment and hasten to repair any wrong their thoughtlessness may have caused. Aimwell and Archer, young and easygoing, show themselves bold in the cause of their love; they are adventurers, like all Farquhar's heroes, and practice deception, but it never goes very far. Comparing them with Vanbrugh's creations, Hazlitt observes:

Farquhar's chief characters are also adventurers, but they are of a romantic, not a knavish stamp, and succeed no less by their honesty than by their boldness. . . . They are real gentlemen and only pretended imposters. Vanbrugh's upstart heroes are "without any relish of salvation", without generosity, virtue, or any pretensions to it. We have little sympathy for them, and no respect at all. But we have every sort of goodwill towards Farquhar's heroes, who have as many peccadilloes to answer for, and play as many rogue's tricks, but are honest fellows at bottom.

In a well-known essay Lamb affirmed that the characters of Wycherley and Congreve inspire no particular sentiment in us because they belong to a world that has no connection with reality. Allowing for the paradox innate in the critic's conception of the "artificial comedy," we can admit that we feel we have little in common with such beings. If they were translated into real life, we should be repelled by the inhumanity of a Horner or even, at times, of Congreve's Mirabel. About Farquhar's heroes there is an absence of calculating cynicism and a fundamental generosity that appeal to us.

The same applies to Farquhar's heroines. Some are merely stage ingenues, innocent and trusting, and destined to be rescued by their lovers from dishonor or from undesired marriages; such are Isabella in *The Stage Coach*, Constance and Aurelia in *The Twin Rivals*. Others, more characteristic, are determined and resourceful; Leanthe, Oriana, and Silvia are ready to confront difficulties and danger, if necessary, in order to remain by their lover's side; witty and audacious, they have been compared to the Rosalinds and Violas of Shakespearean comedy. Like their predecessors they gain a new charm disguised as young men. In them there is a kind of naturalistic philosophy: men are not considered as enemies, as is the case in so many Restoration plays. Lurewell represents an exceptional case: if she sets out to use her beauty to entrap men, it is to revenge her sex for the unjust treatment she herself has received, or believes she has received, at men's hands. But nowhere, among Farquhar's women, do we find a character like the lying, licentious, and vindictive Olivia of Wycherley's *The Plain Dealer*. His conception of womanhood is best illustrated in his last play, with Dorinda, charming, unaffected, direct in thought and speech, and with Mrs. Sullen, a woman who has not been embittered by her unhappy experience and can still believe in happiness.

Precisely because these characters are closer to humanity than most creations of Restoration comedy, we are the more ready to take into serious account the author's presentation of the problem that more than any other preoccupied the writers of the time: the relations of men and women in the contemporary social structures. It was seen by Farquhar's predecessors essentially from the man's point of view, with his age-old right to pleasure; and Farquhar's first plays reproduce this conception, illustrated by Roebuck and Wildair. But, as he proceeds, he moves toward the woman's standpoint. It is expressed directly by Oriana, in *The Inconstant*; and Silvia, in *The Recruiting Officer*, rises against the conventional attitude that allows men a privileged position in the pursuit of love. Already there is a sense of the equality of the sexes and, in the concluding scene of *The Beaux' Stratagem*, we see Squire Sullen and his wife discussing calmly and as admitted equals a situation that they agree is due to faults on both sides. One might imagine such a dialogue in Shaw; and it is no doubt with this in mind that Bonamy Dobrée thinks that, had Farquhar lived to continue his development, he might have been the Shaw of his time. As it is, we are with him on the way to the new "sentimental" comedy of Colley Cibber and Steele, which was to insist on a view of the relationship of the sexes more acceptable to us than that pictured in the Restoration theater.

The new moral dimension in Farquhar's plays is directly linked to his incursion into provincial life and society. Here, too, a significant change is to be noted. One remembers the ridiculous figure cut by the country gentry in the plays of his predecessors. Vanbrugh, in *The Relapse*, had poured scorn on country life, showing us the grotesque Sir Tunbelly Clumsey, his boisterous daughter Hoyden, and their uncouth household. In Farquhar's portrait of Squire Mockmode, and that of young Clincher, some traces of this attitude remain. But, in *The Recruiting Officer*, the Shropshire worthies appear in a completely different light: Balance, Simple, and Worthy are men of culture and good breeding; and Balance's daughter, Silvia, unconventional and outspoken as she is, has nothing in common with Hoyden. Squire Sullen is a reversion to the Restoration type, but without the ridicule attached to him in Wycherley or Congreve; his shortcomings result from temperament rather than from his rural upbringing. In a general way provincial life is portrayed agreeably; the characters are seen in a sympathetic light. Lady Bountiful is a pleasing figure for whom Restoration comedy offers no equal. Farquhar thus breaks the link binding comedy to fashionable London life, with its narrow outlook; he takes us into a pleasanter world, where life is simpler. In *The Beaux' Stratagem* the young gentlemen from London seem like intruders; finally,

they are conquered by the charm of country existence. Farquhar thus carries us back to the joyous, open-air atmosphere of Elizabethan comedy, and he opens the way to Goldsmith, whose inspiration, in *She Stoops to Conquer*, owes something to Farquhar.

Farquhar's plays do not have the robust construction we admire in Wycherley, nor the intricacy that makes Congreve's comedies an intellectual delight. This indifference to a highly mechanized plot Farquhar shares with Vanbrugh. In both cases the story told is full of unexpected turns, but it is rarely complicated. The effects Farquhar seeks are often obtained by the use of all the current, often hackneyed devices of the stage: disguises, hidden identities, unexpected encounters. But he shows great skill in his timing. Cherry, for instance, has been pressed by Bonniface to employ all her wiles to persuade the pseudo footman Archer to reveal his real identity and that of his master; left alone, she indignantly soliloquizes: "This landlord of mine . . . would betray his guest, and debauch his daughter into the bargain—and by a footman, too." And, as she ends, Archer enters. Or Scrub, anxious to deceive Foigard, in whom he detects a rival for Gipsey's favor, tells him: "Gipsey . . . she's dead two months ago." Whereupon Gipsey makes her appearance.

Farquhar's dialogue lacks, no doubt, the glitter and polish of Etherege or Congreve, and the power of Wycherley; but it has an unaffected ease and naturalness often lacking in the work of these writers. It has vivacity and a colloquial ring. The constant straining after wit is replaced by an engaging humor, presented with zest, as Mrs. Sullen's description to Dorinda of life with the squire shows:

He came home this morning at his usual hour of four, wakened me out of a sweet dream of something else, by tumbling over the tea-table, which he broke all to pieces; after his man and he had rolled about the room, like sick passengers in a storm, he comes flounce into bed, dead as a salmon into a fishmonger's basket; his feet cold as ice, his breath hot as a furnace, and his hands and face as greasy as his flannel nightcap. O matrimony! He tosses up the clothes with a barbarous swing over his shoulders, disorders the whole economy of my bed, leaves me half naked, and my whole night's comfort is the tuneable serenade of that wakeful nightingale, his nose. O, the pleasure of counting the melancholy clock by a snoring husband!

(*The Beaux' Stratagem*, II. i)

All the plays, even the earliest ones, are full of such passages, and their cheerful spontaneity more than makes up for the lack of dazzling repartee. They are conceived in the true spirit of "laughing comedy" that Goldsmith was to vindicate later.

In his lifetime Farquhar's reputation was uncertain: his contemporaries, like Oldmixon and a little later Steele, gave praise or blame simply in relation to the success or failure of his plays. In the second part of the eighteenth century, Goldsmith showed himself favorable and suggested that, had Farquhar lived, he would have attained some eminence, while Dr. Johnson affirmed that his plays had "considerable merit." At the beginning of the nineteenth century, Richard Cumberland, in his *British Drama* collection, saw him as "sprightly rather than great," and lacking in outstanding qualities. It was the romantic critics, Lamb, Hazlitt, and Leigh Hunt in particular, who placed him with Wycherley, Congreve, and Vanbrugh and sought to define his position with reference to his fellow dramatists. The opinion of Leigh Hunt deserves to be quoted:

Of the four dramatists of whom we have endeavoured to give some account, it appears to us . . . that Farquhar had the highest animal spirits, with fits of the deepest sympathy, the greatest wish to please rather than strike, the most agreeable diversity of character, the best instinct in avoiding the revolting extravagances of the time, and the happiest invention in plot and situation; and, therefore, is to be pronounced, upon the whole, the finest dramatic genius, and the most likely to be of lasting popularity.

The Victorian era, with its insistent moral preoccupations, could only be hostile to Farquhar and his contemporaries; and Thomas Macaulay's famous onslaught on the Restoration theater found an echo in most of the critics of the time. Toward the end of the century, when the outlook was less biased, Edmund Gosse portrayed Farquhar as a diverting, unsophisticated writer, but remained reticent as to his place in literary history. The twentieth century has proved more generous, and has given Farquhar a position apart from the dramatists with whom he is usually classed. William Archer declared roundly that he "belonged characteristically not to the Restoration, but to the rebellion against it"; Allardyce Nicoll sees him, more justly, as standing between Congreve and Cibber, between the Restoration tradition and eighteenth-century comedy. Present-day criticism has, in general, developed this view.

It is true that Farquhar came at a time of transition, when significant changes were taking place in the social structure of the nation and, as a consequence, in its moral attitudes. He was naturally affected by these changes and, though continuing in many ways the inspiration of the Restoration theater and keeping its essential technique, he gave expression in his plays, particularly in the last ones, to the new outlook, striking a happy balance between the "Old Comedy" and the dawning vogue for sentiment and morality. In so doing, he broadened the sphere of comedy, placed it in a new atmosphere, introduced new types of character. The germs of later transformations are already present in his work. Linked as he is with the past, he is turned toward the future. But at least as important is the highly individual personality that emerges more and more distinctly, more and more confidently, with each of his plays. "He's the only fellow among them," wrote Thackeray delightedly, "something more than a mere comic tradesman"; and it is by his personality, with its never-failing gaiety and verve, its fund of frankness and generosity, its touches of serious feeling, that the young Irish dramatist, prematurely cut off, merits a place to himself, and by no means the least, among the brilliant company of the Restoration playwrights.

SELECTED BIBLIOGRAPHY

Detailed bibliographical information will also be found in the appropriate volume of *The New Cambridge Bibliography of English Literature*, *The Oxford History of English Literature*, and *The Cambridge History of English Literature*.

I. BIBLIOGRAPHY. A. Nicoll, ed., *A History of English Drama, 1660–1900* (rev. ed., London, 1952), vol. I, *Restoration Drama*; vol. II, *Early Eighteenth Century Drama*.

II. COLLECTED WORKS. *The Works of the Late Ingenious Mr. George Farquhar: Containing All His Letters, Poems, Essays and Comedies Publish'd During His Lifetime* (London, 1711), later eds. in 2 vols. (London, 1711, 1714, 1718, 1721, 1728, 1742, 1760, 1772) and in 3 vols. (Dublin, 1775), the last with a "Life" by T. Wilkes; C. Stonehill, ed., *The Complete Works of George Farquhar*, 2 vols. (London, 1930; New York, 1967).

III. COMPLETE PLAYS. *The Comedies of Mr. George Farquhar* (London, 1708), also published as *The Dramatick Works*, 2 vols. (London, 1714, 1718, 1728, 1736); L.

Hunt, ed., *The Dramatic Works of Wycherley, Congreve, Vanbrugh and Farquhar* (London, 1849); A. C. Ewald, ed., *The Dramatic Works of George Farquhar*, 2 vols. (London, 1892).

IV. SELECTED WORKS. *Note*: Farquhar's comedies appear in all the eighteenth- and early nineteenth-century collections of plays, including *Collection of the Best English Plays* (London, 1720); J. Bell, *British Theatre*, 34 vols. (1797); Mrs. Inchbald, *British Theatre*, 25 vols. (London, 1808); T. Dibdin, *London Theatre*, 26 vols. (London, 1815–1818).

L. A. Strauss, ed., *A Discourse Upon Comedy, The Recruiting Officer, and The Beaux' Stratagem* (London, 1904); W. Archer, ed., *George Farquhar* (London—New York, 1906; repr. 1959), containing *The Constant Couple, The Twin Rivals, The Recruiting Officer*, and *The Beaux' Stratagem*.

V. SEPARATE WORKS. *Plays: Love and a Bottle: A Comedy* (London, 1699, [1705], 1735; Dublin, 1761); *The Constant Couple, or, A Trip to the Jubilee: A Comedy* (London, 1700, 1701, 1704, 1710, 1711, 1732, 1735, 1777, 1791); *Sir Harry Wildair, Being the Sequel of "The Trip to the Jubilee": A Comedy* (London, 1701, 1727, 1735, 1779); *The Inconstant, or, The Way to Win Him: A Comedy* (London, 1702, 1703, 1718, 1736), adapted by M. Dumaniant as *Les folles raisonnables* (Paris, 1807), and by K. G. Lessing as *Der Wildfang* (Berlin, 1779); *The Twin Rivals: A Comedy* (London, 1703, 1718, 1736, 1739, 1772); *The Stage Coach: A Farce* (Dublin, 1704, 1705, 1709), published anonymously; *The Recruiting Officer: A Comedy* (London, 1706, 1707, 1714, 1736, 1778, 1786; Dublin, 1722, 1732, 1741, 1786), also by E. Gosse, ed. (London, 1926), by M. Shugrue, ed. (Lincoln, Nebr., 1965), and by A. N. Jeffares, ed. (Edinburgh, 1973); adapted by G. Stephanie as *Die Werber* (Vienna, 1778) and by B. Brecht as *Pauken und Trompeten*; for German original see Brecht's *Gesammelte Werke*, vol. VI (Frankfurt, 1967), English translation in Brecht's *Collected Plays*, R. Mannheim and J. Willett, eds. (New York, 1972); also translated by F. Campenon as *L'officier en recrutement* (Paris, 1823) and by M. Arnaud as *L'officier recruteur* (Paris, 1956); *The Beaux' Stratagem: A Comedy* (London, 1707, 1711, 1715, 1730, 1736, 1748, 1798; Dublin, 1729, 1739, 1766, 1792), also by H. M. Fitzgibbon, ed. (London, 1898), by B. Dobrée, ed. (Bristol, 1929), and by A. N. Jeffares, ed. (Edinburgh, 1972); translated by J. Leonhardi as *Die Stuzerlist* (Berlin, 1782), by M. Constantin-Weyer as *Le stratagème des roués* (Paris, 1921), by J. Hamard as *La ruse des galants* (Paris, 1965), and by A. Lombardo as *Lo stratagemma dei bellimbusti* (Florence, 1955).

Letters: Familiar and Courtly Letters Written by Mr. Voiture (London, 1700), a miscellany containing some letters by Farquhar; *Letters of Wit, Politicks and Morality* (London, 1701), another miscellany containing letters by Farquhar; *Love and Business: In a Collection of Occa-*

sionary Verse and Epistolary Prose not Hitherto Published. A Discourse Likewise Upon Comedy in Reference to the English Stage in a Familiar Letter (London, 1702), entirely by Farquhar.

Other Works: The Adventures of Covent Garden in Imitation of Scarron's City Romance (London, 1699), a short novel published anonymously; *Love's Catechism Compiled by the Author of The Recruiting Officer* (London, 1707), apparently an unauthorized series of excerpts from *The Beaux' Stratagem*; *Barcellona: A Poem, or, The Spanish Expedition Under the Command of Charles, Earl of Peterborough* (London, 1710).

VI. SOME BIOGRAPHICAL AND CRITICAL STUDIES. W. Hazlitt, *Lectures on the English Comic Writers* (London, 1819), containing the essay "On Wycherley, Congreve, Vanbrugh and Farquhar"; C. Lamb, *Essays of Elia* (London, 1823), containing the essay "On the Artificial Comedy of the Last Century"; W. M. Thackeray, *The English Humourists of the Eighteenth Century* (London, 1853); A. W. Ward, *A History of English Dramatic Literature to the Death of Queen Anne*, 2 vols. (London, 1875; rev. ed., 3 vols., 1899); E. Gosse, *Gossip in a Library* (London, 1891), containing an interesting article on *Love and Business*; L. I. Guiney, *A Little English Gallery* (New York, 1894), containing a perceptive study on Farquhar; D. Schmid, *George Farquhar, sein Leben und seine Original-Dramen* (Vienna, 1904), the first well-documented study of Farquhar's life; J. L. Palmer, *The Comedy of Manners* (London, 1913); G. H. Nettleton, *English Drama of the Restoration and Eighteenth Century 1642–1780* (New York, 1914); E. Bernbaum, *The Drama of Sensibility: A Sketch of the History of English Sentimental Comedy and Domestic Tragedy, 1696–1780* (Boston, 1915); W. Archer, *The Old Drama and the New: An Essay in Revaluation* (London, 1923); A. Nicoll, *A History of Restoration Drama, 1660–1700* (Cambridge, 1923), and *A History of Early Eighteenth Century Drama, 1700–1750* (Cambridge, 1925), reissued with preceding item as vols. I and II of *A History of English Drama, 1660–1900* (Cambridge, 1952); B. Dobrée, *Restoration Comedy, 1660–1720* (Oxford, 1924), a good evaluation of Farquhar's work.

J. W. Krutch, *Comedy and Conscience After the Restoration* (New York, 1924); H. Ten Eyck Perry, *The Comic Spirit in Restoration Drama* (New Haven, 1925); K. M. Lynch, *The Social Mode of Restoration Comedy* (New York, 1926); P. Kavanagh, *The Irish Theatre* (Tralee, 1946); W. Connely, *Young George Farquhar: The Restoration Drama at Twilight* (London, 1949), a lively biography that sometimes relies on unverifiable details; J. H. Smith, *The Gay Couple in Restoration Comedy* (Cambridge, Mass., 1948); T. H. Fujimura, *The Restoration Comedy of Wit* (Princeton, 1952); L. Kronenberger, *The Thread of Laughter* (New York, 1952); F. Boas, *An Introduction to Eighteenth-Century Drama* (Oxford, 1953); K. Spinner, *George Farquhar als*

Dramatiker (Bern, 1956), analysis of aspects of Farquhar's dramatic technique; J. Loftis, *Comedy and Society From Congreve to Fielding* (Stanford, 1959); *La ruse des galants* [*The Beaux' Stratagem*] (London, 1965), with intro., translation, and notes by J. Hamard, the intro. offering the best-documented account to date of Farquhar's life and work; E. Rothstein, *George Farquhar* (New York, 1967), a good full-length study; E. N. James, *The Development of George Farquhar as a Comic Dramatist* (Mouton, 1973); R. A. Anselment, ed., *The Recruiting Officer and The Beaux' Stratagem: A Casebook* (London, 1977).